Finger, enzo
Oldani, bruno
Rosenbaum, sarah

Poland

Lenica, jan*
Mlodozeniec, jan
Mroszczak, józef
Palka, julian
Starowieyski, franciszek*
Swierzy, waldemar
Tomaszewski, henryk
Urbaniec, maciej

Russia

Chaika, vladimir
Logvin, andrey*
Surkov, yuri

South Africa

Walker, garth

Spain

Eskenazi, mario
Ferrer Soria, isidro
Huguet, enric
Mariscal, javier
Martín, pablo
Medina, fernando*
Morillas i Verdura, antoni
Pla-Narbona, josep
Ruiz, david
Thomas, patrick
Torrent (Peret), pedro
Vellvé, tomás

Sweden

Beckman, anders
Beckman, per*
Bramberg, lars*
Eksell, olle
Gavler, martin
Jonsson, dan
Kusoffsky, björn
Lindberg, stig*
Melin, john*
Österlin, anders*
Palotai, gábor

Switzerland

Aeschlimann, roland
Andermatt, peter
Baviera, michael
Bertram, polly
Brühwiler, paul*
Brun, donald
Bucher, mayo
Bühler, fritz
Bundi, stephan
Calame, georges
Carigiet, alois
Eggmann, hermann
Eidenbenz, hermann*
Erni, hans*
Falk, hans*
Frutiger, adrian
Gaberthüel, martin
Gauchat, pierre
Geissbühler, k. domenic
Gerstner, karl*
Gottschalk, fritz
Hartmann, hans
Herdeg, walter
Hiestand, ernst
Hiestand, ursula
Hofmann, armin
Honegger-Lavater, gottfried*
Huber, max*
Imboden, melchior
Jeker, werner
Külling, ruedi
Leupin, herbert*
Lévy, jean-benoît
Lutz, hans-rudolf*
Megert, peter
Miedinger, gérard
Monnerat, pierre*
Moser, peter
Müller, lars
Müller-Brockmann, josef
Netthoevel, andreas
Neuburg, hans
Oberholzer, sabina
Odermatt, siegfried
Pesce, giorgio
Pfund, roger
Piatti, celestino
Reinhard, edgar
Robert, jean
Rüegg, ruedi
Schmid, max*
Schraivogel, ralph
Steiner, heiri
Tissi, rosmarie
Troxler, niklaus
Varga, mihaly
Weingart, wolfgang*
Wetli, hugo
Wirth, kurt
Woodtli, martin
Zeugin, mark
Zintzmeyer, jörg*

Turkey

Erkmen, bülent
Karamustafa, sadik

UK

Bawden, edward
Birdsall, derek*
Brook, tony
Brookes, peter
Calman, mel
Calvert, margaret
Carabott, frederick vincent
Coates, stephen
Collins, jeanette
Crosby, theo*
Davis, paul
Dempsey, mike bernard*
Deuchars, marion
Eckersley, tom
Esterson, simon
Facetti, germano
Fanelli, sara
Fisher, jeffrey
Fletcher, alan
Foreman, michael*
Freedman, barnett
Frost, vince
Gentleman, david
Gorham, john*
Gray, milner
Gutiérrez, fernando
Hardie, george
Havinden, ashley
Henrion, f.h.k.
Hillman, david
Him, george
Hogarth, paul*
Hyland, angus
Jones, terry
Keaney, siobhan*
Keely, pat
Kinneir, jock
Kitching, alan
Klein, louis*
Kroll, natasha*
Law, roger
Lewitt, jan*
Lippa, domenic
McConnell, john
McKnight Kauffer, edward
Michael, anthony
Muir, hamish
Myerscough, morag
Nash, stephanie
Neale, paul
Oehler, justus
Pearce, harry
Pelham, david*
Peters, michael
Porter, mark
Rand, michael
Reichert, hans dieter
Rushworth, john
Scarfe, gerald
Schleger, hans 'zero'*
Searle, ronald
Spencer, herbert
Stevens, andrew
Till, peter
Topolski, feliks*
Warren-Fisher, russell
Wolsey, tom*

USA

Allemann, hans-ulrich
Allner, walter
Anderson, charles s.
Antupit, sam
Appleton, robert
Arnett, dana
Bass, saul
Bayer, herbert
Beall, lester
Benguiat, ed
Bezrutczyk, florence a.*
Bielenberg, john
Bierut, michael
Binder, joseph
Blackburn, bruce

Carter, matthew
Casey, jacqueline
Chermayeff, ivan
Chwast, seymour
Cooper, kyle
Cooper, muriel
Crosby, bart
Cross, james
Danne, richard
Danziger, louis
Davis, paul brooks
Dinetz, bob
Dorfsman, lou
Doyle, stephen
Eiber, rick
Federico, gene
Fili, louise
Fong, karin
Forbes, colin
Geismar, thomas h.
Geissbuhler, steff
Gelman, alexander
Gericke, michael
Giusti, george*
Glaser, milton
Godard, keith
Goldberg, carin
Gonda, tomás
Gorkin, baruch
Grear, malcolm
Greenberg, bob
Greiman, april
Guarnaccia, steven
Harak, rudolph de
Hasting, julia
Hess, richard
Hinrichs, kit
Holland, brad
Hurlburt, allen
Ilic, mirko
Isley, alexander
Ives, norman
Kalman, tibor*
Katayama, toshihiro*
Kidd, chip
Kunz, willi
Leibowitz, matthew
Lionni, leo
Lubalin, herb
Lustig, alvin
Mabry, michael
Maeda, john*
Makela, p. scott
Massey, john
Matter, herbert
McCoy, katherine
McGuire, richard*
Miho, james
Miho, tomoko
Miller, abbott
Morla, jennifer
Niemann, christoph
Nitsche, erik*
Paul, art
Peckolick, alan
Pedersen, b. martin
Pineles Burtin, cipe
Pirtle, woody
Probst, robert
Rand, paul
Sagmeister, stefan
Sahre, paul
Saks, arnold
Scher, paula
Schwartzman, arnold
Sebastian, james
Silverstein, louis
Skolos, nancy
Smolan, leslie
Sommese, lanny
Steinweiss, alex*
Sterling, jennifer
Sussman, deborah
Tenazas, lucille
Thompson, bradbury
Troller, fred
Tscherny, george
Valicenti, rick
Vanderbyl, michael
Victore, james*
Vignelli, massimo
Wadden, douglas
Ward, james s.
Winkler, dietmar*
Wissing, benno
Wolf, henry
Woodward, fred*
Wurman, richard saul*
Yagi, tamotsu
Yount, danny
Yu, garson

Venezuela

Pol, santiago
Rodriguez, carlos*
Sotillo, álvaro

** no longer a member of AGI*

This book is dedicated to those AGI members who are no longer among us.

AGI
Alliance
Graphique
Internationale

Graphic Design Since 1950

Edited by Ben & Elly Bos

Thames & Hudson

First published in the United Kingdom in 2007 by
Thames & Hudson Ltd, 181A High Holborn,
London WC1V 7QX
www.thamesandhudson.com

First published in 2007 in hardcover in the United
States of America by Thames & Hudson Inc.,
500 Fifth Avenue, New York, New York 10110
thamesandhudsonusa.com

British Library Cataloguing-in-Publication Data
A catalogue record for this book is available from the British Library

Library of Congress Catalog Card Number:
2006910398

ISBN: 978-0-500-51342-2

Printed and bound in China

Responsible for the publication:
Alliance Graphique Internationale (AGI),
Bahnhofstrasse 11, PF157,
CH-9230 Flawil,
Switzerland.
tel: +41 71 393 58 48
fax: +41 71 393 45 48
www.a-g-i.org
International president of AGI:
Jelle van der Toorn Vrijthoff, Amsterdam
Conceived and edited by:
Ben Bos (AGI) and Elly Bos, Amsterdam
Image research:
Elly Bos
Image editing:
Ben Bos (AGI), Wout de Vringer (AGI)
Project coordination team:
Elly Bos, Erika Rehmund, Ursina Landolt
Translation:
Roz and Hans Vatter-Buck, Doe-Eye, Lasserre
Typeface headings:
BaldingerPro by André Baldinger (AGI), Paris
All other typefaces:
Univers by Linotype
Packaging and production:
VK Projects Cees de Jong, Laren
Telephone: 00 31 35 533 44 55; Email: vk@euronet.nl
Graphic design:
Ben Faydherbe (AGI) and Wout de Vringer (AGI),
Faydherbe/De Vringer, The Hague
Layout:
Wout de Vringer (AGI),
Faydherbe/De Vringer, The Hague
Pre-press & scans:
Colorset, Amsterdam
Sponsored by:
Linotype, André Baldinger

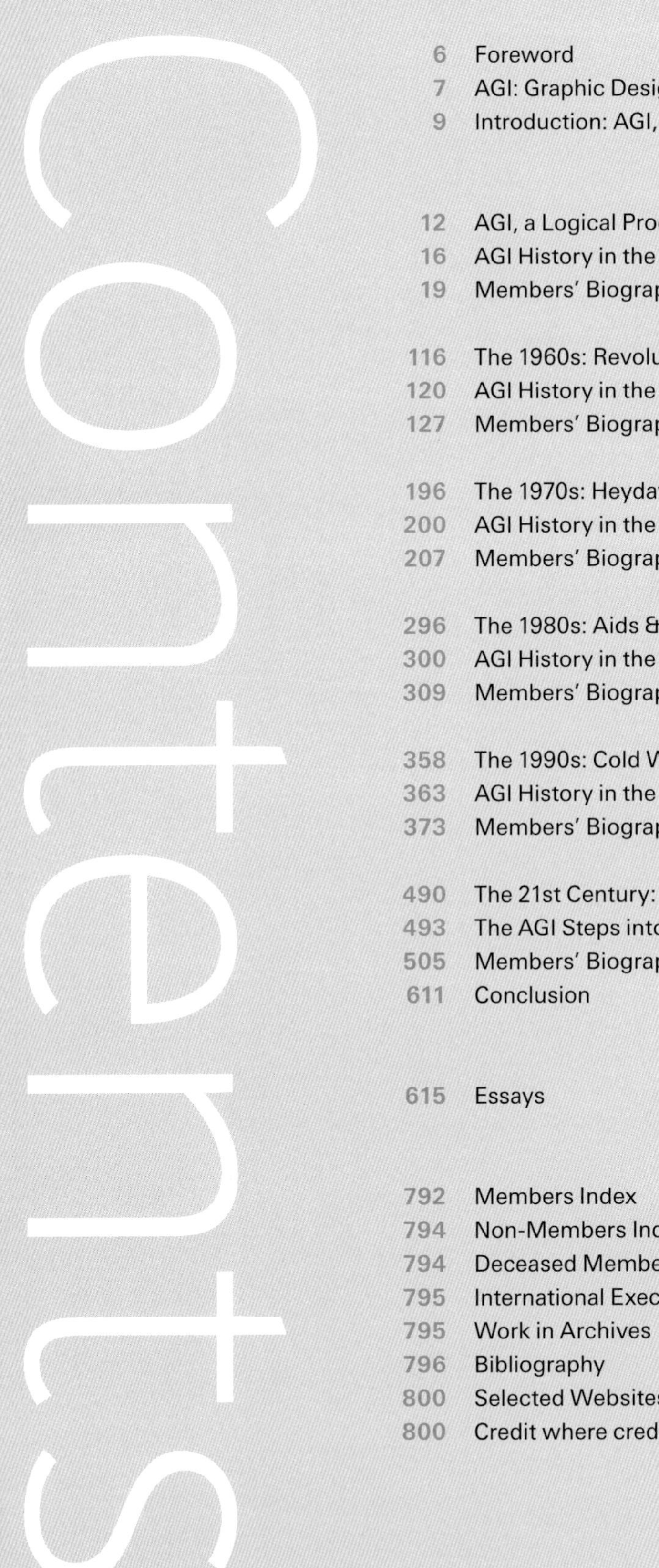
Contents

Foreword

There are many who claim that the book as we know it is disappearing. Just as many point out that the very opposite is true. After all, more dead trees than ever are being pulped to produce paper. Paper is ennobled by ink to create printed matter, some of which is bound into books. This process is many centuries old and constitutes a solid foundation of our culture. There are, however, clear signs that certain forms of printed matter are on their way out. Just as radio was superseded by television, it has been said that the new media will supersede the book. At the same time, though, radio has carved itself a powerful niche in the wall of interfaces that we, as mankind, perceive and which enable us to communicate.

Just as radio will never disappear, neither will the book become extinct. Radio claims its right to existence on the basis that it is not necessary to see a newscaster and that the weatherman, too, can easily remain invisible. Radio is a medium aimed specifically at our ears and nothing else. The book will live on because it is intended for our eyes. As a paradigm, it has remained unchanged from the days when the great library in Alexandria consisted entirely of unique manuscripts to the far-reaching automated production of the huge print runs of our times. The book is one of the most efficient interfaces there is. Tried and tested throughout the ages, repeatedly revised and improved, honed to perfection by legions of designers and typographers over a period of time rivalled by few objects in our daily life.
There will always be books, to present static images. Images that require no movement to justify themselves.

The Alliance Graphique Internationale felt itself able to produce such a book on the work of its members. So much work of this quality has never before been displayed in one single volume. And probably never will be again, in this form. I therefore urge you to possess and cherish this book as a personal treasure, so that many more generations to come can be as amazed as we are now.

Jelle van der Toorn Vrijthoff
International President of the AGI, 2006–
Amsterdam, May 2007

AGI: Graphic Design Since 1950

An 800-page book about some 600 designers who have become members of the Alliance Graphique Internationale, since the organization was founded in 1951. Born in Paris, out of the curiosity of its founders (French and Swiss poster makers and typographers), who were eager to discover and meet the people behind the works they already knew. Some 55 years later that curiosity is intact. Even though the blogs, the websites and the Googlization of the world link us, we still believe that the human being is irreplaceable. It is what this design family cherishes. An extended family, and yet also still a very small one. In 2007 we are 360 AGI designers, in a world of 6 billion human beings.

Once a year we meet in a different part of the world. An international selection committee reviews the work of proposed designers. As you cannot apply for AGI, a godfather proposes you and the international jury votes you in – or not. That is how is this very small group is constituted. Apart from the pleasure of seeing each other, the congress holds a seminar for students and we discover the host country through its national group, which organizes lectures and visits. Cultural institutions welcome us and these exceptional moments help us shed a light on our profession and strengthen the awareness of how valuable graphic design can be.

Someone wrote that the name of our organization sounds like *'a brigade of resistance fighters'*, especially when one hears its full title in French. What a wonderful compliment! Yes indeed, our community of 360 designers does maintain a resistance against marketing, which is so pervasive in the global world. We fight daily to uphold the visual culture we believe in, each in our own country, or in commissions that cross our borders.

AGI has been gathering to confirm this vision for 55 years now, thanks to her members, who now represent 28 countries on six continents. Yes indeed, we will continue *'raising the aesthetic standard'*. *'The public is more perceptive than you think,'* said AGI member Walter Allner, who passed away in July 2006.

We will continue to do our design work for the public, who are citizens, and not just consumers.

The history of AGI in an 800-page book was a project voted for by the members at the 2003 Helsinki General Assembly, presented by David Hillman, who was then the International AGI president.

An editorial committee was formed in December 2004, consisting of Anette Lenz, Leonardo Sonnoli, Jelle van der Toorn Vrijthoff and myself. We proposed Ben Bos and Elly Bos to be the editors and they agreed to take on this immense and wide-ranging task. Later the designers Ben Faydherbe and Wout de Vringer (of course also AGI members) joined the team.

I invite you to take pleasure in discovering the history of the AGI and its present. This is not only a record of the work of the designers who have contributed but also a tool, for the younger generation as well as for the members themselves, as I discovered when we presented the previous AGI book, edited by FHK Henrion, to the French Ministry of Culture for our Paris 2001 Jubilee Congress: the amazement and respect on their faces!

Laurence Madrelle
International President of the AGI, 2003–2006
Paris, October 2006

Introduction: AGI, a Graphic Olympus

The first half of the twentieth century was marked by a quick succession of brief ups and slightly longer, fathomless downs, not only economically and politically, but also on the military front. The euphoria of astonishing discoveries at the beginning, an unprecedented world war, major revolutions, massive inflation, the *'Roaring Twenties'*, a stock market crash and the depression, the threat and reality of World War II, genocide. The history of that time can only be described in the metaphor of a towering pile of ink-black pages. General confusion, oppression, destruction and indescribable suffering. Nonetheless, the sun shone from time to time and there were, naturally, happier moments and more positive developments.

The graphic production of the early decades of the 20th century was dominated by books and newspapers. Plenty of text, lots of black and white, not many pictures. Colour had only really come into style to any extent when the poster made its breakthrough around the illustrious *fin-de-siècle*. For a long time, however, colour remained a costly business. Letter designers and those typographers working for newspaper and book publishers were at the fore of the budding specialism that gradually became known as graphic design, something still being practised on the margins of fine art and architecture. Renowned painters had brought the poster to life. Architects ventured beyond the strict boundaries of their metier, designing not only buildings, but also furniture, magazines and commercial publications. They were even commissioned to create special stamps.

The graphic product itself was often part of the image-determining trends taking root in architecture and the applied arts. The Arts and Crafts movement was quickly followed by Art Nouveau and the Secession, which were again, for a briefer period – and rather less universally – followed by the avant-gardists of Dada, Futurism and Constructivism.

Art Deco, on the other hand, was a movement with a broad foundation, which was also clearly represented in graphic output. The late 1920s and the successive decades saw a great breakthrough for the ideas of De Stijl, the Bauhaus and early notions of New Typography. The Nazis made short work of the Bauhaus, which – in their eyes – was an intellectual breeding ground with a wider reach than just art and design.

The closure of the Bauhaus prompted a stream of emigrants: some to what was for the time being the safer area of Western Europe, some to the USA, where the ideas of the Bauhaus were elaborated upon. An international elite had evolved, of teachers who no longer acted as individual artists, but who together were seeking new expressive forms and techniques.

The contours of the profession vaguely began to emerge. The pioneers from Western, Central and Eastern Europe were experimenting with new forms, with contemporary fonts and unorthodox layout principles. There had also been a breakthrough in photography as a major image carrier.

When World War II broke out, the economy in the occupied war zones came to a standstill. The press was curbed entirely, giving way to propaganda. There was virtually no further international contact. Many young artists joined the resistance, using their skills to forge documents and produce illegal printed matter.

In neutral Switzerland, the further development of New Typography continued undisturbed throughout the war years. In 1944, Walter Herdeg set up *Graphis*, which is still going strong to this day. It must have been lonely at the Swiss top.

Graphic design as we know it now was still a vague concept. Advertising agencies wielded the sceptre, although even their significance and scope was modest. *'Communication'* was not yet an established concept, either.

In both France and Switzerland, the poster had played a considerable role in the years leading up to the outbreak of war. When a number of designers on both sides of the French/Swiss border had the idea of setting up a group, they themselves and the people they knew in their own countries and elsewhere were almost exclusively known for their posters and illustrative work. The group was named *'Alliance Graphique Internationale'*: the true profession, however, still had to wait a while to be invented. In the US, designers were still simply known as commercial artists...

With such a lack of clarity, in the early years it was not unusual for people to be invited to join the AGI who were actually primarily fine artists. The definitions of the profession were still extremely vague. For some members, it soon became plain that this was not the place for them and they opted out of the AGI to follow their path in fine art.

The picture becomes clear when you look at the photographs of the young AGI's first exhibitions: practically pure poster shows, with here and there some associated printed matter, such as a catalogue cover or an advertisement. The second AGI exhibition (London, 1956) was entitled *'AGI Design in Advertising'*, something that would later have been unthinkable.

Thereafter, the designer's operational field rapidly expanded. Posters were no longer primarily devoted to consumption. They also brought culture onto the streets. Museums commissioned catalogues and the layout of their exhibitions. Designers worked for theatres, for concert halls, for films, for social issues. Publishers engaged designers for their periodicals and books. Enthusiastic businesses took on not only industrial designers, but also graphic designers to gear their communications to their innovative products. The AGI's 1962 exhibition in Amsterdam's Stedelijk Museum was therefore entitled *'Graphic Design for the Community'*.

AGI is not a professional organization; it does not protect any interests. AGI is an extraordinary *'club'* of highly qualified designers. Many of them have gained a reputation in a wide cultural hinterland over the years. Some have acquired the status of *'Olympic Champion'*. The criteria for membership are clearly formulated and have been tightened up several times. AGI is still an association with a ballot; prospective members still have to promote themselves, be nominated and accepted. Even an international professional reputation, in itself, is still no guarantee. As was the case when it was established, the AGI is insistent that existing members should feel comfortable with the arrival of a newcomer. An earlier *'unforgivable'* professional conflict – even if strictly personal – can therefore close the door to an otherwise excellent candidate.

AGI is a forum. Colleagues from all corners of the world can get to know each other, meet at the annual congresses, exchange ideas and pieces of work, perform during each other's events, visit each other in far-flung places, support each other in projects, collaborate and confer. AGI is an arena in which you can demonstrate your prowess in the profession. It is a checkpoint where you are confronted with opinions, philosophies, quality, mentalities and ethics. AGI is an honour and a pleasure. AGI is also about respect and is the source of often long-term, *'boundless'* friendships.

It is still a club dominated by men, although these days the male/female ratio is improving slightly. The time of the *'old boys'* is now behind us. Since the early 1990s, the average age of AGI members has dropped considerably. AGI has survived its mid-life crisis. Laurence Madrelle became the first woman AGI President in the 21st century, in an era when women are being elected as national presidents and prime ministers all over the world, generally with good results.

AGI's map of the world still contains many blank patches. There are continents with enormous populations that are barely represented in AGI, if at all. Filling in these gaps is not easy. Icograda, the international council of graphic design associations, has so far had more success in establishing its forum on a worldwide level. AGI still has the task of exploring Asia, Africa and South and Central America largely ahead.

For a long time, AGI failed in what its members were so good at doing for their clients: presenting itself. By holding high-quality seminars and inspiring exhibitions and providing a website, an archive and well-founded publications, AGI is now building on its name, its significance and its future.

Ben Bos, Amsterdam, 2006

Epilogue

In compiling this book, we made grateful use of FHK Henrion's research and extensive knowledge of affairs. His *AGI Annals* (1989) served as the model for this new history. *'Henri'* had to draw on his more than 35-year association with the AGI, his experience in filling numerous board functions in the Alliance and his unceasing influence and presence. His solo marathon was bolstered by correspondence, lengthy long-distance phone calls and the use of the then brand-new, now obsolete fax machine. In compiling our book in 2006, the Internet was a fabulous source of information – although it sometimes needed double-checking. We have made every effort to verify our sources where possible.

Several AGI members have been invited to submit an essay about their favourite subject for this book. AGI is not a dogmatists' organization, but a club of individuals with a high degree of professional expertise. Their contributions will represent a personal view on their specialization. This means that they really speak for themselves, and do not give an opinion that will always and automatically be shared by all of their AGI peers, nor by the AGI Executive Committee.

MACO
The Family of Man
The greatest photographic exhibition of all time – 503 pictures from 68 countries – created by Edward Steichen for the Museum of Modern Art
Prologue by Carl Sandburg

Leo Lionni, USA.

AGI, a Logical Product of the 1950s

The world was catching its breath, although the mess had not yet been cleaned up, by any means. The hopes and expectations cherished during the war had still to be forged into realities. Food was still scarce, the cry for raw materials loud. The allies of 1939–1945 had once again retreated to their respective sides of the Iron Curtain. The echo of the Bomb was still resounding in everyone's ears. New alliances were already in place (NATO, 1949) or in the making (Warsaw Pact, 1955). The Marshall Plan was helping the (western) European countries back on their feet, ready to reassume their role as potential partners in a global market.

The decade was soon shaken by the start of the Korean War. General Eisenhower became the first Supreme Commander of NATO and, a few years later, US President. Nuclear weapons were on the advance: the British got their own atom bomb, the USA produced an H-bomb, a few years later the UK copied them. The French became painfully embroiled in troubles in their Indo-Chinese territories and Algeria. Stalin died. King George VI died and Elizabeth II was crowned while the world watched on television. Anthony Eden succeeded Churchill and the Tories came to power. Harold Macmillan was the next PM. Argentina ousted Peron. Tunisia and Morocco gained independence. Pakistan parted from India and declared itself an Islamic republic. Nasser came to power in Egypt. Israel temporarily occupied the Sinai. War broke out over the Suez Canal. The Soviets invaded Hungary. Adenauer was elected Chancellor of Germany. General de Gaulle became the French premier. Fidel Castro seized power in Havana. Archbishop Makarios, initially exiled, became president of Cyprus. And the Dalai Lama fled Tibet for India. The US launched *Explorer*, the first terrestrial satellite. The French, the Citroen DS. Transistors were developed, as were nuclear power stations and penicillin. Brussels launched its world exhibition in 1958, with – appropriately – the Atomium. Trendsetting architectural structures were rising everywhere: the UN Headquarters and the Guggenheim Museum in New York, Oscar Niemeyer's government buildings in Brazil, UNESCO in Paris, Le Corbusier's Unité d'Habitation in Marseilles and his Chandigarh Plan in India, Buckminster Fuller's domes. Ponti's Pirelli tower in Milan. Too many to mention, in fact. And due to – or perhaps despite – all that, for many the spirit had returned. People wanted to broaden their horizons, to travel and renew old friendships and make new contacts, to find out what advances were being made by professional colleagues elsewhere. Curiosity, openness, willingness to share and exchange, the need for a sounding board. In search of new frontiers, new ideals and new opportunities.

One way of remedying the information deficit, a by-product of the war years, was to establish new international contacts. The world was still big, the means of travelling limited, foreign currency was not easy to come by; in the weaker economies wages and fees were still meagre. Nevertheless, the time seemed ripe for initiatives, such as an *'Alliance Graphique Internationale'*. The founding fathers and the colleagues they wrote to in the European hinterland looked forward to discussion, possible inspiration, recognition and acknowledgment. James Cross, the Californian AGI president from 1988 to 1992, once described the organization as *'a family'*. That was certainly so in the early years, when the number of members was fewer than a village football club. The *'formula'* proved to be an attractive one, however: the opportunities to meet *'the man behind the work'*, the interchange of opinions, the unique sector-oriented exhibitions, the possibility of intensifying contact at the annual congresses *'somewhere in Europe'*.

Swiss colleagues, who had escaped the ravages of war, were able to demonstrate that they had not been idle. By then, the *'Swiss Style'* had gained a clear, theoretical foundation. Former Bauhaus students Max Bill and Theo Ballmer were there at the birth of the arithmetic grid and geometric letter shapes. This masterplan for the Swiss approach, which had rapidly increased in significance, gained a new name, the International Style. Designers of the calibre of Josef Müller-Brockmann, Armin Hofmann, Hans Neuburg and Emil Ruder were instrumental in the further development and promotion of the Swiss design approach. They lectured in Zürich and Basel, published and set examples in their own work. The British and their refugees had been able to make themselves useful in wartime information and were quickly provided with new challenges for their skills in projects such as the 1948 London Olympic Games and the Festival of Britain, in 1951.

The Dutch had had to keep a low profile under German occupation. A number of designers had placed their skills at the disposal of the resistance, producing underground newspapers and forging official stamps and documents. Others were forced to go into hiding or were picked up by the Gestapo, the Nazis' secret police. Will Sandberg prepared the GKf, the organization of Dutch applied artists, for after liberation, when he became its chairman. He was also instrumental in initiating design activities as director of Amsterdam's Stedelijk Museum. Belgium remained for a long time an isolated *'island'* in an ocean of design. For decades, Jacques Richez, a prominent AGI member, strove in vain against the hegemony of the advertising agencies

that totally dominated design in his country.
Italy was steeped in a history unique in Western civilization. The continued presence of the Etruscans, the Roman Empire and Greek heritage, the Renaissance and 20th-century Futurism have perpetually confronted the man in the street with exceptional painters, sculptors and architects.
In this climate, design was easily able to find itself a place. It is remarkable that there were nevertheless no design courses available in Italy until the 1960s. Earlier designers had been trained as painters, architects or sculptors. However, Italian design output did not suffer qualitatively in any way.

Shortly after the war, Germany had other worries. In 1955, OWH Hadank, an influential teacher, was made an *'honorary member'* of the AGI; amazing, actually, as all AGI members were honorary members in a way. Anton Stankowski, who had helped pioneer Swiss design before the war, became an AGI member in 1956. The Swedes had also escaped the direct consequences of war. A design scene had emerged, which was primarily visible in editorial design and early forms of corporate identity. Most French designers with any reputation were born around the *'fin de siècle'* or in the early decades of the new century. Old enough to have played a substantial role as the masters of the poster and therefore promoters of French wine, spirits, tobacco and tourism, but still young enough to pick up their work again after the war. They were able to share in the public recognition that French painters and sculptors enjoyed. That made Paris the obvious choice as the birthplace of the AGI.

In the US, the role of former European *'imports'* was a strong determining factor in the design climate. After all, the US magazine style differed greatly from that in Europe. Many designers were art directors for magazines, a discipline only known in Europe in the advertising world. The Container Corporation of America (CCA) can be seen as a pioneer in corporate design policy, starting as early as 1936. When AGI was established, the reputation of American colleagues was strong enough to cross the still wide Atlantic Ocean. *'The Yanks were coming!'*

Roughly speaking, this was the *'playing field'* of international graphic design in 1951, barely six years after Hiroshima. We have to realize that the number of *'players'* compared with today was extremely limited and therefore easy to manage and oversee. It was the Swiss Heiri Steiner, based in Paris, who brought forward the idea of an Alliance. Actually his compatriot Alfred Girardclos who had suggested it to him.

The five founding fathers met in Paris in 1951: the Frenchmen Jean Picart Le Doux, Jacques Nathan Garamond and Jean Colin, and the Swiss Fritz Bühler and Donald Brun. Then followed the first formal meeting, in which the Swiss Pierre Monnerat, the Englishman Ashley Havinden, George Him and Henrion and the Swede Anders Beckman took part. Cathy Garamond acted as secretary and, in gratitude, was granted *'vice-presidency for life'*. This group initiated the contacts with 'foreign correspondents' who, in turn, approached aspiring members in their own countries.

The first wave of members was characteristic of how vague the meaning of the concept was: what was graphic design before it was known as such? It led to a number of misunderstandings, *'displaced persons'*. They were sometimes akin to talented athletes who had started out as footballers. Fast, perhaps, but without any gift for ball control. Some were tile painters or drew the type of postcard you and I would never dream of buying. And so they departed, to achieve fame and happiness, or otherwise, in their own crafts. The major changes in graphic production that were to mark the second half of the century began to tentatively reveal themselves in the 1950s.
Offset was rattling at the door of relief printing. Photo-setting still had a lot of progress to make before it could undermine traditional wood and lead typesetting. Screenprinting, so crucial to poster production, was becoming more professional and undergoing forms of automation. Repro techniques were evolving rapidly. Other European users were increasingly obtaining four-colour quality from Switzerland. The market was flooded with dry transfer lettering, not always to the benefit of letterspacing.

It was time for graphic designers to roll up their sleeves and get ready for the many dramatic innovations awaiting them.

Ben Bos, Amsterdam, 2006

AGI History in the 1950s

We Want You!

Ben Bos, Amsterdam, 2006

1952: London AGI Assembly. The Founding Fathers and the Invited New Members at their first Assembly. Beckman, Nathan Garamond, Him, Lewitt, Gauchat, Jean Colin, Mrs Garamond, Monnerat. Bühler, Erni, Brun, Heiri Steiner, Havinden, Picart Le Doux, Schleger, Herdeg, Keely.

The Alliance was established at a first meeting in Paris. A dozen designers from France, Britain and Switzerland took the initial steps. Jean Picart Le Doux became the president, Fritz Bühler and FHK Henrion were vice-presidents and Jean Colin became the secretary general. Jacques Nathan Garamond was the treasurer and his wife, Cathy, worked very hard for AGI in its first few years. Those efforts won her the title of honorary vice-president for life.

The founders and a number of *'new members'* met again in London (1952), Paris (1953) and Basel/ Zermatt (1954). In Basel they celebrated the very special local carnival, after which they travelled to Zermatt to enjoy a wonderful time in the mountains. This must have been the very start of a long AGI tradition: a General Assembly, a Congress and an interesting venue in which to enjoy them. In Zermatt a special committee was appointed to prepare and organize the first AGI Exhibition, held at the Louvre in 1955. Jean Carlu took over the presidency of AGI and was also in charge of the Paris exhibition.

1954: Basel/Zermatt, AGI Assembly.

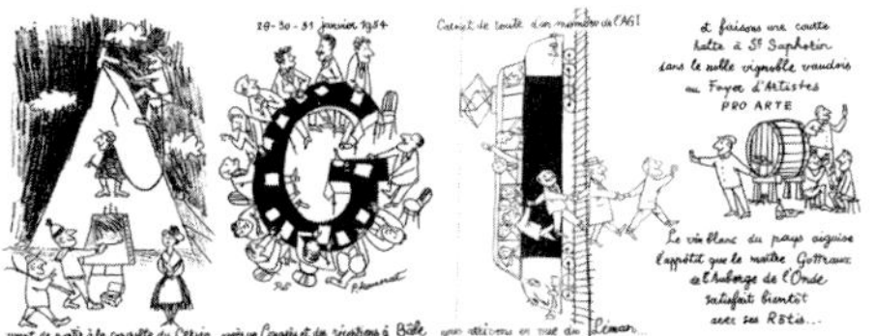

Illustration by Pierre Monnerat.

1955: AGI Poster Exhibition in Helsingborg, Sweden.

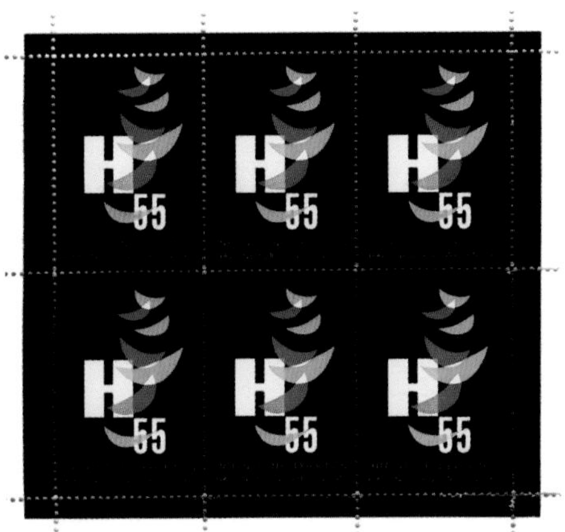

The Swedish member Anders Beckman arranged an AGI poster exhibition during the Industrial Fair H55 in Helsingborg, and designed for this manifestation a comprehensive event style. One of the earliest of its kind.

1956: London AGI assembly and exhibition.

The exhibition was arranged by FHK Henrion, who also designed its logo.

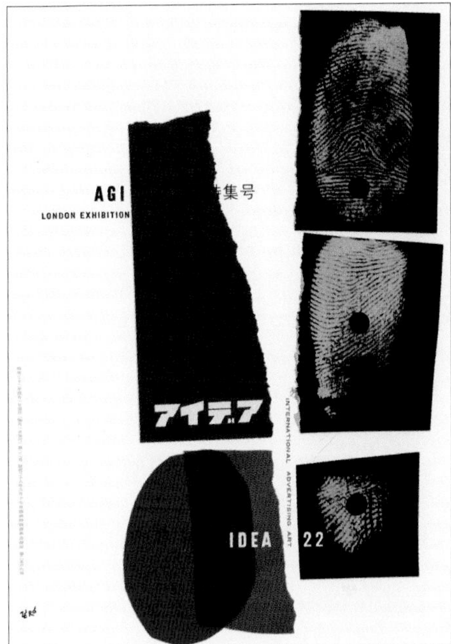

Cover of the Japanese magazine *IDEA*, featuring the AGI London exhibition. Design Hans Schleger.

Logo designed by Nathan Garamond.

1957: *'Graphis 57'* exhibition in Lausanne, Switzerland.

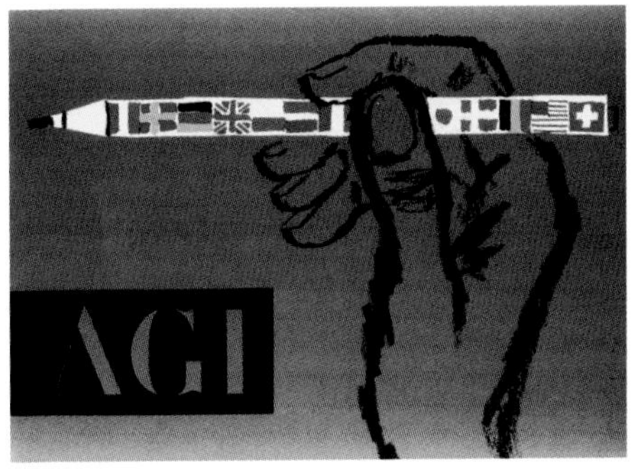

Fritz Bühler designed the catalogue and poster for the *'Graphis 57'* exhibition in Lausanne, in which AGI participated. Bühler's design was for a few years the official AGI emblem.

'Art et Publicité dans le Monde' was the title of that first AGI exhibition in the Musée des Arts Décoratifs on Rue de Rivoli. 74 designers from eleven countries took part, putting AGI on the world map. Numerous ministers and ambassadors from members' countries attended the event. As was typical of the period, the poster was the dominating medium. Issue 58A of Walter Herdeg's *Graphis* recorded the exhibition in detail. In addition to the members' personal works, there were displays of work by AGI members for leading design-conscious companies such as Olivetti, Ciba and Larousse. Also in 1955, the Swedish designer Anders Beckman organized an AGI poster exhibition in the pavilions of the important design and industry show H55 in Helsingborg. Beckman created a city-wide corporate design programme for the occasion, in fact the first ever of its kind.

AGI chose to expand its early reputation with two more exhibitions in the following years. London was the venue in 1956, organized by Ashley Havinden and designed by F.H.K. Henrion. There were no governmental subsidies this time, but solid support from major international companies, clients of the AGI members. A retrospective of the late Edward McKnight Kauffer (an American designer who had worked in England for most of his life) and work by the two Polish designers Jan Lenica and Henryk Tomaszewski and many Japanese, American and Italian designers gave this London show a more global spirit than the previous Paris exhibition, which was dominated by French and Swiss colleagues. In spite of the *'local dialects'*, this exhibition clearly demonstrated the common visual language of quality. London was followed by Lausanne, where the work of 67 AGI members was shown in 1957.

The 1959 Knokke AGI assembly, on the Belgian coast, was a kind of philosophical turning point. Jacques Richez was the host for 20 members. In addition to a day tour to the old town of Bruges, it was a meeting with serious discussion of major professional, social and ethical issues. This time it was not only the work itself that was in the limelight; in Knokke, AGI talked about the men behind the work. Jacques and Heiri Steiner made themselves heard, as they would continue to do throughout their many years in AGI. Heiri had produced a paper on *'The moral mission of AGI'*. The Alliance should, in his words, tackle its true task of acting as a trustee of our profession. He pleaded that designers should have an independent position and attitude because, when they join an agency, they are lost to the profession. Discussing young designers, he wrote: *'It is important for them to realize that our work generates something of higher value and makes it possible for designers to participate more fully in life. We might also perhaps be able to contribute to the human society of the future.'*

Founding fathers 1951:
Brun, donald
Bühler, fritz
Colin, jean
Nathan Garamond, jacques
Picart le Doux, jean

Invited to join 1952:
Andersen, ib *
Beckman, anders
Beckman, per •*
Boucher, pierre
Bramberg, lars *
Brusse, wim *
Carboni, erberto *
Carlu, jean
Dubois, jacques
Eckersley, tom
Eidenbenz, hermann *
Eksell, olle
Elffers, dick *
Erni, hans *
Excoffon, roger
Falk, hans *
Flora, paul •*
François, andré *
Freedman, barnett
Gauchat, pierre
Gavler, martin
Georget, guy •*
Gray, milner
Grignani, franco
Hansen, aage sikker
Havinden, ashley
Henrion, f.h.k.
Herdeg, walter
Hetreau, remy •*
Him, george
Honegger-Lavater, gottfried •*
Jacno, marcel
Keely, pat
Lancaster, eric •*
Leupin, herbert *
Lewitt, jan *
Lindberg, stig *
Malclès, jean-denis
McKnight Kauffer, edward
Monnerat, pierre *
Müller-Brockmann, josef
Munari, bruno *
Pintori, giovanni *
Richez, jacques
Sadolin, ebbe •*
Sandberg, willem
Savignac, raymond
Schleger, hans (zero) *
Steiner, heiri
Treumann, otto
Ungermann, arne *
Villemot, bernard

Admitted 1954:
Bayer, herbert
Beall, lester
Bernard, francis
Binder, joseph
Lortz, helmut

Admitted 1955:
Burtin, will
Carmi, eugenio *
Cassandre, a.m.
Colin, paul *
Dorfsman, lou
Giusti, george *
Hadank, o.h.w.
Kamekura, yusaku
Leibowitz, matthew
Lionni, leo
Loupot, charles
Lustig, alvin
Matter, herbert
Ohchi, hiroshi
Pineles Burtin, cipe
Rand, paul
Steiner, albe
Steinweiss, alex *
Thompson, bradbury

Admitted 1956:
Bawden, edward
Breker, walter
Hayakawa, yoshio *
Lenica, jan *
Manzi, riccardo *
Palka, julian
Searle, ronald •
Stankowski, anton
Topolski, feliks *
Wirth, kurt

Admitted 1957:
Carigiet, alois
Crouwel, wim
David, jean
Imatake, shichiro
Peignot, rémy *
Piatti, celestino
Tomaszewski, henryk

Admitted 1958:
Bass, saul
Bons, jan *
Hartmann, hans
Huber, max *
Kapitzki, herbert w.

Admitted 1959:
Melin, john *
Österlin, anders *

• *no work submitted*
* *no longer member of AGI*

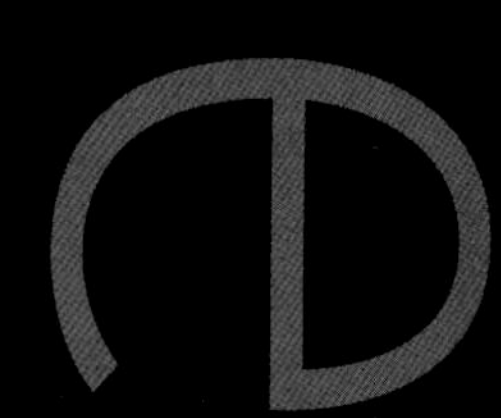

Donald Brun [Switzerland]

1909-1999; born in Basel
Founding Father of AGI, 1951
International President 1970-1972

Donald Brun was the oldest of a small group of designers from Basel, all followers of Niklaus Stoecklin. He was trained in a studio in Basel, at the Allgemeine Gewerbeschule there, and later at the Akademie für Freie und Angewandte Kunst in Berlin (with the professors O.W.H. Hadank and Böhm). He became an independent designer in 1933. This was the beginning of four decades of poster design at the highest level, full of humour, making use of an impressive range of techniques.

He was entrusted the design of his nation's pavilions for the national exhibitions in Zürich 1939 and Lausanne 1964, as well as at the Brussels Expo 1958. He also regularly contributed exhibition stands for the Schweizer Mustermesse in Basel. The chemical industry of Basel was another major client. His painterly approach to poster design was well demonstrated in his series on Swissair destinations. Donald Brun also taught at the Kunstgewerbeschule Basel (1947–74); his contribution there was very influential. His works were honoured with numerous awards and exhibitions and are in the permanent collections of several international museums.

Poster for **Tenta** sun blinds, 1960.

Poster for **Gauloises** filter cigarettes, 1966.

Poster for **Bata** shoes, 1946.

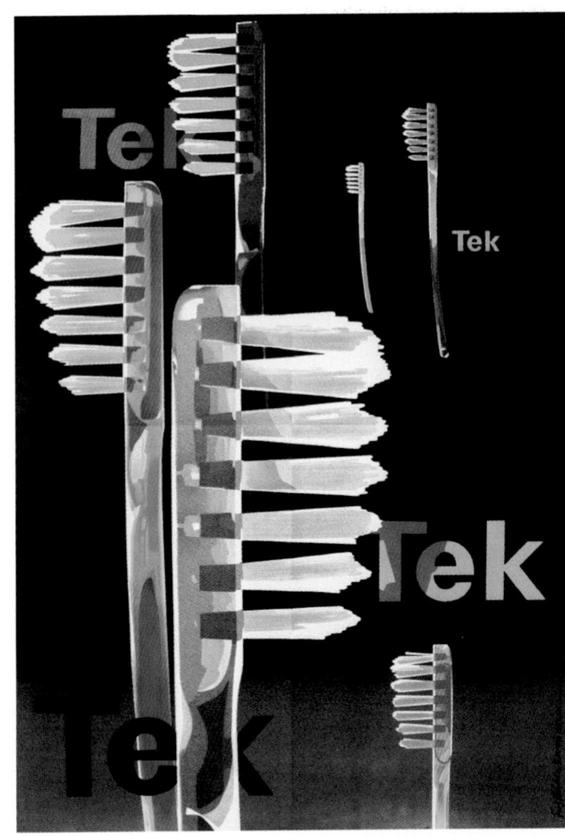

Union, poster for a Swiss fuel company, Zürich, 1943.

Tek toothbrushes, poster.*

Swiss Pavilion, at the World Expo in Brussels, 1958.

**Donated by MAK - Austrian Museum of Applied Arts/Contemporary Art, Vienna.*
Photograph: © MAK/Georg Mayer

Fritz Bühler [Switzerland]

1909-1963; born in Basel
Founding Father of AGI, 1951
International President 1960-1962

Bühler studied in 1925–27 at the Allgemeine Gewerbeschule in Basel, and in the following two years (with O.H.W. Hadank) at the Vereinigten Staatsschulen in Berlin. Then he went to Paris, before working in a Basel agency. In 1933 he opened his own studio in Basel, working with important designers such as Barth and Piatti. He saw advertising as a tool to convert the general public to art. He also gave evening classes at the Gewerbeschule, specializing in graphic design and posters.

Bühler had a great range of activities: he designed posters, periodicals, exhibitions, promotional films and packaging, and excelled in all these areas. His poster for Union Coal became a huge success. He was an illustrator and a painter. His style was sometimes surrealist, but also decorative and with abstract elements. Bühler was for many years an advisor on matters of design for several large companies. He was the fourth president of AGI and devoted much of his energy and love to the organization. He also designed the catalogue for the Lausanne AGI Exhibition 1957; the cover image was used as a giant mural.

Jean Colin [France]

1911-1982; born in Paris
Founding Father of AGI, 1951

Jean Colin was one of the founding fathers of AGI and became its first general secretary. He made name as a poster designer. His work had a lot in common with that of André François, Raymond Savignac and Francis Bernard, all of his own generation. Their posters had a special lyrical quality and often a kind of naive and disarming humour, which appealed to a wide audience. Jean made more than 300 posters. For many of them he received medals and awards, among them one from the Académie de l'Affiche, for the best poster of the year in 1943. He also won a gold medal for the Most Beautiful Poster of 1959.

He worked in his own arts and advertising studio for important clients like Shell, Omo, Pernod and Cinzano. Colin taught at the École Supérieur des Arts Décoratifs in Paris. Anne-Claude Lelieur wrote the catalogue *Jean Colin: Affichiste* (2000).

Berlitz language courses, Vienna, May–August, 1960–69. *

Larousse Encyclopedia, cover design.

Left half of a two-part billboard for **Perrier mineral water**.

** Donated by MAK - Austrian Museum of Applied Arts/Contemporary Art, Vienna.*
Photograph: © MAK/Georg Mayer

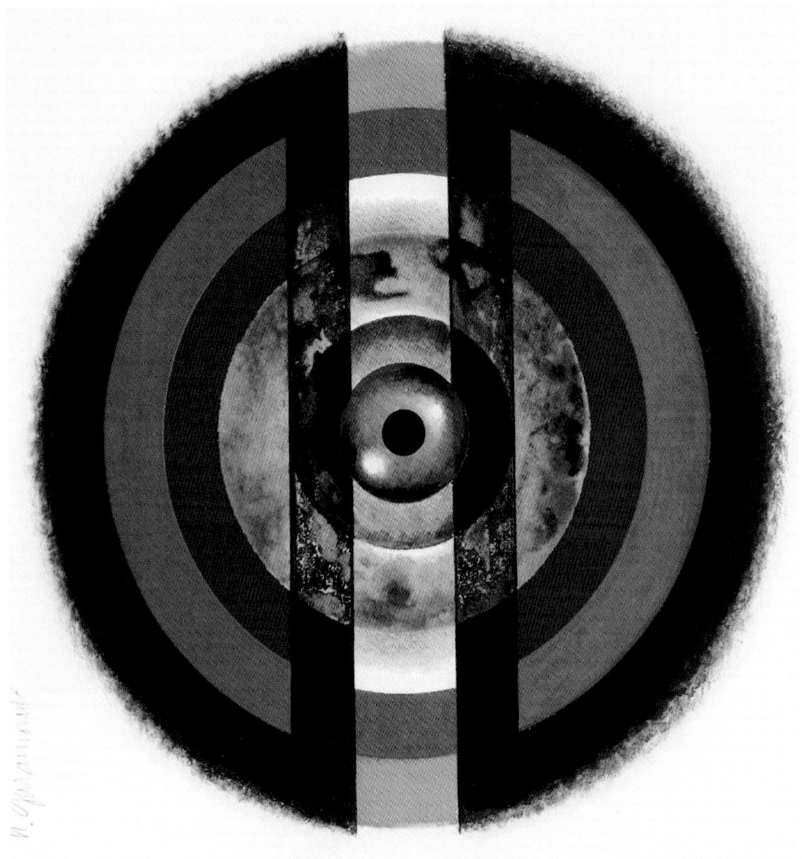

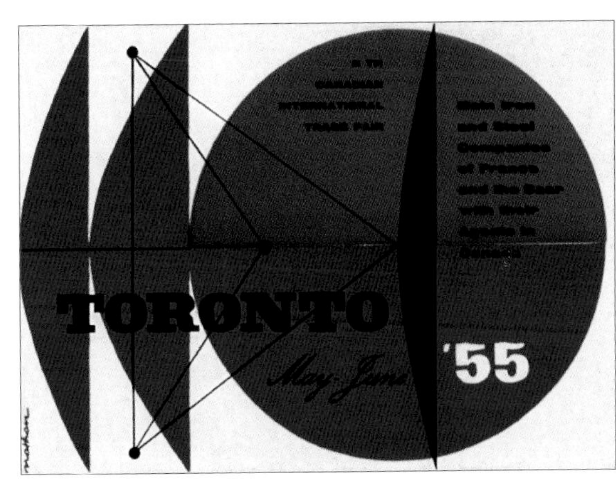

Graphimages, exhibition poster. Chosen as Garamond's favourite piece of work in the book *First Choice* by Ken Cato.

Toronto, May–June '55. One of a series of covers for booklets, listing iron and steel companies of France and the Saar, for a Canadian Trade Fair 1955.

Travel poster for **Air France**, created under the art direction of Jean Carlu.

Jacques Nathan Garamond [France]

1910-2001; born in Paris
Founding Father of AGI, 1951

Born as Jacques Nathan, he *'covered up'* his family name during WW2, using it as a middle name and adding Garamond as his surname. This change was inspired by the threatening actions of the German occupiers. Jacques Garamond, Jean Colin, Jean Picart Le Doux from France and the Swiss Fritz Bühler and Donald Brun founded the AGI in December 1951. Jacques's wife Cathy assisted the young AGI for many years; she was voted an honorary AGI vice-president for life.

He studied at the École Nationale des Arts Décoratifs, and became director of *Architecture d'Aujourd'hui* before setting up as a designer. He did trademarks, packaging, book design, illustrations, posters and corporate identity programmes. Jacques was a teacher at the École Internationale and a professor at the École Supérieure des Arts Graphiques in Paris. His 'Human Rights' poster for UNESCO 1949 was his masterpiece. He designed the symbol for the 1956 London AGI exhibition, and was awarded a gold medal at the 1957 Milan Triennale. Jacques was also a painter. Jacques and Cathy Garamond were both among the guests at the fabulous 1997 AGI congress in Barcelona.

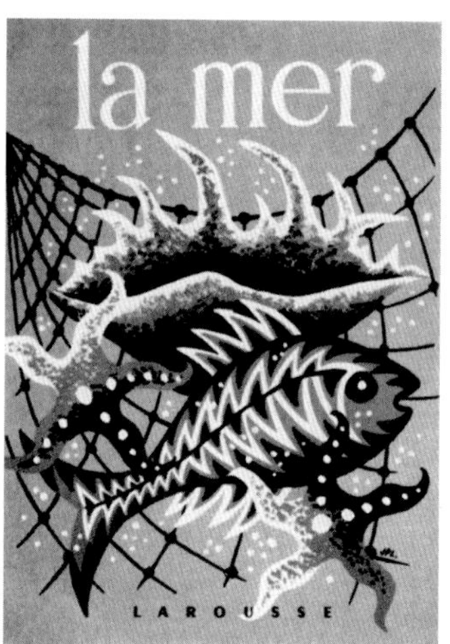

Jean Picart le Doux [France]

1902-1982; born in Paris
Founding father of AGI, 1951
1st International President 1951-1954

Picart le Doux studied art in Paris. Cassandre had a great influence on him, as well as on Raymond Savignac and Jacques Garamond. He made a series of posters, mainly landscapes, for the French Tourist Office. A friendship with Renoir led him from academic art to impressionism. Later on he started to produce tapestries and textile hangings for embassies, museums and public buildings. After WW1, he was commissioned to paint murals on the ocean liner *Normandy*. Picart illustrated the literary works of Paul Verlaine, Colette and Charles Baudelaire.

Throughout his life he had many exhibitions. His work can be found in the collections of many museums like the Musée de Petit Palais, Musée Nationale d'Art Moderne and in the museums of Bagnol, Le Havre and Nice as well as in the Museum of Modern Art in Moscow. In 1950 he was awarded the Legion d'Honneur.

Air France, poster

Winter, an Aubusson tapestry, 2 x 2 m.

La Mer, cover for a book on the sea.

Poster for the Sunday edition of the political newspaper **Politiken**, 1965.

Danish Air Lines, poster, 1945.

Ib Andersen [Denmark]

1907-1969; born in Copenhagen
Invited to join AGI, 1952

Ib Andersen was one of the first Danes to be invited to join AGI together with Aage Sikker Hansen, Arne Ungermann and Ebbe Sadolin. They all had in common their work for the Sunday edition of the political newspaper *Politiken*. Later he became a poster designer. His style was often Art Deco or Cubist. Nowadays some of his posters have been reprinted and are available in Denmark and abroad in poster galleries and auctions. Unfortunately, very little is known about him.

Anders & Per Beckman [Sweden]

Anders 1907-1967 / Per 1913-1989;
Both born in Stockholm
Both invited to join AGI, 1952

Anders Beckman, was a gifted artist, architect and marketing guru. He was the founder of Beckmans College (1939), which is still one of the most important design schools in Sweden today. As a pioneer in Swedish advertising art, he was responsible for many prestigious projects such as marketing for the World's Fair in New York, 1939. He was the designer of the complete identity for the Helsingborg 55 Exhibition. Anders also organized a special pavilion in which the AGI could show its members' work.

After his sudden death, Ashley Havinden wrote: *'Anybody who had the privilege and pleasure of Anders's friendship will never forget his ebullient character and fun-loving zest for life.'*

Per Beckman, Anders's brother, was an artist, graphic designer and author. He was a teacher at Beckmans College of Design and was its director from 1967–80. He worked side by side with his brother Anders. Per was also a book illustrator in a style that made use of Swedish folklore and humour. As a designer and educator, his contribution to Swedish book and poster design was significant. Unfortunately we could not find any examples of his work.

All work shown by Anders Beckman.

Swedish Air Lines, poster, 1932.

Bring your Family, Go to the Cinema, poster, 1952.

Poster for the daily newspaper **Arbetet**, celebrating the installation of the biggest rotary printing press in Sweden, 1950.

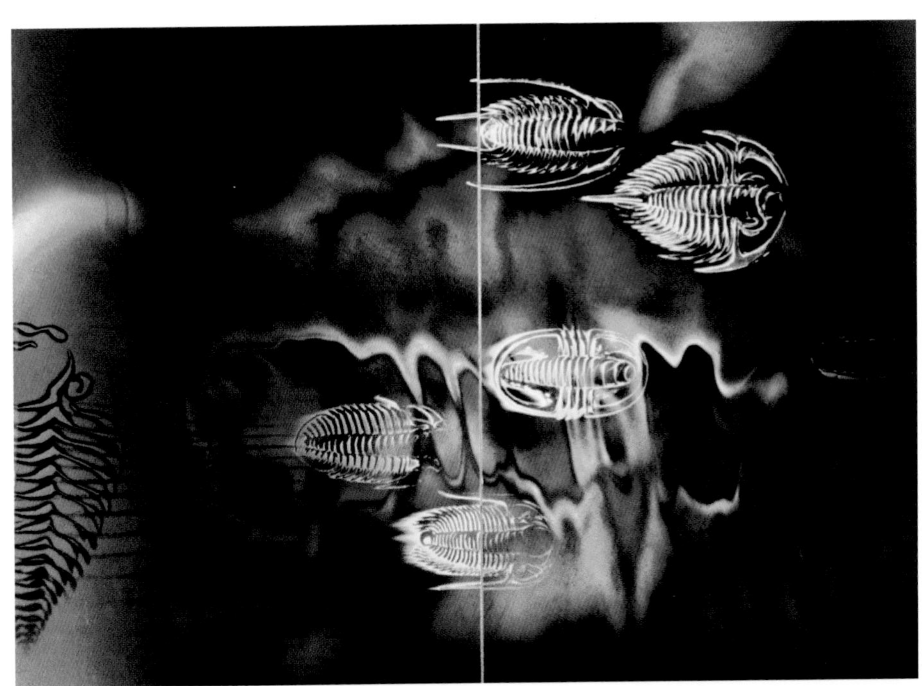

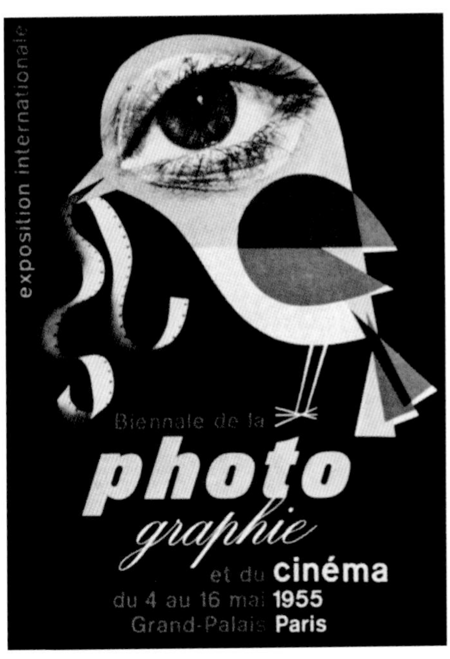

Details (x 2) of a monumental mural for the **Northern Gas Board in Newcastle-upon-Tyne**, 2.1 x 16 m. Chosen by Boucher as his favourite piece of work in the book *First Choice* by Ken Cato.

International Photography and Cinema Biennial, poster, Paris, 1955.

Pierre Boucher [France]

1908-2000
Invited to join AGI, 1952

This pioneer of photomontage, a mixture of two related but quite different media, always remained part photographer, part designer. Often this synthesis resulted in a happy marriage, as in his 1955 poster for the International Photography and Cinema Biennial. He met Herbert Matter at the Deberny et Peignot type foundry, where Charles Peignot acted over many years as a catalyst for new graphic art. Pierre founded *Arts et Métiers Graphiques*, the leading pre-war French design magazine. With friends he also founded the Alliance Photo, experimenting with all kinds of photographic techniques.

He was commissioned to do large murals in France and Great Britain and came up with a technique combining colour graphics and montage. It was a great pleasure to see that he *'re-appeared'* at the 1997 Barcelona AGI congress.

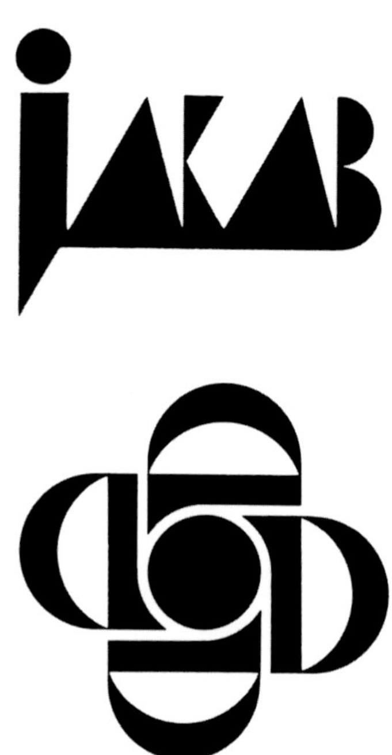

Lars Bramberg [Sweden]

1920-1999; born in Luleå
Invited to join AGI, 1952

Bramberg was initially trained in the applied arts, as a furniture designer. He gained his first graphic experience under Anders Beckman, during two terms at Beckmans College in 1944. He continued his studies, after having worked as a freelance designer for 4 years, in London, the US and Canada. He had a long career, designing posters, exhibitions and corporate programmes for industry and government and social institutions.

In 1951, Bramberg worked together with Willy de Mayo on the Northern Ireland Pavilion for the Festival of Britain. Among his projects are the Rhodes Centenary exhibition, Bulawayo (1953), and the centenary exhibition of the Gilbey wine company, London (1957). Bramberg was chief designer for 'The Parallel', an exhibition in Vancouver, 1958. In 1959 he became design consultant to the Swedish Council of Personnel Administration. One of his major assignments was publicity work for UNESCO. In 1954, Lars Bramberg had a joint exhibition in Stockholm with Fritjof Pedersen. He won several Swedish awards for posters and packaging designs. His works are in the collections of the National Museum, Stockholm, NY MoMA and elsewhere.

Tabletop design, 110 x 80 cm.

Logo for **Sten Jacobsson Konsult**.

Logo for **DUZAN** timberworks, Turkey.

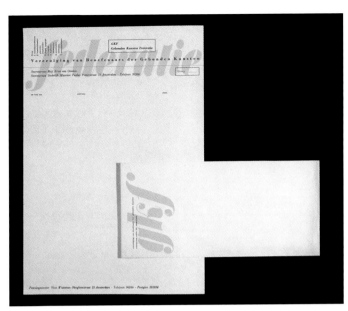

Sculpture in Frederick's Square, poster for an outdoor sculpture exhibition, Amsterdam, 1954.

Stationery for the **Dutch Federation for the Applied Arts**, 1945.

Poster about the **rehabilitation of the Netherlands**, after the liberation of 1945.

Wim Brusse [The Netherlands]

1910-1978; born in Rotterdam
Invited to join AGI, 1952

As the son of a publisher, Wim Brusse was exposed to typography, publicity and printing matters as a child. He studied at the Royal Academy of The Hague. After having worked in a progressive advertising agency, Wim set up his own studio. He worked for the Dutch Post, and was strongly political engaged, caring about the victims of the Sino-Japanese War and the Spanish Civil War. He and Dick Elffers criticized the use of photography in graphic design, as it had become crucial to the leading Dutch pioneers and the Bauhaus adepts. They did this in an issue of the magazine *De 8 en Opbouw*, promoting the value of drawn illustrations. Nonetheless, both Elffers and Brusse married very talented, prominent photographers (Emmy Andriesse and Eva Besnyö). In 1947 Eva and Wim even co-operated on some stamp designs! Brusse made one of the first Dutch postwar posters. He became a teacher at the Rietveld Academy, and designed many books. He was one of the editors of an early postwar avant-garde magazine (with Willem Sandberg, Mart Stam and Gerrit Rietveld). Like his friend Elffers, Wim Brusse resigned from AGI after a few years.

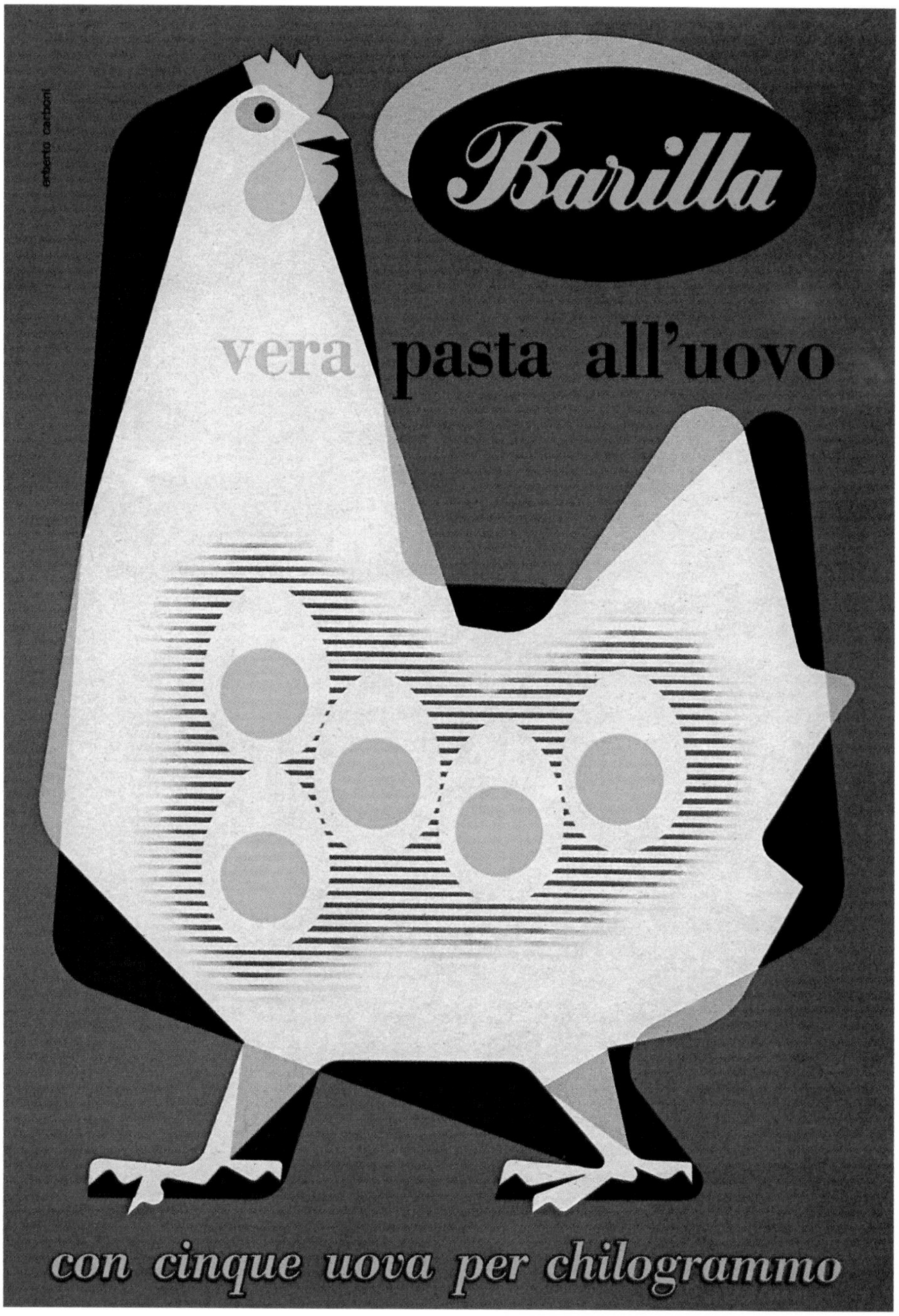

Erberto Carboni [Italy]

1899-1984; born in Parma
Invited to join AGI, 1952

Carboni started his studies in architecture in 1921, but became also interested in graphic and industrial design. His career began at the famous Studio Boggeri, but later he worked on his own. He specialized in exhibitions for trade fairs (Olivetti), interior design and graphics. For many years, Carboni worked for RAI (the Italian radio and TV company), but also for clients who mainly manufactured basic consumer products like Motta (ice cream), Pavesi (bread), Barilla (pasta) and Shell Oil. He presented those clients with a complete graphic line, ranging from packaging to posters.

From 1953 to 1960 he worked for Bertolli, for whom he designed a whole series of magazine ads and posters. He mixed photography, graphics and inventive typography and brought a rigorous modernism into his work. In 1954 he designed the *'Delfino'* (dolphin) chair for Arflex. He wrote several books; *Exhibitions and Displays* (1959), with an illustrated introduction by Herbert Bayer, features his relatively unknown work from the early 1930s through to the late 1950s.

Barilla: Real Egg Pasta with Five Eggs per Kilo, advertising poster, 1958.

Advertisement for **Bertolli olive oil**, 1953.

Advertisement for **Motta ice cream and confectionery**, 1947.

Gellé toothpaste, poster, before WW2.

America's Answer! Production, poster for the Office for Emergency Management, 1945.

Perrier, poster, 1950.

Jean Carlu [France]

1900-1997; born in Bonnières sur Seine
Invited to join AGI, 1952
International President 1954-1956

Originally trained as an architect, he decided to become a graphic designer after he lost his right hand in a traffic accident. He was one of the avant-garde who launched the new European poster. His early works reveal a fascination for geometric forms and minimal text, inspired by cubists like Juan Gris and Fernand Léger and surrealists like André Breton and Yves Tanguy. He also started to try new developments like photomontage (*Atlantis* film poster, 1932) and three-dimensional elements (La Grand Maison de Blanc department store, 1933).

His political and social commitment was evident in his work for the peace movement (*Le Désarmement*, 1932 and *Stop Hitler Now*, 1940). The latter he made in the US, where the French government had sent him and where he lived till 1953. There Carlu created his most famous poster, *America's Answer! Production*. It was voted as poster of the year by the NADC. Back in France (1953) he became art director for Larousse and made a great contribution to commercial art, working for Air France and Firestone France.

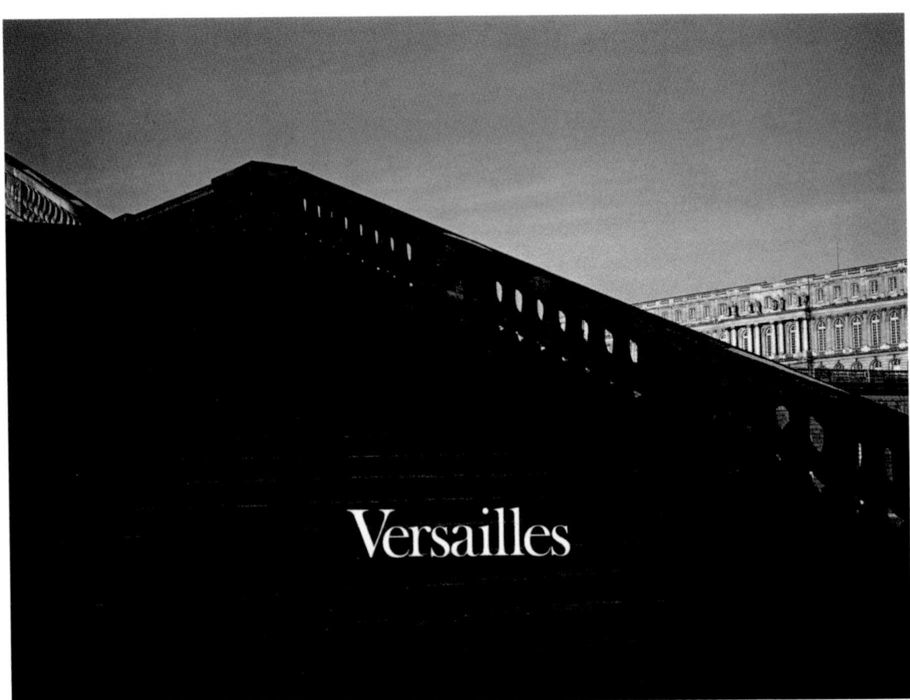

Jacques Dubois [France]

1912-1994; born in Versailles
Invited to join AGI, 1952

Jacques studied at the École Nationale des Arts Décoratifs and briefly at Cassandre's *'private'* school, both in Paris. As assistant to Jean Carlu, he collaborated on the Publicity Pavilion at the Paris Expo 1937. In a large mural he depicted all the well-known advertising characters of the day, including Bibendum the Michelin man, the two St Raphael waiters and Cassandre's Dubonnet man; they *'met'* each other in a surreal mountain landscape. As an excellent photographer he worked in North Africa for a shipping company. During WW2, he produced textile designs and theatre sets.

Dubois was a gifted poster designer, working for the French Tourist Office (1946–68). Other important postwar clients were Vittel, Pathé-Marconi, Longines, Air France, Larousse and Crédit Lyonnais and Van Cleef & Arpels. For his photographs of the 300-year-old Saint Gobain glassworks he won an international award in Genoa 1966. His work is in the collection of the Musée de l'Art Moderne, Paris. His masterpiece is probably *Versailles*, a photo book with a great layout, on the Palace of Versailles over the four seasons. It is very poetic and shows an enormous dedication to this extraordinary place in the city where Dubois himself lived for many years.

Versailles (x 2), photography and book design, 1981.

Dubois was a photographer and designer. For a prestige publication for Braun Druckerei in Mulhouse (Elzas) he took a picture of half an apple and replaced the pips with two identical emeralds. He called it **How to Make an Apple Talk**.

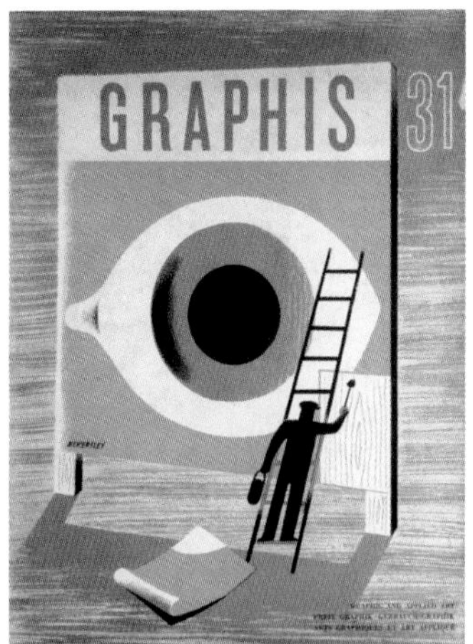

Extension of the Piccadilly Line to Heathrow Airport, poster published by London Transport Executive, 1971.

London Transport Collection, poster published by London Transport Executive, 1975.

Graphis #31, magazine cover, published by Graphis Press, Zürich, 1950.

Tom Eckersley [UK]

1914-1997; born in Lowton, Lancashire
Invited to join AGI, 1952

Eckersley studied at Salford School of Art (1930–34), where he met Eric Lombers. They co-operated in London till the outbreak of the war. They were acknowledged as two of the foremost poster designers in Britain, working for the BBC and the Post Office, Frank Pick of London Transport and Jack Beddington at Shell-Mex and BP. Tom was visiting lecturer at Westminster School of Art (1937–39). During the war he worked as a cartographer for the RAF, also designing many posters for the GPO and the Royal Society for the Prevention of Accidents.

These posters reveal his willingness to engage with modernism to promote progressive social policies and worker welfare. He was given an OBE, elected RDI in 1963, and awarded the CSD medal in 1990. After 1945 he continued his design practice and his involvement in education. In 1970 he was visiting lecturer at Yale University. In 1958–76 he was head of the design department of the London School of Printing (now London College of Communication); the Eckersley archive is now held by this college. His work is represented in many museums: the V&A, Imperial War Museum, NY MoMA and Stedelijk Museum Amsterdam.

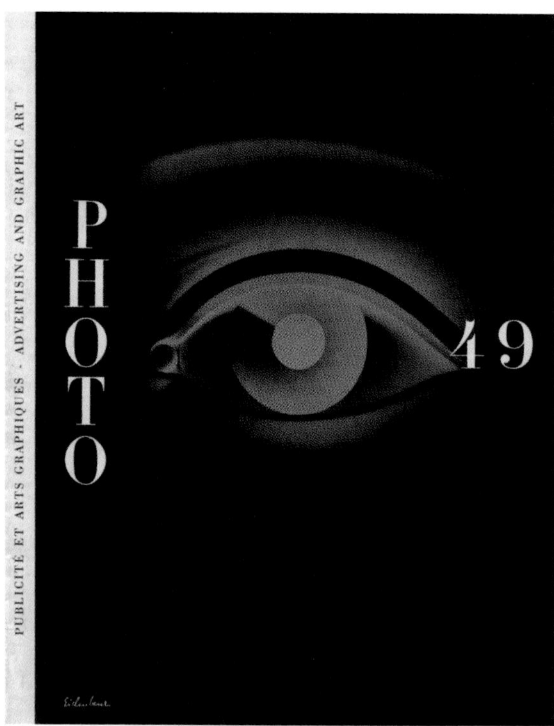

Hermann Eidenbenz [Switzerland]

1902-1993; born in Cannanore, India
Invited to join AGI, 1952

Initially trained at a commercial lithographer, Hermann studied for two years at the Zürich Kunstgewerbeschule and subsequently for three years at the studio of Professors Hadank and Deffke in Berlin. He taught design in Magdeburg, Germany (1926–32) and then went to Basel, where he shared a studio with his brothers Reinhold and Willy.
He worked on the Swiss pavilion at the Paris Expo 1937 and the Milan Triennale of 1940. Hermann later came back to Basel as an educator and also taught in Braunschweig and designed that city's coat of arms. In 1955–67 he was a consultant/designer with the advertising department of the Hamburg cigarette firm Reemtsma.

He also worked as a freelance designer. Hermann produced many posters, logos and the 10 and 20 Swiss franc banknotes. He also won a competition to design banknotes for West Germany. In 1953 he enriched the graphic design profession with his typeface Clarendon (Linotype). When an AGI exhibition was held at the Kunstgewerbemuseum, Hamburg, Eidenbenz made its striking poster. His special AGI logo appeared on the cover of Henrion's *AGI Annals* in 1989. Eidenbenz had exhibitions in Zürich, Hamburg, Basel and New York.

20 Swiss franc banknote, Swiss National Bank, Berne, 1954.

Photo 49, brochure of advertising and graphic art, 1949.

AGI logo, 1964. Later used for the cover of FHK Henrion's book *AGI Annals*.

Logo for **Halag linen trading**, Basel.

Logo for **Swiss Film Archive**, Lausanne.

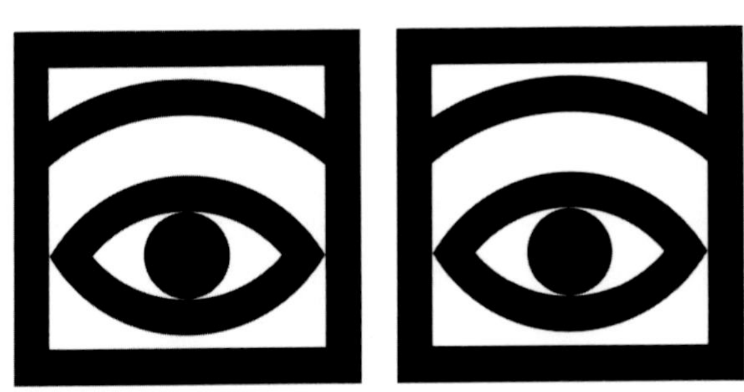

This logo for the confectionery company **Mazetti** was the winner of an international competition, 1955.

Poster for the **Lucerne International Music Festival**, 1969.

Logo for **Nessim carpet stores**, 1958.

Olle Eksell [Sweden]

1918–2007; born in Insjön
Invited to join AGI, 1952

Eksell studied with Hugo Steiner, Prague in 1939–41. He trained at the Art Center College of Design in Los Angeles in 1946–47. In 1947 he organized the first exhibition of American commercial art in Sweden. He was among the few Europeans to be included at the international packaging exhibition at NY MoMA. His work was shown in numerous exhibitions in Paris, London, Lausanne, Helsinki, Jerusalem, Milan, Vienna, and more. His designs featured in magazines, books, newspapers, and radio and television programmes.

He was included in books like *42 Years of Graphis Covers* (1987), *World Trademarks and Logotypes I and II* (1986 and 1987), *First Choice* (1989), and *World Trademarks: 100 Years* (1997). Eksell pioneered corporate identity programmes, worked on book illustrations and advertising, and wrote five books and many articles on design, advertising, architecture and professional training. He was elected to the Platina Academy (a kind of Hall of Fame), is an honorary member of the Society of Swedish Designers, and holds the state-awarded title of Professor. Eksell was the subject of a major exhibition in 1999 at the Malmö Form Design Centre; it later travelled to Vaxsjö and Stockholm. The monograph *Olle Eksell: Swedish Graphic Designer* was published in Japan in 2006.

Dick Elffers [The Netherlands]

1910-1990; born in Rotterdam
Invited to join AGI, 1952

A very versatile man: an exhibition and graphic designer, illustrator, painter, muralist. This wide scope stamped him as a real individualist, who would later despise the concept of design groups. He studied 1929–33 in Rotterdam at the Academy of Art, before becoming an assistant to Paul Schuitema and Piet Zwart. His studio was destroyed by the devastating German air attack on Rotterdam, May 1940. He then moved to Amsterdam, where he became a member of an underground artists' group, who used their graphic skills to forge identity papers.

His Resistance poster (1946) is famous; 40 years later he produced a remake. He also designed national memorial exhibitions in Auschwitz (1980) and Westerbork (1983). He won the H.N. Werkman Award in 1949. Worked for many years on posters and programmes for the Holland Festival (1954–67): his work for the Arnhem Film Festival was equally colourful and strong. Dick designed the graphic industry's annual of 1952. He experimented constantly with printing tecniques. He was the designer of many books and covers, and created several Dutch stamps. He left AGI after a few years. Two monographs were published about him. His work was the first to be included in NAGO, the Dutch Archives of Graphic Design.

Poster for the **Holland Festival**, 1962.

Poster for the **Holland Festival**, 1969.

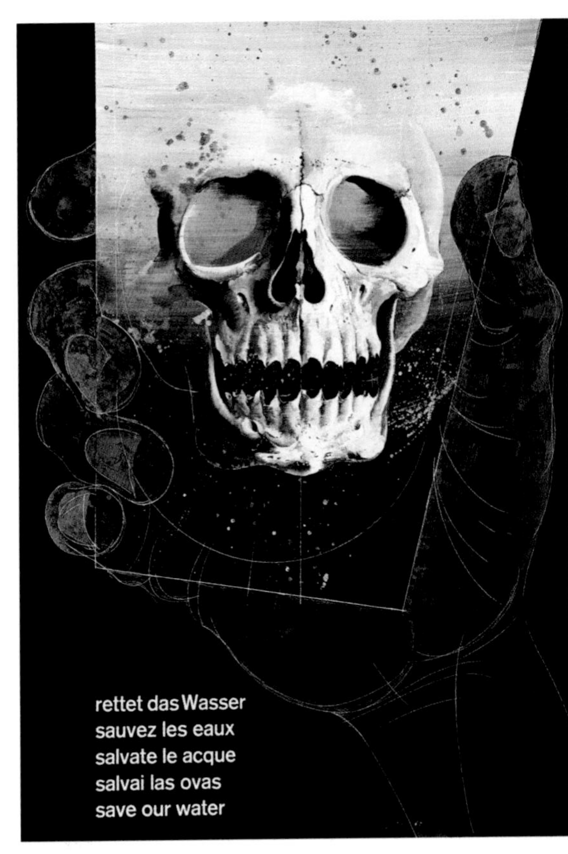

rettet das Wasser
sauvez les eaux
salvate le acque
salvai las ovas
save our water

Berner Oberland, Swiss regional tourist poster, 1956.

Save Our Water, poster, 1961.

Hans Erni [Switzerland]

1909– born in Lucerne
Invited to join AGI, 1952

Erni was closer to fine art than the majority of his colleagues, which does not mean that his applied works were less important than his paintings, murals and prints. He started his career (1924–27) as a surveyor's assistant and an architect's draughtsman, but attended the Lucerne Kunstgewerbeschule, the Académie Julian in Paris and the Berliner Staatsakademie. He travelled the world, lived for some time by turns in Paris and Lucerne. He was impressed by Picasso and Braque, and met Arp, Brancusi, Calder and Mondrian.

Hans Erni made a 100-metre mural for the 1939 Swiss Expo in Zürich, on the theme of *'Switzerland, Holiday Resort for the World'*, depicting nature and mankind coming together. The majority of the 200 posters he designed had an existential message: human rights, the right to vote, pure water, the endangered forests, the nuclear threat, hunger. His work was unique, not only in his fine sensitive lines, but also in his well-chosen subjects. On his optimistic side, he enjoyed the pleasures of horse riding and the circus, but also the beauty of nature and culture. His artistic production was large, and he sometimes used the pseudonym of François Greques.

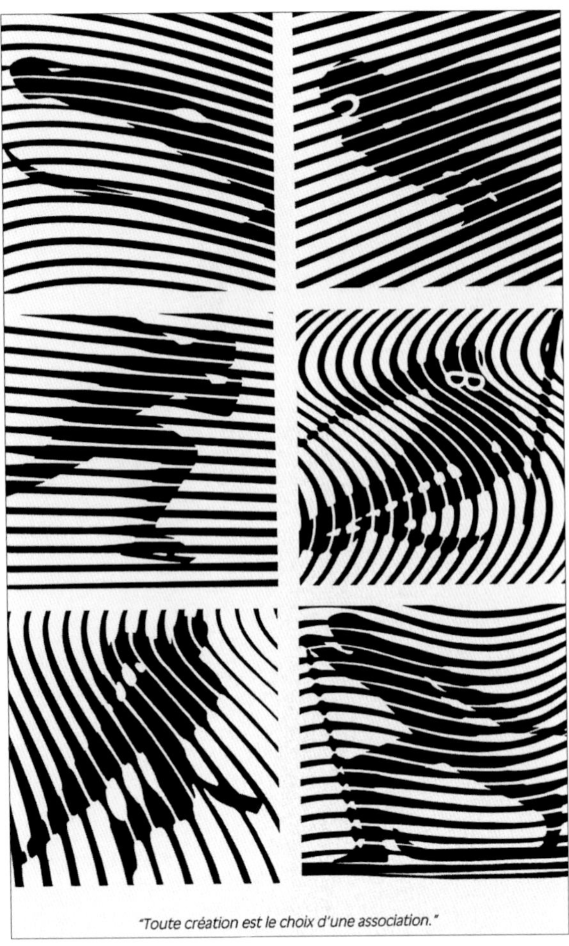

Roger Excoffon [France]

1910-1983; born in Marseille
Invited to join AGI, 1952

Excoffon was not only a graphic designer, but even more a typographer and type designer. Studied law in Aix-en-Provence, but later painting in Paris. He worked as an art director of the Marseilles type foundry *'Olive'*. He opened his own studio in 1947 and founded with others the advertising agency U&O (Urbi et Orbi) in 1957. He specialized in letterforms. His typeface *'Nord'* grew out to be the most famous logotype for Air France.

According to Henrion he was a very elegant man: *"His elegance found constant expression in the line, drawn by pencil or more often brush, to convey a kind of visual shorthand to depict flight, fashion, fowl, figure or fancy, just like the flowing precision of the many typefaces he created: Mistral (1953), Choc (1955), Calypso (1958) and Antique Olive (1962-1966). He was the only western designer to excel in the Chinese brush stroke technique"*. In 1968 he made the designs for the Winter Olympics of Grenoble. He started his agency Excoffon Conseil in 1972. Roger made numerous poster designs for Air France, Bally shoes, Dunlop, SNCF, among others. He received many national and international prizes and honours.

Poster and pictograms for the **Grenoble Winter Olympics**, 1968.

Mistral typeface, 1953.

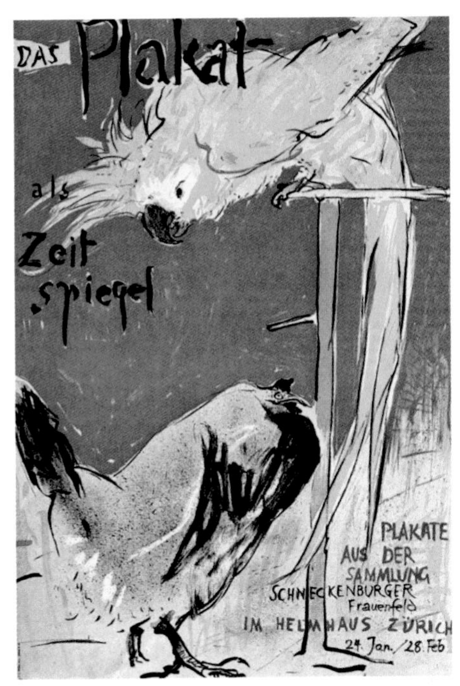

Swiss National Exhibition, Lausanne, poster, 1964.

The Poster as a Mirror of Time, exhibition poster, Zürich, 1949.

PKZ Menswear, advertising poster, 1944.

Hans Falk [Switzerland]

1918-2002; born in Zürich
Invited to join AGI, 1952

Falk was taught by Joseph and Max von Moos at the Kunstgewerbeschule in Lucerne (1935). Educated as a graphic designer by Albert Rüegg in Zürich. Won second prize (among 900 contributions) for the poster of the Swiss National Expo 1939. He was a collaborator of Walter Herdeg, the editor of *Graphis* (1939–41). Shared a studio with his friend Werner Bischof, photographer. Taught at the Zürich Kunstgewerbeschule 1950–55. His many posters were often drawn directly on the lithographic stone. He preferred to work for social causes, political groups, the theatre, tourism and the circus.

In 1957 he stopped working on commercial art in order to concentrate on his painting. However, he still entered his abstract paintings as proposals for the posters of the 1964 Swiss Expo in Lausanne. In spite of their minimal lettering, they were accepted and proved to be an outstanding success. He became a printmaker and painter on the international scene. He lived in Britain, Ireland, New York and the Italian island of Stromboli. He accompanied Circus Knie around Switzerland. In 2002 he created two Europa stamps for Switzerland; these works were exhibited together with 40 other pieces in Zürich.

André François [France]

1915-2005; born in Timisoara, Romania
Invited to join AGI, 1952

Trained at the School of Fine Arts in Budapest, André Farkas moved to France in 1934, where he joined Cassandre at the École des Beaux-Arts in Paris. He changed his surname when he became a French citizen. He lived in the French countryside from 1945 where, in December 2002, his atelier burned down, destroying almost his complete oeuvre. Six months later the Centre Pompidou in Paris exhibited 60 of his earliest works. When in 2002 the famous early poster designer Henri de Toulouse-Lautrec was commemorated with a great show and book, 87-year old André produced his own contribution.

Cartoons, illustrations, (childrens') books, covers, (theatre) posters, stage settings and ballet costumes, animated films, advertisements, paintings and sculptures: François did it all. His prolific, humane, poetic work was witty and innovative, and was admired in exhibitions throughout the world. It was published in *Graphis*, *Punch*, *Lilliput* and *The New Yorker*. He also drew advertisements for Citroën and *Le Nouvel Observateur*. André was made a Royal Designer for Industry and was awarded a doctorate by the Royal College of Art, London (1977). From the early 1960s, the Sunday painter François became a Sunday designer and a weekday fine artist.

Poster for **DOP shampoo**, 1955.

Poster for **Pirelli**, 1960.

God Save Our Queen. Commissioned by Shell-Mex and BP London for the coronation celebrations, 1953.

Circus. Two-sheet poster, published by London Transport Executive, 1937. This poster is a technically complex demonstration of lithography which made use of the most up-to-date inks and effects available.

Barnett Freedman [UK]

1901-1958; born in London
Invited to join AGI, 1952

While spending four years in hospital as a kid, Barnett Freedman began to focus on drawing. In 1916–22 he took evening classes at St Martin's School of Art and was helped to a full-time scholarship at the Royal College of Art. He took a teaching position at the Working Men's College in London, but fell ill again and had to give it up. He then began to illustrate and became a part-time instructor at the RCA and the Ruskin School of Drawing in Oxford. Now trained as a lithographer, he made a series of very individual, colourful and decorative posters, especially for the Post Office, and book jackets.

He worked for Frank Pick at London Transport Board and for Shell-Mex in the 30s, and illustrated for several publishers. In 1936 he designed the stamp for King George V's Silver Jubilee. During WW2 he became an official war artist, creating drawings, watercolours and oil paintings. He illustrated *Jane Eyre*, *Wuthering Heights*, Walter de la Mare's *Love*, *War and Peace* and *Anna Karenina* (for the NY Limited Editions Club). Barnett had many solo and group exhibitions, both during his life and long after.

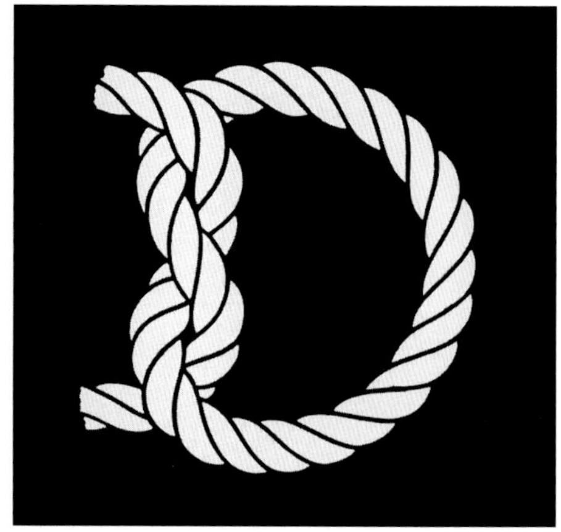

Pierre Gauchat [Switzerland]

1902-1956; born in Zürich
Invited to join AGI, 1952

Gauchat studied at the Kunstgewerbeschule Zürich where he later became a teacher. He also studied in Munich. After his studies he worked for some time as a lithographer. He then became a freelance designer of books, posters (with Bally as his most famous client), stamps, industrial and general advertising.

In 1941 he was the founder of the Swiss Poster of the Year competition, which still exists today. After WW2, the Swiss National Bank held a competition for new banknotes, which Gauchat won with his beautiful 50, 100, 500 and 1000 Swiss franc notes (Hermann Eidenbenz won for the 10 and 20 franc notes). These symbolized values like fertility and motherhood, love of one's neighbour and, rather less optimistically, death. It took a long time before the notes were printed (1956–57) and it is not certain if he ever saw them before he died in 1956.

Poster for **Swiss Tourist Board**, 1940.

Olma St Gallen, poster for agricultural fair, 1950s.

Logo for **Denzler**, ropemakers, Zürich.

Ad for **Crawford's** advertising agency.

Contribution to the **De Jong & Co. Festschrift**, Hilversum, 1971.

Cover for his book **Advertising and the Artist**, 1956.

Ashley Havinden [UK]

1903-1973; born in Rochester, Kent
Invited to join AGI, 1952
International President 1956-1960

A British advertising designer who worked for no less than 45 years at one place: the ad agency W.S. Crawford's. Known by all simply as Ashley, he dominated modernist commercial work in Britain. He believed that *'designers are problem-solvers'*. Influenced by Cubism, Futurism and the Bauhaus, he dared to introduce bold sans serif typefaces into advertising, back in the 1920s. He advocated great freedom in style and typographic choices and an unusual range of illustrative possibilities. His agency served them all: the Milk Marketing Board, Simpson, the GPO, DAKS, Liberty, and Wolsey. For Chrysler, his 1925 campaign showed his dynamic illustrations and heavy block letters, which were later cut as an alphabet for Monotype; as was a brush script he had made. The Chrysler campaign was most successful and had many imitators. Ashley was elected a Royal Designer for Industry in 1947 and in 1951 received an OBE for his services to graphic design. He was president of SIAD in 1953. He was the author of *Line Drawing for Reproduction* (1933, 1941) and *Advertising and the Artist* (1956).

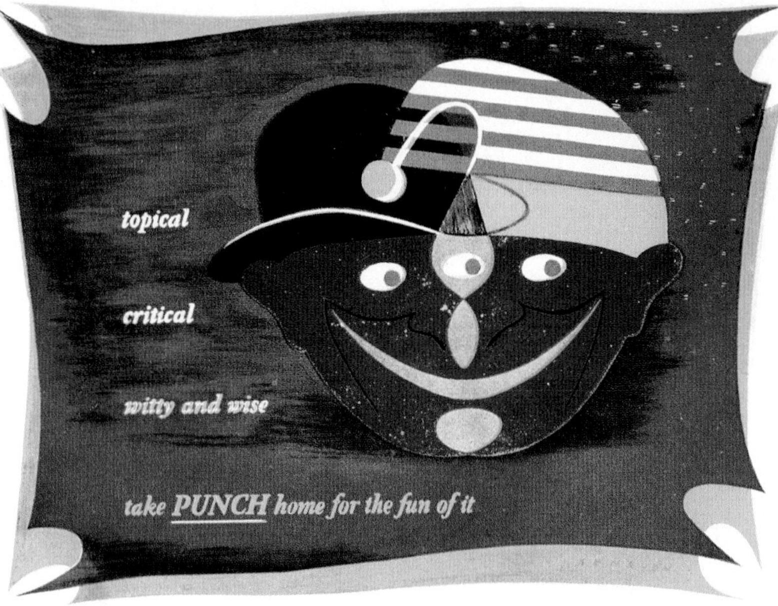

F.H.K. Henrion [UK]

1914-1990; born in Nuremburg, Germany
Invited to join AGI, 1952
International President 1963-1967/1976-1977

Frederic Henri Kay Henrion, or *'Henri'* for short, studied at the École Paul Colin, Paris. He emigrated to England in 1936. Working during WW2 in the UK Ministry of Information and for the US Office of War Information, he designed exhibitions, posters and publications. He was a true pioneer of corporate design in Europe, responsible for the image for KLM Royal Dutch Airlines, British European Airlines, InterRent, Coopers & Lybrand, British Leyland, London Electricity Board. His firm Henrion Design Associates (1951), which became HDA International in 1972, did corporate identity projects for numerous leading international companies.

Henrion wrote an early and much valued book on this *'new'*, complicated subject with his friend Alan Parkin. He was the author/designer of *AGI Annals* (1990), the predecessor of this very book. Taught at the Royal College of Art and the London College of Printing. He was a president and frequently a board member of AGI, SIAD and Icograda. His flair for languages was unique. Henrion organized the annual Icograda Student Seminars in London (1974–90), an eagerly awaited event on the UK college calendar, which also attracted many students from all continents.

Four Hands, 1943. Poster for the US Office of War Information in London.

Punch, 1948. Poster from a series of double faces.

Philips Philishave, one of 14 advertising images from 1957, featuring the Philishave Rotary Man who was introduced in 1955 on Henrion's Philishave poster commissioned by Erwin Wasey for Philips.

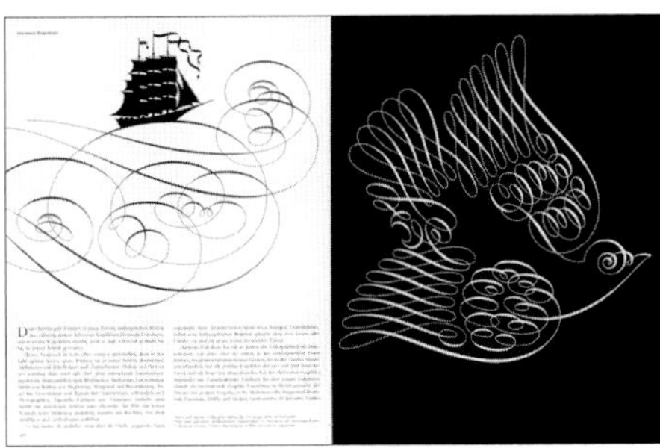

Spread from an article on Hermann Eidenbenz in **Graphis # 206**, 1979.

Logo for **Café Littéraire**, Zürich.

Travel brochure to promote **St Moritz**, 1932.

Walter Herdeg [Switzerland]

1908-1995; born in Zürich
Invited to join AGI, 1952

Walter Herdeg studied at the Kunstgewerbeschule in Zürich and subsequently at the Staatliche Academie für Freie und Angewandte Kunst in Berlin (under O.H.W. Hadank). Continued his studies in Paris, London and New York. His first commission in Switzerland was the design of the visual identity of St Moritz. He opened his own advertising agency and publishing house with Walter Amstutz. Started as the editor/designer of the bi-monthly, authoritative and respected magazine *Graphis* in 1944. He was secretary general of AGI 1975–85.

The annuals came later: *Graphis Annual* 1952, *Photo Graphis* 1966, *Graphis Posters* 1974, *Graphis Diagrams* 1976. The rigid selection of works he published in the magazine and books was no doubt quite subjective; illustrative work seemed to be his preference. Steven Heller wrote: *'He had passionate likes and dislikes, and a few heroes too.'* In 1986 he handed *Graphis* over to B. Martin Pedersen. He was given the Walter Design Award by Parsons School of Design and the AIGA Medal, both in New York, 1987. To quote Steven Heller once more: *'I think these were the two happiest moments in a life that brought insight and inspiration to others.'*

George Him [UK]

1900-1982; born in Lódz, Poland
Invited to join AGI, 1952

After studying religious history (Moscow, Berlin and Bonn), Him went for four years to the Staatliche Akademie für Graphische Künsten und Buchwerbe in Leipzig. Worked freelance for a while in Germany and started a unique, complementary partnership with Jan Lewitt. The two created a wonderful children's book, *Lokomotywa*. They left Poland in 1937 for London. When their work was shown by Lund-Humphries, many advertising commissions followed. During WW2 Lewitt and Him designed posters for ROSPA, the GPO and the London-based Polish Ministry of Information. By late 1942 they were concentrating on children's books, posters and murals for war factory canteens. After the war they designed murals for the Festival of Britain (1951) and the Guinness Festival Clock. The poster for American Overseas Airlines is typical for their joint output. Their work was exhibited in Jerusalem, Tel-Aviv, New York and Philadelphia. In 1954 their partnership was dissolved. George made unique work for Schweppes drinks (creating the land of 'Schweppshire') and co-operated in 1963 with Dutch designer Otto Treumann on the corporate identity of El-Al, designing a logo in both Hebrew and Roman lettering. He was a fellow of RSA and elected a Royal Designer for Industry.

American Overseas Airlines, poster, collaboration between Him and Lewitt, 1946–48.

Advertisement for **Schweppes**. This successful and highly witty campaign ran for some 15 years during the 1950s and 1960s.

Top People Take *The Times* Wherever They Go, poster, 1955.

Festival d'Avignon, theatre poster, TNP.

Paul Foster: *Tom Paine*, theatre poster, TNP.

Rezvani: *Capitaine Schelle, Capitaine Eçço*, theatre poster, TNP.

Theatre National Populaire (TNP), poster. Chosen by Jacno as his favourite piece of work in the book *First Choice* by Ken Cato.

Marcel Jacno [France]

1904-1989; born in Paris
Invited to join AGI, 1952

Marcel Jacno was a self-taught graphic and type designer and typographer. His best-known design was the Gauloises cigarettes package that he produced in 1936 and refined in 1946. Over 70 million of these were printed each week in the 60s. His other major achievement was the design of several fonts for the type foundry Deberny et Peignot. He designed Le Film (1934), Scribe (1937), Jacno (1950) and the stencil typeface Chaillot (1954), used for the logo of the Théatre National Populaire (TNP) and shown on more than 100 TNP posters. Composition, form and typography were completely integrated and his posters were always recognized, even before they were read.

He also designed lettering for movie titles. Among his other clients were Courvoisier, Guerlain and Shell. He taught advertising at the École Technique de Publicité and the École de l'Union des Arts Décoratifs in Paris. Jacno was the author of *Anatomie de la lettre* (1978). Although he received an Oscar de la Publicité in 1968 for his work and many other awards, he remained a modest and self-effacing man.

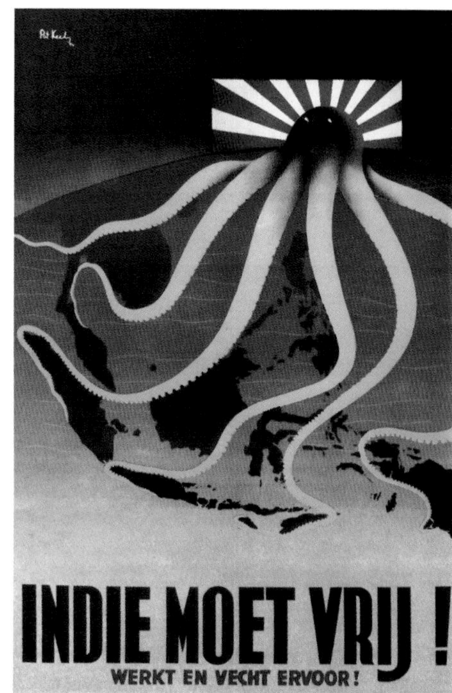

Pat Keely [UK]

(?)-1970; born in Nottingham
Invited to join AGI, 1952

Mostly self-taught, Patrick Cokayne Keely was a distinguished poster designer. Before WW2 he created posters for London Transport, the Southern Railway, the Post Office and British Aluminium Co. During the war, Keely, like Tom Eckersley, George Him, Jan Lewitt and many others, worked for ROSPA, designing posters for accident prevention. He used rich colours, which was rather unusual for that time. His poster *Lookout in the Blackout* (1940) was issued by the Ministry of War Transport and was one in a series in a campaign to reduce the number of accidents in the blackout.

He used only a few objects or symbols that resulted in a strong impact and visual message. Keely said: *'Deliver a message in shorthand, which is nevertheless understandable to everybody.'* He was a member of the Society of Industrial Artists. Part of his work is kept in the National Archives, London.

Join the War Volunteers, poster published by HMSO, London, on behalf of the Free Dutch Government, 1944.

Join Your Savings Group Now, poster published by the HMSO, London for the GPO, 1940 and in subsequent editions

Post Early in the Day, poster published by the HMSO, London for the GPO, 1937.

Liberate the East Indies, poster published by HMSO, London, on behalf of the Free Dutch Government, 1944.

Tribune de Lausanne, poster, 1955.

SSB Super, Swiss Railway poster, 1978.

Rössli Cigars, poster, 1954.

Herbert Leupin [Switzerland]

1916-1999; born in Beinwil
Invited to join AGI, 1952

After a difficult and secluded period of his childhood in his *'father's'* kitchen (his parents owned a restaurant in Augst near Basel), he studied at the Kunstgewerbeschule in Basel (1932–35). He received his practical education with Hermann Eidenbenz. In 1936 Herbert went to Paris to study at the École Paul Colin. In 1938, he started his own studio and designed record sleeves and advertising, but mainly posters. With his lyrical and childlike sense of humour and his lightness of touch he became one of the most distinguished Swiss poster designers.

He received many awards, among them those from the ADC Chicago (1960), Warsaw Poster Biennale (1968) and in 1974 the Ernst Litfass Medal in Kassel. Many exhibitions were held all over the world, including Chicago, Offenbach, Hamburg and his last one, at the Ginza Graphic Gallery (GGG) in Tokyo in 1998, one year before his death. The work shown there was from his most productive years, between 1937–74. Throughout his life he made more than 500 posters. In his later years he illustrated children's books, very successfully. From 1970 on he was also a painter.

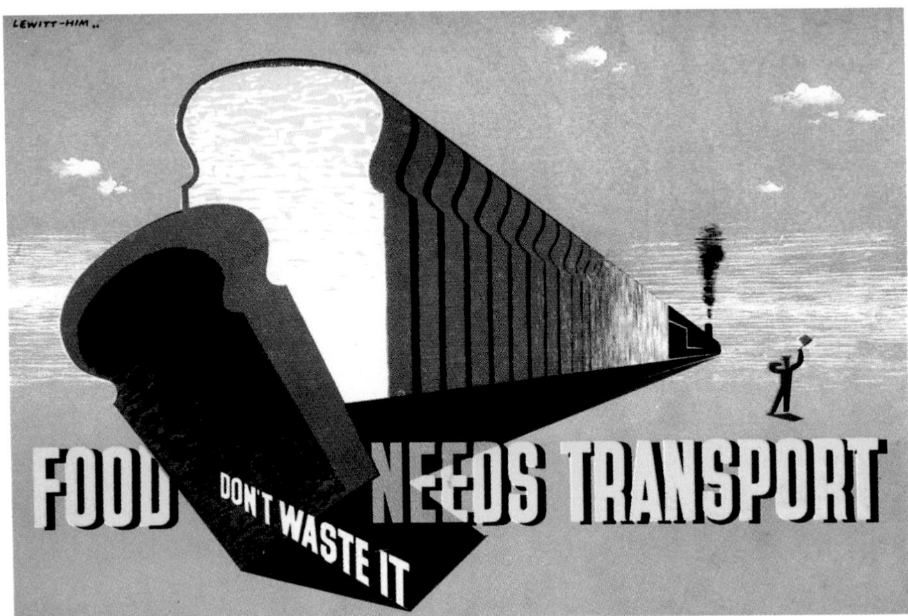

Jan Lewitt [UK]

1907-1991; born in Czestochowa, Poland
Invited to join AGI, 1952

Lewitt was *'the other half'* of a very close partnership with George Him (see also George Him). After his schooling Jan travelled for three years in Europe and the Middle East, and *'tried to make a living in thirteen different occupations'*, but finally began to work as a self-taught graphic artist and designer. In 1925 he designed his first Hebrew typeface, Chaim. When he met George Him in 1933 in Warsaw, they immediately felt like professional twins. In Poland and later in Britain they created wonderful children's books and posters.

After the end of their partnership in 1954, Lewitt decided to concentrate on painting, but he also designed costumes and scenery for Sadler's Wells Ballet, produced tapestries and worked in glass.

American Overseas Airlines, poster, collaboration between Him and Lewitt, 1946–48.

Food Needs Transport, poster, collaboration between Him and Lewitt, 1944.

Contribution to the **De Jong & Co. Festschrift**, Hilversum, 1971.

School mural, 1960s.
Photo: Staffan Larsson.

Stoneware, 1950s.
Photo: Lasse Yrlid.

Wrapping paper for **Gustavsberg** china factory.

Stig Lindberg [Sweden]

1916-1982; born in Umeå
Invited to join AGI, 1952

Stig Lindberg was one of the most important postwar Swedish designers. He studied at the National College of Art, Craft and Design (Konstfack). Soon after his graduation, in 1937, he was hired by Gustavsberg potteries, where he became art director and chief designer. He was responsible for all their china design and utilitarian ceramics, and developed painted decorations for enamelware. He also designed wrapping paper, packaging, witty posters, exhibitions, textiles and children's books. He stayed at Gustavsberg until 1978 and started his own studio in Italy in 1980. His work can still be found in museums and galleries in various countries.

Jean-Denis Malclès [France]

1912-1962; born in Paris
Invited to join AGI, 1952

Thanks to Florence Robert: *'His father was a painter and ornamental woodcarver, so it was natural that he joined the woodcarving department at the École Boulle in 1927. After completing his studies, he began working with the cabinetmaker Ruhlmann before doing his military service in Nancy. He then went to a silk-painting studio where he stayed till 1936. At an exhibition, he met Jean-Pierre Grenier of the Grenier-Hussenot theatre company who commissioned him to design sets for a show that he was preparing for the Libération (Malclès had already worked for the Comedie Française). This meeting was the turning point in his career. He created many sets and costumes (Comédie Française, Ballet des Champs-Elysées, Covent Garden Opera Company, London), as well as posters for stage shows including the mime artist Marcel Marceau and the singing group Les Frères Jacques, for whom he first designed costumes in 1944.'*

Malclès was a man of many talents. He was not only a furniture and textile designer, but also produced sculptures, interior design and typography. He excelled in them all, yet he eventually concentrated on costume and stage design for theatre and ballet in Paris and London. He was elected a member for his outstanding illustrations and posters. (We were unable to find more details about him; even Internet couldn't help us out).

Poster for **Les Frères Jacques**, 1950s.

Poster for **Vidal picture framing**, 1950s.

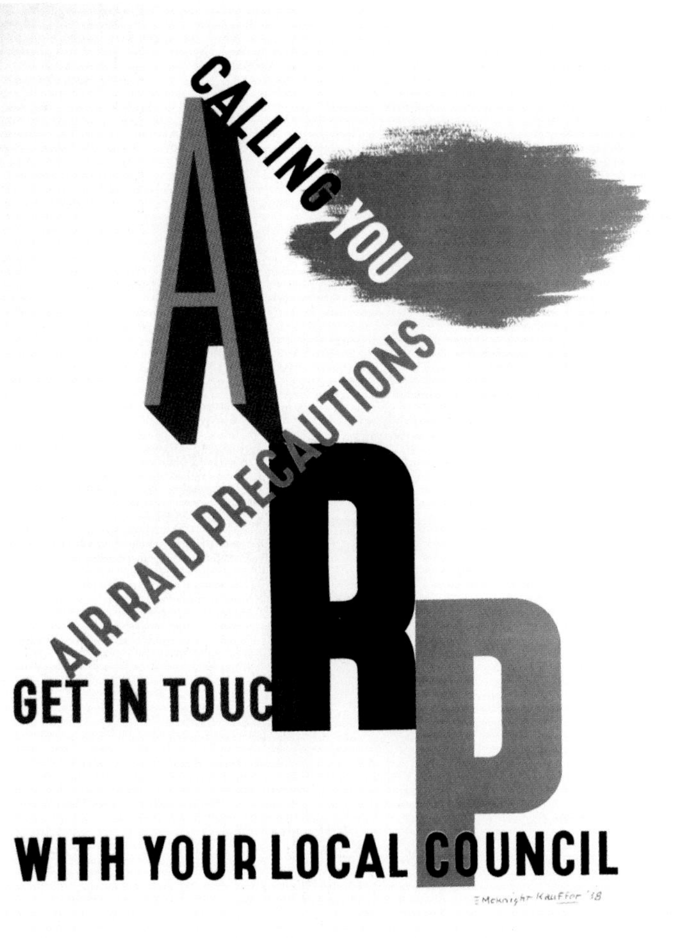

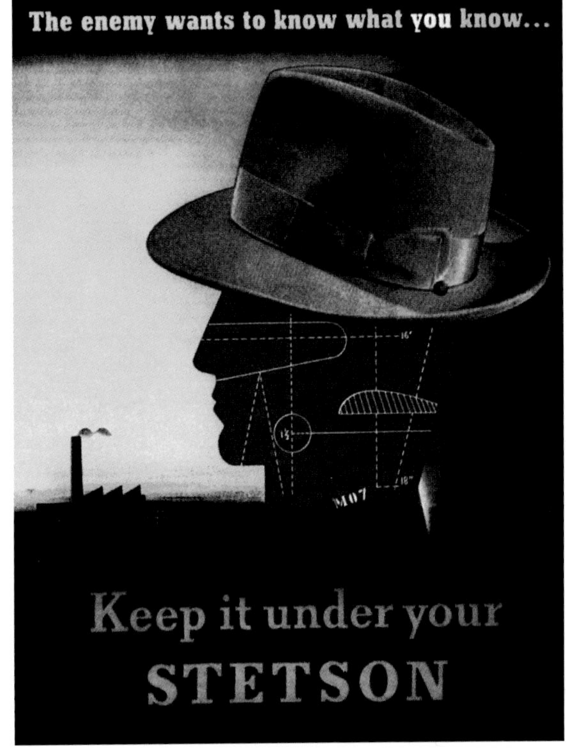

Air Raid Precautions, poster, published by HMSO, London, 1938.

Ask for BP Ethyl. Lorry bill poster published by Shell-Mex and BP, London, 1933.

Keep It Under Your Stetson, advertisement in *Life* magazine, 1947.

Edward McKnight Kauffer [UK]

1890-1954; born in Great Falls, Montana, USA
Invited to join AGI, 1952

Kauffer studied at evening classes in San Francisco, went to Chicago Art Institute and attended the controversial Armory Show. He added 'McKnight' to his name in gratitude to Professor McKnight, who gave him $12,000 to study painting in Paris (1913). He moved to London at the outbreak of WW1 and was commissioned to design the first of more than 140 posters by Frank Pick of the London Underground. For eighteen months he worked for Ashley Havinden at Crawford's. He switched from painter to commercial artist, associated with the Cumberland Market Group and the Vorticists. His painting experience was a great help. His figurative style changed to embrace Cubism, Art Deco and Futurism (the *Daily Herald* poster *'Flight of Birds'*, 1919). Shell, BP, Eastman & Sons were among his clients. Edward was also a book designer, and produced set designs, murals and textiles. He returned to the US and worked in New York. American Airlines and Subway advertising became his clients after the war. In 1937, NY MoMA gave him a one-man show; the Victoria & Albert Museum followed in 1955. A collection of his work is held at the V&A Library, London.

Pierre Monnerat [Switzerland]

1917-(?); born in Paris, France
Invited to join AGI, 1952

At first, Monnerat studied architecture and some time later design in Lausanne at the École Cantonale des Beaux-Arts et d'Art Appliqué, where he himself became a professor 20 years later. From 1940 he worked as a freelance designer in Lausanne, for Swiss and international clients. He made many labels, advertisements and booklets for local firms, such as the wine and cheese industry. He designed posters for Swiss Railways, for tourism and Cinzano, produced layouts and covers for the magazine *Publicité et Arts Graphiques*, and illustrated a children's bible. His style was more French than Swiss, often humorous, always easy and delightful.

Pierre also painted, did murals and sculpture and designed stage sets. Between 1958 and 1964 he was a member of the Organization Committee and Graphic Advisors for the Swiss Expo 1964 in Lausanne. He ran his own École d'Art Graphique Monnerat in Lausanne 1970–74. Monnerat disappeared to South America in the late sixties and later moved to Spain, where he worked on children's books. An article on him was published in *Graphis* # 13.

Cinzano, poster, 1961.

Cover for the graphic design annual **Publicité 11**, 1958.

Say Skiing, Say Switzerland, tourist poster, 1955.

Josef Müller-Brockmann [Switzerland]

Overtaking? If in doubt, never!, poster for Swiss Automobile Association, 1957.

Werner Bischof: The Photographic Work, exhibition poster, Basel Museum of Applied Arts, 1958.

June Festival, poster, Zürich, 1959.

1914-1996; born in Rapperswil
Invited to join AGI, 1952

As there were far too many Josef Müllers in his country, JMB added his wife's surname to his own. Nonetheless, his fame as a designer, typographer, teacher and writer on the International Typographic Style would have easily helped him to single him out. In Zürich he studied at the Kunstgewerbeschule and University (architecture, design and history of art). After an apprenticeship he started his studio in Zürich, specializing in photography, graphics and exhibitions, including the Swiss National Expo 1939. He is particularly famous for his concert posters for the Zürich Tonhalle, beginning in 1951, influenced by Constructivism.

JMB was a founder and co-editor of the trilingual magazine *Neue Graphik* (1968). He taught at the Kunstgewerbeschule, the Ulm Hochschule für Gestaltung and at universities in Japan and the US. He was the European design consultant for IBM (a counterpart of Paul Rand), was responsible for the signage of Zürich Airport, designed the corporate identity for SBB Swiss Railways, and made theatre sets in Munich, Copenhagen and Zürich. Being a great adept of *'the grid'*, he wrote books including *Grid Systems in Graphic Design* (1981), *The History of Visual Communication* (1971), *History of the Poster* (1971) *and Foto-Plakate* (1989).

Bruno Munari [Italy]

1907-1998; born in Milan
Invited to join AGI, 1952

Picasso called him *'the new Leonardo'*. Munari, a self-taught man, was more than a graphic designer. He was an industrial designer, architect, writer, philosopher and educator, a man with a childlike imagination and a lot of knowledge, lucidity and humour, which he shared with everyone who knew him. In the 1920s he became involved in the Futurist movement. He worked as a photographer and graphic designer for Pirelli, Cinzano, IBM and Olivetti. After WW2, he started to work as an industrial and interior designer.

He challenged all conventions and stereotypes, pulling down barriers between architecture and design with his modest creativity and ingenuity. Munari created experimental sculptures that could collapse and fit inside a suitcase, simple but exquisite lamps, animated children's books, unreadable books (*Libri illegibili*), useless machines and many other beautiful artefacts. He wrote many books, and thanks to Edizione Corraini, many of those have been reprinted. He was awarded the Compasso d'Oro in 1954, 1955 and 1979. His advice: *'Take life as seriously as a game.'* One of his teachings: *'See the rainbow from the side.'*

The Tale of Tales, children's book.

In the Dark of the Night, picture book, 1956.

Unreadable book ML1, 1949.

La Pennellessa, art object, 1976.

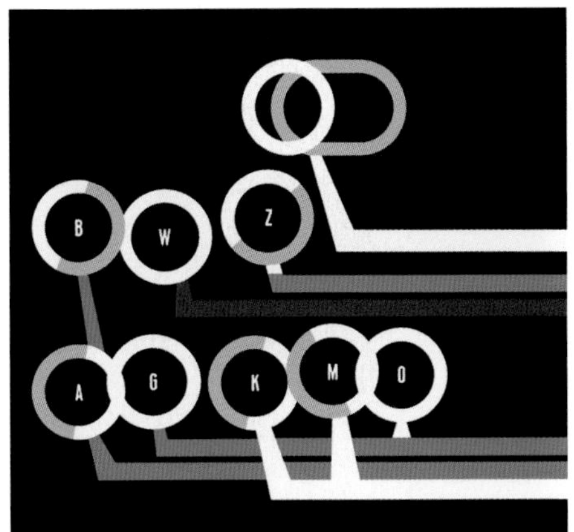

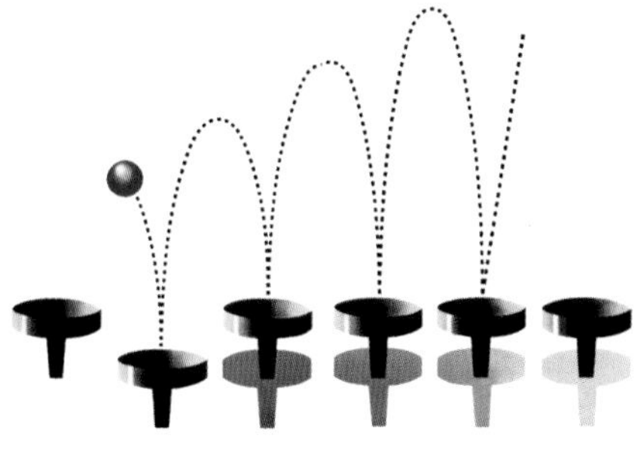

Olivetti Elettrosumma 22

Olivetti Graphika, advertisement, 1958.

Olivetti Lexicon, poster detail, 1953.

Olivetti 84, advertisement detail.

Poster to promote **Olivetti Elettrosumma**, 1956.

Giovanni Pintori [Italy]

1912-1999; born in Tresnuraghes, Sardinia
Invited to join AGI, 1952

After studying at ISIA in Monza in 1936, he started his career with Olivetti. From this time on his name was successfully linked to the Ivrea-based firm. He had a clear and conscious view of the mechanics and problems of graphic design. His work can be characterized as competent, professional, cultural and creative. Pintori designed many posters for advertising campaigns, print and exhibitions. He was, like many others, responsible for Olivetti's reputation all over the world. The Olivetti Exhibition 'Design in Industry', showing Pintori's work, was organized by NY MoMA in 1952. The Louvre in Paris (1955) also filled an entire hall with his work.

He was given the Palma d'Oro by the Italian Federation of Advertising (1950) and many other awards. A lot of articles on Pintori and about his designs appeared in many leading magazines, like *Fortune* (1953–57), In 1969 he left Olivetti, to start working as a freelance designer on projects for Pirelli, Ambrosetti and Gabbianelli. After his career he withdrew from the profession and became a painter. A retrospective exhibition was held in his honour in Nuoro in 2003.

RICHEZ

L'ATELIER RUE STE ANNE PRESENTE
TRILOGIE DU REVOIR
DE BOTHO STRAUSS
DECOR ET COSTUMES: CLAUDE LEMAIRE / MUSIQUE: JEAN-YVES BOSSEUR
REGIE GENERALE: JEAN-MARIE VERVISCH / MISE EN SCENE: PHILIPPE VAN KESSEL
AVEC HENRI BILLEN / FRANCINE BLISTIN / JEAN-CLAUDE DERUDDER / PATRICK DESCAMPS / CLAUDE ETIENNE / HELENE FRIEDLI
MICHELINE HARDY / CLAUDE KOENER / PIERRE LAROCHE / MARIE SYGNE LEDOUX / VINCENT LEMAITRE / FRANCIS MAHIEU / ESTELLE MARION
DENIS PANERAI / JEAN PASCAL / DENYSE PERIEZ / PHILIPPE PETIT / PHILIPPE VAN KESSEL
COPRODUCTION ATELIER RUE STE-ANNE / THEATRE DE LA PLACE
GRANDE SALLE / 75 RUE DES TANNEURS / 1000 BRUXELLES
DU 15 NOV. AU 15 DEC. 1984 / TOUS LES SOIRS A 20 h 15 / RELACHE DIMANCHES, LUNDIS
ET LE 5 DEC. / RESERVATIONS DE 14 A 18 h AU 02/513 19 28

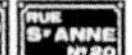

RICHEZ

THEATRE DE LA VIE
LE JEU DU MEDECIN MALGRE LUI
DE JEAN-BAPTISTE POQUELIN, DIT MOLIERE
AVEC MARC BAUDOUX, YANNICK DELULLE, NICOLE DUMEZ, IRENE FABRY,
BERNARD GILLARD ET ALAIN STEVENS / REGIE: SERGE SIMON
MISE EN SCENE: HERBERT ROLLAND
THEATRE DE LA VIE. 100 AVENUE DU HARAS. 1150 BRUXELLES
DU 16 DEC. AU 16 JANV. / DU MARDI AU SAMEDI A 20 H 30, LE DIMANCHE A 15 H 30.
RELACHE LE LUNDI, LE 25 DEC. ET DU 1er AU 5 JANV.
LOCATION: 02/762 71 32

Jacques Richez [Belgium]

1918-1994; born in Dieppe, France
Invited to join AGI, 1952

Richez, largely a self-taught man, had his formal training at the Académie Royale des Beaux-Arts in Mons, Belgium. After WW2, he started his own studio in Brussels where he mostly worked for advertising but also on cultural posters, logos and exhibitions. His reputation was made with the poster and booklet *Bâtir le monde pour l'homme* ('Building the World for Mankind') for the 1958 Brussels Expo. He created the overall design concept for the Kinshasa International Fair in 1969 and two murals for the Osaka Expo in 1970. Besides the fact that Richez was a gifted designer, he was also an excellent draughtsman and an experimental photographer. With his extraordinary skills he added new dimensions to drawing and photography. In 1973 he was chosen as one of the 40 most original artists in experimental photography by Time-Life in their *Photography Annual*. He wrote two books: *Graphic Art Applied to Communication* (1964) and *Texts and Pretexts: 25 Years of Reflecting on Graphic Design* (1980). In 1967 he became vice-president of Icograda and from 1972–76 of AGI, where he indefatigably *'preached'* ethics and professional integrity.

Botho Strauss: *Trilogie des Wiedersehens*, theatre poster for Théâtre de l'Atelier Rue Ste Anne, Brussels, 1985.

Molière: *Le Médecin Malgré Lui*, theatre poster. Chosen by Richez as his favourite piece of work in the book *First Choice* by Ken Cato.

Samuel Beckett: *Waiting for Godot*, theatre poster, 1984.

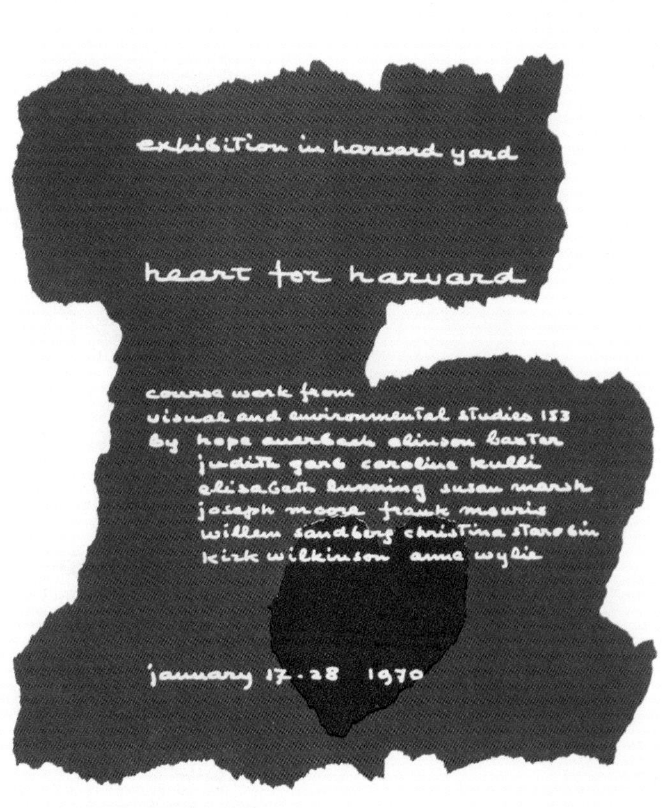

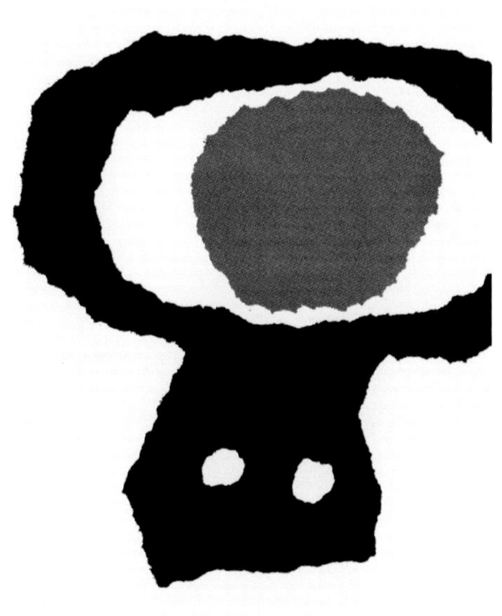

sandberg

die nützlichkeit eines

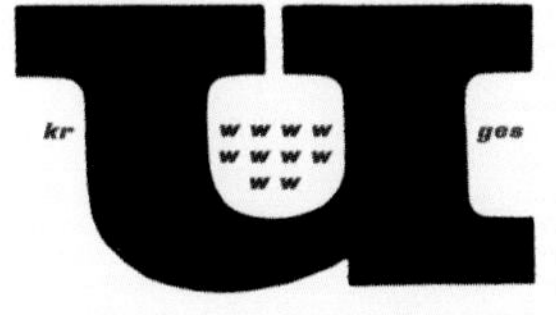

the inner

principle

Heart for Harvard, exhibition poster, 1970.

Open Eye, symbol for an avant-garde magazine, 1946.

The inner and the outer form, a typical Sandberg typographical exercise, 1956.

Willem Sandberg [The Netherlands]

1897-1984; born in Amersfoort
Invited to join AGI, 1952

Sandberg was a graphic and exhibition designer as well as a museum man. Educated at the State Academy of Art in Amsterdam and later in Vienna, with Otto Neurath who worked on Isotype (standardized pictograms), and in Utrecht. Sandberg's design career started with a publishing firm, but he soon was commissioned by the Dutch Post and the Amsterdam Stedelijk Museum. He was a curator at that museum (1937–41) and worked with the resistance against the German occupiers, on the forging of documents. While in hiding he developed the series *Experimenta Typographica*, which went on to influence his main body of characteristic graphic work: 300 catalogues and many posters for the Stedelijk Museum, of which he was the director (1945–62). He worked with roughly torn shapes and letters, coarse paper and stark contrasts. He was the director or advisor of several museums, including the Centre Pompidou, Paris and the Israel Museum, Jerusalem. His awards include: NY Hall of Fame, 1979; Werkman Prize, 1959; Erasmus Prize, 1975. In his position at the Stedelijk Museum he was very active in his efforts to encourage other graphic designers and build up their professional organization.

Raymond Savignac [France]

1907-2002; born in Paris
Invited to join AGI, 1952

When AGI celebrated its 50th anniversary in Paris, Savignac, aged 93, made a fine contribution by designing the logo for the event. There was also a one-man show of his work. In a film shown at the exhibition, he remarked that, at the outset, he was one of the *'perfect'* total of eight AGI members: *'It was more fun before,'* he added. Raymond was a great poster designer, with that typical French painterly style and cartoon-like humour. Educated at the École Lavoisier in Paris, in 1935 he became (after numerous jobs) an assistant to A.M. Cassandre (like André François).

Savignac always tried to find a *'single image for a single idea'*; it made him a true poster designer, with maximum directness: *'A poster is like a visual rape.'* When he produced his first Monsavon poster at the age of 41, he considered himself to be *'reborn'* under the udder of the cow. In another famous poster he protested against the *autoroute* running by Notre-Dame. He was nicknamed *'L'Homme du Choc'*. He also worked for Olivetti, Air France and UNICEF, and against Coca-Cola. His autobiography was entitled *A Man and his Profession*.

Monsavon with Milk, poster advertising soap, 1949.

Cinzano, poster, 1951.

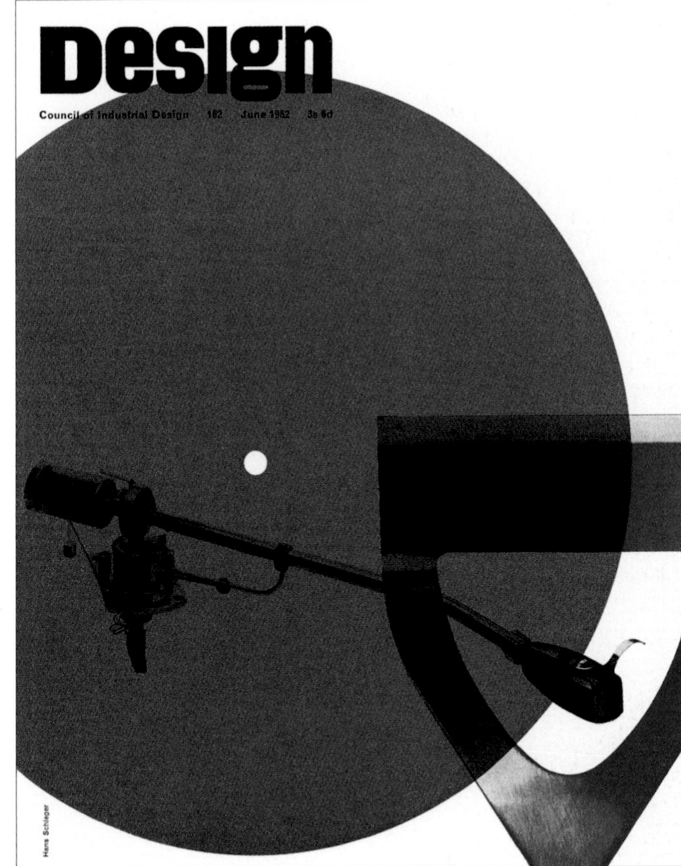

Hudnut cosmetics company sales brochure, 1929–33.

Design magazine cover. The Council of Industrial Design, 1962.

The **Request Bus Stop sign**, with its strong red background, was easy to see at a distance and easily distinguishable from ordinary bus stops, 1935.

Penguin Books, symbol for education imprint, 1968.

Hans Schleger 'Zero' [UK]

1898-1976; born in Kempen, Germany
Invited to join AGI, 1952

Between 1918 and 1921 Schleger studied at the Kunstgewerbeschule in Berlin. He began his career as a publicity and set designer for John Hagenbeck Films. In 1924 he moved to New York where he stayed for five years, establishing his Madison Avenue studio and using the pseudonym *'Zero'*. He then returned to Berlin in 1929 and worked at the German office of London ad agency Crawford's. In 1932 he moved to England and freelanced for major British commercial and industrial corporations, designing posters for Shell-Mex and BP, the wartime ministries, GPO and London Transport, for whom he designed bus stop signs, simplifying the existing circle-and-bar symbol.

Between 1950–62, he worked for the advertising agency Mather and Crowther. Zero's studio became Hans Schleger and Associates in 1953. Schleger was involved in unifying design policies and pioneering the concept of corporate identity for clients like Mac Fisheries, Fisons, British Rail and British Sugar Corporation. He designed the symbol for the Design Centre in 1955, and the corporate identity for the Edinburgh International Festival in 1966. He lectured and had one-man shows in London, New York and Chicago. Ken Garland wrote of Schleger: *'...he was such a youthful designer, wasn't he?'*

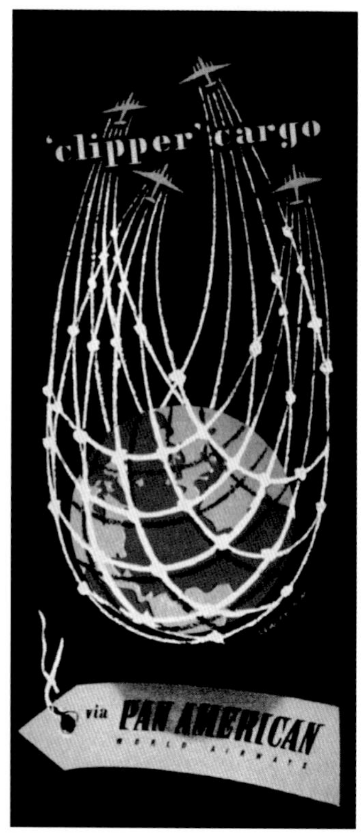

Heiri Steiner [Switzerland]

1906-1983; born in Horgen
Invited to join AGI, 1952

After studying at the Kunstgewerbeschule under Ernst Keller and in Berlin with O.H.W. Hadank in 1929, Heinrich 'Heiri' Steiner started his own studio in Zürich. From 1934–39 he worked together with Ernst Heininger. He was an illustrator, typographer and exhibition designer. Heiri worked on the Swiss Pavillion at the 1937 Poster Exhibition and the Swiss National Exhibition in Zürich. In 1947 he moved to Paris where he was appointed art director for UNESCO publications. He also worked for various publishers on typography and cover illustrations.

According to Henrion he could illustrate the unillustratable, including concepts such as fear, anxiety and the neurotic state of mind – a unique achievement. In 1959 he returned to Zürich, where he designed scientific exhibitions for Zürich University and Zoological Museum. He was a man with ideals and ethics, which one can see in his posters, postage stamps and books. He designed *Exempla Grafica* in 1967. Again, in Henrion's words: *'The subtle mixing of typography, illustration and colours makes this a typical Heiri Steiner.'*

Schauspielhaus, Zürich, poster for a theatre festival, 1946.

Schauspielhaus programme, Zürich, 1955–56 season.

Brochure for **Pan American Airways**.

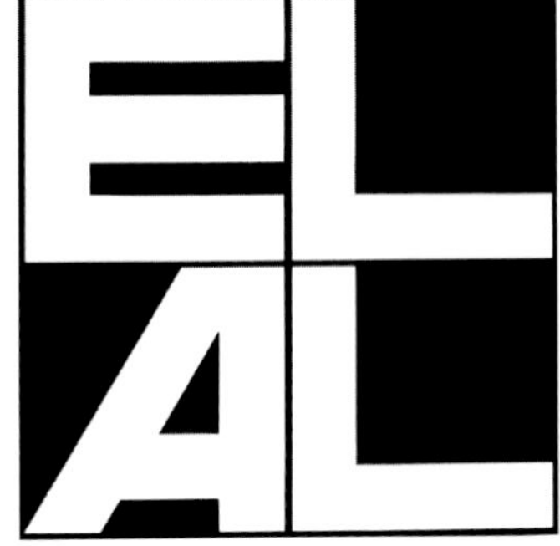

El-Al Airlines logotype, corporate identity project, 1963, in cooperation with George Him.

Poster for the **Dutch Federation of Artists Associations**, 1946.

Resistance movement, stamps for the Dutch PTT, 1965. Otto depicted statues commemorating the Second World War.

Otto Treumann [The Netherlands]

1919-2001; born in Fürth, Germany
Invited to join AGI, 1952

Otto was among the earliest members of AGI and remained one all his life. Migrated to Amsterdam in 1935. Educated at the Graphic College 1935–36 and Nieuwe Kunstschool 1936–40, where he met his wife Jenny, an illustrator. Went into hiding, worked for the resistance movement during WW2. Started his private studio in 1945. Bauhaus and Swiss typography set his rules. Treumann became strongly involved in the designers' national organization GKf. His working field included museum catalogues and posters, logotypes and identity programmes, stamps and editorial design. His most prominent clients were the Dutch Post, Utrecht Trade Fair, Museum Kröller-Müller, Dutch Gas Union, Wolters-Noordhoff publishers, El-Al Airlines (with George Him), Enka Rayon and the Open-Air Museum, Arnhem. Being strongly connected with Jewish society, he taught at the Jerusalem Bezalel Academy 1964–68 and worked on several special projects. Otto received numerous national and international awards, such as the H.N. Werkman Prize, the Frans Duwaer Prize twice, the David Roëll Award for his posters, the BKVB Lifetime Award 1994 and two high Dutch State decorations. He was an honorary member of the graphic designers associations of Israel and the Netherlands. His works were shown in many national and international exhibitions. Monograph: *Otto Treumann, Grafisch ontwerpen in Nederland*, Rotterdam: 010 Publishers, 1999.

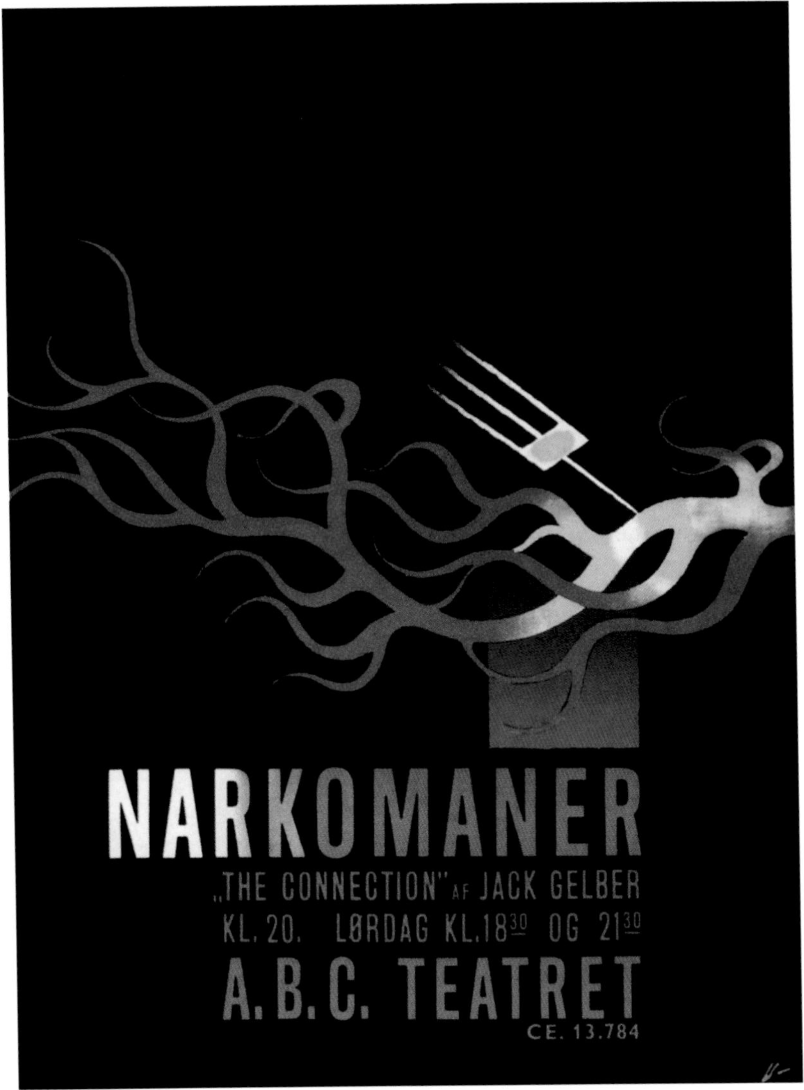

Arne Ungermann [Denmark]

1902-1981; born in Odense
Invited to join AGI, 1952

Arne Ungermann belonged to the AGI's first small group of Danish members. He started his career as a lithographer, but worked throughout his life as an illustrator and cartoonist. From 1924 until his death he worked for the daily newspaper *Politiken*, and for the Sunday supplement *Magasinet* (1922–62). At that time, he also started to create posters, making around 150 during his lifetime. The French poster designer A.M. Cassandre was often his inspiration.

Ungermann was considered a pioneer in book illustrations, especially children's books. He created the illustrations for *Palle alene i Verden* ('Paul is alone in the world') by Jens Sigsgaard, which was published in over 20 countries. He produced many books, showing children that art can help to see the world with fresh eyes. His work was exemplary as far as picture books were concerned. In 1961, he won the Danish Ministry of Culture's Children's Book Prize and in 1979 the Eckersberg medal.

The Connection by Jack Gelber, film poster, 1965. Danish Museum of Art & Design, Copenhagen.

Reklamekunst (Poster Art), exhibition poster, 1945. Danish Museum of Art & Design, Copenhagen.

Illustration from the schoolbook **Min laesebog** (My Reader) by Erik Danielsen, Copenhagen, 1951.

Poster for **Perrier** mineral water.

Greeting card for **Arts Graphiques Bussière**. Chosen by Villemot as his favourite piece of work in the book *First Choice* by Ken Cato.

Wagons Lits Cook, poster, 1953.

Bernard Villemot [France]

1911-1990; born in Normandy
Invited to join AGI, 1952

He was the son of a famous cartoonist and studied at the Académie Julian and the École Paul Colin. In 1936, he set up a Paris atelier with four former Colin students. He started to devote a lot of his time and talents to humanitarian causes: the fight against cancer, work for the Red Cross, children's charities, and returning prisoners of war. He developed corporate identities *'the French way'*: by making series of posters with a clear *'signature'* that became familiar to the public. This he did for Orangina (also designing their labels), Perrier and Bally Shoes. Monsavon soap, for whom he also worked, chose for a different course, by inviting Carlu, Savignac and Villemot to work on different projects. Air France was a similar case: under the art direction of Carlu, twelve AGI designers worked over several years for the airline. In 1949 Villemot shared an exhibition with Raymond Savignac. Between 1952–59 he created film posters for Gaumont, Pathé and UGC. His posters, he said, were influenced by Matisse, De Stael, Colin and Cassandre. He lectured in Chicago (ADC) in 1954. He had a solo exhibition at the Musée des Arts Décoratifs in Paris, 1963. He warned: *'The country is being occupied by the armies of marketing!'*

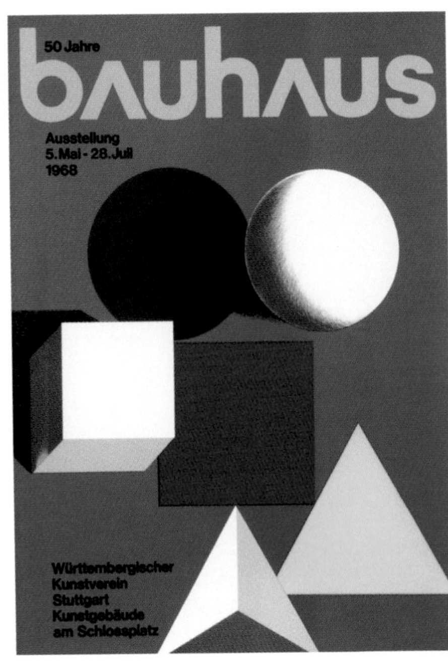

Herbert Bayer [USA]

1900-1985; born in Haag, Austria
Admitted to AGI, 1954

Graphic and exhibition designer, architect and landscape designer, photographer, painter. A great man who was a pioneer of modernism in European and US design. Apprenticed to the architect Schmidthammer in Linz and worked for Emanuel Margold in Darmstadt. Studied 1921–23 at the Bauhaus in Weimar under Kandinsky and Moholy-Nagy. Designed bold typographic banknotes in 1923. When the Bauhaus had moved to Dessau, Herbert was placed in charge of typography and advertising. Advocated the use of sans serif typefaces, produced a geometric alphabet (1925), and proposed the abolition of capital letters. Set up a Berlin studio in 1928, where he exercised all of his specialist skills. He was art director of German *Vogue* magazine. Co-operated with Gropius, Moholy-Nagy and Breuer on a Berlin exhibition of the Werkbund and the Workers Union. Berthold produced his typeface Bayer in 1933. Moved for political reasons to New York, becoming an art director for leading agencies during the war. Initiated and designed the 1938 Bauhaus exhibition at NY MoMA. Moved to Aspen in 1946, to become a leading educator at the Aspen Institute, for which he designed several buildings. Was initiator of the Aspen Design Conferences. Worked for CCA and later became chairman of its design department.

Poster for exhibition of **German art at the Grand Palais**, Paris, 1929.

50 Years of the Bauhaus, exhibition poster, 1968.

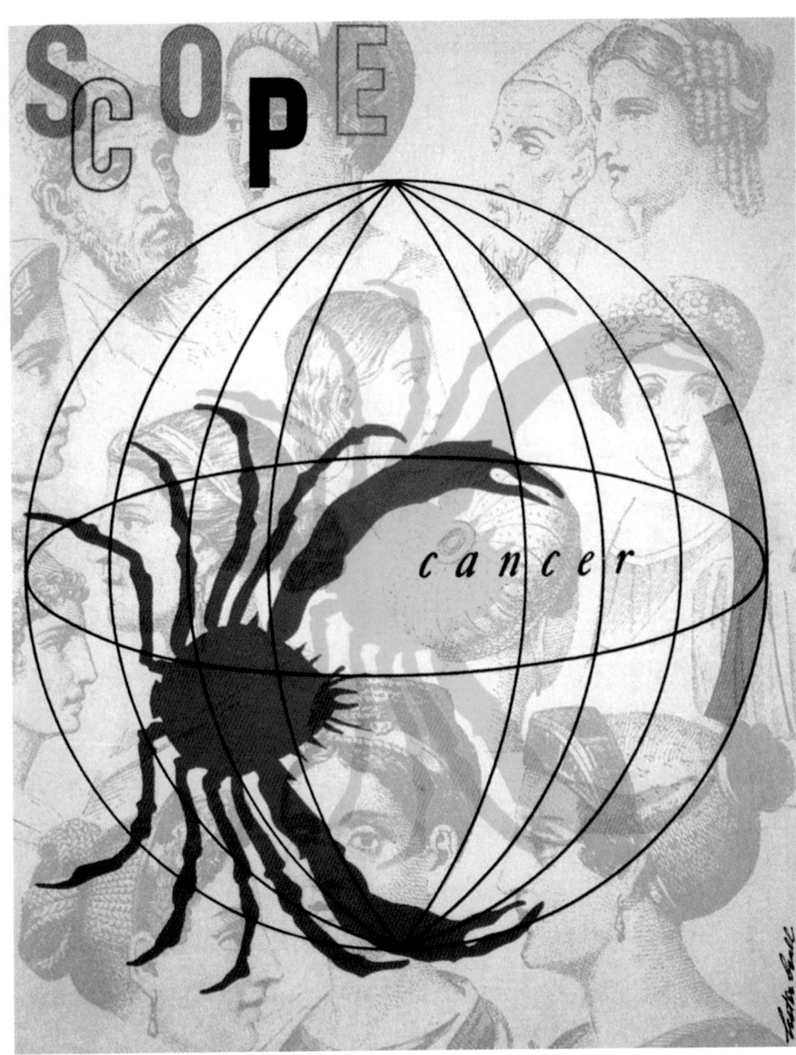

Logo for **International Paper Company**, 1960.

Cover for **Scope**, Upjohn Company, 1948.

Logo for **Caterpillar Tractor**, 1967.

Logo for **Titeflex**, industrial springs.

Lester Beall [USA]

1903-1969; born in Kansas City, Missouri
Admitted to AGI, 1954

A self-taught graphic designer who grew up in Chicago and freelanced there (1927–35), before moving to New York. He has been called a *'trailblazer of American design'*. Was the first to receive a one-man exhibit at NY MoMA (1937) and posthumously a Lifetime Award by the AIGI in 1993. He did it all: identities, advertising, packaging, product styling, posters, books, reports, magazines, murals and interiors for clients like the Rural Electrification Administration, *Scope* magazine for Upjohn Pharmaceuticals, International Paper, Martin Marietta, Container Corporation of America (CCA), Connecticut General Life Insurance, the US Government, *Chicago Tribune*, *Collier's* and *Time* magazine. In 1955 he moved his studio to Dumbarton Farm in Brookfield, CT. Lester read a lot, and blended Jan Tschichold's New Typography with Dada's intuitive placement of elements and also made playful use of 19th-century American wood type. He applied strong flat colours, geometric shapes and enduring images. He was an early innovator in the development of the design manual as a major tool in corporate identity programmes. Lester was a man of high principles, a favoured lecturer in professional and educational circles. On top of all this, he was the chief proponent of the American modernist design movement.

Francis Bernard [France]

1900-1979; born in Marseille
Admitted to AGI, 1954

Francis Bernard studied at his local art and business school. Afterwards he went to the École des Beaux-Arts in Paris. In 1945 he became head of the advertising department of RTF, the French radio and television company, where he remained in charge until his retirement. Besides his position at RTF he worked as a freelance poster designer. He and colleagues like Cassandre, Loupot, Colin and Carlu often worked for the same clients.

Although he was a modest man, hiding away from honours and the media, most of his posters for Nicolas, the major French wine distributor, Pernod, La Menthe Pastille, Gervais and L'Oréal are still sought after by collectors. Photography was a medium he liked to incorporate into his designs. His annual posters for the Art Ménagers exhibition always involved unexpected variations on a theme.

Visit Morocco, tourist poster, 1930.

Two of his annual posters for the **Arts Ménagers exhibition** in Paris.

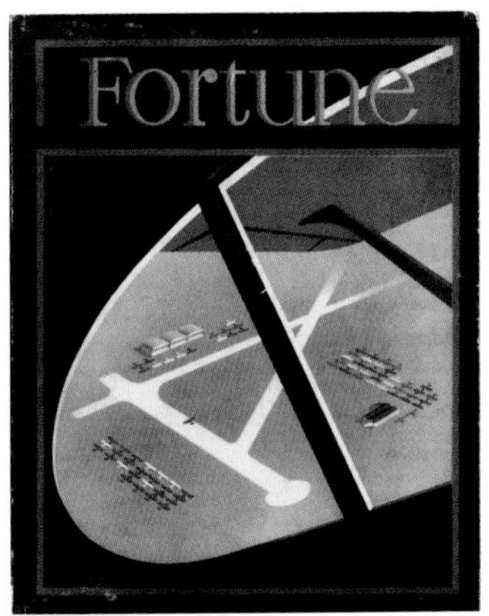

Poster for the **Association of American Railroads**, 1952.

Cover for **Fortune** magazine, 1930s.

Meinl Coffee, poster, 1924.

Joseph Binder [USA]

1898-1972; born in Vienna, Austria
Admitted to AGI, 1954

Trained as a lithographer, Joseph entered the Vienna School of Arts and Crafts in 1922. In 1924 he founded the studio Vienna Graphics and made his name with posters and advertisements. He was one of the founding fathers of the association Design Austria, which still organizes a competition for the Joseph Binder Award. As a student he created award-winning posters for the American Red Cross; this allowed him to work for two years in the US. In 1933–35 he was guest lecturer at the Chicago Art Institute and the Minneapolis School of Art.

Represented in poster exhibitions in New York and Tokyo, obtaining first prizes in competitions fron NY ADC and NY MoMA, his reputation grew. In 1936 he left definitively for New York, and became a US citizen in 1944. He worked with simplified geometric forms, contrasts and high-impact colours. Clients included American Railroads, American Airlines, A&P Iced Coffee. He designed covers for *Fortune* and *Graphis*. The US Navy appointed him their art director and designer. In the sixties he turned away from commercial work and produced abstract art, which was shown in NY MoMA and the Museum of Applied Art in Vienna.

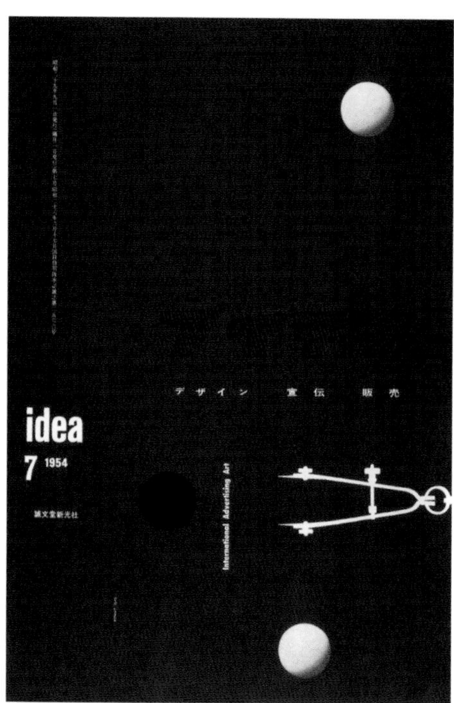

Helmut Lortz [Germany]

1920–2007; born in Schneppenhausen
Admitted to AGI, 1954

After an apprenticeship as an ivory-carver, sculpture studies and military service, Lortz started a voluntary job at a printer in Reutlingen in 1946. In 1948 he was commissioned to design book covers for Rowolt, Desch, Insel and DVA. In 1949 he worked at the graphic department of the US Headquarters in Frankfurt; he also designed a building exhibition in Nuremberg. He became the first German AGI member. Lortz taught at Darmstadt Art School (1952–59) and received the Art Award of Darmstadt (1956). In 1957 he became a founder member of the graphic group Novum. Designed the exhibit *'Sight'* for Expo 58, Brussels.

In 1959 he became a professor at Berlin Hochschule für Bildende Kunste; he designed its logo in 1975. Novum exhibited in Tokyo in 1960. Lortz designed the German section at Italia 61, Turin. He made the IAA poster for the Frankfurt International Motor Show, 1963. Designed *Blauwelt Fundamente*, a series of books. Darmstadt honoured Lortz with the Johann Heinrich Merck Award, 1970. Between 1972 and 2004 fourteen books were published on Lortz as an illustrator, draughtsman, photographer, teacher, friend, photomontage artist, portraitist, sketcher and human being.

New Darmstadt Secession, exhibition poster, 1967.

Packaging for **Jena Glas**.

Cover for the graphic design magazine **Idea #7**, Japan, 1954.

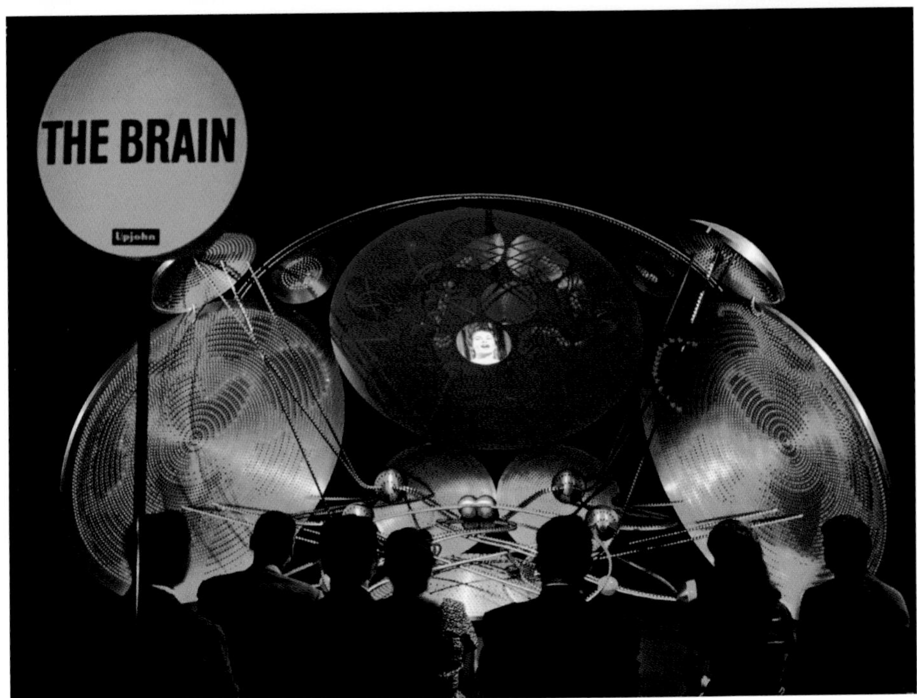

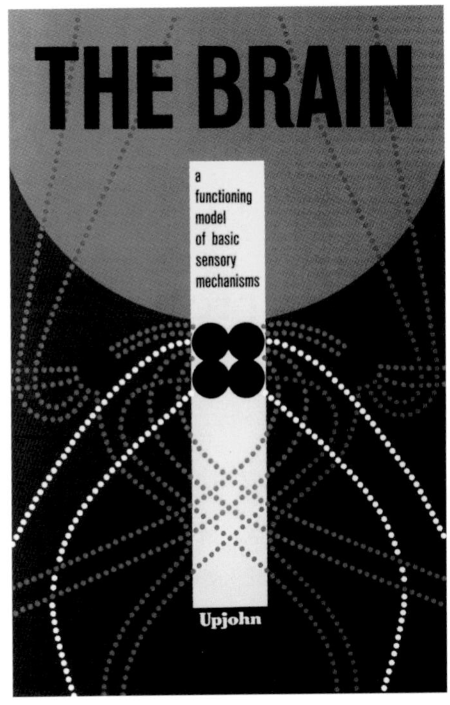

Cell, exhibition display for Upjohn.

Cover of **Defense of Life**, exhibition booklet for Upjohn.

The Brain, exhibition display for Upjohn.

Promotional poster for **The Brain** exhibition.

Will Burtin [USA]

1908-1972; born in Cologne, Germany
Admitted to AGI, 1955

Education: until age 14. Studied typography at Handwerkskammer Köln while apprenticed, 1922–26; then studied art/graphics at Cologne Werkschulen. Established Entwurfe Burtin (Designs by Burtin), 1927–38. Taught in Berlin, marrying his student Hilde Munk, 1932. Hitler demanded Burtin become design director of the Propaganda Ministry (1938). Instead, he took his Jewish wife to New York, winning Federal Works Agency contract for 1939 World's Fair. Freelance design for Time-Life, others. War work: OSS, designed aerial gunnery manuals. Art director for *Fortune* magazine, 1945–49. From 1949 Will Burtin, Inc. served corporate clients, including Upjohn. Renowned for scientific models: *Cell*, *Brain*, *Uranium Atom*, others. Burtin organized and chaired the conferences Vision 65, and Vision 67. After Hilde's death he married Cipe Pineles. Will Burtin pioneered the fields of scientific visualization, information design, corporate identity and multimedia (he called it *'Integration'*). His large models foreshadowed computer-assisted virtual environments (CAVE). He promoted Helvetica in North America. Affiliations, appointments: AIGA, Aspen co-founder, programme chair, 1955–56, medallist, director, solo exhibitor; AGI, president of American Sector; Type Directors Club; Art Directors Club; Icograda, vice-president, 1968–72. Awards from ADC, AIGA, American Medical Association Gold Medal, and others. Pratt Institute, faculty member for 30 years, professor; Harvard's Carpenter Center, research fellow.

Eugenio Carmi e Umberto Eco
LA BOMBA E IL GENERALE
Bompiani

Eugenio Carmi [Italy]

1920– born in Genoa
Admitted to AGI, 1955

After studying to be a painter in Turin under the direction of Felice Casorati, he moved over to graphic art. From 1958 till 1964 he was consultant to Italsider, Italy's nationalized steel industry. He experimented with enamels on steel and work in welded steel. As a painter, he combined 'art' and 'industry' by inviting noted artists like Calder and Chadwick to make monumental steel sculptures. These were put up in the streets as part of the Spoleto festival. In 1963 he founded the Gruppo Cooperativo di Baccadasse. He worked with artists like Max Bill, Victor Vasarely, photographers, critics and architects. One of the most significant stages of his artistic career was the Venice Biennale in 1966. He published many books; his first, *Stripsody*, was produced with Cathy Berberian and Umberto Eco. He did early experimental television work for RAI in 1973–74. In the same period a book was published, *Eugenio Carmi, una pittura di paesaggio* by Umberto Eco.

11th Milan Triennale, poster, 1957.

The Bomb and the General, children's book by Eugenio Carmi and Umberto Eco, 1966.

BAM, 1966.

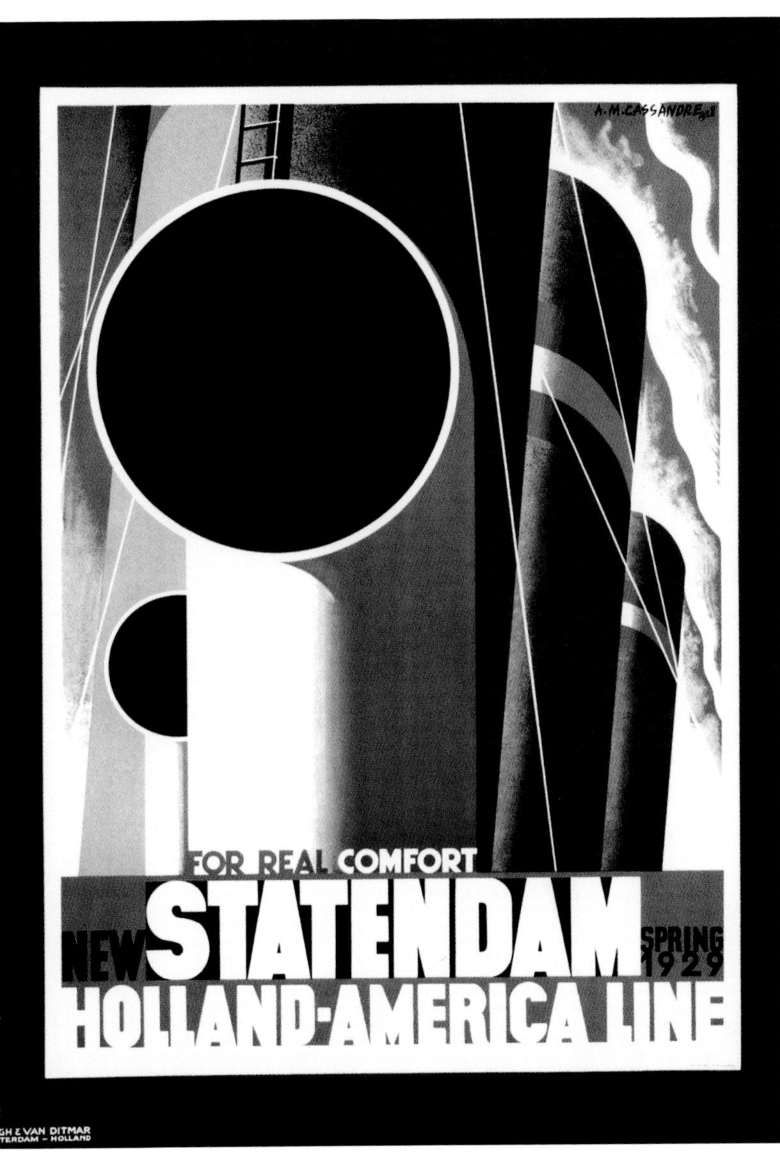

Foire de Paris, poster, 1957. This small poster is not listed in the official catalogues of Cassandre's work.*

Statendam, poster, 1928.*

Bifur, a typeface for Deberny et Peignot, 1929.*

A.M. Cassandre [France]

1901-1968; born in Kharkov, Ukraine
Admitted to AGI, 1955

Henrion wrote: *'Cassandre was the greatest and most influential poster designer of this century.'* Adolphe Mouron left the Ukraine in 1915 for France and studied briefly at the École des Beaux-Arts and the Académie Julian. Cassandre was his artistic pseudonym. In 1923–36 he produced an enormous and stunning range of posters for clients in France, the Netherlands and Great Britain. A painter at heart, he was strongly influenced by Derain and Léger. Cassandre called posters a kind of telegram between the company and the public. His work was powerful and lyrical at the same time.

Trains and their tracks, ocean liners, *Dubo-Dubon-Dubonnet*, Nicolas wine merchants, tobacco, tourist destinations, Philips, Van Nelle: all these came from his Paris studios. He also worked for the theatre and became a teacher. After a retrospective exhibition at NY MoMA, he signed a contract with *Harper's Bazaar* and spent two winters in New York. Influenced by Balthus in 1936, he then devoted much of his energy to painting. Cassandre made three exclusive typefaces for his friend Charles Peignot: Acier, Bifur and Peignot. In 1959 he created typefaces for Olivetti. Became an Officier de la Légion d'Honneur in 1962.

Paul Colin [France]

1892-1985; born in Nancy
Admitted to AGI, 1955

Colin studied painting, but became famous as a poster designer. He was often called one of the three Cs: Cassandre, Carlu, Colin. During his life he made more than 2,000 posters and more than 100 stage sets. Paris of the 1920s and 1930s was often referred to as *L'Epoque Paul Colin*. His first poster was for La Revue Nègre at the Theatre des Champs-Élysées, which was an opportunity to make a name for himself. It brought him his muse, lover and long-time friend Josephine Baker, the most famous jazz singer and dancer of her time.

In 1927 Colin produced a portfolio, in an edition of 500, in tribute to her and the other African-American performers who appeared in Paris in the Roaring Twenties. He used a time-consuming technique called *pochoir*. It required a separate stencil for every colour and a special brush, called a *pompon*. Paul Colin ran his own school from the early 1930s until the 1960s. Henrion, at one time, was his lettering assistant because Colin was not interested in typography. Sometimes there was no space for lettering and Henrion asked: *'But where?'*, only to be answered: *'That's your business.'*

Tabarin, cabaret poster, 1928.

Arts Ménagers, Grand Palais, exhibition poster, 1939.

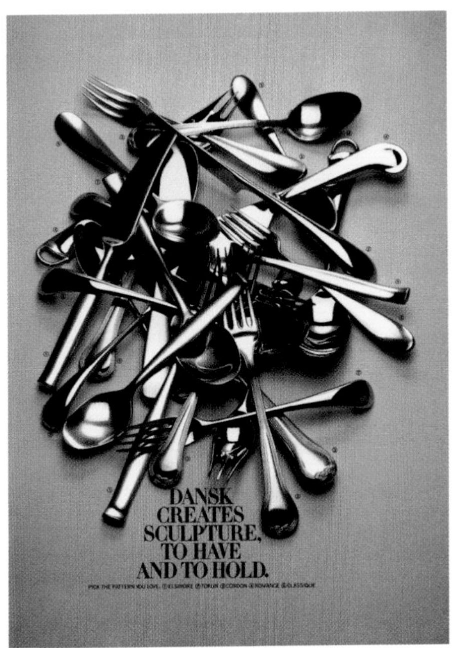

CBS Masterworks, logo.

Dansk Cutlery, single page advertisement.

Mural in the CBS cafeteria.

Lou Dorfsman [USA]

1918– born in New York City
Admitted to AGI, 1955

Dorfsman graduated from the Cooper Union School of Art and Architecture. While a student he created exhibitions for the 1939 New York World Fair. He joined CBS in 1946 and never really left: after 41 years of being *'Mr CBS'*, Dorfsman is still around. Today he can be found at the Museum of Television and Radio, NY, living and working with all those familiar artefacts of a lifetime in this audiovisual world. Lou started as a staff designer and graduated to become Vice President and Creative Director of Corporate Advertising and Design.

He disliked the word *'designer'* when it was used for cosmetic changes. A designer should be a *'master planner'*, and that was what Lou was for CBS. He was responsible for advertising, print, film titling, marketing, book design, direct mailing, television promotion and environmental design. In all these fields he set and maintained award-winning standards. During his years at CBS, television grew to its maturity and radio made a strong comeback. Lou has been honoured with numerous Gold Medals from NY ADC, has been inducted into the Art Directors Hall of Fame, served as President of the ADC, and received three honorary degrees from colleges and universities, and AIGA's coveted Gold Medal.

George Giusti [USA]

1908-1990; born in Milan, Italy
Admitted to AGI, 1955

George got his training at the Accademia di Belle Arte di Brera, Milan. He had a Swiss father and an Italian mother and worked in advertising agencies in Milan, and Lugano, Switzerland. Opened his own studio in Zürich between 1930–37. Emigrated in 1938 to the United States, where he started his own studio in New York. Worked on the Swiss Pavilion with Herbert Matter for the NY World's Fair 1939. Also worked for the US Departments of Agriculture, the Army Corps and the Office of Strategic Service, designing posters, exhibitions and publicity material.

For twelve years he was a design consultant for Geigy Pharmaceuticals; the work he did for them is characterized by a simplified, symbolic style. In 1960 he joined the guiding faculty of the Famous Artists School in Westport, CT. Giusti also taught at Cooper Union. He was elected Art Director of the Year 1958 and awarded the Gold T-Square. Giusti was elected to the ADC Hall of Fame in 1979. His cover designs for *Fortune*, *Time* and *Holiday* were outstanding.

Cover for **Graphis Annual 63/64**.

Two covers for **Fortune magazine**, May 1948 and November 1941.

Advertisement for the **Davison Chemical Corporation** of Baltimore, 1950.

Bookplate for Dr Hermann Neuerburg.

Pelikan logotype.

Cigarette box design for Haus Neuerburg.

Horch 8, car design, 1929.

O.H.W. Hadank [Germany]

1889-1965; born in Berlin
Admitted to AGI, 1955

In 1907, O.H.W. (Oskar Hermann Werner) started his studies at the Unterrichtsanstalt des Kunstgewerbemuseums in Berlin. He was not only a graphic designer but also a painter. Between 1912–17 he worked for publishers such as Cotta, Phönix-Druck, Scherl and Ullstein. In 1919 he co-founded the Bund der Deutschen Gebrauchsgrafiker (BDG). He was professor of commercial art at the Hochschule für Freie und Angewandte Kunst in Berlin (1919–49). Hadank was well known, not only in Europe but also in the US, as a pioneering packaging designer, especially for the cigarette company Haus Neuerburg, and also for his own brand of cigarettes (!) marked HDK.

In the 1930s, he designed cars for Horch, a brand that is now known as Audi, which was at that time Germany's most beautiful automobile. One of his other clients was Pelikan in Hanover. Over his life he made around 70 logos, labels for spirits manufacturers and a broad spectrum of commercial artwork. Since the heyday of his career was in an earlier design era, Hadank was granted honorary membership of AGI. After his death, Bruno and Ruth Wiese took over and updated his tradition.

Yusaku Kamekura [Japan]

1915-1997; born in Niigata
Admitted to AGI, 1955

He studied at the Institute of New Architecture and Industrial Arts in Tokyo, specializing in basic composition theory. Founding member (1960) and later director of Nippon Design Centre. Chairman of the Japan Graphic Designers Association. He was the art director of *Nippon* magazine, which introduced the country's culture to the world. Kamekura worked freelance from 1962. He was a great adherent of the International Typographic Style. The use of Japanese aesthetics, combined with geometric and linear forms and dramatic photography, enabled him to communicate effectively with an international audience.

His posters for the 1964 Tokyo Olympics were honoured with the Grand Prize of the Ministry of Education. Kamekura also acted as the design director for those Games. He received numerous awards and had international solo exhibitions. The Tokyo ADC honoured him with four gold, five silver and several bronze medals. He designed posters for Expo 70 (Osaka), Interski '79 and Rayon and Synthetic Fibres of Japan (1961), the 1972 Sapporo Winter Olympics and Expo '89 (Nagoya). An important client of his was Nikon Camera Company. Kamekura designed for advertising, corporate identities, symbols, books and packaging. Moreover he was an active writer on design.

Nikkor lenses, poster for Nikon cameras, 1955.

1964 Tokyo Olympics, poster, 1964.
Photo: Osama Hayasaki.
Photo director: Jo Murakoshi.

EXPO '70 Osaka, poster. Designed in 1967.

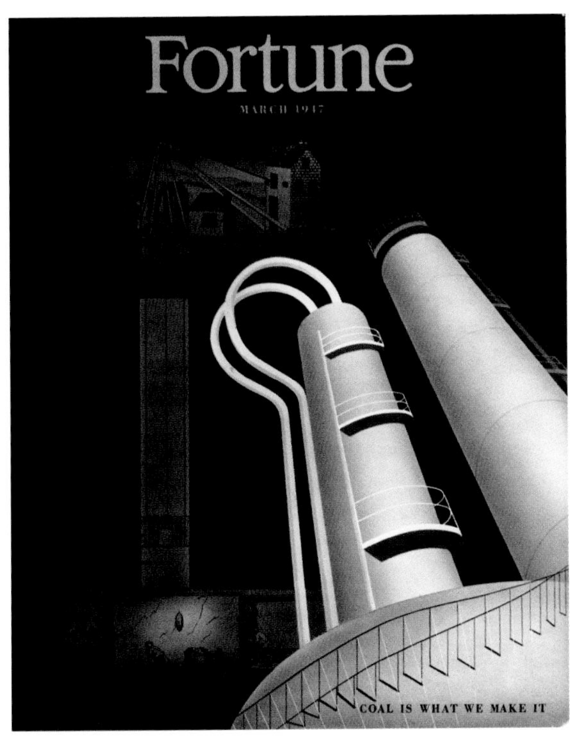

Fortune, magazine cover, March 1947.

Brochure cover for **Sharpe & Dohme**, c. 1945.

Matthew Leibowitz [USA]

1918-1974; born in Philadelphia, Pennsylvania
Admitted to AGI, 1955

Leibowitz attended the Philadelphia Museum School of Art from 1936–39. He worked for three years as an art director for the Philadelphia Advertising Agency, before setting up his own firm. Matthew became a consultant/designer for many major firms, like IBM, RCA Victor, Sharp & Dohme, Spalding, Container Corporation of America (CCA), General Electric, N.W. Ayer & Son, the International Red Cross and others. No doubt, Lester Beall's example was of great influence on his early work. He excelled at very sensitive designs, dynamic and yet balanced, with exemplary typography.

Between 1941 and 1959 he received no less than 163 gold medals and other awards. His work is in the collections of NY MoMA, Denver Art Museum and Musée National d'Art Moderne, Paris. His archive is kept by Rochester Institute of Technology.

Leo Lionni [USA]

1910-1999; born in Amsterdam, The Netherlands
Admitted to AGI, 1955

Moved to Italy and took his PhD in Economics in Genoa, 1938. Leo was a very charming, self-taught designer. Was active in Milanese circles, doing paintings, sculpture, graphics and writing reviews. Worked for Motta. He emigrated to the US in 1939. Art director of N.W. Ayer advertising agency until 1947. Succeeded Will Burtin as art director of *Fortune* in 1949. He developed a distinctive visual identity, utilizing photography and illustration. Was a design consultant for Olivetti and CCA.

His famous cover of the *Family of Man* exhibition catalogue for NY MoMA (1955) is a 20th-century classic. *'I felt the only way to reach my goals was by doing painting, sculpture, writing and graphics the way I wanted to do it.'* In his 50s he lived alternatively in Italy and New York. He was a co-editor of *Print* and an extremely productive and most original author/designer of 40 children's books that conquered the world. Won the AIGA Gold Medal 1984, was a four-time winner of the Caldecott Medal. *'One time I was jolted out of a near-slumber by the words "the mouse that didn't exist". I am sure they will eventually become the title of a book.'*

Keep 'Em Rolling!, propaganda poster for the Office for Emergency Management, 1941.

Cover and spread for the children's book **Frederick**, 1974.

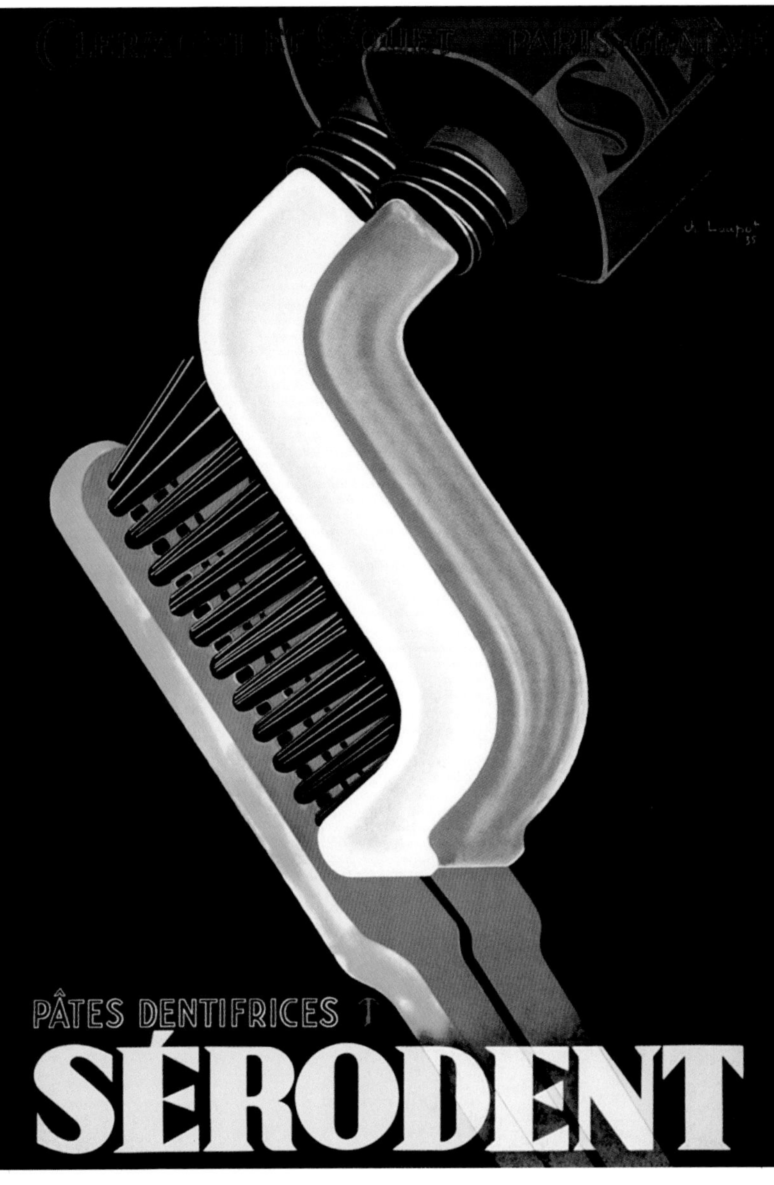

St Raphaël Quinquina, 1950. The stylized image of the two waiters was painted over and over again on walls along the roads of France; the shape of the two figures went through many changes over the years.

Poster for **Sérodent** toothpaste.

Charles Loupot [France]

1892-1962
Admitted to AGI, 1955

Loupot, another pioneer of the French modern poster, had his own special, personal style, characterized by simplicity and synthesis of ideas. He worked for 5 years in Switzerland as a typographer and was very successful with his posters. In 1923 he was called back to Paris by a French printer. In 1930 he, Cassandre and Maurice Moyrand founded their own studio, Alliance Graphique. The apéritif St Raphael became his most important client (1936) and this co-operation lasted far into the 1960s. One could say that he was the designer of their corporate identity *'avant la lettre'*.

In 1945, Loupot designed the famous St Raphaël waiters and used them as a logo on transport, advertisements and posters. He also turned them into murals; three thousand of these were hand-painted onto the sides of houses across the whole of France. *'A prestigious red and white ballet,'* Cassandre called it. Other clients included Peugeot, Nicolas, Twinings and Sato cigarettes, for whom he used elegant female figures. His DOP poster, an outcome of a new technique, appeared in the streets of Paris like *'a smile in the everyday grey'*, according to Henrion.

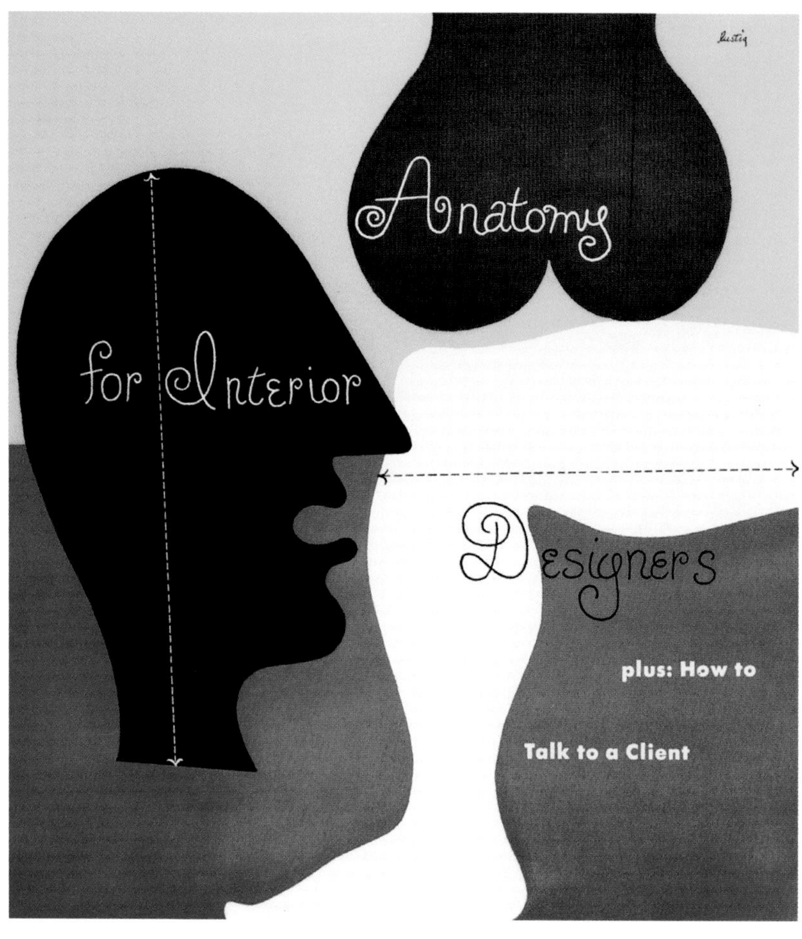

Alvin Lustig [USA]

1915-1955; born in Denver, Colorado
Admitted to AGI, 1955

Alvin Lustig was *'one of the most promising, gifted and sensitive designers of his generation'*. These words were Henrion's, written in his *AGI Annals* about young Lustig, who completely lost his sight before he died from diabetes. Lustig was educated in Los Angeles at the Community College and the Art Center School, followed by a brief period with Frank Lloyd Wright. By 1937, Alvin opened the first of the many design studios that he had during his brief career. His work was innovative. He worked for a book publisher and several LA clients. In 1944 he left for New York to become the Director of Visual Research at Look Magazine. In 1946 he went back to LA. Soon he turned to architectural and interior design, did commissions for lighting fixtures, fabrics and furniture. He also continued to design numerous covers for books and periodicals.
He redesigned *Arts and Architecture* completely (1942). In 1951 he moved back to New York, where he continued to produce 3D works. Josef Albers invited him to form a new graphic design department at Yale University. Lustig worked for Girl Scouts of America, American Crayon, *Industrial Design* magazine. Lustig taught at the Art Center School and Yale University.

Cover for **Fortune magazine**, 1952.

Growth of the Soil by Knut Hamsun, book cover, 1940s.

Anatomy for Interior Designers, book cover, 1948.

Cover for **Arts & Architecture**, 1946.

Advertisement for **Knoll Furniture**, 1948.

Engelberg Trübsee, tourist poster, 1935.

Herbert Matter [USA]

1907-1984; born in Engelberg, Switzerland
Admitted to AGI, 1955

Matter studied painting in Geneva and with Fernand Léger in Paris and worked with Cassandre, Le Corbusier and at Deberny et Peignot. Having returned to Zürich, Matter made his reputation with his early travel posters for the Swiss National Tourist Board, which won him international acclaim. He pioneered photomontage, combined with type. He came to the US in 1936, where he freelanced for *Harper's Bazaar*, *Vogue* and other periodicals. He became the staff photographer for Condé Nast publishers. Matter also worked for the Swiss and Corning Glass pavilions at the NY World's Fair 1939. He was a design consultant for Knoll (1946–66). Yale appointed him a professor of photography (1952–76). He was a master technician who created much of his work in the darkroom, cropping and retouching in unexpected ways. For ten years he was design consultant to the Guggenheim Museum in New York and the Museum of Fine Arts in Houston. Herbert Matter had exhibitions in LA, at Yale, at the Zürich Kunsthalle and NY MoMA. He was elected to the NY ADC Hall of Fame (1977), received a Guggenheim Foundation Fellowship in photography in 1980 and the AIGA medal in 1983.

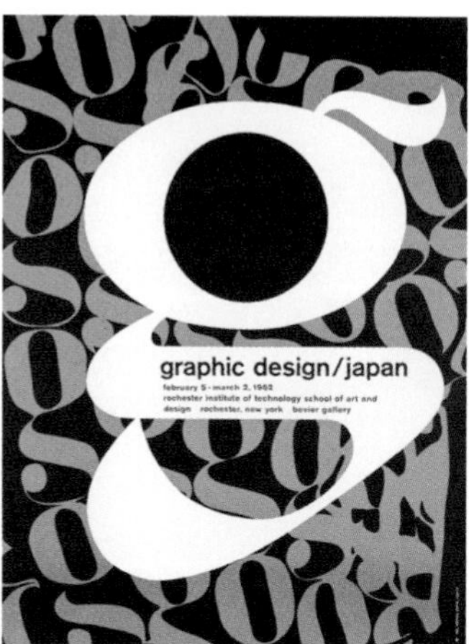

Hiroshi Ohchi [Japan]

1908-1974; born in Tokyo
Admitted to AGI, 1955

Ohchi was trained at the Tokyo School of Fine Arts. His career started before WW2. In 1953 he became the first art director of *Idea* magazine, a position he held until his death. He was an educator and a designer of posters, packaging and exhibitions, working freelance in Tokyo. Hiroshi Ohchi wrote no less than 33 books and many articles on design.

Ohchi was professor of Tokyo University of Education, Jissen Women's College and Kanazawa College of Arts and Technology. His contribution to design education was remarkable and he helped to bring many up-and-coming talents into the design community. He was the first president of the Japanese chapter of AGI.

Poster to promote **Japan**.
Client: Japan Tourist Association.

Don Cossack Chorus, concert poster.
Client: Art Friends Association.

Graphic Design/Japan, exhibition poster, New York.

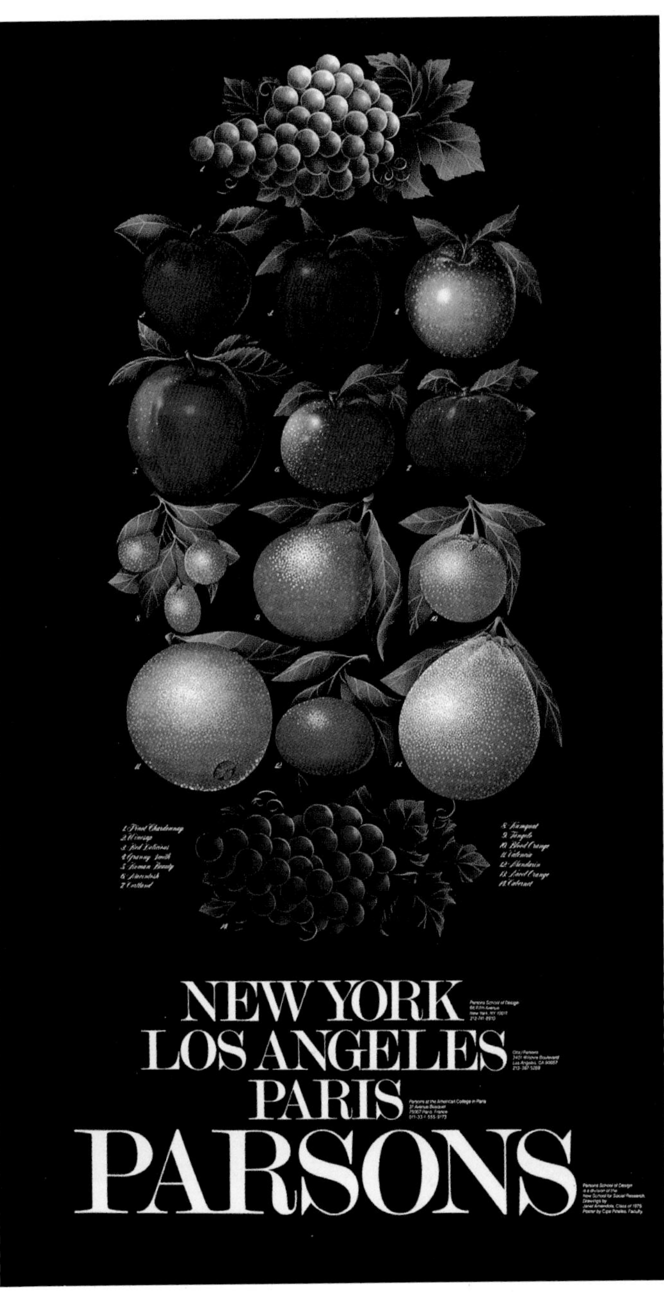

Cover of **Seventeen**, July 1949.
Photograph by Francesco Scavullo.

Poster for **Parsons School of Design**, 1955.

Cipe Pineles-Burtin [USA]

1908-1991; born in Vienna, Austria
Admitted to AGI, 1955

Cipe Pineles emigrated to the USA in 1923 and was awarded a scholarship to Pratt Institute, NY, 1927–31. Started off in an industrial design practice, but joined Condé Nast Publications in 1933. There, Dr M.F. Agha taught her the principles of magazine art direction through the 30s and early 40s. She was the first female art director for mass media, the first woman in the all-male NY ADC and AGI. The first also, to hire fine artists to illustrate the publications. She was also the first woman elected to the NY ADC Hall of Fame (1975).

She worked with Dr Agha on *Vogue* and *Vanity Fair* and was appointed as art director of *Glamour* in 1942, collaborating with famous photographers, designers and artists. After WW2 she art-directed *Seventeen* and *Charm*. Cipe not only addressed her readers on fashion matters, but also on values and changing roles in society. In 1959 she became a freelance designer, working mainly for Will Burtin; they married in 1961. She was the art director of Lincoln Center 1965–72. Cipe played an important role in Parsons School of Design, NY, teaching and designing the school's promotional material.

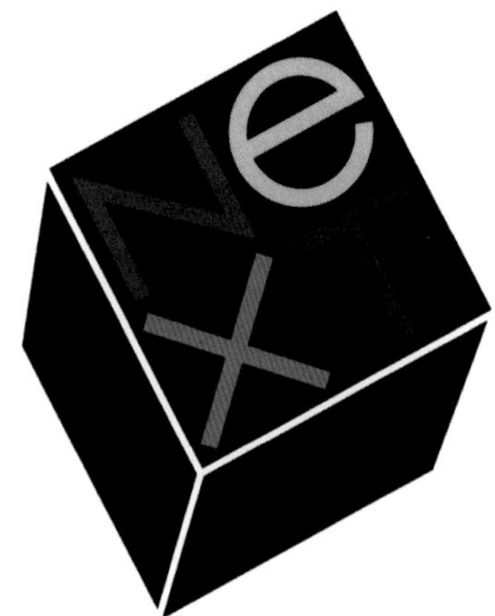

Paul Rand [USA]

1914-1996; born in Brooklyn, New York
Admitted to AGI, 1955

Born Peretz Rosenbaum, one half of twins, Paul started to draw at the age of 3. He was educated at Pratt Institute NY, 1929–32, followed by two years at Parsons and another two years at the Art Students League, with George Grosz. His design *'background'* of Cubism, Constructivism and De Stijl led him to his unique American graphic language. Wit, simplicity and Bauhaus principles made Rand a great art director for *Esquire* and *Apparel Arts* magazines. He was a book designer and illustrator, and also created children's books, made posters and did a lot of editorial design.

In 1938–45 he created covers for *Direction*. For 15 years he worked with Weintraub Advertising Agency, before starting as a freelancer (1955). He then became consultant/designer for IBM, Westinghouse and NeXT. The IBM logo dates from 1956. He created corporate identities for UPS and ABC Television. Paul Rand taught at Cooper Union and from 1956 at Yale. He wrote significant books and many articles on his work and was a fearsome critic. He was an honorary professor at Tokyo Tama University, an AIGA gold medal winner,and the first to be elected in the NY ADC Hall of Fame, among other honours!

AIGA cover/poster, 1968.
Paul Rand made this for free.

IBM's logotype by Paul Rand could stand some playing around.

NeXT, a logotype for a fee of $100,000; educational computer firm, 1986.

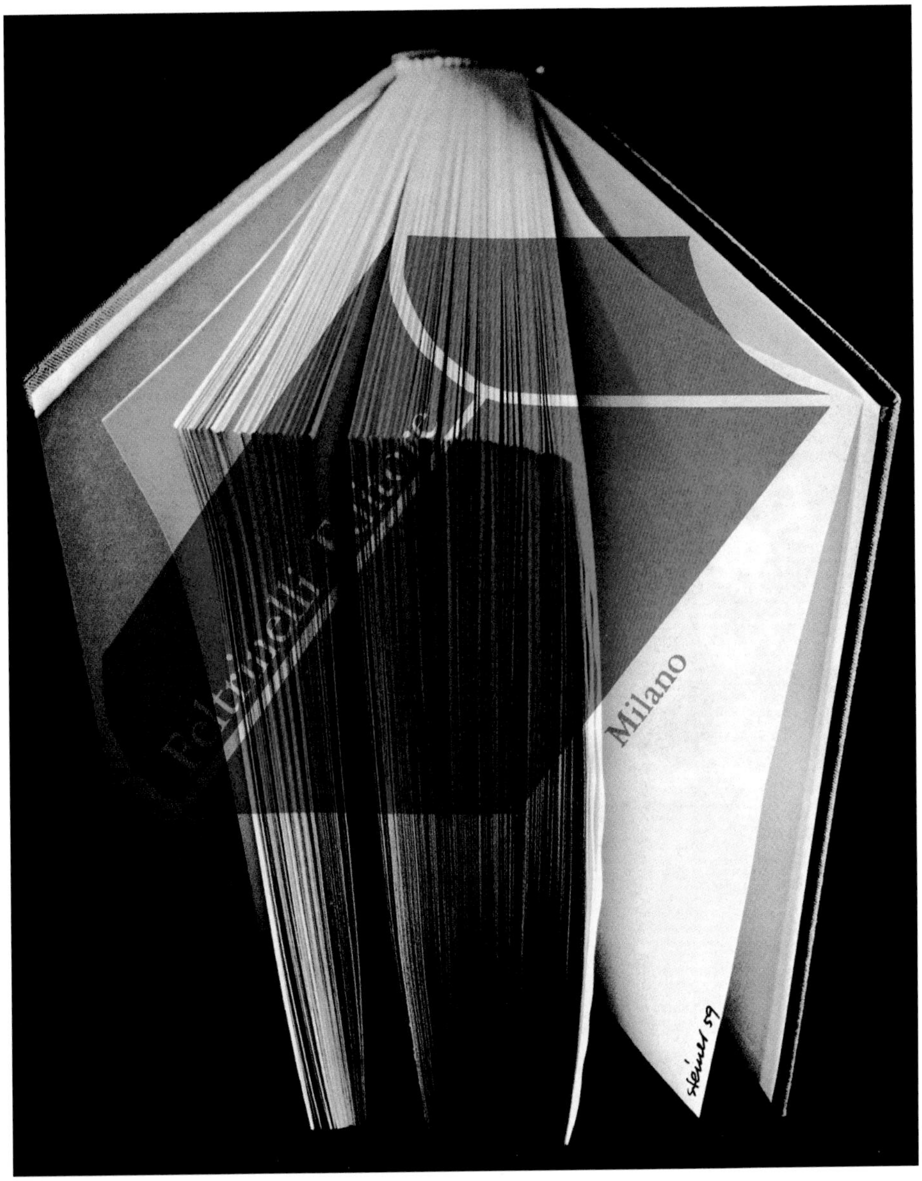

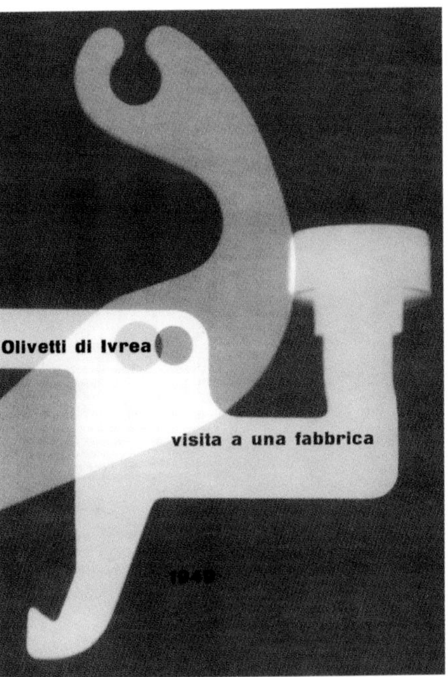

Advertisement for the publisher **Feltrinelli**, 1959.

14th Milan Triennale, exhibition poster, 1968.

Brochure for **Olivetti**, 1949.

Albe Steiner [Italy]

1913-1974; born in Milan
Admitted to AGI, 1955

Self-taught as an artist, Steiner showed great versatility and ingenuity. For him design was a way of life. Albe was idealistic and politically motivated. Started off as a textile designer, but made his name as an art director, exhibition and industrial designer, technical editor and display manager. Taught the history and technique of graphic art at the Scuola Rinascità from 1949, was art director of Feltrinelli publishers, Milan. Won a Triennale Grand Prix and silver medal in 1951, a Triennale gold medal in 1954 and another at the Milan Fair of 1956.

He loved to experiment in two and three dimensions. Wrote in trade magazines. With his students, he designed an identity for the historic town of Urbino. Designed, wrote, illustrated a plan for an illustrated publication, which he presented at an AGI assembly in Warsaw 1974. He had hoped that it would become an educational tool about design, understanding and appreciation. In Carpi he designed the interior and the displays for a commemorative museum for and about Nazi victims, deportation, camps and extermination. Albe Steiner also designed many political publications and newspapers.

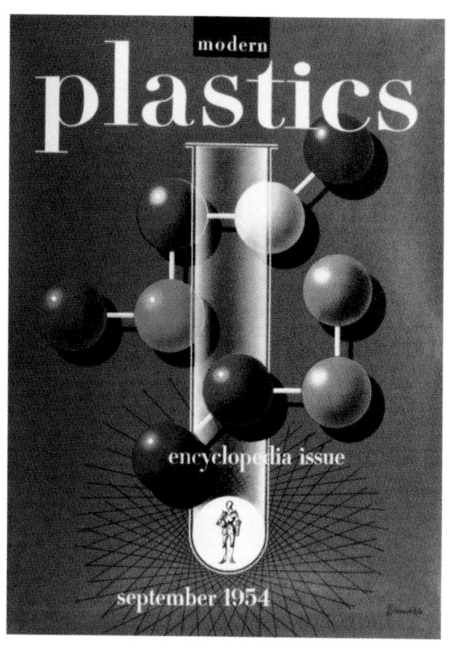

Alex Steinweiss [USA]

1917– born in Brooklyn, New York
Admitted to AGI, 1955

In 1930, Steinweiss went to the Abraham Lincoln High School under Leon Friend, his art teacher, who formed the so-called Art Squad. They designed school publications and posters and were encouraged to enter competitions. At 17, the promising Steinweiss was published in *PM* magazine. He won a scholarship to Parsons in 1934. Started his career as an assistant to Joseph Binder in 1937 and became the first art director of the newly formed Columbia Records at the age of 23. His first cover was for a collection of songs by Rogers and Hart in 1939. In all he designed more than 850 covers for Columbia, Decca, London, Everest, Remington and RCA Victor records.

He had a unique style, using geometric patterns, folk art symbols and hand-drawn lettering that became known as the *'Steinweiss Scrawl'*. During WW2 he designed information posters and displays for the US Navy. He also worked for National Distillery, Schenley Distributors, *Print* and *Fortune* and various other clients. Steinweiss has won numerous awards for design, including the ADC gold medal. He moved to Florida in 1974 where he started to work as a painter, but also designed posters for community and cultural events.

Budapest String Quartet, album cover for Columbia.

Cover for **Modern Plastics** catalogue, 1954.

Poster for **Sarasota Jazz Festival**, 1984.

Quick as a wink,
a typeface can express the
creative mood and spirit of a
graphic arts idea printed
on fine paper

WESTVACO

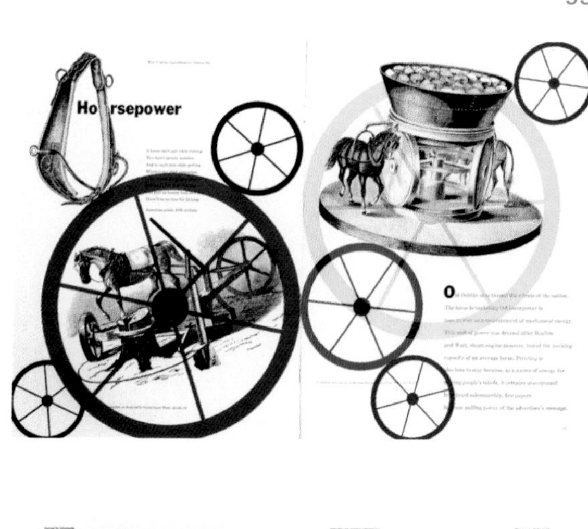

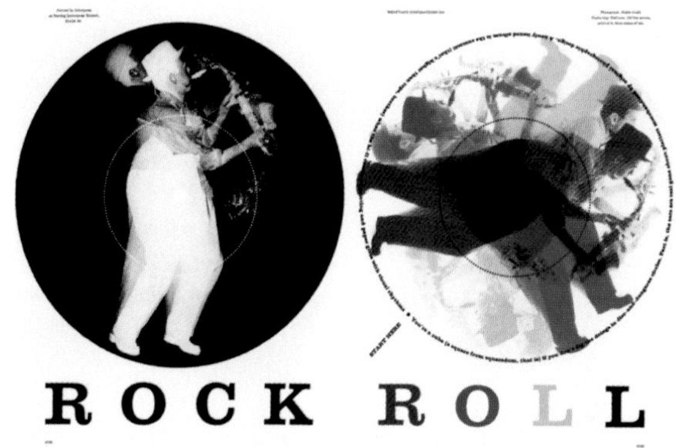

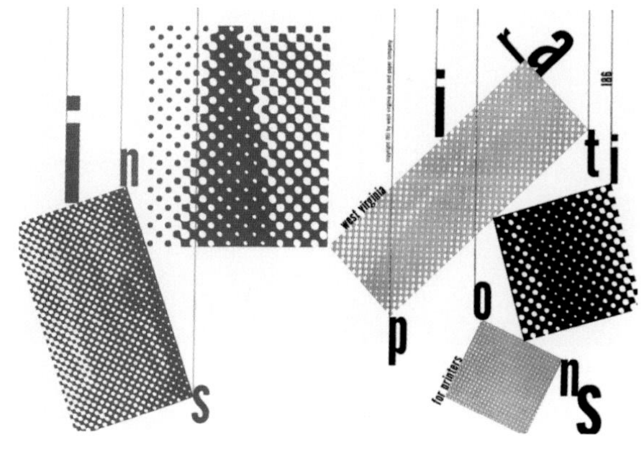

Cover for **Westvaco Inspirations** brochure, 1988.

Spreads from **Westvaco Inspirations**, 1952, 1958, 1951.

Bradbury Thompson [USA]

1911-1995; born in Topeka, Kansas
Admitted to AGI, 1955

Thompson studied in his hometown Topeka at Washburn College (1934). From 1938–62 he designed the innovative journal of the West Virginia Pulp & Paper Company, *Westvaco Inspirations for Printers*. He sought to inspire printers with his imaginative typography, graphics, and ingeniously appropriated paintings and engravings, employing colour separations and enlarged screens. During WW2 he served as art director of the Office of War Information. From 1945–72 Thompson served as art director for *Mademoiselle* as well as the influential *Art News Annual* and *Art News* magazine. He designed 35 magazines over the course of his career, including *Smithsonian*.

Alphabet 26 was an experiment to simplify and improve our current alphabet system by breaking with the tradition of differentiating capitals and lower-case letters. He designed 130 US postage stamps and many limited edition books. His *Washburn Bible* (1969) is a landmark in contemporary book design. From 1956 until his death he was on the faculty of Yale University. Among his numerous major awards, Thompson received the National Society of Art Directors 'Art Director of the Year' (1950), AIGA Gold Medal (1975), and the Art Directors Hall of Fame award (1977).

Edward Bawden [UK]

1903-1989; born in Braintree, Essex
Admitted to AGI, 1956

Bawden studied at the RCA in the early 1920s. Was greatly influenced by the ideas of Paul Nash. He soon started to work for Curwen Press, making his prints in lithography or linocut. Became close friends with Eric Ravilious; they influenced each other strongly in their ways of using line and shape. Bawden had a versatile talent. He did book illustrations, murals and advertising material. He painted and also made copper engravings. His work was typically English, with a sharp, introverted wit. His war sketchbooks were widely published in the UK and US.

He was made *'an honorary member of AGI'* (which is not so unusual, considering the fact that the membership itself is a kind of honour). Henrion visited him once when he was about to print a large linocut. Edward had put the block on the floor on top of the special paper, and walked up and down across the lino to obtain a perfect print. He also taught at the RCA – David Gentleman, one of his students who became a friend, remembers him as an inspiring and friendly if exacting teacher. He continued printmaking and painting to the end of his long life and was working on a linocut on the day he died.

The Battle of Qadisiya: detail from a double-page illustration from *The Arabs*, Puffin Books, lithograph, 1947.

Liverpool Street, linocut, 1960.

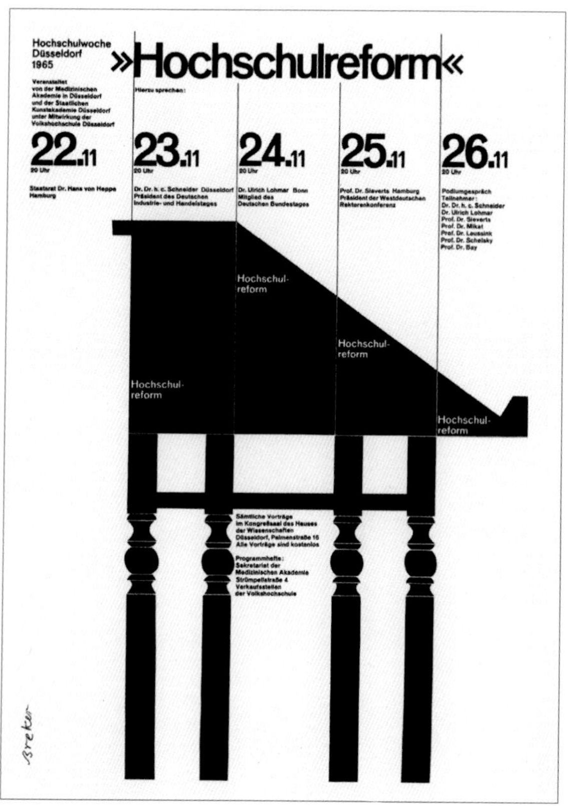

Highschool Week 1965, poster for a lecture series about educational reform, Düsseldorf.

Mind and Matter, Highschool Week 1964, poster for a lecture series, Düsseldorf.

Walter Breker [Germany]

1904-1980; born in Bielefeld
Admitted to AGI, 1956

Trained as a lithographer (1918–22), he switched over to a design education at the Kunstgewerbeschule in Bielefeld till 1925. He worked as an art director in Frankfurt, Minneapolis, Lotz and Berlin. In 1930 he was appointed director of the Magdeburg Kunstgewerbeschule, before becoming head of the department of applied arts at the Krefeld Werkkunstschule. He left in 1954, to become a professor at the Kunstakademie in Düsseldorf. Apart from teaching, he worked for various commercial clients and designed numerous, mainly typographical posters.

He was the author of many books on the Dutch design profession, co-operating with colleagues Dick Dooijes and Pieter Brattinga. Among his titles: *Industrial Design in the Netherlands*, *60 Plakate*, *9 Holländische Grafiker*, *Influences on Dutch Graphic Design 1900–1945*, *The Activities of Pieter Brattinga* and also *Sandberg*, the latter in collaboration with Ad Petersen.

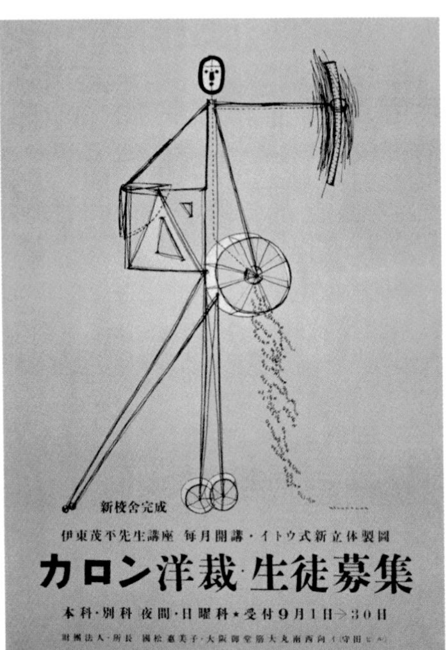

Yoshio Hayakawa [Japan]

1917– born in Osaka
Admitted to AGI, 1956

Hayakawa, as well as his colleagues Kamekura and Hara, set themselves to the formidable task of matching the design skills of the post-war Western countries, or even surpassing them. While in the 20s and the 30s the Japanese could feel quite comfortable with Cubism, Futurism, Constructivism and Bauhaus principles, they had to retrieve their creative course after the devastation of WW2. The status of designers was at the time very low, and their printing technology could not match that of the Western industrialized world.

Hayakawa was trained in Osaka and worked for design teams at department stores and the city's cultural section. He designed displays, advertising, posters, stage sets, and taught at the Kyoto University of Arts. He took part in exhibitions all over Japan, the US and Europe. He won several awards with his works, which used traditional Japanese imagery in strong, unorthodox, contemporary ways: a fresh approach for the time.

Poster for personal exhibition **The Face**, 1968.

Poster for the **5th Biennial Exhibition of Prints** in Tokyo, 1966.

Poster for **Caron Dressmaking School**, 1953.

Jan Lenica [Poland]

Il Bidone (The Swindlers), poster for the Federico Fellini movie, 1957.

The Locomotive, children's book cover, early 1960s.

Verdi: *Otello*, thetare poster, an award-winner at the International Poster Biennale Warsaw, 1979.

1928-2001; born in Poznan
Admitted to AGI, 1956

Jan studied music at Poznan College and later architecture at Warsaw Polytechnic (1947–52), but then became a painter. He produced cartoons for a satirical journal, before turning to poster design. His work has simplicity of expression and an abstract use of line and colour. He received the Polish State's award for lithography (1955). In the 50s and 60s he designed numerous posters and won prizes for his film posters (1961) and the first prize at the Warsaw Biennale 1966. In 1972 Lenica designed posters for the Munich Olympics. He experimented with film, first in collaboration with Borowczyk, later alone. He produced an enormous body of work.

Lenica worked in a unique style on surreal illustrations, graphic art, children's books, stage designs, satirical cartoons and animations, exploring the complex relationship between the individual and the state. As a poster designer he was strongly influenced by his countryman Henryk Tomaszewski. Lenica was an author and a professor at Harvard (1974) and the Berlin Academy of Fine Arts (1986–94); from 1963 he worked in Paris. More awards came from Versailles (Toulouse-Lautrec Grand Prix 1961), Karlovy Vary, Katowice, Catania, Bologna. He had numerous exhibitions throughout Europe and the US.

Riccardo Manzi [Italy]

1913-1993
Admitted to AGI, 1956

Henrion wrote of him: *'Manzi trained in Naples. He worked for the editorial departments of various papers in Rome and Milan. His experience in the newspaper world inspired him to do a series of cartoons portraying the contemporary world. His approach is frequently humorous, as in his advertisement for a Milanese restaurant. Later he devoted much of his time to painting and advertising. Since 1953, his work has been exhibited at various galleries in Milan, Rome, Modena, Parma and La Spezia.'*

Advertisement for **Luigi Franchi**, a Milanese restaurant, 1964.

Vivere in Due, book cover, published by Feltrinelli, 1961.

Advertisement for **Pirelli**, 1957.

Les Enfants du Paradis, movie poster, 1955.

Napolitani a Milano, movie poster, 1954.

L'Appel du Destin, movie poster, 1954.

Julian Palka [Poland]

1923-2002; born in Poznan
Admitted to AGI, 1956

Palka was one of the leading figures of the Polish poster school. He produced some of the famous posters for the French and Italian *'new wave'* movies, which were so important in Poland's cultural life in the fifties. Palka was a great personality, but always remained a modest and warm man. He studied at the Warsaw Academy of Fine Arts until 1951. Two years later he was employed by the Academy, where he served twice as rector. He was one of the pillars of that institution; even when retired, he still frequented the diploma shows. He also lectured at the European Academy of Art.

He won the Gold Medal at the Warsaw International Poster Biennale 1968 and the All-Poland Biennial in Katowice 1967. He was involved with exhibitions and designed Polish pavilions at international fairs. His commemorative posters for the Auschwitz victims are an outstanding achievement. Palka collaborated on the design of the Auschwitz memorial and the monument for the 1939 defenders of Warsaw. He died after a long illness. Palka and Tomaszewski were truly two of a kind.

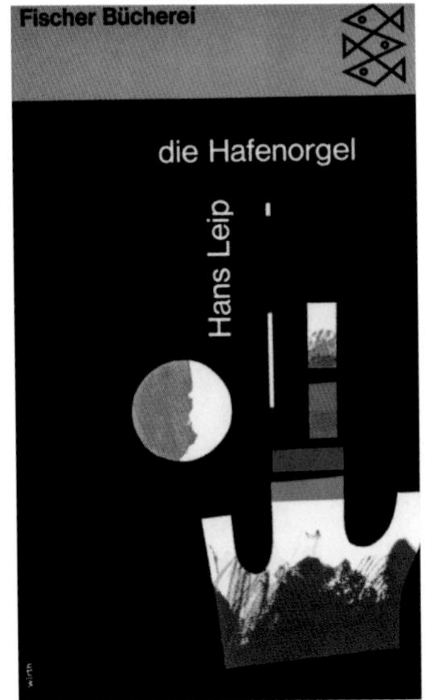

Kurt Wirth [Switzerland]

1917-1996; born in Berne
Admitted to AGI, 1956

For three years Wirth was an apprentice with Hans Fischer and other designers and took courses at the Berne Gewerbeschule, before opening his own atelier in 1937. He illustrated books, newspapers and periodicals. He designed 180 book covers for Fischer Verlag of Frankfurt, and produced promotional material for the pharmaceutical industry. In 1955 he was one of the four artists who founded Tim (Team). For five years they created murals and paintings in all techniques. Kurt Wirth was a great draughtsman, who wrote excellent books about the techniques of this art; he won a gold medal at the Israel Biennale for art books 1977. Wirth taught at the Berne Kunstgewerbeschule. He was the president of the VSG, the Swiss designers association, 1956–59. He had solo exhibitions in Berne, Zürich, Frankfurt and London. But aside from all that, he was an excellent poster designer, who contributed strongly to the great Swiss reputation. He worked for Swiss Railways, for book promotions, sports and Swissair. He was also the designer of a corporate programme for that airline. The images and type in his posters were very well matched. Kurt was a true AGI member, with strong, valuable opinions.

Swissair brochure, early 1960s.

Jack Richardson: ***The Prison Life of Harris Filmore***, book cover, S. Fischer Verlag.

Hans Leip: ***Die Hafenorgel***, book cover, S. Fischer Verlag.

Au Grand Passage, poster, c. 1940.

Greetings from Switzerland, tourist poster, 1937.

Graubünden, Switzerland: The Holiday Paradise, tourist poster, 1937.

Alois Carigiet [Switzerland]

1902-1985; born in Trun
Admitted to AGI, 1957

After an apprenticeship in visual art, Carigiet trained in Zürich in an advertising agency (1923–27). He then started his own practice and got assignments to design posters and stage sets. He was co-founder of the Cabaret Cornichon for which he produced sets, costumes and the publicity. His pre-war posters are classics. The Zürich men's fashion firm PKZ was an important client. His reputation opened the doors of AGI: he was chosen as what AGI dubbed at the time *'an honorary member'*.

In 1939 Carigiet moved back to his native mountains and focused on painting. He later also created several successful children's books. He received the Hans Christian Andersen Award for illustration in 1966. He had many exhibitions in Switzerland, Germany and Canada, and became well known in Japan and the USA.

'In my own tiny first flat (1956), I had one major piece of art: a Carigiet Swiss lake-and-mountains landscape.' – Ben Bos

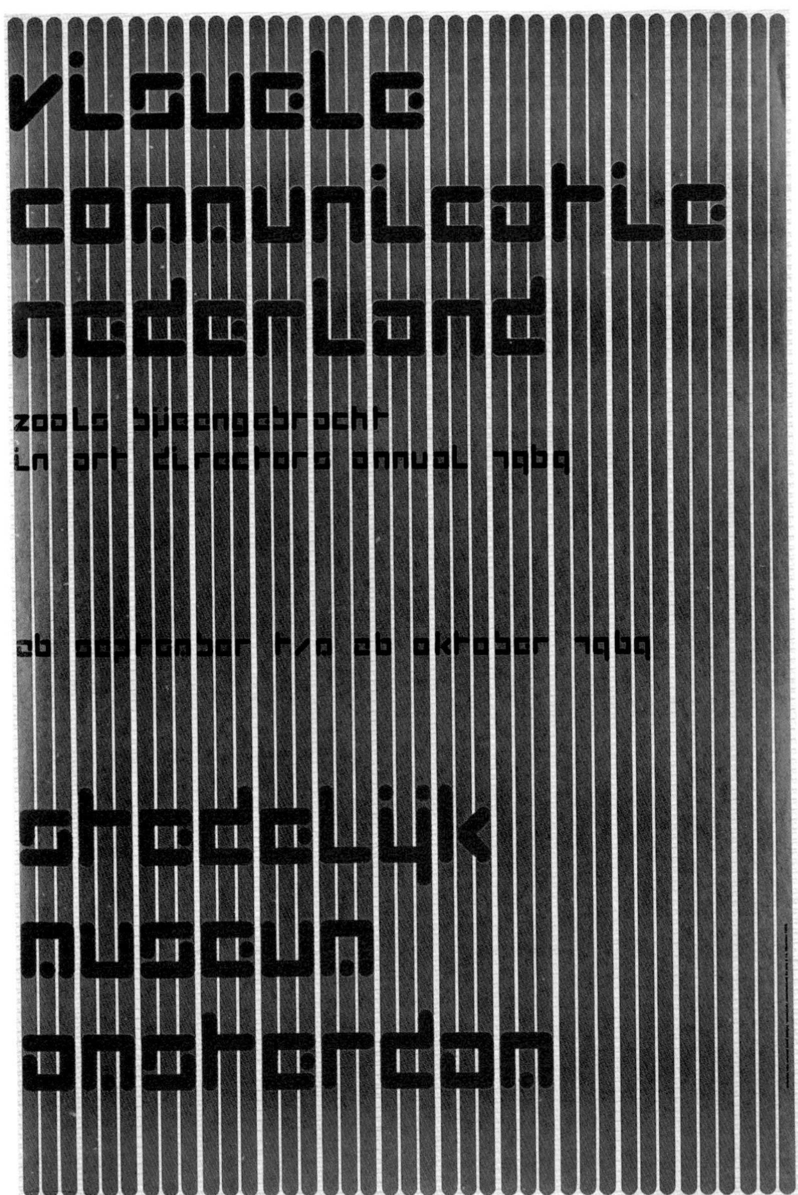

Wim Crouwel [The Netherlands]

1928– born in Groningen
Admitted to AGI, 1957
International President 1980-1983

Studied fine art (1946–49) at the Academy Minerva in Groningen. Joined an exhibition design firm (1962) where he gained his first experience in graphic design. Inspired by Swiss design, he started a freelance practice in Amsterdam (1964). In 1956 Crouwel set up a studio with industrial designer Kho Liang Ie; they collaborated on 3D and graphic design projects. He experimented with letterforms, graphic systems and a rigorous examination of the grid. During the 50s he met with leading Swiss colleagues and witnessed the emerging International Style. Became the first general secretary of Icograda (1963). In that year with Benno Wissing, Friso Kramer and the Schwarz brothers he founded the first multi-disciplinary Dutch design group, Total Design, which was to become a dominant force in the Netherlands. He designed the standard Dutch postage stamps and produced extensive work for the Stedelijk Museum (1964–85). Wim extended the grid to become a matrix within which he constructed his New Alphabet. At Delft University Crouwel became a part-time professor (1972) and, after leaving Total Design (1980), a full-time professor. Was appointed director of Museum Boijmans-van Beuningen, Rotterdam (1985). He received the British OBE, is a RDI, Knight of the Dutch Lion, Officer of Orange Nassau. Received the Oeuvre Award 2004 from the Dutch Fund for Fine Arts, Design and Architecture.

Visual Communication in the Netherlands, poster, 1969. Dutch Art Directors Club.

Edgar Fernhout, exhibition poster, 1963. Van Abbemuseum, Eindhoven.

The New Architecture, exhibition poster, 1982. Architectural Institute, Amsterdam.

Travel by ZIM ship, tourist poster, 1960.

Visit Israel, one of a series of posters for Government Tourist Office of Israel.

Jean David [Israel]

1908-1993; born in Bucharest, Romania
Admitted to AGI, 1957

From 1927–33, Jean David studied at the Académie Julian and at the École des Beaux-Arts in Paris. He fled from Romania to Palestine in 1942. He was interned by the British in Cyprus, but fought later in the British Navy. From 1948 on he worked as a painter and graphic designer in Tel-Aviv. He made murals for public buildings, including the university campus in Jerusalem, as well as for the Israeli pavilions at the Brussels and Montreal world fairs. His posters for the Ministry of Tourism won the gold and silver medals at the Milan Triennale 1954. El-Al, the New Tel-Aviv Museum, Rothschild Hospital and the Jerusalem Theatre were among his clients. Also, David worked on the interiors of seven Israeli passenger ships, including two 50-metre stained-glass windows for the *Shalom*. His one-man exhibitions were held in Paris, London, New York, Mexico City, Johannesburg and Bucharest. In 1967 he designed the poster for an AGI congress that did not take place, because of the Six-Day War with Egypt.

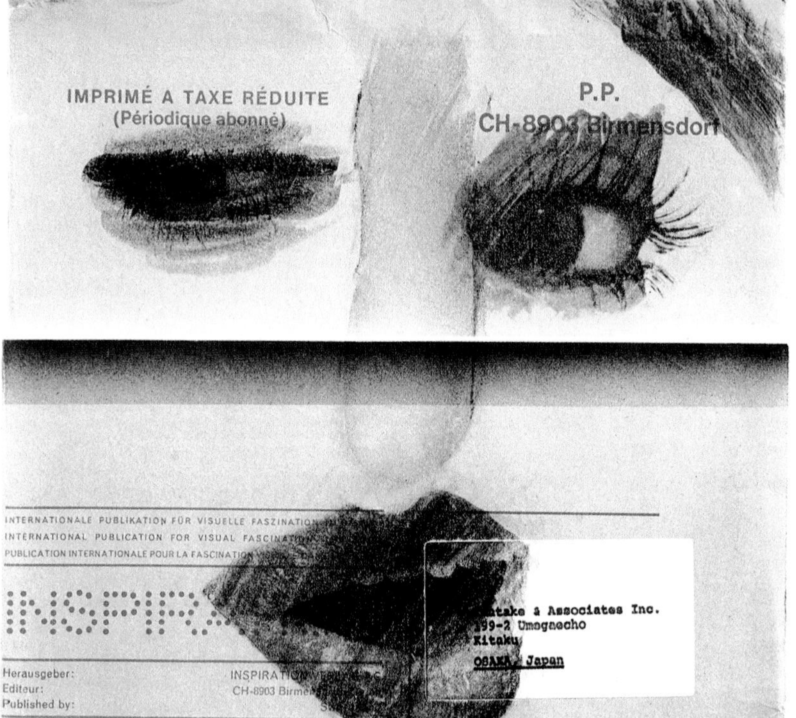

Shichiro Imatake [Japan]

1905-2000; born in Kobe
Admitted to AGI, 1957

When he started his activities in the profession, in the mid-twenties, Imatake concentrated on literature, films and music. But he also became involved with advertising for Kobe Daimaru Department store, for which he worked from 1927 till 2000. (At his age of 94! This looks like information for the *Guinness Book of Records*.) He foresaw the worldwide rise of media art. Imatake was strongly influenced by Bauhaus and tried, with the help of their theories, to bring *'zu-an'* (pattern) design into the 20th century. He was a leader and promoter of the modernist movement in Japan. Apart from being a designer, Imatake was also a painter.

He designed the logotype for a Japanese *'wonder cream'*, Mentholatum. After the war he worked for Sumitomo Bank, designing posters that carried a peace message. He also designed a cover for an early edition of *Idea* magazine.

Original design for cover of weekly magazine **Asahi Journal**, 1971.

New Dimension False and Real Image, frottage on relief, 1977.

Magazine cover, **Idea #12**, 1955.

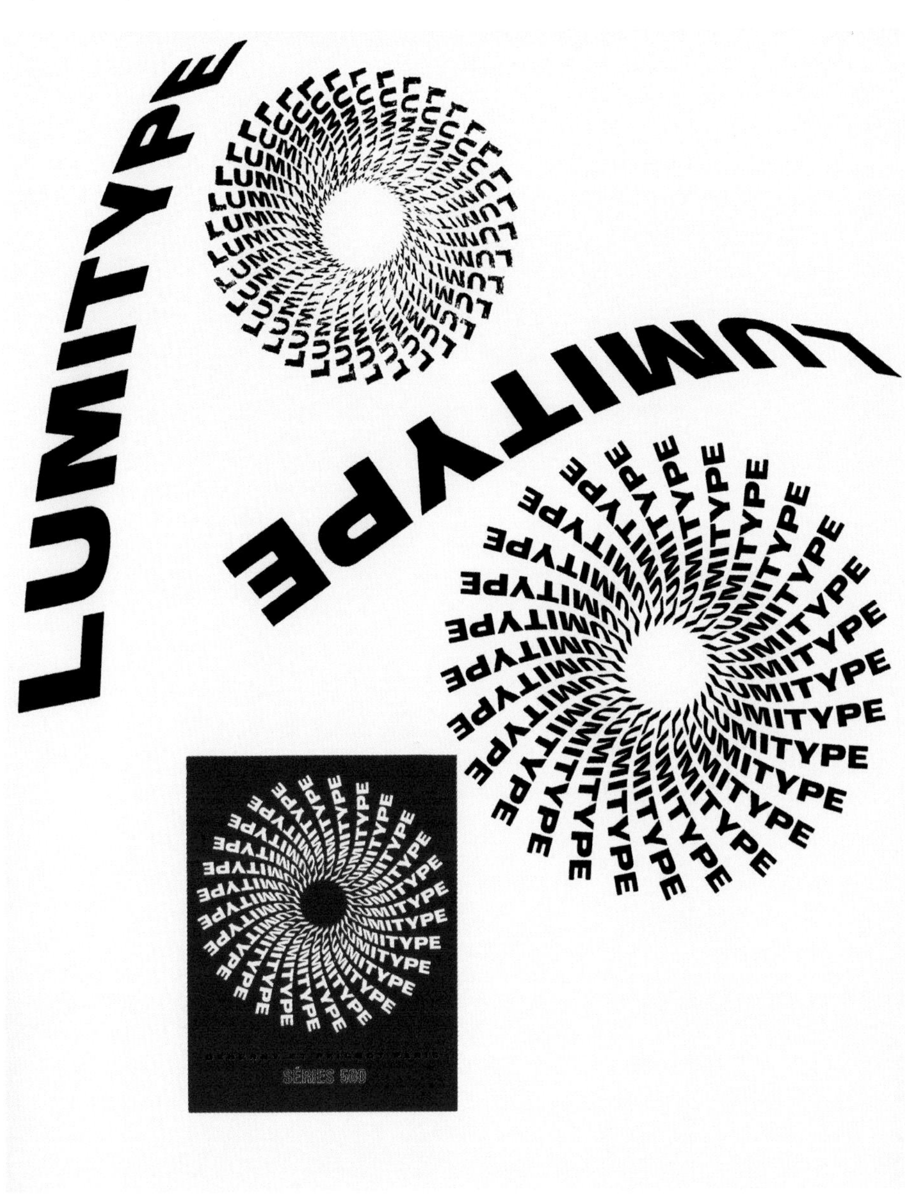

Trademarks for the photo typesetting machine **Lumitype** designed for Deberny et Peignot, Paris, early 60s.

Rémy Peignot [France]

1924-1986; born in Paris
Admitted to AGI, 1957

Rémy was the grandson of George and the son of Charles Peignot, from the famous Deberny et Peignot type foundry. He studied at St Gallen art college in Switzerland, before he started to work for his father's firm. In 1955, Rémy designed the typeface Cristal, which was very important because it became part of the first set of typefaces to be printed on a dry transfer paper called Typophane.

Later, after the installation of the first Lumitype photo typesetting machine, Peignot produced fascinating type compositions, made possible by this new technology. For three years, he also was the art director of the magazine *En Direct*. In 1968 he set up his own studio.

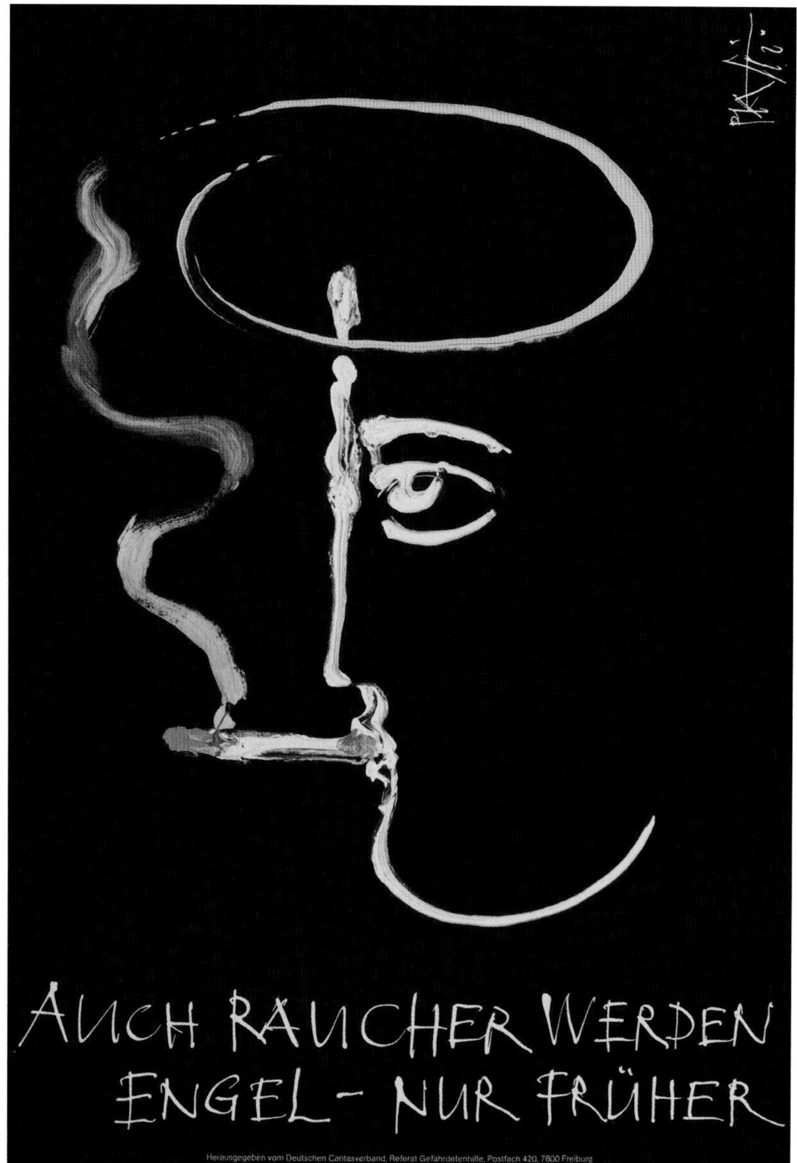

Celestino Piatti [Switzerland]

1922– born in Wangen
Admitted to AGI, 1957

Piatti studied at the Zürich Kunstgewerbeschule from 1937 and had an apprenticeship 1938–42 with the Fretz Bros, Zürich. He opened his own studio in 1948, and later also one in Paris.He was a successful poster designer with an international reputation, who worked in a clear personal style. Was also involved in publicity campaigns and for 30 years was responsible for the artistic and typographic design and publicity for the German publishers DTV. 5,000 paperbacks came through his hands with a distinct brand image. White covers with black type (Akzidenz Grotesk) and mostly colourful illustrations. Some 300 million books were printed. DTV founded the Celestino Piatti Prize for graphics in publishing (1983). Piatti worked for the Swiss encyclopaedia publishers Mengis + Zier and for Ciba AG in Basel, as well as the Swiss Pavilion at the 1967 Montreal Expo. He also did murals and created monumental stained glass. He designed and illustrated seven children's books, which were translated into 12 languages. From the mid-60s he became socially engaged, designing many posters for Caritas Germany (1967–2005) and socio-critical illustrations. Piatti also created Swiss stamps, packaging and animations. Later he turned to fine art: oil paintings, watercolours, drawings and prints. He was honoured with many one-man exhibitions and awards, at home and abroad.

Even Smokers Become Angels – Only Sooner, charity poster, 1981.

Cover for children's book **The Golden Apple**, Japanese edition, 1970.

100 Years of the Animal Protection Society 1897–1997, charity poster, 1997.

Poster for exhibition of paintings by Tomaszewski's wife **Teresa Pagowska**, 1988.

Cat illustration, used for a birthday calendar and for the cover of **Graphis #186**, 1976.

Peter Shaffer: ***Amadeus***, theatre poster, 1981.

Gitanes, advertising poster, 1991.

Henryk Tomaszewski [Poland]

1914-2005; born in Warsaw
Admitted to AGI, 1957

Henryk was the founder of the Polish Poster School. The Dutch newspaper *NRC* wrote an obituary in which it was said that *'Poland lost probably his most important post-war artist'*, and *'He taught his people to think.'* Tomaszewski came from a musical family, but chose to abandon his violin. In the harsh Communist period there was only a place for political posters. Henryk: *'Politics are like the weather: something you have to live with.'* When Stalin died, things became a bit more relaxed.

His 1959 poster for a Henry Moore exhibition was an absolute hit. Unequalled simplicity, strong colours and *'catching the whole story in one image'* were his recipe. Polish posters became an artform in the sixties. The authorities were pleased that they could show their *'liberal'* attitude towards the arts. He only spoke Polish, his wife was the interpreter for the many (often French) students (later famous themselves), who were attracted by the maestro. He was *'a thinking artist, his spontaneous utterances were the outcome of observation, thought and experience.'*

Read about his student Alain Le Quernec elsewhere in this book. Henryk died after a long illness.

Saul Bass [USA]

1920-1996; born in New York City
Admitted to AGI, 1958

Saul studied 1936–39 at the Art Students League and 1944–45 at the Brooklyn College, New York. Had his own design and art direction practice in New York, 1936–46. Saul was the principal of Saul Bass & Associates, Los Angeles (1946–80), later renamed Bass Yager & Associates. Bass worked as a graphic designer, animator, photographer and film director. He designed trademarks/logos and corporate identity programmes for AT&T, Bell Systems, United Airlines, Minolta, Alcoa, Warner Communication, Exxon and many more major companies.

Bass changed the world's approach to movie titles and trailers with his innovative titles for more than 40 movies including *Exodus*, *The Man with the Golden Arm*, *Bonjour Tristesse*, *Vertigo* and *Psycho*. Saul Bass scored an Oscar and a Moscow Film Festival gold award for his documentary *Why Man Creates*. He also directed special sequences in feature films. Designed posters and graphics for the LA Olympics 1984. Was US Art Director of the Year (1957). Elected in 1978 to the NY Art Directors' Hall of Fame. Got a Lifetime Achievement Award (1988) from the ADC of Los Angeles. Saul was an amiable personality, and always present at AGI congresses.

Title sequence for **Vertigo** by Alfred Hitchcock, 1958.

Film poster for **The Man with the Golden Arm** by Otto Preminger, 1956.

Title sequence for **Anatomy of a Murder** by Otto Preminger, 1959.

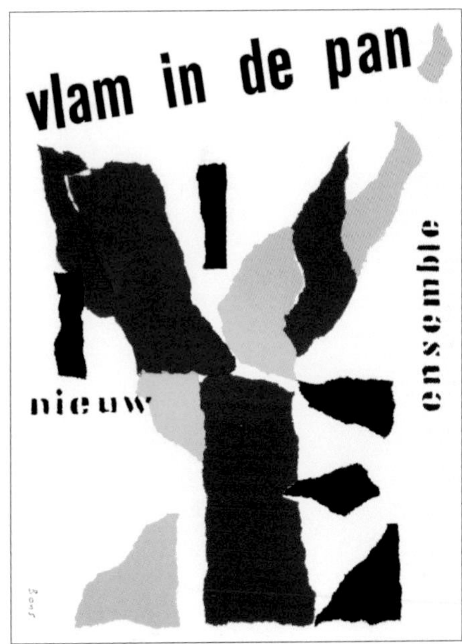

Het oordeel van Paris, poster for the Appel theatre group.

Life on a String, poster for the Nieuw Ensemble theatre group.

Vlam in de Pan, poster for the Nieuw Ensemble theatre group.

Jan Bons [The Netherlands]

1918– born in Rotterdam
Admitted to AGI, 1958

Studied at the Royal Academy in The Hague (Paul Citroen, Paul Schuitema and Gerard Kiljan), before switching to the Nieuwe Kunstschool. His teachers got him involved in exhibition design for the Stedelijk Museum Amsterdam, where he met Sandberg and Duwaer. Bauhaus teacher Johannes Itten was a visiting professor. His first designs were for the Spanish anti-fascists, refugees and the Vigilant Committee. Co-operated during WW2 with Frans Duwaer on illegal booklets and with Dick Elffers on identity papers.

With nine other painters, he took part in an exhibition on Defensible Democracy (1946), where he met architect Gerrit Rietveld, with whom he collaborated till Rietveld's death in 1964. In 1947 he won second prize in the international UN poster competition *'One World or None'*. Also created monumental art for an Amsterdam cinema. In 1952 he painted a 76-metre mural for a Mexican exhibition *'Así es Hollanda'*, curated by Rietveld. Designed emblem for the Dutch pavilion at Expo 58 and objects for Rietveld's Hall of Textiles. From 1962 he created the posters for Studio Appel Theatre group and later for the IDFA film festival. Awarded the Werkman Prize 1969, the Lifetime Award 1992, KVGO culture prize 1993, Piet Zwart award 2003. Honorary member of BNO. Left AGI after a few years.

Hans Hartmann [Switzerland]

1913-1991; born in Villnachern
Admitted to AGI, 1958

Hartmann worked for two years in the advertising department of Bally Shoes and then attended the Zürich Kunstgewerbeschule (1932–36). He shared an atelier with Hans Fischer in Berne, then started his own in 1938; later on, Hartmann moved to Köniz. He was a designer of many effective logos and posters for important firms and institutions, such as Swiss Railways, the Swiss National Council for Road Safety, and Swissair. For the Swiss PTT he designed several stamps. He received a Certificate of Merit from NY ADC.

The Swiss Federal Department of the Interior granted him five awards for posters and three in a competition for books and stamps to promote an anti-malaria campaign. He designed posters and folders for the Ministry of Transport. He had the unique visual power and clarity that allowed him to come up with posters that could work well without text (practical in his country, with its four languages). Hartmann also designed the cover for *Graphis* #28, 1949.

Poster for the **Swiss Road Safety Council**, 1964.

Logo design for **SBB Swiss railways**, 1972.

Swiss National Exhibition, Lausanne, 1964.

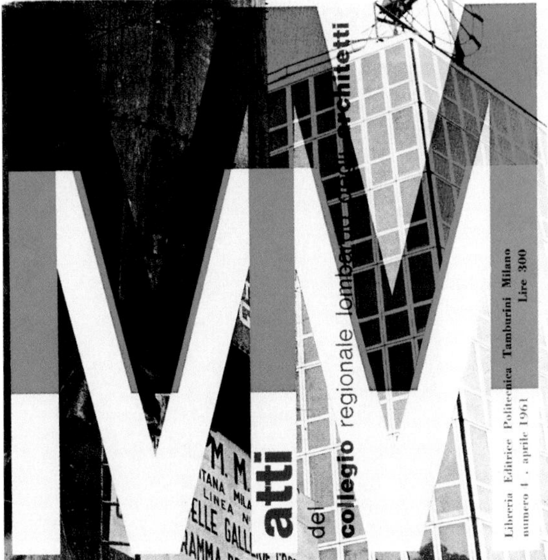

Poster for the **Milan Triennale**, 1947.

Cover for the **Regional College of Architects of Lombardy**, 1959–63.

1000 km at Monza, poster for a motor-racing event, 1968.

Max Huber [Switzerland]

1919-1992; born in Baar
Admitted to AGI, 1958

From 1935 Huber studied at the Zürich Kunstgewerbeschule and then did an apprenticeship. In 1937 he joined an advertising company. After a short period in the Swiss Army, he started in 1940 at Studio Boggeri in Milan, and also continued his studies at the Accademia Brera. In 1942 he returned to Switzerland, working for *Du* magazine. He joined the modern artists of the Allianze group. During the war he worked for socialist organizations and publishers. He returned to Milan after the war. Huber taught for two years at the Scuola Rinascità.

He worked for RAI (Italian radio and TV), ENI, La Rinascente, Olivetti, Einaudi, Milan Triennale, Automobile Club of Italy and Montecantini, and made posters for the Monza car races. He designed exhibitions, many jazz record covers and book covers. Huber got several international awards. He taught for years in Milan and Lugano, and had many exhibitions at home and abroad as a constructivist and concrete artist. His redesign of the logos for La Rinascente and Essolunga supermarkets made the general public more aware of graphic design. He had a life-long partnership with Achille Castiglioni. His widow Aoi Kono created the m.a.x. museo in Chiasso, where his and her work and archives are held.

Herbert W. Kapitzki [Germany]

1925-2005; born in Danzig
(now Gdansk, Poland)
Admitted to AGI, 1958

Kapitzki's studies started in Danzig and Hamburg and were completed at the Stuttgart Academy of Fine Arts 1948–52. In graphic design he was, however, self-taught. Starting an inquiry into theory and practice of design in mass communication, he became freelance in 1953. He was a real educator: running a department at the Ulm Hochschule für Gestaltung, becoming head of the Institute of Visual Communication at Frankfurt (1969), and a branch of the Institute of Environmental Design. Moving to Berlin in 1970, he was appointed as professor at the Hochschule der Künste, where he taught until 1990. During the 1970s he worked intensely on changes to the name and the curriculum of this school. He pioneered the development of functional design, pictograms and international standards for orientation systems. A systematic approach to design always remained a central theme in the teaching he offered to his many German and international students. His lasting legacy can be traced in their later works. Kapitzki redesigned the Frankfurt Historical Museum in 1971. The German pavilion for the Montreal Expo 1967 was one of his many exhibition designs. He wrote several books about grids *'underneath design'*, and also worked for SWF television and did the visual identity for Schering AG.

LGA, exhibition poster, 1962.

LGA Centre: Design, exhibition poster.

Jahrbuch 57, Baden-Württemberg.

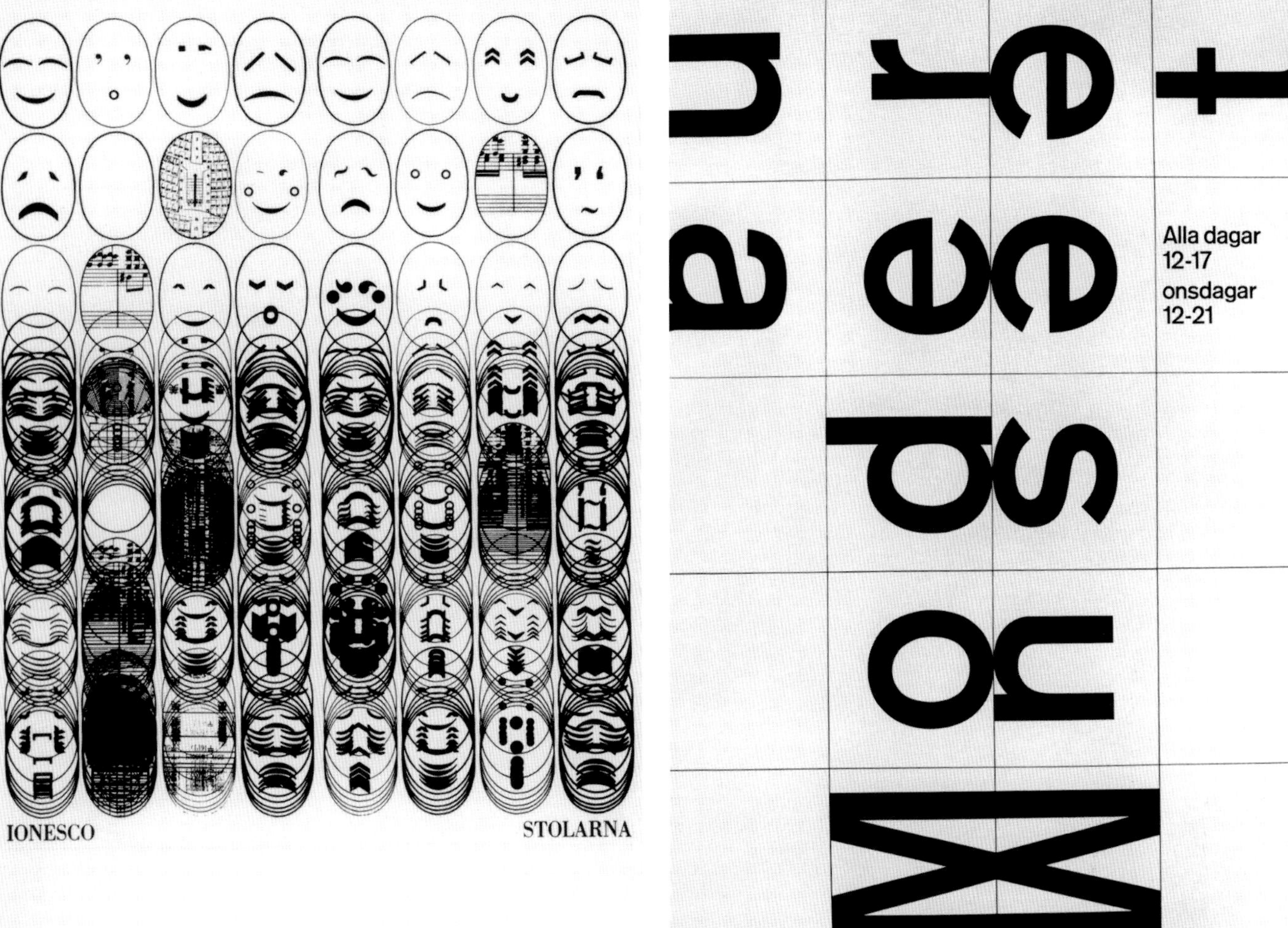

Ionesco: *The Chairs*, theatre poster, 1960.

Poster for the **Moderna Museet**, Stockholm, 1963.

John Melin & Anders Österlin [Sweden]

John: 1921-1992; born in Malmø
Anders: 1926– born in Malmø
Admitted to AGI, 1959

John Melin and Anders Österlin were partners in advertising, described as *'gurus'* of the 60s and 70s. Melin became famous for creating the Moderna Museet's first graphic profile, which looked Swiss-inspired. The ideas were John's, the drawing Anders's. They co-operated, and they were actually known as *'anden'* and *'handen'* (the spirit and the hands). As directors at the advertising and design agencies Svenska Telegrambyrån and Arbman, together they created brilliant and accurate designs, full of wit! John Melin's ability to find new surprising solutions for commercial as well as everyday projects has few counterparts within Swedish graphic design. Under the signature *'M&Ö'*, they designed posters, books, catalogues, cardboard packaging and paper cartons. The catalogues were for artists like Jean Tinguely, Niki de Saint-Phalle and Andy Warhol. For NY MoMA they made a very special one, called *The Machine*, which was a piece of metal. One poster, made for Stockholm Moderna Museet, had text printed in moist glue, sprinkled with cress seeds that sprouted, grew green and then wilted. As well as all this, Anders is also a painter, who started a Swedish art group called Imaginisterne. In 1947 he became involved with the Cobra group, with Appel, Corneille, Jorn and Constant.

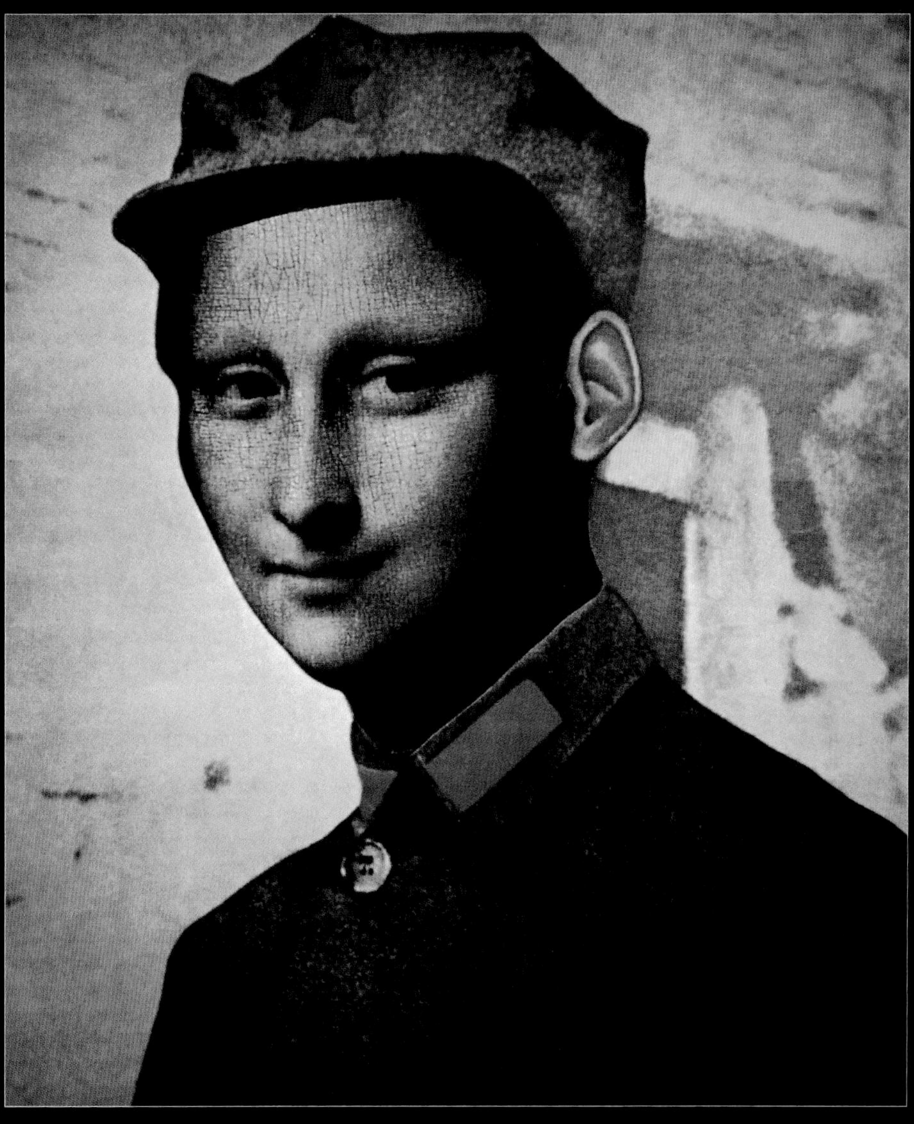

Mona Tse Tung, Roman Cieslewicz, France.

60s

The 1960s: Revolution in the Air...

Fifteen years had passed since **'Little Boy'** exploded, the bomb that wiped Hiroshima from the map and brought an end to WW2. Years in which the world licked its wounds and worked flat out on reconstruction. After all that suffering, the 1960s were welcomed as a new decade of optimism, of chances and change. But the world would not be the world if everything progressed smoothly and painlessly. It was still business as usual...

The bloodbath of Sharpeville, the assassinations of John and Robert Kennedy, of Congo's Lumumba, of Malcolm X, of South Africa's Verwoerd, of Martin Luther King; war (and protests against it) in and outside Vietnam, peace perhaps in Algeria, but war enough between Israel and Egypt. A religious civil war broke out in Northern Ireland. And there was the surprise attack on Czechoslovakia, which, in the true spirit of the sixties, was attempting, in vain, to celebrate the more liberated political atmosphere of Prague Spring.

Young people everywhere were protesting against the established order and authoritarian leaders. There were student uprisings in Paris and elsewhere in Europe. In Amsterdam there were '*happenings*', with the Provos cleverly exposing and challenging the weaknesses of the authorities. Their protests were given their own graphic language, which could be read on the banners outside their squats. More extreme were the German Baader-Meinhof group and the Italian Red Brigade. One word sums them up. Ruthless. Nor should we forget the astonishing behaviour of the young Chinese Red Guards during the Cultural Revolution (1966–69) orchestrated by Mao Tse Tung, whose actions were totally humiliating and destructive towards everyone and everything.

This was the decade of frequent partings. Nelson Mandela was *'buried alive'* on Robben Island. The famous truly deceased included such politicians as Winston Churchill, Pandit Nehru, Konrad Adenauer, Dwight Eisenhower and Clement Attlee. Soviet leaders also came and went. And we said goodbye to Marilyn Monroe.

The Russian, Yuri Gagarin, followed the dog Laika into space as the first human cosmonaut, in Vostok I. The American Alan Shepard was hot on his heels. The space race became a prestigious political billion-dollar game. It was also the decade in which the astronauts Neil Armstrong and Buzz Aldrin set foot on the Moon, broadcasting television images and bringing back moon rocks. Men space-walked on thin umbilical chords. Satellites criss-crossed the heavens by the dozen. The supersonic British/French Concorde took its first test flights. At the same time, the Pope banned all forms of birth control. The South African Dr Christian Barnard performed the first heart transplant. And so a handful of mortals, in their own way, played God.

But how lively the 1960s were! Federico Fellini produced his *Dolce Vita*. Macho James Bond, Agent 007 appeared, with all his high-tech violence. On the other hand, you could opt for Alpine meadows with the sugary *The Sound of Music* and the tearjerker *Bambi*. Minimal Art, Conceptual Art and Op Art filled the galleries and museums: revolutions on canvas. The decade of The Beatles and The Stones: a rift in society that will only heal once the last witness has passed away. *All You Need is Love* and *Satisfaction*. Pop and hippies, keywords for the 1960s. Biba and Carnaby Street, Mary Quant, swinging London! Colourful facades, lots and lots of Union Jacks. Anything and everything went: mini skirts, flower power, and long hair, loads of long hair. Men in fur coats and too many rings. Even television, by now an accepted part of life, was suddenly in colour. And, in London's Fulham Road, Terence Conran opened the first of his Habitat and Conran stores, which were later to spread worldwide; when he retired in 1990 he had an empire of 1,000 outlets.

Immediately prior to the beginning of this decade, Frank Lloyd Wright paid his last visit to the building site of his almost completed Guggenheim Museum next to Central Park in New York. Three weeks later, he was dead.

Alvar Aalto continued to build, enriching his Finnish fatherland. Marcel Breuer pulled out all the stops for the Whitney Museum in New York. Buckminster Fuller created his gigantic Dome for the Montreal Expo 67. Mies van der Rohe produced the National Gallery in Berlin. Charles and Ray Eames constructed the US Pavilion for the New York World Fair. The governments of India, Bangladesh and Brazil commissioned Le Corbusier, Louis Kahn and Oscar Niemeyer to create major government buildings. Eero Saarinen gave TWA its unique terminal at New York's Kennedy Airport and repeated the performance for Dulles International in Washington. Kenzo Tange and Frei Otto provided the spectacular Olympic arenas in Tokyo and Munich. Jørn Utzon created the fabulous Sydney Opera House. The list is, naturally, far from complete: the world was anxious to show that the war was now really behind us. Good times were on the horizon.

Graphic design itself underwent turbulent developments. At the simple level of the studio and the drawing boards, designers switched from wet to dry photocopiers and dry transfer lettering. They sometimes even had a heading setter in their own darkroom. One gadget followed another. Letraset and Mécanorma were doing booming business. Dry transfer typography, having *'escaped'* from the iron grip of the lead diktat, often had extremely narrow letterspacing and was an absolute abomination to the orthodox typographer. The vertical camera in the studio enabled designers to rapidly enlarge and reduce. Computers were still only used for the storage and organization of information. It was not until the late 1980s that they were to invade the profession as tools in the design and realization process.

Offset rapidly improved in quality and density in the 1960s, gaining ground at the expense of letterpress. Rotation presses were capable of churning out large numbers. (Colour) lithography started to oust the metal image carriers, the clichés. Screenprinting was often automated and produced increasingly higher quality, which greatly benefited poster designers. Generations of photosetting machines entered the fray against the established order in the *'lead'* composing rooms. Enormous investments were made but, in the end, photosetting proved to be nothing more than a transitional phase. One example of the speed with which systems followed one after another was the essay that Wim Crouwel published in 1967 in one of the *Kwadraatblad* editions issued by publisher/designer Pieter Brattinga. The booklet – now a desirable object amongst collectors – was entitled *New Alphabet: An Introduction for a Programmed Typography*. The alphabet in question aimed to provide a solution to the limited possibilities of the cathode ray tube in setting apparatus at that time. A lot has been published on that *'new alphabet'* even as late as the 21st century but, in retrospect, this was primarily due to the daring, unorthodox nature of the letters and characters. Things progressed far more quickly in reality, and this speed was not uncommonly paired with a loss of quality, as was the case when enlarging letter images from too small an original.

The design profession itself was on the move, as a result of entirely new demands from governmental, commercial and organizational sectors, in particular. The profession split up into the individually exercised craft on one hand and, on the other, practices in which various designers worked together, sometimes supported by commercial advisors and managers. The rise of the design agencies was strongly stimulated by the call for identity programmes and other complex systems that were above the capabilities of the majority of individual designers. The soloists (sometimes assisted by an apprentice or a few work placement students) remained primarily active in poster, book and type design, in illustration and other specialisms demanding a strictly personal signature. Designers such as the Dutchman Dick Elffers talked of *'the enemy'*, as they felt their prospects were being threatened. The enemy, in other words, was the design agency! But those same *'professionalized'* colleagues set developments in motion towards better rules and rates and towards a more mature working relationship with clients and governments.

Increasingly large agencies spread like oil stains throughout the graphic design sector. At the same time, the profession was starting to organize itself better. National professional organizations joined together under the umbrella of Icograda, the International Council of Graphic Design Associations, which held congresses annually and developed many educational programmes. In Ulm, the Hochschule für Gestaltung was set up and seen as the successor of the Bauhaus, which the Nazis had closed on 11 April 1933 for being *'corrupt'*.

This was the dawn of richly decorated annual reports, internal newsletters and company brochures. The arrival of 'wide-body' aircraft required architectural innovations to create increasingly larger airport buildings, which also demanded new systems for routing passenger flows. Benno Wissing *'opened the dance'* with Schiphol Amsterdam in 1967, in collaboration with architect/designer Kho Liang Ie.

This approach was much emulated, all over the world. Jock Kinneir and Margaret Calvert enriched the UK with an innovative, extremely practical and legible signing system for the road network. The London agency Fletcher/Forbes/Gill quickly became Crosby/Fletcher/Forbes and then Pentagram: the beginning of a massively influential factor in international graphic, industrial and spatial design. And all this in one decade.

Ben Bos, Amsterdam, 2006

1962: AGI congress and exhibition in Amsterdam, The Netherlands.

Hilversum, Steendrukkerij De Jong & Co. Pieter Brattinga staged an exhibition of Japanese children's toys in the canteen of this printer's firm. Hans Schleger, Will Sandberg and Walter Herdeg.

Donald Brun, Otto Treumann, Piet and Mrs Zwart, Olle Eksell, Mrs Sandberg, Jean Colin, Jacques Richez, Gérard Ifert, Tom Eckersley and many other (inter)national graphic design celebrities.

AGI exhibition 'Print Around the Clock' in the Stedelijk Museum.

Hugo Wetli, Celestino Piatti, Kurt Wirth, Josef Müller-Brockmann.

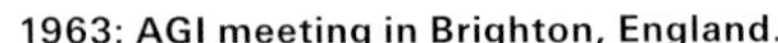

1963: AGI meeting in Brighton, England.

Roger Excoffon, AGI's secretary general.

guided by logic, art by inspiration. They are two ends of a continuous spectrum, a kind of rainbow spectrum with no sharp boundaries in between.'

By 1966 AGI had matured so much that it was able to cross the Atlantic: that year New York was the venue for the congress and for two exhibitions, one at the AIGA and the other in the new Lincoln Art Center. Milton Glaser designed the publicity planned by Walter Allner; George Tscherny, Will Burtin and his wife Cipe Pineles designed the shows. Henrion pleaded in favour of attracting younger members, a plea that would again become topical in the early 1990s. At the same time, however, a proposal had been tabled suggesting that the national presidents should nominate their own members and that membership should be restricted to five or six per country! Discussions, on the other hand, were mainly about finding and retaining members of the highest quality. The acceptance requirement of *'how well known is the candidate?'* was discussed. Tscherny commented that *'fame and reputation'* are not easily measured. By this time, AGI was sporadically publishing a *Bulletin*. Issue 3 in 1967 included the first obituary. The Swede Anders Beckman had died and his stormy, colourful life was depicted with verve.

In the same year, the book *Exempla Graphica* appeared as the first prestigious AGI presentation, a kind of manifesto. Heiri Steiner was responsible for its conception and production. 78 AGI members were given a double spread. In the afterword, Henrion remarked (after five years as chairman): *'Each professional association and especially a self-selected elite, as we are sometimes called, must be concerned with education. My personal opinion is that today too much time is spent on nurturing talent and not enough on developing an intellectual, analytical approach.'*

In 1967, AGI met in Nice. Germano Facetti, recently admitted as an AGI member, immediately became the new international president. The term lightning career is certainly applicable here! The renowned Galerie Maeght in St Paul de Vence was the main attraction of this meeting, of which the annals make little further mention. Facetti is, in any case, featured in many of the photographs of the event.

The following year, Rigi in Switzerland was the venue. It was decided not to invite any speakers, but to examine the changes in the profession in a round table discussion. Heiri Steiner instigated the theme: *'What does design mean today? What does the profession mean to everyone personally and to the world in general?'* One of the responses was that, although the designer has little influence on society, society strongly influences the designer, particularly as economics had surpassed the significance of religion. People were modelling themselves on the ever-changing fashion image the mass media rapidly helped permeate everywhere, which was accepted – often, to be rejected just as quickly but always with the chance of making a comeback. Serious design is not about incidental style, nor personal expression, but high-quality information transfer.

AGI concluded its second decade in London. The content of the meeting was again largely determined by a major philosophical speech from the Belgian, Jacques Richez, *'AGI's conscience'*. In his statement, Jacques invoked both the here-and-now and the future, right up to the 21st century. He harked back to George Him's reaction during their conversation on the flanks of the Rigi Mountain. Him: *'Our duty is to bring order and beauty into a world which would be dull and empty without our participation. We should fulfil this task to the best of our ability: this is the justification of our existence and the reason for our professional pride.'* Cassandre had once preached a credo: *'The duty of a designer is to deliver a message as clearly and as swiftly as possible. His own personal opinion is of no concern.'* Richez, however, considered those words outdated: *'Competition is setting the tone in society and rages the most wildly in those countries with the highest material standards. As designers, we should be aware of the results and consequences of our activities at a social level.'*

These words preceded the presentation of the UNESCO figures, which Jacques quoted, reflecting the expected rapid growth of the world population, the increase in university education and the role of the intellectual elite of the coming 21st century, the future *'boosters of further intensification of competitive relationships'*. He foresaw an explosive market for systematically produced *'goodies'* aimed at accommodating the wishes and driving forces of a living climate strongly determined by those young people: *'production in order to produce'* and *'consumption for its own sake'*.

1964: AGI congress in Alpbach, Austria.

Henrion and George Him.

1966: AGI exhibition in Hamburg, Germany.

1967: AGI congress in Nice, France.

Members visiting the famous Galerie Maeght. Bob and Mrs Noorda, Benno Wissing, Germano Facetti.

1966: First AGI congress in the USA.

Logo by Milton Glaser.

1967: *Exempla Graphica*, AGI. Heiri Steiner designed this wonderful book, showcasing the histories of 78 AGI members.

1968: AGI congress at Rigi-Kaltbad, Switzerland.

The 'Alpine' poster exhibition.

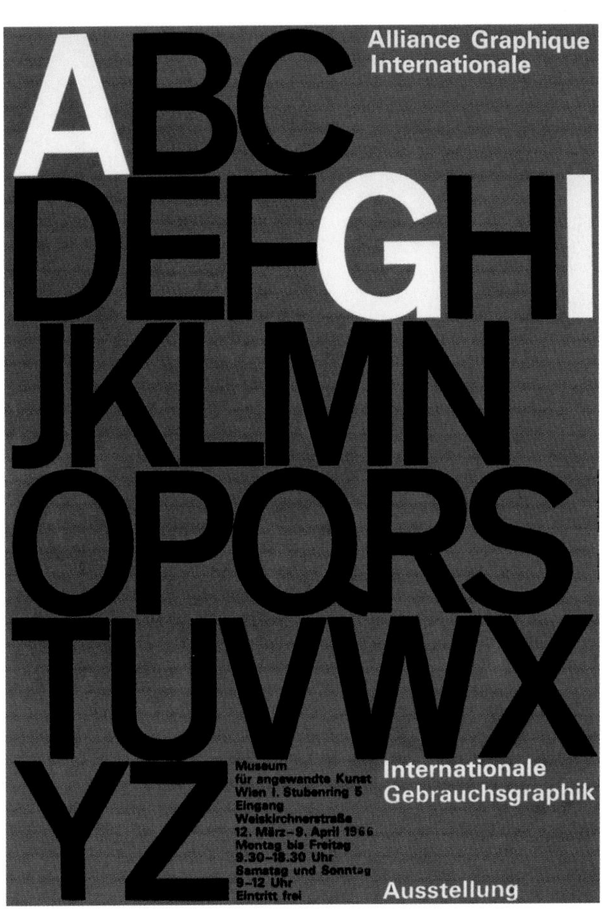

Poster by Hans Fabigan for the AGI 1966 exhibition in Vienna.*

**Donated by MAK - Austrian Museum of Applied Arts/Contemporary Art, Vienna. Photograph: © MAK/Georg Mayer*

Admitted 1960:
Federico, gene
Gerstner, karl *
Lubalin, herb
Zimmermann, wolf d. •*

Admitted 1961:
Hillmann, hans
Kono, takashi *

Admitted 1962:
Allner, walter
Olyff, michel *

Admitted 1963:
Harak, rudolph de

Admitted 1964:
Blase, karl oskar
Edelmann, heinz
Kieser, günther
Nitsche, erik *
Pla-Narbona, josep
Schmid, georg
Ward, james s. •*

Admitted 1965:
Fabigan, hans
Tscherny, george
Vignelli, massimo

Admitted 1966:
Akira, uno •*
Awazu, kiyoshi •
Birdsall, derek *
Calabresi, aldo *
Cieslewicz, roman
Crosby, theo *
Facetti, germano
Fletcher, alan
Forbes, colin
Hara, hiromu *
Hosoya, gan •*
Huguet, enric *
Itoh, kenji *
Morillas i Verdura, antoni
Mroszczak, jósef
Mykkänen, martti
Nagai, kazumasa
Noorda, bob
Ohashi, tadashi •*
Rastorfer, hermann
Schlosser, wolfgang •*
Schrofer, jurriaan
Spencer, herbert
Starowieyski, franciszek *
Swierzy, waldemar
Tanaka, ikko
Wissing, benno
Wolf, henry
Wolsey, tom •*
Yamashiro, ryuichi *

Admitted 1967:
Bongard, hermann *
Calame, georges
Confalonieri, giulio
Hartmann, niels •
Hofmann, armin
Hoyrup, paul •
Ives, norman
Kroll, natasha *
Massey, john
Neuburg, hans
Oksen, jørgen •*
Schmid, max *
Tovaglia, pino
Vellvé, tomàs
Wetli, hugo
Zeugin, mark

Admitted 1968:
Carabott, frederick vincent
Geissbühler, k. domenic
Hiestand, ernst
Hiestand, ursula
Katzourakis, michalis
Külling, ruedi
Saks, arnold
Svoboda, josef

Admitted 1969:
Andrews, gordon *
Hogarth, paul *
Klein, louis *
Kovàr, stanislav
Silverstein, louis
Wollner, leo •*

• *no work submitted*
* *no longer member of AGI*

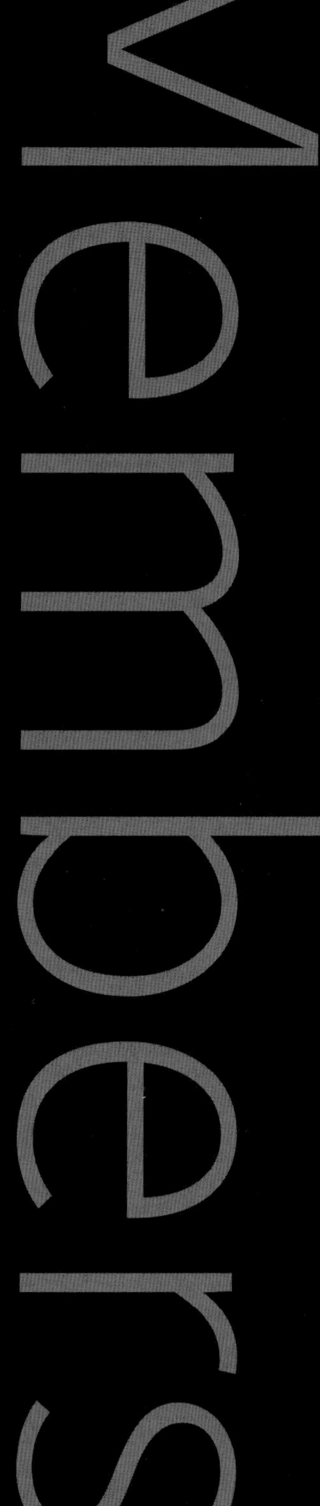

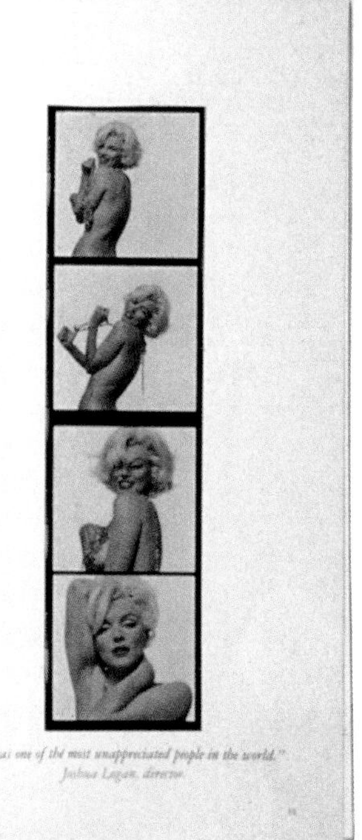

Herb Lubalin [USA]

1919-1981; born in New York City
Admitted to AGI, 1960

Herb graduated from Cooper Union School NY (1939). Was art director (1945) and vice-president (1955) at Sudler & Hennessy. Left in 1964 to set up the design consultancy Herb Lubalin Inc. From 1969 on he led various partnerships with designers such as Tom Carnese, Tony DiSpigna, Seymour Chwast and Alan Peckolick. Herb was an influential, typography-driven and experimental designer. Together with Bradbury Thompson he was a pioneer in extending the role of typography into advertising and visual communication. *'He wrote fluently with pictures and text, using words as images and images as words,'* wrote Ellen Lipton of the Lubalin Study Center.

He founded and designed the magazine *U&lc* for ITC, which was distributed worldwide. As an editorial designer he was in charge of *Saturday Evening Post*, *Eros* (1962), *Fact* (1967) and *Avant Garde* (1968). They were platforms for his creative energy. The masthead of *Avant Garde* led him to design a type family of the same name. Furthermore he created the Serif Gothic typeface. He was the subject of many exhibitions and was awarded internationally. Herb was elected to the NY ADC Hall of Fame (1977) and awarded the AIGA medal in 1981. He was vice-president of AGI and organized the NY AGI Congress 1979.

Spread from **Eros**, a Ginzberg publication.

Cover of **Avant Garde**.

Cover of **U&lc magazine** for an article on American jazz.

Chosen by Hillmann as his favourite drawing in the book **First Choice** by Ken Cato. *'I chose this illustration because I think its idea works with a minimum of effort to achieve its effect.'*

It doesn't hurt, Ma'am. Illustration for an article on drawing.

Hans Hillmann [Germany]

1925– born in Nieder-Mois, Silesia
Admitted to AGI, 1961

Studied from 1948–53 at the Werkakademie Kassel, then worked as a freelance designer in Kassel and Cologne. He has lived in Frankfurt am Main since 1957. From 1961–89 he taught at Kassel University as a full-time professor of graphic design. He has designed film posters, picture stories and illustrations for books and magazines.
Since 1956, his work has been acknowledged by international publications, exhibitions and awards.

Takashi Kono [Japan]

1906-1999; born in Tokyo
Admitted to AGI, 1961

Graduated from Tokyo Academy of Fine Arts (now Tokyo National University of Fine Arts and Music) in 1929. His early work included posters, advertisements, costume and set designs for plays and movies (Tsukiji Little Theatre, Shochiku Kinema). Worked for Nippon Kobo from 1934 to 1939 as art director, established DESKA in 1959, and worked on book designs, magazine covers, packaging, advertisements, stage sets, displays, textiles and monumental designs. Taught design at Musashino University, Tokyo National University of Fine Arts and Music, Joshibi University of Art and Design, and Aichi Prefectural University of Fine Arts and Music, where he later served as president. Lectured at the Ulm School of Design in 1963. Became the Japanese AGI president in 1961. Presiding judge at the International Warsaw Poster Biennale in 1968. Was appointed a Royal Designer for Industry (UK) in 1983, and was elected to the Tokyo ADC Hall of Fame in 1986. He held his first solo exhibition in 1967. A posthumous solo exhibition was held at Ginza Graphic Gallery (GGG) in 2003 and the National Museum of Modern Art, Tokyo in 2005. Published *Package Design* in 1956, and *Takashi Kono: My Momentum* in 1983.

NIPPON no. 7, 1935. Magazine cover. Photo by Yonosuke Natori.

Sheltered Weaklings: Japan, exhibition poster, 1953.

Tanko, 1955. Poster for tea art magazine. In the permanent collection of the NY MoMA.

Poster (one of a series of eighteen) for a **World Theatre Festival**, Cologne, 1981.

Cabaret, theatre poster, 1986.

Arthur Miller: *The Crucible*, theatre poster, 1986.

Heinz Edelmann [Germany]

1934– born in Ústí nad Labem, Czech Republic
Admitted to AGI, 1964

In 1958, with a not completely rewarding and not very promising career as a janitor and museum guard compromised when he managed to drop a Rembrandt, a Van Gogh and a Felix Vallotton, Heinz Edelmann was looking for something less humdrum, more challenging and adventurous, and decided to take up graphic design (at the time, design – much like digging ditches – did not seem to call for any special talents, skills or abilities).

In this quest for new thrills he was, however, fated to be cruelly disappointed: even though he produced a fair amount of posters (theatre, film, radio and TV) and designed numerous books and book jackets, illustrated about 50 books (including some for children) worked in advertising (communications, canned vegetables, computers) and for magazines (mostly as a freelance illustrator) and dabbled in animation, true excitement forever eluded him. Reliable observers unanimously describe him as crouching in a cluttered cubbyhole for 45 years, unnaturally immobile, hardly ever getting up, barely breathing, occasionally catching a fly with a lightning flick of his tongue.

Günther Kieser [Germany]

1930– born in Kronberg
Admitted to AGI, 1964

1981–92: professor of communication design, University of Wuppertal. 1955–on: designed tour posters for major jazz and rock musicians, including Ellington, Basie, Miles Davis, Coltrane, Peterson, Grateful Dead, Zappa, Hendrix and others; 1965–99: Jazz Festival Frankfurt; 1968–2000 Berlin Jazz Days; 1962–80: American Folk Blues Festival in Europe; 1960–93: poster artwork for Frankfurt radio and TV. Also designed posters on social and political issues and for operas, ballets and movies. *Solo exhibitions:* Lincoln Center, NY; Mexico City; Wuxi, China; Torun, Poland; Kornhaus Forum, Berne; Poster Museum, Essen; Museum of Arts and Crafts, Frankfurt, and others.

Awards: gold medal, Toulouse-Lautrec awards, 1983; silver medal, Warsaw Biennale, 1984; gold medal, Salon International Lodz, 1985; gold medal, Brno Poster Biennale, 1986; Litfass Award, 1991. Dr Stefan Soltek: *'Günther Kieser is engaged in poster design, laying out clear principles of form and colour. Bound to strict aesthetic approaches, these posters are Kieser's way of making contact with people and leading them to a responsible form of creation and interaction. Postermaking can be both a matter of power and a delightful and intelligent method of liberal communication. Instructive, not destructive – that is the central issue of his art.'*

Exile, poster, 1994.

Jazz Festival Frankfurt, poster, 1999.

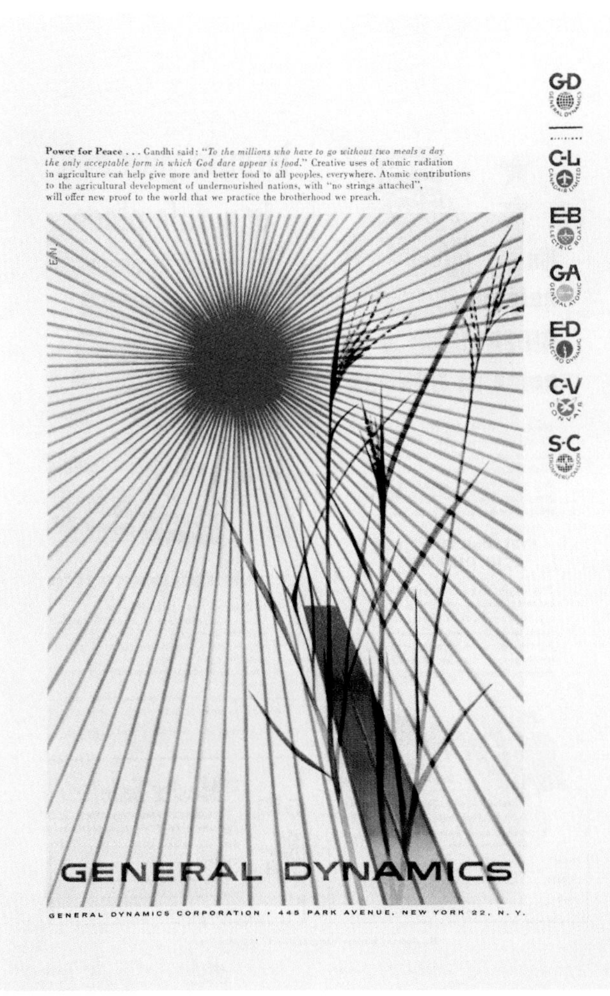

Ads (x 3) for General Dynamics:
Power for Peace, 1956.
Exploring the Universe: Control of Weather, 1958.
Undersea Frontiers, 1961.

Tchaikovsky, Piano Concerto no. 1, record sleeve, 1952. Nitsche designed numerous record sleeves for Decca Records (1950–54). Their highly complex images give the impression of having been designed by computer.

Erik Nitsche [USA]

1908-1998; born in Lausanne, Switzerland
Admitted to AGI, 1964

In *Print* (1999) Steven Heller wrote an obituary entitled *'Erik Nitsche, The Reluctant Modernist'*, calling Nitsche the equal of Lester Beall, Paul Rand and Saul Bass. Paul Klee was a family friend who had a great influence on young Erik. Yet Nitsche did not study at the Bauhaus, but went – after a short period at the College Classique in Lausanne – to the Kunstgewerbeschule in Munich, where he won a prestigious poster award. He worked in Cologne and Paris; there he was employed by the Draeger Bros and Maximilien Vox.

Aged 26 he moved to New York, where he was appointed art director for Saks Fifth Avenue. His list of clients included Orbachs, Bloomingdales, Decca Records, Filene's, 20th Century Fox, NY MoMa, CCA, NY Transit Authority and Revlon. He could have done the corporate identity for IBM that went to Paul Rand, but he turned that job down. As art director for General Dynamics he produced a famous poster series. Nitsche designed covers and artwork for American fashion and decoration magazines, and books for US and Swiss publishers. He was a consultant to commercial and industrial corporations and museums. Nitsche was inducted into the ADC Hall of Fame. Considering himself to be asocial, he soon left AGI.

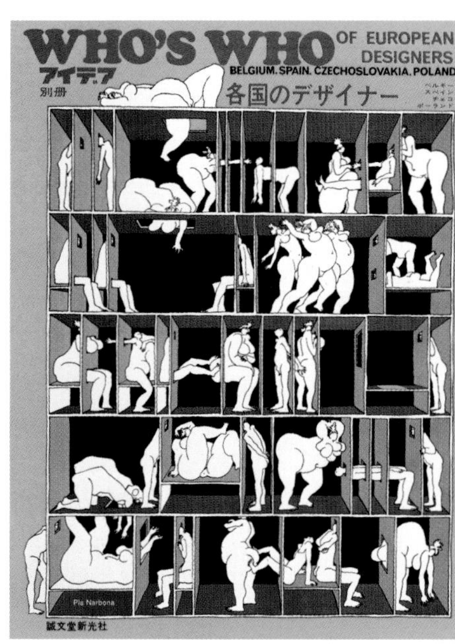

Josep Pla-Narbona [Spain]

1928– born in Barcelona
Admitted to AGI, 1964

Studied art at the Barcelona Art and Craft School 1945–49, then spent two years working in Paris. Returned to Barcelona in 1958 to set up his own studio and by 1961 had been twice awarded the San Jorge prize for drawing. Appointed professor of advertising and plastic art at the Massana School, and elected first chairman of the Grafistas Agrupación FAD (now ADG-FAD). In 1962, Pla-Narbona studied typographic techniques in Switzerland and worked with the advertising agency Adolf Wirz of Zürich; also produced a series of lithographs for ARTA Zürich. He has been frequently honoured with exhibitions, awards and grants for his art and design work.

International exhibitions include the 1st Warsaw Poster Biennale, the inauguration of the Lincoln Center and the NY AIGA. His work is in MoMA's graphic art collection (1972). He designed posters for the 25th Olympic Games and the Spanish Pavilion at Expo 92 in Seville. He is currently AGI chairman for Spain. He has been featured in many publications, including *IDEA*, *U&LC*, and M. Muller's *The Haunted World of Josep Pla-Narbona*. He received the LAUS Award 2000 from ADG-FAD, the Design Award from the AEPD (Asociación Española de Profesionales del Diseño) in 2001 and the Spanish National Design Award 2004.

Barcelona Olympic Games, gouache, 1992.

International Theatre Congress of Catalonia, unpublished, oil on canvas, 1985.

Cover design for **Idea Magazine**, Japan, watercolour, 1970.

Georg Schmid [Austria]

Bertolt Brecht: *The Good Person of Sezuan*, set design.

Untitled illustration, postcard for AGI Congress 1994, Cambridge.

No to an Atomic State, political poster, 1983.

1928-1998; born in Vienna
Admitted to AGI, 1964

After studying architecture and painting at the Academy of Fine Arts in Vienna, Georg started his own studio with his wife Epi Schlüsselberger, a costume designer, in 1955. His work was mainly cultural, social and political. For ten years he was responsible for all the design for the Museum of 20th-Century Art in Vienna and for the Europe publishing house. Schmidt was head of the Institute of Graphic Design, Ornamental Script and Heraldry at the Vienna Academy (1969–72). As well as his graphic work, he was also a set designer for theatre and opera in Austria, Switzerland and Germany.

His imaginative, lyrical and sometimes satirical designs were very well known in Austria as well as in Switzerland and Germany. He was involved in a series of animated films for Austrian Television. In the 1980s, he worked for the Vienna People's Party, designing all their posters, printed matter and promotions. His imagination and originality made him an intelligent designer who made optimal use of his creativity. There have been many international, individual and group exhibitions of his work. He received numerous awards for exhibition, poster and book design, and Austria and Vienna honoured him with prizes and medals.

Hans Fabigan [Austria]

1901-1974; born in Vienna
Admitted to AGI, 1965

Hans Fabigan received his education at the Graphische Lehr- und Versuchsanstalt, Vienna. He was not only a leading poster designer before the fifties but also well known on the Viennese marketing scene. In 1927 he moved to Berlin where he gained a reputation as a fashion designer, cartoonist and graphic artist. In 1935 he returned to Vienna, where he became head of the graphic department at the Institut für Werbung. He also taught at the Modeschule and several universities. In 1948 he worked on a new identity for the Austrian government and the city of Vienna, to celebrate the anniversary of the 1848 Revolution.

New Advertising, exhibition poster, 1963.*

From the Lives of Working People, exhibition poster, 1951.*

Give Blood, Save Your Own Life, promotional poster, 1965.*

**Donated by MAK - Austrian Museum of Applied Arts/Contemporary Art, Vienna.*
Photograph: © MAK/Georg Mayer

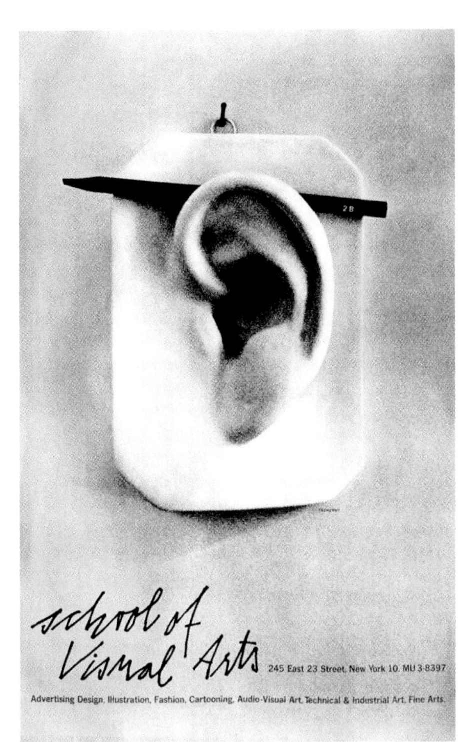

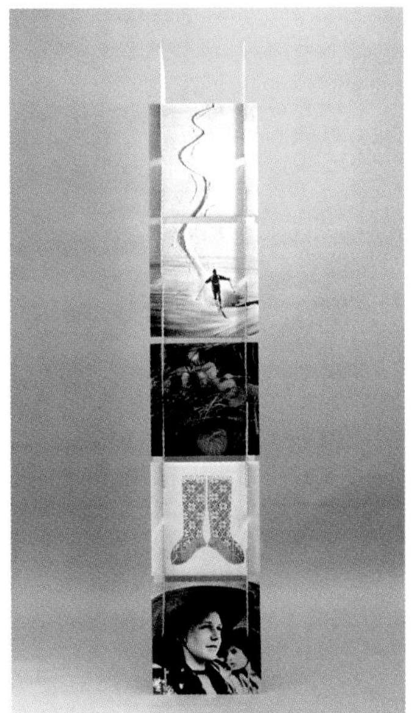

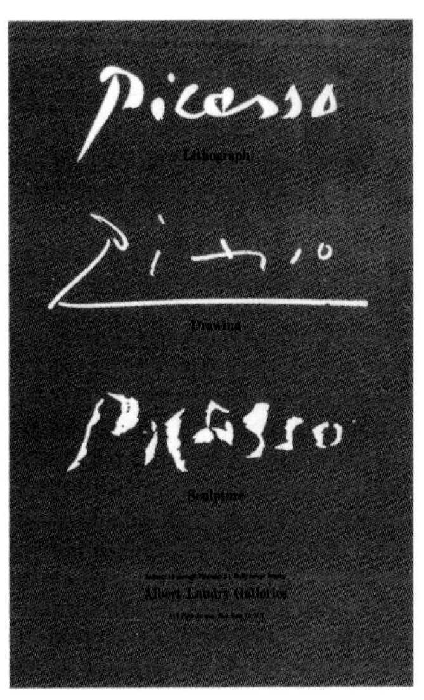

One of a series of **Modular Display Towers**, 1971.
Client: Pan American Airways.

School of Visual Arts, subway poster, 1959.
Client: School of Visual Arts.

Picasso, exhibition poster, 1957.
Client: Albert Landry Galleries.

George Tscherny [USA]

1924– born in Budapest, Hungary
Admitted to AGI, 1965

George began his professional career as a designer with Donald Deskey & Associates in 1950. He joined George Nelson & Associates as a graphic designer in 1953 and became an associate and head of the graphics department before leaving in 1955 to open an independent design office. Tscherny served two terms as president of the American Institute of Graphic Arts (AIGA). In 1988 the American Institute of Graphic Arts awarded him their annual medal, *'in recognition of distinguished achievements and contributions to the graphic arts'*.

In 1992 the Visual Arts Museum, NY invited Tscherny to mount a one-man retrospective of his work in 'The Masters Series: honouring the great visual communicators of our time'. In 1997 Tscherny was inducted into the Art Directors Hall of Fame. A 164-page book, covering 5 decades of Tscherny's work, was published in 2004 by Southeast University Press, China. His posters are in the collections of NY MoMA; Cooper-Hewitt Museum NY; Library of Congress, Washington DC; and the Kunstgewerbemuseum, Zürich. An extensive selection of his work is deposited in the print archive and the electronic database of the Cooper Union School of Art. Over 100 posters and other examples of his work are included in the archives of the Bibliothèque Nationale de France.

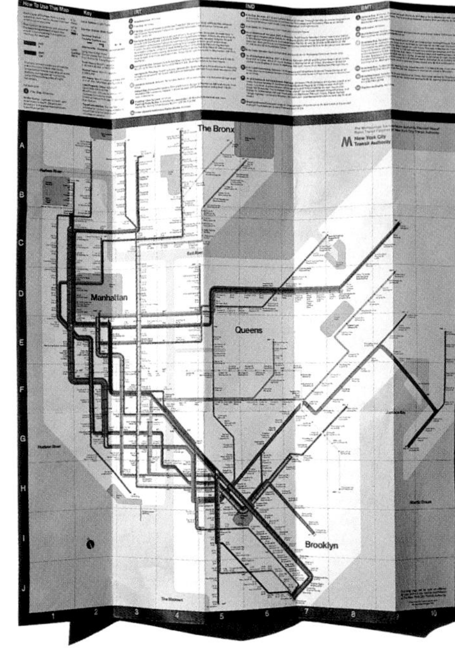

Massimo Vignelli [USA]

1931– born in Milan, Italy
Admitted to AGI, 1965
International President 1985-1988

Massimo Vignelli studied architecture in Milan and Venice. President of Vignelli Associates, New York. His work includes graphic and corporate identity programmes, publication designs, packaging, architectural graphics, exhibition, interior, furniture, and consumer product designs for many leading American and European companies and institutions. Vignelli's work has been published and exhibited throughout the world and entered in the permanent collections of several museums. He is a past president of the AGI and the AIGA, and a vice president of the Architectural League of New York.

A major exhibition of Vignelli Associates' work toured Europe's most important museums between 1989 and 1993. Vignelli is the recipient of many important national and international awards: seven honorary doctorates in fine arts; the 1982 ADC Hall of Fame; the 1983 AIGA Gold Medal; and the 1985 US President's Design Excellence Award. In 1996 he received the Honorary Royal Designer for Industry Award from the Royal Society of Arts, London. Lella and Massimo Vignelli received the 2003 National Design Award for Lifetime Achievement, and in 2005 received the Architecture Award from the American Academy of Arts and Letters.

Piccolo Teatro di Milano graphic programme, 1964. The project included programmes, posters and publications.

MTA Subway Map, New York, 1970.

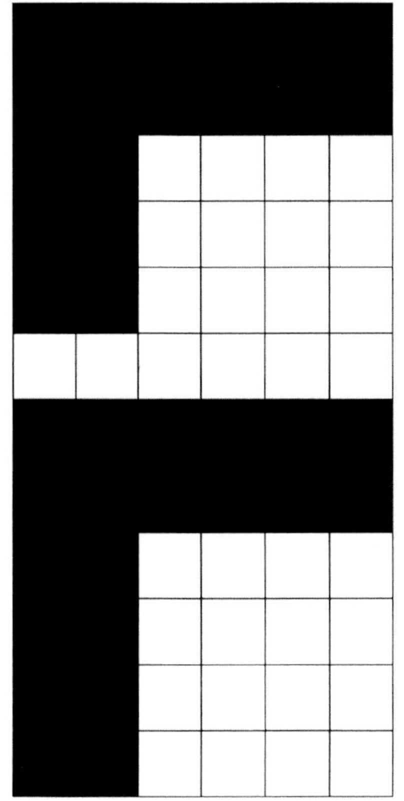

Colophon for **Frances Lincoln Ltd**, 2005.

Information pack for **AGI 69 congress**, held in London.

Windscreen de-icer pack for **Pirelli**, 1963.

Derek Birdsall [UK]

1934– born in Yorkshire
Admitted to AGI, 1966

He studied at Wakefield College of Art and at the Central School of Art under Anthony Froshaug. In his career, spanning more than over 40 years, Derek Birdsall has become one of the most distinguished graphic designers in Britain. He designed the first Pirelli calendar in 1964. Among his clients were Mobil Corporation, HRH The Prince of Wales School of Architecture and the Church of England. His work has included also the Monty Python books and numerous paperback covers for Penguin Books.

Derek Birdsall also was a consultant art director of the first *Independent Magazine* (1988) and he designed magazines like *Nova*, *Town* and *Twen*. In 2000 he did a complete redesign of the Church of England's *Book of Common Worship*. Among his works are award-winning catalogues for artists like Mark Rothko and Georgia O'Keeffe. He has set the standard for book and magazine design. His style accentuates the beauty of typography and has often been described as economical, elegant and minimal. In 2005 he was awarded the Prince Philip Designers Prize, handed to him by the Duke of Edinburgh.

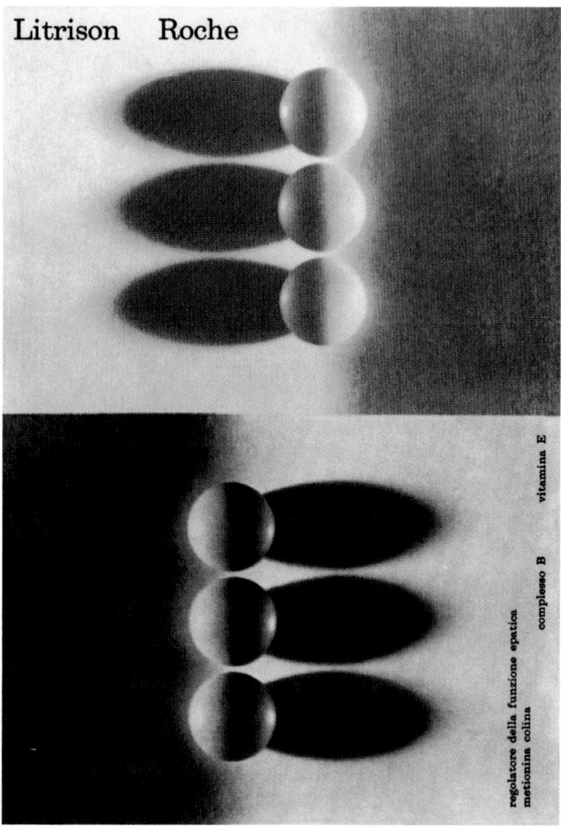

Aldo Calabresi [Italy]

1930-2004; born in Adiswil, Switzerland
Admitted to AGI, 1966

Aldo Calabresi studied at the Kunstgewerbeschule in Zürich. During the same period he was apprenticed to a firm of printers. From 1950–51 Calabresi was employed as a designer in the Zürich branch of PKZ, gentlemen's outfitters. From 1951–52, he worked in Gérard Miedinger's studio in Zürich. He then went to Paris where he freelanced for six months. From 1953, he worked as a graphic artist at Studio Boggeri, Milan, which had a well-earned reputation for its artistic awareness and for the high quality of its work.

In 1963, together with Umberto Capelli and Ezio Bonini, Aldo established CBC, Calabresi, Bonini, Capelli Advertising Agency. Mayor clients: Agfa, Alfa Romeo, Bassetti, Milan Fair, Superga, Total. He retired in 1983, moving to Panarea, the smallest island of the Aeolian archipelago.

Ravizza, package design, early 1960s.

Ahrend-Cirkel, logo for a factory making steel furniture, early 1960s.

Litrison, advertisement for the Roche pharmaceutical company, 1961.

KAFKA

PROCES

Roman Cieslewicz [France]

Paradise Lost, opera poster, Grand Theatre Warsaw, 1980.

Cover for **Opus, international art review**. Theme: *'Objects'*, 1968.

Franz Kafka: ***The Trial***, theatre poster, 1964. Originally commissioned by the Warsaw Drama Theatre, before Roman left for Paris. Published in 1968 in France by Georges Fall.

1930-1996; born in Lvov, Poland
Admitted to AGI, 1966

In 1955 Cieslewicz graduated from the Academy of Fine Arts in Krakow. He was predominantly a (politically conscious) poster designer. He and his colleagues Julian Palka, Waldemar Swierzy, Jan Lenica, Henryk Tomaszewski and others made more than 200 Polish film posters a year.
He migrated to France in 1963 and was naturalized in 1971. As well as posters he designed books, magazines and displays. He was art director of *Elle* and *Vogue* and of the advertising agency Maffia. By using photography, collage, screen-printing, typography and other media, he created a new vocabulary of graphic expression.

He designed for the magazines *Opus International* (1967–69) and *Kitsch* (1970–71). The Musée des Art Décoratifs, Galeries Lafayette, Hachette, the Centre Pompidou, and the Musée Picasso were among his clients. His exhibitions were held in major cities all over the world. Throughout his career, Cieslewicz received many medals and honours. He commented on modern posters in an interview with Margo Rouard-Snowman in 1993: *'Posters need powerful occasions and significant subjects, which they can't find at the moment. As a means of communication they belong to another age and have very little future.'*

Theo Crosby [UK]

1925-1994; born in Mafeking, South Africa
Admitted to AGI, 1966

Crosby's studies (1940–47) at the University of Witwatersrand, Johannesburg were interrupted by WW2 military duties, and were continued in London at Sir John Cass School, the Central School of Art and Crafts and St Martin's School of Art (1947–56). He worked for five years in a London architects' group and was technical publisher of *Architectural Design* from 1953 to 1962. 1962 found him in charge of the Taylor Woodrow Construction Company, and creating a special design group, employing the six founders of the Archigram movement that dominated the architectural avant-garde through the 1960s and early 1970s.

Theo joined Fletcher/Forbes/Gill (1965) in the design partnership that would become Pentagram, of which he was a co-founder. He taught at RCA, and held fellowships with RIBA, SIAD, the Berlin Academy of Arts and the Royal Academy. His numerous awards include the 1963 Gran Premio of the Milan Triennale, the 1965 Warsaw Biennale and the 1973 Architectural Heritage Year Award. He had several exhibitions and commissions including planning, conservation and interiors, at home and abroad, throughout the 70s and 80s, with larger building appointments in the 90s. Arguably Theo's achievement of greatest renown was his intensive involvement in the reconstruction of Shakespeare's Globe Theatre in London.

Reconstruction of the **Globe Theatre**, London, 1980s and early 1990s (x 2).

Interior design for **Unilever House**, London (x 2).

Michael Shanks: *The Stagnant Society*
Homer: *The Odyssey*
Bertolt Brecht: *Threepenny Novel*
Book covers designed by Germano Facetti for Pelican Books, Penguin Classics and Penguin Modern Classics.

Germano Facetti [UK]

1928-2006; born in Milan, Italy
Admitted to AGI, 1966
International president 1967-1970

As a member of the armed Italian resistance, 15-year-old Germano was arrested by the Germans and deported to the Mauthausen camp in Austria. The documents he kept secretly in a small box that had held photographic paper provided the title for a short film by Anthony West: *The Yellow Box: A Short History of Hate*. Germano studied architecture in Rome and Milan. His values are directed towards one ethical purpose: *'Building a society.'*

Germano married a British architect and moved to London in 1950, where he worked as an art director/designer and consultant to cultural institutions and publishers. He spent some time working in France, then went back to England in 1960 to work as an art director for Penguin Books until 1972, redesigning a whole series of paperbacks. He worked for Time-Life, Rizzoli, Olivetti and the National Film Institute. In 1972, Facetti went back to Italy and was an art director for Fabbri, publishers of children's books. He lectured graphic design at the Bath Academy of Art, Manchester Polytechnic, London College of Printing, the Grafiska Institut Stockholm and Yale University. In 1999 he was given an exhibition of 100 covers of his Penguin books at the Galleria Aiap in Milan.

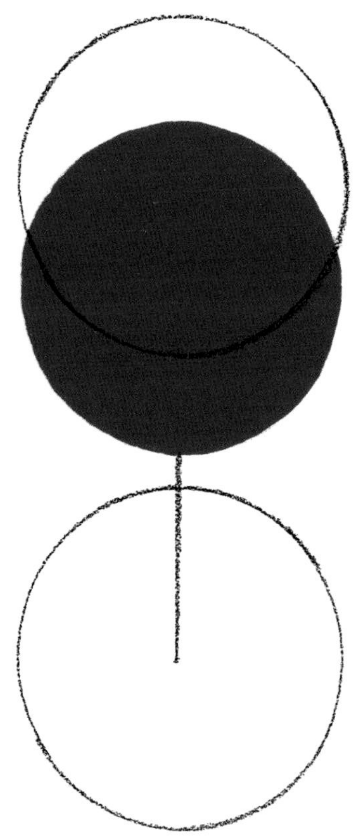

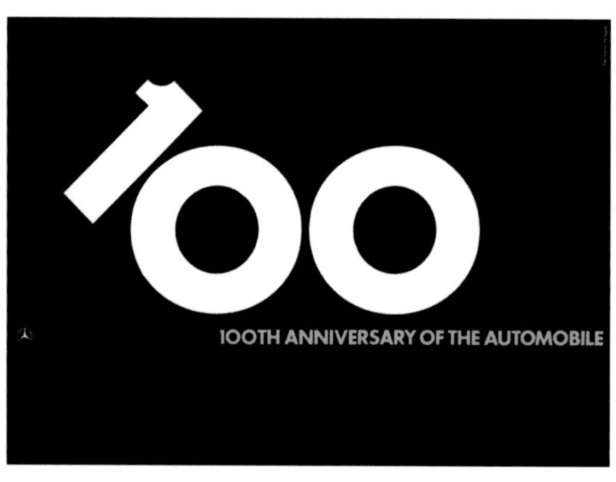

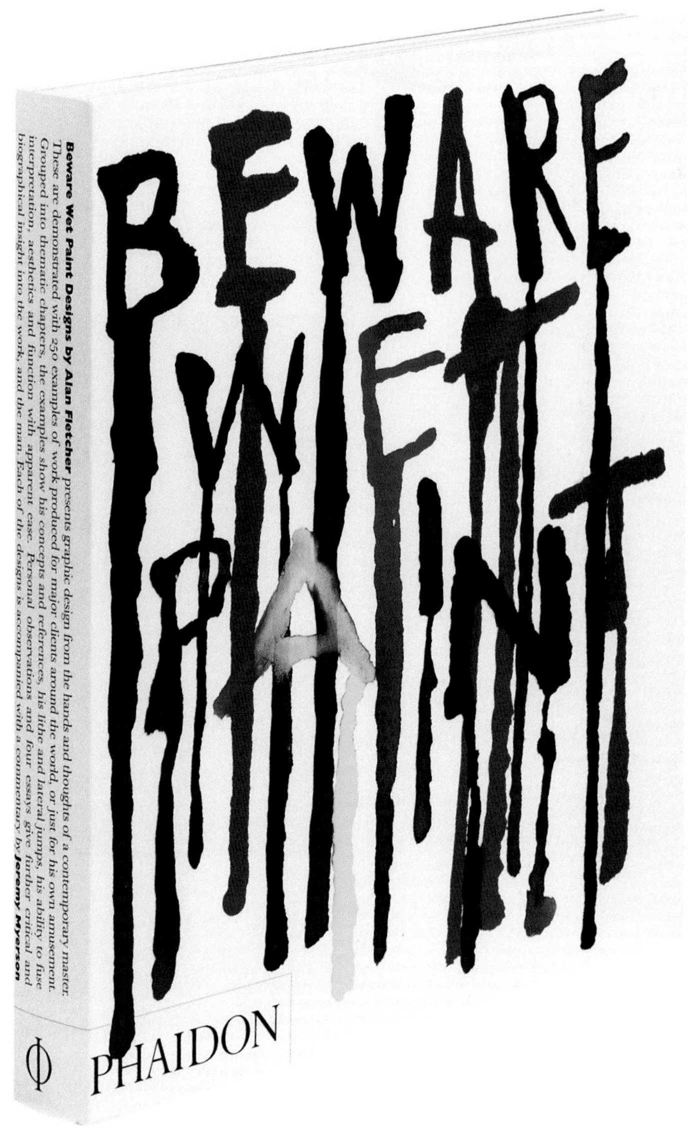

Alan Fletcher [UK]

1931-2006; born in Nairobi, Kenya
Admitted to AGI, 1966
International President 1982-1985

1949: Hammersmith School of Art.
1950: Central School of Art.
1952: teaching in Barcelona, Spain.
1953-56: Royal College of Art.
1957: Yale School of Art and Architecture.
1958–59: *Fortune* magazine, New York.
1960: returned to London to work freelance.
1962: co-founded Fletcher/Forbes/Gill.
1972: co-founded Pentagram.
1973: president of D&AD.
1992: freelance.
1993: Prince Philip Prize for Designer of the Year.
1994: inducted to American ADC Hall of Fame.

Jeremy Myerson in 1996:
'Alan Fletcher belongs to that elite international group of designers who have transcended the conventional boundaries of their craft. In a long and distinguished career, he has tackled every facet of design – from corporate identities to posters – with a style and a purpose that has marked him out as one of the most admired designers of his generation. There is perhaps nobody else who inhabits the world of ideas and ironies, of wit and ambiguity in graphic design in quite the same way. Thus he has been depicted as the man who took all that serious less-is-more, form-follows-function dogma and somehow found a way to, well, relax.'

Glass of Beaujolais, personal work, 1994. The glass (also a cover for *Idea*, the Japanese magazine) presented itself over a drink one evening.

In 1986 Daimler-Benz celebrated their **100th anniversary** with an international poster competition. This poster was the joint winner and was the basis of the anniversary symbol.

Beware Wet Paint. Marcel Duchamp used the phrase *'Beware Wet Paint'* to remind us that it takes time to judge the worth of work. This provided both the title and cover design for a book on Alan's work.

We, the undersigned, deplore and oppose the Government's intention to introduce admission charges to national museums and galleries

Write in protest to your MP
and send for the petition forms to
Campaign Against Museum Admission Charges
221 Camden High Street
London NW1 7BU

Campaign Against Museum Admission Charges, poster, 1970.

Logo for **zinc diecasting conference**, 1966.

Poster for **Designer's Saturday**, 1983.

Colin Forbes [USA]

1928– born in London, England
Admitted to AGI, 1966
International President 1977-1980

Colin Forbes studied at the Central School of Arts and Crafts. After a period as a freelance designer and lecturer at the Central School he became an art director with an advertising agency. He was subsequently appointed head of the graphic design department at the Central School. In 1960 Colin established his own practice, and soon afterwards joined with designers Alan Fletcher and Bob Gill to form the partnership of Fletcher/Forbes/Gill. In the early 1970s the development and expansion of the partnership resulted in the formation of Pentagram, and in 1978 Colin moved to New York to establish the first Pentagram office in the United States.

His work has included corporate identity programmes and other projects for clients including Pirelli, Lucas Industries, British Petroleum, American-Standard, Neiman Marcus, Nissan and Kubota. He has served as a member of the British Design Council, as International President of the Alliance Graphique Internationale and as president of the American Institute of Graphic Arts (AIGA). He was elected Royal Designer for Industry by the Royal Society of Arts in 1973. He received the President's Award of the Designers and Art Directors Association (D&AD) in 1977 and the AIGA Medal in 1992.

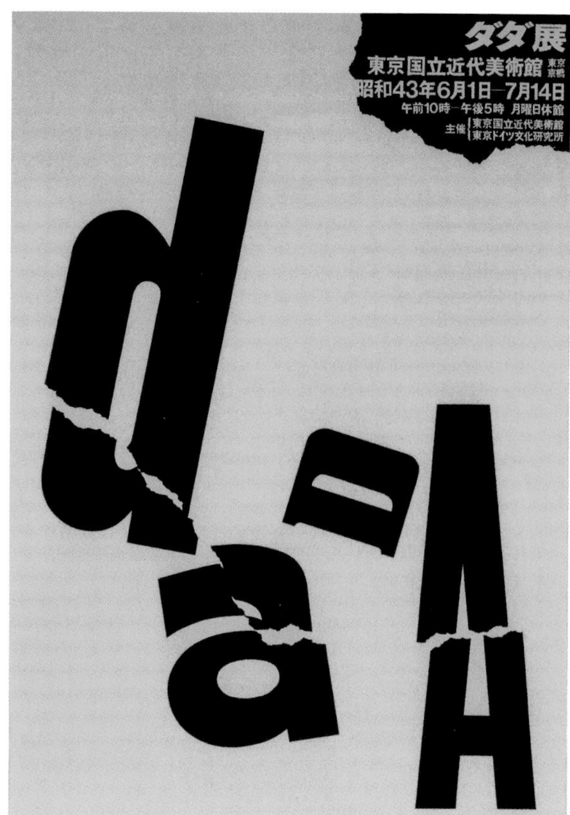

Hiromu Hara [Japan]

1903-1986; born in Nagano
Admitted to AGI, 1966

Hara graduated from the Tokyo Prefectural School of Technology and taught there from 1922–41. He got acquainted with the work of László Moholy-Nagy, Herbert Bayer and El Lissitzky, before he started his design career. He had contact with Tomoyoshi Murayama and other members of the Sankakai group of painters, which influenced him in his later design. He started a studio with the photographer Kimura. Together they made a giant photo mural for the Japanese pavilion at the Paris Expo, 1937. He used montage and collage techniques which were formerly unknown in Japan.

He had the philosophy that graphic design was the sum of planning and organization, typography, production methods and materials. His theories and book designs changed the out-of-date concepts of the Japanese publishing world. Hara was one of the founders of the Japan Studio (Nippon Kobo). In 1951, he was a founder member of the Japanese Advertising Artists Club. At the age of 82, he was made professor emeritus at Musashino Art University. He was also honoured by being elected president of the Nippon Design Centre. Ginza Graphic Gallery gave him a retrospective exhibition in 2001.

Shino, book cover, 1967.

Dada, exhibition poster, 1968.

Japanese Typography, exhibition poster, 1959.

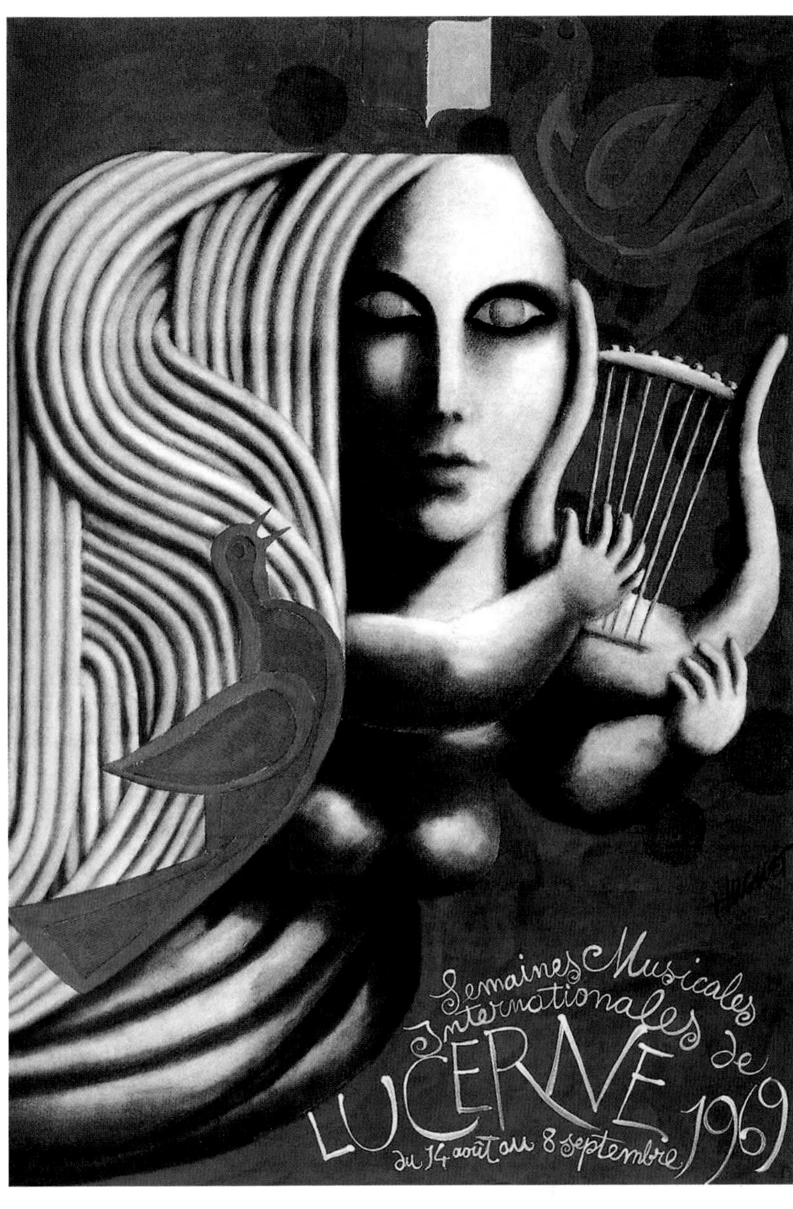

Poster design for **Semaines Musicales de Lucerne**, 1968. (Group exhibition, Rigi-Kaltbad, AGI Congress.)

Enric Huguet [Spain]

1928– born in Barcelona
Admitted to AGI, 1966

Huguet is founder of Grafistas Agrupación FAD (ADG-FAD) and an honorary member of the Collegi Oficial de Dissenyadors de Catalunya. He was a graphic design professor at the Escola Massana (1963–93) and design professor at the Escola Oficial de Publicitat (1967–69). Huguet worked for Generalitat de Catalunya, Fira de Barcelona, International Olympic Committee, Autopista CESA, Santiveri, Roca Radiadores, and more.

He has had solo exhibitions of his works and has been honoured with several awards. His work has been featured in articles and regularly reproduced and discussed in the best-known international design publications, and exhibited in museums and galleries around the world.

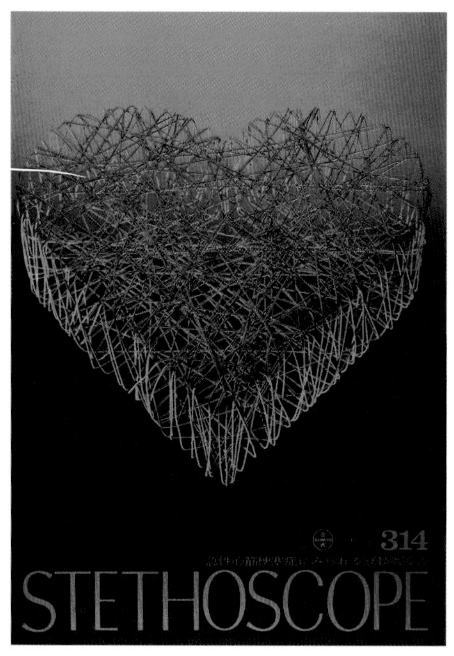

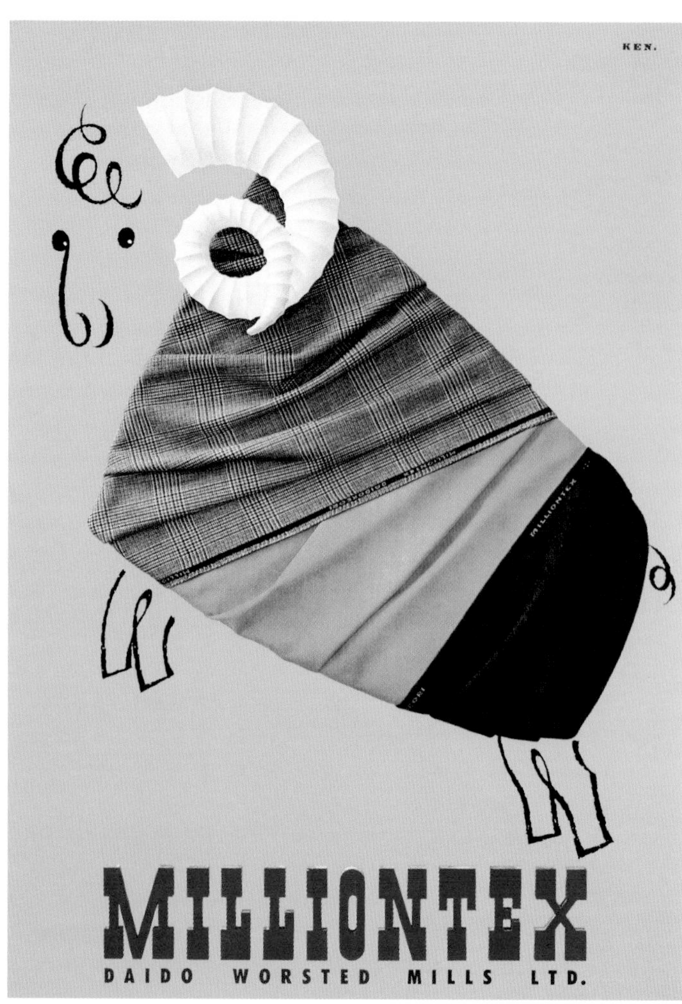

Kenji Itoh [Japan]

1915-1998; born in Tokyo
Admitted to AGI, 1966

Kenji Ito studied at the Tokyo High School of Technical Arts (now Chiba University School of Technology). He is considered one of the masters of post-war design. According to the Ginza Graphic Gallery, which presented a retrospective exhibition of his work in 2000, *'Itoh is a marathon performer in the design world.'* Over 48 years (1953–2000) he designed 560 covers for *Stethoscope*, Sankyo's monthly medical journal: a unique achievement. He created posters and also the Canon logo (1953), the Kappa novels, packaging for Nescafé coffee and window displays for the Wako department store (1956–82).

Poster for **Canon cameras**, 1954.

Stethoscope, monthly magazine for Sankyo Co., 1993.

Poster for **Milliontex**, 1954.

Signage programme for the **New York Subway**.

Poster for the **33th Venice Biennale**.

Poster for **Pirelli Tyres**.

Bob Noorda [Italy]

1927– born in Amsterdam, The Netherlands
Admitted to AGI, 1966

Studied design and graphic communication in Amsterdam under architect Gerrit Rietveld. From 1956 he worked in Milan, collaborating with Pirelli Tyre Corporation; he became Pirelli's art director 1961–62. He then set up his own studio for graphic and interior design, packaging, product design and signage. In 1963 he started working with Albini to design the interiors and signage system for the Milan Metro, followed by the signage system for New York City Transit Authority (1970) and the São Paolo Metro. Co-founder of Unimark International (1965), with offices in Chicago, New York, Milan and London, focusing on corporate identity design. Worked for oil companies Agip and Total, Dreher Beer, Stella Artois, and Truman Beer. Packaging designs for Olivetti, Shiseido and Sunstar. He founded Noorda Design in 1985. Has designed over 150 trademarks, many for public companies: AEM, Amsa, the crest of the Regional Government of Lombardy, corporate identity for Enel (National Electricity), and more. Noorda has won 4 Compasso d'Oro awards, and several prizes for typography and packaging. Member (1961) of ADI (Association of Industrial Design); is an honorary member since 2001. Was awarded an honorary degree in industrial design from Milan Polytechnic (2005).

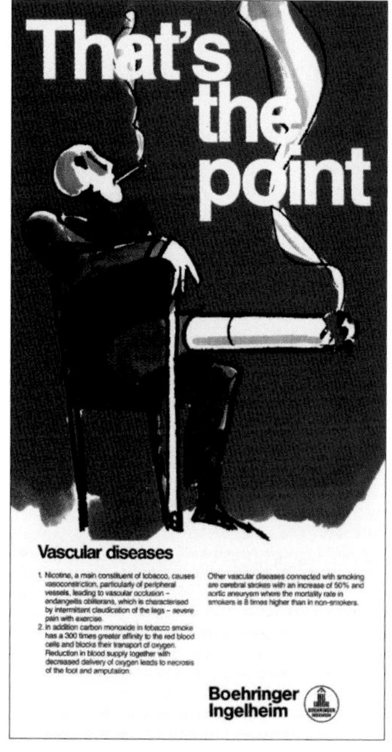

Hermann Rastorfer [Austria]

1930– born in Salzburg
Admitted in AGI, 1966

After the Meisterschule für Kunsthandwerk, Salzburg (1944), Rastorfer was a visiting student at the Kunstgewerbeschule and gained practical experience at a printer in Salzburg (1945–50). His first exhibitions took place in 1950 and 1951. He gained further practical experience in a local gallery. Worked for two years in an advertising agency in Frankfurt, before starting his own studio in Munich. He worked for national and international enterprises, institutes and publishing firms on graphic and industrial design projects, photography and film (1967–93).

Since 1978 he has also painted and made sculptures. In 1980 Rastorfer designed the bibliographical work *Harlekin-Zyklus*. In 1993 he returned to Austria. He has had several solo exhibitions in London, Munich, Wiesbaden and Bad-Ischl. As a sculptor he has been commissioned for prestigious projects by Salzburg Airport, the Museum Carolinum Augusteum and the *'Haus für Mozart'* at the Salzburger Festspiele. His works are in private collections throughout Europe and the US, and have been published in many books, design magazines and brochures. In 2001 he became an honorary member of Design Austria.

A VW is a must, 2 posters for Volkswagen, 1961.

Advertising for **Angina Pectoris medicine**, 1977.

That's the point, anti-smoking poster for the pharmaceutical industry, 1975.

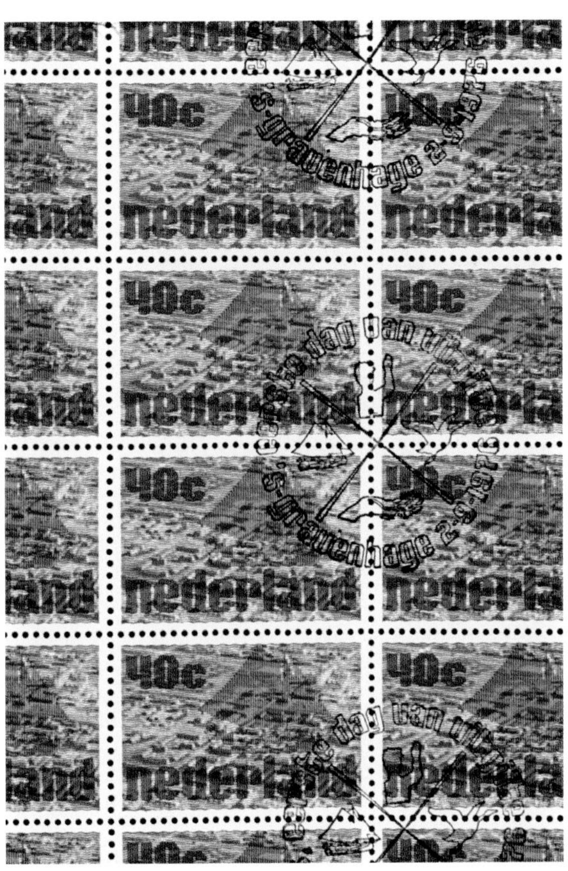

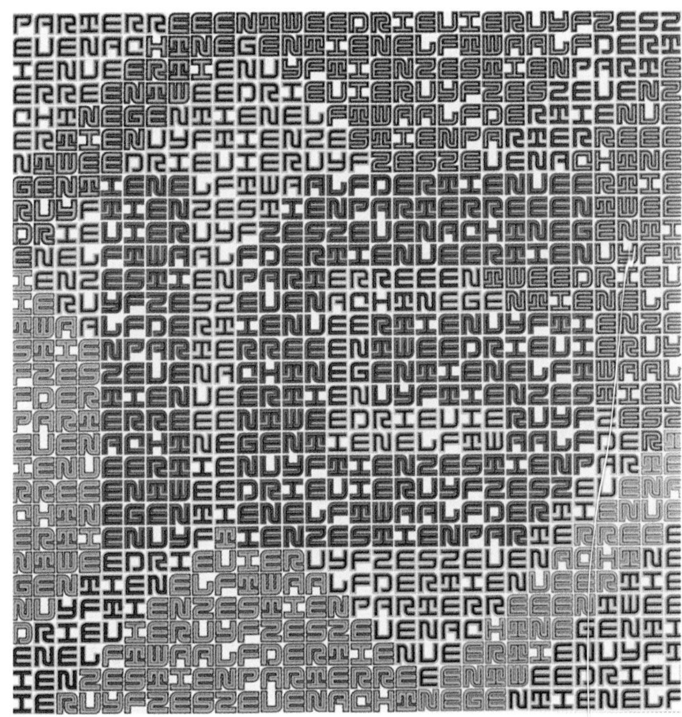

Dutch postage stamps on the theme of land reclaimed from the sea, 1976.

Floor signage in Postgiro Building, Leeuwarden, 1975.

Dutch Telephone Company, promotional book. Photography: Paul Huf.

Jurriaan Schrofer [The Netherlands]

1929-1990; born in Scheveningen
Admitted to AGI, 1966

Jurriaan was a very strong, sophisticated personality, politically engaged, with an original approach to everything he got involved in. His career started as an assistant to Dick Dooyes, a Dutch typographic designer. He had close contact with all the leading designers and photographers of the early postwar years. From 1951 he worked for a long period with Meyer Printers, producing many company photography books. Film, photography and typography were his main predilections. He was an advisor to the department store De Bijenkorf, the Dutch PTT and the Koninklijke Hoogovens steelworks, for which he designed a logo.

His many experimental typefaces were inspired by his great interest in mathematics and technique; they can be seen on numerous book covers, posters, stamps and signage systems. These original and often complex typefaces, although hand-made, often looked digital. Jurriaan was a great teacher and a leading figure in design organizations such as the Art Directors Club, the graphic designers' group GKf, and the Federation of Artists. He was always active in seeking positive change. He was co-ordinator of art for the Amsterdam Metro, a board member of Total Design and the director of the Arnhem Academy.

The Book of Numbers

Herbert & Mafalda Spencer

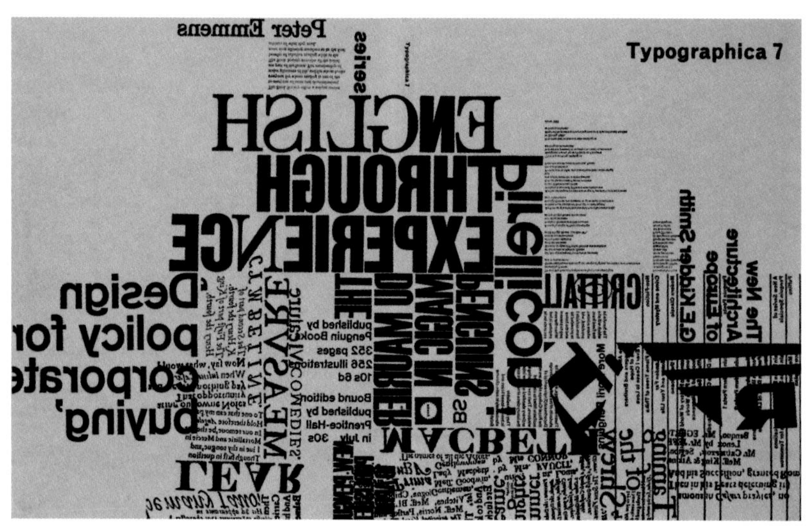

Herbert Spencer [UK]

1924-2002; born in London
Admitted to AGI, 1966
International president 1972-1974

Spencer was a typographic designer, author, educator, researcher, photographer, editor, consultant and painter. This very versatile man opened his own London studio in 1948. Books, catalogues, timetables, reports and logos were his output. He was a lecturer at the Central School of Arts and Crafts in London (1949–67), taught at the Royal College of Arts, where he became a professor of graphic arts (1978–85) and also a senior research fellow. The Post Office made him a consultant to their Stamp Design Committee (1968).

He was the editor of *Typographica* magazine (1949–67) and *Penrose Annual* (1964–73). Herbert introduced modern European typography developments to the UK. Lund Humphries appointed him director of their publishing division in 1970. He designed for British Rail, the Imperial War Museum, WHSmith, the Tate Gallery, the Royal Institute of British Architects and Leeds University. He was deeply involved in legibility research in information publishing. Herbert wrote several important books, including his famous *Pioneers of Modern Typography*, *The Visible Word* and *The Liberated Page*. He was master of the faculty of Royal Designers for Industry (1979–81).

Pioneers of Modern Typography, book cover, 1951.

The Book of Numbers, book cover, 1977.

Typographica no. 7, front and back cover, 1963.

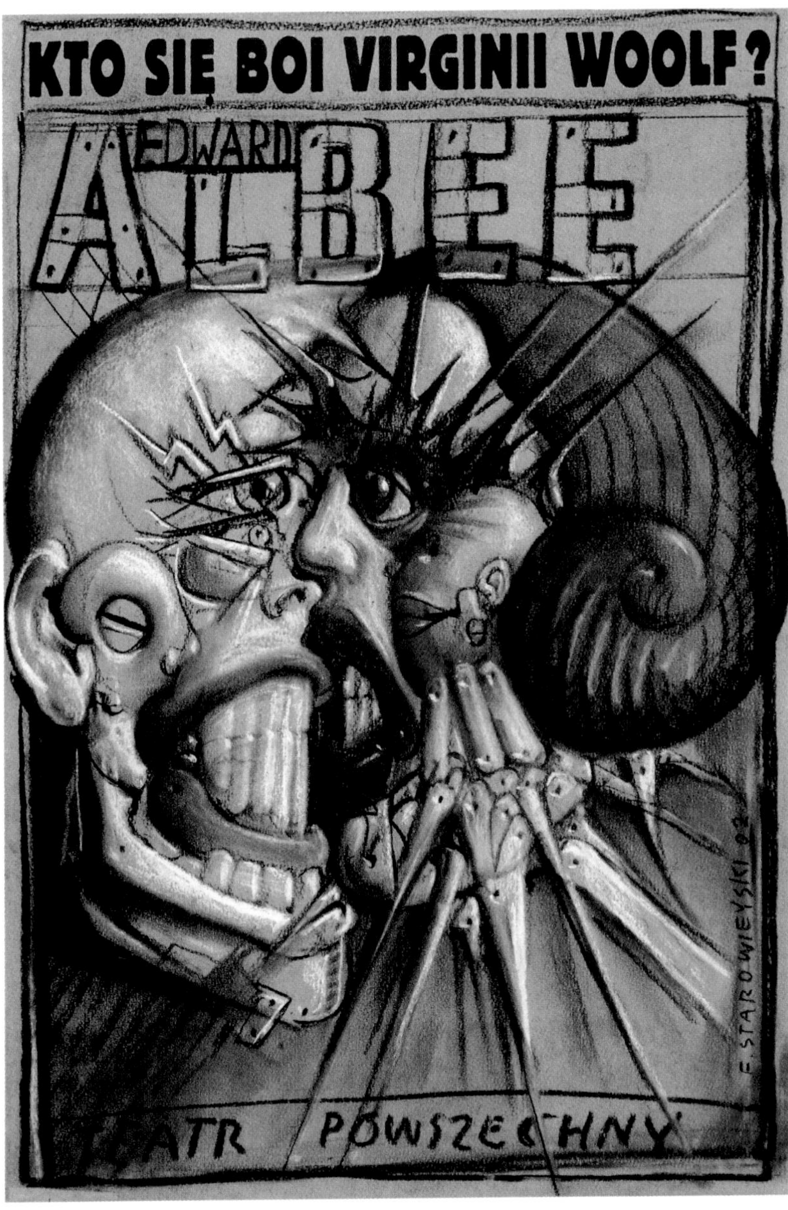

Faust, theatre poster, 2003.

Edward Albee: ***Who's Afraid of Virginia Woolf?***, theatre poster, 2002.

Franciszek Starowieyski [Poland]

1930– born near Krakow
Admitted to AGI, 1966

He studied at the Academies of Fine Art in Krakow and Warsaw, 1949–55. He is very versatile: as well as being another great Polish poster designer who produced more than 200 posters, he is a baroque calligrapher, a painter, a draughtsman who, in his own words, *'lives in the 17th century'*, a stage designer, TV and theatre set designer and a maker of TV films. Fame brought him a film poster award in Cannes (1974), a gold medal at the Film Festival of Chicago (1979), two prizes at the Warsaw Biennale, and the Silver Hugo award (1982).

Franciszek works with richly ornamental brush-strokes. His favourite motifs are the passing of time, death and the edges of civilization. He impresses spectators with his consistency, power, and intellectual impact. Some of his work is signed Jan Byk. (It's not said why, but it is no doubt easier to read and pronounce.)

ALFRED HITCHCOCK
FILMY Z LAT 1929 - 1938
INSTYTUT BRYTYJSKI
FIMOTEKA NARODOWA
DKF KINEMATOGRAF '75
PRZEGLĄD ◆ WYSTAWA
MAJ - CZERWIEC'88

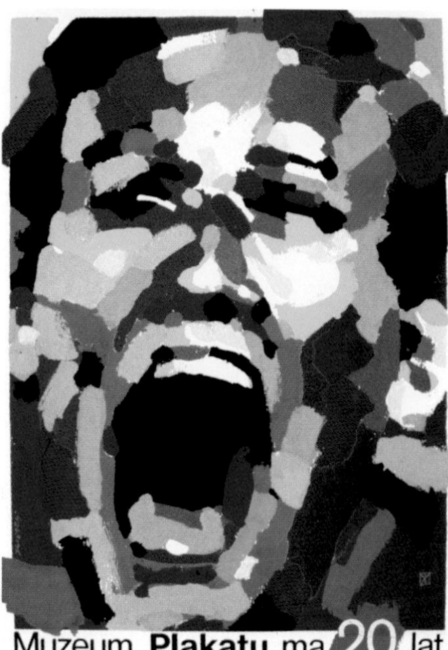

Muzeum Plakatu ma 20 lat

Waldemar Swierzy [Poland]

1931– born in Katowice
Admitted to AGI, 1966

Waldemar graduated 1952 from the Cracow Academy of Fine Arts/Graphic Arts, after also studying in Katowice. He then moved to Warsaw, where he first worked for the WAG publishing house and CPW film distributors. He then became a freelance graphic and poster designer. Swierzy is the author of more than 1,000 posters. The human head features in his posters in seemingly endless variations. Swierzy also illustrated books and designed a number of exhibitions in Warsaw and elsewhere for the Polish Chamber of Commerce.

Since 1965 Waldemar has been a professor at the Academy of Fine Arts in Poznan and since 1994 a professor at the Academy of Fine Arts in Warsaw. His work is represented in several leading and specialized museums worldwide. In 1978 he was appointed president of the Warsaw Poster Biennale. The list of his international awards, Grand Prix, gold and silver medals, solo and group exhibitions is one of the longest and most impressive in the profession. Since 1959 his work has been shown at a huge number of biennials, triennials, galleries and museums, and published in many leading design annuals, magazines and books.

Alfred Hitchcock, poster for a film festival.

The Dogs of War, film poster.

Poster Museum, 20th Anniversary, exhibition poster.

999 Books–5

National Cultural Festival, poster, 1986.

Ikko Tanaka GGG Books: 5, book cover.

Purple Iris, mural, 1992.

Ikko Tanaka [Japan]

1930-2002; born in Nara
Admitted to AGI, 1966

Tanaka graduated from Kyoto City College of Fine Arts (now Kyoto City University of Arts) in 1950. He joined Kanegafuchi Spinning Mills as a textile designer, Sankei Press in Osaka (1952–57) and later Nippon Design Centre in Tokyo employed him as a graphic designer and art director. He started his own design studio in 1963. Tanaka worked for the 1964 Tokyo Olympics and the Osaka World Expo 1970, where he designed the Japanese historical pavilion. His fabulous poster career began in 1954, when he made the first of his 30 years of Noh posters for the Kanze Noh theatre in Osaka.

He combined traditional Japanese calligraphy and aesthetics with *'western'* geometric images and bright colours. Many leading Japanese theatres commissioned him to design their posters. He was widely considered to be a *'father of graphic design in Japan'*. He collaborated with fashion designers like Hanae Mori, Kenzo and Issey Miyake, and had solo exhibitions around the world. His work is in the permanent collections of NY MoMA and Stedelijk Museum Amsterdam. In Toronto, Halifax, Calgary and other cities, he exhibited works in which he expressed his global concern for humanity (2000-2001). AGI lost a great, fine man when Ikko's heart gave up.

Benno Wissing [USA]

1923– born in Renkum, The Netherlands
Admitted to AGI, 1966

Benno Wissing studied fine arts at the Rotterdam Academy (1941). Started his career in 1949 as an independent designer, working for cultural and industrial clients, as well as department stores. The Museum Boijmans-van Beuningen, Rotterdam was an early important client of his; he designed their posters, catalogues and many exhibitions (1949–63). In 1963 he was a co-founder of Total Design, Amsterdam. His early corporate identity programmes for PAM, SHV, Makro and Calpam were exemplary.

Wissing worked on signage projects for theatres, concert and exhibition venues, including Martini Hall, Groningen; Ahoy, Rotterdam; de Doelen, Rotterdam. His comprehensive signage system for Amsterdam Schiphol Airport (1967) set an example for almost all early international airports that were equipped for the first generation of jumbo jets. He also worked as an architect and a product designer. He had his own design offices in Amsterdam (1972) and later in Providence, Rhode Island. There he worked for many major companies and produced more signage projects, including a terminal at Raleigh-Durham Airport. Benno designed for the Holland Festival before and after he moved to the USA. In the early 1980s he taught as a professor at the Rhode Island School of Design, Providence.

Signage system for **Schiphol Airport**. Wissing was the first designer to work with a new airport signage system back in the sixties.

Gino Severini, exhibition poster, Museum Boijmans van Beuningen, 1963.

Poster for the **Doelen concert and conference centre**, Rotterdam, 1966.

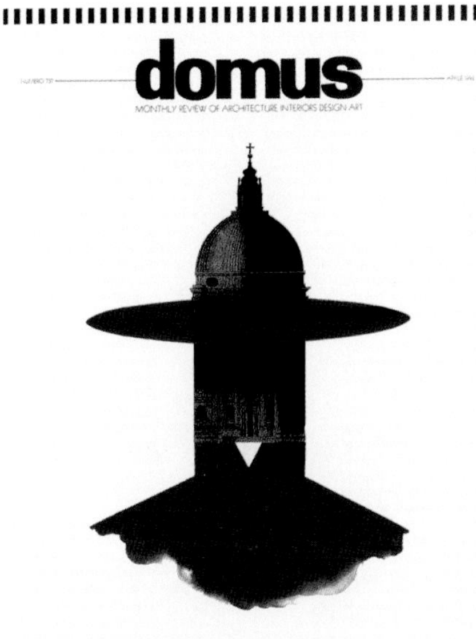

The Impact of Excellence, poster for lecture series, Rochester Institute of Technology, 1980.

The Kosher Hassidic and Pork Chop Temptation. Postcard for AGI Cambridge Congress 1984, on the theme of *'Humour'*.

Cover of **Domus** for an article on the Vatican, April 1992. Chosen as Wolf's favourite design in the book *First Choice* by Ken Cato.

Henry Wolf [USA]

1925-2005; born in Vienna, Austria
Admitted to AGI, 1966

Henry studied in France and, after emigrating to New York (1941), he took courses in design and photography with the famous Alexey Brodovitch. He received further education at the NY School of Industrial Art. After starting in an advertising agency, he soon became an art director for the US State Department. Art direction was indeed his prime activity; it was certainly one of the most important US graphic design specialisms of the 20th century.

He was appointed art director of *Esquire* magazine, changing the format, using bold photography and a lot of white space. He went on to succeed his teacher Brodovitch at *Harper's Bazaar*. He later worked for *Show* magazine and various agencies. In 1971 he founded Henry Wolf Productions Inc. Henry was an outstanding photographer and designed film titles. The Manhattan department store Bloomingdales was one of his favourite clients. He taught in New York for almost 50 years: at Cooper Union, the School of Visual Arts and the Parson School of Design. He was recipient of the AIGA gold medal (1976) and inducted in the NY ADC Hall of fame. He became a Royal Designer for Industry in 1990.

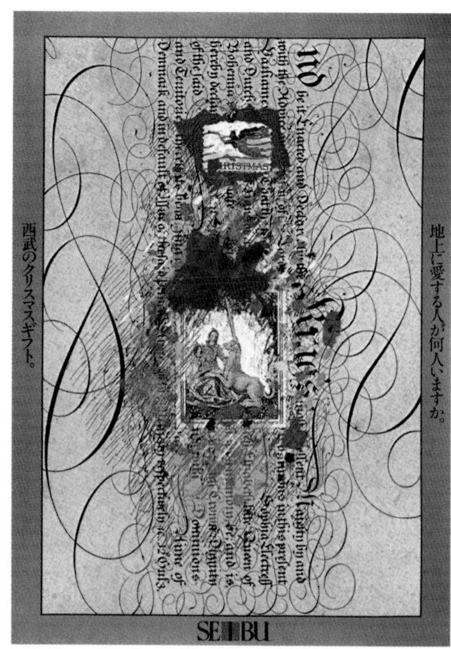

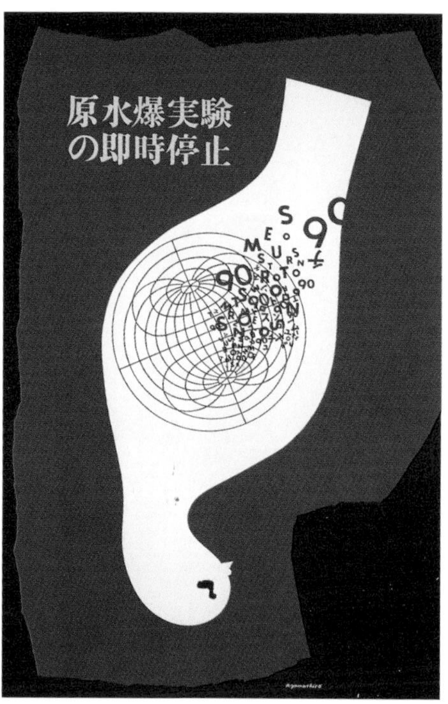

Ryuichi Yamashiro [Japan]

1920-1997; born in Osaka
Admitted to AGI, 1966

Yamashiro graduated in 1938 from the design department of Osaka Municipal Polytechnic. He worked in the advertisement department of Hankyu and Tokyo Takashimaya department stores and helped to establish the Japan Design Centre in 1959. In 1952 he had already started a freelance practice, working for Toshiba Electrical Works, Toyota Automobiles, Daiwa Securities, Nippon Kogaku, Fuji Steel Mills and others. In 1973 he founded Communication Arts R.

His awards include the Asahi Advertisement Award, Mainichi Industrial Design Award, ADC Silver and Bronze Awards, Dentsu Advertisement Award. In 1985 he was honoured with the Purple Ribbon Medal and in 1993 with the Fourth Order of Merit, Cordon of the Rising Sun. He had solo exhibitions of his paper collages, paintings and illustrations, and designed and illustrated books. In 1966 the Japanese Post and Telecommunications Ministry commissioned him to design the stamp for *'Letter Day'*. His works are in the collections of NY MoMA, Stedelijk Museum Amsterdam and Toyama Prefectural Museum of Modern Art. He was a trustee of the Tokyo ADC, a member of Japan Designers Association, Tokyo Illustrators Society and a director of Nippon Design Centre.

Poster for the **2nd International Print Biennale in Tokyo**, 1960.

Poster for **Seibu Department store**, 1969.

Against Nuclear Testing, poster, 1957.

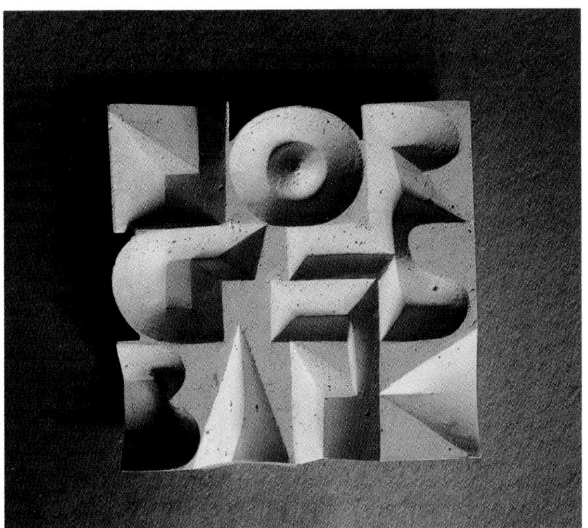

Plaster model for a relief designed for the **Norges Bank**, 100 x 100 cm, depth 20 cm, 1985.

Decanters. Produced by Hadelands Glassverk, 1951. Gold medal at the Milan Triennale, 1954. Museum of Applied Art, Trondheim.

Hermann Bongard [Norway]

1921-1998
Admitted to AGI, 1967

Bongard studied at the National College of Art and Design, Oslo (1938–41). From 1947–55 he was employed by Christiana Glassmagasin and Hadeland Glassworks and from 1957–63 he worked for Figgjo Fajanse. He was artistic director of Plus Workshops (1960–64) and J.W. Cappelens Publishers (art director 1966–68). Bongard designed glass, ceramics, weavings, graphics, silver and stainless steel objects and furniture and plastics. The Norwegian Ministry of Foreign Affairs commissioned him in 1965 to design an exhibition on Norway, which travelled to many countries.

He won the design competition for Norwegian banknotes in 1958. From 1971–85 he taught as professor at the National College of Arts and Design, Oslo. Exhibitions include: Milan Triennale (1954 and 1960); 'Scandinavian Design in the USA' (1954 and 1957); World Expo Brussels (1958); and 'Norwegian Design', New York (1964).
A retrospective exhibition was held at the Oslo Museum of Arts and Crafts (1971). In 1954 he won the gold and silver medal at the Milan Triennale (1954), the Lunning Prize (1957) and the Jacob Prize (1982).

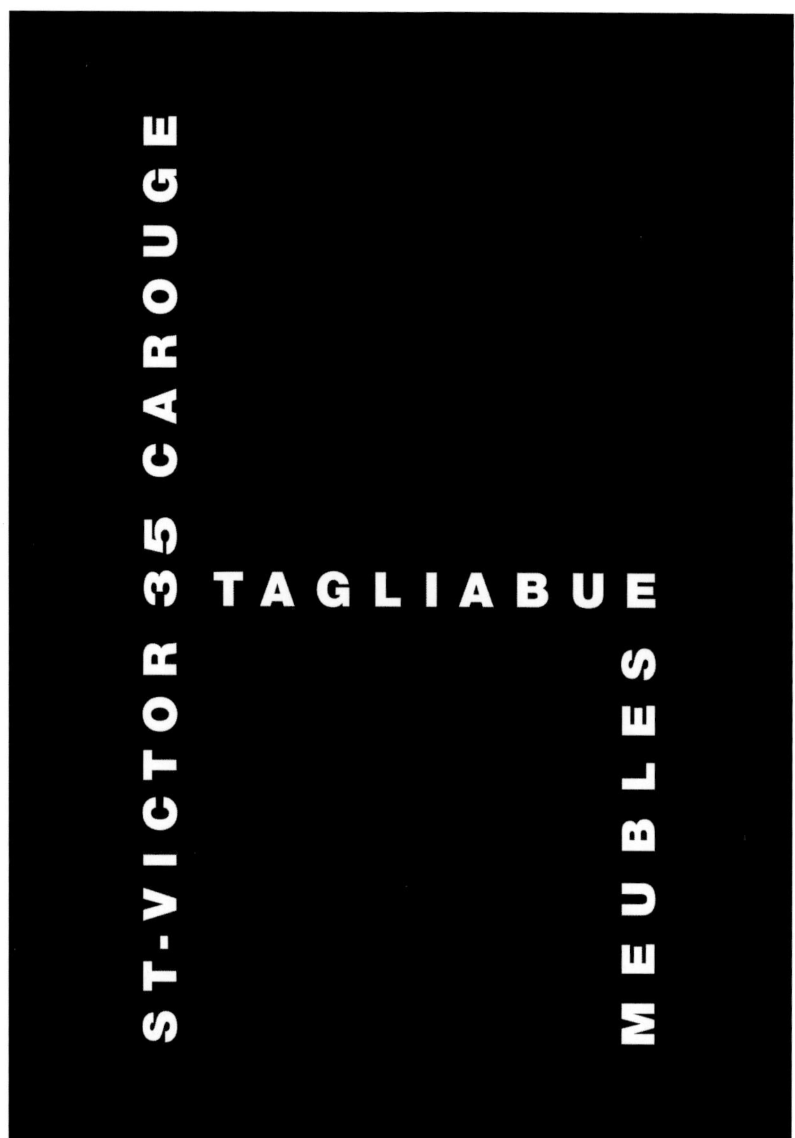

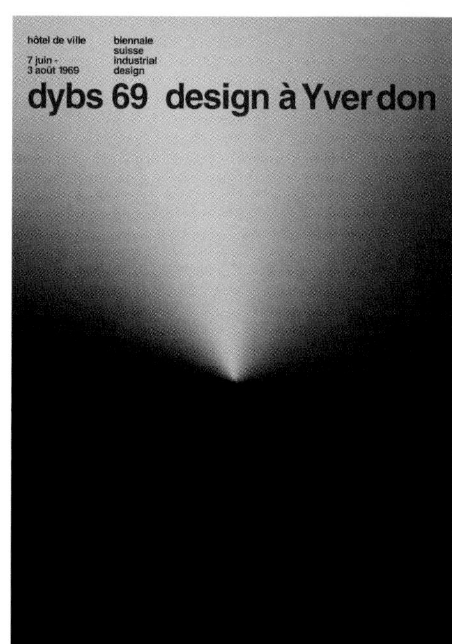

Georges Calame [Switzerland]

1930-1999; born in Geneva
Admitted to AGI, 1967

Georges spent some time in Paris, before opening his own graphic design studio in Geneva, 1953. In exhibition design he received major commissions: the Italian pavilion at 'Graphic 1957', pavilions at Swiss Expo 1964, Lausanne, at the Montreal World Fair 1967, the Swiss pavilion in Brno and a project for the Milan Triennale. From 1969–75 he was art director of the Pakistan Design Center in Karachi, but also designed the 'Dybs 69' design biennial and the travelling exhibition 'Swiss Graphic Design'. From 1975 to 1993 he created the visual identity of the BCG bank and harmonized the look of all its branches.

In 1979 he designed the logo for Palexpo (Geneva Congress and Exhibition Centre) and its signage programme. He worked for major Belgian, Japanese, Luxembourg and Swiss clients. His posters for 'A Japanese Summer in Geneva' (1983) aimed to connect East and West as well as the past and the present. His posters were selected 15 times at the 'Best Swiss Posters of the Year' event. In 1998 he received an award at the Brno Biennale for his powerful and simple design for the Geneva furniture shop Tagliabue, which had been a client over 30 years.

Poster for a **furniture store**, 1994. Awarded a prize as one of the 12 best Swiss posters in 1994.

Gas, advertising poster, 1958. Awarded a prize as one of the 24 best Swiss posters in 1958.

Design in Yverdon, exhibition poster, 1969. Awarded a prize as one of the best Swiss posters in 1969.

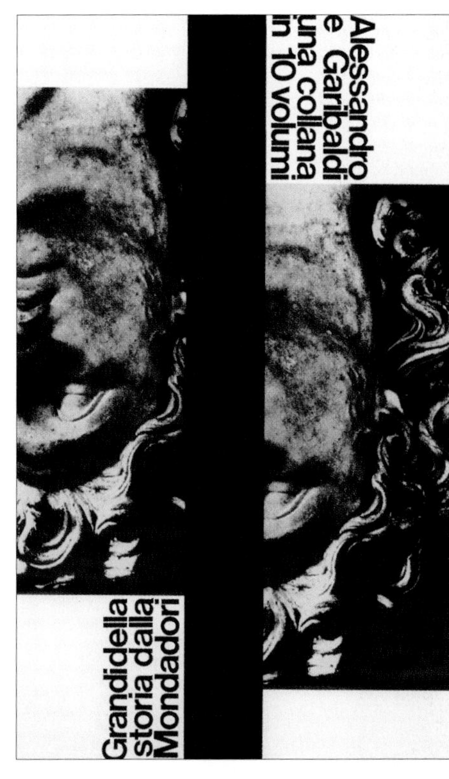

Poster for a **jazz concert**, 1977.

Advertisement for **I grandi delle storia** book series for the Mondadori publishing house, 1969–71.

Advertisement for **Cassina interior design**, 1961.

Giulio Confalonieri [Italy]

1926– born in Milan
Admitted to AGI, 1967

Confalonieri studied in Switzerland, Germany, Italy and India. He was mainly active in the field of graphic production for publishing and industry. He worked as a collaborator at *Domus*, was art director at Lerici and for others including *FMR*, *Art Esquire*, and *Marcatrè*. He was responsible for advertising campaigns for Valextra, Tecno, Boffi, Block and Pirelli. Confalonieri's work was presented at the 11th and 15th Milan Triennale. Meanwhile he taught at the Design Institute of Milan Polytechnic.

Among the prizes he has received are gold medals at the Milan Triennale XI and XV, the Premio Viareggio, the diploma of honour from the ADC NY and the Premio Bodoni. He has exhibited in Zürich and Milan (1969), at the Visual Art Gallery in New York, in London, Amsterdam (1973), Copenhagen (1971), the Musée de l'Art Moderne, Paris (1970), the International Poster Biennale in Warsaw (1968), in Ljubljana (1968–73), in Zürich (1970) and in Barcelona. Alongside his professional work, his graphic design experiments resulted in one of the first examples of visual poetry: *Immagine di un libro*.

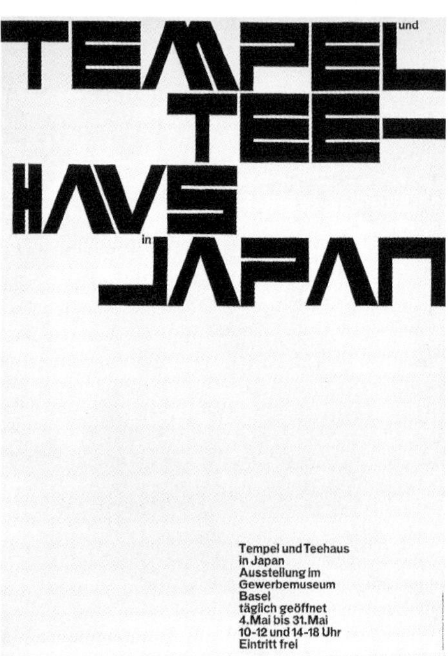

Armin Hofmann [Switzerland]

1920– born in Winterthur
Admitted to AGI, 1967

Between 1937–38, Hofmann attended the foundation course at the Kunstgewerbeschule in Zürich, after which he completed apprenticeships in both draughtsmanship and lithography printing in Winterthur. He worked as a lithographer and designer at Frobenius AG and in the studio of Fritz Bühler, Basel. Hofmann started his teaching career in 1947 at the Allgemeine Gewerbeschule (AGS) in Basel. He held visiting professorships at both the Philadelphia College of Art and Yale University and was advisor and lecturer at the National Institute of Design in Ahmedabad, India.

Two books on his teaching and design work have been published: *Graphic Design Manual* (1965), and *Work, Quest and Philosophy* (1989). Together with Emil Ruder, Hofmann established an advanced class for graphic design at the AGS that brought students from all over the world to study in Basel, and ignited his international reputation as both a designer and educator. Hofmann's work included posters, logos, exhibitions, colour concepts, signage systems and art-in-building projects. He retired in 1986. Armin Hofmann has received numerous honours for his work: an honorary doctorate from the Philadelphia University of the Arts in 1987, honorary membership of the Royal Society of Arts, London in 1988, and the City of Basel Culture Prize in 1997.

William Tell, Basel Open-Air Performances, photolithograph, 1963.

Lace, exhibition poster, Basel Museum of Applied Arts, photolithograph, 1969.

Temple and Teahouse in Japan, exhibition poster, Basel Museum of Applied Arts, linocut, 1955.

Norman Ives [USA]

Collage, mixed media, 1959.

H (Hotel Corporation), trademark study.
This simple *H* is made active by double perspective and by the fact that the triangles read both as horizontal and vertical planes.

Centaur, 1973. Screenprint, edition of 75.

BT (Bankers Trust), company trademark.
This linear composition solves the visual problem of combining an asymmetrical *B* with a symmetrical *T*, so that the *B* reads first.

1923-1978; born in Panama Canal Zone
Admitted to AGI, 1967

Norman Ives was a member of the first graduate class in graphic design at Yale University under the direction of Josef Albers and was invited to join the faculty in 1952, his graduation year. Ives became a full professor in 1972. He was an artist, designer, teacher, and publisher. Letterforms were the constant imagery in both his personal and professional work. His individual graphic work encompassed logos, symbols, book jackets, and posters. In 1960, a partnership with his student colleague Sewell Sillman established the publishing company Ives-Sillman, Inc. The firm produced limited editions of screenprints and portfolios faithfully translating into ink on paper the detail and colours of works from numerous artists including Ad Reinhardt, Willem De Kooning, and Josef Albers. Throughout his 28 prolific years, Ives's primary passions were letterforms and typography. By fragmenting type forms Ives reduced their literal value and raised their formal value. These parts of letters became brushstrokes for his paintings, prints and collages. Many of his finest pieces were architectural commissions for murals and bas-reliefs in banks, schools, and theatres, constructed from letter fragments. Ives also published *Eight Symbols*, in which he dissected and choreographed the figure/ground relationships of his trademarks and symbols.

Natasha Kroll [UK]

1916-2004; born in Moscow, Russia
Admitted to AGI, 1967

Natasha Kroll studied at the Reimann School of Art in Berlin. When the school moved to London in 1936 she was appointed to teach window display. Natasha was one of the first female AGI members. Kroll's early window display commissions included Rowntree's department stores in Scarborough and York. She soon won a more prestigious post as display manager for Simpsons in Piccadilly (1941–55). In 1954, Hugh Casson described Kroll as *'one of the most skilful and imaginative display designers in the country.'*

In 1956, she joined the BBC and made a great impact in production design. As a member of Richard Levin's design department she had a particular ability to devise innovative settings for discussions and factual programmes, becoming an expert in creating contemporary studio designs. In 1966 Kroll was elected to the Faculty of Royal Designers for Industry and it was in this year that she left the BBC to work freelance, specializing in period dramas. Her drama credits include *Eugene Onegin* (1967), *Macbeth* (1970) and *The Wood Demon* (1974). Kroll went on to gain credits as a production designer on films including *The Music Lovers* (1971), directed by Ken Russell, and *The Hireling* (1973), directed by Alan Bridges, for which Natasha won a BAFTA for Best Production Design.

The Wood Demon, BBC Play of the Month, November 1974.

Poster for **Barcelona Motor Show**, 1983.

Poster for the **Barcelona Olympic Games**, 1992. *'This is my first choice because it has received several mentions in the design industry. On a personal level, I felt very satisfied with it and rejoiced when I completed it.'* Published in *First Choice* by Ken Cato.

Tomàs Vellvé [Spain]

1927-1998
Admitted to AGI, 1967

In 1942, Vellvé started to work in Barcelona as a draughtsman, gaining experience in printing and reproduction techniques, while studying drawing, typography, photography and printmaking.
In 1948 he moved to Madrid, continuing his studies in graphic and applied arts. He was also a type designer and got his first commission in 1970. His typeface Jambage Sec Ibérique was later renamed Vellvé. He designed several typefaces, including his first digital one: a very special sans serif that stands between the geometry-based Futura and the industrial sans serifs like Helvetica. Perhaps a bit confusingly, this one is also called Vellvé.

He had several exhibitions in Barcelona, Canada, the US, eastern and western Europe, Israel and Brazil. Vellvé represented his country at the International Congress of Montreal in 1965. He received numerous awards for his posters, graphic design and his art. His work is in collections in Berlin, Honolulu, Warsaw, Barcelona, Belgrade, Brno, New York and Dublin.

Hugo Wetli [Switzerland]

1916-1972; born in Berne
Admitted to AGI, 1967

Wetli initially trained as a technical draughtsman, but then took an apprenticeship at a private graphic studio. From 1936 till 1946 he worked as a painter and draughtsman in Berne and Geneva. Meanwhile he travelled a lot in Europe, Africa and the USA. At the same time, he also produced posters and book illustrations. In 1947–48 he studied at the Académie de la Grande Chaumière in Paris. A gentlemen's fashion firm in Olten employed him in 1949–56. After that he opened his own graphic studio. He also continued to paint, and was commissioned for murals by Swissair in Milan and for the Swiss Expo 1964 in Lausanne. Wetli illustrated and wrote a book about Greece. He designed posters for cultural and travel organizations, as well as for industry.

Persil washing powder, advertising poster, 1947.

By Coach to the Hiking Trail, poster, 1966.

Co-op Coffee, illustration and hand-drawn lettering, 1960.

Ear Protection Is Self-Protection, safety poster, 1964.

Sörenberg, tourist poster, 1955.

Isal, Rotating Windows, brochure, 1961.

Mark Zeugin [Switzerland]

1930-2003; born in Berne
Admitted to AGI, 1967

Zeugin studied in Lucerne at the Schule für Gestaltung and as a trainee in a graphic studio (1948–52). He started his practice in Basel and became an art director in a Lucerne advertising firm (1954–57). From 1958 he worked independently from his own studio and in 1965 turned it into a design and advertising agency, operating with a number of employees. He was the president of the Bund Graphischer Gestalter der Schweiz (1963–1972) and of the Arbeitsgemeinschaft Schweizer Graphiker (1972–75).

Mark taught graphic design at the Kantonale Schule für Gestaltung in Biel. He created many award-winning posters, for CSIO in Lucerne, Caritas Schweiz and the Lucerne region (*'Vaterland'* with a big red V) among other clients. He also designed very effective logotypes. His painting took up a lot of his leisure time. He also had many exhibitions of his work.

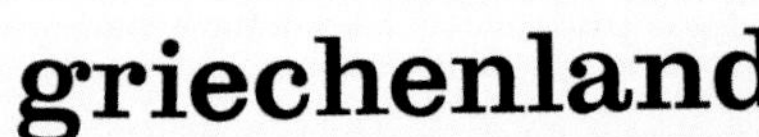

OUR EXPERTISE...
IN STEEL

The large steel structures fabricated by METKA continue to make a not inconsiderable contribution to Greece's electrification programme. The Company manufactures electro-mechanical systems such as lignite mills and electro-static filters; main and auxiliary steel structures for 300 MW thermo-electric stations and much of the equipment needed for the country's hydroelectric projects, as well as lattice towers for the 32, 66, 150, and 380 kV power distribution lines. In addition, the Company produces towers for use in telecommunications and for radio and television transmitters.

Boiler support

Air-ducts

Lignite mills

Frederick Vincent Carabott [UK]

1924– born in Athens, Greece
Admitted to AGI, 1968

Is of mixed Anglo-Greek parentage. Studied 1950–53 in London at Chelsea School of Art and St Martin's School of Arts and Crafts. Returned to Greece and in 1957 became art consultant to Aspioti-Elka Graphic Arts and *Pictures* magazine, both of Athens. Has since acted in the same capacity for many other organizations, including until 1967 the Greek Tourist Board, which was awarded the 1962 Golden Tulip from the International Advertising Association for work done largely under his direction.

His poster designs, with a strong colourful style, have been very influential. In 1962, he co-founded K+K Athens Publicity Centre (now K+K/Univas). Director of studies and lecturer at Hellenic American Institute of Graphic Arts (since re-named Homer/Omiros), 1968–71. Awarded prize at 1962 Livorno International Tourist Poster Exhibition and Rizzoli awards in 1964, 1965, 1966 and 1968. The King of Greece awarded him the Golden Cross of the Order of the Phoenix, in recognition of outstanding contribution to graphic design. He now works as a freelance and has written several books.

Poster for **Eden Beach Hotel**, Peloponnese, 1978.

In-house magazine for **METKA Steel Construction**, 1983.

Greece, German poster for the Greek Tourist Board, 1961.

Paul Hogarth [UK]

Drawings from the book **Graham Greene Country**, 1986.

Grand Hotel Oloffson, Haiti.

Street scenes, Port au Prince.
'The drummers became more reckless as the night advanced. They no longer troubled to muffle the beat.'

1917-2001; born in Kendal
Admitted to AGI, 1969

Paul simplified his real name just a little: he was born as Arthur Paul Hoggarth. He won a scholarship to Manchester College of Art in 1933, but his father called it *'that bloody art school'*. This *'original angry young man'* (in the words of his friend Ronald Searle) went to Spain to join the Republicans in the civil war, but was sent home when they discovered that he was only 17. Back home he resumed his studies at St Martin's College of Art in London. Being a member of the Communist Party, he was not allowed to join the forces in WW2, but worked instead at the Ministry of Propaganda. After the war he went to eastern Europe.

Working at the Central School of Art he challenged his principal to send him to China. It was the end of his job at the school, but he went anyway, as the first British artist to set foot in China (1953). He was an illustrator and graphic designer for Shell and an art director for various magazines. Hogarth travelled the world. He produced magnificent illustrations for the work of Graham Greene, *Jane Eyre*, and *London à la Mode*. ARA 1974, RA 1984, RDI 1979, RE 1988, OBE 1989.

Louis Klein [UK]

1932– born in Czechoslovakia
Admitted to AGI, 1969

Graduated from Cooper Union and Yale University, to become art director for *Interiors* magazine and Time Life in New York. Moved to London to work for Grey Advertising, before returning to New York where he founded Gips & Klein design group. He was a consultant for Time Inc., New York, and became design director for Time Life Books Intl, London and later for Time Life Books USA, developing new products, supervising content of books on computers, space, history and DIY and creating promotion.

As an executive member of D&ADA he designed their Pencil Award. Louis is a fellow of RCA, and was a fellow of SIA&D. His work covered a wide range of design, corporate identities, magazine styling, book design and editorial consulting. Was invited to have a one-man show at the Institute of Contemporary Arts, London. Klein conducted degree courses at the School of Visual Arts, NY and RCA London. He was a visiting professor and acting head of graphic design at Yale University; visiting critic at the RCA, Hounslow Borough College, and Nene College; senior lecturer in graphic design and advertising at Buckinghamshire College. Louis Klein has always remained a very sensitive, versatile designer, in spite of his involvement in mass publications.

Cover for **Interiors magazine**, 1959.

Book cover for **Design & Art Direction**, 1966.

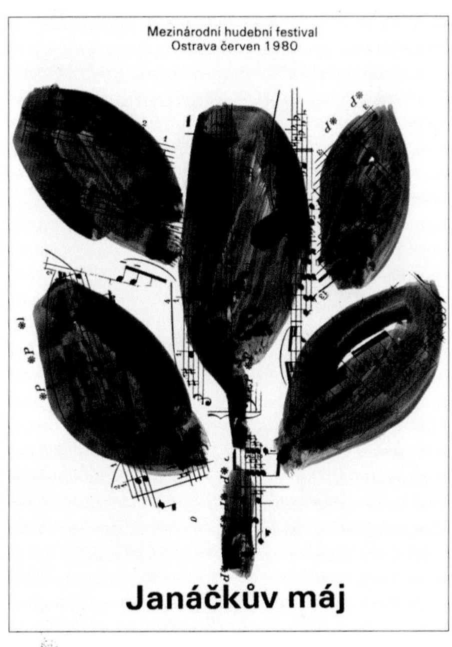

Mezinárodní hudební festival
Ostrava červen 1980
Janáčkův máj

Autoprogress '76, poster for a motor show in Brno, 1976.

Janácek's May, poster for the Janácek Music Festival in Ostrava, 1980.

Export-Import Motokov Czechoslovakia, 1981. Advertising poster, photomontage.

Stanislav Kovàr [Czech Republic]

1921-1985; born in Prague.
Admitted to AGI, 1969

Studied at the School of Applied Graphics in Prague and began to work for experimental theatre, before joining a group that worked to promote culture and industry. At the end of the forties he started to be involved in the promotion of Bohemian glass art, and held exhibitions in Moscow and Montecarlo. He designed for the Brno Biennial, for exhibitions in Ostrawa, and the Czech pavilion at the Montreal Expo 1967. Worked with a group called Horizont on several international exhibitions. He also received various international awards.

He was at the Icograda conference 1968 in Eindhoven when the Russian army invaded his country, to end the Prague Spring. He decided to return immediately. He refused to join the Communist Party, which did not make things easier for him and his family. As the president of the Czech AGI, he nevertheless organized a warm 1981 AGI Congress in cold, occupied Prague.

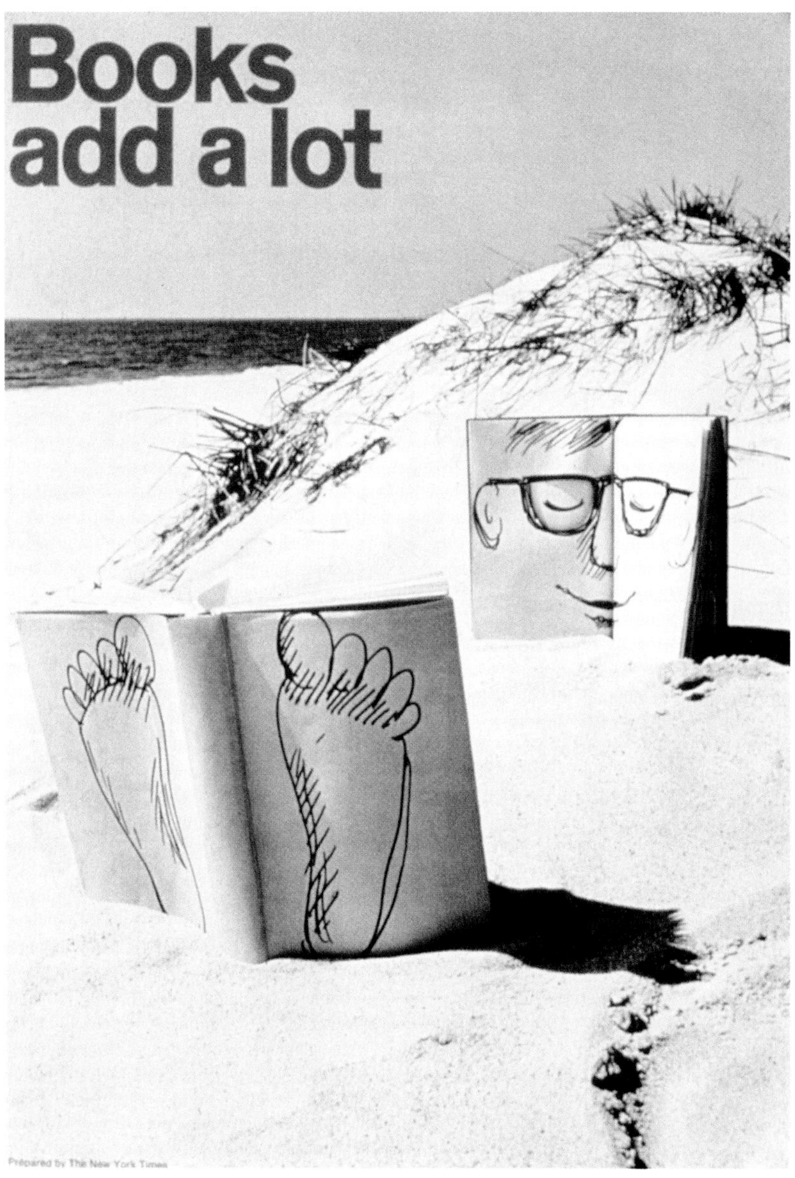

The New York Times
THE
Home
SECTION

Three Different Apartments– One Classic Style

Instant Furniture Boom: The Latest Look Is Sophisticated, The Assembly Is Easy Page C4

A solar house brings heating costs down to earth in Connecticut 8

Television: Lynn Redgrave talks about her new career 29

Books: A look at human behavior and Virginia Woolf 32

White House Acquisitor

How to cope with your unfinished apartment. By Joan Kron, page C6.

JANUARY 25-31 The New York Times

The Guide

Television/5-12

Dining Out/2

Art/21

Critics' Choices	3
Television Week	3
Radio	13
Film	18
Music	19
Dance	20
Photography	22
Children	23
Talks	23
Sound	25
Recordings	26

Opera/19

Theater/16

SUNDAY, JANUARY 25, 1981

Louis Silverstein [USA]

1919– born in New York City
Admitted to AGI, 1969

Early work included book and fashion advertising. Art director for US State Department. Designed the prize-winning Russian language magazine *Amepuka*. Made film strips for labour organizations. Was a successful Promotion Art Director for *The New York Times*, then became Corporate Art Director of the NY Times Co., overseeing the design for the newspaper and 34 affiliated companies, such as WQXR. He became assistant managing director and held both jobs, corporate and editorial, for many years. Took *'the grey lady of US journalism'* to its commanding position. *NYT* was named in 1984 as *'best-designed US newspaper'*.

His influential work affected the entire industry, and the many special sections he created were widely honoured. *HQ* wrote that Silverstein had changed the way newspapers were produced. His honours include the NY ADC gold medal for the creation of the Op-Ed page, two Pulitzer Prizes, lifetime awards from the Society of News Design and Society of Publication Design. Elected to the NY ADC Hall of Fame, 1984. Silverstein was designer and executive editor of *The Earth Times*, a fortnightly, associated with the UN. He taught at the School of Visual Arts NY and has lectured widely in the US and Europe. His one-man show at Cooper Union travelled to Canada and Florida. Silverstein is also an author.

Books Add A Lot, poster, 1960s. One of a series of point-of-sale promotional aids for booksellers produced by *The New York Times*.

The New York Times: Home Section, first issue, 1977. One of 5 daily new magazine-like broadsheet sections introduced.

The New York Times: The Guide, front page of a tabloid-sized entertainment section, 1980.

It’s time
to fly to Hanoi

The 1970s: Heyday?

Later, realization dawns and you think: **'Was it really true? Has the world indeed never been a happier place than it was in the seventies?'** There was really quite a lot to rejoice at. It was a period of great challenges. We bought our homes, gardens and new cars. We travelled. Some positive sides of science fiction had come true. The dreaded Chinese hadn't come west. The malicious Russians had invaded Hungary already in the fifties, and seemed to stop in Czechoslovakia. Bad enough, but...

Yet, this planet of ours has never been a place without its conflicts, confusions, conspiracies, cruelty, fights, hunger, betrayal and catastrophes. So when you only look a bit closer at the reality of those seemingly quiet 70s, you can't escape from the conclusion that, even in those years, **'nothing to complain about'** was once more just a shallow illusion. Maybe this decade was altogether another **'ordinary'** one.

Well okay, General de Gaulle died. So did the Egyptian president Nasser. Left-winger Salvador Allende became president of Chile, but was killed when Pinochet's military junta attacked his palace. Swiss women finally gained the right to vote. War broke out between India and Pakistan. The British joined the Common Market. Arab terrorists murdered 13 Israeli athletes at the Munich Olympic Games. After the dirty napalm war in Indochina spread to Laos and Cambodia, a ceasefire was finally achieved and later an end to the conflict in Vietnam. Israel, October 1973: the Yom Kippur War. An oil crisis quadrupled fuel prices. The Turkish invaded Northern Cyprus. King Feisal of Saudi Arabia was assassinated. Richard Nixon was re-elected as US president, but was brought down by the long drawn-out Watergate scandal: impeachment. Juan Peron regained the presidency of Argentina in 1973 and died in 1974.

Bloody uprisings in Soweto, South Africa. Plane hijackings became the order of the day. Spain celebrated its first elections since 1936 and PM Adolfo Suárez came to power. In Camp David (USA) the Egyptian and Israeli leaders Sadat and Begin attempted to take the first steps towards peace. Pope John Paul I died only 33 days into his papacy; John Paul II was his successor. The Japanese premier Fukuda (now, where do we know that name from?) resigned. The Shah of Persia was forced to flee and was succeeded by Ayatollah Khomeini. Bhutto, the leader of Pakistan, was deposed and condemned to death. Israel and Egypt signed a peace treaty. Margaret Thatcher became the UK's first woman prime minister. Bloody Sunday in Belfast; three storeys of London's Post Office Tower blown up. Major disasters with full aeroplanes colliding. The *Queen Elizabeth* ocean liner burned out in Hong Kong. Pol Pot's regime killed 3 million people in Cambodia: the Killing Fields. Peace was, alas, still no more than a perverse illusion.

The VIP list again contained numerous casualties: Pablo Casals, Coco Chanel, Ezra Pound, Janis Joplin, Jimi Hendrix, Pablo Picasso, Igor Stravinsky, Louis Armstrong, Agatha Christie and Maurice Chevalier.

Theatres and cinemas were showing *Jesus Christ Superstar* and Liza Minnelli in *Cabaret*. Nobel prizes for the authors Heinrich Böll and Alexander Solzhenitsyn. The Christos built their *Valley Curtain* project. Osaka held an Expo. Computer art made its entrance. *Love Story*, *Last Tango in Paris* and *The Godfather* appeared on the silver screen. Science-fiction escaped the boundaries of print and became visual *'reality'*. The immeasurable space in which sci-fi is often set was to know no peace. Americans and Russians stormed the Moon, Venus, Mars and Jupiter in manned and unmanned craft. Skylab was launched. Concorde became operational, for the fortunate few: supersonic travel in the stratosphere on board a long, slim cigar. Caviar and champagne. From Paris or London to the New World in three hours. The first test-tube baby entered the world in the UK, to be immortalized immediately with the new video camera. Some mothers were walking round in hot pants.

Architects were seeking greater and greater heights. Bruce Graham and the SOM agency build the highest skyscraper, the Sears Tower in Chicago. The Hancock Center, also in the windy city, was the highest apartment building so far (also by SOM, with F. Khan). Minoru Yamasaki designed the twin towers for the World Trade Center in Manhattan. Richard Rogers and Renzo Piano wrote architectural history with Paris's Centre Pompidou. These were busy times for the architects of many governmental buildings, theatres and museums. The names of Ricardo Bofill, Louis Kahn, Frank O. Gehry, Hans Hollein, Philip Johnson, Lucien Kroll, Richard Meier, Oscar Niemeyer, Aldo Rossi, Robert Venturi and Frei Otto shine out amongst innumerable others who gave the urban landscape a new look in the 1970s.

It was a time of acceleration, expansion and *'up and up'*. Graphic design played along, becoming to a large extent the *'visual mouthpiece'* of growing economies and the new affluence. Marketing gained increasing influence, often to the irritation of the designers. The day of strict corporate identities with their inevitable manuals had dawned. The West set up design agencies to meet the demand for this new, complex specialism. AGI continued to grow on the wave of the enormous demand for information and imagination.

The Swiss and International Styles still strongly predominated. Clarity, structure (grids) and simplicity were the key concepts. There is a lot of white to be seen on the pages and mostly primary colours, entirely sans serif typography with a certain touch of classicism. Akzidenz Grotesk, Adrian Frutiger and the late Giambattista Bodoni played the main roles. Frutiger's Univers font programme did indeed conquer the universe, but remained in constant conflict with the Helveticas, like the rift between fans of The Beatles and The Rolling Stones. Designers gained increasing control of the pre-print processes.

In the meantime, it was not solely the modernistic principles of Swiss design that dominated the 1970s. Wolfgang Weingart, who lectured in Basel alongside none other than Armin Hofmann, was preaching a totally different approach to design and gaining an international following. In the UK, punk came on the scene. In Dutch design a *'new wave'* emerged, which, aided by technological innovations, liberated form from its rigid constraints, although this was sometimes accompanied by a loss of accessibility to the information and a blurring of the borders with free art. In 1974, together with Jon Naar and author Norman Mailer, Mervyn Kurlansky published the book entitled *Watching My Name Go By*, which identified the tags of 800 early graffiti artists, who saw their names racing over the rails of the New York subway, from *'A.G.'* (it's only missing one letter...) to *'Zip'*. The visual world was being enriched with graffiti and was never again deprived of that beauty – or its inexorable excrescence.

Ben Bos, Amsterdam, 2006

AGI History in the 1970s

A Time of Consolidation

Ben Bos, Amsterdam, 2006

AGI congress in Barcelona. During the assembly: Carabott, Forbes, Pla-Narbona, Brun.

AGI had got through its adolescence. The 1970s were characterized by consolidation. We knew what we wanted from the Alliance. Donald Brun, one of the AGI's five Founding Fathers, had taken over the chairmanship, the registered office moved from Paris to Zürich and the articles of association were re-formulated in accordance with the solid rules of Swiss law. That was all organized in a formal meeting in Ulm, in southern Germany, which, with its Hochschule für Gestaltung (HfG) had become the temporary capital of Functionalism. Unlike the Bauhaus, the link from modernistic theory to industrial practice had been fully made in the instruction at the HfG (1953–68). Based on the *'dream'* of Universal Human Rights (UN: 1948), *'all people are essentially equal'*, the HfG focused on the Ideal Product, intended for Everyone. Design should not be for an elite public. Averse to all trimmings, it should simply work on the idea of *'less is more'* and therefore be as accessible and affordable as possible.

New AGI memberships in the 1970s were only partly a reflection of *'Ulm'* functionalism. And no wonder. Although functionalism was (and still is!) practised regularly in AGI circles, nowhere is it to be found in the biographies that anyone studied in Ulm. The condition in AGI's selection policy that prospective members had to have proved themselves on the international platform was a delaying factor, certainly at that time. Most newcomers were at least in their mid or late forties. They had already acquired their functionalistic ideas much earlier. The AGI *'harvest'* of this decade has nevertheless proved valuable. Many newcomers from those years formed a loyal hardcore of active members that survives to this day.

After Ulm, it was planned to meet somewhere in Switzerland, although this did not work out. The next congress (1971) was held in Barcelona. Pla-Narbona was an extraordinary host: in his vast private cinema, AGI members watched their friend's religious documentaries in astonishment. The actual Middle Ages on celluloid. Once they had recovered from the shock, they set to writing the new articles of association for the AGI. The following year Henrion received an invitation from Hiroshi Ohchi to speak to his students in Tokyo. Henri took advantage of the opportunity to exhibit the work of all 9 British AGI members at the Tokyo Trade Center.

In 1972, Herbert Spencer became AGI President. That year's congress was held in Amsterdam. Wim Crouwel played a major role in taking the AGI guests to the Stedelijk Museum, where he had set up an exhibition and introduced them to the works of art in Turmac's Stuyvesant Collection. There were 80 participants (including guests) from 12 countries. The evening boat trip along Amsterdam's canals and the reception followed by dinner in Amsterdam's Historical Museum were the climax of the programme.

Jerusalem was planned for 1973, but the Yom Kippur War proved to be of higher priority to the young state of Israel. The congress was organized by Dan Reisinger and Jean David. Pentagram had prepared a thematic exhibition. In showing works from the 1950s, 1960s and early 1970s, the idea was to make it clear what graphic design can do for international, national and local governments, politics, cultural and charitable organizations and education. It was not only a historical overview; the intention was to show the style differences and the breadth of activities. On one hand, the strength and unity of the *'Swiss'* International Style came to the fore and, on the other, the personal, more painterly work of designers from Poland and Czechoslovakia. The exhibition was shown in Amsterdam, but ended up in the Israel Museum in Jerusalem in 1974, after all, where it remained in the permanent collection, as a gift from AGI. Illustrative poster available from Reisinger!

In 1974, AGI travelled to Warsaw, on the occasion of the 4th Poster Biennale. The Polish capital had opened the first specialized poster museum in the world in 1968. Josef Mroszczak was the driving force behind that initiative. During the Biennial, there were special one-man exhibitions for the three winners in 1972. The company was then invited to Mroszczak's dacha, somewhere in the interior of Poland. The coach got lost, meandering for four hours through the countryside. But it was certainly a memorable event!

A major exhibition of the work of 107 AGI members was made possible by sponsor Olivetti. The show travelled from Milan (1974), via Brussels (1975) and Montreal (1976) to Stuttgart (1977). Franco Grignani wrote the foreword to the accompanying book. He identified a number of significant changes since the previous AGI exhibition in Milan, 13 years earlier. *'This exhibition of communication graphics should be seen as the most complete and important in the world. It introduces a new character language, visible in numerous "exhibits" and various media: posters, logotypes, trademarks, advertisements, layouts, magazine design, stands, textile designs, etc. ...Yesterday, Cubism gave us a new concept of the synthesis of form. Today, it would appear, in its turn graphic design is inspiring free art. With the common denominators in their work and through their personal experience, 107 AGI members from the USA to Japan are setting objective rules for visual information and visualization. Naturally, it is not possible to make conclusive regulations for a field where discovery and innovation are such primary factors. But there is a practical basis, which derives its validity from its general acceptance. AGI has now become a platform for the exchange of professional experience and areas for concern. There is an awakening of the conscience of intellectual and social responsibility.'*

The congress of 1975 started off in Athens and continued on to the Cyclades islands. The annals are rather vague on that point. Walter Allner took over the AGI chairmanship briefly, but stepped back within a year. Henrion was charged with the task of keeping the AGI ship afloat on the seven seas as interim captain.

The Mediterranean was evidently in mode. The next AGI congress was held in Palma de Mallorca, in October 1976. We had had to say farewell to two highly praiseworthy members; Hans Schleger (who often signed with his pseudonym Zero) and Josef Mroszczak, the driving force behind Warsaw poster museums, had died.

1971: AGI congress in Barcelona.

In Pla-Narbona's own private home cinema the AGI visitors were shown Spanish religious horror films.

General Assembly in the Ritz Hotel.

1973: *'The AGI conference that wasn't'*.

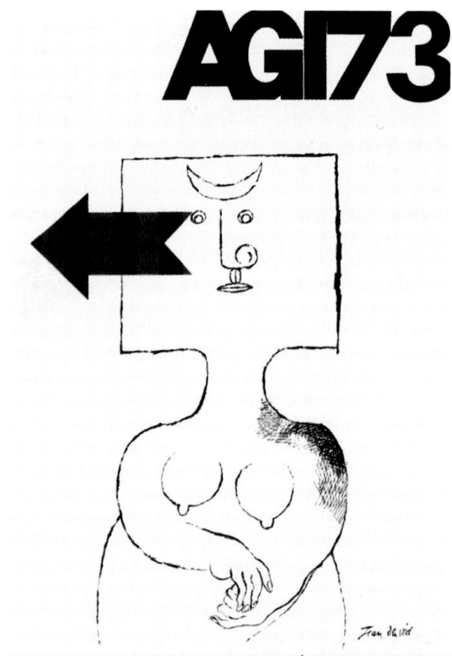

Planned to take place in Jerusalem, but cancelled owing to the 1973 war in the region. Poster designed by Dan Reisinger, illustration by Jean David (both from Israel).

1974: AGI exhibitions in Brussels, Milan, Montreal and Toronto.

Henrion, who gave the memorial speech, was also obliged to announce that his attempts to bring Jean-Michel Folon back to the fold had been to no avail. The Belgian maestro excused himself in his *'defence'* by explaining where his numerous wonderful priorities lay. We will not repeat them here. Suffice to quote the final words: *'I lead my life far from dinners, prizes, talks, discussions about work, exhibitions* [he had dozens more after that...], *mutual compliments and meetings of more than three people, otherwise I would be afraid of becoming a really serious person. Please excuse me. My best wishes, Folon.'*

Naturally, you can also live perfectly well like that. For Henrion, on the other hand, the AGI meant meeting old friends, making new friendships within the profession and periodically restoring the balance of this earthly existence, in which joy and despair appear to be inseparable. In Palma, Colin Forbes became the next international president of AGI. Newly installed members of the board are the harbingers of AGI's continued future, warming up for a three-year chairmanship.

Venice, the venue for the congress of 1978 (AGI was now 25 years old!), was also washed with water from the same Mediterranean sources. The big turnout was unprecedented: 118 participants, of whom more than half were members and the rest their guests.

Also in 1978, Tomaszewski showed a collection of Polish posters at an exhibition in *'Henrion's'* London College of Printing. That year, the AGI congress was held in Bath, England. We were surrounded by history, following the traces of Roman rule, complete with the eponymous Roman baths. There was also, however, a wonderful American Museum in Claverton and the museum of the photographic pioneer, Fox Talbot. Michael Foreman gave a great party in his studio and Tony and Edne Rudd served us an excellent lunch.

The surrounding countryside boasts a wealth of prehistoric finds, so all in all there were lots of things to enjoy. Peter Smithson gave a lecture on Bath, its history and its stylish architecture, Henrion spoke of McKnight Kauffer and his poster work from the pre-war years. Theo Crosby talked about the Neolithic finds. Elizabethan music delighted the ears. Arnold Schwartzman showed us Venice and was so successful that the audience demanded an *'encore'*. Many wonderful, dear people completed the picture in the atmospheric setting of Bath. Ray Eames, recently widowed, was invited as guest of honour (see also the essay *AGI Honoris Causa*).

In 1979, a new AGI tradition was established. The decision made in Bath by the annual general members' meeting to link a student seminar to the congresses, if possible was implemented. The gathering of so much talent and design success at the AGI congresses should surely make it possible to provide a number of extremely informative days for students. SUNY University in New York hosted the première. Richard Hess, Jelle van der Toorn Vrijthoff, Armin Hofmann, R.O. Blechman, Matthew Carter, Henryk Tomaszewski, Tom Geismar, Félix Beltrán, Michael Peters and Paul Davis formed the company of guest lecturers. Ten leading figures from six countries; that is more than most design congresses can offer. There was a film evening with work by AGI members and, naturally, a dazzling party to round it all off. 28 international academies from 13 countries had sent out a delegation. SUNY's Visual Arts Department had organized it all magnificently and the US government provided the necessary simultaneous translators. The success of the seminar called for more. A wish was expressed to continue the seminars, possibly in consultation with Icograda.

The AGI congress was skilfully put together by Herb Lubalin. The first glasses were raised in Lubalin's design group's former fire station. There were great *'side events'* such as a dinner in the famous Park Plaza Hotel, where Will Sandberg was installed in the NY ADC Hall of Fame. And then there were the festivities celebrating the AIGA Gold Medal for the partners of Chermayeff & Geismar, in a stylish club for the greats of New York's theatre world. It was an Indian summer, with its kaleidoscope of colours. The beautiful, glowing countryside around Lakeville in NY State was the backdrop. There was a visit to Norman Rockwell's studio, to the respectable, attractive Hancock Village, populated by the Shakers, and the French studio in Stockbridge. 101 guests had a fantastic time. The fact that the coach broke down not once, but twice, was the only minus point in such a paradise of hospitality and superior technology. AGI concluded its third decade in style.

1977: AGI congress in Venice.

The crowd (with Allner, Fleckhaus, Lubalin, Kurlansky, Dorfsman, Him, Miho, the Rüeggs, Collins, Pla-Narbona. Hiestand).

1975: AGI congress in Athens and the Cyclades, Greece.

Marion Wesel and FHK Henrion (UK).

Ursula Hiestand (Switzerland) and Jacques Richez (Belgium).

1978: AGI congress in Bath, England.

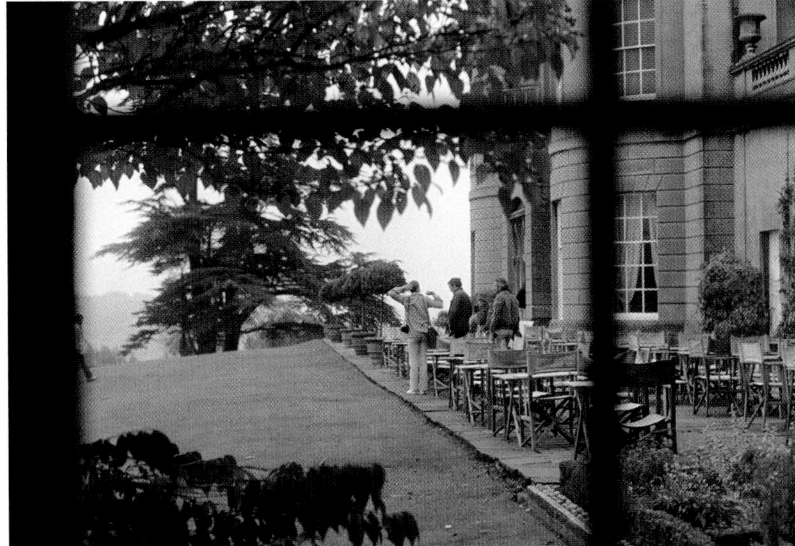

The American Museum at Claverton.

Jacqueline Casey (USA), Henrion (UK), Mr & Mrs Brun (France), Mel Calman (UK).

Zeugin (Switzerland), Fletcher, Foreman, Pelham (UK).

1979: AGI congress in New York/Lakeville.

Cipe Pineles, Arthur Paul (USA), Jean Morin (Canada).

Lou Danziger (USA), Fritz Gottschalk (Switzerland).

AGI Bulletin.

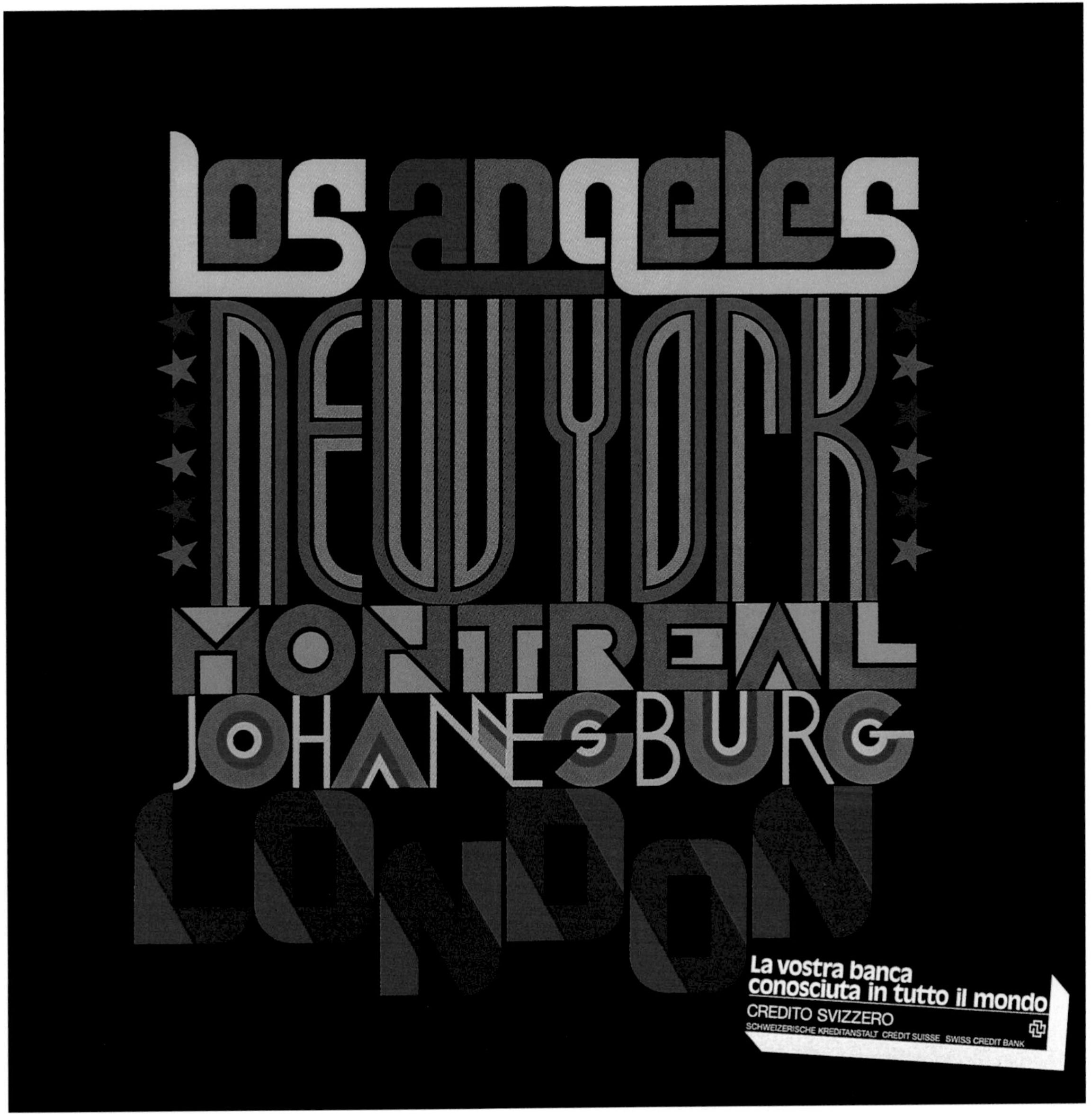

Credit Suisse: Your Bank, Known All Over The World, poster, 1978.

Gérard Miedinger [Switzerland]

1912-1995; born in Zürich
Admitted to AGI, 1970

Miedinger was educated at the Zürich Kunstgewerbeschule 1928–32 and then at the Académie Ranson in Paris. He worked in Zürich with Orell Füssli and an advertising agency, before he opened his own studio there. He created logotypes, posters, packaging, corporate identities and exhibitions for industry and government. In 1945 he was commissioned to work on a social programme for the charity Winterhilfe. Miedinger also contributed to the Swiss entries for the Brussels Expo 1958 and Montreal Expo 1967. For 25 years he designed window displays for Credit Suisse, Zürich.

In 1968–72 he was a member of the jury for the best Swiss posters of the year. In the same period he was president of the Verband Schweizer Graphiker (later ASG).

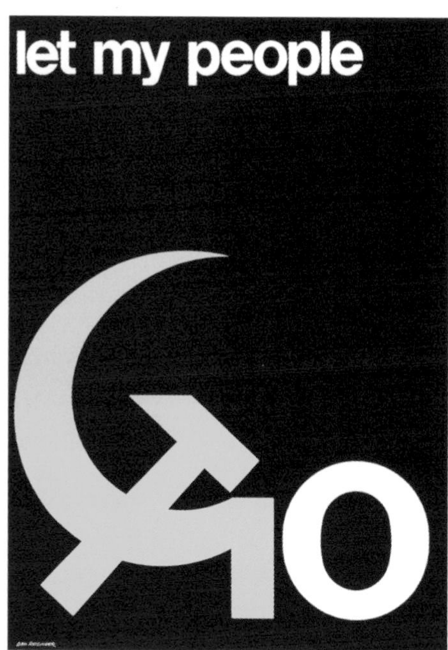

Dan Reisinger [Israel]

1934– born in Kanjiza, Yugoslavia
Admitted to AGI, 1970

Emigrated to Israel in 1949, studied painting, sculpture and poster design at Bezalel Academy, graduated with distinction and continued to study 3D design and painting at the Central School of Art, London. His international reputation was launched at the Brussels 1958 Expo, where his poster for the science pavilion won first prize. In the words of Dr Gaon, curator of the Israel Museum Design Pavilion, Reisinger has a keen ability to absorb international trends and translate them into his own idiom. His work – environmental, 3D and graphics – defies identification with any specific style which would stamp or classify him. If anything, his trademark is colour.

Reisinger was the first Israeli designer to hold a one-man exhibition at the Israel Museum, the Tel-Aviv Museum (1977) and the NY ITC Centre (1991); his posters are in major international collections and he is frequently invited to participate in international forums and juries. In 1998 Reisinger was awarded the Israel Prize for his contribution in the field of design and in recognition of *'his mark on the visual language of Israel for over 40 years'*.
In 2004 Hungary awarded Reisinger the Order of the Knight's Cross. The Hungarian government also honoured him with a retrospective exhibition at the National Museum of Applied Arts, Budapest.

AGAIN?, warning against the rise of neo-fascism in former socialist states, 1993.

EL-AL, airline corporate identity programme, 1971.

Let My People Go, an appeal to the Soviet government to allow Jews to leave the USSR, 1969. Self-published silkscreen.

Winterhilfe, poster, 1959.

Artists Masked Ball Zürich, poster, 1977.

New York City Ballet, poster, Zürich City Theatre, 1962.

Peter Andermatt [Switzerland]

1938-2005; born in Zürich
Admitted to AGI, 1971

Peter studied at the Kunstgewerbeschule in Zürich, graduating with honours. He became a head designer at Studio Müller-Brockmann and was for seven years a partner in MB&Co, Zürich. Peter taught for 19 years at the Art and Design School in Berne. In 1989 he was appointed a professor and director at the Institute for Communication Design (later University of Applied Science) in Konstanz, Germany. His friend Michael Baviera had urged him to take the post. Peter was a driven man with a mission. Caring, warm-hearted, sometimes beyond his own strength. From 1975 he had his own studio in Zürich.

Andermatt was an editor of the magazine *Idée...à jour*, and a visual designer, painter and illustrator. As a young man he dreamed of becoming a farmer, but a severe accident kept him in hospital for several years and during that time he discovered his creative destination and passion. He became the youngest AGI member at the age of 33. He was dedicated to *'letting something good grow out of everything you do'*. In his obituary, his friend Harri Ihring quoted the words of another friend: *'Andy burned the candle of his life at both ends.'* Andermatt made posters, illustrated magazines, designed a chess game for Alusuisse. And painted and drew. And drew and painted. And cared.

Opernhaus Zürich

medea

Oper von Luigi Cherubini
Erstaufführung
in italienischer Sprache
Samstag, 19. Februar 1972
20 Uhr

Musikalische Leitung:
Nello Santi
Inszenierung:
Günter Roth
Bühnenbild/Kostüme:
Max Röthlisberger
Chöre: Hans Erismann

Besetzung: Antigone Sgourda,
Carol Smith, Costanza
Cuccaro, Elisabeth Promonti,
Alexandra Kunošiková;

Glade Peterson, Aurelian
Neagu, Gejza Zelenay

m

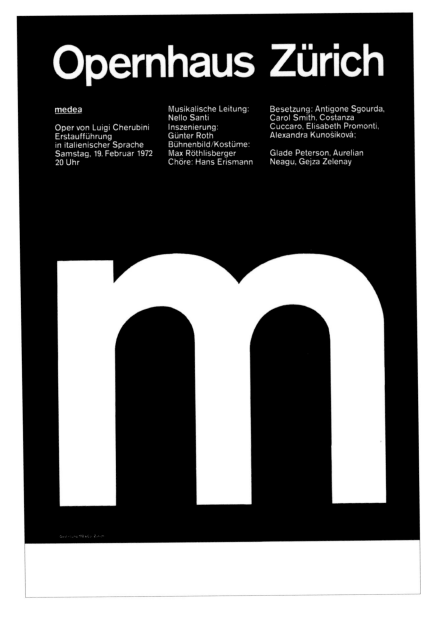

Ruedi Rüegg [Switzerland]

1936– born in Zürich
Admitted to AGI, 1971

Education: Zürich Design School with Josef Müller-Brockmann and Hans Finsler. 1963: went to the US as assistant to Paul Rand; study trips to Mexico and the US. 1964–65: employed by Nakamoto International Agency, Osaka. 1967–76: co-owner and director of Müller-Brockmann & Co., Zürich. 1973–80: juror for the Best Swiss Posters of the Year. 1974–80: president of Hombrechtikon Kindergarten. 1976–81: president of AGI Switzerland. 1977–83: Baltis & Rüegg Zürich. 1981–2000: member of the International Executive Committee of AGI. 1984: Designalltag Zürich Ruedi Rüegg. 1996–2000: International Secretary of AGI.

Teaching background: 1968–88: visiting professor of graphic design, Ohio State University, Columbus. 1983–89: lecturer at Kent State Summer Workshop, Switzerland. 1984–2006: teaching at School of Design, St Gallen. Various guest lectureships and workshops in Europe, the US and Mexico. Several awards for posters and books, including AGI's Henri Award, 2000.
Clients: Zürich Airport, signage and corporate design; Swiss Post & Telegraph, corporate design and identity; Mäser Austria, CD and CI; Westinghouse Design Center USA, CD and CI; Rockwell International, CD and CI. Tonhalle Zürich, Opera Zürich, Zürich City and State.
Secrets: married to Anni, They have 3 children and 2 grandsons.

Orte, cover design for a literature magazine, c. 1985.

Who's Who in Graphic Design, book design, 1994.

Poster for the **Zürich Opera**, 1972.

David Gentleman [UK]

Mural at Charing Cross station, London underground, 1979. Wood engravings, enlarged and screenprinted on melamine, depict the construction of the medieval Charing Cross which once stood where the station now is.

Bliar: Stop the War, placard for a protest march against the Iraq War. One of a series designed for the Stop the War Coalition from 2003–2006.

Montmartre and **Bir-Hakeim bridge** , water-colours from David Gentleman's *Paris*, 1991 (x 2). Other books in the series were on Britain, the British coastline, India and Italy.

1930– born in London
Admitted to AGI, 1972

David Gentleman, the son of artist parents, studied at the Royal College of Art from 1950–53. Since then he has worked on his own as watercolourist, wood engraver, illustrator, lithographer and designer. His early commissions ranged widely: engravings for books and press ads, drawings for newspapers and magazines, designs for fabrics and wallpapers, watercolours for Shell, illustrations for New York limited editions and for Penguin and Faber paperbacks. In 1962 the Post Office issued the first of his hundred postage stamps. In the seventies he made many lithographs, designed and took the photographs for a series of environmental posters for the National Trust, and designed a platform-length mural at Charing Cross tube station. The eighties and nineties were largely taken up with his most extended work, writing and illustrating *David Gentleman's Britain* and five subsequent books about London, the coastline, Paris, India and Italy. *Artwork*, a book on his designs and illustrations, was published in 2002. Since then he has made lithographs of Suffolk, painted watercolours of London, Brazil and India, and designed coins for the Royal Mint and placards protesting against the Iraq War. There have been many solo exhibitions of his paintings and lithographs. He was elected a Royal Designer for Industry in 1970.

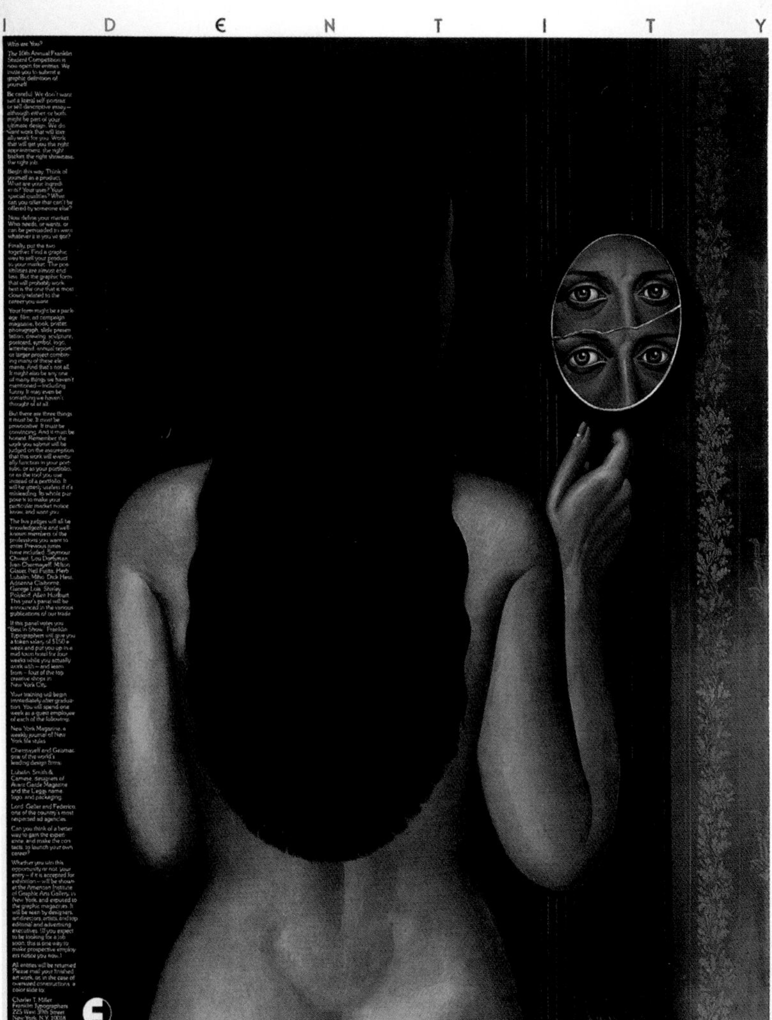

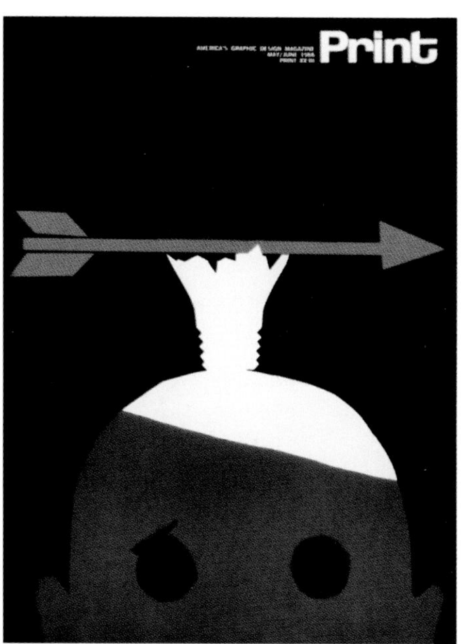

Richard Hess [USA]

1934-1991; born in Royal Oak, Michigan
Admitted to AGI, 1972

Although Richard won a scholarship to Pratt and briefly attended the University of Michigan, he was mainly a self-taught designer. His first experience was at the Palmer Paint Company, where he painted originals for the first paint-by-number sets. In 1955, at the age of 21, he became art director at Walter J. Thompson. It took him 11 years, working at various agencies, before he started his own Hess Design, a graphic and film art consultancy.

Hess was an influential graphic designer who worked on annual rapports, corporate magazines and identity systems for clients including Champion International, AT&T and Washington Post. He also worked for CBS, PepsiCo, IBM, Xerox, DuPont and *Esquire*, *New York* magazine and the *New York Times*. When he was designing *Vista* for the United Nations, he started to illustrate, something he hadn't done for 17 years. His chief pleasure was painting covers for *Time*, featuring famous but sometimes controversial figures.

Poster competition announcement for **Franklin Typographers**,1974.

New York, magazine cover painting, 1973.

Print, magazine cover.

Cover of Hurlburt's book **The Grid**, 1978.

Cover of Hurlburt's book **Publication Design**, 1976.

Allen Hurlburt [USA]

1910-1983
Admitted to AGI, 1972

He graduated in economics from the University of Pennsylvania in 1932, and wanted to become a cartoonist, but his reputation was made as a magazine art director. During the postwar years (1953–68), Hurlburt worked for NBC and *Look* magazine, where his page designs were awarded with a dozen gold medals in the Advertising and Editorial Art and Art Directors Club annual exhibitions. He was design director for Cowles Communications (1968–72). His graphic design scope included advertising and corporate art direction.

In 1965, he was named Art Director of the Year and he received the gold medal of the American Institute of Graphic Arts (1973). He was elected president of the AIGA from 1968–70. Hurlburt was a newspaper addict. He wrote many books, among them *Publication Design* (revised 1976), *Layout: The Design of the Printed Page* (1977) and *The Grid: A modular system for the design and production of newspapers, magazines and books* (1978). He was coordinator at Parsons and lectured at the London College of Printing.

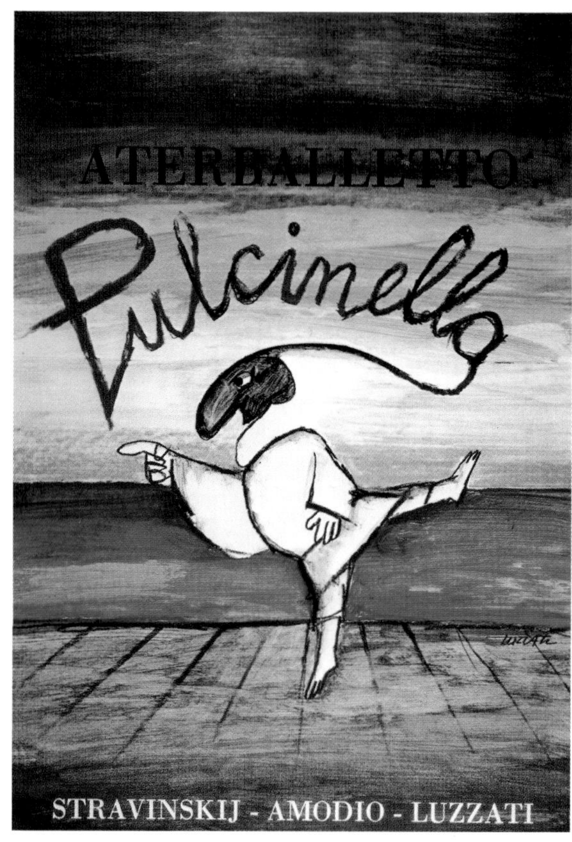

Emanuele Luzzati [Italy]

1921-2007; born in Genoa
Admitted to AGI, 1972

Luzzati studied at the École des Beaux-Arts in Lausanne. He was a painter, illustrator, graphic designer and ceramicist. After graduating he began his creative activity in Albisola, designing wall panels and unique pieces that allowed him to win the first prize for ceramics in Cannes (1955) and the Rosa d'Oro (1979). In addition he created panels and tapestries for ocean liners. Afterwards he devoted his skills to building stage sets and designing costumes for some of the most important national and international theatre companies.

He designed approximately 200 stage sets for plays, operas and ballets, in Italy and abroad. In some cases he also produced programmes and posters for these performances. In the 1960s, he turned his attention towards illustrations and animated films. The best known, *La gazza ladra* and *Pulcinella*, received two Oscar nominations. The Museo Luzzati, showing his oeuvre, is located in his hometown of Genoa. His interest in the emotional and cultural world of childhood led him to write and illustrate some books for children in which the world of art and play merge perfectly. In the context of visual communication he was mainly involved in publishing and experimental graphics, exhibiting in 1972 at the Venice Biennial.

Stage set design.

Eugene Ionesco: *The Bald Soprano*, theatre poster, 1982.

Pulcinella, poster for the Spoleto Festival, 1993.

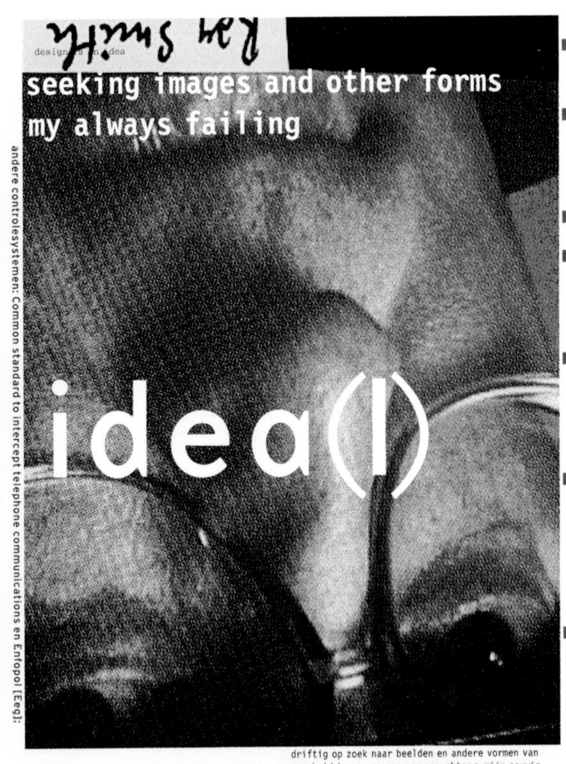

Double page from Jan van Toorn's book **Design's Delight**, from the chapter *'Design is a good idea'*, Rotterdam, 2006.

Museumjournaal 4, magazine cover, 1979.

Jan van Toorn [The Netherlands]

1932– born in Tiel
Admitted to AGI, 1972

Lives and works in Amsterdam. He studied graphic design at the IVKNO (later Gerrit Rietveld Academy) in Amsterdam (1950–53). He has been a freelance designer since 1957. Among others he worked for the Stedelijk van Abbemuseum Eindhoven, the Dutch Ministries of Culture and Public Works, the Dutch PTT, Rosbeek Printers and 010 Publishers. Jan van Toorn's radical teaching and practice were highly influential on the younger generation of Dutch designers. For many years he taught visual communication at various academies and universities in the Netherlands and abroad, including the Gerrit Rietveld Academy (1968–85), the department of architecture at Eindhoven Technical University (1982–83) and the multimedia department of the State Academy of Fine Arts, Amsterdam (1987–89). From 1991–98 he was director of the Jan van Eyck Academy in Maastricht, a postgraduate centre for fine art, design and theory. In this context he organized *Design Beyond Design: Critical Reflection and the Practice of Visual Communication*, a conference devoted to the discrepancy between the sociocultural and symbolic reality of the information economy (1997).Since 1989 he has been associate professor in the MA programme of RISD, Providence. He has received the Werkman prize from the city of Amsterdam (1965 and 1972); the Piet Zwart prize (1985); and the Athena award for career excellence. (New York, 2004).

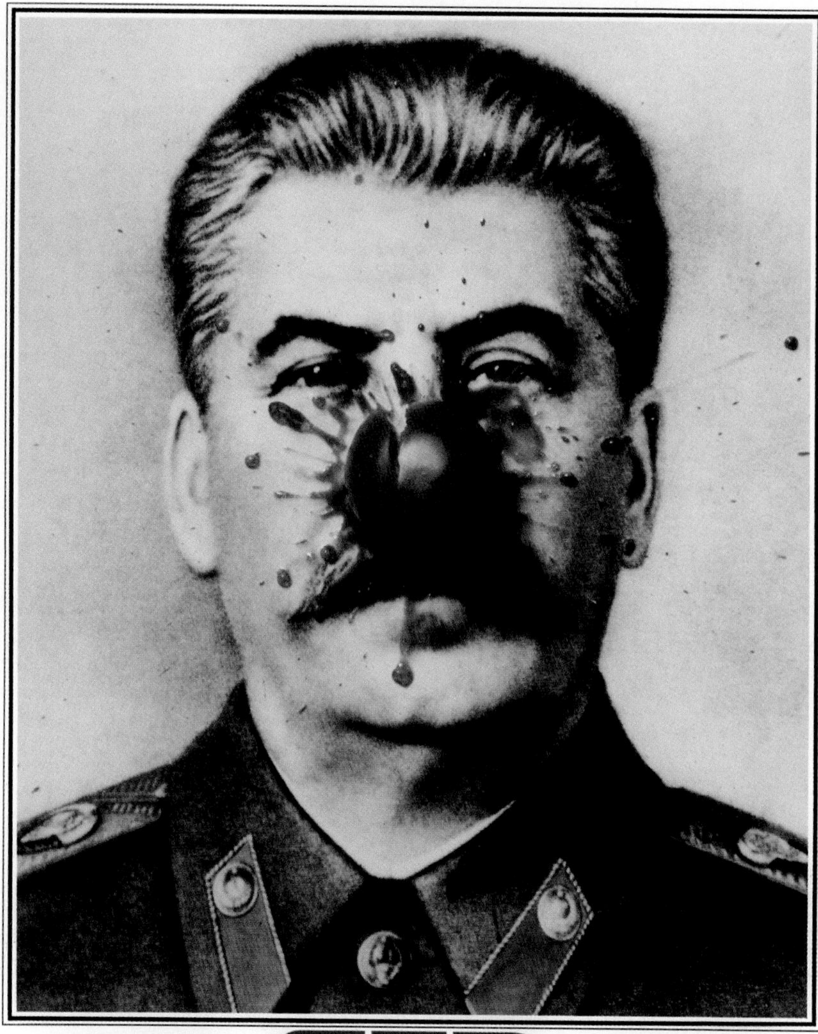

COLIN BLAKELY
DAVID SUCHET
SPECIAL APPEARANCE BY
CARROLL BAKER

EXECUTIVE PRODUCER
DAVID PUTTNAM
SCREENPLAY BY
CHARLES WOOD
BASED ON THE STORIES OF YURI KROTKOV
PRODUCED BY
GRAHAM BENSON
DIRECTED BY
JACK GOLD

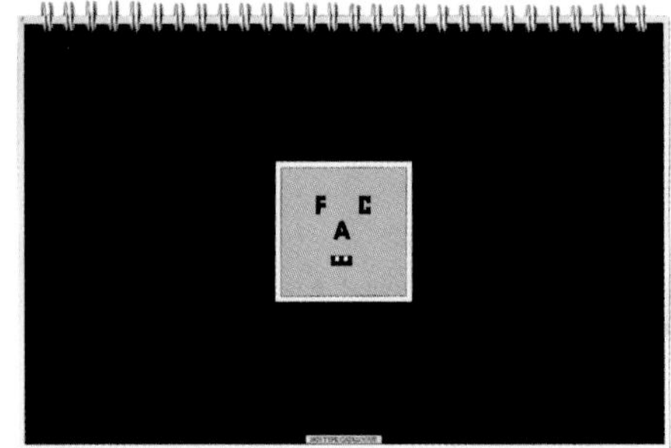

John Gorham [UK]

1937-2001; born in Hillingdon
Admitted to AGI, 1973

After an erratic education due to poor health, John started work as an apprentice in a silkscreen company, followed by periods in two art studios. In 1963 he joined the *Daily Mirror* publicity department as a graphic designer, leaving in 1965 to work in the marketing department of the *Sunday Times*. He then went to the advertising agency CR Cassons as an art director. He became a freelance designer in 1967. Success came almost immediately, as his originality, purity of ideas, humour, faultless execution and general freshness of approach were quickly recognized. His range of work was phenomenal, covering both advertising and design, including packaging, identity design, direct mail, posters, stamps, book design, book jackets and film graphics. He was a consummate craftsman, renowned for his masterly lettering design, typography and illustration. Clients included top advertising agencies and design groups, and the magazines that were setting the graphic pace at any one time. He also had strong relationships with the Royal Mail, WHSmith, Penguin Books, film producer David Puttnam and directors Alan Parker and Hugh Hudson. During the late 1970s and early 1980s John taught at the RCA. His work gained him many British, American and European awards. In 1993 D&AD honoured him for his lifetime achievement with the President's Award.

Poster for black comedy film **Red Monarch**, 1978.

Poster for **Torbay Tourist Board**, 1984.

Cover for **Face Type Catalogue**, 1976.

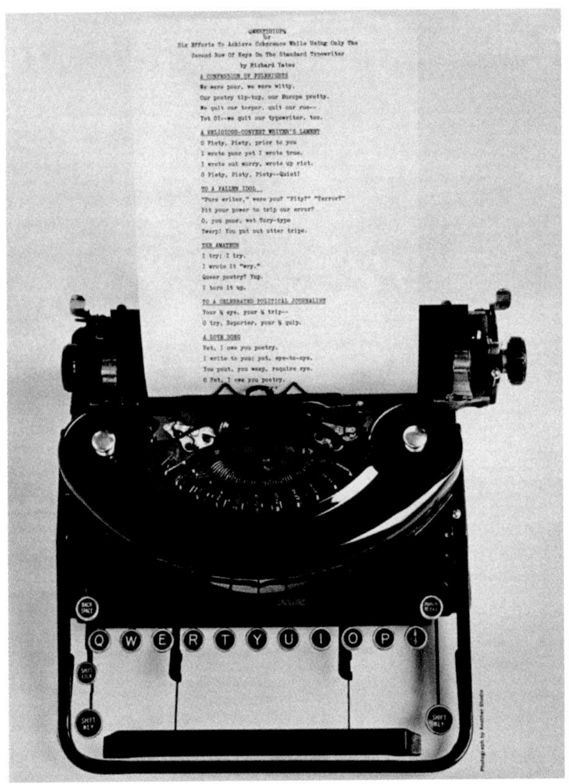

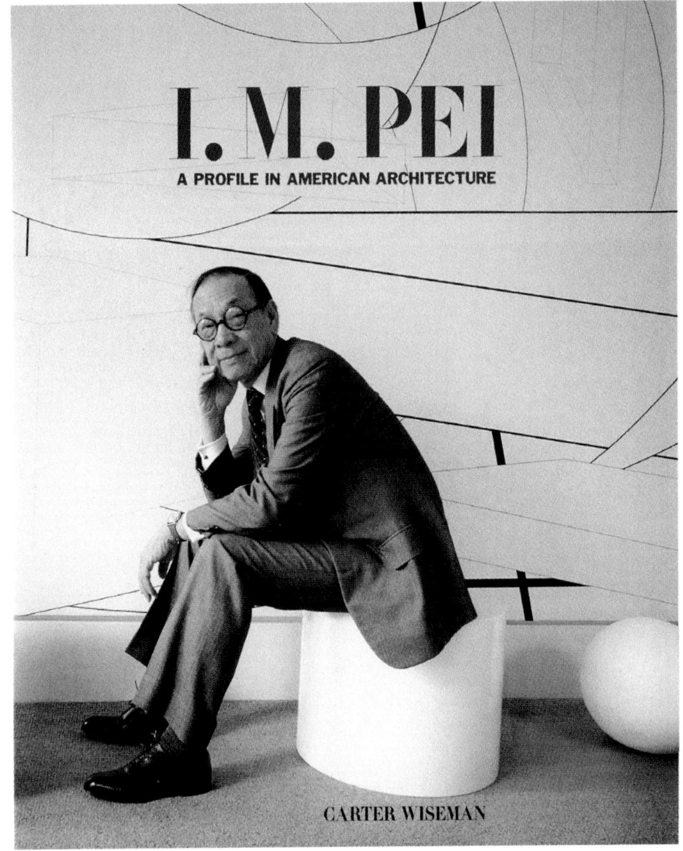

Poems by Robert Brown from *Esquire* using only the top row of typewriter keys, photo by John Paul Endress, 1968.

Prison: Interviews by Leonard J. Berry, book cover, Grossman, 1972, photo by UPI.

I.M. Pei: A Profile in American Architecture, book cover, Harry N. Abrams, 1990, portrait by Marco DeValdivia.

Samuel Antupit [USA]

1932-2003; born in Hartford, Connecticut
Admitted to AGI, 1974

He graduated 1954 from the Yale School of Design and Architecture, and followed a graduate programme where he studied with Paul Rand, Josef Albers and Herbert Matter. In 1958 he worked for Henri Wolf and later assisted Alexander Liberman. He designed and art directed for *Harper's* magazine and *New York Review of Books*; in all, he art-directed more than 100 magazines and papers. In 1963 Sam became a member of Push Pin Studios. Antupit was the chief art director of *Esquire* (1962–68). From 1968–70, he established Hess and/or Antupit and in 1970 Antupit & Others, which consulted to book and magazine publishers.

In 1972 he started Subsistence Press and from 1978–81, he was executive art director of the Book-of-the-Month Club. He also served as director of art and design at Harry N. Abrams for 16 years, with scores of books including monographs on Monet, Lichtenstein and Katz. In 1995 Sam established CommonPlace Publishing, dedicated to creating quality-illustrated books. But his major interest and heart, for over 40 years, lay in his private print shop Cycling Frog Press, operated from his basement. Sam received an N.E.A. American Fellow Grant in 1994 and the AIGA Medal in 2001.

Stuart Ash [Canada]

1942– born in Hamilton
Admitted to AGI, 1974

Ash is a founder and principal of the strategic graphic design firm Gottschalk+Ash International. Stuart Ash and Fritz Gottschalk established G+A in Montreal in 1966, with a shared enthusiasm for design that is both functional and creative. G+A has built an international reputation for creating powerful, successful communications driven by the vision, values and strategic imperatives of our clients. Our offices in North America and Europe service companies around the globe to deliver solutions that shape public perceptions.

G+A Toronto and Calgary offices have recently become part of DW+Partners – a network of best-of-breed creative companies that further extends our reach and complements our already formidable range of skills. Stuart Ash has broad-based experience in all aspects of graphic design. He is a graduate of the Ontario College of Art (1964).
His work has been exhibited in the Mead Library of Ideas in New York, the National Gallery of Canada and the Montréal Museum of Fine Arts. He has been published in most major design magazines in Japan, the United States and Europe. Stuart Ash is a member of the Society of Graphic Designers of Canada, the Society of Environmental Graphic Designers, the American Institute of Graphic Arts, and the Royal Canadian Academy of the Arts.

G+A rebranded the **Schulich School of Business** with a lean, contemporary identity to convey the image of an institution devoted to educating the nation's business leaders.

Boston Convention and Exhibition Center (BCEC), wayfinding programme.

G+A created the identity and positioning for a dynamic part of Toronto's city core. We named the area **DownTown** (featuring the call to action *'DO TO'*) and developed and image which captures the edge and excitement of Toronto's main street.

Canadian Centennial, symbol.

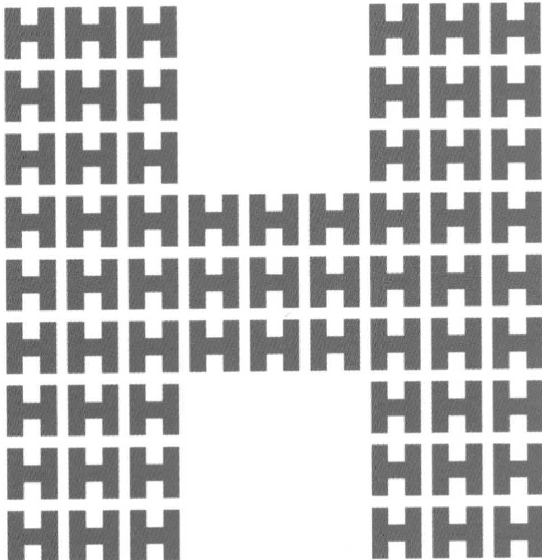

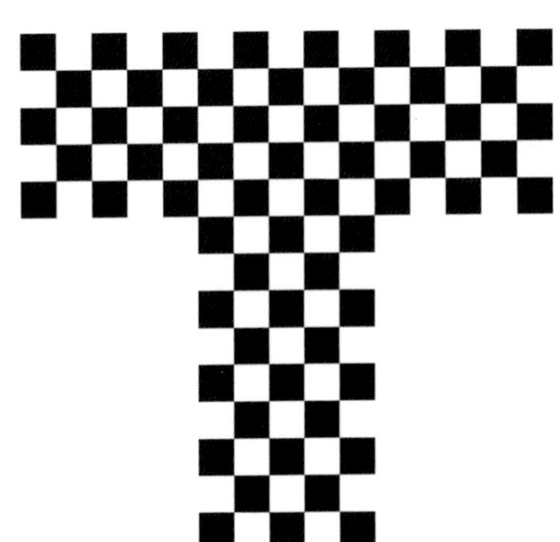

Hotel logo, 1956. The balconies of the building resembled an *'H'*.

Invitation to a film presentation, 1998.

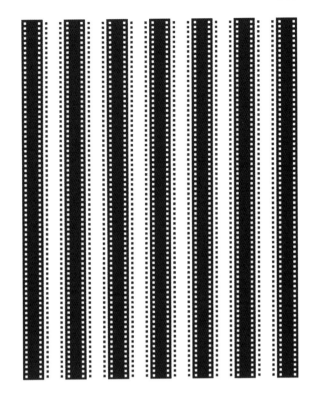

Logo for a manufacturer of modular panels for exhibitions, 1975.

Táxis Nacionales, taxi logo to be marked on the vehicles, Havana, 1973.

Félix Beltrán [Mexico]

1938– born in Havana, Cuba
Admitted to AGI, 1974

In 1956 Félix Beltrán travelled to the United States where he studied at the School of Visual Arts, the American Art School, and the Art Students League, New York. He was awarded scholarships from the New School for Social Research, Graphic Art Center of the Pratt Institute, and from the Council of International Exchanges of Scholars, Washington DC. His works have been included in 478 group exhibitions, 69 solo exhibitions and in the collections of 60 national and international museums. He has written four books, as well as many articles for national and international publications.

He has received 132 awards in national and international competitions and a honorary Doctorate from the International University Foundation, Delaware. He has been on juries for 103 national and international competitions. He appears in reference works including *Who's Who in American Art* (New York), *Who's Who in Art* (London), *International Profiles* (Cambridge), *Who's Who in Graphic Arts* (Zürich), *Personaggi Contemporanei* (Milan), and *Dizionario del Grafico* (Milan), among others. He is a professor at the Universidad Autónoma Metropolitana, Mexico.

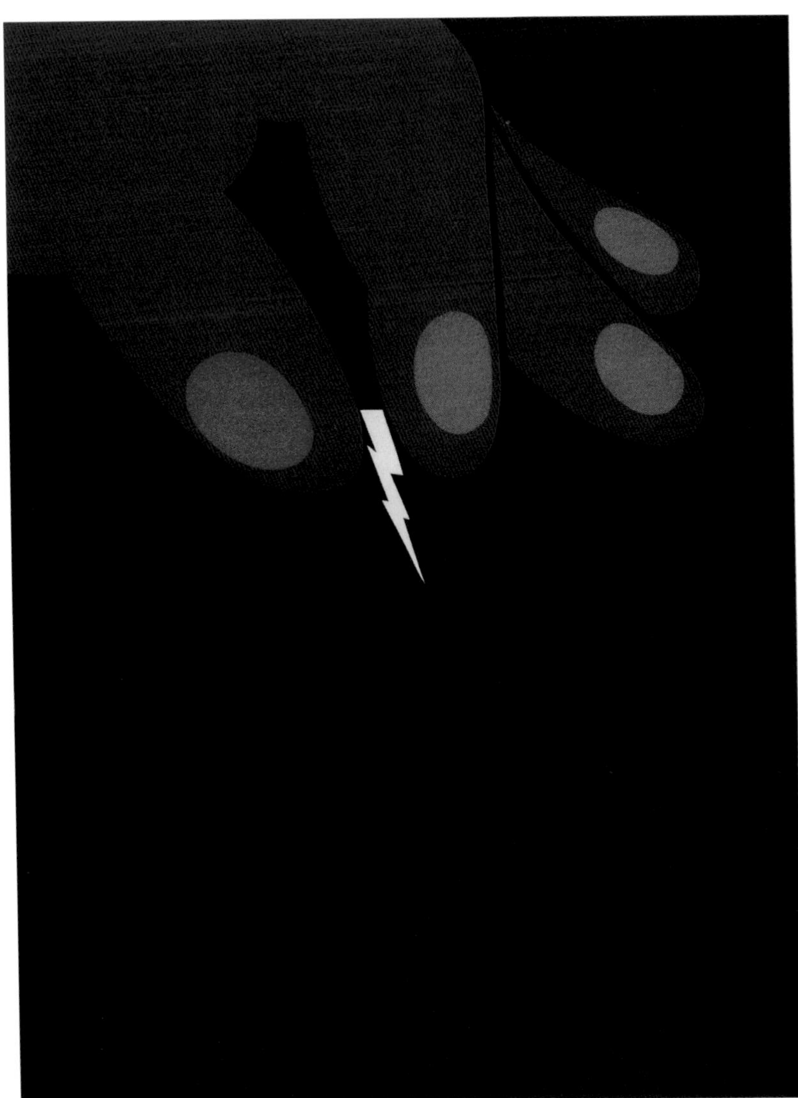

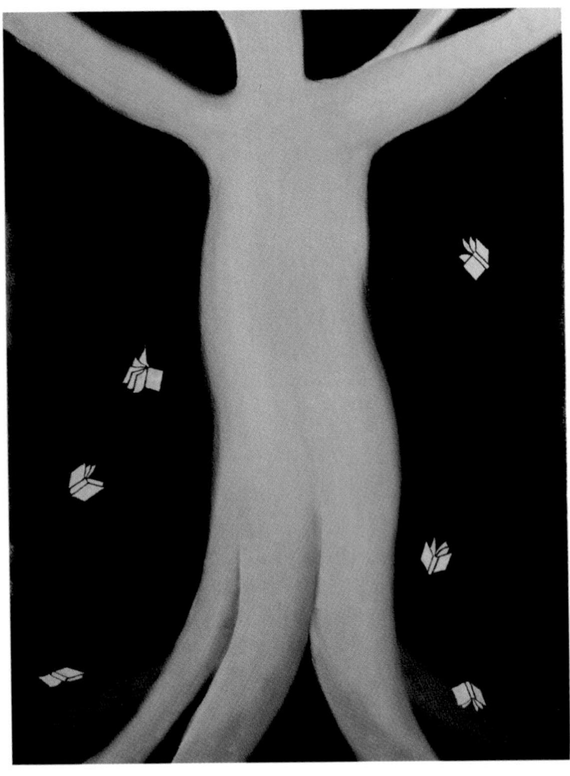

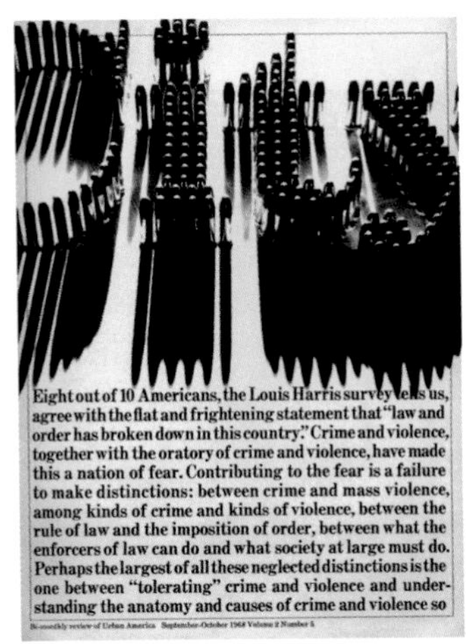

Peter Bradford [USA]

1935– born in Boston, Massachusetts
Admitted to AGI, 1974

Trained at the Rhode Island School of Design, Peter worked for I. M. Pei Architects, Time Inc., Whitney Publications, and CBS Television, New York, before opening his own office in 1965. Those were the hard years for America. His first projects dealt with the violence of the civil rights and anti-war movements, with work for Urban America Inc., Ford Foundation, NAACP Legal Defense Fund, and the Population Council. He used his highly subjective graphics to tweak the noses of television (ABC Emmy Awards), social welfare (the film *View from the Bottom*), stagnant public education (Ginn's reading textbooks), and corporate cultures (Hitachi of Japan).

His love of classic typography appears in over 30 monographs of master photography for Aperture, Inc. His urge to clarify data produced an electronic encyclopedia for Macmillan, and ultimately led to the book *Information Architects* with Richard Saul Wurman for Graphis Press. His work has won over 300 design awards, and been placed in the permanent collections of the Library of Congress and Smithsonian Institute. His urges have now morphed to writing. Recently he has produced books about storytelling (*Jackie Tales*), and the creative process (*The Design Art of Nicos Zographos*). Next: his illustrated *Guide to Idiomatic Language*.

Hitachi, signature image for 14 ads for electronic products, 1984.

American Institute of Geographic Arts, poster for an annual book design show, 1975.

City, cover for a periodical, on the theme of crime and violence, 1968.

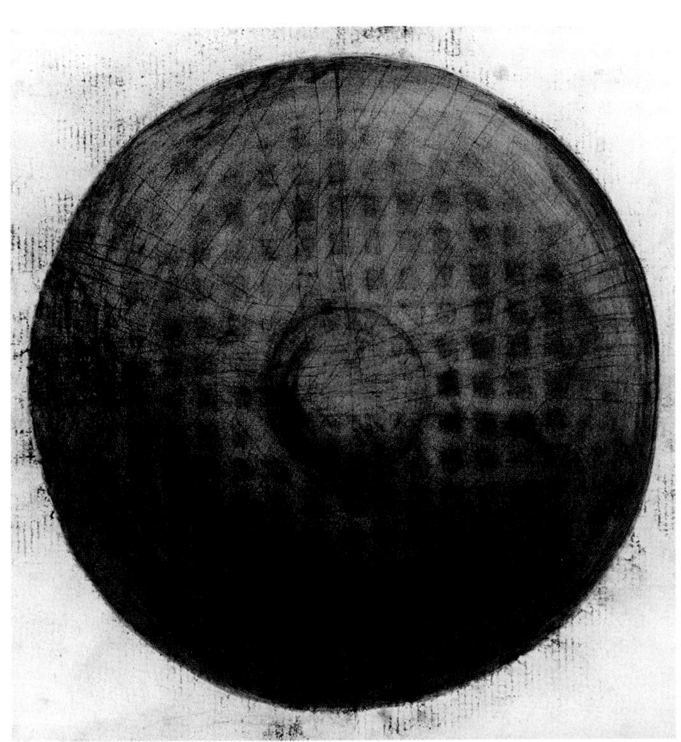

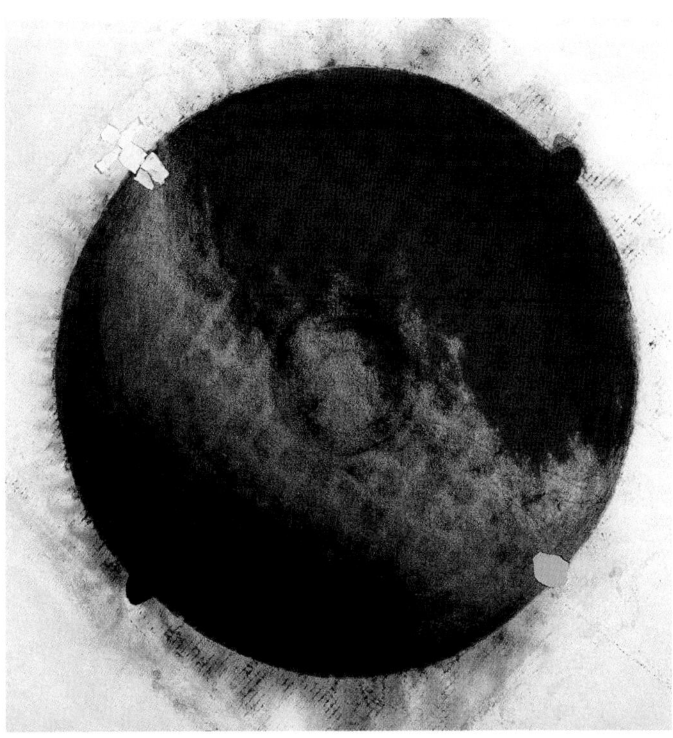

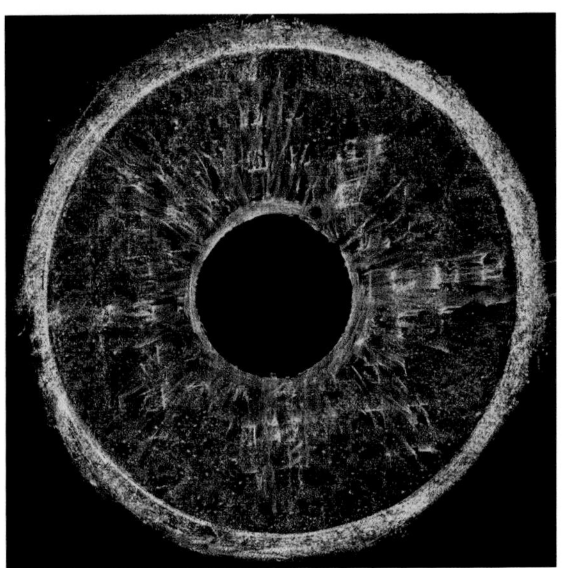

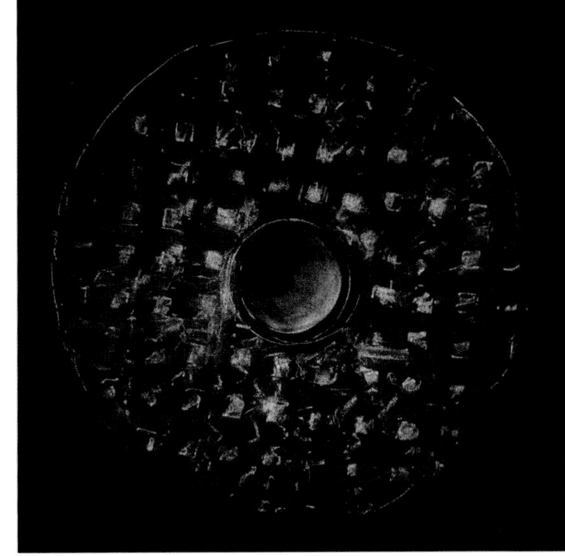

Robert Burns created a very unusual series of artworks based on, of all things, a manhole cover on the street outside the hostel where he was living in downtown Toronto, 1998. The works were made by hand-rubbing sheets of various materials, including paper, canvas, linen and silk onto the manhole cover, using various substances for colours, including powdered pigments, chalk, gold leaf, wax, and shoe polish. A Toronto gallery staged an exhibition of 88 of these works called **Recovering the Ground**. Later, nine of them, which Robert called *'urban mandalas'*, were reproduced as 12-colour lithographs on fine paper, with all copies signed and numbered by the artist.

Robert Burns [Canada]

1942-2005; born in London, England
Admitted to AGI, 1974

Born (then adopted) in 1942 and raised in working-class London, Robert entered the RAF as a teenager. He left to train as a graphic artist, before migrating to Canada in the late 1960s. His first job was at a TV station in Toronto, but he soon set up his own design firm, which later evolved into a personal and business partnership with Heather Cooper. In the early 1970s, Burns & Cooper became rising stars on the Toronto design scene and attracted the attention of many, including Jim Hynes, who first became a B&C client, then joined the partnership as a copywriter to create Burns Cooper Hynes.

BCH continued to grow in both size and reputation into the 1980s, with many of Canada's leading corporations and institutions as clients. Robert's vital contribution to the firm's success was his inspirational leadership, which challenged all to make what he called *'an assault on perfection'*. His influence is still evident in the work of dozens of designers in Toronto who once strove to meet the Burns standard. For the last two decades of his life, Robert struggled with addiction problems that severely limited his design work. He died in Toronto in May 2005.

Mel Calman [UK]

1931-1994; born in Hackney
Admitted to AGI, 1974

'A man widely known in the UK and abroad for his wit, force, originality and distinction,' wrote FHK Henrion. He studied at Perse School, Cambridge and did illustration at St Martin's School of Art and Goldsmith College. In a time span of 37 years (1957–94), he created cartoons for the *Daily Express*, *Sunday Telegraph*, *Observer*, *Sunday Times* and *The Times*. He also worked for *Cosmopolitan* and *House & Garden*.

Mel was a cartoon art addict and founded The Workshop, later called The Cartoon Gallery, where exhibits were held of original cartoons, illustrations and graphics. He created a short, striking animated cartoon, *The Arrow*, and has drawn for television. He used simple graphic means, with 4B or 5B pencil for the main illustration. He said that his *'little man'* was influenced by James Thurber and is not autobiographical. He published many books including *Calman and Women* (1968), *Couples* (1972) and *How About A Little Quarrel Before Bed?* (1981). In 1986 he wrote his autobiography, called *What Else Do You Do?*
I'll never forget and often use, when applicable, the text of his cartoon *'I hope my eating doesn't spoil your cigar!'* Thanks, Mel! – *Ben Bos*

I want to design a client..., postcard for AGI Congress Cambridge, 1994.

AGI Bulletin #6, cover, 1978.

26th London Film Festival, poster, 1982.

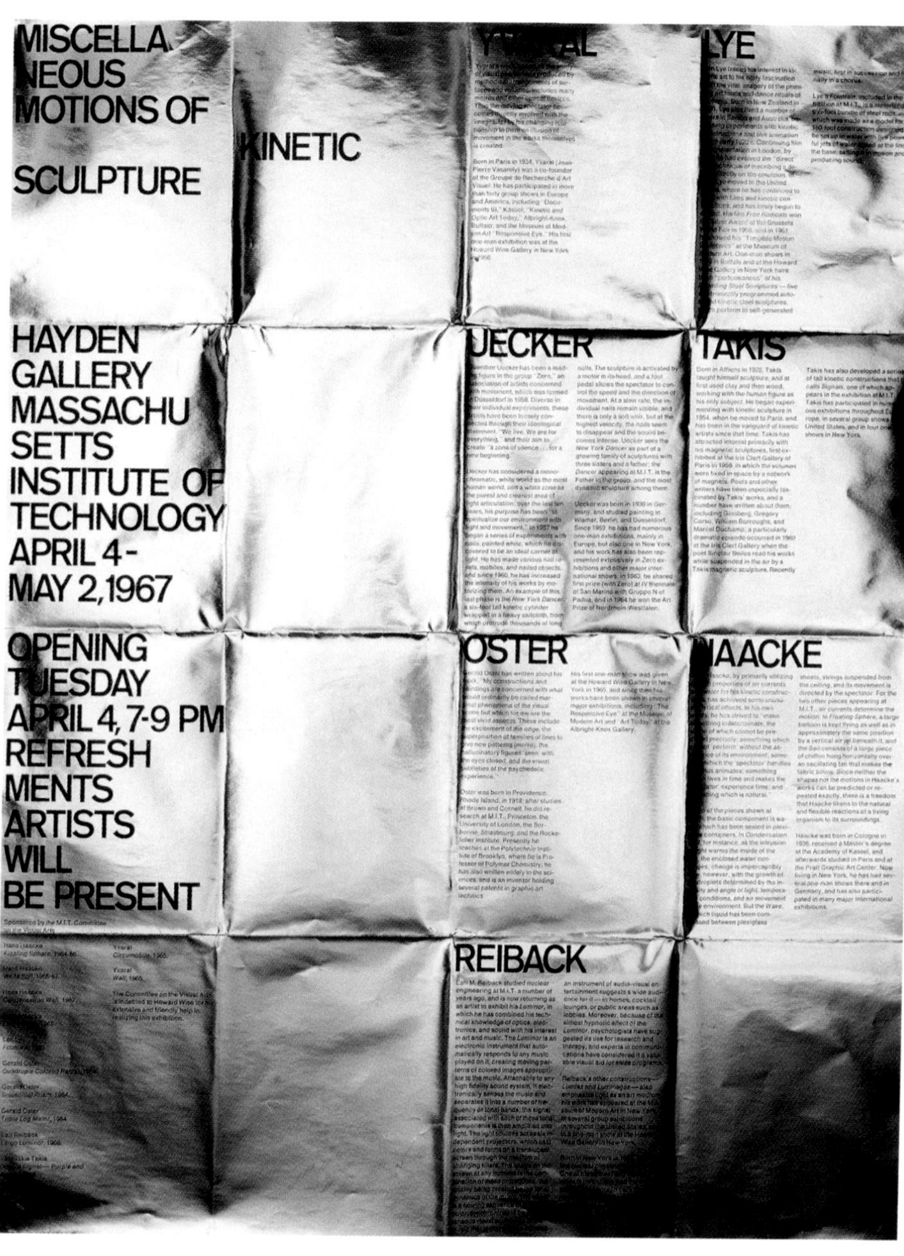

Miscellaneous Motions of Kinetic Sculpture, exhibition poster, MIT Committee of the Visual Arts, 1967.

Jacqeline Casey [USA]

1927-1992; born in Quincy, Massachusetts
Admitted to AGI, 1974

Jacqueline Casey = MIT Press. She worked there for 30 years. Her studies were at the Massachusetts College of Art. She became the design director of MIT in 1955. In 1982 she was given the Design Leadership Award by the AIGA. She developed a highly individualistic graphic style, consistent in itself, yet capable of the greatest variety. Her control of all visual communication material for MIT created a powerful yet appropriate and well-known image for the university.

She wrote: *'My job is a constant learning experience. While MIT has its roots in tradition, the university represents all that is experimental, exciting and future-orientated. For me designing is highly personal and private. Before I start designing, I research the subject so that my work will be representative of it. I always try to use colours and materials that relate to the subject and the typeface must fit the whole design. Quite simply, my objective is to design a product with an accurate visual and verbal message that can be understood by the audience.'*

Richard Danne [USA]

1934– born in Kingfisher, Oklahoma
Admitted to AGI, 1974

Richard studied music and art in Oklahoma before attending the Graduate School of Design, UCLA. He began his independent career in Dallas, Texas in 1959. He moved to New York City in 1963 and served as design consultant to clients such as AT&T, DuPont, Fashion Institute of Technology, Seagram and NASA. He also taught at the School of Visual Arts. Richard has won many national and international design awards. As a partner in the firm Danne & Blackburn, he accepted one of the first Presidential Awards for Design Excellence from President Reagan.

Richard was elected President of the American Institute of Graphic Arts, and later served as founding Chapter President of AIGA/New York. He was also pleased to serve as President of the AGI/USA delegation for many years. Danne participated on numerous design juries and lectured at design conferences and universities. Articles about his work have appeared in various publications including *Communication Arts*, *Print*, *Idea*, *Metropolis*, and *Industrial Design*. He has been the subject of several one-man design exhibitions in the US. In early 2006, after over 40 years in New York City and Massachusetts, Danne relocated his design practice, grand piano, and primary residence to Napa, California.

World Flight was researched and designed for Pratt & Whitney. The book offers a visual chronology of Amelia Earhart's attempt to circle the globe, and the re-creation of that flight, 1997.

Poster for **DuPont** announcing a major scientific conference on the 50th anniversary of their nylon fibre, entitled *'Celebrating the Past – Shaping the Future'*, 1988.

Dedication poster for the **Woods Hole Research Center's new headquarters**. The Center is focused on global warming and the preservation of our world's great forests, 2003.

Samuel Taylor Coleridge on language and the mind

"Language is the armory of the human mind; and at once contains the trophies of its past, and the weapons of its future conquests."*

Container Corporation of America

*(Biographia Literaria, XVI, 1817) Great Ideas of Western Man . . . one of a series Artist: Louis Danziger

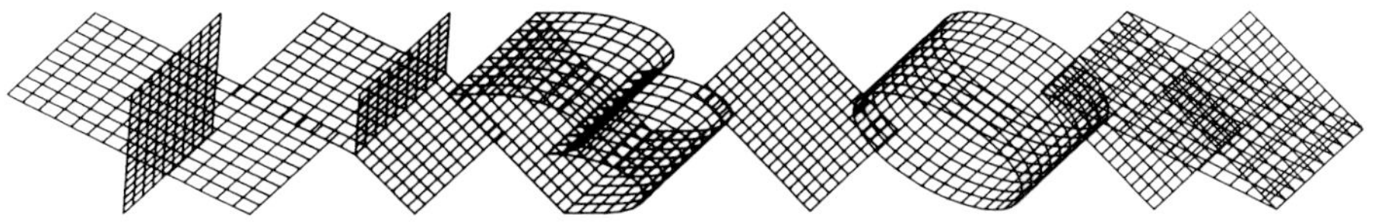

Louis Danziger [USA]

The New York School, poster and catalogue cover for an exhibition at Los Angeles County Museum of Art, 1965.

Magazine advertisement for the Container Corporation of America **Great Ideas of Western Man** series, 1958.

Xybion Corporation, 1975. Logotype from an identity programme for a very high tech company. Possibly the first identity design programme done on a computer. This was a decade before graphic designers began to work on computers.

1923– born in New York City
Admitted to AGI, 1974

Danziger's design education began in high school and Federal Art Project classes, 1938–42. During 1946–48 he continued his education, studying with Alvin Lustig and Alexey Brodovitch. His design practice began in Los Angeles, 1949. Work includes: art direction, advertising concept and design, books, catalogues, ephemera, exhibition designs, identity programmes, packaging, photography, posters, and more. His work has been widely published and clients have ranged from minuscule enterprises to major international corporations. He has been a creative consultant (1975–86) to the Federal Government Design Improvement programme, the 1984 Los Angeles Olympics, LA County Museum of Art, Atlantic Richfield (Arco), Microsoft and others. A design educator for over 50 years, he currently teaches at Art Center College of Design in Pasadena, has taught at Chouinard Art Institute, was director of the design programme at California Institute of the Arts and taught at Harvard University, Carpenter Center (1978–88). He has also given lectures and workshops at major US universities, as well as Canada and Japan. Most notably he pioneered the teaching of graphic design history in the US. He has received the Distinguished Achievement Award from the Contemporary Art Council of the LA County Museum of Art (1982), Distinguished Designer Fellowship Award from the NEA (1985), and the AIGA Medal 1998. His wife adds: *'He's a good person.'*

Paul Brooks Davis [USA]

1938– born in Centrahoma, Oklahoma
Admitted to AGI, 1974

Student of Phil Hays, Robert Weaver, George Tscherny at SVA. First illustrations published in *Playboy* in 1959. Joined Push Pin Studios in December 1959. Freelance in 1963. Work has appeared in major publications worldwide, including *Life*, *Look*, *Time*, *Esquire*, *Rolling Stone*, *The New York Times*, *The New Yorker*, *Fast Company*, *Wired*, *Vanity Fair* and *GQ*. Art director for Joseph Papp's New York Shakespeare Festival, founding art director for *Wig Wag* and *Normal* magazines. Recent clients include *GQ*, *New York Times*, WNYC and Saatchi & Saatchi. Work has been the subject of exhibitions in galleries and museums in Europe, US and Japan. Member of the faculty of the School of Visual Arts, fellow of the American Academy in Rome, member of the ADC's Hall of Fame. Honorary Doctor of Fine Arts from School of Visual Arts, 1990. Medal from AIGA and Lifetime Achievement Medal Academy of Arts, Guild Hall, East Hampton, 1990. Doctor of Fine Arts degree, Maryland Institute College of Art, 2005. Retrospective of drawings, paintings and posters at Complesso Museale Santa Maria della Scala, Siena, Eurotopia gallery, Museo di Porto Romano, Milan, 2005 and Torre Avogadro, Lumezzane, 2006. *Paul Davis: Show People*, text by John Lahr, was published by Nuages, 2005. Poster exhibition in Vicenza at LAMEC gallery, September 2006.

Che Guevara, art for *Evergreen* magazine cover and subway poster, *'Che Guevara Lives'*, 1967. The magazine offices were firebombed when the poster appeared, presumably by right-wing Cubans. Art director: Ken Deardoff.

Poster for **Streamers**, produced by Joseph Papp and directed by Mike Nichols, 1976. Art director: Reinhold Schwenk.

Poster for **The Threepenny Opera** produced by Joseph Papp and starring Raul Julia, 1976. Opened at the Delacorte theatre in Central Park and then moved to Lincoln Center. Art Director: Reinhold Schwenk.

gilles fiszman
Commémoration du 25e anniversaire
du soulèvement du Ghetto de Varsovie
Palais des Beaux-Arts de Bruxelles
Mercredi 24 avril 1968 à 20 h 15
Avec la Participation de Anne Marev et Charles Kleinberg
Les mouvements de Jeunesse Juive
Orateurs
Aba Kovner, Commandant de la révolte du Ghetto de Vilno
M. Hougardy, Sénateur, résistant armé
Prix des places : 100 f. - 50 f.
Billets en vente : Palais des Beaux-Arts / Centre d'Information de Bruxelles
Comité Juif Unifié et toutes les Organisations Juives de Bruxelles

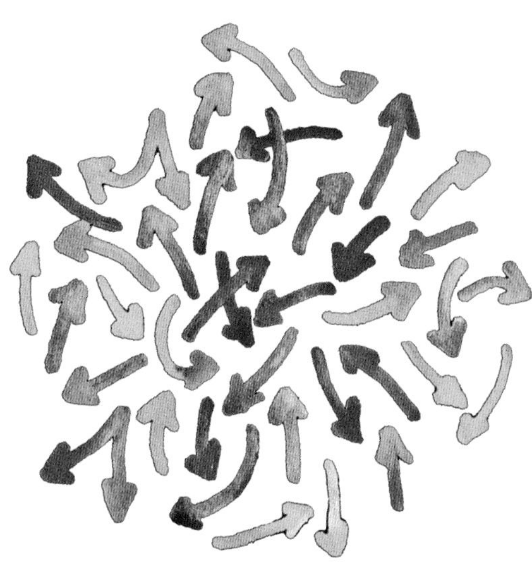

Standardized emblem and visual identity for **Belgium's French Community**.

Logo for the **Family Studies and Human Systems Institute**. A graphic evocation of the principle of interactions within an open system.

Poster for the **25th Anniversary of the Warsaw Ghetto Uprising**.

Gilles Fiszman [Belgium]

1932– born in Brussels
Admitted to AGI, 1974

Studied drawing at the Academy of Fine Arts in Brussels (1951) and painting at the Academy of Fine Arts in Warsaw (1952–57). After returning to Belgium, Gilles got involved in a wide range of creative work, such as commercial window displays, exhibition stands at trade fairs, setting up exhibitions, etc. (1957–60). He was an art director at the André François advertising agency (1960–63). Interested in matters of visual identity and institutional communication, he practised as a graphic designer (1963–82).

Fiszman was the president of CBG, the Belgian Chamber of Graphic Designers (1975–78). He was a professor of graphic information processing at ENSAV (National High School of the Visual Arts), La Cambre, Brussels (1983–89). He set up the Axion Design Partnership in Montreal and San Francisco and Axion Fiszman & Partners, Brussels in 1982.

Allan Robb Fleming [Canada]

1929-1977
Admitted to AGI, 1974

As a 12-year-old, Allan Robb Fleming knew that art would be an important part of his life. He studied at Western Technical School in Toronto and at 16 did his apprenticeship with several advertising agencies. Between 1953 and 1955 he went to London to study typography. When he came back to Canada he established himself as a freelance design consultant. He taught typography at the Ontario College of Art and Design, designed the History of Typography exhibition for the Royal Ontario Museum in 1957 and joined Cooper & Beatty as typographic director and designer. At the height of his career he entered publishing. In 1962 he completely redesigned *Maclean's* magazine, which increased its circulation. With his design for the book *Canada: A Year of the Land*, Fleming experienced a critical and commercial triumph, prior to joining University of Toronto Press as chief designer. He not only did book design (more than 100 covers) but also stamps, art posters and logos including Ontario Hydro, the Ontario Science Centre and his famous logo and identity programme for Canadian National Railway. He received the Royal Canadian Academy of Arts medal.

The corporate identity programme for **Canadian National Railway**, designed in 1959, was Fleming's most celebrated design achievement. Almost fifty years later, the trains still feature the elegant symbol that combines the initials with the *'track'*. Pieter Brattinga gave the CN programme a solo exhibition in Steendrukkerij de Jong & Co's gallery (Hilversum, 1963).

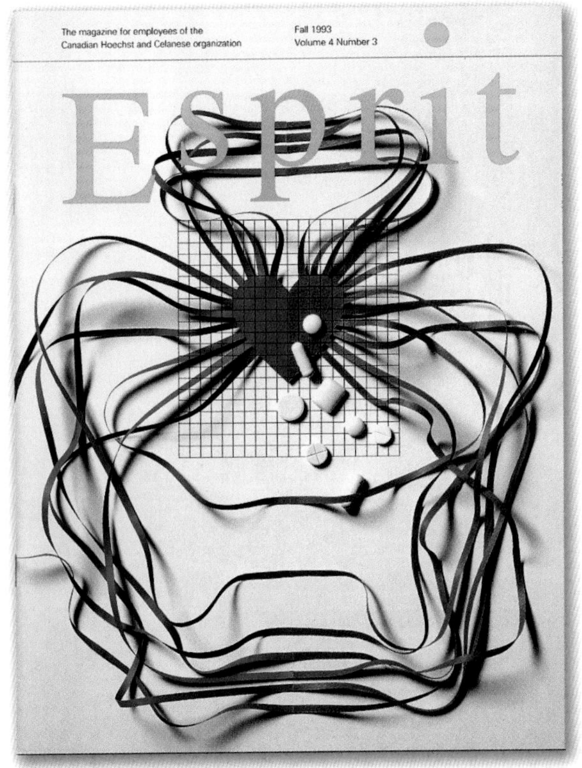

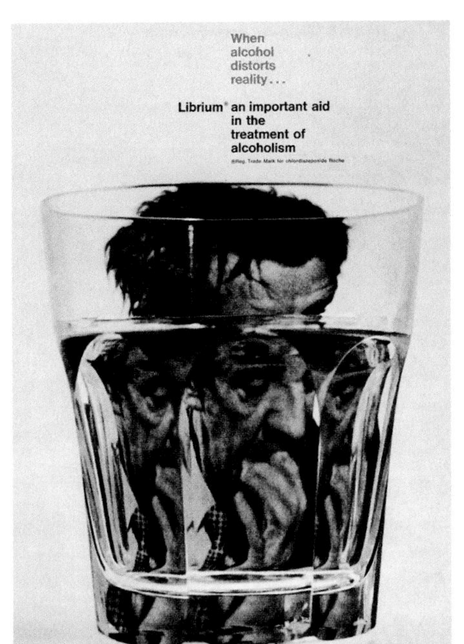

Rolf Harder [Canada]

Esprit, 1993. Cover for quarterly in-house magazine, the feature in this issue being the safety of clinical trials. Client: Hoechst Celanese Canada.

Sun, 1973. Illustration for La Roche calendar. Client: Hoffmann-La Roche, Montreal.

When alcohol distorts reality, c. 1963. Advertisement for medication to combat alcoholism. Client: Hoffmann-La Roche, Montreal.

Peace, c. 1987. Poster design for international competition in Moscow (special prize).

1929– born in Hamburg, Germany
Admitted to AGI, 1974

Professional education at the Hamburg Academy of Fine Arts (1948–52). Designer and art director in German and Canadian agencies and studios (1952–59). Opened graphic design office in Montreal (1959–65). Co-founder and principal of Design Collaborative, Montreal/Toronto (1965–77). Founder and principal, Rolf Harder & Assoc. (1977–present). Member of Royal Canadian Academy of Arts and AIGA. Fellow of the Society of Graphic Designers of Canada. Major projects for industry, government and cultural institutions. Designed over 70 Canadian postage stamps. Numerous international design awards and prizes, including World Logo Design Award 1998 (International Trademark Centre, Belgium), and special prizes at Biennale of Graphic Design, Brno, and Peace Poster Competition, Moscow. Travelling exhibition (together with Ernst Roch), sponsored by the Canadian Government, shown throughout Canada, in the US, Germany and Yugoslavia. Participant in group exhibitions across Canada, US and Europe; in Japan, South Korea, Russia, South America, Australia. Represented at the 36th Venice Biennale (Experimental Graphic Design). Work appeared in professional publications in Canada, US, Great Britain, Germany, Switzerland, Austria, Italy, France, Czechoslovakia, Australia, Japan, Korea, South America. Co-organizer of the exhibition 'The Visual Image of the Olympic Games', Museum of Fine Arts, Montreal (1972).

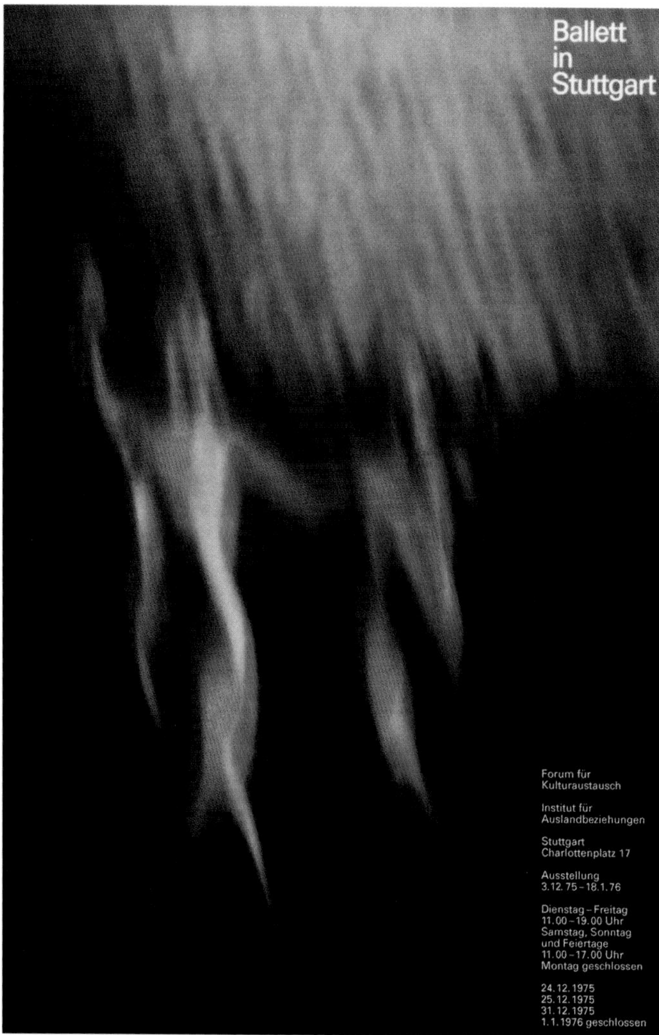

Hans Peter Hoch [Germany]

1924– born in Aarau, Switzerland
Admitted to AGI, 1974

Trained as repro-photographer. Attended the Höhere Fachschule für das Grafische Gewerbe and subsequently studied painting at the Akademie für Bildende Künste Bernstein and Stuttgart. Since 1950 he has run an independent studio for graphic design, photography and visual communication. His work encompasses the design of publications and exhibitions for the Institute for Foreign Cultural Relations (IFA), promoted by the Federal Foreign Office.

Other projects include: design and realization of the German Resistance Memorial Centre, Berlin (permanent exhibition 'Resistance to National Socialism'), design and visualization of literary museums as G.W.F. Hegel, Bertolt Brecht, Martin Heidegger, Hermann Hesse and Max Eyth, as well as the reading room of the library of the Erzabtei Kloster Beuron. In 1985 Hoch was appointed professor by the state of Baden-Württemberg. In 1988 he won the Stankowski Foundation award for lifetime achievement in art and design. Hoch has received various honours in national and international contests. He lives and works in Baltmannsweiler near Stuttgart.

Ballet in Stuttgart, poster, 1969.

German Resistance Memorial Centre, Berlin, 1998. Themed display on *'Resistance from the Labour Movement up to 1939'*.

20 July 1944, commemorative stamp, 1994.

Die Brücke, postage, stamp, 2005.

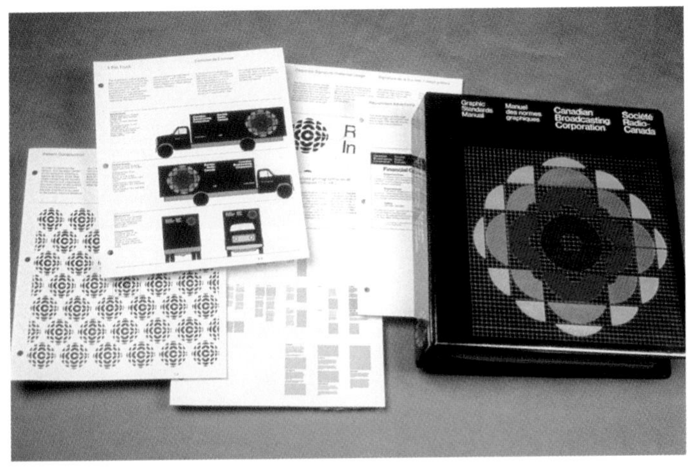

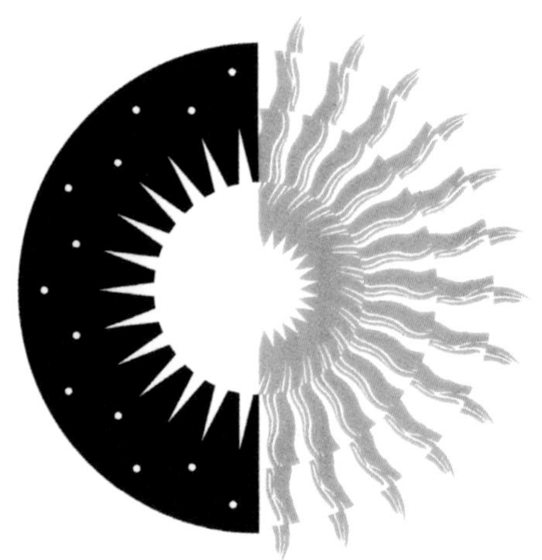

CBC (Canadian Broadcasting Corporation), logo and visual identity manual, 1975.

Children's Mental Health, logo and identity programme, 1998.

McLaughlin Planetarium, poster, Toronto, 1968.

North American Life Centre, logo, identity programme and sculpture, Toronto, 1988.

Burton Kramer [Canada]

1932– born in New York City, USA
Admitted to AGI, 1974

Kramer studied at the Institute of Design, Chicago (BSc. 1954) and Yale University (MFA 1957).
He started his career in the NY office of Will Burtin and at Geigy Pharmaceuticals under Gottfried Honneger. He moved to Zürich in 1961, where he was chief designer at the E. Halpern Agency; his work received publicity and awards. In 1965 Kramer moved to Toronto to work on graphics and signage for Expo 67. In 1967 he founded Kramer Design Associates Ltd, creating visual identity programmes for the Royal Ontario Museum, Ontario Educational Communications Authority and many educational, art, cultural and corporate organizations.

Kramer created the well-known logo and visual identity programme for the Canadian Broadcasting Corporation (1974). His logos and corporate identity designs have been included in numerous books and international design journals. He received a lifetime achievement award from Arts Toronto (1999).
In 2002 the Province of Ontario awarded him the Order of Ontario, its highest honour, *'for his contributions to the cultural life of the Province'*.
In 2003, in recognition of 21 years of teaching, the Ontario College of Art and Design granted him an honorary doctorate (D.Des). Kramer's geometry-based, lyrical, colourist paintings have been shown in galleries in Europe, the US and Canada.

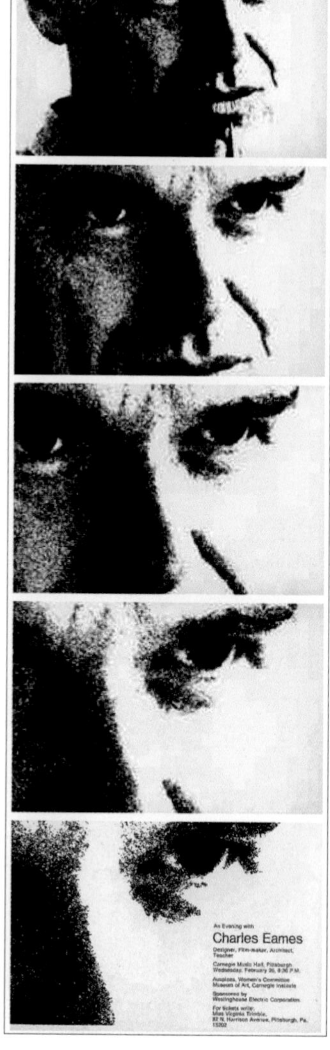

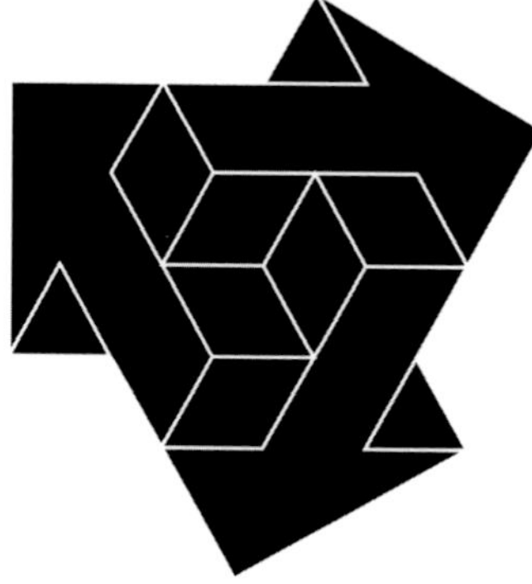

Peter Megert [Switzerland]

1937– born in Berne
Admitted to AGI, 1974

Peter Megert, living and working in Columbus, Ohio, was exposed early on to the creative lifestyle and design of Europe. He was educated in Switzerland, with graduate studies in France and the United States. In 1960 he founded Studio M in Switzerland. His work covered all aspects of graphic design, including visual identities, print graphics and exhibit design. In 1968, invited by Paul Rand, Peter Megert became the advisory graphic designer at the Westinghouse Corporate Design Center in Pittsburgh. In 1970, he was appointed professor of visual communication design at Ohio State University.

In 1988 Peter Megert founded visual syntax/design, a international design consultancy, specializing in planning and design of visual images and their communication content. Megert received three federal awards for design excellence in Switzerland, twice for one of the best Swiss posters of the year. He also received an annual design award from the Ohio Arts Council. In 2004 he was nominated by the Cooper-Hewitt Museum for a national design award. Peter Megert is affiliated with design firms in Europe.

Light and Movement, exhibition poster, Kunsthalle, Berne, 1965.

Charles Eames: Filmmaker, poster, Carnegie Institute, 1969.

Visual syntax/design inc., logo design, 1988.

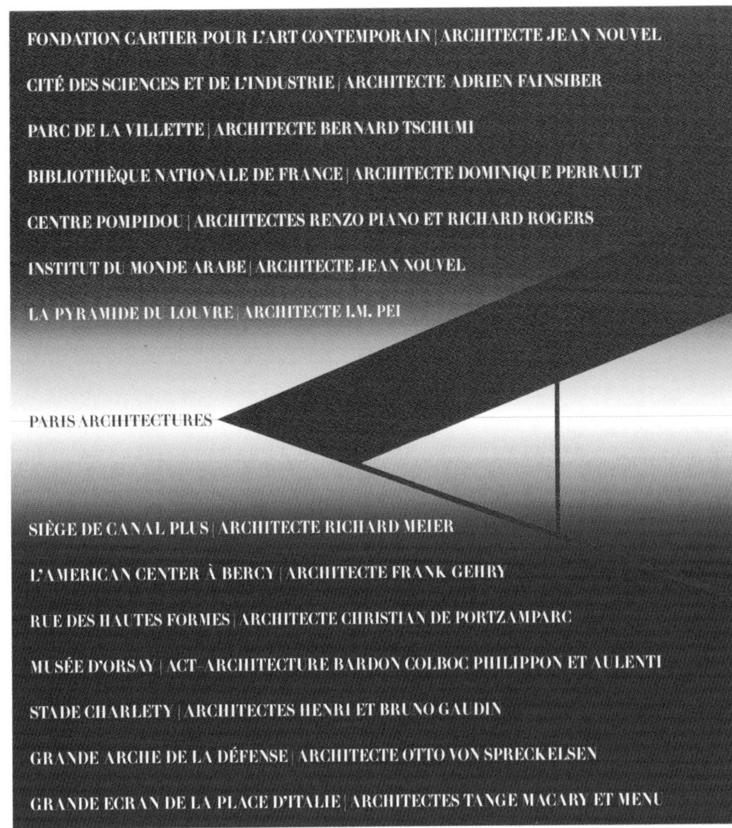

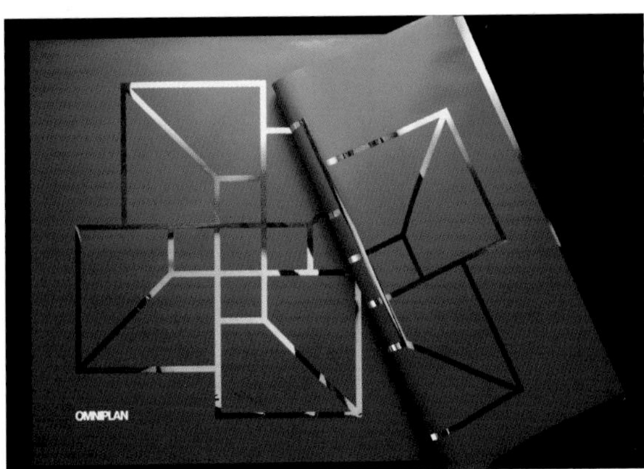

Great Architecture in Chicago, poster promoting the cultural aspects of the city of Chicago, 1967. One in a series sponsored by Container Corporation of America. Silkscreened on silver foil.

Paris Architectures, poster for the fiftieth anniversary of the AGI Congress in Paris, 2001.

Omniplan Architects, poster, Dallas, 1970. Logo design in silver mylar with silkscreened background. Set of four colours (blue, red, yellow, green) individually presented in a clear plastic tube.

Tomoko Miho [USA]

Born in Los Angeles
Admitted to AGI, 1974

Tomoko Miho currently designs print communication materials, environmental graphics and signage. Representative clients include: NY MoMA; Herman Miller; Isamu Noguchi Foundation and Garden Museum; Kodansha International; Museum of Cycladic Art, Athens; Aveda, and Willem de Kooning Foundation. As a partner of Miho Inc., designed graphics for Champion International Corporation and Smithsonian Institution, National Air and Space Museum. Previously with the Centre for Advanced Research in Design in Chicago and New York, created designs for Herman Miller, ARCO, Neiman-Marcus, and Omniplan Architects.

Designer and later head of the graphics department of George Nelson & Company, designing for Herman Miller and Champion Papers.
Recipient of many awards, notably the American Institute of Graphic Arts Gold Medal in 1993.
Member of the AIGA Board of Directors 1979–82.
Poster designs are in the permanent collection of MoMA, touring in exhibitions worldwide, and the collections of the Library of Congress, Museum für Gestaltung, Zürich, and Victoria & Albert Museum.
Subject of articles in AIGA's *Graphic Design USA: 15* and *HQ High Quality*. Graduated from the Art Center School (now Art Center College of Design) and previously studied at the Minneapolis School of Art.

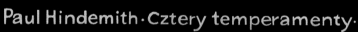

Jan Mlodozeniec [Poland]

1929-2000; born in Warsaw
Admitted to AGI, 1974

Mlodozenic was one of the many famous Polish poster designers; his work simply couldn't have come from anywhere else. He studied in Henryk Tomaszewski's department of graphic arts and posters at the Warsaw Academy of Fine Arts (1948–55). He created drawings, book and publication designs and illustrations. He made over 400 posters, some of those uncommissioned.
His colleague Franciszek Starowieyski said of Jan: *'He is in the same class as Matisse; nobody else has such understanding of colour.'*

He had solo exhibitions around the world, and his work features in all major museum collections.
He received many of the highest awards in Warsaw, Katowice, Vienna and Lahti. When Poland was placed under martial law (because of the Solidarity movement) in 1981–84, many designers stopped working for the government in protest. Jan, however, turned an innocent poster into a *'silent'* political manifesto and everybody immediately got the meaning. The main colour used was that of the uniforms of the hated secret police. His posters tended to be abstract, yet strangely subject-related. Type was often an integral part of the image.
He didn't care about money, just about his art.

The Four Temperaments, ballet poster, 1962.

Jane Avril, Moulin Rouge, decorative silkscreen print, 1993.

Marek Hłasko: *A First Step in the Clouds*, book cover, 1956.

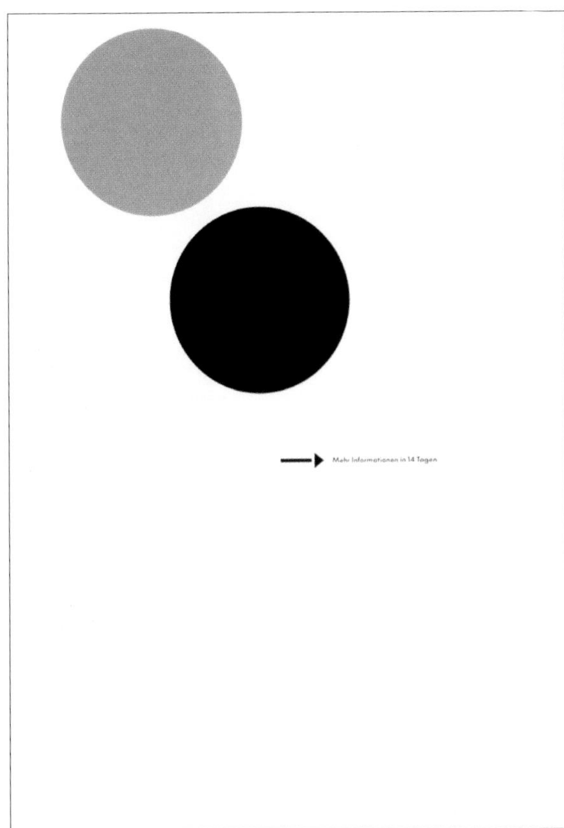

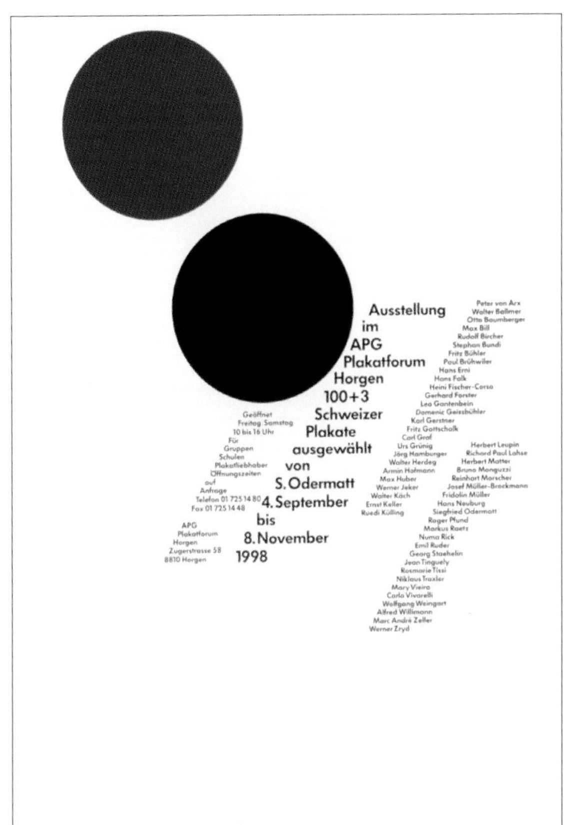

100+3 Swiss Posters, exhibition posters, 1998 (x 2). The second poster contains all the information about the exhibition.

Change of address card, 1991.

Siegfried Odermatt [Switzerland]

1926– born in Neuheim
Admitted to AGI, 1974

Odermatt calls himself a self-taught graphic designer, although he attended various courses at the School of Applied Arts in Zürich. From 1943–46 he was a freelance collaborator with the painter Hans Falk. He then started to work independently. Since 1968 he has run a studio with Rosmarie Tissi. Both have a reputation as pioneers in graphic design. Odermatt has received numerous international distinctions and awards. His books have several times been among the Best Swiss Books (1986, 1987, 2000). In 1987 his work was among the World's Most Beautiful Books (Leipzig).

In 1993 he won the poster and corporate identity competition for the Kieler Woche 1994 sailing festival. He has shared exhibitions with Rosmarie Tissi in Offenbach, New York, Zürich, Essen and Tokyo. On the occasion of their poster exhibition at the German Poster Museum in Essen Sigi and Rosmarie's hand and footprints were marked in concrete. He designed the book *Odermatt & Tissi, Graphic Design* (1993), showcasing their work, and *100+3 Swiss Posters* (1998), containing a selection from his comprehensive and excellent poster collection. It also served as the catalogue for the *100+3* exhibition in Horgen (1998), Essen (2000), London (2002), Tehran (2004) and Chiasso (2006).

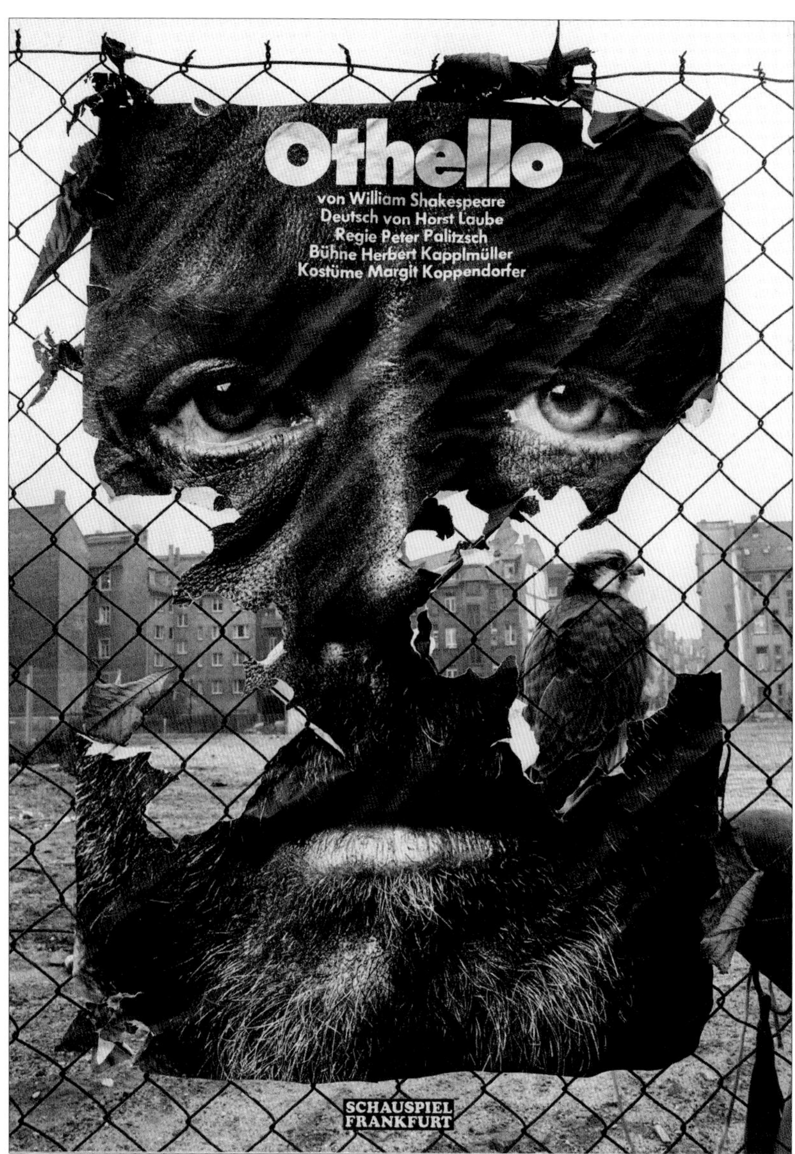

Gunter Rambow [Germany]

1938– born in Neustrelitz
Admitted to AGI, 1974

Hans Hillmann was Rambow's professor and taught him his sense of form. In the Rambow and Lienemeyer studio community (1961–86), Rambow created numerous photo books and designed posters on the themes of literature, theatre and social issues. This work now continues in the Studio Rambow + van de Sand. The Bibliothèque Nationale, Paris, the Akademie der Künste, Berlin, the Deutsches Plakatmuseum, Essen, the Art Museum of Shanghai and many other institutions have dedicated large solo exhibitions to his work.

He has won many silver and gold medals at poster festivals, biennials and triennials in Warsaw, Chaumont, Lahti, Brno, Toyama and other places. Between 1974 and 2004 he taught as a professor for visual communication at the University of Kassel and the Staatliche Hochschule für Gestaltung Karlsruhe. During this time numerous books of his projects were published by renowned publishers. Rambow is very glad that so many former students are successful in practice or are now even active as teachers. In 2004, as emeritus professor, he bought the former mansion house of Count von der Lühe, built in 1583, in the town of Güstrow. He lives and works there and manages a poster gallery.

Othello, theatre poster, Schauspiel Frankfurt, 1978.

Der Freischütz, opera poster, Badisches Staatstheater Karlsruhe, 2006.

Orpheus & Eurydice, theatre poster, Hessisches Staatstheater Wiesbaden, 1998.

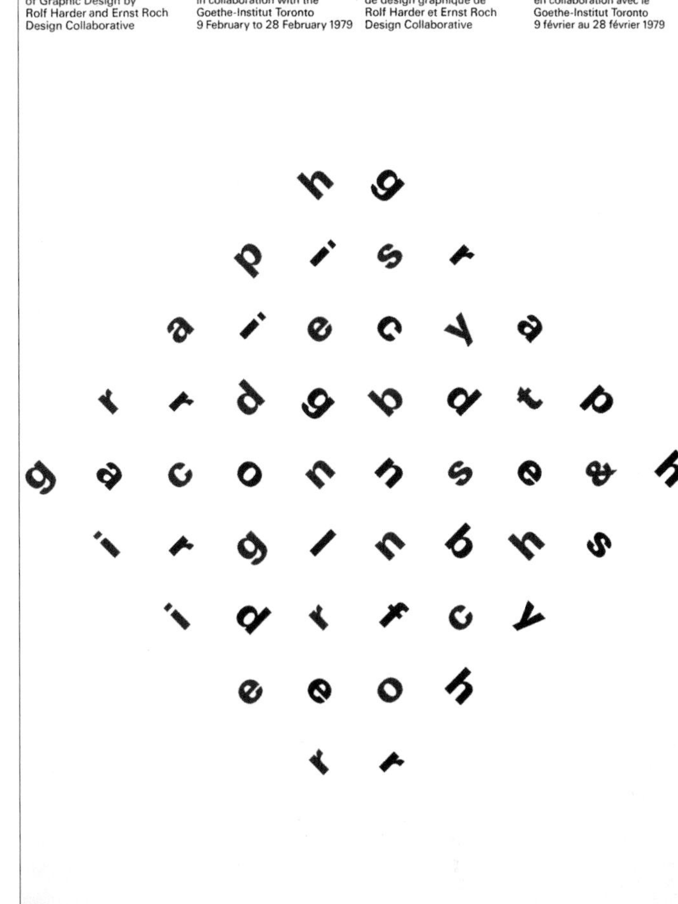

Exhibition
of Graphic Design by
Rolf Harder and Ernst Roch
Design Collaborative
Art Gallery of York University
in collaboration with the
Goethe-Institut Toronto
9 February to 28 February 1979
Exposition
de design graphique de
Rolf Harder et Ernst Roch
Design Collaborative
Art Gallery of York University
en collaboration avec le
Goethe-Institut Toronto
9 février au 28 février 1979

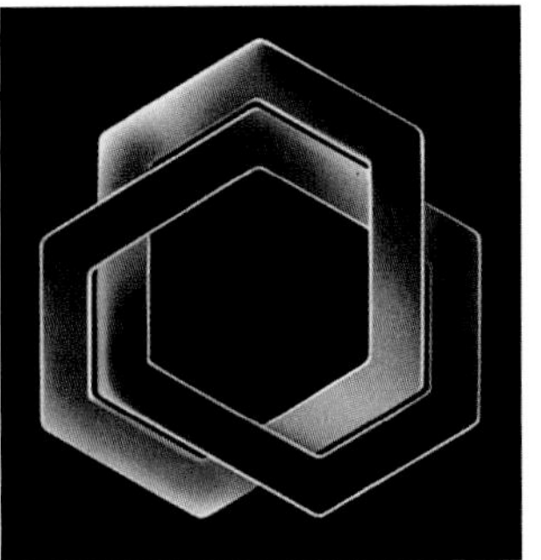

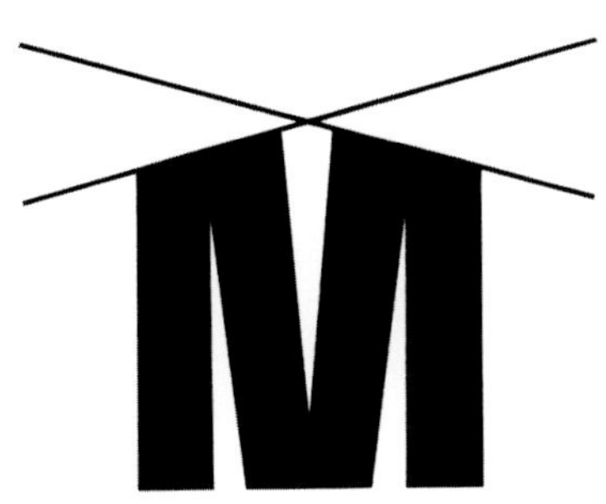

Ernst Roch [Canada]

Canadian unity campaign, poster for Imasco Ltd. Chosen by Ernst Roch as his favourite piece of work for the book *First Choice* by Ken Cato.

Ernst Roch and Rolf Harder Design Collaborative, poster for touring exhibition, 1977.

Symbol design for **National Arts Centre** in Ottawa.

Symbol design for **Marquesa Knitwear**.

1928-2003; born in Osijek, Croatia
Admitted to AGI, 1974

From 1948–52 he studied in Graz at the Staatliche Schule für Angewandte Kunst. He migrated to Canada in 1953, where he became one of the pioneers of Canadian 'International Style' graphic design. His craftsmanship was outstanding, as was his imagination. He worked for various studios before he founded his own company Roch Design (1960–65) and later Design Collaborative with Rolf Harder (1965–77). After that he had his own firm again. Ernst Roch was involved in all fields of graphic design, trademarks, posters, packaging, books, security and architectural graphics as well as complete identity programmes, such as the National Arts Centre, Ottawa (1965).

He designed many stamps, including the 1–5 cents 'Queen Elizabeth' series (1962–63) and 'Early Canadian Locomotives' (1983–86). He also organized and designed the exhibition 'Munich Olympic Games' (1972) and produced the official poster for the Montreal Olympic Games. Over the years he lectured in Montreal, Halifax and Columbus. Ernst deservedly received many national and international awards and honours. The legacy of his works is in the Canadian National Archives in Ottawa and in the Library of Congress in Washington DC.

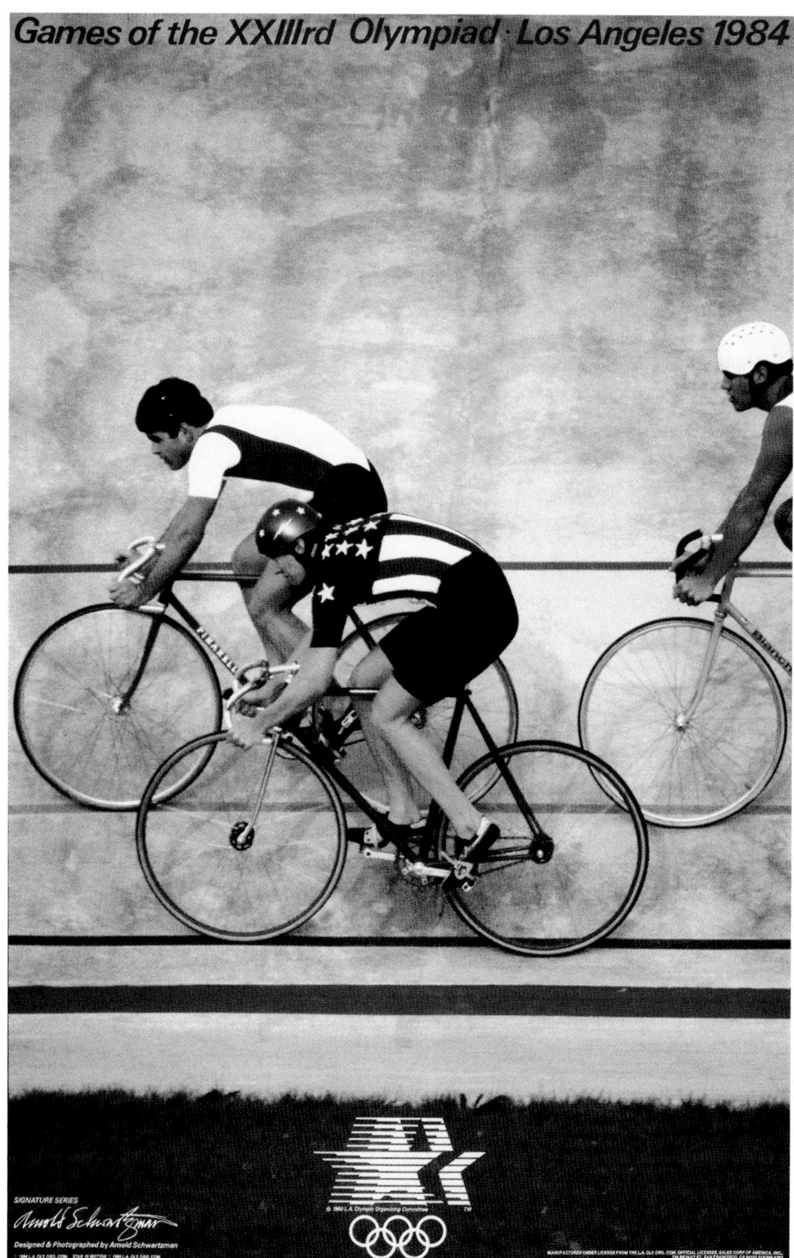

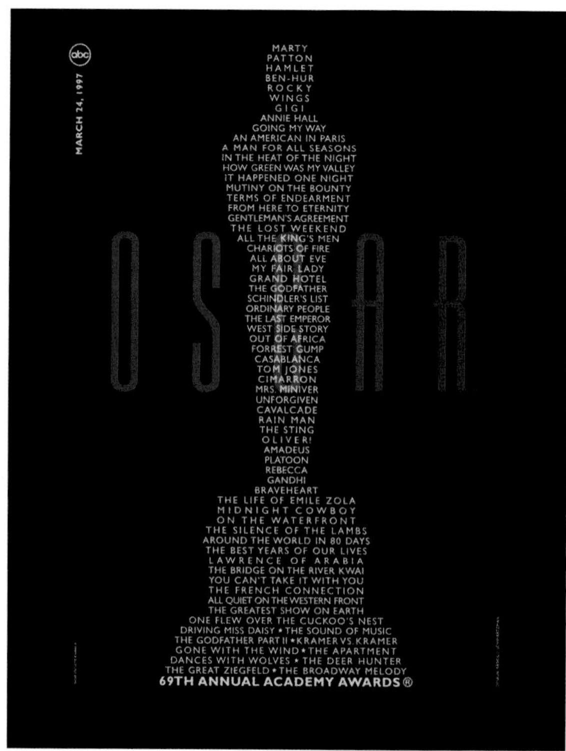

Arnold Schwartzman [USA]

1936– born in London, England
Admitted to AGI, 1974

Studied at Thanet School of Art and Crafts, and Canterbury College of Art, England (1951–55). Began his career as graphic designer in television broadcasting, became an art director for Erwin-Wasey Advertising, London, and later joined the board of directors of Conran Design Group. A long-time illustrator for the *Sunday Times*, also designed the *Sunday Times Magazine*'s 'Eureka' and 'The Facts of Life' series. In 1978, became design director for Saul Bass & Associates, Los Angeles, and later produced and directed the feature documentary *Genocide* (1981), which garnered him an Oscar®.

In 1982, he was appointed director of design for the 1984 Los Angeles Olympic Games. Since reverting to his own design consultancy, his commissions have included a number of commemorative posters, related print collateral and cinema trailers for the Annual Academy Awards®; multiscreen video exhibits for the Museum of Tolerance and the Skirball Cultural Center in Los Angeles, and a *Time Line* mural for the Skirball. He is the author/photographer of a score of books, and has lectured extensively throughout the world. Recipient of numerous film and design awards, including three D&AD Silver awards. Appointed an Officer of the Order of the British Empire (OBE), 2002. Elected a Royal Designer for Industry, 2006.

Official poster for the **Los Angeles Olympics**, 1984. The bicycle wheels form the Olympic rings.

Commemorative poster for the **69th Annual Academy Awards®**, 1997. The Oscar® statuette is made up of the titles of the previous 68 winners of the Best Picture award.

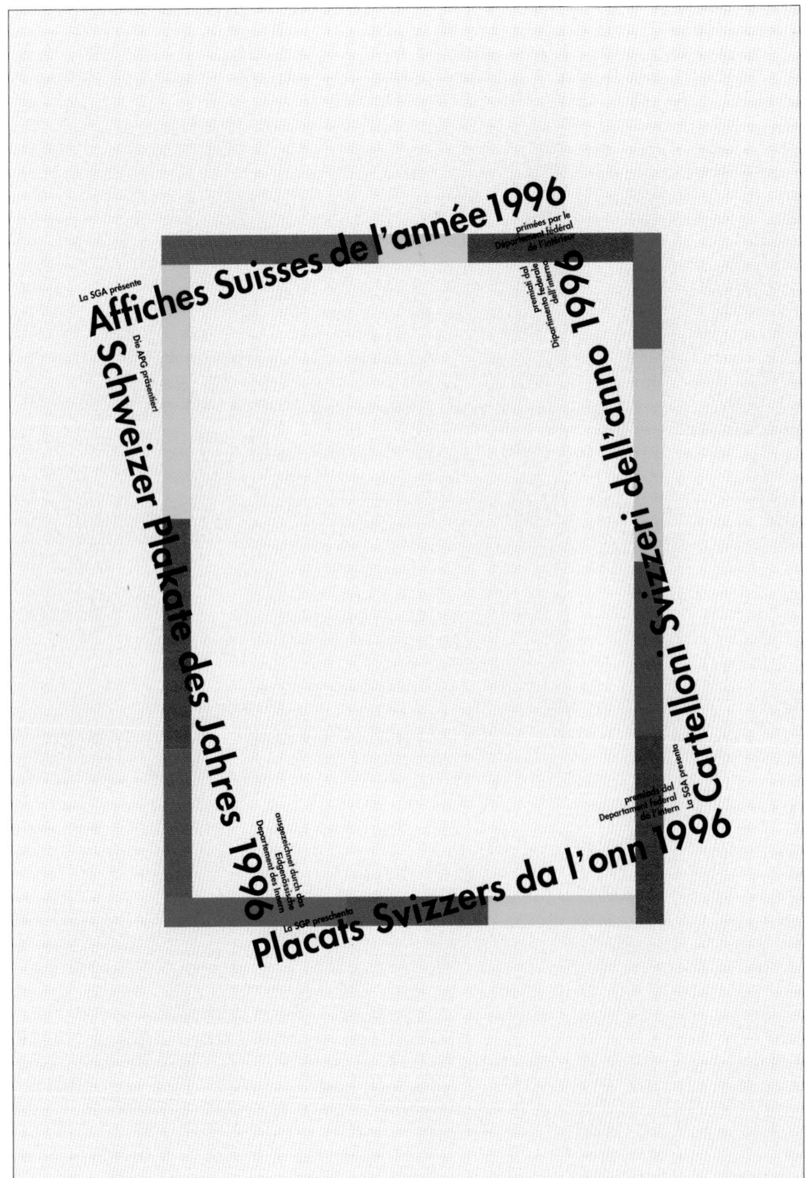

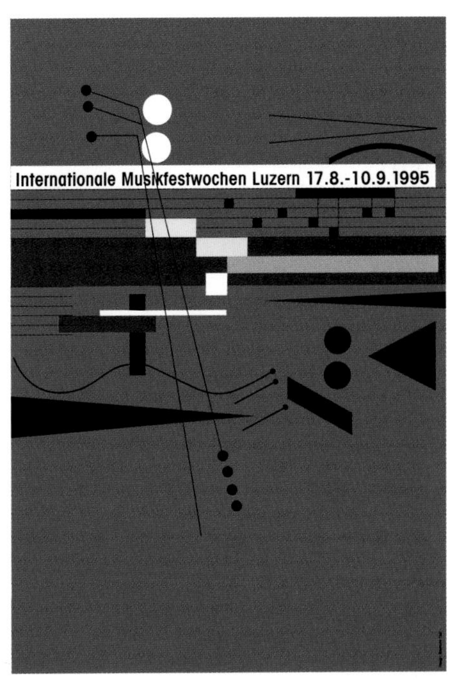

Swiss Posters of the Year, exhibition poster, 1996.

International Music Festival Lucerne, poster, 1995.

Invitation to the **2nd International Design Conference in Acapulco**, Mexico, 1994.

Rosmarie Tissi [Switzerland]

1937– born in Schaffhausen
Admitted to AGI, 1974

Rosmarie Tissi trained as a graphic designer in Zürich. She shares a studio with Sigi Odermatt in Zürich. Distinctions and awards include: first prize and gold medal, 11th International Poster Biennial, Warsaw, 1986; second prize, competition for new Swiss banknotes, 1989; Henri de Toulouse-Lautrec silver medal, 6th International Poster Triennial, Essen, 1990; bronze medal, 4th International Poster Triennial, Toyama, 1994.

Lectures: 2nd International Design Conference, Acapulco, Mexico, 1995; International Congress of Architecture and Graphic Design; La Salle University in Mexico City, 1996; AIGA Conference, San Diego, 2000; Society of Typographic Designers, London, 2002; and Tehran Poster Biennial, 2004. *Exhibitions* (together with Sigi Odermatt): Reinhold-Brown Gallery, New York, 1992; German Poster Museum, Essen, 1996–97; Ginza Graphic Gallery, Tokyo, 1998.

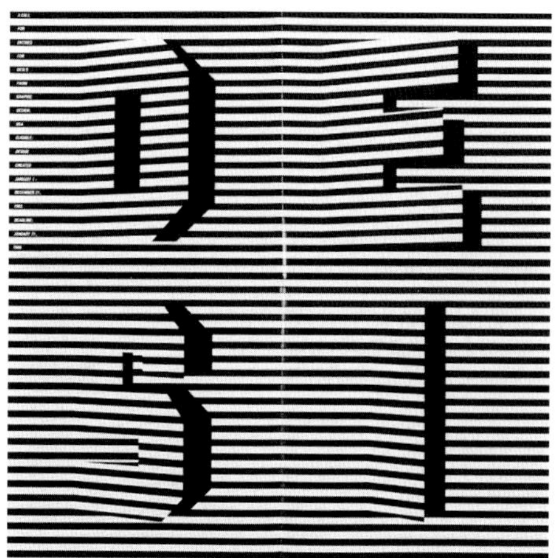

Fred Troller [USA]

1930-2002; born in Zürich, Switzerland
Admitted to AGI, 1974

Massimo Vignelli said: *'Fred Troller's designs successfully combined Swiss rigour with American vitality.'* In his *New York Times* obituary, Steven Heller called Troller *'champion of bold graphic style'*. Fred taught at the Kunstgewerbeschule Zürich after he graduated. In 1954 he worked for motion picture producer Louis de Rochemont. He headed his own design studio in Zürich and became design director for Geigy Corporation USA in 1960. From 1966 on he worked in his Rye, NY studio, designing for major corporations like General Electric, Exxon, IBM, Westinghouse and Doubleday.

He created posters for American Airlines, the United Nations and the Whitney Museum. In addition he taught at the School of Visual Arts and Cooper Union in NYC, the State University of New York, Purdue University, Philadelphia College of Art, Ohio State, Southeastern University, RISD, and lastly he was chairman of design at Alfred University, NY. He was a critic in the Studio Seminar for Federal Designers/Writers at Yale and the 8th Studio Seminar for Federal Designers in Washington DC. Troller received awards from AIGA, ADC, TDC and others. His work was exhibited at the Composing Room, NY Art Directors Show, AIGA, Whitney Museum's Color Show, and elsewhere.

American Airlines, poster, 1969.

Panamericana 1996, poster for design conference in São Paulo, Brazil, 1996.

DESI Design Awards.

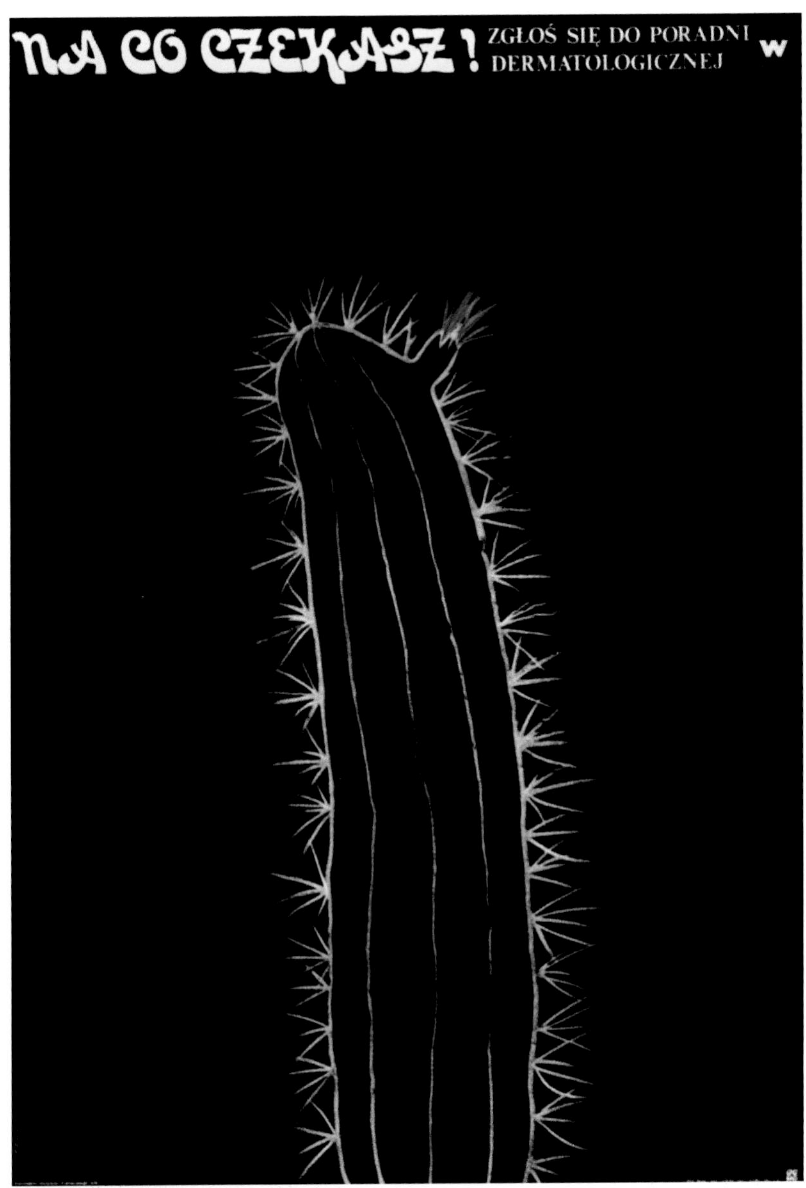

What Are You Waiting For?, poster for the AGI Cambridge congress, 1994, on *'Humour in Design and Photography'*.

Zawsze z pomoca, poster, c. 1960.

Cyrk, circus poster, 1970.

Maciej Urbaniec [Poland]

1925-2004; born in Zwierzyniec
Admitted in AGI, 1974

Born as Maciej Zdzieblan, he used *'Urbaniec'* as a pseudonym during the Warsaw Uprising in 1944, and chose to keep it. He studied at the National Academy in Wroclaw (1952–54) and subsequently with Henryk Tomaszewski at the Poster Studio in the Warsaw Academy of Fine Arts (1954–58); he graduated with honours. Urbaniec taught as assistant professor at the National Academy of Wroclaw (1970–75) and took charge of the graphic design studio of the Warsaw Academy of Fine Arts (1975). He created utility graphics, posters, illustrations and book designs.

For many years he collaborated with the State Publishing Institute on a popular science book series. His design awards include countless Best Book prizes, medals at IBA Leipzig and the Biennial of Graphic Art in Berne; the list of his other prizes and distinctions is most impressive. Urbaniec was one of the outstanding designers of the Polish *'golden age of posters'*. His works were exhibited the world over and can be found in the permanent collections of the leading specialized museums. In his early posters he showed his great painterly skill. Later he turned often to pastiche after Italian maestros, 17th-century Dutch art and German expressionism. He also worked with photographic props and installations, yet always remained aware of his quest for unity of form and content.

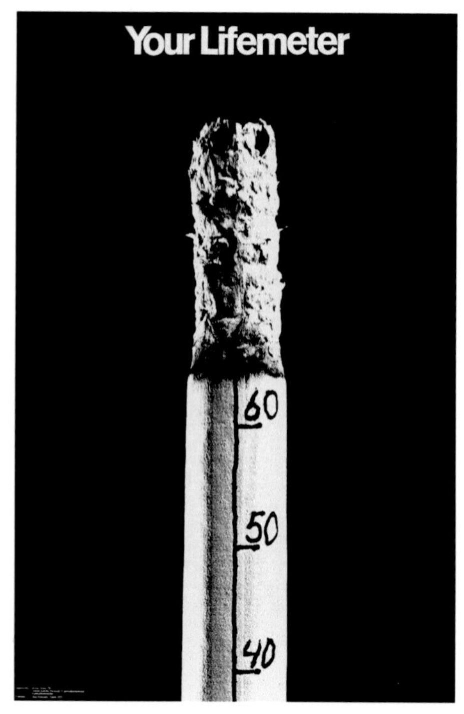

Kyösti Varis [Finland]

1933– born in Joensuu
Admitted to AGI, 1974

Attending typography courses and working at printers in Finland and Germany, I started in advertising in 1957. In 1959 I joined SEK Advertising, worked in the studio, later became an art director and was finally made responsible for the agency's artistic output. In 1968 I decided to ease my workload and started a one-man operation. Over a ten-year period, however, this endeavour grew to comprise 50 people, with a reputation for over-the-par creative thinking. New personal developments were to follow. In 1988, together with Esa Ojala, we began on our own again as V&O, listing Nokia as one of our principal clients.

At the turn of the millennium I once more shed the responsibilities of agency management, since then doing consultative work and freelance advertising art, and calling this operation Varis Original. I have received about 200 prizes for my work and 24 of my posters were selected amongst the year's best in Finland. Internationally I cherish my awards from Warsaw and Brno. My aim has always been to design posters, which can communicate without words. Yusaku Kamekura has described my posters as being *'full of clear-cut humour, like Herbert Leupin's, yet totally of its own brand and breed.'*
In 1983 I received the honorary title of professor.

Pori Jazz, festival poster, 1982. Year's Best Poster, Finland, 1982.

Your Lifemeter, health poster, 1970. Honourable Mention, Warsaw Biennale, 1970.

The Dangers of Driving, road safety poster.

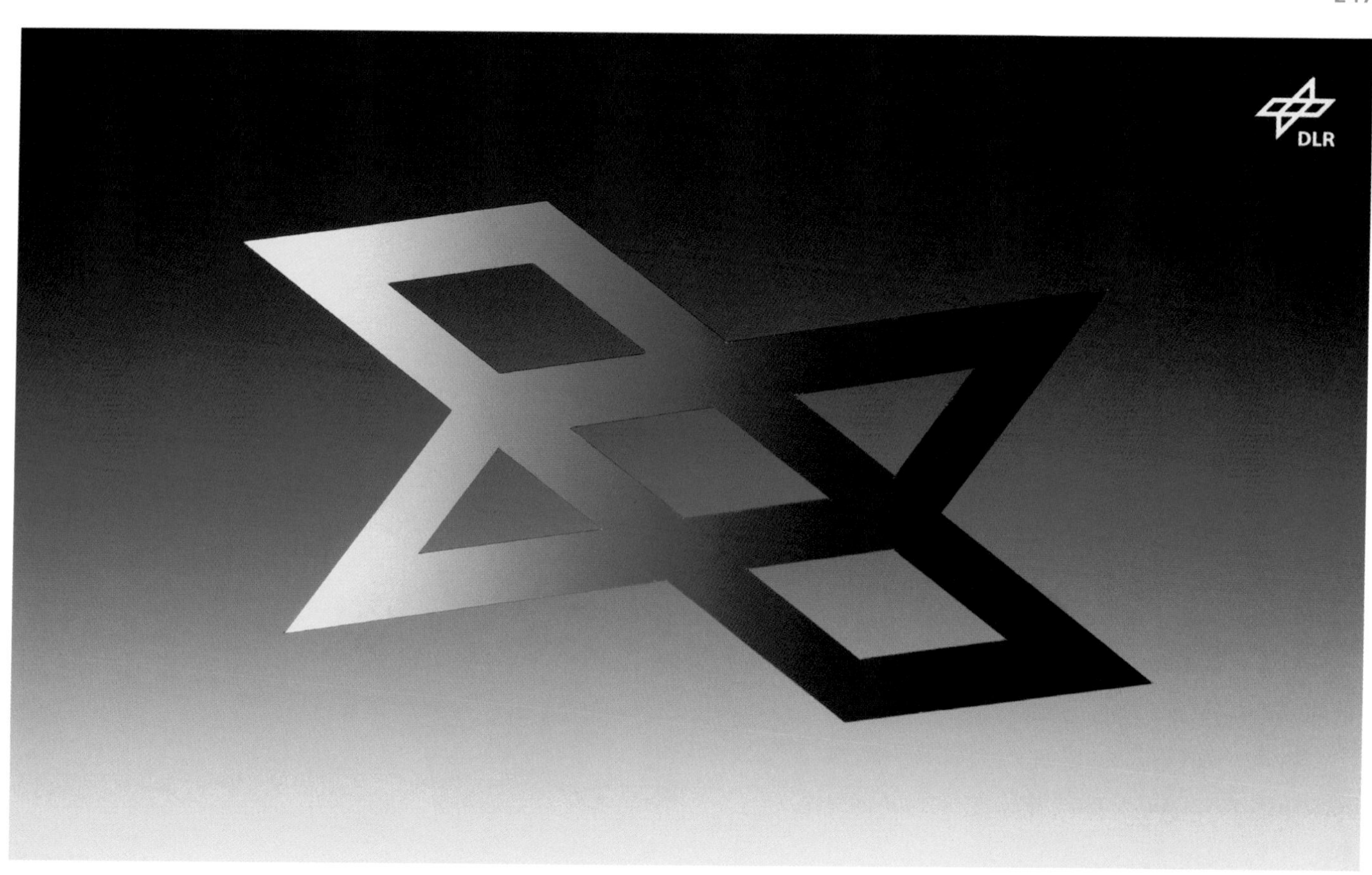

DLR (German Aerospace Centre), conceptual model of a logo that can be used for TV screens or giant-size projection. Tilted at a special angle, the logo captures the image of a flying object, and can also be made to move, if necessary. Originated in 1975. Application for TV screen 1997.

Bruno K. Wiese [Germany]

1922– born in Berlin
Admitted to AGI, 1974

Wiese studied at the Staatliche Hochschule für bildende Künste in Berlin under O.H.W. Hadank (1945–49). After graduation he worked as an assistant in Hadank's studio before establishing his own studio (1954) with his wife Ruth in Hamburg. They did a lot of packaging design for the German tobacco industry. Wiese has been a lecturer (1978–80) and a professor (1980–87) at the department of communication design at the Fachhochschule in Kiel. He designed almost 40 stamps for the German Bundespost, and two for the United Nations: 'Combat Racism' (1971) and one for UN Peacekeeping Operations (1980).

In 1996 he was invited to join the Arts Council of the German Ministry of Post and Telecommunications. Wiese has been awarded many prizes: for packaging for Henkell Sekt in 1970; for a logo for the German Aerospace Centre in 1975; for the Kieler Woche sailing festival in 1971 and 1977; a first prize in the Industrial Design Society of America Award Competition in 1983. In 1987 he was awarded the Arts and Crafts Prize from the City of Hamburg. Bruno has been a member of the jury for the Kieler Woche for many years. Along with his colleague Fritz Seitz, Wiese was responsible for the event's visual presentation.

R.O. Blechman [USA]

1930– born in Brooklyn, New York
Admitted to AGI, 1975

As a teenager I attended a special high school in New York, the High School of Music and Art, which offered courses in music or art along with a full academic programme. This had a profound influence on me, although at the time I had no thought of becoming an artist. I went on to college, majoring in history and literature. Immediately after graduation (1952), I published my first book of text and illustrations, *The Juggler of Our Lady*. The following two decades saw me pursuing a career in illustration (with forays into graphic design).

In 1978 I formed an animation studio, The Ink Tank. Among my films was a version of Igor Stravinsky's *Soldier's Tale*. Animation and illustration (especially graphic stories) have remained the two poles in my creative life. Along the way I had exhibitions of my artwork in Galerie Delpire, Paris (1968), Graham Gallery, NY (1978) and Galerie Bartsch & Chariau, Munich (1980, 1990, 1999). In 1999 I was elected to the Art Directors Hall of Fame. In 2000 my animated films were given a retrospective at the NY MoMA.

The New Yorker: **City Lights**, cover illustration.

The New Yorker: **Eustacia Tilley**, cover illustration.

Story magazine: Winged Elephant, cover illustration.

Story magazine: Don Quixote, cover illustration.

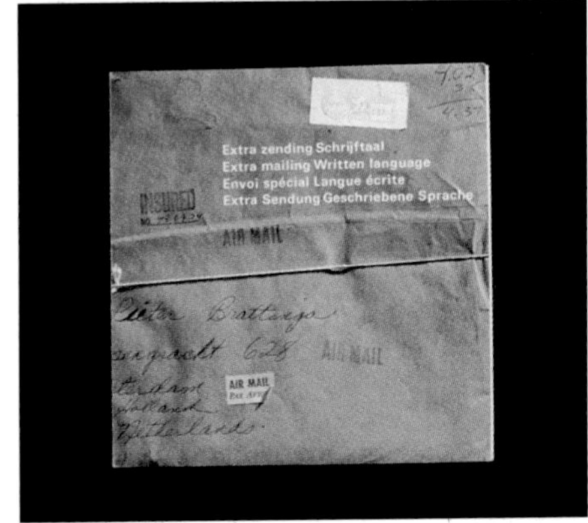

Design and Aerial Photography, exhibition poster, 1960. De Jong Printers' gallery.

Christo: Surrounded Islands, exhibition poster, Kröller-Müller Museum, 1985.

Extra Mailing: Written Language, text and drawings by Henry Miller, from the *Kwadraatbladen* series, 1967.

Pieter Brattinga [The Netherlands]

1931-2004; born in Hilversum
Admitted to AGI, 1975

A gifted designer, organizer, promoter, cosmopolitan, educator and author. Studied in Leiden, Paris and London. Director of design at his family's printing house Steendrukkerij de Jong & Co, Hilversum (1951–74). There he had his first own small gallery, where he held exciting exhibitions about the (inter)national graphic design scene. At the same time he published his renowned *Kwadraatbladen*, a series of square brochures on various design or art-related subjects, including Wim Crouwel's *New Alphabet* and Anthon Beeke's *Nude Alphabet*. Chair of visual communication at Pratt Institute, Brooklyn (1980–82), visiting professor at the Technical University of Eindhoven. Secretary General of Icograda and later, board member of AGI. President of the Dutch ADC. From 1972 he had a new print gallery in the basement of his Amsterdam home. He designed logos, book covers, symbols, exhibitions. Main clients included the Kröller-Müller Museum in Otterlo, DSM Chemicals and the Dutch PTT, for which he created many stamps. He was also, with his firm Mercis, the well-dressed businessman behind the global success of Dick Bruna's work. He wrote books about the history of Dutch posters and made a documentary on Willem Sandberg.

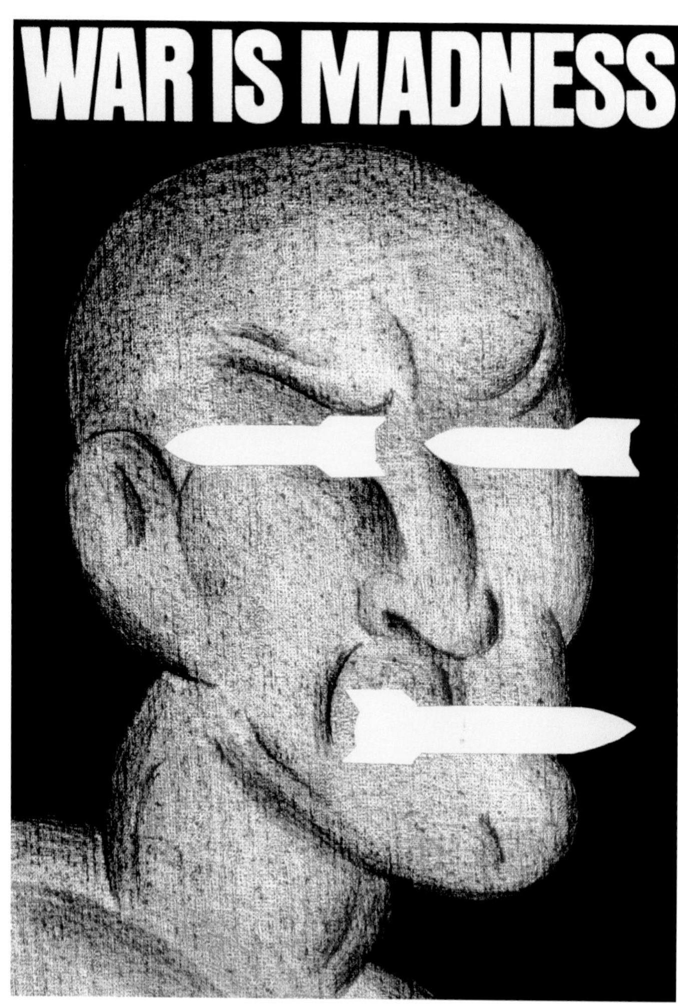

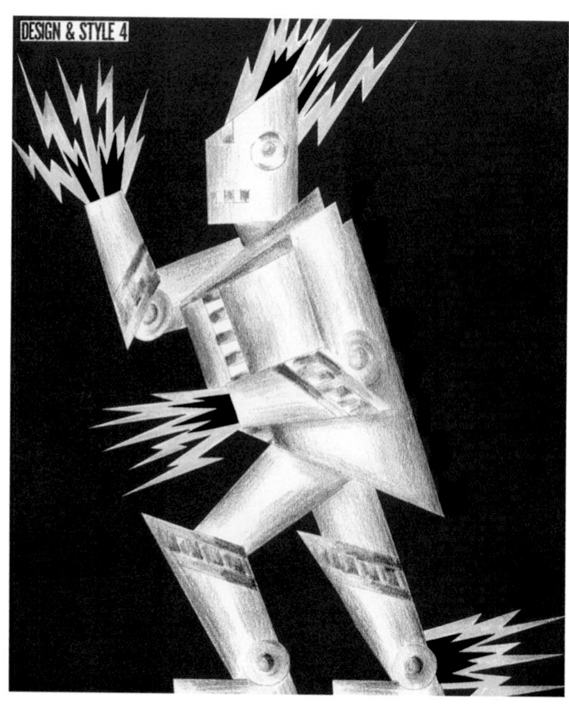

Seymour Chwast [USA]

1931– born in New York City
Admitted to AGI, 1975

Chwast graduated at the Cooper Union. He is a founding partner of Push Pin Studios, whose distinct style has had a worldwide influence on visual communications. In 1981 the studio's name was changed to The Pushpin Group. His clients have included leading corporations, advertising agencies and publishing companies both in the US and abroad. Chwast's designs and illustrations have been used in advertising, animated films, corporate and environmental graphics, publications, posters, packaging and record covers. He has designed and illustrated over thirty children's books and has developed several typefaces.

The studio published *The Push Pin Graphic*, (1957–81) and now *The Nose*, with Steven Heller. Chwast works in a variety of styles and media. His works featured in major galleries and museums in the US, Europe, Japan, Brazil and Russia. He has had one-man shows of his paintings, sculptures and prints in the US and elsewhere. His posters are in the permanent collection of NY MoMA, the Cooper-Hewitt Museum (Smithsonian Institution), the Library of Congress, the Gutenberg Museum and the Israel Museum, among others.He has an honorary Ph.D in Fine Arts from Parsons School of Design and is in the AD Hall of Fame; he was awarded the AIGA medal 1985. He became a Royal Designer for Industry in 2005.

War is Madness, anti-war poster.

Cover for a brochure on **Futurism** for a paper mill.

The South, one of a series of illustrations about the civil rights movement in the Deep South.

Silvio Coppola [Italy]

Poster from a series for book publisher, 1969.

One of a set of posters for a restaurant. It highlights his originality in problem solving.

1920-1985; born in Brindisi
Admitted to AGI, 1975

Coppola graduated from Milan Polytechnic and began his career as an architect, like many other Italian designers. In 1955, he worked with the European Development Fund and was responsible for four residential complexes for students in Zaire. Between 1956–58, he designed department stores and offices in Baghdad, and residential houses in several Italian towns. In 1960 he started to be involved in industrial design, making a name for himself with his innovative designs for motor vehicle bodywork, made of fibre glass. He also worked for Berni, Alessi, Artemide and Cassina; many of his designs still feature in their collections. As a freelance designer and consultant, Coppola worked for major Italian and European firms like Bayer Italia, Monteshell, Montecatini Edison and Cotonifici Cantoni. In 1967 he formed a group to explore exhibition design with Bruno Munari, Franco Grignani, Pino Tovaglia and Giulio Convalieri. He had exhibitions in Copenhagen, Barcelona, Madrid, Milan and other major cities. His work is in the permanent collection of the NY MoMA.

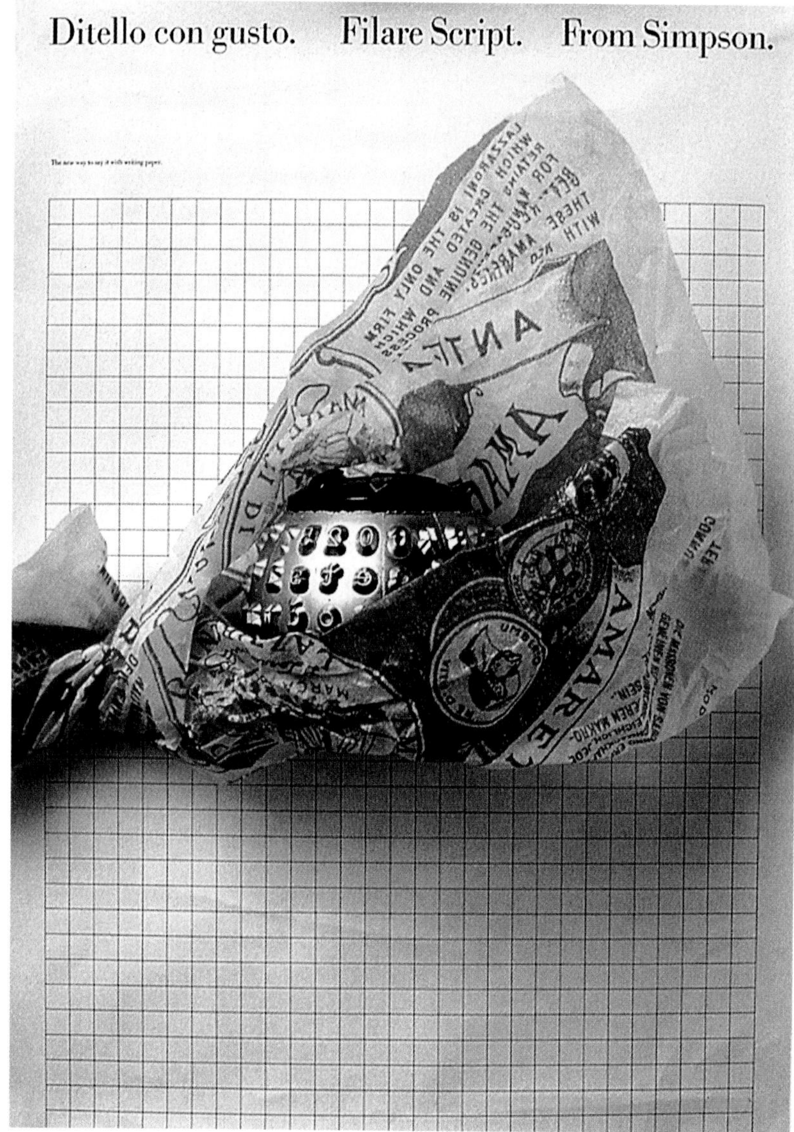
Ditello con gusto. Filare Script. From Simpson.

PANZA

James Cross [USA]

1934– born in Los Angeles
Admitted to AGI, 1975
International President 1988-1992

James Cross is a graduate of UCLA School of Fine Art. He opened Cross Associates design firm in 1963, eventually having offices in Los Angeles, San Francisco and Newport Beach, California. His work was described in *Graphis* as *'influencing and shaping the visual appearance of major corporations where he gained an international reputation for design conveying simplicity, clarity, depth and integrity.'* He has served on the board of directors of the International Design Conference in Aspen and the American Institute of Graphic Arts.

He received the Lifetime Achievement Award from the Los Angeles Art Directors Club and the AIGA Legacy Medal. He has taught at UCLA, Arizona State University and the Portland School of Art in Maine. In 1988 Cross Associates was purchased by Saatchi & Saatchi, LLC. Jim is presently consulting and creating packaging for the wine industry in the Napa Valley, California where he and his wife, Sue, live.

Simpson Filare Script, poster for a line of fine printing papers.

Trademark for American **Honda's Acura Division**.

Package design for **Panza wine**.

Thomas H. Geismar [USA]

National Aquarium in Baltimore, 1980.

We Are One, poster, 2001.

Peace, poster, 1985.

1932– born in New Jersey
Admitted to AGI, 1975

Tom Geismar is a founding principal of Chermayeff & Geismar, and widely considered a pioneer of American graphic design. During the past four decades he has designed more than a hundred corporate identity programmes. His designs for Xerox, Chase Manhattan Bank, Best Products, Gemini Consulting, PBS, Univision, Rockefeller Center and, most notably, Mobil Oil have received worldwide acclaim. Tom has also been responsible for many of the firm's exhibition designs and pavilions. Burlington Industries' 'The Mill' was a major NYC tourist attraction for 10 years as today are the Ellis Island Immigration Museum, the Statue of Liberty Museum, and the recently opened Truman Presidential Library. He has received all the major awards in the field, including one of the first Presidential Design Awards for helping to establish a national system of standardized transportation symbols. Tom Geismar concurrently attended the Rhode Island School of Design and Brown University. A Phi Beta Kappa graduate of Brown, he received a masters in graphic design from Yale University, School of Art and Architecture.

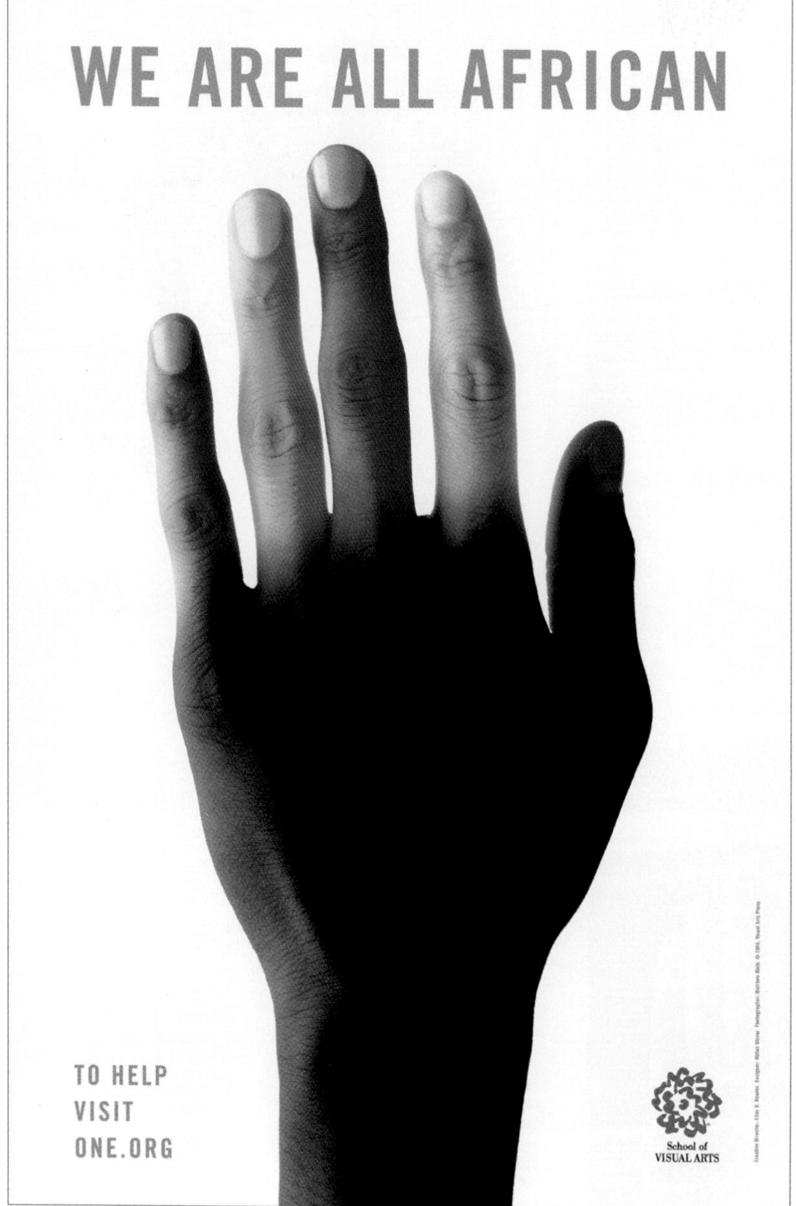

Milton Glaser [USA]

1929– born in The Bronx, New York
Admitted to AGI, 1975

Milton Glaser is among the most celebrated graphic designers in the US. He has had the distinction of one-man-shows at the MoMA and the Centre Pompidou. In 2004 he was selected for the lifetime achievement award of the Cooper-Hewitt National Design Museum. As a Fulbright scholar, Glaser studied with the painter Giorgio Morandi in Bologna. He is an articulate spokesman for the ethical practice of design. In 1974 he opened Milton Glaser, Inc., and continues to produce an astounding amount of work in many fields of design to this day.

To many, Milton Glaser is the embodiment of American graphic design during the latter half of the 20th century. His presence and impact on the profession and design education internationally is formidable. Immensely creative and articulate, he is a modern renaissance man: one of a rare breed of intellectual designer-illustrators, who brings a depth of understanding and conceptual thinking, combined with a diverse richness of visual language, to his highly inventive and individualistic work. Glaser has been a prolific creator of posters and prints. He also is a renowned graphic and architectural designer with a body of work ranging from the iconic logo to complete graphic and decorative programmes for the restaurants in the New York WTC.

We Are All African, poster, 2005. A social awareness campaign, to bring recognition of our solidarity with African people today.

I Love NY More Than Ever, 2001. Created directly after the attacks of September 11, almost a million copies of this version of the classic *I Love NY* circulated around the city, turning up on windows, lampposts, subway walls and wrapping the *New York Daily News*.

New York magazine: Gossip, 1976. One of many covers Milton designed after founding the magazine with Cley Felker in 1968.

Fritz Gottschalk [Switzerland]

SZU: Zürich Public Transport.
Design of a total transportation system, consisting of trains, buses, funicular trains, station design and collateral material.

Coninx Museum Zürich, poster, positioning and branding for private museum containing over 10,000 works of art. Task: naming, designing posters and exhibitions.

Exhibition design: **Swiss Federal Institute of Technology, Zürich, Faculty of Architecture**. Annual presentation of graduation work.

1937– born in Zürich
Admitted to AGI, 1975

Founder/principal of Gottschalk+Ash International. 1954–58: apprenticeship as typographer at Art Institut Orell Füssli, Zürich. Studied at Kunstgewerbeschule Zürich and Allgemeine Gewerbeschule Basel. 1961–64: Fritz received three awards for excellence from the Swiss Department of the Interior. After freelancing in Paris (1959–60) and working for industry in London (1960–63) he moved to Canada. After having worked for Paul Arthur & Associates and Expo 67 he opened his own studio with Stuart Ash in 1966. He was a juror of *Spectrum '75*, the Royal Canadian Academy Art Exhibition for the 1976 Olympic Games in Montréal. 1976–78: he built up the G+A New York office in collaboration with Ken Carbone and Leslie Smolan, now Carbon Smolan Agency. Returned to Zürich (1979) and concentrated on communication design, corporate identity and architectural graphics. 1982–89: also responsible for the Milan office in collaboration with Walter Ballmer. 1983–89: faculty member of the Kent Summer Graphic Design Workshop in Rapperswil, Switzerland. 1985–91 Secretary Treasurer for AGI. 1990–2000: Graphis Publishing, member of board of directors. 1991–on: member of board of trustees, Coninx Museum, Zürich. Lecturer at Ohio State University, Kent State University, Washington University and Yale University. Gottschalk+Ash today has offices in Toronto, Calgary and Zürich. Total staff: 25–30.

Galleria Colonna

NAPOLI

A poster commissioned by
NAPOLI 99 Foundation as a contribution
towards the cultural image of the city

John McConnell [UK]

1939– born in London
Admitted to AGI, 1975

John was director of Pentagram Design for 31 years before re-establishing McConnell Design in 2005. John is involved in all areas of graphic design for a broad range of clients including corporate identity, packaging and signage programmes, to posters, books and print. This work has been complemented by a number of design consultancies such as Boots, Halfords, the Co-operative Group and the John Lewis Partnership. From 1983 to 1990 he was a board director responsible for design for Faber & Faber. John has also been a non-executive director of Cosalt Plc and is a member of the Royal Mail Stamp Advisory Committee.

John has won many international awards including gold and silver D&ADs and the President's Award for outstanding contribution to design, plus an American Art Directors Club award and a gold medal at the Warsaw Biennale. He served as President of the D&AD in 1986, a Fellow of the Chartered Society of Arts, and is a Royal Designer for Industry. In December 2002 John was awarded one of only two special commendations for the Prince Phllip Designers Prize.

Galleria Colonna, 1990. Symbol for a retail and business development in central Rome.

Napoli 99 Foundation, 1985. Poster for promoting the conservation of the city's cultural heritage.

Hydro-Québec, visual identity programme update, 1994. The original was designed in 1965. As a member of the conceptual team with James Valkus, Charles Gagnon, Robert P. DeVito and James McElheron, Jean Morin (who had just finished his education in Switzerland) was asked to define the exact shape of the symbol.

Bell Canada, visual identity programme, 1976.

Norman Bethune commemorative stamps for Canada Post Corporation, 1990. Issued in Canada and the Republic of China. Illustration: Liu Xiangping.

Jean Morin [Canada]

1938– born in Quebec City
Admitted to AGI, 1975

Studied advertising art at the École des Beaux-Arts in Quebec. One of the first French-Canadians of his generation to study in the field of graphic design, he attended classes at the Kunstgewerbeschule in Zürich in 1960–61. Was involved early in his career in the design of such well-known identities as CN, Hydro-Québec, and Voyageur. In 1975, with his partner, he was responsible for the design of the signage system of the Montréal Olympic Games. In 1976, Jean was retained for the corporate rebranding of Bell Canada, which won the Design Canada Award of Excellence.

In 1982, as a founder of Axion, he worked with his partner on the re-identification of Petro-Canada, Musée des Beaux-Arts, Montreal, and Hydro-Québec (1994). Was responsible for the design of many postage stamps for Canada Post, such as the centennial of the Royal Canadian Mounted Police (1973), a series on heritage artefacts (1982–87), and Norman Bethune (Canada and China, 1990). Elected member of the Royal Canadian Academy of Arts in 1981. Jean was elected an honorary member of the Quebec Graphic Designers Association in 2006. Jean is grateful for having had the good fortune to be in the right place at the right time, surrounded by talented people and supportive clients and family.

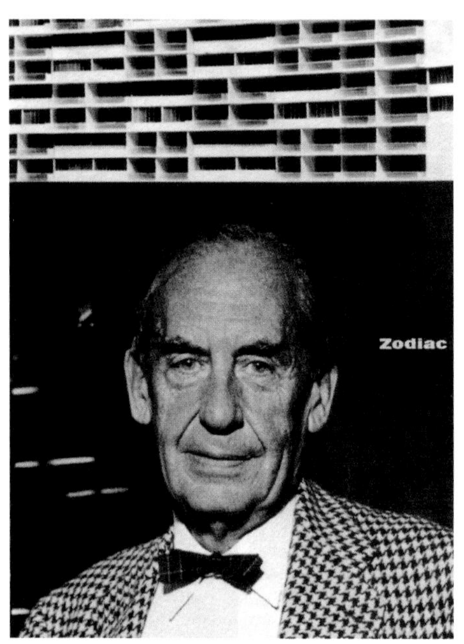

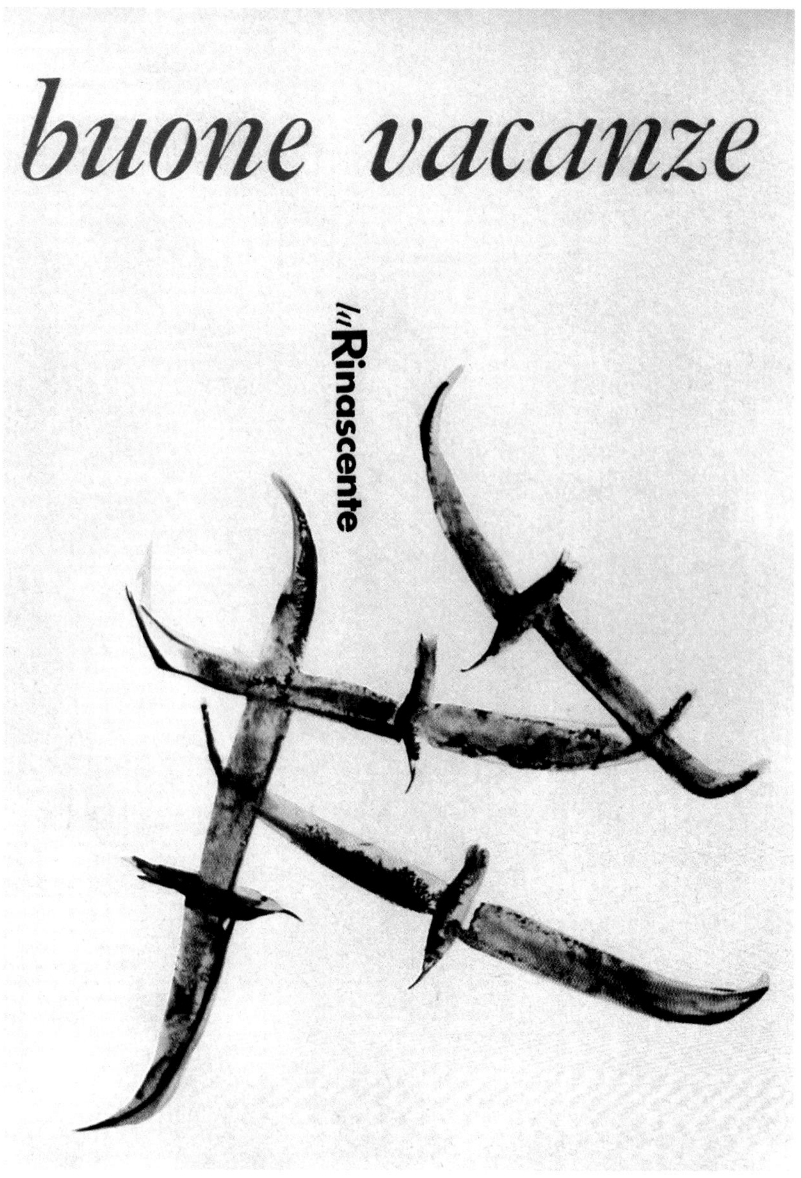

Roberto Sambonet [Italy]

1924-1995; born in Vercelli
Admitted to AGI, 1975

Roberto studied architecture at Milan University, but soon dedicated himself to painting. After his great successes in Europe and Brazil, he switched over to design and opened a studio in Milan. He met Alvar Aalto, with whom he formed a life-long friendship and collaboration. Sambonet was a graphic consultant for Pirelli, Alfa Romeo, Renault, Touring Club Italiano, RAI, Tobu Tokyo department stores, Feltrinelli and Einaudi Publishers. He was art director of the architecture review *Zodiac* from 1956 to 1960.

As an industrial designer, he worked on projects for La Rinascente, Baccarat, Bing&Grondhal, Richard Ginori, Seguso Murano and Tiffany, working in glass, crystal and porcelain. He designed exclusive stainless steel dinner sets for his family's firm; some of these objects are in the permanent collection of NY MoMA. He was awarded the Compasso d'Oro, 1956, 1970, 1979, 1995, and Milan Triennale Grand Prix, 1960. His art was shown at solo exhibitions in São Paulo, Milan, Helsinki, Lugano, then in Stockholm, Venice, Rio de Janeiro, Chicago, New York, Turin and Paris. His final years, spent between Milan and New York, were devoted to painting, ranging from portraits to landscapes to abstract works.

Pinacoteca di Brera, after Piero della Francesca, poster, Milan (with Bruno Monguzzi), 1972.

Zodiac magazine no. 1 , cover with portrait of Walter Gropius, Olivetti, Ivrea, 1958.

Buone Vacanze (Happy Holidays), poster for La Rinascente department store, Milan, 1960.

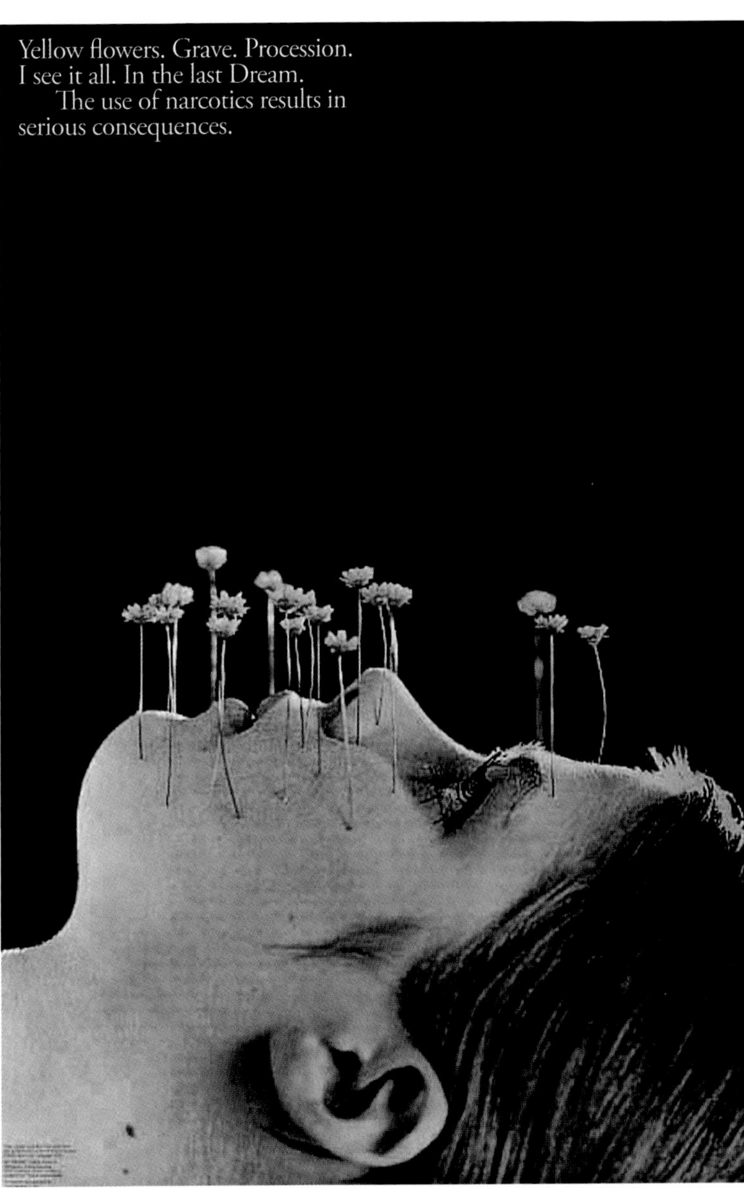

Yellow flowers. Grave. Procession.
I see it all. In the last Dream.
The use of narcotics results in serious consequences.

Homage to Toulouse-Lautrec, poster designed for a poster exhibition on the theme of 'The Grandchildren of Toulouse-Lautrec', 2001.

Anti-drugs poster. It won a gold medal in International Poster Biennale in Warsaw.

Jukka Veistola [Finland]

1946– born in Helsinki
Admitted to AGI, 1975

Jukka Veistola studied at the Atheneum Art School in Helsinki, graduated as the best student and received the teachers' scholarship in 1969. He has won medals of all colours in international poster biennials and other international competitions. He has also been successful in other fields of graphic design. His works are featured in several books, including *Graphic Design of The World, Vol. 1* (Japan, 1993), *The Modern Poster* (NY MoMA, 1988) and *The 100 Best Posters from Europe and the United States* (Japan, 1995). He has served as a jury member at international poster biennials and design competitions, including Warsaw, Colorado, Paris, Mexico City, New York and Helsinki.

As a speaker he has given lectures in international design congresses in Helsinki, Argentina, Brazil, the US, Mexico and elsewhere. The lectures are mostly based on the themes of creativity, posters, symbols and logos, packaging and graphic design. Today Jukka Veistola runs his own design firm in his hometown Helsinki. He is a member of the Federation of Finnish Enterprises; Grafia Finnish Graphic Designers; Helsinki Chamber, Finland; JCA (Japan Creators Association); NYADC (honorary member); Ornamo Finnish Industrial Designers; and Sauna Academy, Independent Art Association.

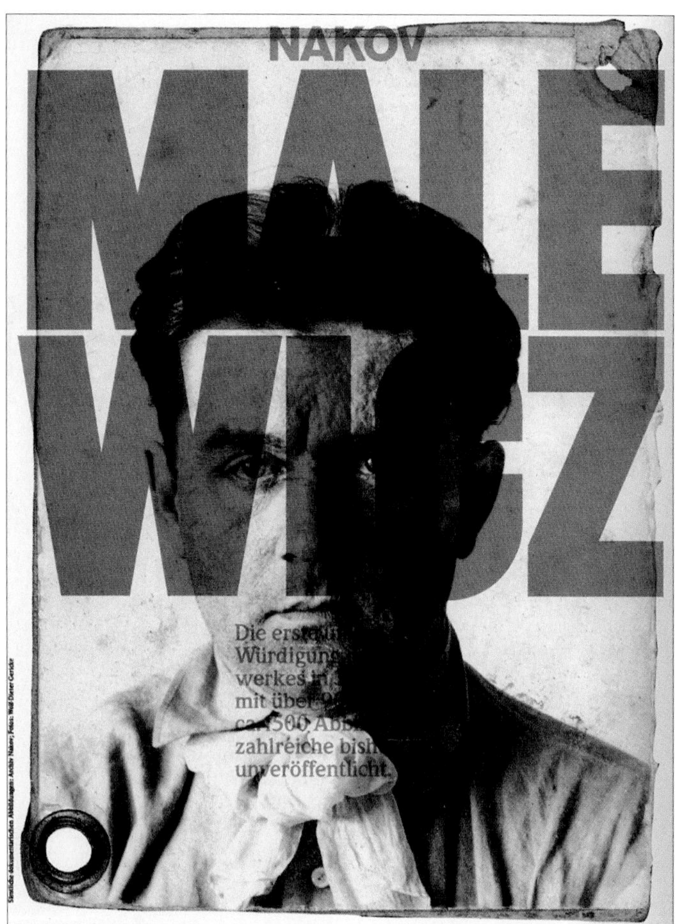

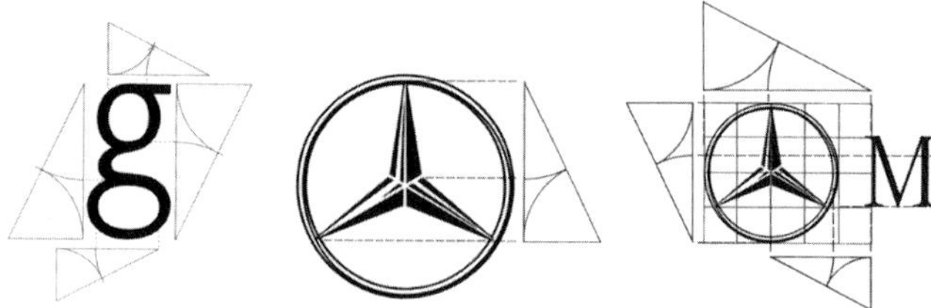

Kurt Weidemann [Germany]

1922– born in Masuren
(East Prussia/now Poland)
Admitted to AGI, 1975

Kurt graduated 1940 from high school in Lübeck. 1941–45: military service in Russia. 1945–50: prisoner of war in Russia. 1950–52: apprentice typesetter. 1953–55: studied book graphics and typography at the State Academy of Fine Arts in Stuttgart. 1955: started a freelance practice as a graphic designer, advertising consultant and copywriter. 1956–63: was sub-editor and type manager of *Der Druckspiegel*. Weidemann worked for several leading firms like COOP, Zeiss, Merk, Mercedes-Benz, Daimler-Benz, Deutsche Aerospace, Deutsche Bahn and Bundespost. He also designed for several publishing companies.

Has worked on corporate identity programmes since 1961. Weidemann was a professor at the Academy in Stuttgart, 1965–85. Started teaching at the Koblenz School of Corporate Management in 1983. From 1987 he was corporate identity consultant for Daimler-Benz. Re-designed Porsche's corporate identity in 1990. The next year he started teaching at the Hochschule für Gestaltung in Karlsruhe. He won the Lucky Strike Design Award (Raymond Loewy Foundation) in 1995 and Germany's Order of Merit in 1996. His font designs include Biblica (1979), ITC Weidemann (1983) and Corporate A.S.E. (1985–89). His most important publications are *Wo der Buchstabe das Wort führt* and *Wortarmut*. Uta Brandes wrote the monograph *Kurt Weidemann. Das Nachbild auf der Netzhaut* (1995).

Andrei Nakov: *Malevich*, brochure for a three-volume publication, Pfälzischen Verlagsanstalt, 1987.

Deutsche Bundesbahn (German Railways), logo, 1993.

Enerplan, logo, 1978.

Mercedes-Benz logo, demonstrating the use of the Golden Section, 1988.

Glasgow Airport identity for British Airports Authority.

British Airports Authority signing system.

British Rail lettering with integrated spacing system.

Margaret Calvert [UK]

1936– born in Durban, South Africa
Admitted to AGI, 1976

Margaret Calvert studied illustration at Chelsea School of Art in the 1950s. After leaving Chelsea, she was invited to join Jock Kinneir (her tutor), to assist on the design of signs for Gatwick Airport. Attended evening classes in typography at the Central School of Arts and Crafts in 1958. Worked with Jock on the UK's road signage system. Mainly responsible for the font Transport and several pictograms. Practice eventually established as Kinneir Calvert Tuhill (now works independently). Major projects included designing an integrated lettering and signing system for British Rail, British Airports, and the Tyne and Wear Metro.

Collaborated with Monotype to produce the typeface Calvert, released in 1981, based on lettering designed for the Metro and later adapted for the Royal College of Art, 1992. Designed the typeface A26 (based on traffic signs), for *FUSE*, 1994. Won a D&AD Silver Award for the David Hockney book *Travels with Pen, Pencil and Ink*, 1978. Has contributed to several books and exhibitions including Lucienne Roberts's *Drip Dry Shirts* (AVA, 2005). She taught part-time at the Royal College of Art (1966–2001) and was head of graphic design at the RCA (1987–91). She is a senior fellow of the RCA, fellow of the University of the Arts, London and an honorary doctor of the University of Brighton.

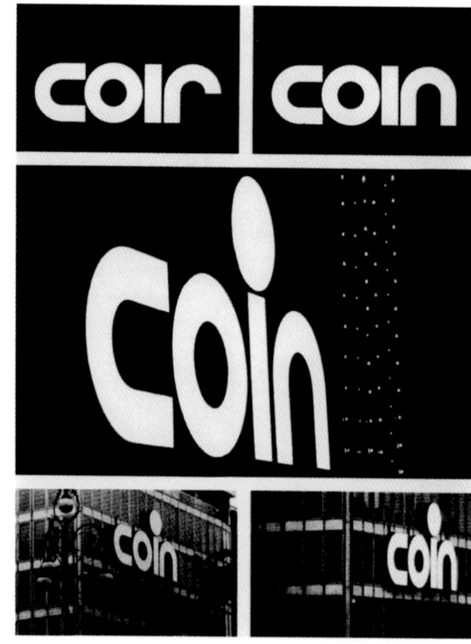

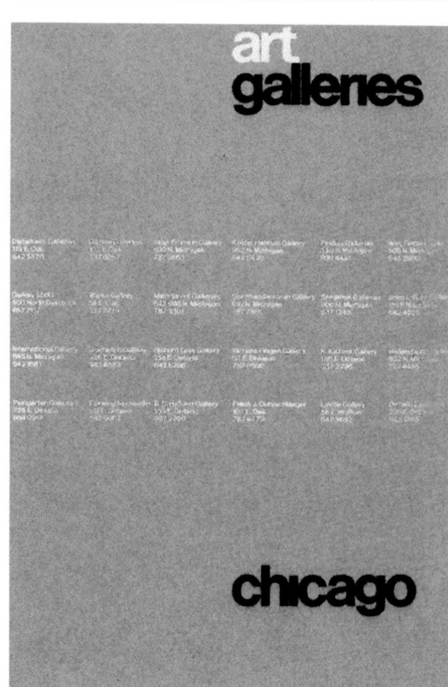

Giulio Cittato [Italy]

1936-1986; born in Venice
Admitted to AGI, 1976

After he graduated from the Venice University in 1963, Cittato spent two years working as a designer with La Rinascente in Milan. He moved to the USA in 1965, where he worked for Unimark International, the Center for Advanced Research in Design and the Container Corporation of America. In 1971, Cittato returned to Italy and from 1971–74 he taught visual design at the Corso Superiore di Disegno Industriale and the International University of Art in Venice. He was involved in a wide range of design projects, corporate programmes and signage, which he taught at the University of Urbino from 1978–80.

A one-man exhibition was held at the Smithsonian Institute in 1969. Clear colourful compositions were typical of his work. More exhibitions were held in Milan, Montreal and Venice. Samples of his work can be found in the NY MoMA, as well as in museums in Italy and other countries.

Photography Courses, poster, 1983.

Coin department store, logo, 1971.

Art Galleries Chicago, poster, 1967.

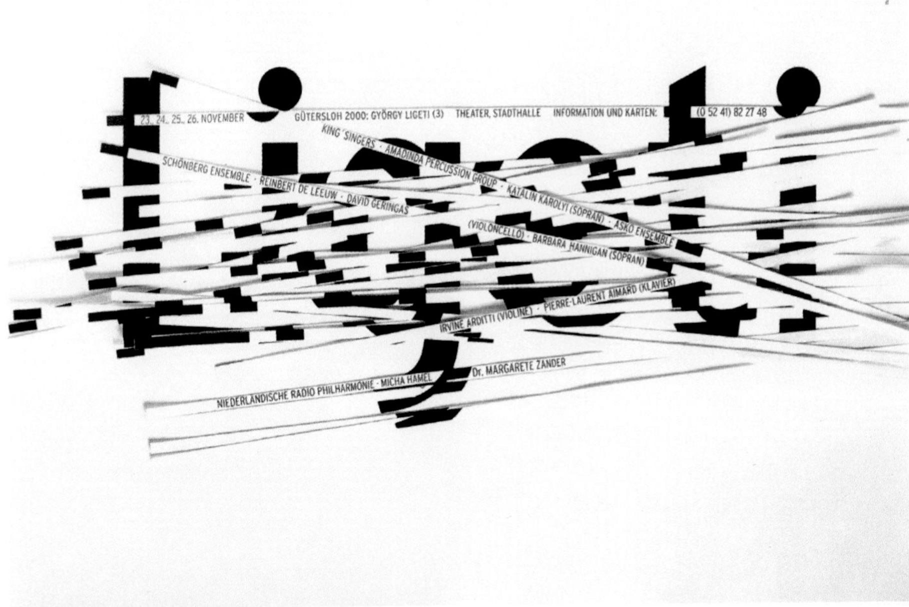

Poster for German AGI Members Exhibition in Osaka, Japan, 2005.

György Ligeti, poster that pays tribute to a contemporary composer, 2000.

We don't only have football in our heads. Theatre poster to coincide with the 2006 Soccer World Cup in Germany.

Giuseppe Verdi: *Don Carlos*, opera poster, 1992.

Holger Matthies [Germany]

1940– born in Hamburg
Admitted to AGI, 1976

Matthies was an apprentice in colour lithography from 1957–61. In 1961–62 he studied at the Fachhochschule für Gestaltung and from 1962–66 he attended the HfBK in Hamburg. His freelance graphic design career started in 1966. He became guest professor at the Fachhochschule für Gestaltung, Hamburg and several other institutions. In 1994 he was appointed professor of visual communication at HfBK Berlin. His posters have gained recognition worldwide. Holger has held 60 solo poster exhibitions in 40 different countries.

Awards include: gold medal, German Poster Museum, Essen, 1976; gold medal, International Poster Biennale, Warsaw, 1980; Edwin Scharff Prize, Hamburg; bronze medal, International Poster Festival, Colorado, 1981; silver medal, NY ADC 1987; Henri de Toulouse-Lautrec medal, German Poster Museum Triennial, Essen, 1990; gold medal, Warsaw Biennale, 1990; Merit Award, NY ADC, 1993; silver medal, International Poster Biennale, Brno, 1994; silver medal, International Poster Biennial, Mexico, 2000; silver medal, Hong Kong International Poster Triennial, 2001.

Isolde Monson-Baumgart [Germany]

1935– born in Munich
Admitted to AGI, 1976

Isolde Monson-Baumgart studied graphic design with Hans Leistikow and Hans Hillmann at the Kassel Hochschule. While still a student, she was commissioned to design film posters and established a reputation by winning awards in national and international shows. In 1959 she went to Paris to study engraving and colour printmaking with S.W. Hayter (Atelier 17). As a freelance designer, she worked in Frankfurt and Paris with emphasis on posters, postage stamp design and magazine illustration. Isolde moved to the USA in 1976 and settled in New England.

From 1980–84, she taught at the University of Connecticut, Storrs. Other teaching assignments followed: in 1984–86 at the Merz Akademie, Stuttgart and in 1987–89 as a guest professor at Kassel University. In 1996 she moved to France. Her work has been shown in major shows and biennials in Europe, Japan and the US. Her posters and prints are part of various collections, including the Art Institute of Minneapolis, Bibliothèque Nationale de France, Die Neue Sammlung, Munich, Kunstbibliothek Berlin, National Gallery Oslo and Staatsgalerie Stuttgart.

Cactus, multimedia print, 2003.

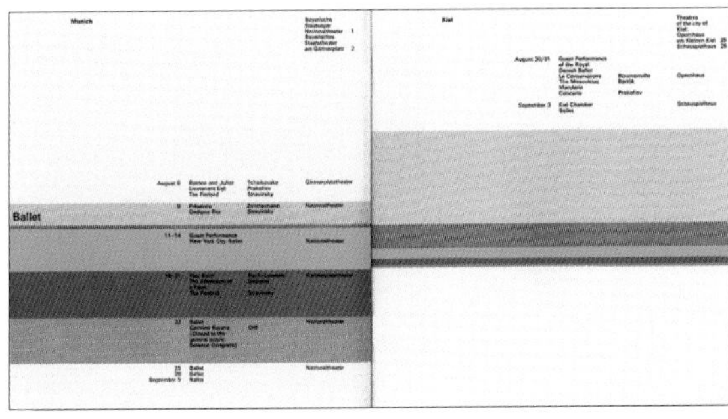

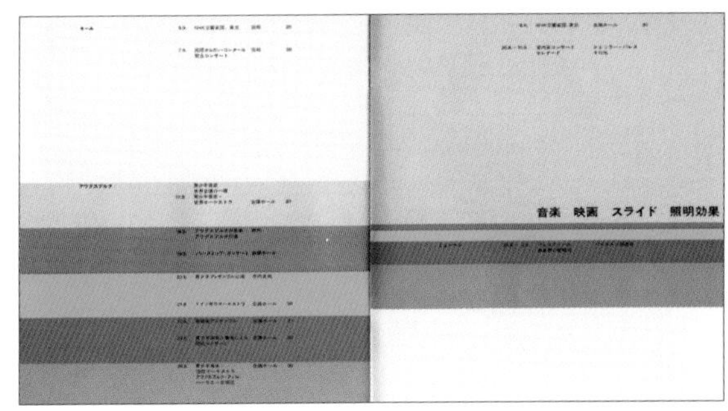

Münchner Volkshochschule, poster for an educational programme, 1978.

SOS Children's Villages, poster for an international charity organization, 1998.

German and Japanese spreads from a brochure advertising cultural events during the **1972 Olympic Games**. This brochure was published in 16 different languages.

Rolf Müller [Germany]

1940– born in Dortmund
Admitted to AGI, 1976
International President 1992-1994

Four years of studying, three of them at the Hochschule für Gestaltung, Ulm, one at Josef Müller-Brockmann, Zürich. At the age of 24, I opened my own studio in Ulm, mainly working on corporate design. In 1967–72 I worked with Otl Aicher on the corporate design of the 1972 Munich Olympic Games and was the deputy chief. After that, I reopened my own studio in Munich, where I still live and work.

For more than 25 years I worked with 8 employees and was engaged in many fields of graphic design: posters, books, magazines, exhibitions, signage systems, town planning; but mostly corporate design for companies, public institutions and major events. Like many AGI members, I won prizes in competitions and got several awards. I never taught full-time, but gave lessons and seminars in Canada, the US, Great Britain, Switzerland, Austria and Germany. I was a member of the AGI board for around eight years and I personally organized the AGI Congresses twice (1980 and 1989).

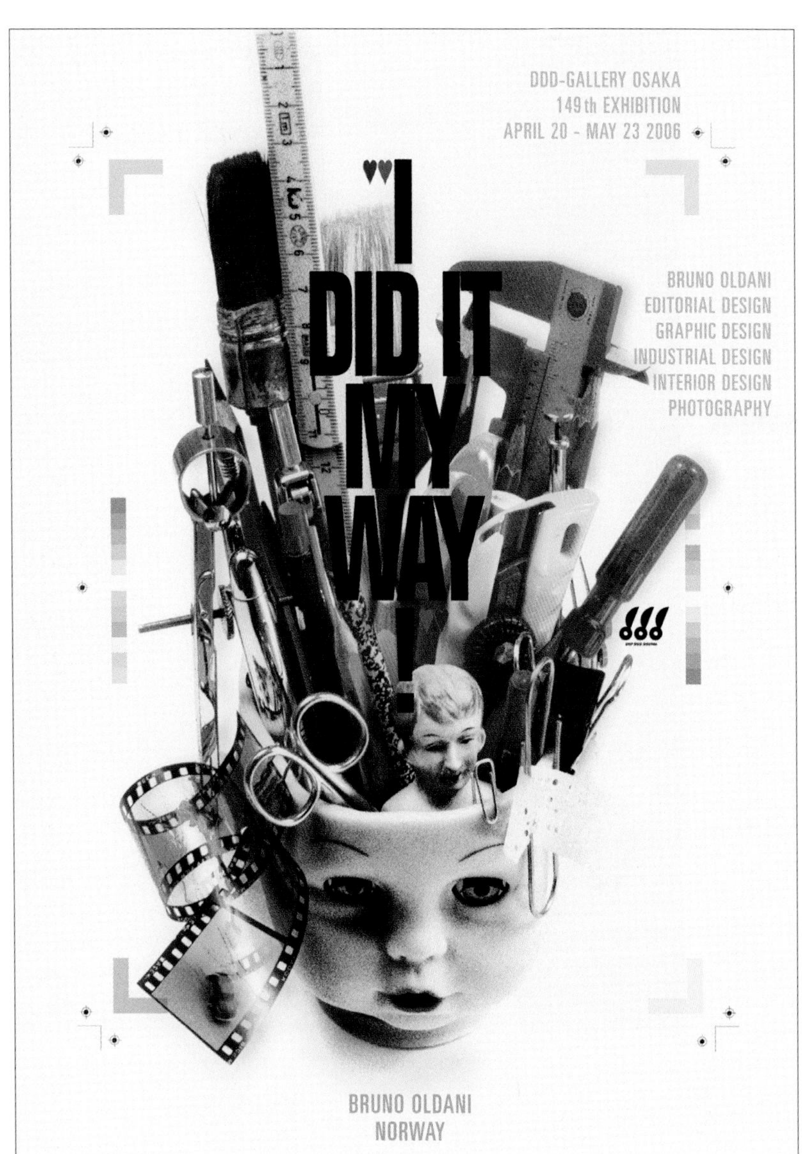

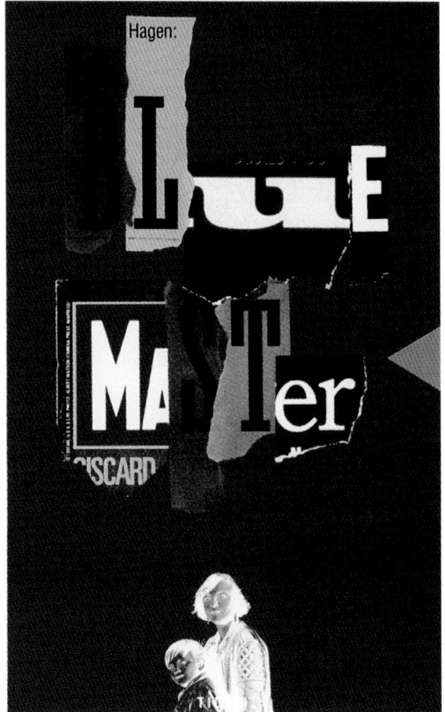

Bruno Oldani [Norway]

1936– born in Zurich, Switzerland
Admitted to AGI, 1976

After graduating from the Kunstgewerbschule in Zürich, Oldani moved to Norway in 1958. In 1965 he started Norway's first design bureau, specializing in industrial and graphic design and photography. He was a professor in graphic design and illustration at the National College of Art and Design in Oslo (1988–94). Oldani has worked within many disciplines of design. He has received, among other national and international awards, an international gold medal for ski design, many Norwegian book design awards, the Jacob prize (Norway's highest-ranking award in design) and the Classic Award from the Norwegian Design Council. Bruno Oldani plays a leading role in the Norwegian design scene, especially in graphic design. In 2005, major parts of his lifetime oeuvre were collected in a 300-page illustrated book, published in China in Chinese and English, as part of a series on international masters of design. In April–May 2006, the renowned DDD Gallery in Osaka featured 270 Oldani works, from throughout the last 40 years, in a dedicated exhibition under the musical title *I Did It My Way*. (It must have looked as good as it sounded – a glorious visual Oldani opera. – *Ben Bos*)

I Did It My Way, poster, postcard and flyer for solo exhibition at the DDD Gallery, Osaka, 2006.

Golden Pencil, trophy in steel, iron, brass, gold plate and acrylic for Kreativ Forum, an organization for art directors, graphic designers, photographers and copywriters, 1996.

Jan Hagen: *Blue Master*, book cover, Tiden Publishing, Oslo, 1990.

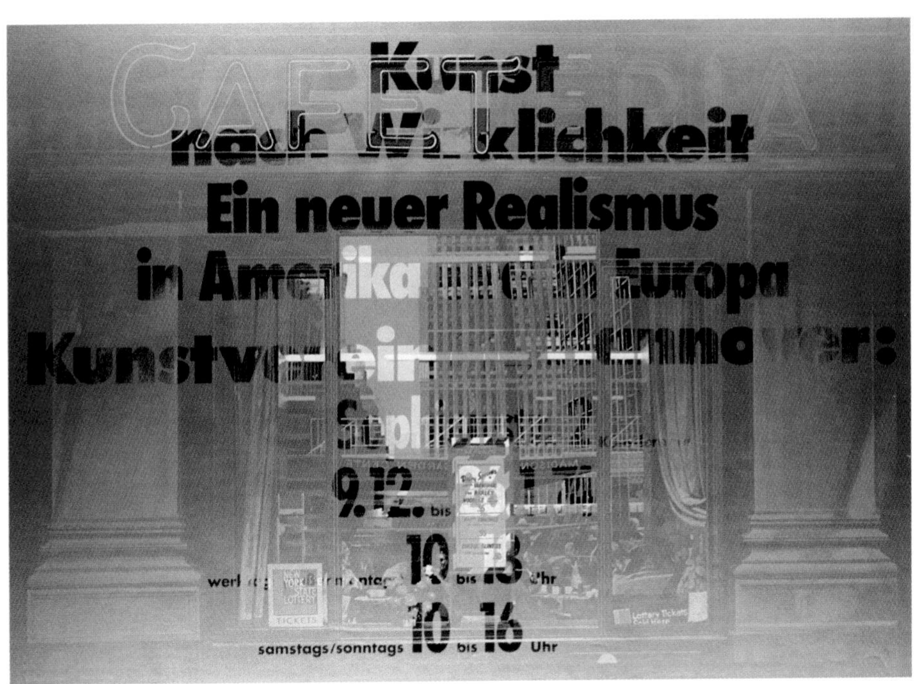

With itself, 45°, poster, limited edition of 50 copies, 1982.

Art After Reality: A New Realism, exhibition poster, 1973.

Das Neue Mainz, cover for a brochure on town planning, 1961.

Helmut Schmidt-Rhen [Germany]

1936– born in Cologne
Admitted to AGI, 1976

Schmidt Rhen worked as a bookseller before embarking on his studies in art, painting and design at the Kunstakademie in Kassel. He was art director for GGK in Basel/Switzerland (1961–65) and later of *Capital* magazine in Cologne (1967–68). He then ran his own design studio in Cologne, and since 1980 in Düsseldorf. Schmidt Rhen was appointed professor at the design department of Fachhochschule Düsseldorf in 1976, a post he held until 1993. In 1984 he co-founded the Forum Typografie.

He has received numerous national and international awards. Schmidt Rhen closed down his design studio in 1994 and moved to Hamburg, setting up Labor Visuell in 2001, which is dedicated mainly to art and painting.

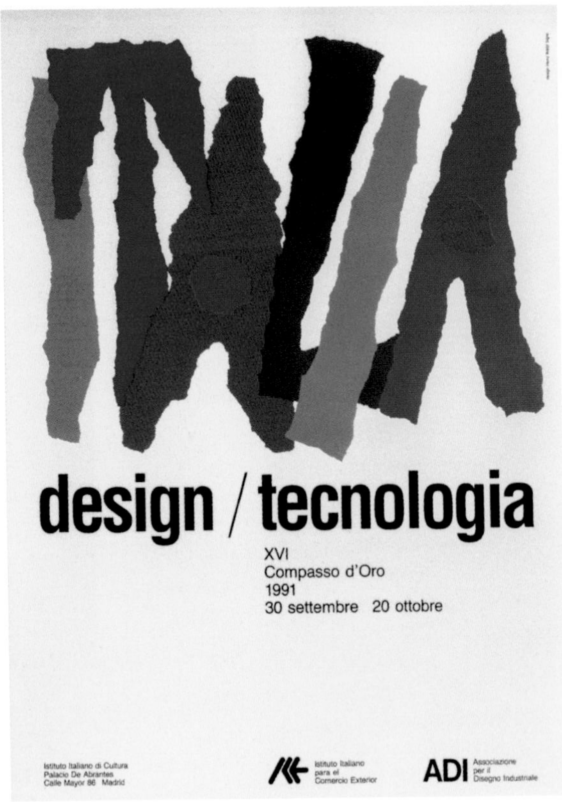

design / tecnologia
XVI
Compasso d'Oro
1991
30 settembre 20 ottobre
ADI

Heinz Waibl [Italy]

1931– born in Verona
Admitted to AGI, 1976

Degree and two-year course in architecture at Milan Polytechnic. 1950–54: apprentice and later assistant to Max Huber, with whom he starts graphic courses at the Umanitaria school in Milan (1959–63). As Huber's assistant he prepared the futuristic RAI pavilions at the Milan Fair, designed by the architect Castiglioni. He also designed posters and printed matter for RAI, Italia Nostra, La Rinascente, Atkinsons, Montecatini, Olivetti and Pirelli. Heinz joined Unimark International, Chicago (1967–71) and worked for J.C. Penney, Levi's and Transunion, among others.

After returning to Milan in 1971 he founded Signo, together with Laura Micheletto, soon gaining customers such as Cinzano, Max Meyer, Venini Venezia, Nava Milano, BTicino. He is also head of visual design at the Scuola Politecnica di Design. Became president of AGI Italy in 1994. 1980–2000: he designed the BTicino pavilions for the Intel fair (1985, 1987, 1989, 1990); a logo for the Emilia Romagna region; a poster and catalogue for the 16th Compasso d'Oro exhibition in Madrid; the pavilion and catalogue for the Compasso d'Oro/ADI exhibition in Moscow. In 1998 he created the signage and visual identity for the Civitella di Chieti Archaeological Museum, Abruzzo.

Visual identity for the **Civitella di Chieti Archaeological Museum**, Abruzzo, 1998.

Italy: Design/Technology, poster for the 16th Compasso d'Oro exhibition, Italian Cultural Institute, Madrid, 1991.

Atkinson's perfume line, product and packaging design, Milan, 1965.

Yves Saint Laurent, fashion advertisement from the magazine *Jardin des modes*, 1960s.

Observatoire International des Prisons, poster, 1992.

Tourist signs, with pictogram sign preceding a sign with the place name. French highway system, 1972.

Jean Widmer [France]

1929– born in Frauenfeld, Switzerland
Admitted to AGI, 1976

Jean Widmer studied at the Kunstgewerbeschule, in Zürich, under Johannes Itten. He arrived in Paris 1953 and studied at the École des Beaux Arts. For him functionalism took precedence over decoration, characterized by reductive design and very simple forms. From 1955–70 he worked as art director and photographer for the agency SNIP, the Galeries Lafayette department store and the fashion magazine *Jardin des Modes*. In 1960 he joined the faculty of the École Nationale Supérieure des Arts Décoratifs, where he remodelled the graphic design curriculum, stressing mastery of typography and colour as fundamental skills.

In 1970 he founded his own agency Visuel Design with his wife Nicole. His field was visual identity systems for cultural institutions and public infrastructure projects. In the early 1970s Widmer designed the first tourist signage system for French highways. He produced the identity programme for the Centre de Création Industrielle and the total identity for the Centre Pompidou, and the same for the Musée d'Orsay in the 1980s, in collaboration with Bruno Monguzzi. Next followed the Institut du Monde Arabe and in 1994 the Bibliothèque Nationale de France. Since the early 1990s he has taught at the Atelier de la Recherche Typographique. In 2001 he received the distinction of Commandeur des Arts et des Lettres.

THE TIMES

UP AND AWAY

Fashion by Prudence Glynn

I have a theory about holiday makers and holiday wardrobe planners. I believe that there are those who sweep aside the crumbs of the Christmas cake to unfold their summer travel brochures and who start thinking on Boxing Day what they will be wearing when they meet *him* in August. Then I believe that there are those who live through the spring toying with a few tentative plans but secretly convinced that the S and B (or subsequent and better) idea is just around the corner.

Suddenly it is June and other people want to *know* if and when one is going to be away. What is more, I do not think I am by any means alone in this latter category. It's not just me and a few absconding bank-cashiers who leave for Beirut at short notice. It's lots of people, and these people need clothes.

You would not think so to look at the shops. Although the posher department stores which keep cruise and swimwear all the year round usually have something to offer, the chances of finding a good selection of interesting and cheap bathing suits now is just about nil. All you will find are the much-handled, grubby and stretched leavings of more prudent holiday makers. Indeed, wait a while and you will be able to get the same items for a minimal price in the sales, a policy which I strongly advocate anyway for last minute holiday shoppers: the most careful planning in the world does not necessarily mean that a striped zoot suit which is a wow in the Costa Brava is going to be very useful for a suburban weekend. You will probably be heartily sick of stripes.

Marks and Spencer have new deliveries of bathing suits until the end of July and their value is unbeatable if you do not mind being one of a crowd. While on the subject of M and S bathing suits by the way, the reader who wrote to me about the problem of shopping when you are pear-shaped might like to know that the St. Michael brand name embraces no illusion about out national shape. The hip measurements are always on the generous side and I think she would find that the size 34" bust bikini would accommodate a 34½" bust and 37½" hips quite comfortably.

One item of holiday gear which should never be bought at the last minute is shoes. More sunshine hours have been clouded over by sore feet than ever have by sunstroke, I am certain. More views from the Acropolis at sunset have been missed for ever, more picnics cut short, because someone's feet are pinching and she cannot walk another step, than ever have by a touch of gippy tummy. Always take well-broken in shoes with you and practise wearing them over bare feet. This is particularly vital with sandals. Once your feet are blistered any pair of shoes will be painful even through sticking plaster (though take lots of sticking plaster with you anyway).

One of the pleasures of having a car with you on holiday is that you can snatch a bathe whenever a tempting beach appears. But this poses the problem of getting into and – far harder – out of your bathing suit. Fine of course if the beach is deserted or you can run to the luxury of a cabin. But for many impoverished tourists it means an unseemly struggle under a bathing towel on the sea front or, worst of all, back in the car. To peel off wet, tight bikini pants in a hot car, sitting down, I think would have taxed the ingenuity of a Houdini.

If you are going to make a regular practice of swimming en route then it is worth investing in a garment designed to facilitate changing—a sort of dressing bag. I have never actually seen one of these things on sale now that I come to think of it, but the basic principle is so simple that you can easily make one for yourself. You merely need two pieces of towelling shoulder to floor length. Dressing shifts *must* be full length. Nobody wants to know what colour your knickers are. You seam up the sides, run a cotton cord drawstring around one end of the resultant tube and there you are. If you feel ambitious you can leave openings in the side seams to put your arms out through but if you feel especially nervous of the lascivious glances of *bambelone* salesmen or the beach police do not bother. You step into your towelling tube, pull the drawstring tight around your neck and you are clad in a cloak of impenetrable respectability equal to that which those two incompetent brothers in Milton's "Comus" confidently assumed surrounded their sister.

What you do inside your dressing shift is your business. Of course you can dry yourself in it and with it, you can then sunbathe lying on it and the garment is bisexual.

On the other hand, if your off-car bathing is more in the nature of a desperate determination to get in the very first and the very last swim of the holiday before the coastline disappears for ever, Georgina Lindhart has the answer. She has designed a pair of bikini pants which un-popper down either or both sides. The poppers are the stout sort which will not come undone until you want them to and the idea is a brilliant solution to a boring scramble.

Clothes above, left to right: Baltrik culottes dress, called Kasha, in soft stretch towelling costs seven guineas, sizes 10–16, in navy, sky, cerise, old gold, white, moss green or orange. Green towelling hat with stitched brim, two guineas by Bermona • Bolero top by Baltrik, called Chopp, costs three guineas in super quality stretch towelling. Choice of lilac, white and yellow; apple green, yellow and white; melon, chocolate and beige; chocolate, melon and orange, sizes 10–16. Bikini pants from a duo called Gidding by Baltrik, which costs four guineas, colours and sizes as for bolero top. Yellow towelling beret, 32s. 6d.; navy floppy towelling hat price 2 guineas. All by Bermona • Cotton chenille velvet wide legged trousers by Baltrik, called Bardin, with a halter top in Trevira called Gai. Trousers cost seven guineas, top 50s. Sizes 10–16, in navy, moss green, turquoise, brown or gold. Yellow zipped canvas beach bag, price 69s. 11d. from all branches of Susan Handbags or from their mail order department at 5–11, Worship Street, E.C.2. • Stretch towelling jumper top with popper-up shoulders and brief shorts with popper-up sides by Georgina Lindhart. The set costs five and a half guineas, and is called Tee-Off. Sizes 10–14, in navy, green, turquoise or scarlet. Purple plastic sunspecs with protruding lenses, three guineas. Please write to The Times Fashion Department for further details and stockists' names.

Any holiday beauty routine needs to be simple and quick, particularly if there are men involved. Many a promising mixed-party romance has been nipped in the bud by the irritation of having every expedition delayed while one female member gets her face on straight. How many seeds of marital discord have been sown by the discovery on the honeymoon that an idyllic early morning swim means no breakfast until after a lengthy period of restoration? While you are laboriously pinning up your wet hair the baby will have smashed up somebody else's sand castle, the singing in the cafe will have finished and the parade will have passed by. So start by having your hair really well cut. Have it styled very simply so you can manage it yourself; if necessary have a light perm so that you will not need to take a whole salon full of hairdressing bits and pieces with you. Make sure that your mascara is water and sun-oil proof. Lipstick colours should be brown or straight pink toned. Steer clear of scarlet or blue reds which look harsh under bright skies. Lancôme have two beautiful browns, Maya and Yucatan, either of which looks fabulous on a skin which is at any stage of tan.

You can afford to be a little more exotic on holiday, so try Cyclax's gold or silver eye shadow for late-night lid-fluttering, or use the gold to stipple freckles on shoulders and upper arms —sensational on the brown skin revealed by a bare back dress.

Colour by East Midland Litho Printers Ltd., Oundle Road, Peterborough.

WORKING WOMAN

NOVEMBER £1.25

MAKING OFFICE POLITICS PAY

THE 'TINY' TROUBLES OF HOUSE OF FRASER

WHO'S LEFT HOLDING THE BABY?

CHECKING UP ON HEALTH CHECK-UPS

LIFE BEYOND THE BUSINESS SUIT

TRAVELLING ON TICK

'NEVER DILUTE YOUR IMAGE'

ANITA RODDICK
FOUNDER OF THE BODY SHOP

COMPANY PROFILE

Behind the image

Britain's major companies now package themselves as carefully as their products. But do they live up to their glossy annual reports? You may buy their shares but would you work for them? By Patience Wheatcroft

ICI

Paternalism + progress the battle continues

Jeanette Collins [UK]

1939– born in Woodford
Admitted to AGI, 1977

Jeanette Collins qualified in graphic art at the Central School for Arts and Crafts, London. 1960: she began her career as assistant to Tom Wolsey on *Town* magazine. 1962: art editor of news magazine *Topic*. 1963: worked for the Illustrated London News group of magazines, which included *Tatler* and *The Illustrated London News*. 1965: art editor of *London Life* magazine. Joined *The Times* in 1966 to art-direct the new pioneering woman's pages edited by Suzanne Puddefoot. The *'Collins-Puddefoot axis'* was described as *'the best thing in British journalism'*. Eventually art-directing the whole paper, she redesigned *The Times* in 1970.

The scale of the broadsheet pages offered a new freedom and her 12 years at *The Times* were her most creative period, during which she was able to express her life-long passion for illustration. Working with designer John Pym, she won the D&AD Silver Award for most outstanding design for a newspaper feature (1969, 1973, 1975), and the D&AD Silver Award for the most outstanding artwork for a newspaper feature (1973). She art-directed the news magazine *Now* (1979), *Working Woman* (1981); The Illustrated London News Group (1982–2000), including *The Illustrated London News*, *Orient Express* and *E&O*.

The Times Women's page, fashion feature, 1969. Won the D&AD Silver Award for the most outstanding design for a newspaper feature. Illustration by Barry Zaid.

Working Woman, magazine cover featuring Anita Roddick, founder of Body Shop, 1981. Photograph by John Carter. Illustration by Paul Allen.

Working Woman, magazine spread. One of a series of articles assessing corporations as employers of women, 1981. Illustration by Paul Allen.

نخستین نمایشگاه هنر گرافیک آسیا ـ تهران
مهر ماه ۲۵۳۷
FIRST ASIAN GRAPHIC DESIGN BIENNALE_TEHRAN
organized by: Asian Cultural Documentation Center for UNESCO, Tehran
Sep. 23 to Oct. 13, 1978
مرکز اسناد فرهنگی آسیا

Al-Khwarizmi, poster to celebrate the 1,200th anniversary of the birth of this Islamic mathematician and scholar.

First Asian Graphic Design Biennale, poster.

Morteza Momayez [Iran]

1936-2005; born in Tehran
Admitted to AGI, 1977

His friend and admirer Alain Le Quernec wrote: *'Morteza was the first Iranian AGI member. It is difficult to find a single man who had such a great influence on the creation and development of modern graphic design in his home country. Morteza studied at the Paris Decorative Arts School (1968). He had a particular interest in Swiss design, for its perfectionism, and the Polish poster school, for its innovative nature and ability to break the rules. Back in Iran, he developed these influences to create his own form of expression, Iranian culture already being rich in its illustrative traditions and calligraphy.*

He introduced modern graphic design, without losing the identity of his culture. The second face of this man was the challenge of getting graphic design recognized and taught at universities. Morteza was a leader who brought together the talents of other designers and established the Iranian Graphic Designers Society (IGDS), which is one of the strongest and best organizations of its kind worldwide. He also promoted the enthusiastic engagement of the new generation of graphic designers who were willing to be modern, creative and internationally recognized. Talent and ambition are not enough to build such a body of work. Above all, Morteza was deeply human. Without that quality he could not have succeeded.'

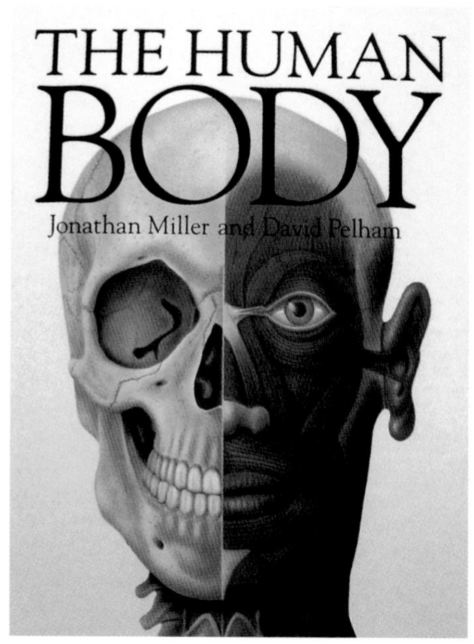

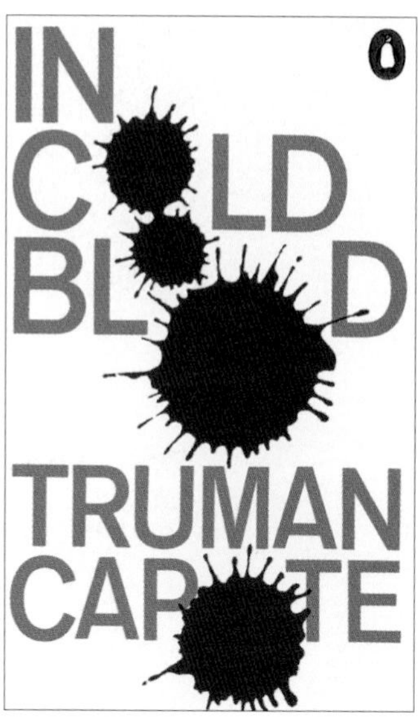

David Pelham [UK]

1938– born in Gloucestershire
Admitted to AGI, 1977

David Pelham graduated from St Martin's School of Art, London in 1958. Specializing in editorial design he went on to become art director of *Harper's Bazaar*. Later, as art director of Penguin Books, he was responsible for the new look of Penguin covers in the early 1970s. During his twelve years at Penguin he wrote and designed his award-winning bestseller *The Penguin Book of Kites* (1976).
In 1982, in collaboration with Dr Jonathan Miller, Pelham designed and co-authored *The Human Body*, the world's first seriously intentioned pop-up book, which sold almost three million copies.

During the mid-1980s Pelham created numerous pop-up books as creative director of Intervisual Books in Los Angeles. In 1989 he designed his famous *Dimensional Man*, a life-size pop-up anatomical wall chart. He is author/designer of over thirty children's books; a more recent project is a pop-up wall sculpture, *Leaf Pool*, published in an edition of 500 copies and created in collaboration with the distinguished sculptor Sir Anthony Caro. Among his many awards are three D&AD Silver Awards (1977, 1982, 1984) for the most outstanding book; the D&AD gold award (1982) for a complete book, and the gold award of the Art Director's Club, New York (1985).

Leaf Pool, folding wall-mounted card sculpture and slipcase in collaboration with Anthony Caro, 30 x 60 cm, 1996.

The Human Body, pop-up book in collaboration with Dr Jonathan Miller. First published by Jonathan Cape, 1983.

Anthony Burgess: *A Clockwork Orange*, book cover, Penguin Books, 1972.

Truman Capote: *In Cold Blood*, book cover, Penguin Books, 1970.

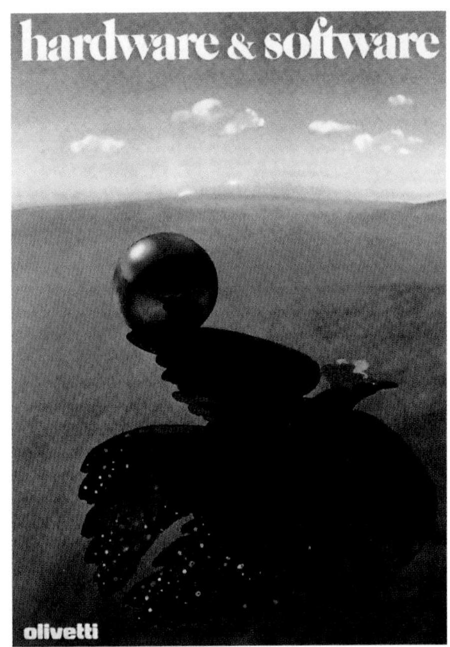

Don't Waste Energy, poster for Olivetti, 1980.

One of a series of covers for **Urbanistica magazine**. Chosen by Bonfante as his favourite piece of work in the book *First Choice* by Ken Cato.

Hardware & Software, poster for Olivetti, 1976.

Egidio Bonfante [Italy]

1922-2004; born in Treviso
Admitted to AGI, 1978

During and after his studies at the Brera Academy and the Architecture School of Milan Polytechnic, he became involved in the artistic movements of the 1940s. He was one of the signatories of the Realism Manifesto in 1946. In 1948 Adriano Olivetti appointed Bonfante as graphic designer, because he recognized that his great artistic potential could be used in many publications and exhibitions. Bonfante worked for several legendary magazines including *Urbanistica* and *Comunità*.

He was commissioned to design exhibition stands for major events including the Rome Olympics, Formula 1 championships and the Olivetti art and technology exhibitions outside Italy. He was the author of many books on painting. Later in life he himself became a painter in Treviso and Venice, the places where he grew up. He created architectural landscapes, especially churches. In 2003 the Archivo Storico Olivetti produced a catalogue for the exhibition of his work in Ivrea, which gives a very useful oversight of his work.

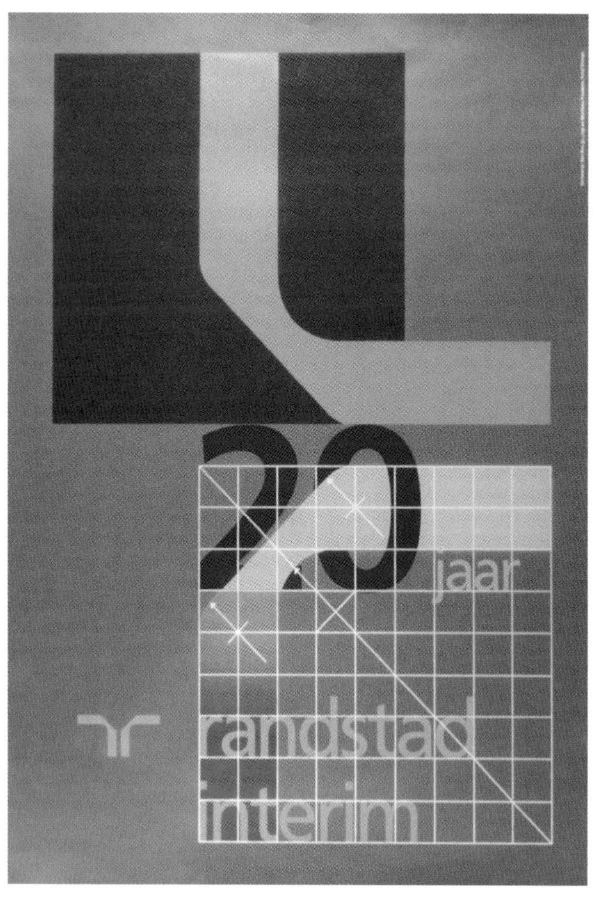

Ben Bos [The Netherlands]

1930– born in Amsterdam
Admitted to AGI, 1978

Studied at the Amsterdam Graphic College and Rietveld Academy with Wim Crouwel (1955–62). Worked for Ahrend, first as a copywriter, later as their art director. Within Total Design and 2D3D and finally as a freelancer, Ben was a designer/consultant for that firm for 50 years. Last job: creating their in-house museum. He was the first employee of Total Design in 1963, and became a creative director; he left TD after 28 years. He specialized in corporate identity. Major clients: Randstad Employment Agency (1966–97), Furness Logistics Group (1968–94), Belgian General Bank.

At his retrospective exhibition (Breda, 2000), there was a special show of more than 100 logotypes. He won several international prizes (Ljubljana, Stuttgart, Brno, and a World Logotype Award 1998). Honorary member of Dutch Designers Association BNO and Brno Biennale. Ben lectured and taught all over Europe, the US, Israel and Japan. *Eye* #59 said: *'He is a Renaissance man: designer, journalist, copywriter, photographer, studio manager, initiator and chairman of the Nederlands Archief Grafisch Ontwerpers.'* He also now paints and is the author of several books, including this AGI book (together with his wife Elly). His monograph *Design of a Lifetime* (2000) is available in Dutch and English editions.

Poster for **Randstad Interim** employment agency, Belgium, 1989. The corporate identity programme for this group dates from 1967 and is still, slightly updated, in full swing worldwide.

Invitation for the relaunch of the **Ahrend Revolt chair** (designed by Friso Kramer), 1993.

Huisstijl, cover of Ben Bos's most recent publication, a book on corporate identity and house style, 2002.

Dick Bruna [The Netherlands]

The Apple, Bruna's first published book, 1953.

Miffy the Musical, silkscreen, 2002.

Poster for railway stations to promote the Zwarte Beertjes (Black Bear) book series, 1966.

1927– born in Utrecht
Admitted to AGI, 1978

From a young age Dick had a passion for drawing. His father wanted him to become a publisher, just like himself. Visiting London and Paris, he saw paintings by artists like Picasso, Braque, Léger and Matisse. Their works made a great impression upon him. For years he illustrated paperback covers for the Zwarte Beertjes detective series, and produced posters and advertisements for books from the Bruna publishing house. Miffy the rabbit was born in 1955. Bruna always uses very simple outlines. Only the most essential part of a subject appears in his pictures. He works with pencil, brush, poster paint, scissors and glue. You will always see a thick, black line around his characters.

Dick has always used the same bright colours: red, blue, yellow, white and green – the true Bruna colours. Between 1958 and 1975 Bruna won many prizes for his posters, for the Zwarte Beertjes range among others, and for his work as an illustrator and designer. In more recent years he has also won awards for his picture books. He has designed posters for many charity organizations, including UNICEF, the Asthma Foundation, the Dutch RSPCA and the Ronald McDonald Children's Foundation. Since 2006, the world-famous Dick Bruna has his own museum in Utrecht.

Ken Cato [Australia]

1946– born in Brisbane
Admitted to AGI, 1978
International President 1997-2000

A designer with an international reputation, Ken is chairman of Cato Purnell Partners, established in Melbourne in 1970 and with offices in Sydney, Brisbane, Perth, Wellington, Buenos Aires, Barcelona, Santiago, Guadalajara, Mexico City, Singapore and representative offices in London, Mumbai, New York, Tokyo, Taipei, Dubai and Guangzhou. Cato Purnell Partners is the largest design company in the southern hemisphere. Cato's work encompasses all facets of corporate and brand management and design. His philosophy of design is dynamically holistic, providing the synergistic solutions that produce positive results.

His work has earned him an international reputation, winning numerous international and Australian design awards, and is represented in museums and galleries throughout the world. The world's largest student design conference was founded by Ken Cato in 1991. Now approaching its 17th year, AGIdeas annually attracts over 2,500 young designers from around the world. Ken was awarded the first Australian Honorary Doctorate of Design from Swinburne University (1995) and was inducted into the Hall of Fame at the inaugural Victorian Design Awards. Ken is a foundation member of the Australian Writers and Art Directors Association, a member of AIGA, Icograda, Design Institute of Australia, Australian Marketing Institute, Industrial Design Council of Australia, and Patron of the Australian Academy of Design.

Seven Network, external signage for a television broadcasting station.

T'Gallant, wine label for T'Gallant winery.

AGIdeas, still from AGIdeas presentation.

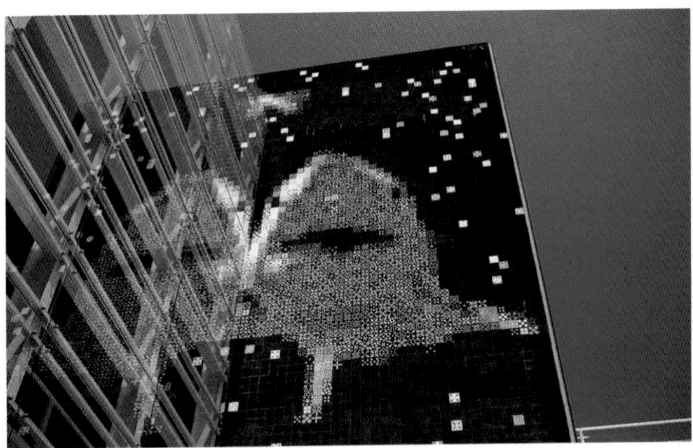

9 West 57th Street, 1972.

US Pavilion, 1967.

Lisbon Aquarium Tile Mural, 1996.

Ivan Chermayeff [USA]

1932– born in London, England
Admitted to AGI, 1978

Ivan Chermayeff studied at Harvard University, the Institute of Design in Chicago, and graduated from Yale University, School of Art and Architecture. A prolific designer, illustrator and artist, Ivan Chermayeff has a lyrical, expressive style that has resulted in iconic images for literally hundreds of clients. As a founding partner of Chermayeff & Geismar, he has played a significant role in establishing the firm's worldwide reputation. His trademarks, posters, publications and art installations for contemporary buildings are widely recognized and have received nearly every award bestowed by the profession, including gold medals from the American Institute of Graphic Arts and the Society of Illustrators. He received the Yale Arts Medal, the President's Fellow Award from the Rhode Island School of Design, and the Industrial Art Medal from the American Institute of Architects. A past president of the AIGA and member of the Art Directors Club Hall of Fame, he also was a trustee of the Museum of Modern Art for two decades and served on the board of Parsons School of Design and New School University for14 years.

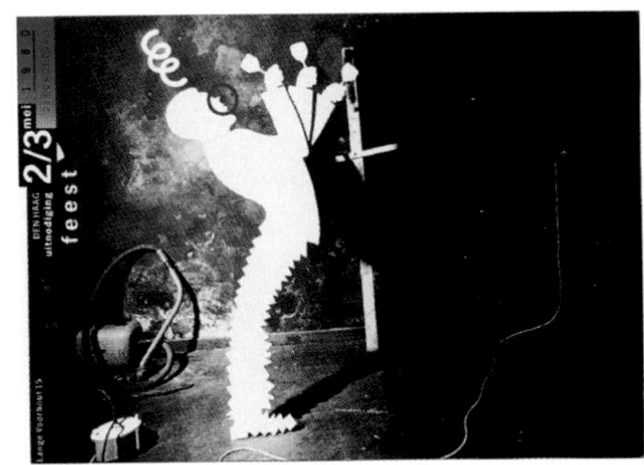

Gert Dumbar [The Netherlands]

1940– born in Jakarta, Indonesia
Admitted to AGI, 1979

Dumbar's career spans more than 30 years, and he has consistently sought to raise the standard of graphic design and visual communications, both at home and abroad. He believes graphic design derives its authority from the quality of thought that informs the deed rather than from the deed itself. He was raised in Indonesia, and the resulting dichotomy of place has impacted his views and responses to the world ever since. He studied graphic design at the Royal Academy of Fine Arts, The Hague, and concluded his studies in the postgraduate graphic design programme at the RCA, London.

Dumbar has held several academic posts, including visiting professor at the RCA, the University of Bandung, Indonesia, Cranbrook Academy of Art in Detroit, DesignLabor in Bremerhaven and the Royal Academy in The Hague. He has served on a number of influential juries, together with, among others, I. M. Pei, Alessandro Mendini, and A.R. Penck.
He has received honorary degrees from Humberside Polytechnic and Southampton Institute and is a member of the ADG Buenos Aires, the British D&AD, and the Dutch BNO. He is co-founder of the progressive Zeebelt Theatre, The Hague, a podium for experimental artistic expression.
He is a family man.

Mondriaan, exhibition poster, Haags Gemeentemuseum, 1971. Photo: Lex van Pieterson.

Dutch Design for the Public Sector, exhibition design for the Dutch Ministry of Culture, 1978. Photo: Lex van Pieterson.

Invitation card for Studio Dumbar, 1980. Photo: Lex van Pieterson.

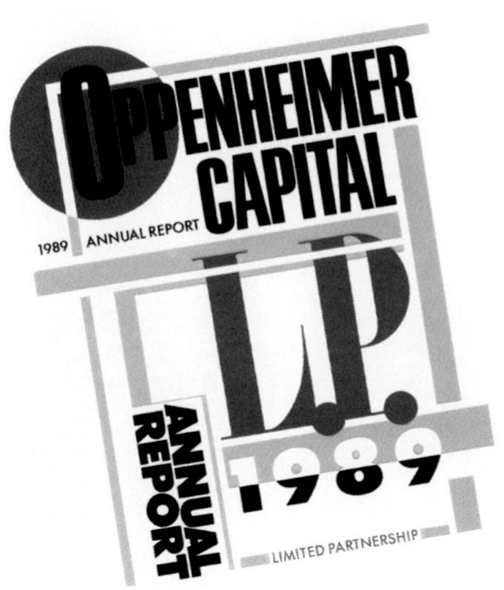

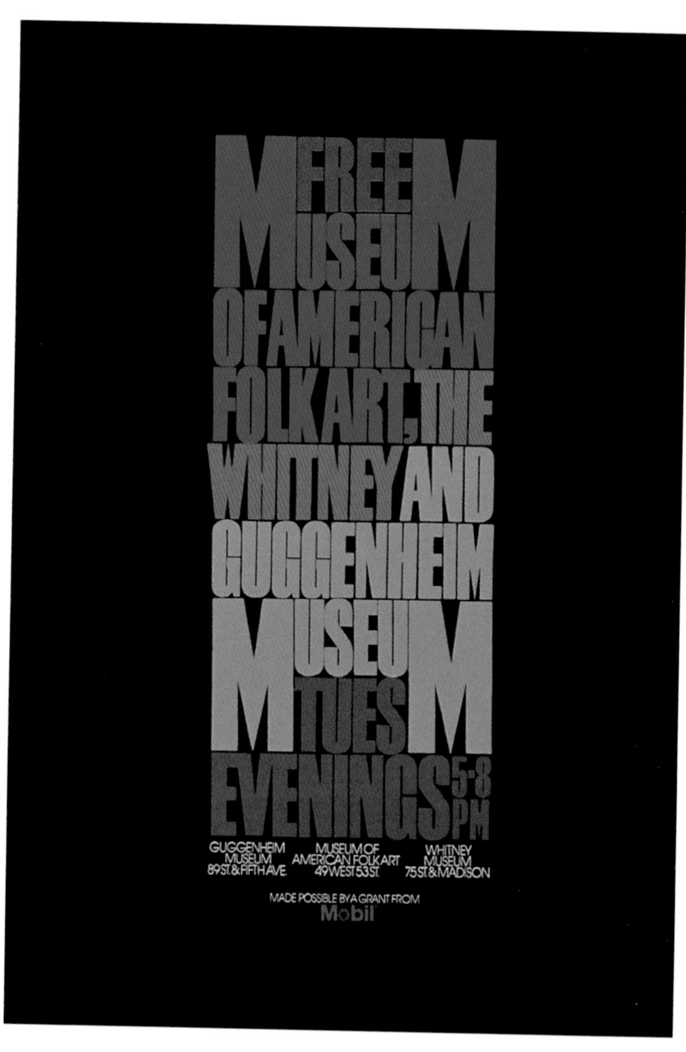

CENTER
FOR JEWISH
HISTORY

Alan Peckolick [USA]

New York Type Directors Club annual, jacket and book design.

Annual report for **Oppenheimer Capital**.

Poster for **Mobil Oil Company**.

Logo for **Center for Jewish History**.

1940– born in New York City
Admitted to AGI, 1978

Alan Peckolick has enjoyed a 35-year career as an internationally recognized graphic designer. His projects include logos, posters, packaging, annual reports, and corporate identities. Peckolick's poster for Mobil Oil hangs in the permanent collection of the Gutenberg Museum in Mainz. He has lectured internationally. A graduate of Pratt Institute, Peckolick and Herb Lubalin were partners for two decades. Peckolick's work has appeared in *Graphis*, *Art Direction*, *Idea* magazine and *Graphics Today*.

Since 1988, he has been listed in *Who's Who in America* and since 1991, in *Who's Who in Graphic Design*. In 2002, Peckolick was invited to donate his archives to New York University's Fales Library where he was the subject of a career retrospective in spring 2005. Peckolick has been painting since 1999. He has had shows in the United States and Europe, and is in numerous private collections.

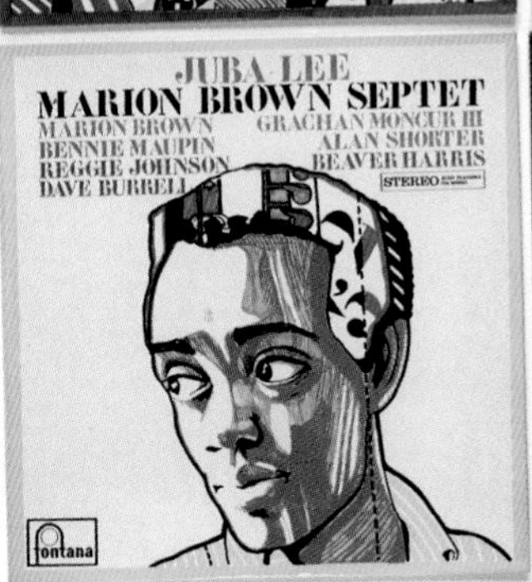

Marte Röling [The Netherlands]

1939– born in Laren
Admitted to AGI, 1978

Marte studied drawing and painting at the State Academy of Fine Arts in Amsterdam, 1956–62. One of her teachers was Professor G.V.A. Röling, her father. From the age of 19, she has held over 150 group and solo exhibitions in museums and galleries throughout Europe and the US. Her work is used in art schools and has been published widely. Her frequent appearances on TV and radio made her into a well-known figure in her own country. She works on a very wide range of projects, including huge sculptures and monumental works of art, commissioned for government buildings, or by private companies and art collectors, in all kinds of techniques. Her portraits of Queen Beatrix, Prince Claus, the Duke of Gloucester and his family, the Mayor of Amsterdam and several captains of industry, have won acclaim. Her unique style enables her to reach maximum recognition through the minimum of lines. She has designed album covers for Philips, stamps for the Dutch PTT, theatre sets and costumes, fashion, posters, videos, films, lithographs, a 50-guilder coin, paintings, and glass designs. Her works are on display in numerous public buildings and on cruise ships. She has worked in collaboration with Wanda Werner, Adrienne and Alissa Morriën, and her beloved, deeply missed Henk Jurriaans, who passed away in 2005.

Jazz album covers for Philips, 1963.

Red Cross stamps for the Dutch PTT, 1970.

Portrait of Henk Jurriaans, acrylic on linen, 2006.

Marte in Max, fashion illustration for the newspaper *Het Parool*, 1981.

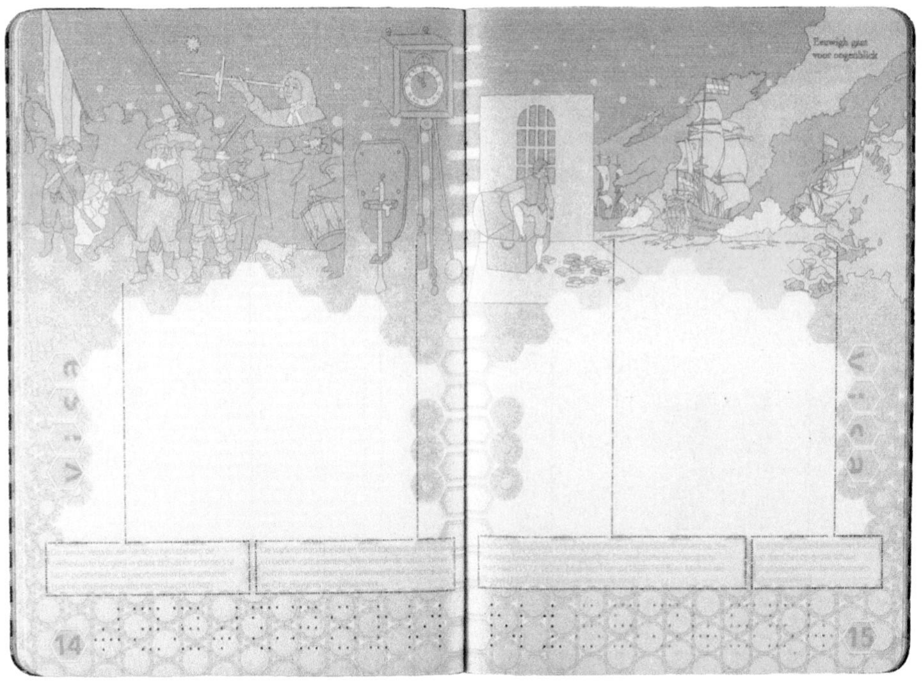

Postage stamp to commemorate **400 years of the Dutch flag**.

Dutch Constitution Law, book spread.

Design of the **Dutch national passport**, depicting the history of the Netherlands.

Jelle van der Toorn Vrijthoff [The Netherlands]

1946– born in The Hague
Admitted to AGI, 1978
International President 2006 –

1962–66: Royal Academy of Art, The Hague, graphic design and Communication (final exam cum laude; Esso Award). 1967–68: freelance graphic designer. 1969–72: further graduate study at the Royal College of Art, London, department of graphic design and communication. 1972: computer-aided design programming at the Imperial College of Science and Technology, London. 1972: science research fellowship at the Experimental Cartography Unit, London. Lecturer at the Middlesex Polytechnic, London, teaching instructional graphics. Freelance graphic designer and scientific illustrator in London. 1973: returns to the Netherlands and works with designers Gratama and De Vries, The Hague. 1976–82: creative director in the design department of the Dutch Government Printing and Publishing House. 1974–90: part-time teaching at the Royal Academy of Art in 's-Hertogenbosch, the Gerrit Rietveld Academy in Amsterdam and the Willem de Kooning Academy in Rotterdam. 1982–2002: creative director of the Total Identity Group in Amsterdam, formerly known as Total Design. His experience as a project director and design manager extends to large-scale design projects in the Netherlands, France, the Middle East and Hong Kong. After having left the Group in July 2002, he founded his own independent consultancy under the name QuinX Design Management and Consultancy.

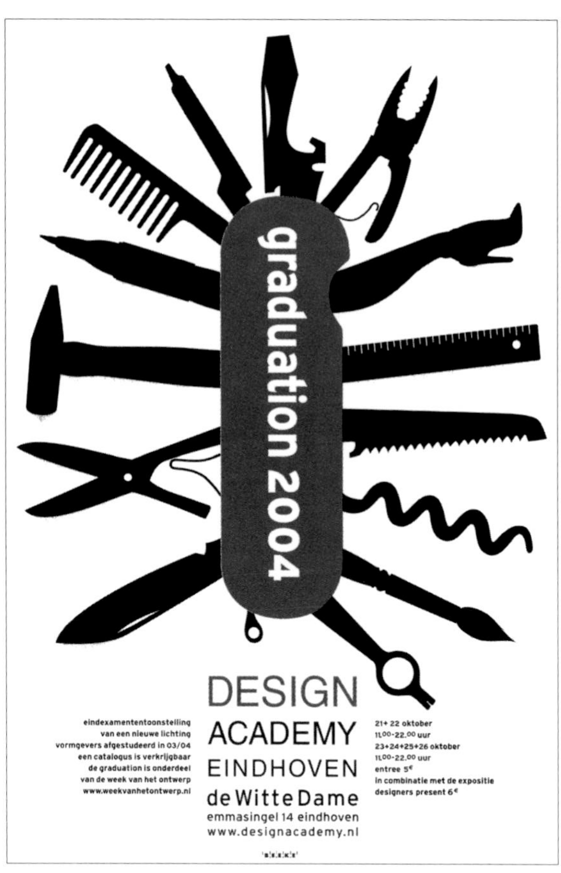

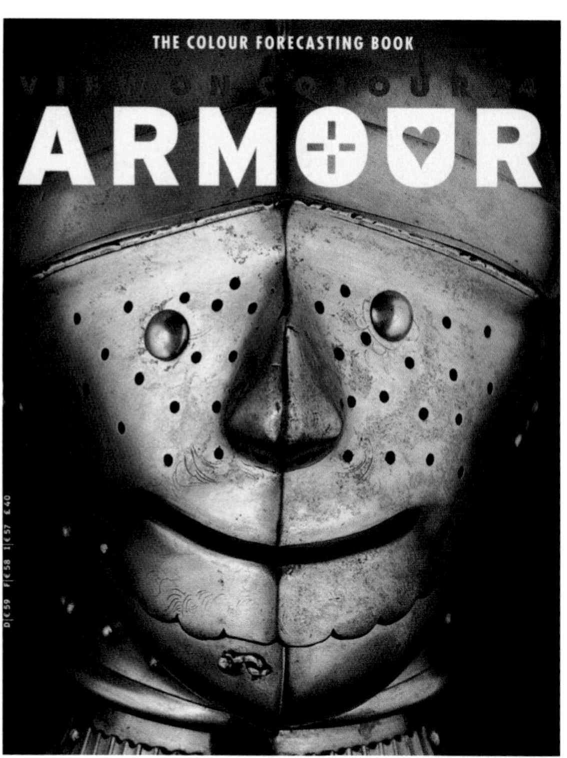

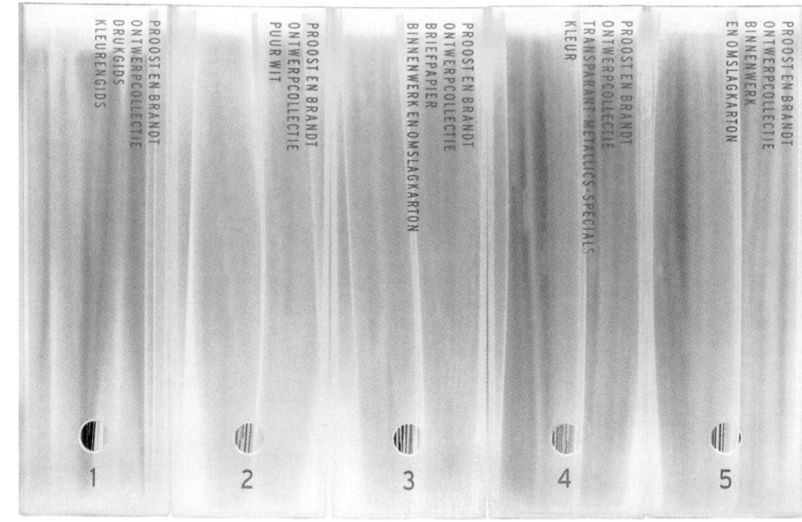

Anthon Beeke [The Netherlands]

1940– born in Amsterdam
Admitted to AGI, 1979

Anthon Beeke had no formal training. He educated himself and learned graphic design while working as an assistant to Ed Callahan, Jacques Richez and Jan van Toorn. He started up as an independent designer in 1963. In 1976 he became a partner in the well-known group Total Design in Amsterdam. In 1989 he set up his own design agency, Studio Anthon Beeke. Beeke's clients come from both the cultural and the commercial sectors. His posters are much discussed and world-famous. Beeke produces two trend-forecasting magazines on colour and horticulture together with Lidewij Edelkoort: *View on Colour* and *Bloom*.

He has several publications to his name, among them *Nude Alphabet* and *Dutch Posters 1960–1996*. He has devised exhibitions, furnished museums, designed books, magazines, house styles, logos, postage stamps, catalogues, TV commercials, packaging, children's games, ad campaigns and posters. Most of these designs have won awards one way or another. He gives lectures and workshops all over the world. He has been a member of many juries and had many exhibitions. Anthon has taught at several academies in the Netherlands and abroad. He is chief lecturer of the 'Man and Humanity' course at the Design Academy in Eindhoven.

One from a series of posters for the yearly graduation show at the **Design Academy Eindhoven**, a prestigious academy with a conceptual and project-oriented approach to industrial design education.

View on Colour magazine, which Beeke has published together with trend forecaster Lidewij Edelkoort since 1991, and for which he also provides the art direction and layout.

Design of a **paper collection for designers** for Proost en Brandt, one of the largest paper wholesalers in Holland. The classification is based on a 'tactile scale'.

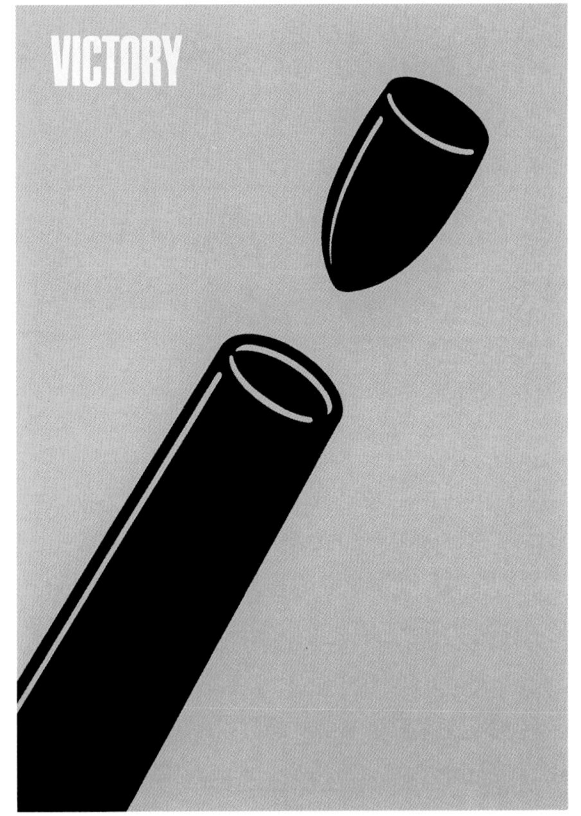

Look 1, poster, 1984.

Victory, poster, 1945.

You May Art, poster for Shigeo Fukuda solo exhibition, 1995.

Shigeo Fukuda [Japan]

1932– born in Tokyo
Admitted to AGI, 1979

Fukuda was educated at the Tokyo National University of Arts and Music in 1956 and joined Ajinomoto Co. till 1958. He then started working freelance. His most important fields of activity are graphic design and 3D design. He created the official poster for the Osaka Expo 1970, the Toyama Expo 1991, as well as the logo for the National Cultural Festival 1986. He was invited to create an international poster to commemorate the 200th anniversary of the French Revolution. Fukuda taught at the Tokyo University of Fine Arts and Music (1972–2002) and at the Graphic Department of Yale University (1982–84). He has had solo exhibitions in New York (1967), San Francisco (1987), Quimper (1991), Buenos Aires (1993), Toyama (1995), Warsaw (1995), Tokyo (1997), and China (2002, 2003, 2004). He won the gold medal at the 1972 Warsaw Poster Biennale, was inducted into the NY ADC Hall of Fame (1987), won the first prize at the 1993 Biennale of Graphic Design in Brno, the UNESCO Grand Prix in Paris (1995), and the Grand Prix at the Lahti Poster Biennial (1995). He is the president of the Japan Graphic Designers Association and a member of JADC. He was elected Royal Designer for Industry, Great Britain (1986).

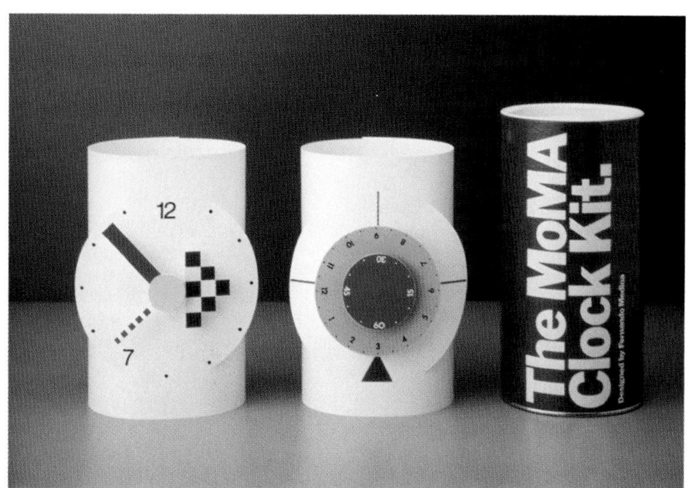

Fernando Medina [Spain]

1945– born in Cadiz
Admitted to AGI, 1979

Fernando Medina has lived and worked in Canada, Japan, the US and France, as well as in his native Spain. His many commercial clients include the CN Pavilion at EXPO 86, Vancouver; NEOCON 22, Chicago; EXPO 92, Seville; Polaroid; and Arjo Wiggins Fine Papers. For the NY MoMA he designed, exclusively, two clocks in kit form, which were sold at the MoMA Design Store for seven years. In 1995 he conceived and designed 'Paper Time', an exhibition of 50 unique clocks, each made of paper.

His most recent projects include 'Traces of Soul', an exhibition of 250 African symbols painted in black ink on crumpled sheets of white synthetic paper, and 'Snowing Ink', an exhibition of his personal musings with brush and ink on specially folded paper. He currently lives in Fontainebleau, France.

Poster for **NEOCON 22**, Chicago, 1990.

EGO R.I.P. symbol for a book cover, 2006.

The MoMA Clock Kit, designed exclusively for the Museum of Modern Art, New York, 1987.

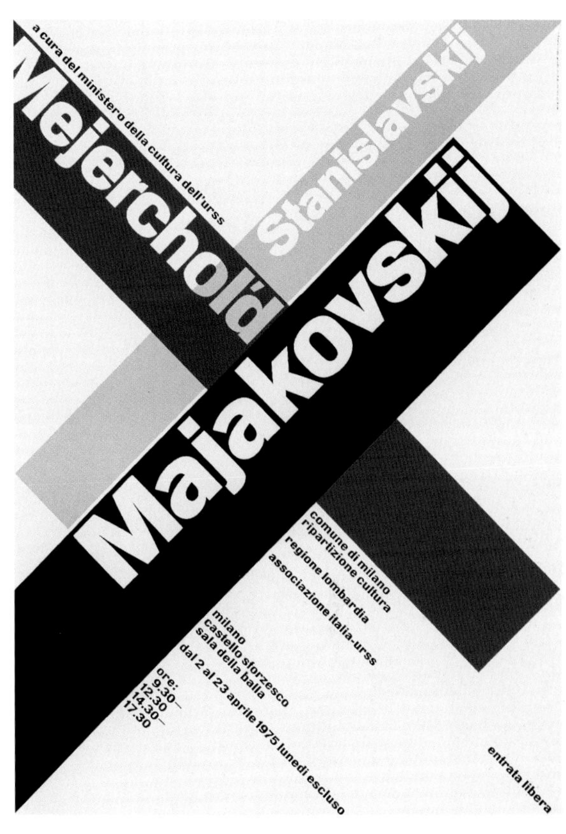

Bruno Monguzzi [Italy]

Musée d'Orsay, poster for the museum opening, 9 December 1986.

Mayakovsky, Meyerhold, Stanislavsky, exhibition poster, Castello Sforzesco, Milan, 1975.

Igor Stravinsky: ***Les Noces***, poster, Museo Cantonale d'Arte, Lugano, 1989.

1941– born in Chiasso, Switzerland
Admitted to AGI, 1979

After studying graphic design in Geneva, typography, photography and gestalt psychology in London, Bruno began his career at Studio Boggeri, Milan (1961). Moved to Montreal (1965) to design nine pavilions for Expo 67. Back in Milan (1968), he reconnected with Antonio Boggeri and collaborated on an independent basis till the closing of the studio in the early 1980s. In the early 1970s, with Anna, Boggeri's daughter, he settled in the secluded town of Meride and began his long teaching career, first in Lugano and later around the world. In Milan he began his association with Roberto Sambonet on exhibition design projects.

In 1981 Bruno was the curator and designer of the Studio Boggeri retrospective at the Milan Triennale. In 1983, in association with Visuel Design Jean Widmer, he won the competition for the signage system and identity for the Musée d'Orsay, Paris. In 1986–91 he was art consultant for *Abitare* magazine. In 1987–2004 he was the sole designer for Museo Cantonale d'Arte, Lugano. *Major exhibitions:* Villeurbanne, 1992; Zürich, 1993; Baltimore, 1999; Tokyo, 2000; Winterthur, 2001; London, 2003; Chaumont, 2006. *Awards:* Premio Bodoni, 1971; Gold Medal, NY ADC, 1990; Yusaku Kamekura Award and Gold Medal, Toyama Poster Triennial, 2000. Became a Royal Designer for Industry in 2003.

Michael Peters [UK]

1941– born in Luton
Admitted to AGI, 1979

In his work as a designer and strategist, Michael Peters has become a pioneer of the design industry, consistently emphasizing the importance of aesthetic quality applied to the highest standards of creative thinking. His name is synonymous with British design, having been at the forefront of the industry for more than 30 years. Michael studied graphic design and typography at the London College of Printing and later graduated with a masters from the School of Art and Architecture at Yale, studying under Paul Rand and Josef Albers.

In 1970 he established Michael Peters and Partners, which revolutionized the role of packaging design in the marketing of consumer products. In 1983, he led the company onto the London Stock Exchange, and by 1989 it had an annual turnover in excess of £45m, working with clients such as the BBC, British Airways and the Conservative Party. In 1990 Michael was awarded the OBE for his services to design and marketing. Two years later, he founded The Identica Partnership in London, now one of the world's leading international brand design consultancies. Major clients include Universal Studios, Johnnie Walker, National Power, Levis, Martell, Vodafone, Nike, Aeroflot and Roust Inc.

Universal Studios, corporate identity programme.

Winsor & Newton, art materials packaging design.

Johnnie Walker, brand identity.

Woods Bagot Architects 125th anniversary, promotional gift, 1993.

Entry banners for Marine Village, Sanctuary Cove Resort, Gold Coast, Queensland, 1988.

Chain of Ponds, three Italian wine varieties, 2006.

Barrie Tucker [Australia]

1937– born in Adelaide
Admitted to AGI, 1979

Although Barrie Tucker attended art school in Australia as a boy and as a teenager, he had no formal education in design. He travelled to Europe in 1966 and learnt design *'on the job'* at Reust Propaganda in Zürich. In the three years he was there, he worked on projects for Renault Suisse, Shell Chemie and Baumgartner Papier, while after hours he worked hard at illustration. Later on Barrie went to London, where he illustrated (freelance) for *The Times* and Penguin Books. Back in Australia (1970), first in Melbourne and then to his home city, Adelaide, where he set up Barrie Tucker Design, creating work for the South Australian Theatre Company.

The year 1980 brought large design commissions in the hospitality industry, including major resort development, Sanctuary Cove and two new Hilton International Hotels. However, Barrie Tucker is best known internationally for his designs for wine packaging and bottle design remains his major creative activity today. Major awards: first prize, International Cultural Section, Lahti Poster Biennial, 1987; World Star Pack Award, International Packaging Awards, 1995; 3 gold and 2 silver Clio awards for wine packaging, 1995, 1996. The exhibition 'The Design World of Barrie Tucker' took place at the Axis Gallery, Tokyo in 1991.

FOR THE LOVE OF LIFE
SUPPORT AIDS RESEARCH

Tom Geismar, USA.

80s

The 1980s: AIDS & Computers 'marching in'

Two phenomena mark this decade. HIV/Aids came as a many-headed monster, a plague that would affect the lives of millions and proved extremely difficult to combat. It took several years to develop the first Aids treatments, and these were and are far too expensive for poor countries and poor individuals. This inheritance from the 1980s would be here to stay for quite some time – if not forever.

The other keyword, albeit of a completely different nature, was computer technology. The fax machine and the word processor married with the computer were the harbingers of a changing professional practice. The design computer was still an extremely scarce commodity in the 1980s. A Dutch invention, the Aesthedes computer, was a bulky, expensive hunk of furniture, with a control panel that required long arms. Before the decade was out, it was already being seriously threatened by early versions of the Apple Macintosh, which rapidly equalled or exceeded the tricks of the Aesthedes. The term *'desktop publishing'* was attributed to Paul Brainerd, founder of the Aldus Corporation. The *'desktop'* is a metaphor for a virtual desk provided by the computer equipment. You could use it to design publications, initially on a smal scale, at a *'home'* level. Typographical tours de force were not yet possible, giving amateurish horrors all the more rein. Publishers used fairly simple layout programs. Lithography underwent major developments.

Sony introduced the Walkman. NASA launched space shuttles. Aids was diagnosed. The Mir space station became permanently inhabited. The Russian cosmonauts stayed away for seven months at a time. The *Titanic* was rediscovered. The Polish formed the protest movement Solidarity.

Gro Harlem Brundtland became the first female prime minister of Norway. Prince Charles married Diana. The UK experienced miners' strikes, hooligans and yuppies. The Eastern Block boycotted the Los Angeles Olympics. Fatal attacks on Archbishop Romero of San Salvador and the Beatle John Lennon. President Reagan and Pope John Paul II were injured in attacks, but lived to tell the tale. For an attack on a mosque in Mecca, 63 people were beheaded. General Sharon ordered slaughters in Lebanese refugee camps. In Bhopal an industrial gas leak at Dow Chemical cost the lives of 2,500 people and thousands went blind; twenty years later, fury at the disaster is still raging. 1986 saw the explosion in the Chernobyl nuclear power plant. The effects were dramatic, long term and covered a vast area. Aeroplane hijackings remained numerous. Accidents at sea and in the air affected hundreds of travellers. There were massive volcanic eruptions and earthquakes, particularly in Mexico and South America.

Meanwhile, in the world of the mighty and their peoples: Rhodesia became independent, thereafter to be known as Zimbabwe. Egypt and Israel opened the border alongside the Sinai. The Israelis invaded Lebanon. Iraq and Iran started a terrible war with enormous losses to troops.

François Mitterand became president of France. Israel destroyed an Iraqi nuclear power plant and went on to annex the Golan Heights. Egypt's president Sadat was assassinated. A state of siege in Poland. Argentina invaded the Falklands and Margaret Thatcher answered with war. Egypt regained possession of the Sinai. Helmut Kohl became the German chancellor, Daniel Ortega president of Nicaragua. Reagan began a second term of office as US president. The British and the Chinese signed an agreement for the future of Hong Kong. Reagan and Gorbachev met in Iceland. The Swedish premier Olaf Palme was murdered; the culprit will forever remain untraceable. Duvalier (Haiti) and Marcos (Philippines) were forced to leave the political stage. Corazon Aquino became president of the Philippines. After a second ballot, Kurt Waldheim became president of Austria, but his evil war record later brought him down after all. Willy Brandt retired as chairman of the SPD, Hu Yaobong as China's party leader. Gorbachev launched his *Glasnost* and *Perestroika* politics. George Bush Sr. was elected as American president. The *Voyager* probes set off to explore space. A cocaine war was raging in Colombia. A civil war broke out in Lebanon. Chinese students, protesting in Tiananmen Square, discovered that the eternal peace implied in its name did not exist for them. A major earthquake hit California.

Eastern Europe began its advance towards the end of Communist dictatorships. Protests and strikes undermined the failing power of the regimes in Prague, East Berlin, Sofia and Bucharest. The DDR leaders resigned, the Germany-to-Germany borders were opened, the Berlin Wall was smashed to pieces and sold as souvenirs. The Americans invaded Panama. The Romanian dictator Ceausescu and his wife, the inhabitants of the second largest building in the world, were executed. Gorbachev visited the Pope. Playwright Václav Havel became president of Czechoslovakia.

Euphoria in the Western world. To many, the bankruptcy of the ideologies and accompanying dictatorships in Eastern Europe felt like a hopeful beginning to world peace and prosperity. The hard, greedy, Western economic model, however, was at odds with an equally necessary improvement in North–South relationships. Religious tensions, flaring up everywhere, were to quickly form an expanding replacement for the melted East–West icebergs and the related fear and apprehension.

An international audience followed the protracted goings-on in *Dallas*, a *'role model'* of the might of Texan oil magnates. Windsurfing was a new sport. Princess Grace of Monaco suffered a fatal car crash. *Gandhi* won 8 Oscars. Spielberg produced *ET.* Madonna started her career. It was goodbye to Christopher Isherwood, Bernard Malamud, Benny Goodman, Otto Preminger, Henry Moore, Danny Kaye, Andy Warhol, Rita Hayworth, Andrés Segovia, Primo Levi and Fred Astaire.

Gae Aulenti created the magnificent Musée d'Orsay. Norman Foster built Stansted Airport and the Hong Kong & Shanghai Bank. Atlanta gained Richard Meier's High Museum, Frankfurt am Main its Museum für Völkerkunde. Germany further enriched itself with museums, such as those in Mönchen-Gladbach (Hans Hollein) and Frankfurt (Ungers: the Architecture Museum). In Paris, Bernard Tschumi and Adrien Fainsilber worked on the great scientific and cultural project, La Villette. Jean Nouvel built its Institute Arabe, Paul Chemetov executed the largely underground project Les Halles. Venturi, Rauch & Scott worked on London's National Gallery. A fatwa was issued, condemning writer Salman Rushdie and declaring him an outlaw. Athlete Ben Johnson (Canada), world record holder for sprinting, admitted to taking drugs and lost his record and medals. Issey Miyake was much talked about, as were Versace and Paul Smith. The miniskirt was back. The streets were full of colourful mohican hairdos. Comme des Garçons and Ralph Lauren's Country Style appeared on the catwalks.

Graphic designers stood by and watched, going with the flow and sometimes making a highly concerned comment.

Ben Bos, Amsterdam, 2006

AGI History in the 1980s

New Waves Violating Old Rules

Ben Bos, Amsterdam, 2006

AGI congress in Alpbach (Austria) in 1989.
Creative assignment: head-gear (produced on the spot).
Bruno Monguzzi (photo James Cross).

Although Munich was the host city of the 1980 AGI meeting, the informal meetings were held in the little village of Isening, in the countryside outside the metropolis. Rolf Müller was the organizer and his achievements were commendable. The main dish on the menu was the personal presentation without words with, as *'non-speakers'*, Shigeo Fukuda, Franco Grignani, Marte Röling, Arnold Schwartzman and Anton Stankowski. The advantage of these performances was that work had to speak for itself in the absence of the usual ex-Babylonian exercises from word-wizard Henrion. This form was often repeated in subsequent years. Arnold turned it into a small-scale life story, to the accompaniment of music.

Fukuda's slides portrayed him clearly, with all his crazy, inventive ideas. Grignani and Stankowski made it plain how many wonderful things a long career in our profession can generate. Marte stole the show: her *'flying team'* had rushed over from Holland in one night and built up a battery of multimedia equipment in the arena of the congress complex in the blink of an eye – she gave her astonishing presentation – and the *'helpers'* took everything down again just as quickly and rushed off home again, leaving everyone utterly astounded. There was a prefab exhibition set-up, where all the members could exhibit the works they had brought with them. And a new ingredient was added to the congress recipe: the members were required to produce an instant piece of work. Masks were the chosen theme for this première. On the spot, often with a hand from Günther Kieser, the designers *'constructed'* their own mask, which was captured on Polaroid, later to be seen again in *Graphis*. That was a wonderfully inspiring event in itself.

1981: back together in Prague. With Russian occupiers still in the oppressed city and an economy plagued by the strictly controlled borders, hosting the AGI congress in the beautiful, but dejected city was a major feat for our Czech friends, under the direction of Stanislav Kovár. Despite the oppression, the congress participants were able to see the rich cultural treasures from better times. Baroque architecture galore, ecclesiastical grandeur, gothic, Prague Castle with its museum full of fantastic antiques. The walkway to the old Jewish cemetery in the middle of the city took on the fleeting ambiance of dark skies and a heavy rain shower. There was an excursion to a Museum of the Book, which was some way away; the coach was not allowed to go faster than 70 km/h and no amount of promises on our behalf to pay any speeding fines fell on deaf ears. Yet more baroque in a little church designed by the famous architect Jan Santini. That year's silent slide-shows came from Heather Cooper, Ernst Roch, Richard Hess and me. In general, they were about more than just design. Herb Lubalin had died in the spring of 1981 and was remembered warmly.

At the end of the congress, there was a big surprise: Josef Svoboda of the *'Laterna Magika'* and his unbelievable theatrical techniques finally appeared from the wings. None of the foreigners had ever had a chance to meet him. Worse still, some people thought he didn't exist and was merely one of his own magical creations! Walter Allner called out: *'So he is real!'* That evening we were treated to a visit to his enchanted theatre and a glass of his wine. Wine, real Pilsner, and lots of rich food in dark cellars are among our recollections of Prague, except in those cases where these were enjoyed to the point where there were those who have no idea how they got back to the hotel, let alone how we managed to leave Prague in good health.

This was the decade of seminars. Paris 1981: an audience of 350 (80 percent students) from 20 design schools listened attentively to Paul Davis and Saul Bass (USA), Alan Fletcher and FHK Henrion (UK) and Shigeo Fukuda (Japan), leaving a varied impression of our many-faceted profession. A year later, it was Paris's turn again. This time, the École Supérieure des Arts Graphiques was the venue. Otl Aicher (Germany), Adrian Frutiger (Switzerland), Seymour Chwast (USA) and Bruno Monguzzi (Switzerland) performed under Henrion's direction.

In 1982, the AGI congress was held in Montreal. Prior to the event, 500 students in Toronto saw and heard a string of prominent AGI members over the space of three days, organized by Robert Burns (Canada), in collaboration with York University. James Cross, Wim Crouwel, Alan Fletcher, Shigeo Fukuda, Henrion, Richard Hess, Woody Pirtle, Henry Steiner, Massimo Vignelli, Jim Donoahue, Rolf Harder and Burton Kramer lectured on design. The Montreal congress was the excellent handiwork of Rolf Harder, Ernst Roch and Jean Morin. The 'slides without words' were presented this time by Walter Allner (*'from Bauhaus to Fortune'*), Fukuda (with Kabuki theatre masks) and Rolf Müller, who took us on a virtual trip to his studio in Munich. There was a coach tour through Montreal, with a visit to the Olympic sites, and a champagne *déjeuner sur l'herbe* in the garden of the National Museum, laid on by the city. Everyone signed the guest book. The AGI poster show hung in the lobby of Place Ville-Marie. The collection, old and new and from half the world, inspired Rudi de Harak's *AGI Poster Book 1960–1985*, published in 1986. The National Film Board of Canada showed films and Gunter Rambow projected posters by Rambow, Lienemeyer and Van de Sand.

In 1983, AGI, Icograda and the Amsterdam Gerrit Rietveld Academy cooperated in a huge seminar. Again a full house of 500 students, listening to heavy discussions on form and content. On the stage were greats from design education: Jurriaan Schrofer, Wim Crouwel, Jan van Toorn, Ootje Oxenaar, Anthon Beeke and Simon den Hartog (The Netherlands), flanked by the great Swiss innovator Wolfgang Weingart, the German Gunter Rambow and the Pole Waldemar Swierzy. These teachers' objectives and ideals often differed dramatically. Where, with Crouwel, the emphasis was on exact

1980: AGI congress in Munich.

Saul Bass.

Ulla Fleckhaus.

Evelyn Schwarz.

'The creative assignment' to make masks (instantly) yielded some wonderful results. Photographed by a king-size Polaroid camera, these masks were presented in *Graphis* magazine 214.

1981: AGI congress in Prague.

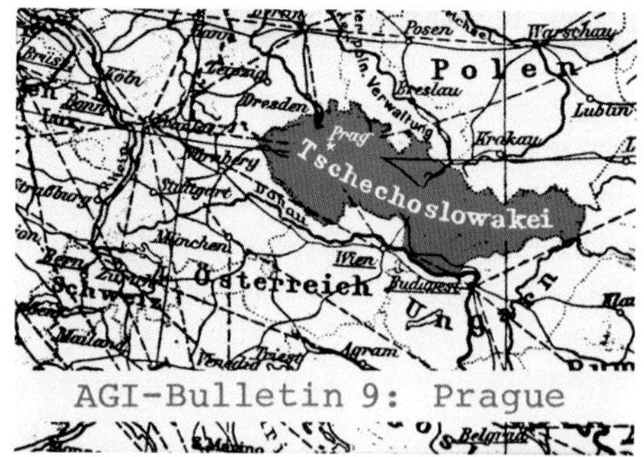

Ben Bos with congress organizer Stanislav Kovár.

1982: AGI congress and student seminar in Montreal/Toronto.

Fukuda in one of his many disguises.

Programme of the Toronto AGI Student Seminar.

On the steps of Montreal city hall...

designing (developing skills, theory and general knowledge), Van Toorn attached the greatest importance to the social context of working in this profession. They did, however, agree about the responsibility of the designer. Rambow felt it is the designer's task to discover forms of *'Utopian hope'*. At the conclusion of the discussion, Van Toorn made it clear that it is important to listen to people with a different view. It is then up to the student to make his or her own decisions. Beeke focused on the process, which is more important while studying than the presented result. Oxenaar was anxious that technology should not get in the way of creativity. On the other hand, there is no reason to fear new techniques, which provide a vast source of surprises. Schrofer stressed the generous dose of intellect the discipline demands: *'A designer must be an Uomo Universale'*.

Gargonza welcomed AGI '84 in the early spring. The members and their guests gathered in a 13th-century castle village on a hilltop in the magnificent Tuscan countryside. Alan Fletcher was now Chairman. Unfortunately, the capacity of the construction was insufficient to accommodate the numerous delegates and some had to repair to hotels in Arezzo, which was no hardship, incidentally. The Belgian artist Benoît Jacques made a drawn report, which was later published as a souvenir sketchbook, with the support of a number of sponsors, including Pentagram. Milton Glaser confessed to the many *'quotes'* in his work; elaborations on the exemplary work and ideas of great predecessors. Gert Dumbar showed his studio's work. Hans Hillmann, Waldemar Swierzy, Heinz Waibl and Massimo Vignelli gave presentations. The *'compulsory contribution'* to this congress was a self-concocted flag. These were hung in the *'knights' hall'*, plentiful, colourful and quite lovely to behold, and were auctioned off at the end. I did not really agree with the F.C. Barcelona club flag – after all, that was not a true AGI design. Olivetti sponsored a wonderful little book, *12 grafici dell'AGI*.

Alisal was the name of the Californian ranch where AGI pitched its annual camp in 1985. The nearest neighbour was none other than Ronald Reagan! The starting shot was fired beforehand in LA, where the local branch of the AIGA provided us with a seafood dinner. A reception at the Temporary Contemporary Museum, where the AGI projected its works of art over the heads of the 300-strong audience, concluded the opening evening. Many of the participants used the following day to travel through the lovely county of Santa Barbara to Alisal. The real work began with Woody Pirtle's slide show on the lifestyles and work of US AGI members. Over the days that followed, there were talks by Schwartzman, Federico, Wolf, Medina, Blechman, Pla-Narbona, Geissbuhler, Peters and Henrion. The exhibitions were of the posters from the Napoli 99 projects and the self-portraits requested specially for the occasion. Participants were challenged to sketch each other during their stay at the ranch. All this was washed down with a great variety of Californian wines and Mexican cocktails and accompanied by barbecue and chilli dinners and plenty of loud folk music!

One of the breakfasts was only accessible if you climbed on a horse and trudged through the hills to the campfire. I had just discovered that getting older means there are things you resolve never to attempt. Like learning Finnish, taking cello lessons or even going horse riding. After signing a document declaring that I would not sue anybody if the horse threw me, driven by hunger I plucked up the courage for the ride there and back again. And at my time of life, that is the end of it. Oh, and I almost forgot, during our warm welcome at Saul and Elaine Bass's studio, the car Jelle and I had hired was stolen. The LA police helped us get a new one within the hour. During the congress we sketched each other. The harvest was presented in a nice little booklet.

1986 was the year of frequent plane hijacks and the enormous ecological drama of Chernobyl. The destructive nuclear rains also washed away numerous US tickets to AGI Holland; there were some 40 no-shows! Amsterdam's Stedelijk Museum devoted a small honorary exhibition to Willem Sandberg, who had died in 1984. It was there that the starting shot was fired for that year's congress. We were transported in a steamboat that had once belonged to Queen Wilhelmina to Weesp, where the mayor and the fanfare were awaiting us on a red carpet leading to the big Marte Röling & Co. studio, for a candle-lit Indonesian meal and piano accompaniment from maestro Louis van Dijk. The nocturnal trip to a hotel in Oosterbeek. The Kröller-Müller Museum, with its vast sculpture garden and the nearby monumental St Hubertus

Admitted 1980:
Benguiat, ed
Bonnell, bill •*
Frutiger, adrian
Geissbuhler, steff
Goffin, josse •*
Gonda, tomás
Ljorring, flemming
Mendell, pierre
Pirtle, woody
Steiner, henry
Winkler, dietmar •*
Zapf, hermann

Admitted 1981:
Blackburn, bruce •
Castellano, mimmo
Flejšar, josef
Igarashi, takenobu
Jonsson, dan
Lupi, italo
Milani, armando
Pfund, roger
Rajlich, jan sr.
Rostoka, vladislav •*
Sura, jaroslav •
Ziegler, zdenek

Admitted 1982:
Reinhard, edgar
Vardimon, yarom

Admitted 1983:
Cooper, muriel

Admitted 1984:
Katsui, mitsuo

Admitted 1985:
Cerri, pierluigi •
Greiman, april
Nakamura, makoto
Sussman, deborah

Admitted 1986:
Aeschlimann, roland
McCoy, katherine
Robert, jean
Vanderbyl, michael
Wurman, richard saul •*

Admitted 1987:
Asaba, katsumi
Bernard, pierre
Ishioka, eiko
Okamoto, shigeo •*
Paris-Clavel, gérard •*
Pedersen, b. martin

Admitted 1988:
Aoba, masuteru
Brookes, peter
Gassner, christof
Loesch, uwe
Matsunaga, shin
Pericoli, tullio •*
Pospischil, hans-georg •
Sato, koichi
Scarfe, gerald •
Schmid, helmut
Smitshuijzen, edo

Admitted 1989:
Bierut, michael
Jeker, werner
Jordan, alexander
Knapp, peter
Le Quernec, alain
Mari, enzo
Troxler, niklaus

• *no work submitted*
* *no longer member of AGI*

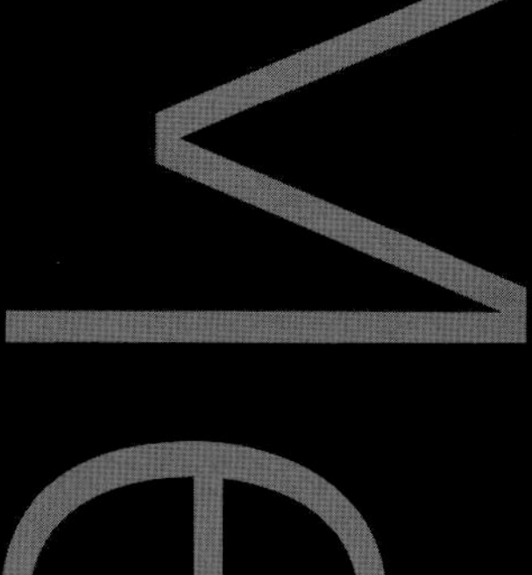
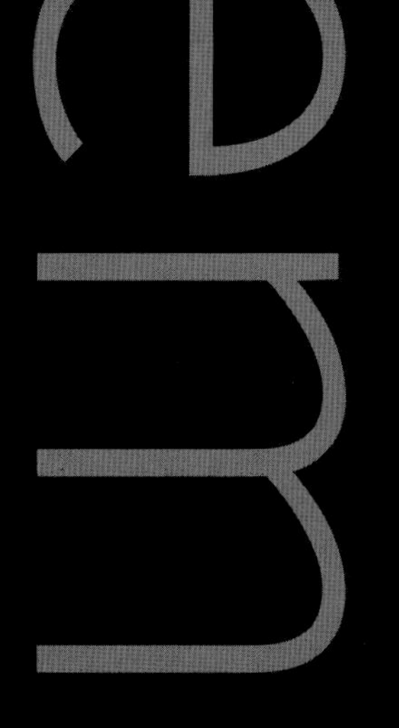
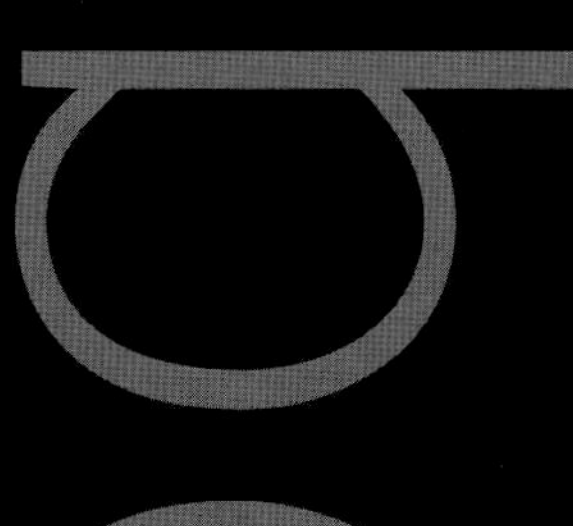
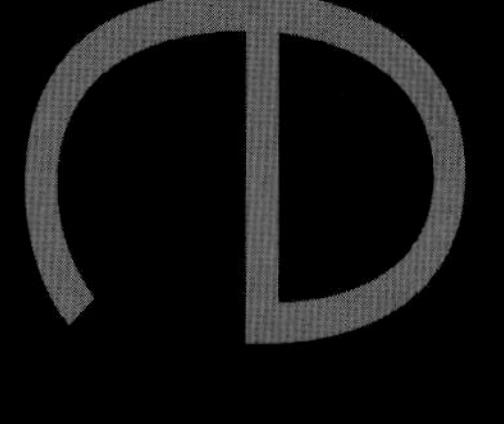

Ed Benguiat [USA]

1927– born in New York City
Admitted to AGI, 1980

Ed Benguiat is a type designer and calligrapher who studied at Columbia University and the Workshop School of Advertising, New York.
In 1953 he was appointed associate director of *Esquire* magazine. In 1962 he became a typographic design director of *Photo-Lettering*, a position he held for decades. He joined ITC International Typeface Corporation and was made a vice-president. With Herb Lubalin he worked on the in-house magazine *U&LC*. He has created many logotypes for leading publications: *The New York Times*, *Playboy*, *Esquire*, *Look*, *Readers' Digest* and *Sports Illustrated*.

He was a long-time teacher at the School of Visual Arts, NY, and he also taught at Columbia University. Among the several hundred typefaces which he (partly co-) designed are: Souvenir, Avant Garde Gothic Condensed, Korinna, Tiffany, Bauhaus, Bookman, Benguiat, Barcelona, Modern, Caslon, Panache, Century Handtooled, Cheltenham Handtooled, Garamond Handtooled, Edwardian Script. Most of these typefaces are part of the ITC Collection.

The Uses of Typefaces, poster, 1985.

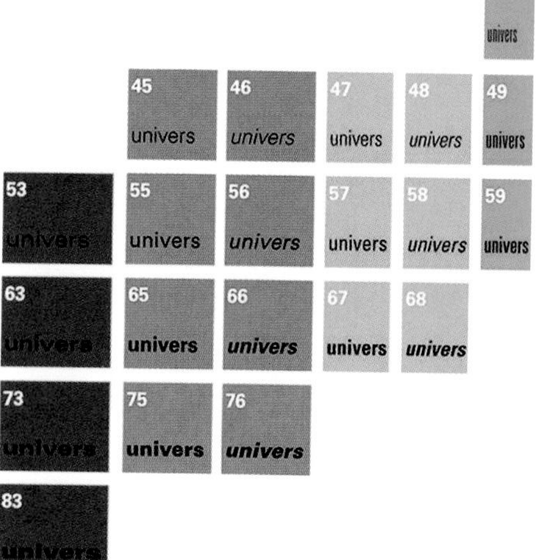

Univers, typeface, 1957.

Adrian Frutiger [Switzerland]

1928– born in Interlaken
Admitted to AGI, 1980

Adrian Frutiger needed know-how and meticulous skill to attain the crucial knowledge that legibility and beauty are brothers. *'Reserved'* type design will not be recognized as such immediately, but will be subconsciously realized by the reader. Good type brings the spirit of the author and the reader closer together. In this Frutiger found his life's goal.
'The students of 1968 left the craft aside in their impatience and tried to solve problems using only their intelligence. I myself couldn't manage with the word alone, without hands and tools.'

He is fascinated by the simplification of signs, symbols and characters: signature expressions, trademarks, sounds, images. He began his career working with lead type, then was confronted by the evolution of printing techniques and the revolutions in type production created by light and electronics. Assignments to create the signage for airports and the Paris Metro gave him experience of legibility in all type sizes. Frutiger then got involved in Indian scripts and discovered the underlying connections of Indo-European culture. He could only try to convey the western experience of 500 years of type and printing techniques and leave the further implementation to his professional friends in India.

Steff Geissbuhler [USA]

1942-born in Zofingen, Switzerland
Admitted to AGI, 1980

Steff Geissbuhler is among America's most celebrated designers of integrated brand and corporate identity programmes. His work also includes posters, brochures, books and illustrations. He has designed architectural graphics and sign systems for various institutions, environmental graphics and exhibitions. Geissbuhler's work has been honoured with the American Institute of Graphic Arts Medal for his sustained contribution to design excellence and the development of the profession. He is also the recipient of the US Federal Achievement Design Award, and several awards from Art Directors Clubs and International Poster Biennales.

He served as the US president of the AGI and has been a member of the board of the American Institute of Graphic Arts. He is also past president of AIGA's New York chapter. Steff Geissbuhler received his diploma in graphic design from the School of Art and Design, Basel, Switzerland in 1964. He has taught at the Philadelphia College of Art, Cooper Union, Yale University, and also lectures throughout the country. Prior to forming C&G Partners in 2005, he was at Geigy Pharmaceuticals, Basel; Murphy Levy Wurman Architects, Philadelphia; Anspach Grossman Portugal, New York, and a partner and principal at Chermayeff & Geismar Inc. for more than 30 years.

AIGA Competitions and Exhibitions. Promotional poster for the American Institute of Graphic Arts.

Alvin Ailey Dance Theater, poster. 25th anniversary tour and new brand identity.

NBC, logo. Complete brand identity programme for parent network company, divisions, stations and affiliates.

Lufthansa. Gonda's work for the airline, from the early 1960s on, placed him at the forefront of comprehensive corporate identity programmes for a globalized planet.

Ng3, Argentina, 1960. One of a series of guides Gonda designed for machinery and equipment, regardless of the primitive state of printing reproduction in Argentina at that time.

Foto Grafika, Hungary, 1946. A hand-made ad for a photo design firm.

Tomás Gonda [USA]

1926-2005; born in Budapest, Hungary
Admitted to AGI, 1980

An immensely dedicated and complex figure, Tomás Gonda's peripatetic life involved him in the formulation of design on a global scale. Born in 1926, Gonda spent his early years in Hungary and after the war in Argentina. As he matured, with years spent in Ulm, Milan and New York, together with his ongoing fascination with Asia, these many influences evolved into a diverse and engaging body of work at the forefront of design innovation. Tomás Gonda is credited with a major role in the critical establishment of graphic design in Argentina and important contributions to the Ulm School of Design in Germany.

His teaching programmes at Ulm and in the US at Carnegie Mellon University and Ohio State University were equally notable. Gonda was an important, though under-recognized, influence in late 20th-century design. Simultaneously, Gonda produced a substantial body of fine art, which informed, and was informed by, his design interests and became an outlet for his ruminations on the minimal nuances of colour, light and form. Tomás Gonda died in New York in 1988.

(Written by Philip Meggs before he too passed away.)

Flemming Ljorring [Denmark]

1939– born in Copenhagen
Admitted to AGI, 1980

Henrion wrote of him:
'He was trained as a lithographer in Copenhagen from 1956–60. He then worked as a layout artist in Sweden. Afterwards he studied creative design at Den Grafiske Hojskole in Copenhagen. In 1964, he opened his own studio, specializing in graphic design, photography, book design, typography, packaging and interior design.'
He is a past president of Icograda (1977–79).

Advertisement for menswear. A bold symphony of abstract and kinetic textures make up a tie and shirt.

All Men Are Equal Before God, anti-racism poster, 1995.

Toleranz, pro-tolerance poster, 2002.

Japanese Posters 1960 to Today, exhibition poster, 1989. Die Neue Sammlung, Munich.

Pierre Mendell [Germany]

1929– born in Essen
Admitted to AGI, 1980

Pierre Mendell studied graphic design with Armin Hofmann at the College for Design in Basel, and founded the Studio Mendell & Oberer in Munich with Klaus Oberer in 1961. He founded the Pierre Mendell Design Studio in January 2000. Mendell has been awarded the Gold Medal from the Art Directors Club Germany, the Gold Medal from the Art Directors Club New York, Best German Poster, Grand Prix Internationale de l'Affiche, Paris, City of Munich Design Prize, Corporate Design Prize, Forum of Industrial Design, Hanover, German Poster Grand Prix, first prize at the International Triennial of Stage Posters, Sofia, and first prize at the International Biennial of Theatre Posters, Rzeszów. His work has been exhibited in Munich, Berlin, Güstrow, Milan, Warsaw, Istanbul, Buenos Aires, Mexico City, New York and Osaka, and is represented in the graphic design collection of the NY MoMA. The exhibition 'L'art pour l'art, Pierre Mendell, Design for Cultural Institutions' was sponsored by the Goethe Institute and has been shown around the world. Pierre Mendell taught from 1987 to 1996 at the Yale University Summer Design Programme in Brissago, Switzerland. He is an Honorary Royal Designer for Industry of the Royal Society of Arts, London.

Woody Pirtle [USA]

1944– born in Corsicana, Texas
Admitted to AGI, 1980

In 1978 Woody established Pirtle Design in Dallas. Over the next 10 years the firm produced some of the most important and celebrated work of the decade, for a broad spectrum of clients. In 1988 Pirtle Design merged with Pentagram. For almost 20 years Woody was a partner in their New York office working on some of the firm's most prestigious projects. In 2005 he left Pentagram to re-establish Pirtle Design. Recent projects include: identity and website redevelopment for the international law firm Wachtell Lipton Rosen & Katz; identity and/or signage programmes for: the American Folk Art Museum, Virginia Museum of Fine Art, Brooklyn Ballet, Rizzoli International, Callaway Golf, Amnesty International, Hudson Valley Preservation Commission, international publisher Graphis, and design development of architectural and graphic components for the William Stafford Centre in Portland, Oregon. Woody's work has been exhibited worldwide and is in the permanent collections of NY MoMA and the Cooper-Hewitt Museum, Victoria & Albert Museum in London, Die Neue Sammlung in Munich, and Zürich Poster Museum. He has taught at the School of Visual Arts, lectured extensively, and has served on both the Texas and National boards of the AIGA. In 2003 he was awarded the AIGA Medal for his contribution to the design profession.

UCLA Summer Sessions 1989, poster and catalogue cover.

Hot Seat, poster for a chilli cook-off at Knoll International's Dallas showroom to celebrate the introduction of a new line of seating.

Mr and Mrs Aubrey Hair, personal logotype.

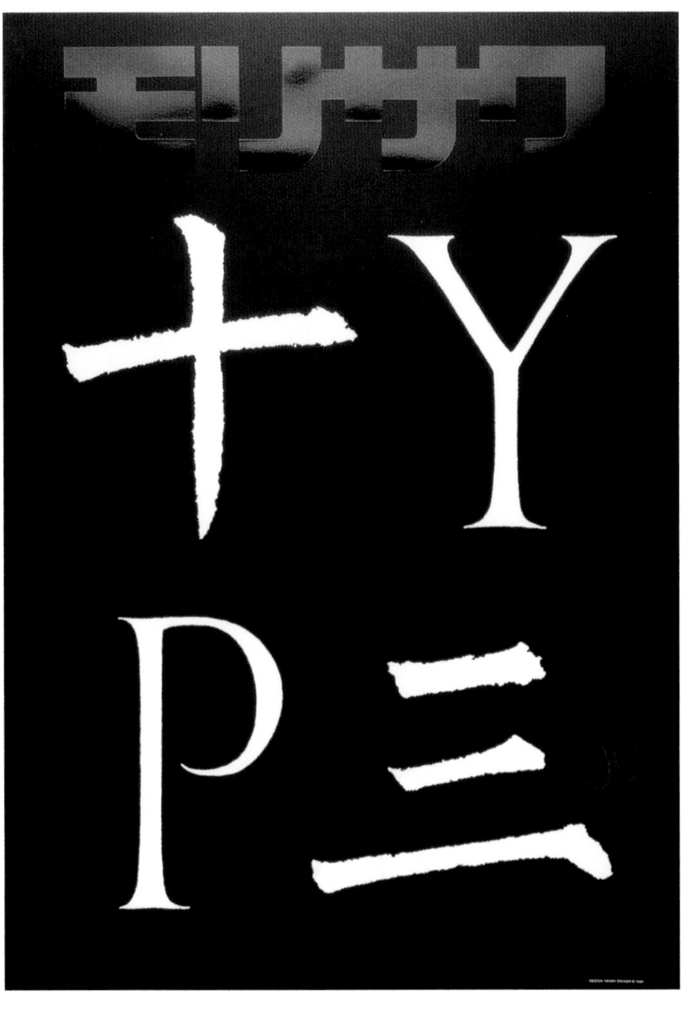

Henry Steiner [China]

TYPE, Japan, 1991. Poster for the Japanese typesetting company Morisawa; their logotype is in Japanese katakana lettering. The white letters suggest stone engraving common to both Chinese and Roman writing systems.

Standard Chartered Bank banknote series, 2004. Fourth and latest iteration of a series of notes first designed in 1979. The denominations are identified by a hierarchy of Chinese mythological animals.

Conserve Nature, Hong Kong, 1992. This poster for recycled paper shows a wooden plate rack protecting a cloud. The inspiration is partly derived from a monumental column at the Forbidden City in Beijing.

1934– born in Vienna, Austria
Admitted to AGI, 1980
International President 1994–1997

His family escaped Vienna in 1939. Henry grew up in Manhattan. At Stuyvesant High School he learned to revere science, but it was not his vocation. At Hunter College, despite studying with masters like Robert Motherwell, he found that he was not a painter. Finally, at the Yale School of Art under Paul Rand, he discovered that the artwork he had been doing for school newspapers, yearbooks and theatre sets was called *'graphic design'*. He received a Fulbright scholarship to the Sorbonne, Paris. Then in 1961 Henry landed in Hong Kong for a nine-month assignment as *The Asia Magazine*'s first Design Director.

In the heart of Asia he found a home and is still there. Highlights of Steiner & Co.'s practice include eighteen years as consultant to HSBC, which produced many groundbreaking annual reports and the bank's famous brand identity. A long-running series of banknotes based on Chinese mythological creatures for Standard Chartered Bank is still in circulation. A member of many international design organizations, Henry has been named Hong Kong Designer of the Year, a World Master by Japan's *Idea* magazine, and one of Icograda's Masters of the 20th Century. Henry received an honorary doctorate from Hong Kong Baptist University and is honorary professor at two Hong Kong Universities.

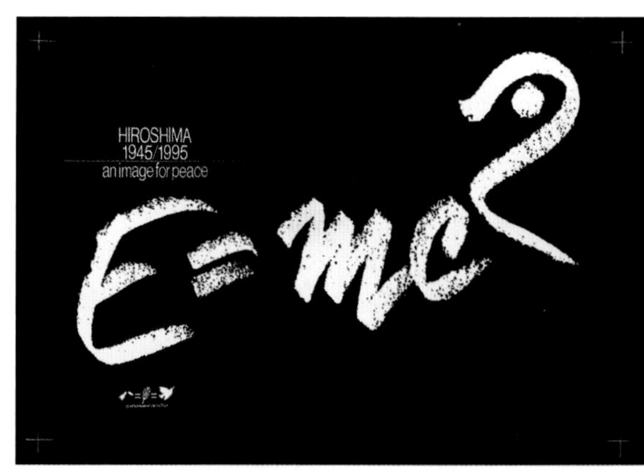

Josef Flejšar [Czech Republic]

1922– born in Nový Bydžov
Admitted to AGI, 1981

He studied at the State School of Applied Arts with Prof. Jaroslav Benda (1941–43) and Prof. Antonin Strnadel (1945–47). During the intervening war years he worked in the chemigraphical department of the State Printing House. After graduation Flejšar co-operated with a group of promotional graphic designers to form Tvar (Shape), the association of visual artists. Between 1956 and 1959 he and Josef Raban provided the creative leadership of the Promotion Cooperative. He was a co-founder of Bilance, a group of visual artists.

He participated in design work for the Czechoslovak Chamber of Commerce in Vienna, Helsinki, Leipzig, Kiev, Damascus, Paris, Brussels, Zagreb, Moscow, Poznan and Budapest. He designed the Czechoslovak exhibitions for the Brussels and Montreal Expos and the International Trade Fair in Düsseldorf 1975. He co-operated with the foreign trade organization Jablonex on exhibition designs for Montreal (1969) and Leningrad (1970).
He regularly participates in significant national and international poster exhibitions, such as the biennales of Brno, Warsaw, Fort Collins, Lahti and the Triennials in Toyama, Mons, Sofia; and the Chaumont Poster Festival.

Contemporary Czechoslovak Posters, exhibition poster, 1990.

Hiroshima Anniversary, poster, 1995.

Hamlet, theatre poster, 1984.

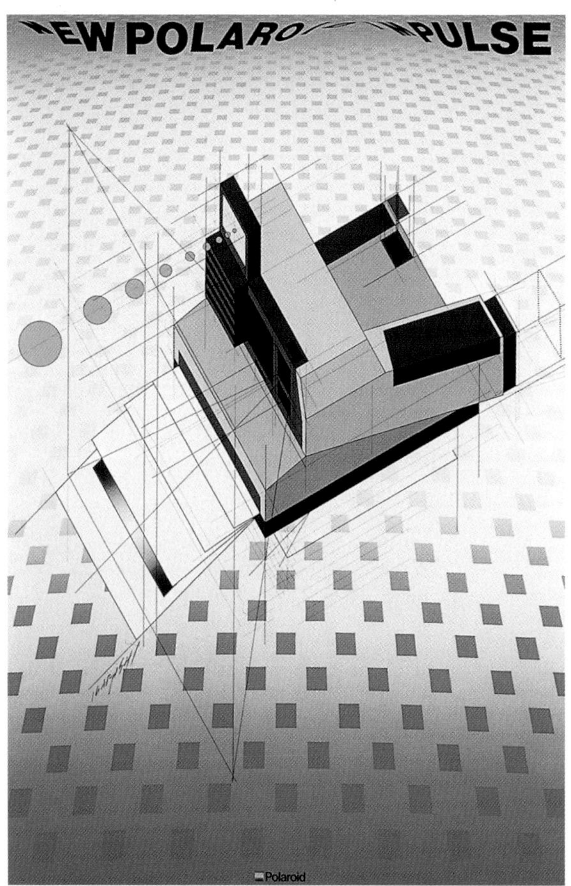

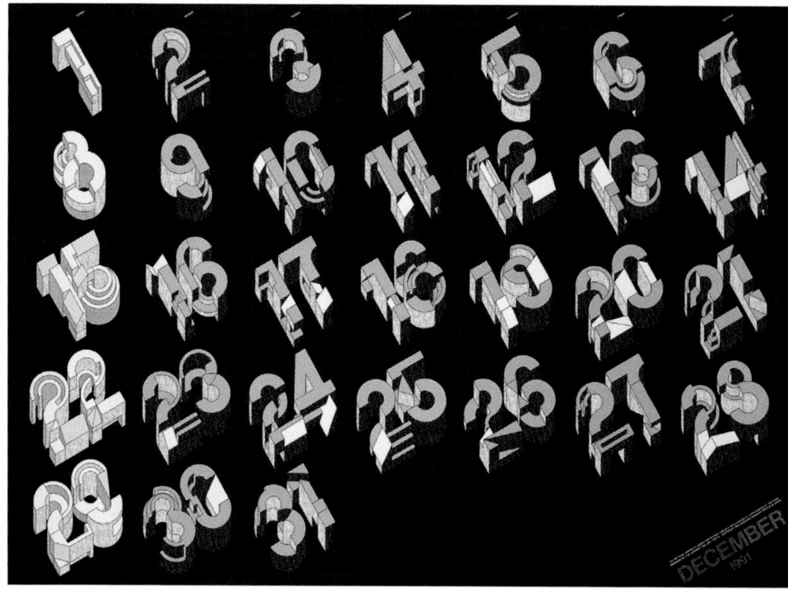

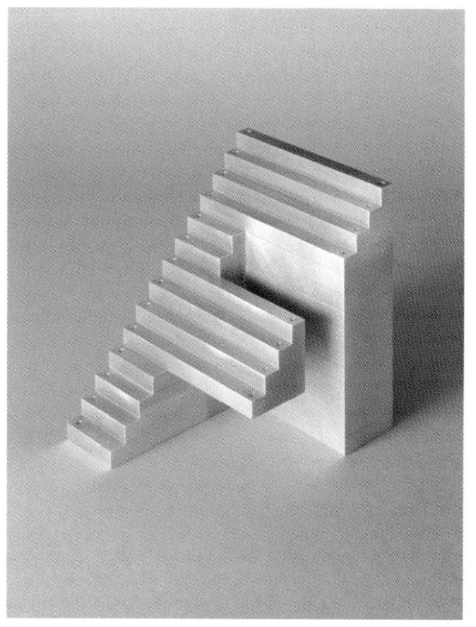

Polaroid Impulse, advertising poster, Pentagram London, 1988.

MoMA NY, calendar, 1991.

Suntory Ltd, logo, 1990.

Alphabet sculptures for Igarashi Studio, 1983. Material: aluminium. Size: 120 x 140 x 140 mm. Size can vary depending on the letterform.

Takenobu Igarashi [Japan]

1944– born in Hokkaido
Admitted to AGI, 1981

Educated at Tama Art University, Tokyo, and UCLA, Takenobu Igarashi is one of Japan's most outstanding, original and prolific designers. His major sculptures and graphic projects for clients worldwide have made him one of the most visible graphic designers on the international scene. He is best known for his three-dimensional letterforms for posters, calendars and sculptures. Today he concentrates on large-scale architectural and sculptural projects in Japan and USA. He has used natural materials such as wood, stone and ceramics for recent abstract sculptures.

Igarashi's philosophy about his work is best summed up in these words:
'My approach to design and sculpture has always wavered between my wish to do something useful for society, and my desire to create something beautiful with my own hands. In my opinion there are three essential things in work: passion, challenge and discovery. Without that, work gets boring; with that, work is enjoyable. And artwork that is enjoyable also results in success.'

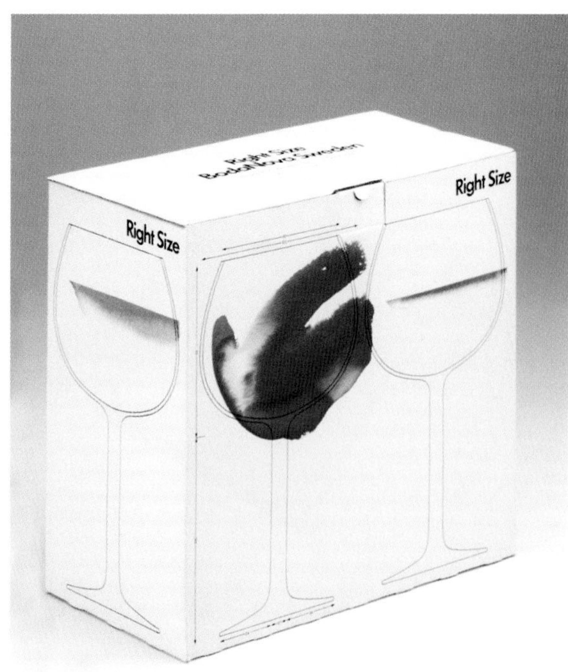

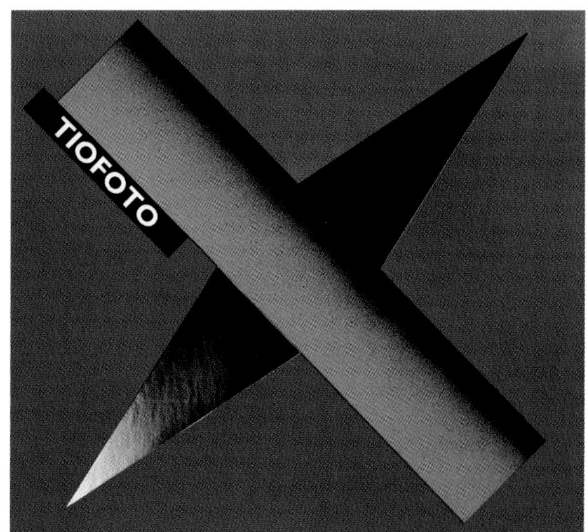

Dan Jonsson [Sweden]

1933– born in Sundsvall
Admitted to AGI, 1981

Dan Jonsson studied graphic design and illustration at Konstfack University College of Arts, Crafts and Design in Stockholm (1954–58). For a short period, in 1959 he was a student of Armin Hofmann and Emil Ruder at the Kunstgewerbschule in Basel. Dan started his career as art director at various advertising agencies in Stockholm, while also working as a freelance illustrator of books. In 1965 he started his own studio with an emphasis on graphic design and illustration. Among his clients were large companies like Astra Zenica and Scania, banks, magazines such as *Femina*, the daily newspaper *Dagens Nyheter* and several publishers.

In the late 1980s and early 90s, Dan taught as a professor at Konstfack, Stockholm. He has been awarded several Golden Eggs (Swedish Association of Advertising), participated in numerous poster biennials, and won the 1995 Icograda Excellence Award, London. His work is represented at the National Museum of Fine Arts, Stockholm.

Solo exhibition poster, 1992.

Packaging design for **Boda Nova**.
Golden Egg Award 1983 from the Swedish Association of Advertising Agencies

X, Tiofoto (the work of ten photographers), 1997.
Catalogue and CD cover.

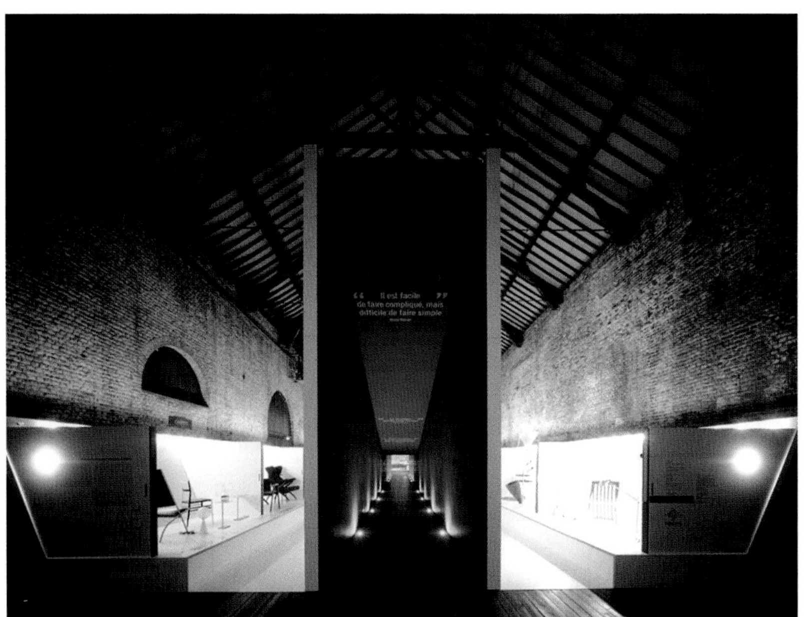

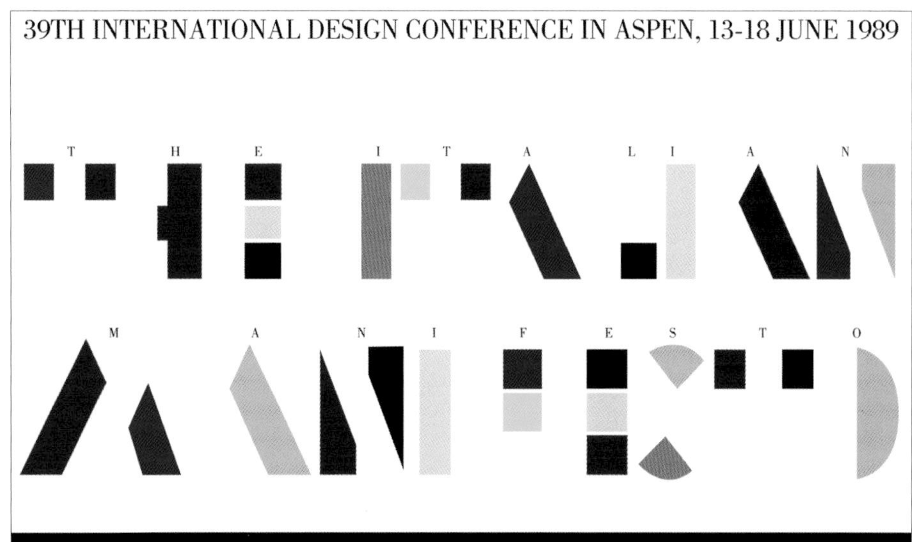

Maestri, 2003. Exhibition on Italian design (the Triennale Collection) held at the Museum of Grand Hornu, Belgium.

Venice, 1997. Logo for the exhibition 'Venezia e la sua laguna'.

Pompeii, 2000. Logo for the Archaeological Sites of Pompeii (proposal with Marina Del Cinque).

Aspen, 1989. Cover for the International Design Conference in Aspen: 'The Italian Manifesto'.

Italo Lupi [Italy]

1934– born in Cagliari
Admitted to AGI, 1981

Graduated in architecture from the Polytechnic of Milan. Was formerly art director of *Domus*, and in charge of the Milan Triennale's image; now both editor-in-chief and art director of *Abitare*. He is involved in national and international projects in graphic design, visual identity, communication, sign systems, museums and exhibition layouts. (Milan Triennale, Palazzo Grassi in Venice and Turin, Palazzo Pitti in Florence, Palazzo della Pilotta in Parma, Palazzo Reale and Arengario in Milan, Grand Hornu in Belgium, the Museum of Contemporary Arts in Tokyo).

Exhibitions of his work have been held in Tokyo, Osaka, New York, Grenoble and Echirolles.
A recent project is the 'Look of the City' design for the 2006 Winter Olympic Games in Turin (with Migliore and Servetto). He is an honorary Royal Designer for Industry and honorary member of Milan Art Directors Club, and has received awards and honorable mentions from Milan Art Directors Club, Prague's Typomundus, the 13th Brno Biennial, the Compasso d'Oro award (1998) and the Pen Club Award (2001) for Editorial Graphic Design.

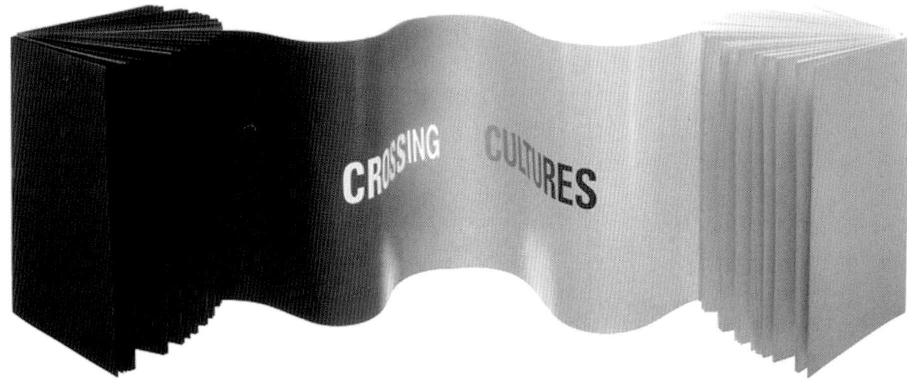

Armando Milani [Italy]

1940– born in Milan
Admitted to AGI, 1981

After studying with Albe Steiner at the Società Umanitaria in Milan, Armando collaborated with important Italian design studios such as Studio Boggeri. In 1970 he founded a studio in Milan, and in 1977 he moved to New York where, after a collaboration for two years with Massimo Vignelli, he opened his own studio. He designs logos, corporate identities, books, and cultural posters. Armando also organizes design seminars and workshops in his olive mill in the south of France.

In 1995 he won an award in NY from Mayor Giuliani, for the poster *New York City: Capital of the World*. In 1997 he designed the book *Double Life*, capturing the sense of humour and creativity of 80 AGI designers. In 2000 he won an award in Italy for the poster for the Promosedia International Chair Show. In 2004 another poster for Promosedia won the Compasso d'Oro award at the Milan Triennale, and he also designed a peace poster distributed worldwide by the United Nations. In 2006 he designed the poster *The Light of Culture* for the Bibliotheca Alexandrina, Egypt.

War/Peace, NY, 2004. Of all my works this poster has received the most recognition around the world. The UN decided to use it for the celebration of their 60th anniversary. It was also turned into t-shirts, tote bags, watches, magnets, pins and umbrellas.

Smoke is poison, Milan, 2005. Ideal communication: this wordless poster can be understood all over the world. It was used at the Policlinico Hospital, Milan.

Crossing Cultures, NY, 2003. The only solution to war is dialogue. I created this image in which the two opposing cultures are depicted in black and white, yet encounter the solutions to this dramatic problem in the greyscale centre.

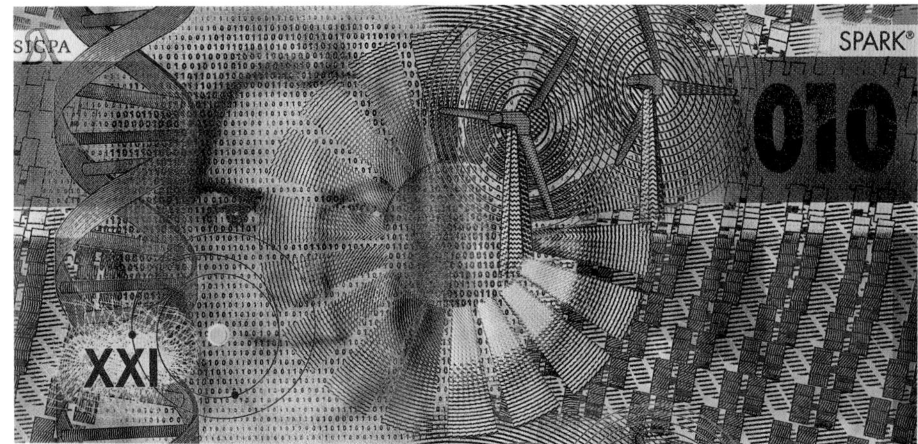

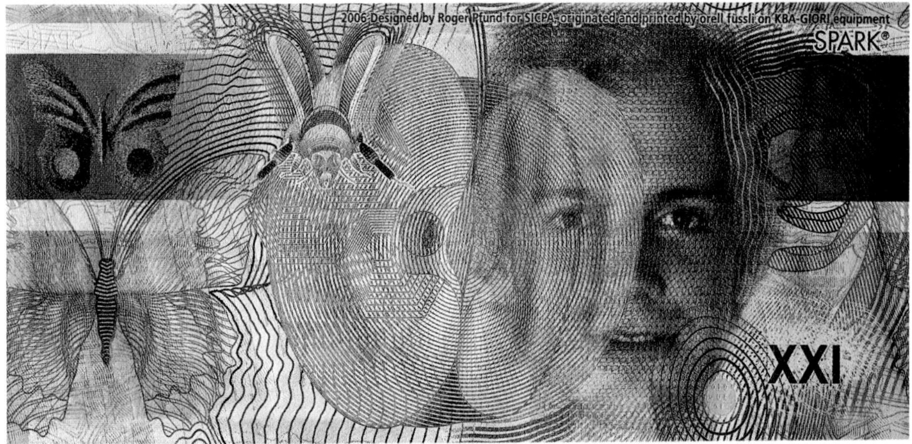

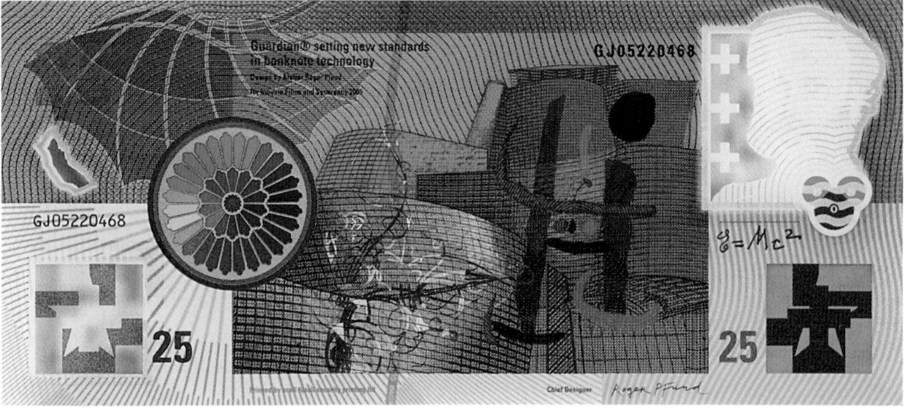

Roger Pfund [Switzerland]

Specimen banknote for SICPA Spark® (x 2), 2006. Design for a new generation of optical security, front and reverse side.

Eurostar specimen, printed on Guardian® for Innovia film and Securency, 2005. Theme: Europe illustrated through its great achievements, artists and intellectuals.

1943– born in Berne
Admitted to AGI, 1981

Pfund is a painter, graphic artist and designer who holds Swiss and French passports. Atelier Roger Pfund Communication Visuelle in Carouge, Geneva, specializes in graphic design, communication, architecture and design. In 1971 he was awarded first prize in the Swiss National Bank's banknote design competition and given the mandate for the creation of the reserve series of Swiss banknotes. On a European level, Pfund is one of today's top specialists in banknote design and security techniques. Since 1971: collaborations with Orell Füssli Security Printing: research and development of security techniques. 1982–97: final banknote series for Banque de France. Since 1987: adviser/member of Swiss National Bank's working group. 1996: first prize, European Monetary Institute's Euro Banknote competition. 2000–3: creation of new Swiss passport. Awarded Officier des Arts et des Lettres. Works on global communication campaigns, corporate identities, annual reports, posters and books. Designed book for 50th anniversary of Universal Declaration of Human Rights. Worked for International North-South Media Festival; International AIDS Congress; Grand Théâtre Geneva; official Alinghi book. Other projects: 700th anniversary of Swiss Confederation; International Red Cross and Red Crescent Museum, Geneva; 50th Anniversary of UN (1945–95) urban exhibition on human rights; Swiss Transport Museum, Lucerne; FIFA trophies; Geneva International Airport; Jaeger-LeCoultre watches.

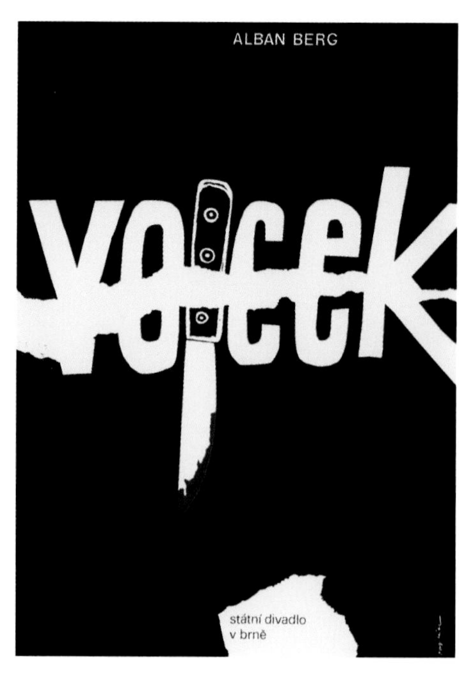

Jan Rajlich Sr. [Czech Republic]

1920– born in Dirna
.Admitted to AGI, 1981

Studied 1939–44 at the Skola Umeni in Zlin, a private university-level art school. Has freelanced as a graphic designer and painter in Brno since 1950, designing posters, logotypes, pictograms, layouts, murals and mosaics. He did corporate identity projects for Brno Trade Fairs and Hotel Morava Pohorelice. Jan lectured in graphic design and semiology at the Brno VUT University of Technology (1983–88) and became head of the visual communication department there (1992–94). He writes for design magazines, has had over 40 solo exhibitions and taken part in more than 300 (inter)national exhibitions, including: Venice, 1972; Brno Biennale, 1964–2006; Warsaw Biennale, 1968–2004; Trnava Triennial, 1994–2006. He has won over 40 awards, including: Icograda Excellence Awards, Nice, 1985 and Brno, 2002; Euro-Design Award Oostende, 1994; Czech Design Prestige Award, 1996; City of Brno Prize, 1995; elected to the Hall of Fame, Czech Exhibition Design, 2002. Rajlich founded the International Biennale of Graphic Design Brno in 1963 and remained its president until 1992. He is a member of ISGD (USA) and the Czech Art Association 'Q'. A monograph on his work was published in 1999. He is also the author of *All Men Are Brothers: Designer's Edition* (Berlin and Shanghai, 2006).

Anton Chekhov: *The Seagull*, theatre poster, 1975. Client: Brno State Theatre.

Alban Berg: *Wozzeck*, opera poster, 1976–84. Client: Brno State Theatre.

Set of orientation pictograms, designed for a research institute, Brno, 1986.

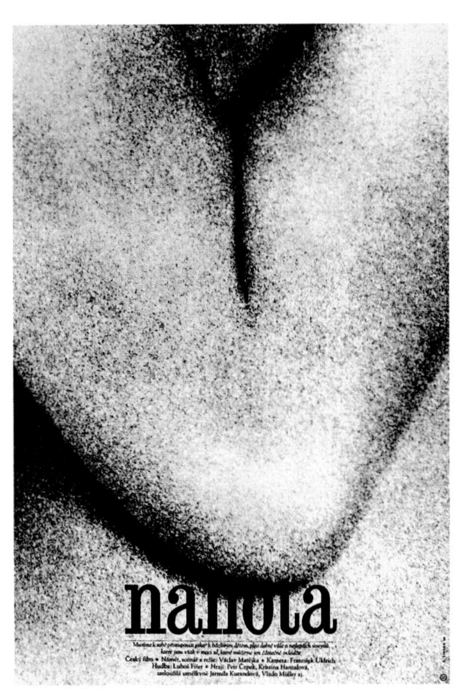

Indian Summer, poster, 2003.

Nakedness, poster, 2002.

Czech Cubism, stamp, 2002.

Zdenek Ziegler [Czech Republic]

1932– born in Prague
Admitted to AGI, 1981

Ziegler studied at the Prague Academic High School (1943–51) and the School of Architecture, Czech Technical University, Prague (1955–61). His activities include poster, book and magazine design, visual communication, industrial design of art exhibitions and interiors, and graphic art. He is a member of Typo & and TDC Prague. He has been a juror in Brno, Warsaw, Fort Collins, Paris, Vienna, Budapest, Leipzig and Trnava. Since 1990 he has taught at the Academy of Art, Design and Architecture in Prague, and also served as rector (2000–2003). Ziegler has taken part in group exhibitions in Prague, Brno, Warsaw, Ljubljana, Helsinki, New York, Montreal, Fort Collins, Havana, Lahti, Wuppertal, Zürich, Los Angeles, Toyama, Ogaki, and more. *Solo exhibitions:* Frankfurt (1970), Tabor (1979), Stuttgart, Prague, Mnichovo Hradiste and Orlova (1980), Kladno (1981), Cheb (1982), Olomouc (1988), Prague (1993 and 2003), London (1998). *Awards:* first prize, Brno Biennale, 1964; honorary awards at Poster Exhibition Karlovy Vary and Typomundus, Montreal; silver medal, Colombo, 1966; Most Beautiful Czech Book: 1969, 1970, 1973, 1991, 2005; bronze medal, Brno Biennale 1978; Gold Hugo, Movie Posters Chicago, 1978; Bronze Hugo, 1983; Merit Award, NY ADC, 1987; Czech Republic TDC Prize 1997, 2005.

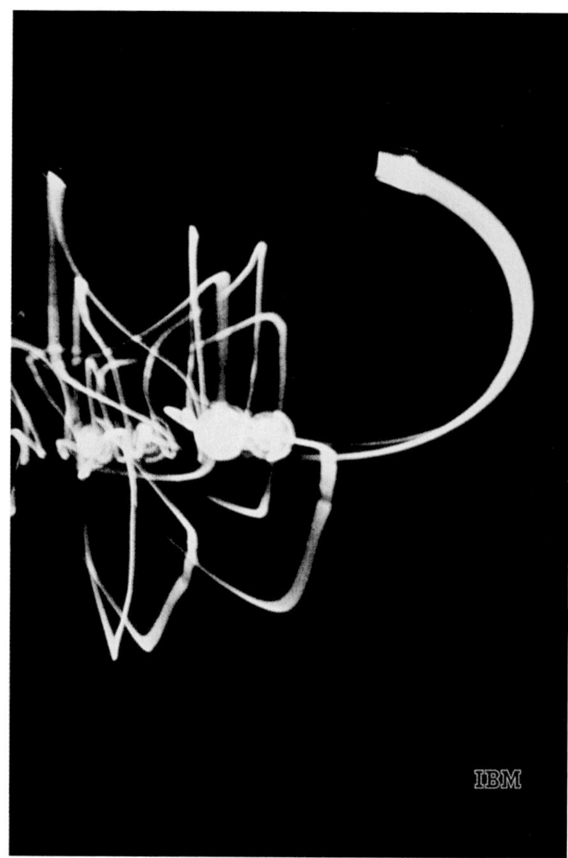

Edgar Reinhard [Switzerland]

1942– born in Thun
Admitted to AGI, 1982

Edgar Reinhard trained as a lithographer. He started his design career in advertising, subsequently specializing in three-dimensional design. He opened his own studio in 1971. His clients include multinational corporations such as IBM, Toyota and Dow Chemical, along with numerous European companies. He has broken completely new ground in exhibition design with his use of new materials and new technology. His Geneva Telecom pavilion showed a bold architectural concept in volume, colour and materials, suggesting a utopian image of the future evolution of the media.

Reinhard has influenced the quality and development of exhibition design ever since. Since 1995, he has passed on his experiences and unique methods as a professor in the Interior Design Department of Lippe Detmold University of Applied Art in Germany.

Dow Chemical, 1971.
Exhibition on water purification.

IBM Pavilion, at Telecom, World Exhibition of Telecommunication in Geneva, 1983.

IBM, poster, 1965. The hieroglyph shows the path followed by an IBM Typewriter golf ball when typing a line.

Left Right Left Right Left Right Boom!, poster about political extremes, 1991.

Airlines, environmental poster, 2006.

Yad Vashem Holocaust Memorial, 2005.

Hadassah Medical Center, Jerusalem. Mother and Child Pavilion/Atrium, 1996. (Now being extended.)

Yarom Vardimon [Israel]

1942– born in Tel Aviv
Admitted to AGI, 1982

Studied in England at the LCP (University of the Arts), Chelsea College of Art and the University of Westminster. His clients include leading Israeli industrial firms, banks, medical centres, academic institutions and museums. Design distinctions include: recipient of the Icograda Design Excellence Award; Fellow of the International Design Conference, Aspen; Honorary Member of the Art Directors Club of New York; recipient of the Design Excellence Award, International Design Conference, Mexico Design Year 2005; past president, GDAI, and past vice-president, Icograda. He has been a professor of visual communications since 1980, was in charge of the submission of the undergraduate and masters degree design programmes to the Council of Higher Education in Israel; has been head of graphic design at Bezalel Academy in Jerusalem; head of the Design Workshop at Tel-Aviv University School of Architecture, and presently, he is vice-president for Academic Affairs and Dean of the Faculty of Design at Shenkar College of Engineering and Design, Ramat Gan. He has judged many international design events and has won many design awards. His work is represented at major international exhibitions and in the permanent collections of museums in Europe, the USA, Japan and Israel.

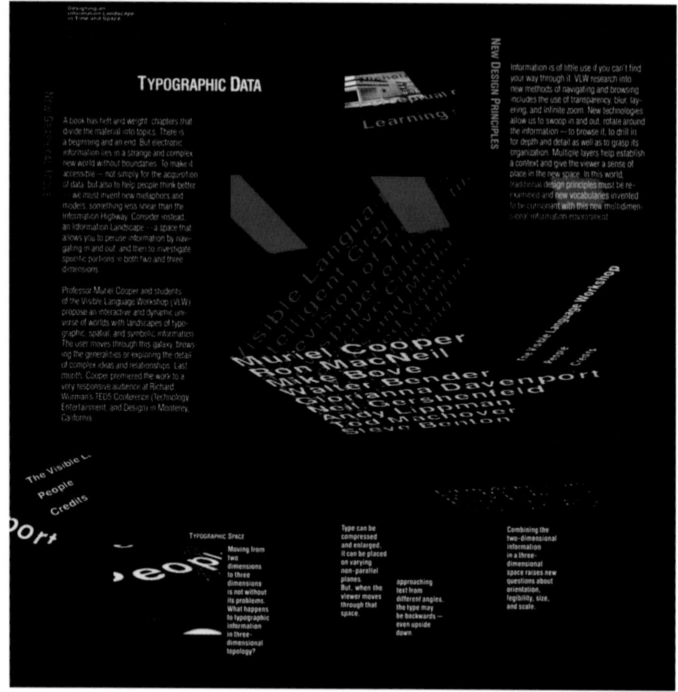

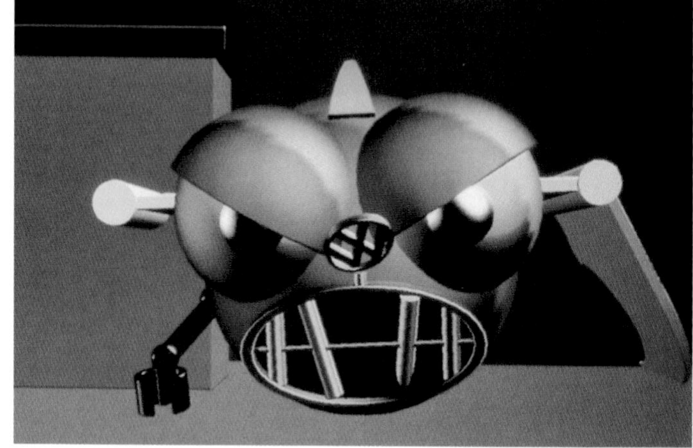

MIT MEDIA LAB

Muriel Cooper [USA]

1925-1994
Admitted to AGI, 1983

Muriel Cooper taught at the Boston Museum School, Simmons College, Massachusetts College of Art and the Universities of Boston and Maryland. From 1952–58 she was design director of MIT Publications, and subsequently media director of MIT Publications. From 1981–87, she was associate professor of visual studies, MIT Department of Architecture. In 1988 Muriel was appointed Professor of Visual Studies. Amongst the groups, she established was the Visual Language Workshop Media Laboratory. Together with her associates she conducted seminar work.

'The goal was to structure a group that could respond creatively to change where research and practice could inform one another... The Workshop was a unique laboratory in which the content, quality and technology of communication may be explored and tested... providing a learning triangle of experience, theory and application.'
As a book designer, Muriel worked for MIT Press and designed and art directed hundreds of books that became award-winners, like Hans Wingler's *BAUHAUS* (1969) and *Learning from Las Vegas* by Robert Venturi (1972). Muriel was awarded the AIGI Design Leadership Award 1986. She was principal of Muriel Cooper Media Design, Cambridge. She also did a wonderful, inspiring presentation at the 1993 AGI Congress in Montauk, NY.

MIT Summer Session announcements, 1985.

CG animation stills produced at the **Visible Language Workshop** during the 1980s.

MIT Media Lab rendered as Soft Type, 1990.

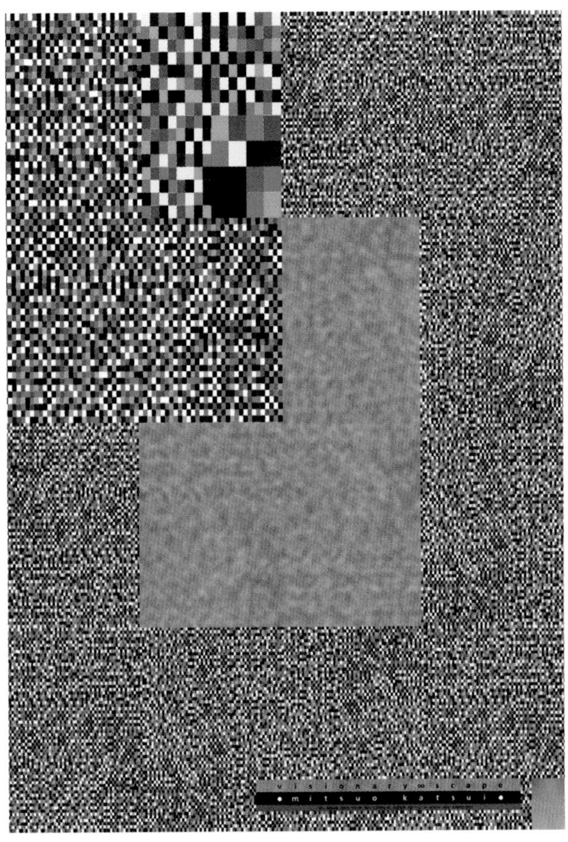

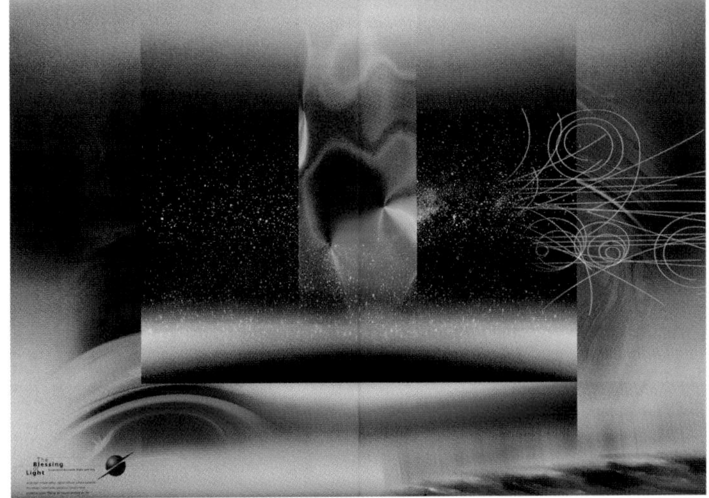

Mitsuo Katsui [Japan]

Visionary∞Scape, 2004.
Client: Katsui Design Office.

The 200th Anniversary of Sharaku, 1995.
Client: Mainichi Shinbunsha.

Yu, The Blessing of Light, 1993.
Client: Ginza Graphic Gallery.

1931– born in Tokyo
Admitted to AGI, 1984

Katsui graduated from the University of Tokyo Department of Education in 1955. He has worked in all fields of graphic design, including providing the art direction for the Osaka International Expo in 1970, Okinawa Ocean Expo in 1975 and the Tsukuba Science Expo in 1985. His work strives to open a new realm of communication through the modes of expression that technology provides. He is the recipient of the JAAC Award, the Mainichi Industrial Design Award, the Kodansha Cultural Publishing Prize, the Minister of Education Prize for the Arts, a Purple Ribbon Medal, as well as numerous gold prizes from international organizations and events such as Brno Book, the Warsaw, Lahti, and Mexico Poster Biennials, and the NY ADC. He is an emeritus professor of Musashino Art University, a JAGDA director, and member of the Tokyo and New York Art Directors Clubs. Group CG exhibition: 'Ape Call from Tokyo', New York, 1990. Solo exhibitions: Warsaw, 1996; Beijing and Shanghai, 1998; 'Mitsuo Katsui: Visionary∞Zone', Museum of Modern Art, Toyama, 2004. He is the author of *Mitsuo Katsui: Visionary∞Scape* (published by Sendenkaigi, 2003).

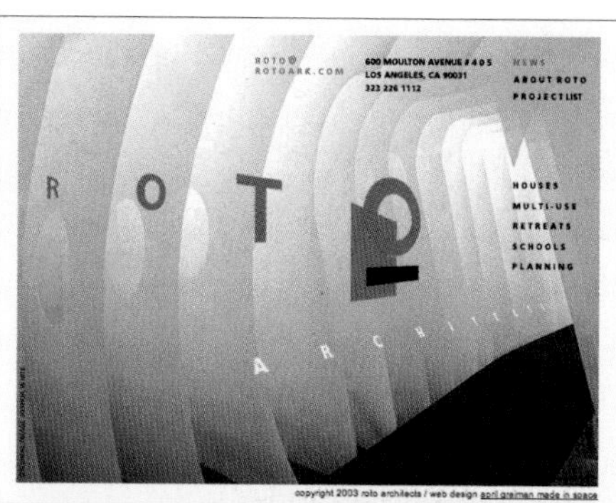

April Greiman [USA]

1948– born in New York City
Admitted to AGI, 1985

April Greiman has been instrumental in the use of advanced technology in problem-solving since 1982. She pioneered digital design with the Mackintosh computer. Clients whose projects have become legendary include Esprit, US West, Walker Art Center, and SCI-Arc. A growing interest in the built environment has led to close collaborations with Barton Meyers, Frank Gehry and RoTo Architects. Projects range from signage, exhibitions to colour, and materials palettes, for clients such as AOL, TimeWarner, Sears, Amgen, Dosa and the new Prairie View School of Architecture, Texas. Among her prestigious awards are: Hallmark Fellowship; American Institute of Architects; AIGA Gold Medal, and the Chrysler Award for Innovation. Her work has appeared in articles and media broadcasts ranging from *Domus* and *Time* to *NY Times* and *USA Today* to CNN and PBS ESPN. Published books: *April Greiman: Floating Ideas into Time and Space* (1998); *It's Not April What You Think It Greiman Is* (1996); *Hybrid Imagery: The Fusion of Technology and Graphic Design* (1990); and *Something from Nothing* (2002). April was Director of the Visual Communications programme at Cal Arts and is presently an instructor at Southern California Institute of Architecture. April Greiman moved from the Metropolitan NYC to Los Angeles in 1976, establishing her multi-disciplinary design practice, currently called Made in Space.

Art Walls Commission/ Wilshire Vermont Housing and Subway Station, Los Angeles Commission; 700 m², 2006.

Warehouse C, Nagasaki, Japan, Roto Architects; colour, surfaces and materials commission, 1996.

Roto Architects, brand identity, website and animation, 1996–present.

MAK Center @ the Schindler House, identity/www.makcenter.org, 1985–present.

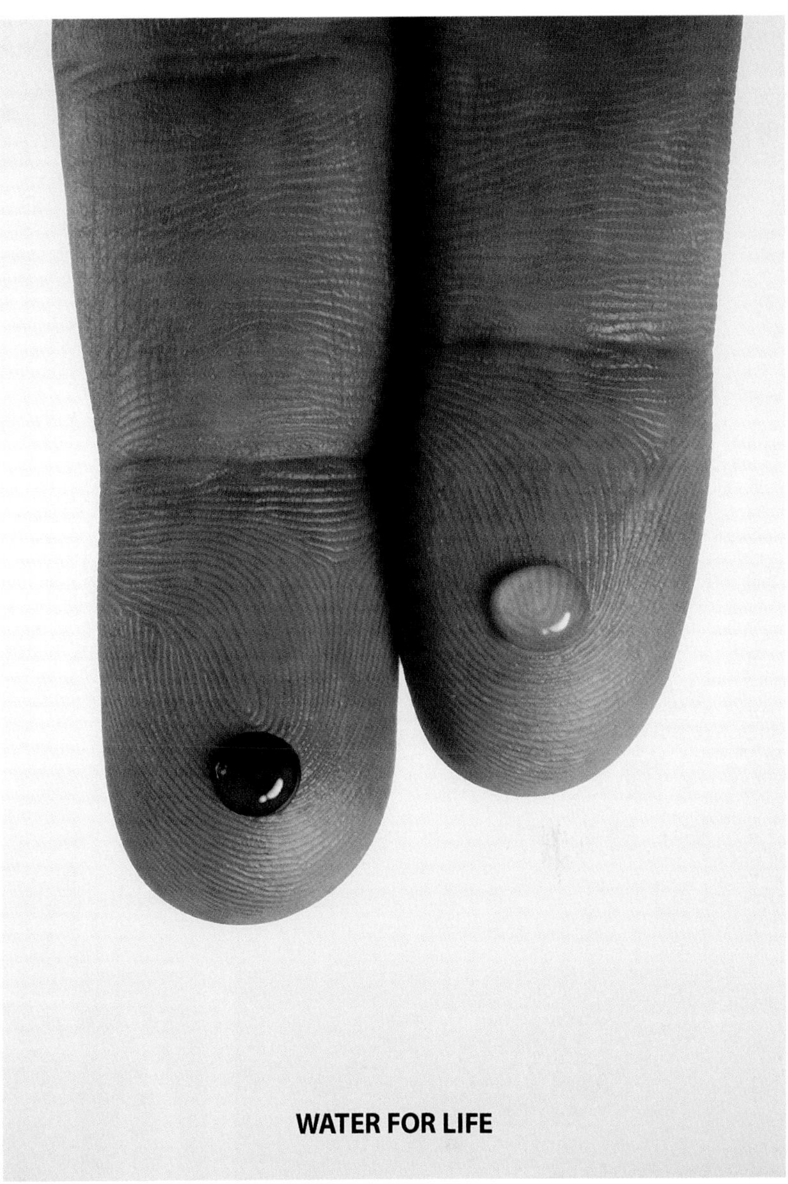

Shiseido Nail Art & Shiseido Flash Eyes, poster, 1973. Gold award, International Poster Biennale, Warsaw, 1976.

Japan, poster, 2001.
Grand Prize, JAGDA Poster Exhibition 2001.

Water for Life, poster, 2005.
JAGDA Poster Exhibition 2005.

Makoto Nakamura [Japan]

1926– born in Iwate
Admitted to AGI, 1985

After graduating from the Design Department of Tokyo Art University in 1948, he joined the advertising department of Shiseido in 1949 and served as an executive director of the advertising division and chief of the production division. Since 1967 he has been a consultant to Shiseido and also currently works as a freelance designer. Received the JAAC Special Award in 1953, Tokyo ADC Award in 1963, gold and silver prizes at the Warsaw Poster Biennale in 1976, grand prize at the JAGDA Poster Exhibition in 2001, and many other awards.

He was inducted into the Tokyo ADC Hall of fame and received the Purple Ribbon Medal, given by the Japanese government to honour a major contribution to society in the field of science or the arts. His works are collected by many museums, including the Centre de Création Industrielle, Palais du Louvre, Paris, the NY MoMA, Wilanów Poster Museum, National Museum of Modern Art, Tokyo, the Stedelijk Museum Amsterdam, and others.

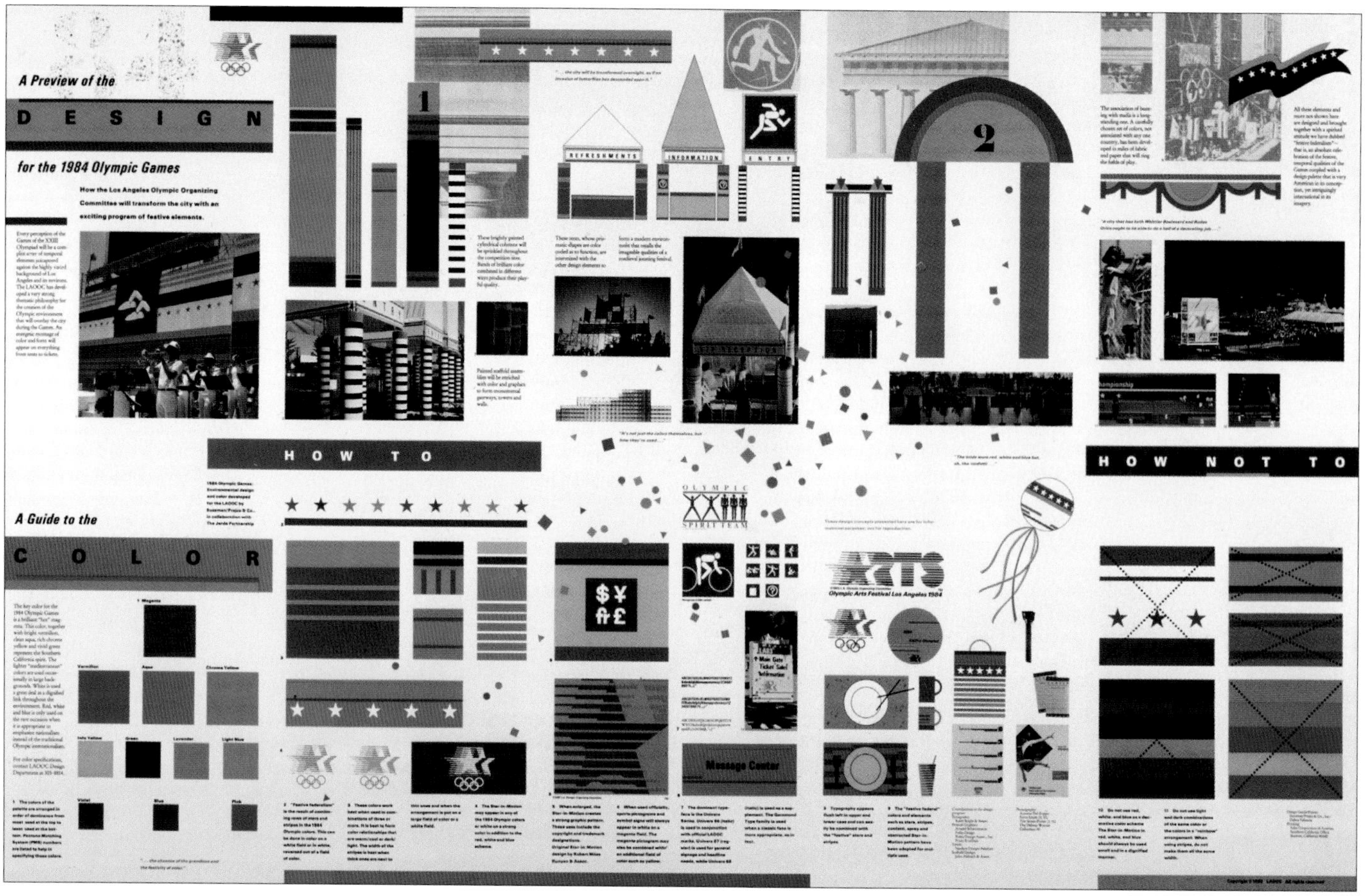

Deborah Sussman [USA]

1931– born in Brooklyn, New York
Admitted to AGI, 1985

Deborah Sussman is a pioneer of environmental graphic design. Her passion for the marriage of graphics and the built environment, fuelled by her early career at the Eames Office, led to extensive collaborations with urban planners, architects and multi-disciplinary teams. Her work is informed by perceptive observation and rigorous investigation of communities and cultures. It appears in civic spaces, cultural venues and commercial developments around the world. In 1980 her firm incorporated as Sussman/Prejza & Co., with husband Paul Prejza. Deborah has led the team in designing such notable projects as the *'look'* of the 1984 Olympics (winner of *Time* magazine's award for 'Best of the Decade'); identity and corporate interiors for Hasbro Inc.; branding and wayfinding systems for Walt Disney Resorts and the cities of Philadelphia and Santa Monica. Recent works include: interiors of the Seattle Opera (McCaw Hall) and identity and exhibits for the Museum of the African Diaspora in San Francisco. Honours include: Doctor of Humane Letters, Bard College; medallist, American Institute of Graphic Arts (AIGA); honorary member, American Institute of Architects (AIA); Fellow, Society of Environmental Graphic Design (SEGD). Her work has been featured in numerous design publications and books, *The New York Times*, and *Time* magazine.

Design Guide for the 1984 Los Angeles Olympics. The kit of parts shown was applied to all aspects of the programme including 28 sports venues, 42 cultural venues, the streets of Los Angeles, its airports, athletes' villages and uniforms.

Façade of the Cincinnati Convention Center, 2003–2006. Sign becomes building becomes sign.

The Gas Company of Southern California, brand/logo for the largest gas company in the US. S/P designed the total programme for print, sculpture, exhibits and vehicles, 1988–93.

Museum of the African Diaspora, as seen from Mission Street, San Francisco, 2001–2005.

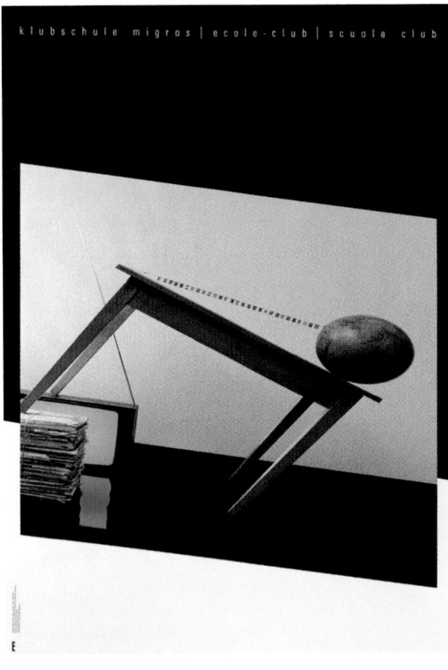

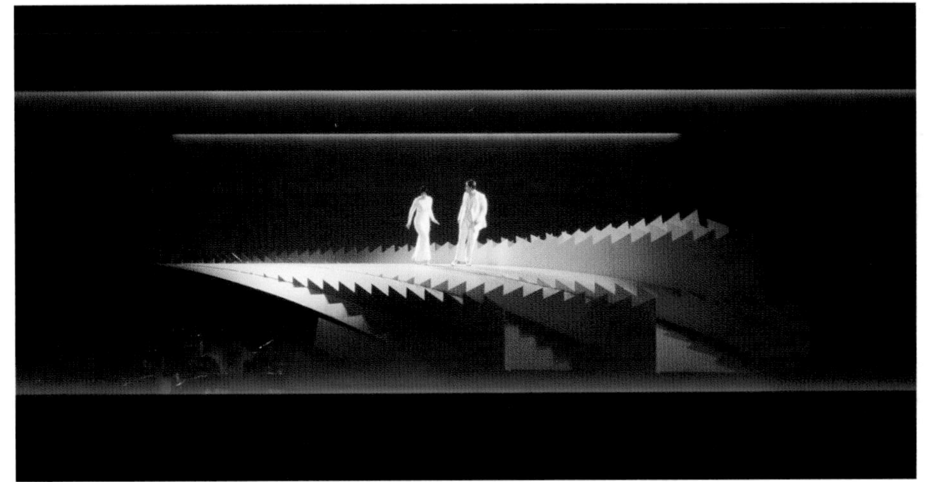

Klubschule Migros, poster.

Set design for the ballet **Daphnis et Chloé** by Maurice Ravel, Grand Théâtre, Geneva.

Luci mie traditrici, opera by Salvatore Siarrino, Théâtre Royal de la Monnaie, Brussels.

Roland Aeschlimann [Switzerland]

1939– born in Biel-Bienne
Admitted to AGI, 1986

Started his career in 1959. Designs and exhibition conceptions for Geigy Basel and other firms. Collaborated with Josef Müller-Brockmann's team. Was an art director in Osaka, Japan. Various activities in the Japanese theatre: Noh, Kabuki, Bunraku. Collaboration with interior architect for Westdeutschen Spielbank Duisburg, as well as for Patek-Philippe Watches, Geneva. Collaborates in the conception and realization of the Red Cross Museum in Geneva. Since 1972: works in the opera and theatre fields, designing sets and costumes for following operas: Geneva, Zürich, Leipzig, Wiesbaden, Dortmund, Hanover, Frankfurt, Mainz, Stuttgart, Karlsruhe, Warsaw, Düsseldorf, Essen, Deutsche Staatsoper Berlin, Deutsche Oper Berlin, Bordeaux, San Francisco, Nuremberg, Paris, Brussels, as well as the following festivals: Montpellier, Vienna, Schwetzingen, Lucerne, Festspielhaus Baden-Baden, Festival d'Aix-en Provence, Glyndebourne, Lincoln Festival, the Händel Festival Halle and the Trisha Brown Company NY. Since 1976: other design work for the Geneva Opera including design of programmes and posters, organization of art exhibitions, art book design. Since 1980: posters for Le Cabinet des Estampes, Geneva, Musée des Beaux-Arts, Berne, the Berlin, Bonn and Stuttgart operas, the University of Cologne and Whitney Museum, NY.

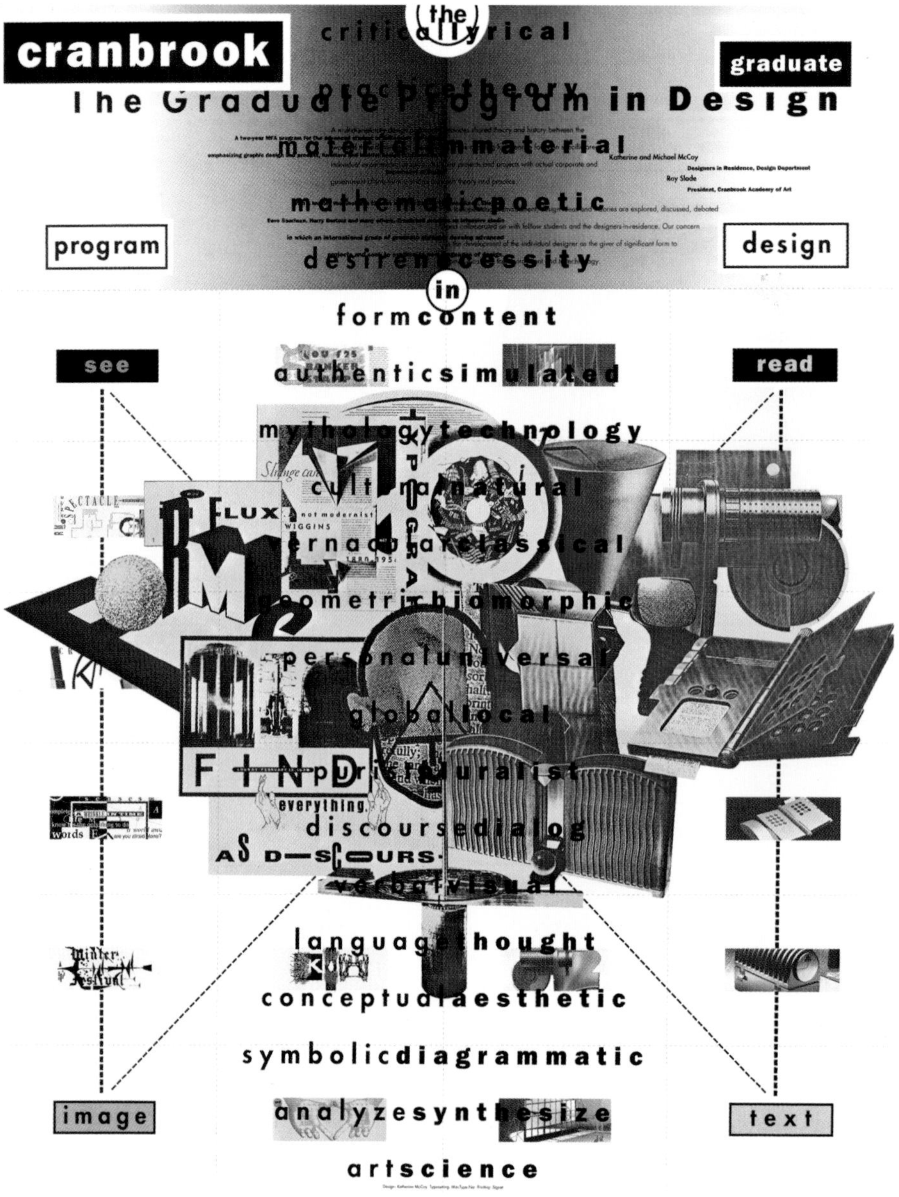

Katherine McCoy [USA]

1945– born in Decatur, Illinois
Admitted to AGI, 1986

Katherine McCoy was educated in industrial design and began her career at Unimark International. She was co-chair of Cranbrook Academy of Art's Design Department (1971–95), a senior lecturer at Illinois Institute of Technology's Institute of Design (1995–2004), and a Royal College of Art Distinguished Visiting Professor. Katherine is a medallist of the American Institute of Graphic Arts and holds an honorary doctorate from Kansas City Art Institute. She is a fellow and past president of the Industrial Designers Society of America, past president of the American Centre for Design, and served as an AIGA national vice-president.

With Michael McCoy, she received the Industrial Designers Society of America Education Award and the Society of Typographic Arts Educator Award. They were jointly awarded a Chrysler Award for Innovation in Design, and in 2005 the first Design Minds Award by the Smithsonian Museum's National Design Awards. Her communications design practice focuses on cultural, educational and environmental clients. She writes on design criticism and history, co-produced the television documentary on Japanese design *Future Wave* and chaired the first ACD Living Surfaces Conference on interactive electronic communications design. She collaborates with her husband Michael on High Ground professional programmes and the High Ground Design Conversation.

Cranbrook Graduate Program in Design, 1989. A photo collage of recent student work is overlaid with a communications theory diagram and a scrolling list of opposing words.

Fluxus Selections, exhibition poster, 1989. For an exhibition of the neo-Dada art movement, the Fluxus Manifesto is collaged into a typographical structure.

Cranbrook Academy of Art, 1978. To indicate the nine unique viewpoints of the nine Cranbrook departments, nine boxes or rooms each look out on the world through a different leaded-glass window by architect Eliel Saarinen.

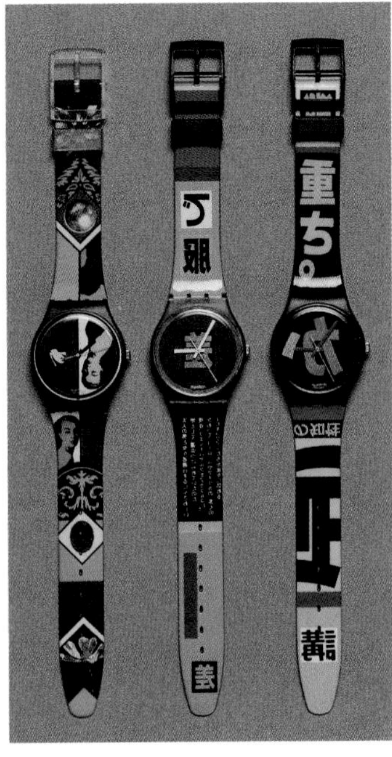
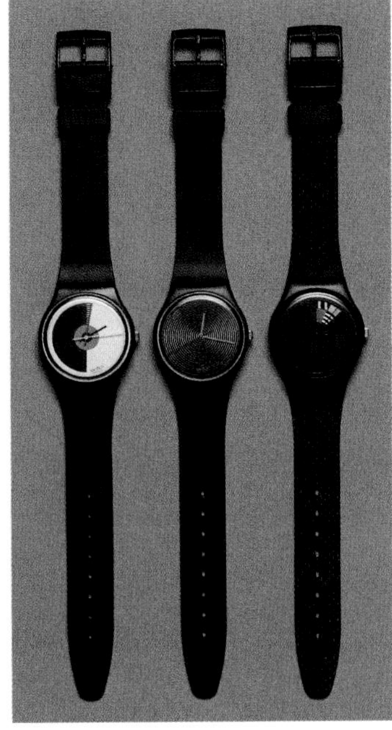

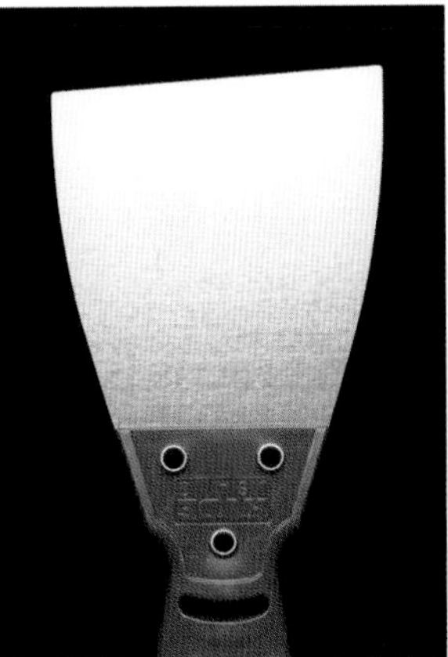

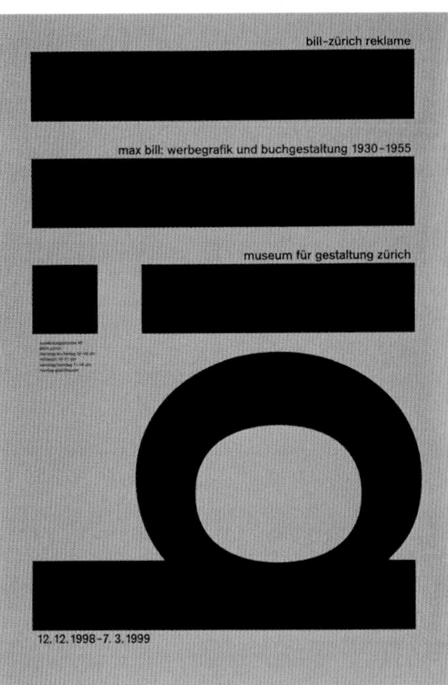

Swatch designs, a selection from more than 350 different models, 1983–89 .

Face to Face, sample pages from a book documenting the 'faces' of everyday objects, 1995.

Max Bill, exhibition poster, Museum of Design, Zürich, 1998.

Jean Robert [Switzerland]

1945– born in La Chaux de Fonds
Admitted to AGI, 1986

After working for Pirelli in Milan (1968–72) and for Pentagram Design in London (1972–76), Jean returned to Switzerland to establish a design studio in Zürich with his partner Käti Durrer. A small product with a big name cemented the Robert-Durrer reputation: Swatch Watches. From 1983 to 1989, under Jean's direction, Robert-Durrer created the now famous Swatch style by designing the first 350 Swatch models. These watches revolutionized the watch industry, with sales rising from 100,000 to 100,000,000 between 1983 and 1990.

Since 1990, Jean has focused his energies on art and culture, designing books and corporate identities as well as posters for renowned private and state museums, publishers, and cultural institutions including the Kunsthalle Zürich, the Fotomuseum Winterthur, the Swiss Foundation of Photography, and the Museum of Design Zürich. In 1995, together with his brother, photographer François Robert, Jean published *Face to Face*, in which everyday objects, from cameras to handbags, are shown to contain faces with an astonishing range of *'expressions'*. Jean has taught at Ohio State University as well as the Zürich and Lucerne Schools of Design.

Michael Vanderbyl [USA]

1947– born in California
Admitted to AGI, 1986

Michael Vanderbyl has attained international prominence as a design practitioner, educator and advocate. Since establishing Vanderbyl Design in 1973, the San Francisco studio has become a multi-disciplinary practice comprising graphic design, product design and interior architecture. He has worked extensively in the contract and residential furniture industry, designing for Baker Furniture, HBF, Bernhardt, Bolier and Company, Henredon, McGuire and Teknion, Inc. Additional clients include the AIA, AmericaOne/America's Cup Challenge, Barbara Barry, Inc., The Blackstone Group/LXR Luxury Resorts, Walt Disney, IBM, Luna Textiles, Napa Valley Vintners Association, Oakland Museum, Robert Talbott Company, SF MoMA and Waterford Wedgwood USA. Michael has served as President of the national AIGA (2003–2005) and in 2000, received the AIGA Gold Medal. At the San Francisco Museum of Modern Art, he sits on the Design Advisory Board and Architecture and Design Accessions committee. At California College of the Arts, he presides as Dean of Design. Michael's work resides in the permanent collections of the Cooper-Hewitt National Design Museum, Library of Congress, SF MoMA and Die Neue Sammlung, Munich. His work appears internationally in books and periodicals, including *Abitare*, *Direction*, *Idea*, *Graphis*, *Communication Arts*, *ID*, *Interiors*, *Metropolis* and *The New York Times*.

Les Enfants Terribles, bus shelter poster for a 1993 lecture series featuring French designers, sponsored by SF MoMA and AIGA San Francisco.

AmericaOne, identity and hull graphics for the America's Cup Challenge, St Francis Yacht Club, 2000.

Teknion Chicago Showroom, 2001.

California College of Arts and Crafts, 2001–2003. School catalogue.

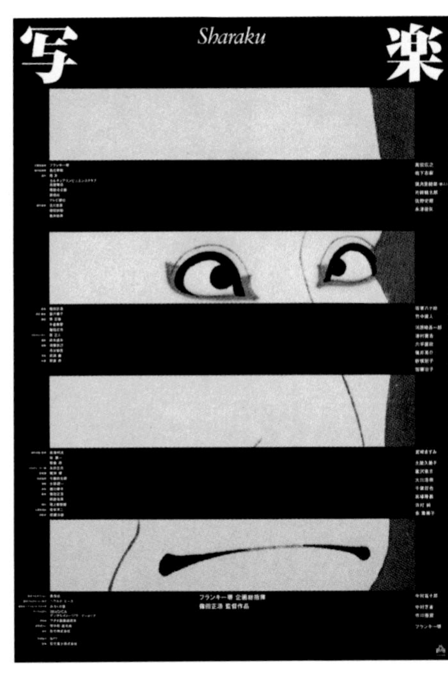

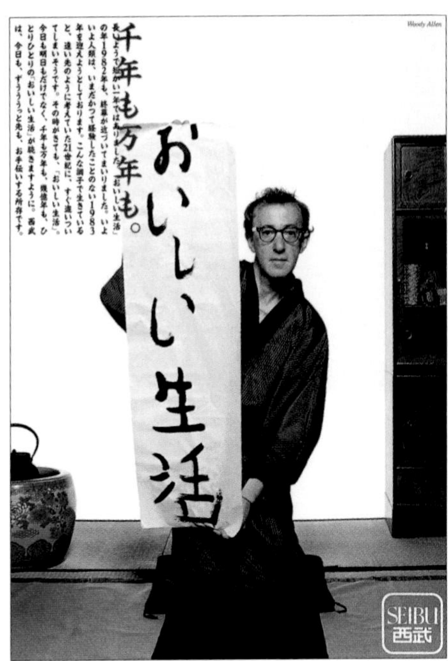

Katsumi Asaba [Japan]

Water for Life, 2005.
Poster for Japan Graphic Designers Association.

Sharaku, 1994. Poster for a movie directed by Masahiro Shinoda.

Tasty Life, 1982. Poster for Seibu department stores.

1940– born in Kanagawa
Admitted to AGI, 1987

Graduated from Kuwasawa Design School. After working for Light Publicity Inc., he established Asaba Design Co. Ltd in 1975. Since then he has taken an active role at the forefront of Japanese design industry. Representative works of his include pieces for Seibu Department Stores, Nissin Food Products, Takeda Chemical Industries, TV titles for *24 HOUR TELEVISION* and packaging designs for Kirin Beverage Corp. He is chairman of Tokyo Type Directors Club and maintains an interest in the Asian culture of written characters, pursuing the relationships between written scripts and visual expression.

In 1999 he held an exhibition featuring the Dongba script, the last surviving hieroglyphs on earth, in Lijuang, Yunnan, China. The exhibition went on to the US and attracted great attention. Awards he has won include Tokyo ADC Award Grand Prize, Tokyo TDC Award, the Good Design Award, Japan Academy Prize, Purple Ribbon Medal, and others.

B. Martin Pedersen [USA]

1937– born in Brooklyn, New York
Admitted to AGI, 1987

Switched from an engineering interest to advertising and ultimately graphic design. First job in Benton & Bowles ad agency and later D'Arcy, with night classes at the School of Visual Arts. Later became Corporate Design director for American Airlines. Last job was with Geigy Pharmaceutical Co. as both advertising art director and designer. In 1968 started Pedersen Design Inc. Clients included: American Airlines, Bell Labs, VW, Hopper Papers, Dow Jones & Co. In 1976 founded a magazine on boating called *Nautical Quarterly*.

In 1986 purchased Graphis Press from Walter Herdeg. Has taught at SVA and the Syracuse University graduate design programme.
Past president of the Type Directors Club, and served multiple terms on the Boards of Directors for the Art Directors Club and the AIGA. Elected into the Art Directors Hall of Fame in 1997, and in 2003 was the recipient of the AIGA Gold Medal.

Early promotional calendar series for **S.D. Scott Printing Co. company**.

The American Way, the first airline magazine for American Airlines.

Animal, cover for book of animal portraits by James Balog for Graphis.

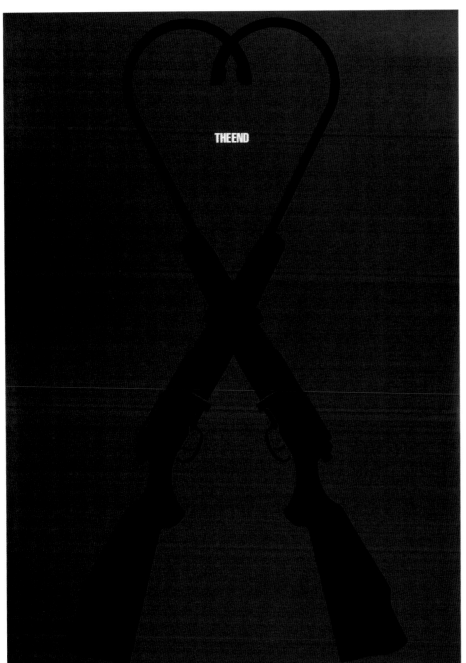

The End, poster, 1981.

All Flesh Is Grass, posters, 1998 (x 2).

Masuteru Aoba [Japan]

1939– born in Tokyo
Admitted to AGI, 1988

Masuteru graduated 1962 from the Kuwasawa Design Research Institute. He then joined Orikomi Co. Ltd. In 1969 he established the A&A Masuteru Aoba Design Office. His works have been awarded frequently, at home and abroad: ADC Award, 1972; gold, silver and bronze awards at the Japan Magazine Advertising Awards; second prize, International Graphic Design Biennale, Lahti, 1980; Grand Prix, International Biennale of Graphic Design, Brno, 1982; gold award, International Poster Biennale, Warsaw, 1987; NY ADC International Exhibition Gold Award, 1992; design of the first official poster for the 1998 Nagano Winter Olympics, 1993; bronze award, 5th International Poster Triennial, Toyama, 1997; bronze award, 5th International Biennale of the Poster, Mexico, 1998; second prize, Trnava Poster Triennial, 2000. Masuteru has also been honoured with solo exhibitions in Tokyo, New York, Los Angeles, Canada, Chaumont, Poland and elsewhere.

Peter Brookes [UK]

1943– born in Liverpool
Admitted to AGI, 1988

Brookes was educated at Heversham Grammar School, Westmoreland; RAF College, Cranwell (BA London Ext.); Manchester College of Art; Central School of Art & Design, London. He has been a freelance illustrator and cartoonist since 1969, and political cartoonist for *The Times* since 1993. Stamp designs for Royal Mail: 1995, 1999, 2003. Contributor to: *The Sunday Times*, *The Spectator*, *New Statesman*, *Radio Times*, *Times Literary Supplement*, *Time*, *The Week*.

Illustration tutor at the Central School of Art & Design, 1977–79, and Royal College of Art, 1979–89. FRSA, 2000; Royal Designer for Industry, 2002.
Awards: Political Cartoonist of the Year, Cartoon Art Trust Awards 1996, 1998, 2006; Cartoonist of the Year, British Press Awards 2002; D&AD Silver Award 2000; Cartoonist of the Year, BBC *What the Papers Say* Awards 2005.
Publications: Nature Notes, 1997; *Nature Notes II: The New Collection*, 1999; *Nature Notes III*, 2001; *Peter Brookes of The Times*, 2002; *Nature Notes IV*, 2004 (all published by Little, Brown & Co Ltd).

Cost of War in Afghanistan, 2006.

President Bush campaigns, 2004.

Israel's Prime Minister Ariel Sharon incapacitated by illness, 2006.

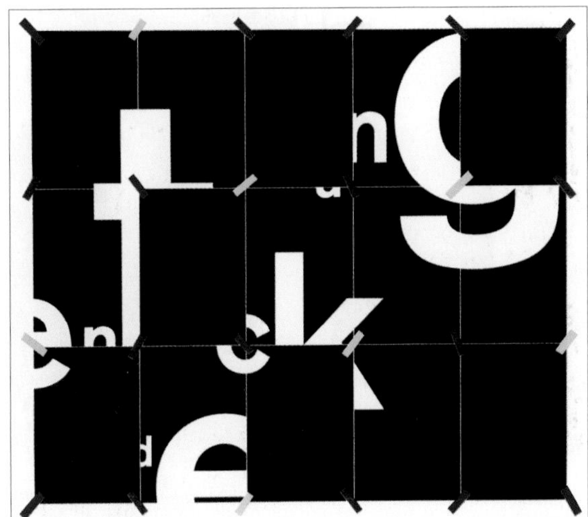

ZDF Matinee, poster for ZDF TV, 1979.

Seeing with Hands, stamp to celebrate 200 years of the Berlin School for the Blind, Bundesministerium der Finanzen, 2005.

Entdeckung (Discovery), poster for the Litfass Art Biennial, Munich, 1994.

Christof Gassner [Germany]

1941– born in Zürich, Switzerland
Admitted to AGI, 1988

Educated at the Kunstgewerbeschule Zürich under the guidance of Walter Binder, Walter Käch and Josef Müller-Brockmann. Followed by various industry and publishing assignments. Then starting in 1966, set up own graphic design studio in Frankfurt am Main; relocated to Darmstadt in 1992. The design studio specializes in editorial design, corporate design, typography, poster, book and stamp design. Important projects in the 1970s: PR work for the German TV channel ZDF, cooperation with Letraset (exhibitions in Darmstadt, Zürich and Krems) and development of typefaces.

In the 1990s: ecological projects, co-founder and art director of *Öko-Test Magazin*, relaunch and art direction of the magazine *Natur*. Designed visual concepts for the Kieler Woche festival in 1993, Deutscher Evangelischer Kirchentag in 1998 and Hessisches Landesmuseum Darmstadt in 2003. During the period between 1974 and 1988, close collaboration with Canton Hifi Electronics. Design of seventeen German stamps for the new millennium. 1986–92: professor of graphic design and typography at the Fachhochschule Darmstadt, 1993–2006: teaching at the Kunsthochschule Kassel. *Major awards:* Biennale Brno: Gold Medal and Icograda Excellence Award (1986), Design Prestige Award (1994); Deutsches Plakatmuseum: Dr Rudolf Brandes Prize (1994).

Koichi Sato [Japan]

1944– born in Takasaki
Admitted to AGI, 1988

Koichi studied in the design department of Tokyo National University of Fine Arts 1965–69. After two years at the advertising division of Shiseido, Japan's leading cosmetics company, he started to work freelance and gradually became known as one of the foremost explorers of traditional Japanese aesthetics in modern design. He won first prize in the MoMA International Poster competition (1988), received the Mainichi Design Award (1991) and Japan's Education Minister's Prize for outstanding artist (1998).

He has been recognized at international events, such as the International Biennial for Communications Design, Essen (1995, 1996 and 1999), Warsaw Poster Biennial (1996 and 1998), Golden Bee at Graphic Design Biennial, Moscow (1996, 1998 and 2000). Other prize-winning competitions include Brno (1994), Helsinki (1995), Mexico City (1996), Lahti (1997), Trnava (1997), Colorado (1977), Sofia (1998), and Hong Kong (1998). Koichi's mysterious and graceful works are in the permanent collections of museums all over the world. He lectured at the AGI congress in Paris (2001) and has been a professor at Tama Art University in Tokyo since 1995. He also enjoys writing haikus.

Fading Japan, exhibition poster, 1988.

Europalia Japan, poster, 1989.

Concert poster, 1974.

Typography Today (new edition), Seibundo Shinkosha, Tokyo, 2003. Cover and spread (x 2).

Pocari Sweat, isotonic soft drink. Otsuka Pharmaceutical, Tokyo, 1980.

Energen, energy drink. Otsuka Pharmaceutical,. Tokyo, 1993.

Helmut Schmid [Germany]

1942– born in Ferlach, Austria
Admitted to AGI, 1988

Rolf Müller called Helmut Schmid a *'musicus typographicus'*. Schmid studied under Emil Ruder, Robert Büchler and Kurt Hauert at the AGS Basel. He has worked in Berlin, Montreal, Vancouver, Stockholm and Düsseldorf (for the Social Democratic Party, the German government, and its chancellors Willy Brandt and Helmut Schmidt). Since 1977 he has been resident in Osaka. His brand identities for Otsuka Pharmaceutical (Pocari Sweat) and logomarks for Shiseido (Elixir) have had a long life.

He is a contributor to *Typographische Monatsblätter* (*TM*), *Idea* magazine and *baseline*, and has given lectures or workshops in Xian, Munich, Bombay, Seoul, Mainz, Zürich, Beijing, Basel and Tokyo. In 1978 the Print Gallery Amsterdam showed his *'Politypographien'* and in 2006, the *schmid today* project by the Fachhochschule Düsseldorf was shown at Seoul International Design Plaza. Helmut Schmid also teaches typography at Hongik University, Seoul.

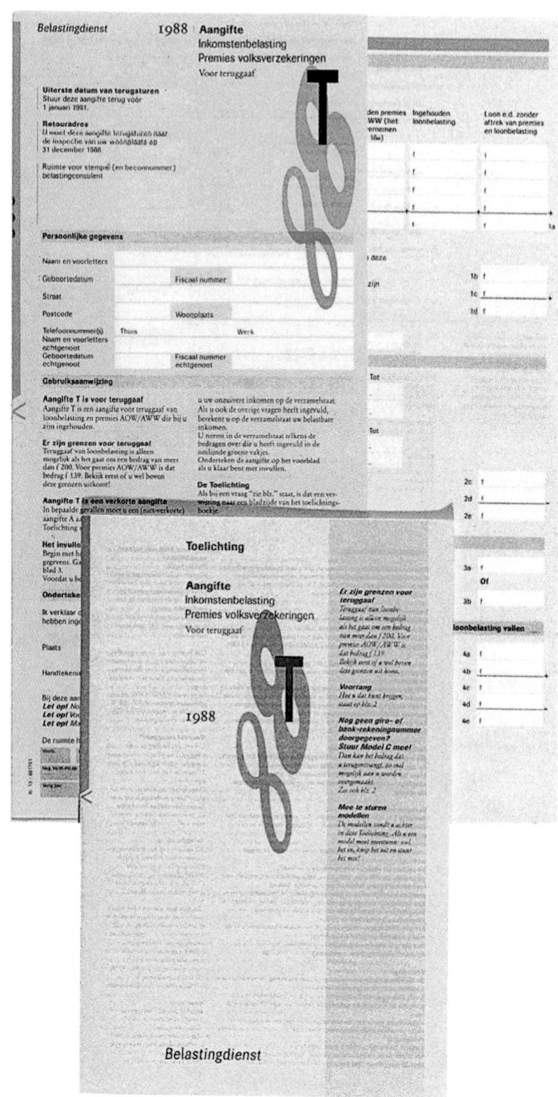
Belastingdienst
1988 Aangifte
Inkomstenbelasting
Premies volksverzekeringen
Voor teruggaaf

Persoonlijke gegevens

Naam en voorletters
Geboortedatum
Fiscaal nummer
Straat
Postcode
Woonplaats

Gebruiksaanwijzing

Toelichting

Aangifte
Inkomstenbelasting
Premies volksverzekeringen
Voor teruggaaf

1988

Belastingdienst

Edo Smitshuijzen [The Netherlands]

1944– born in Amsterdam
Admitted to AGI, 1988

Studied graphic design at the IVKNO, now called the Rietveld Academy in Amsterdam. Started as a freelance designer working for a large Dutch publishing house. Joined (1977) a small design partnership that grew out to be one of the largest design studios in the Netherlands after merging (1987) with an established group of interior architects and industrial designers. Became director of professional development of the new partnership, BRS Premsela Vonk. Worked as design principal in many major and comprehensive corporate design and/or signage commissions for Dutch governmental bodies and multinational companies, like the Ministries of Justice, Economic Affairs, Transport and Water Management, Home Office, High Courts, Court of Audit, Council of State, Tax and Customs, Central Bank, Royal National Library, National Archive, Open University and the city of The Hague. The partnership, nicknamed in the Netherlands *'the Ministry of Design'*, made a major contribution to the Dutch government's perspective on (graphic) design, which is still surprisingly unparalleled in other countries. He invented and developed a modular sign panel system (mss 0.5) now produced under licence in various countries around the world. He left the design partnership in 1994 and is currently an independent designer and writer on design.

Logo for the association of **Dutch Health Insurers**, reflecting the Dutch consensus-based society, 1994.

Dutch Tax Form, 1988. The Dutch Inland Revenue reaped great financial benefits as a result of improved efficiency after starting its comprehensive corporate identity programme in 1983.

mss 0.5. This modular sign panel system started as a spin-off from a signage project for the Royal Dutch National Library (1979). The system was then developed further and is now marketed worldwide.

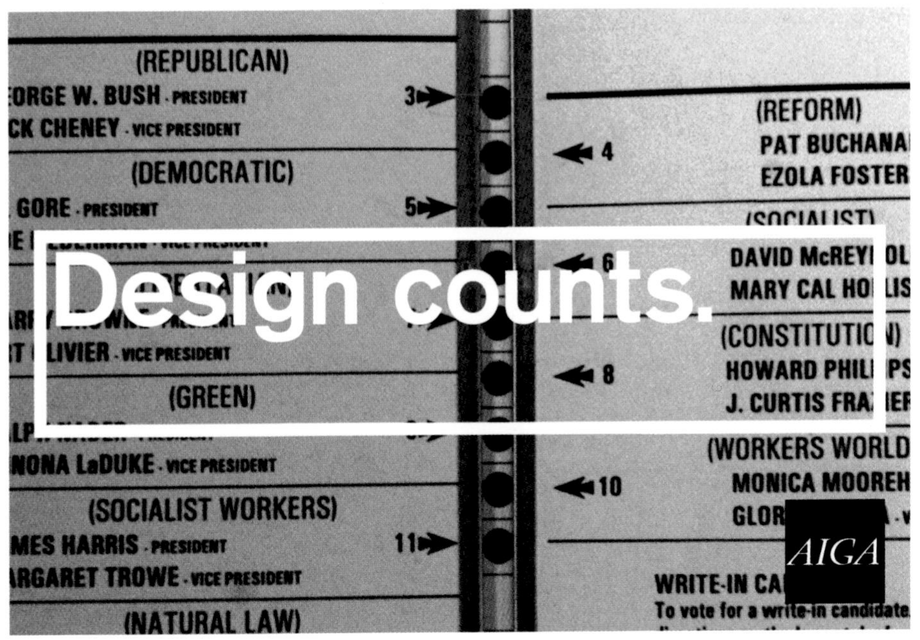

Light Years, poster for the Architectural League of New York, 1999.

Streetscape signage for Lower Manhattan, 2001. Client: Alliance for Downtown, New York. Photo credit: Peter Mauss/Esto.

Design Counts, poster for the 2001 AIGA National Design Conference, 2001.

Michael Bierut [USA]

1957– born in Cleveland, Ohio
Admitted to AGI, 1989

Michael Bierut studied graphic design at the University of Cincinnati's College of Design, Architecture, Art and Planning, graduating summa cum laude in 1980. Prior to joining Pentagram in 1990 as a partner in the firm's New York office, he worked for ten years at Vignelli Associates, ultimately as vice-president of graphic design. At Pentagram, Michael has created identities, packaging, publications and environments for clients that have included the Brooklyn Academy of Music, Harley-Davidson, Saks Fifth Avenue, Princeton University, *The New York Times* and the William Jefferson Clinton Foundation.

His work has ranged from brand standards for the New York Jets football team, to signage for a new town in central Florida, to serving as design consultant to United Airlines. Michael was president of the American Institute of Graphic Arts (AIGA) from 1998 to 2001. He was elected to the Art Directors Club Hall of Fame in 2003 and received the AIGA Medal in 2006. Michael is a senior critic in graphic design at the Yale School of Art, co-editor of the anthology series *Looking Closer: Critical Writings on Graphic Design*, and a co-founder of the weblog DesignObserver.com.

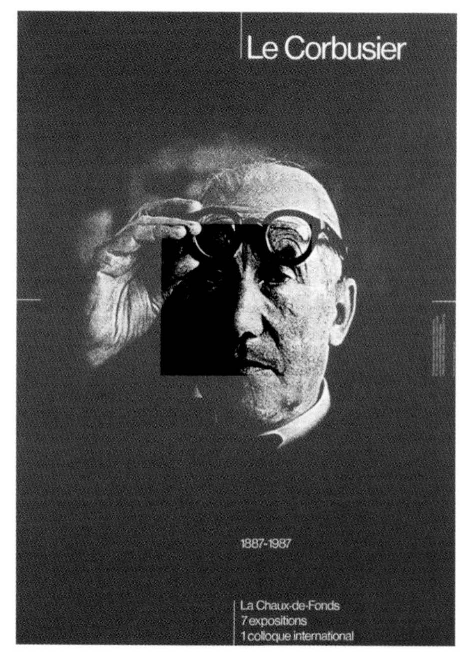

Werner Jeker [Switzerland]

1944– born in Mümliswil
Admitted to AGI, 1989

1965–onwards: has his own atelier in Lausanne. 1972–86: professor, School of Art and Design, Lausanne. 1974–86: head of graphic department. 1983: foundation of the community Les Ateliers du Nord with the industrial designers Cahen/Frossard, Lausanne. 1995–97: professor, State College for Design, Karlsruhe. 1997–98: visiting professor, École Supérieure des Arts Décoratifs (ENSAD), Paris. Since 2003: co-head of studies in visual communication, Berne University of the Arts. *Clients include*: cultural, social, commercial institutions: Théâtre Vidy-Lausanne, Swiss Foundation for Photography, Cinémathèque Suisse, Collection de l'Art Brut, Musée de l'Elysée, Musée des Arts Décoratifs, FNAC Galeries Photo, Cité de la Musique, Magnum Photo. *Selected projects:* corporate design for Weimar '99, European City of Cultural, 1999; Foundation Schloss Neuhardenberg, Berlin, 2001; Institut National du Patrimoine (INP), Paris, 2002; Signalschmerz Pavilion, Swiss Expo '02, 1998–2002.
Awards include: Swiss Department of the Interior awards for Best Poster of the Year, 1975–97; Award for Exceptional Use of Photography in Graphic Design, International Center of Photography, New York, 1988; first prize, new banknote series design, Swiss National Bank, 1989. A great number of his posters have won prizes at the Warsaw, Lathi and Toyama poster festivals, and feature in collections worldwide.

Noir/Black/Schwarz/Nero, exhibition poster, 1999.

Le Corbusier, exhibition poster, 1987.

Man Ray, exhibition poster, 1988.

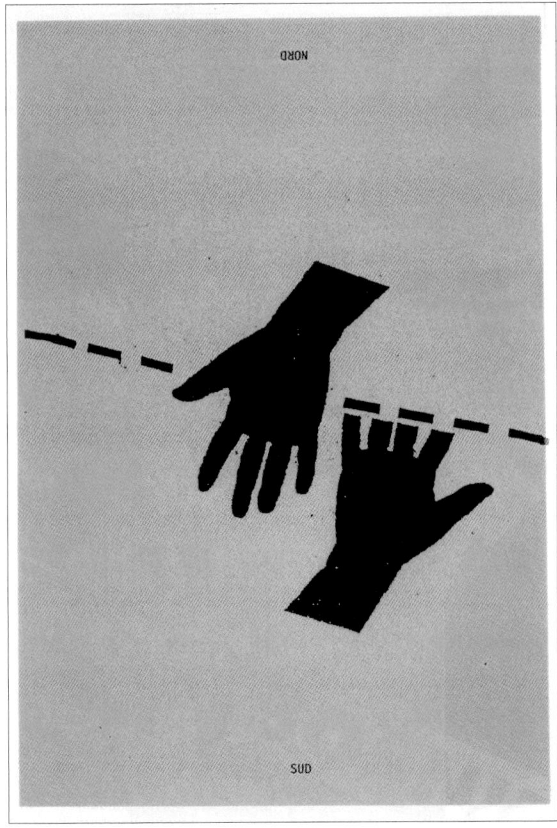

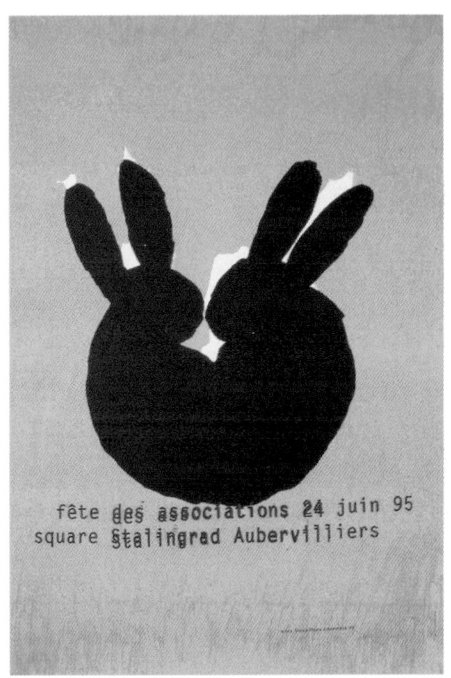

Image for a Grapus/NTE exhibition about the US–Mexican border.

Against the soft dictatorship in Tunisia, NTE, 1997.

Street festival poster, NTE, 1995.

Alexander Jordan [France]

1947– born in Winterkasten, Germany
Admitted to AGI, 1989

Alex Jordan is a graphic designer, photographer and professor. 1966: university entrance diploma. 1966–70: studies at the Kunstakademie, Düsseldorf (Academy of Fine Arts). This was followed by his first steps as an artist, husband, father, teacher and photographer. 1976: arrives at the graphic studio Grapus in Paris. Learns about graphic design, in exchange for his own creative and political talents. 1985: founded the photo agency Le Bar Floréal. 1989: foundation of the group Nous Travaillons Ensemble, as a part of Grapus (current members Sebastien Courtois, Elodie Cavel, Valérie Debure, Isabelle Jégo, Ronit Meirovitz). 1990: National Graphic design award for Grapus (Pierre Bernard, Gérard Paris-Clavel, Jean-Paul Bachollet, Alex Jordan). Break-up of the group. 1993: appointed to the communications and design department, Kunsthochschule Berlin-Weisensee. Since 2000: member of the Art Direction team, International Poster Festival, Chaumont, France. Board member for 100 Best Posters from Germany, Austria and Switzerland.

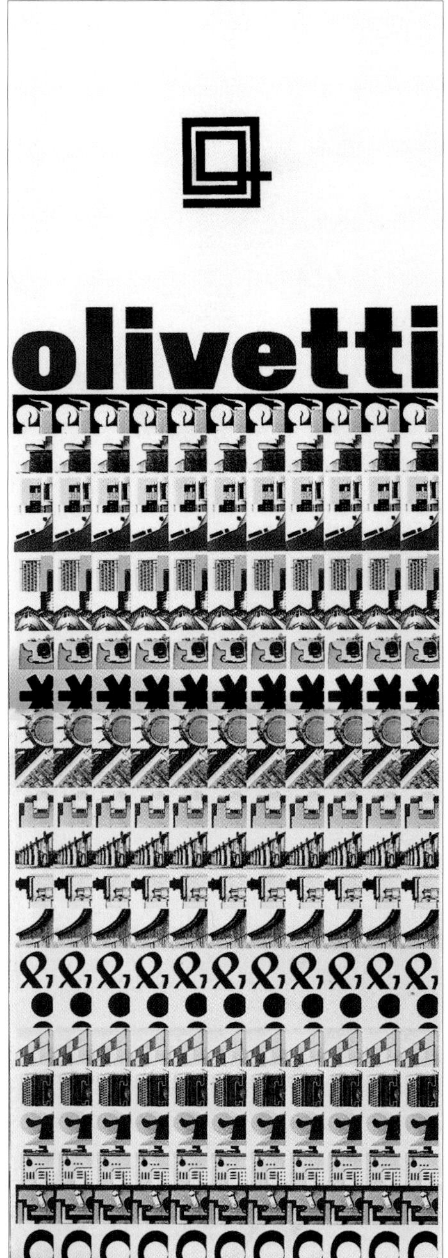

Enzo Mari [Italy]

1932– born in Novarra
Admitted to AGI, 1989

He attended the Brera Academy of Fine Arts in Milan, and dedicated his attention to research *'into the psychology of vision and the methodology of design'*. As a true philologist of the language of visual arts he is aware of the necessity of maintaining high standards of quality when designing for mass culture. He has created nearly 2,000 projects for Italian and international companies such as Alessi, Artemide, Danese, Driade, KPM, Olivetti, Zanotta, Magis, MUJI, Gebruder Thonet, Zani & Zani, Robots, Daum.

His works have been exhibited at Schloss Charlottenburg in Berlin, the International Museum of Ceramics in Faenza, and at the Venice Biennale and Milan Triennale. Examples of his art and design work are to be found in the collections of many museums, including the CSAC in Parma, the National Gallery of Modern Art in Rome and the NY MoMA. He has won more than 40 prizes, including four Compasso d'Oro awards. His books include *Progetto e Passione* (2001) and *La valigia senza manico* (2004).

Advertisement for **Olivetti**, 1965–68.

Universale Scientifica (Universal Scientific), book series, Boringhieri, 1965.

Formosa: perpetual wall calendar with movable plates, 1962, and **Timor: perpetual desk calendar**, 1966. Produced by Danese.

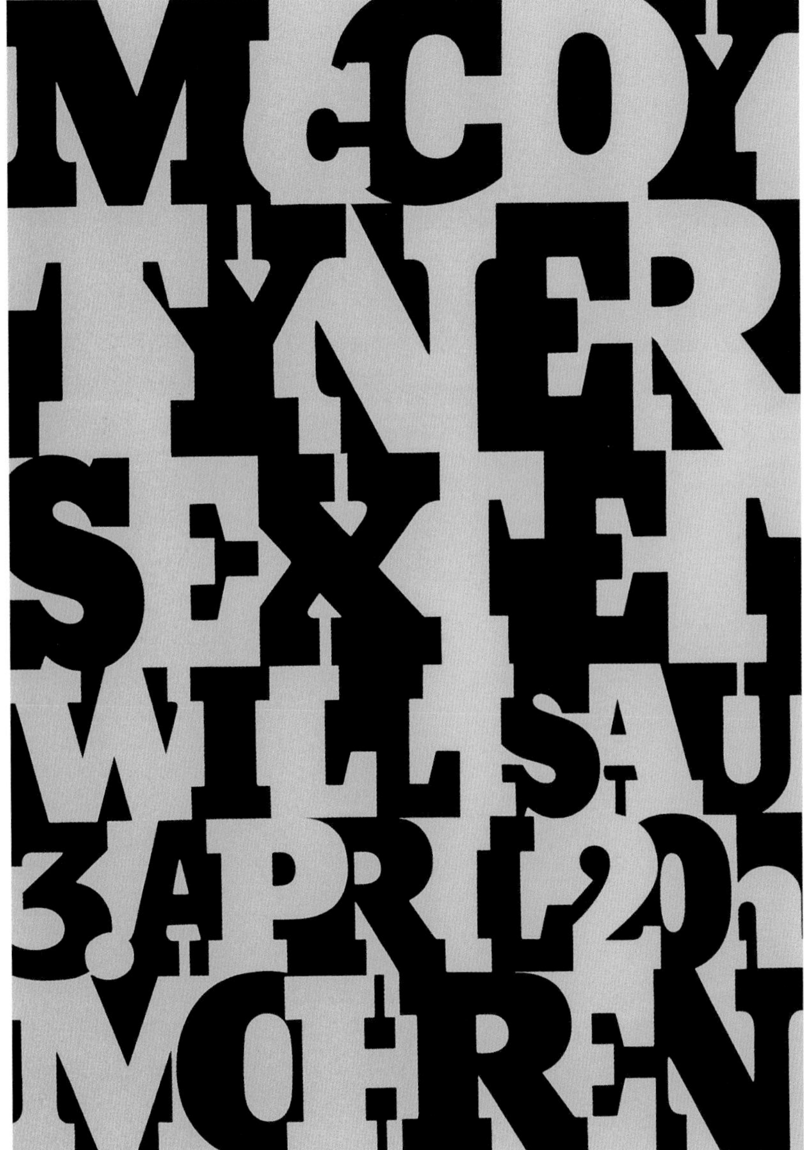

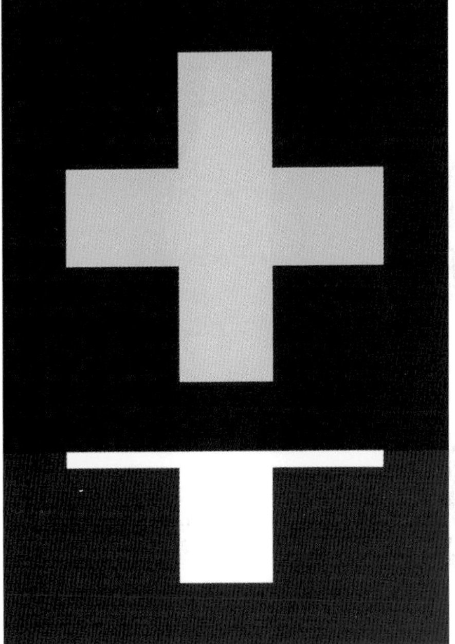

McCoy Tyner Sextet, concert poster, 1980.

Dead Trees, poster, 1992.

CH-EU, political poster, 1996.

Niklaus Troxler [Switzerland]

1947– born in Willisau
Admitted to AGI, 1989

Troxler studied graphic design at the Art School of Lucerne. He became an AD in Paris, and founded his own studio in 1973. He has been a professor at the State Academy for Art and Design in Stuttgart since 1998. He works for clients in the commercial and cultural fields, producing posters, CD and book covers, illustrations, typography, and more. Exhibitions in NY, Minneapolis, Mexico, Caracas, Paris, Berlin, Warsaw, Tokyo, Beijing. Many important international and national design and poster awards.

Books: *Jazz Blvd: Niklaus Troxler Posters* (Lars Müller), *A Designer's Design Life* (Wang Xu), *Niklaus Troxler Jazz Posters* (Oreos), *Niklaus Troxler: Master of Design* (Hesign).
His works are in many important design and poster collections, including NY MoMA, Minneapolis Institute of Arts, Stedelijk Museum Amsterdam, Wilanówa Poster Museum, Zürich Poster Collection, and Deutsches Plakat Museum Essen.

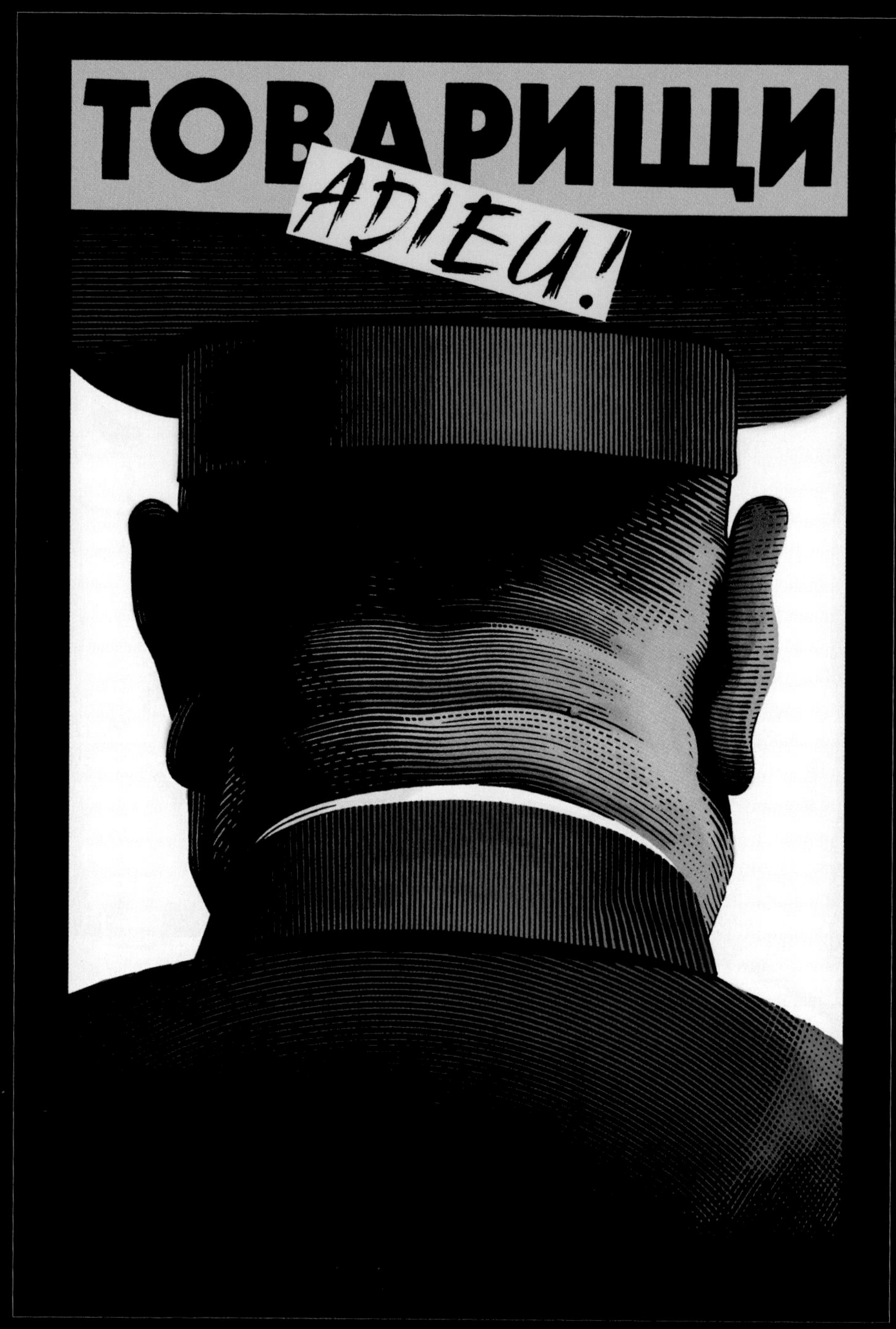

István Orosz, Hungary.

90s

The 1990s: Cold War Exits

Graphic design is a true companion to sociocultural life. It is a way to communicate culture, business and political contexts, to provide information and comment. The great changes in international society during the 20th century have demanded and created a real avalanche of visual communication. With it has come a great variety of often entirely new media. The young design profession has had little time to create proper education for its members and little time to grow up. It is a profession that has had to be invented and developed often simply by way of unexpected challenges initiated by society.

The Mother of Arts works overtime

Acknowledging the theory that architecture is the mother of the (applied) arts, my predecessor FHK Henrion (who wrote a similar book in the 80s) always referred, in his introductory texts to the decades, to the architectural scene. Looking at the built environment, one cannot evade the feeling that the economic peaks of the nineties have led to tremendous changes in urban landscapes, not only in the Western world, but also in Asia, from the Emirates to the cities of Bangkok, Jakarta, Kuala Lumpur, Singapore, Hong Kong, Seoul, Beijing and Shanghai (to mention just a few metropolises). New and often extravagant palaces of capitalism were built all over the globe, demonstrating extreme levels of luxury and scale. Astonishing new concepts, fabulous technical and aesthetic structures.

In Alpbach (Austria) the boxes were opened and Henrion personally handed out his AGI history books to the members attending the 1989 Congress. Just a few months later we witnessed a true political spring. Prague, Warsaw, Budapest and East Berlin staged massive demonstrations for freedom and democracy. On 10 November, the Berlin Wall was demolished. Gorbachev visited the Pope and met with the US president George Bush Sr. on a cruise ship in Malta harbour, proclaiming that the time for peace, after all those years of Cold War, was here to stay. Revolutions swept across large parts of the Communist areas of Eastern Europe. We witnessed dramatic changes in the world's political climate, causing huge waves of optimism and new prosperity. Nelson Mandela was set free, the Germanies reunited. The fragments of the Berlin Wall seemed to be the raw material for a new world of positivity. The palace of the megalomaniac Romanian leader was deserted. New palaces were built elsewhere, for the mighty leaders of the economic world.

The skylines of many important capitals changed dramatically in the early nineties. The Sheikh of Dubai transformed his small capital in the Arabian desert into a futuristic, super-luxurious, and even green New Manhattan of the Near East. He began extending his territory by creating artificial islands in the Gulf. Only a handful of decades ago, Dubai was a sleepy desert town with a population of a few hundred thousand people. It is now on its way to 3.5 million inhabitants. Among the developments are the plans to build the Palm Jebel Ali, a centre of commerce and tourism with golden towers, in the shape of a huge palm tree. Royal Haskoning is the architectural group that submitted the winning pitch for this marvel.

A confession: the eternal, old-fashioned modernist in me is heaving a sigh. *'Isn't more less?'* A great deal of the glamour of many structures in the oil-state capitals looks a lot like a blown-up set for a TV song festival. We can only hope that some of these architectural works will yield a few valuable laboratory results. The vast majority of the world's building cranes seem to be found in that area and in Shanghai.

Corporate headquarters and government centres top the bill in the irrepressible growth of the industrial world. Numerous new art museums have been built all over the globe. Frank O. Gehry first demonstrated his own, individual style in the Vitra Design Museum in Weil (Germany) and enhanced it in the design of the Bilbao Guggenheim. To some extent, Mendini's Groningen Museum also followed a kind of *'chaotic'* approach, but this was in fact a belated product of the 1980 Memphis concept. Everywhere, large vacated industrial buildings and whole harbour districts have been put to new purposes. Berlin, the capital that made its comeback, built a new centre and reputation. Rem Koolhaas, Herzog & De Meuron, Jean Nouvel, Richard Meyer, Norman Foster, Steven Holl, Ben van Berkel, Richard Rogers, Alonso Balaguer, Santiago Calatrava, Henning Larsen are just a few of the architects leading the dance.

Architects hate to be compared with fashion designers, as fashion is something that is quickly superseded, whereas buildings are meant to last for several decades, at least. Looking at many recently erected buildings, however, one cannot escape the impression that the liberated drawing boards (replaced by computers) are a source of oblique lines, recesses and curves. We see buildings ending in sharp, uninhabitable angles. The vertical facade is no longer axiomatic; nowadays so many buildings are leaning over that *'fashion'* would seem, indeed, to be evident. A new kind of town was created: the intercontinental airport. These not only accommodate airlines, but are also shopping malls, with all the visual glamour that goes along with the insatiable urge to consume luxury goods. The big airports have hotels, conference facilities, banks and other offices, warehouses and maintenance halls. Ten thousands of commuters are finding employment in these daytime towns.

Rick Poynor, the design critic who founded *Eye* magazine, observed of a chic shopping mall in Kent that it was, in fact, almost a small town for *'the happy many'* who share one passion, shopping, *'retail therapy'*. Poynor writes and lectures on the designer's responsibility in our *'spectacular society'*. Wise words.

The Cold War ends

The euphoric emotions caused by the end of the Cold War were not to last for long. Peace was soon disrupted by Iraq's invasion of Kuwait and the reaction of the US and its allies in 1991. The Middle East, Afghanistan, Somalia, Uganda, Sudan, Rwanda, Congo and the Balkan countries remained explosive political areas, which denied any immediate hope for real world peace. Many countries in South America remained also a permanent battleground in an internal cocaine war. Parts of the former USSR got into serious conflicts with each other or with Moscow. Peace was frequently at stake at the Kashmir borders of India and Pakistan; Sri Lanka is confronted with its Tamils. Apartheid in South Africa ended in 1993, however, and a year later Nelson Mandela became its first black president. In the former USSR, Mikhail Gorbachev made way for Boris Yeltsin.

The computer in charge

Computers have caused an unrivalled revolution in design. Drawing boards and slide rules disappeared rapidly after the mid-nineties. Screens, keyboards, scanners and printers took their place. Precision at pixel level meant the end of such traditional instruments and tools as the Rotring pen and rubber cement. External type shops and type catalogues were soon out of the picture. Many designers, starting with the young ones, took control of the total pre-press process. This new equipment speeded up the design process tremendously. Clients with their own computers for office work wanted quicker results and more alternatives. Naturally, fast equipment does not help reduce the time needed for analysis, inspiration and creation. Machines only help to produce rapid visualizations almost as perfect as a final printed result.
The majority of the (older) AGI designers present at the Amalfi congress of 1995 confessed that they, themselves, did not yet work with a computer. They either did not have one, or they left that work to their assistants or specialized operators.

Computer software opened the gates wide to graphic media. For many designers, this meant they could broaden their field of activity, entering the market for websites and film (also aided by the video camera). Old-fashioned, static slide presentations could be replaced by much more effective Powerpoint shows. Designers have replaced traditional typesetters. They can now work with their own selection of numerous fonts.

The Internet, the original concept of which was developed in the early 1960s, had already become reality in December 1969, when the four host computers of universities in California and Utah were interconnected. During the 1990s, the Internet gained momentum. In 1991, NSFNet was opened for commercial purposes. Online shopping arrived in 1994 and online banking via the Internet in 1999. In 1993 the Lycos search engine had some 800,000 webpages, by May 2005 Google had more than 8,000,000,000. These days, which designer or communicator can manage without frequently consulting the Internet and without those fast and frequent email contacts?

The stunning technological innovations have also dramatically affected the entire graphic industry. The complete content and design of books can now be transferred by CD-Rom or simply via the Internet. Printed matter can also be produced straight from computer to press.

Today's clients are very different from those of the mid-20th century. In those days, management could be design-conscious and even idealistic. The new generation is university-educated, often in marketing or communication sciences, and target and profit-driven. For many young designers with an art school background, these clients are sometimes of too high an intellectual level.

Do more designers necessarily mean greater quality?

The number of people leaving art schools to attempt to earn their living in our profession has seen unprecedented growth. It may be another side effect of the handy design tool, the computer, that so many youngsters were lured by the charms of design. They work for the arts world, for commercial clients, for authorities, but less often for political, social or ideological purposes. If you compare the developments in graphic design with those I mentioned in architecture, you will see a great similarity. The huge population of graphic designers lives under the pressure of harsh competition and – since the persistent economic depression in the early years of this century – is often faced with a real battle for professional survival. A world of more designers does not necessarily mean that standards have risen. We are seeing many desperate attempts to come up with original design solutions, which unfortunately fail to communicate properly. Typography is now sometimes used as a kind of wallpaper pattern that is not really meant to be read at all. The results may look attractive and intriguing but have, in my humble opinion, little to do with the fundamental tasks of graphic design. They are of solely decorative value; it is fine art, with the shape of letters as a motif. Illegible, *'dyslexic'* texts in an apparently non-existent language are the results.

I know that many people are intrigued by this approach, but it is simply not my cup of tea.
It would be quite wrong to compare that approach to graphic design with the projects of Dada, the Futurists, the Constructivists and De Stijl. Those movements were strongly connected with and part of contemporary, heated social revolutions. Yet many works that were produced under those umbrellas also often suffered from illegibility. While the technical limitations and material shortages of the 1920s played a role in those designs, the opposite seems to have happened in the late 1990s: the computer strongly facilitated the development of what I referred to as *'dyslexic'* typography. There was no longer any idealism, no higher objective to be served. We had left behind all the constraints of the old typographical tools. The computer assured total freedom. That also explains why that same computer serves as the perfect tool for enabling hordes of people to instantly develop useless alphabets: typefaces that seem to serve no purpose other than giving brief satisfaction to their creator.

Ben Bos, Amsterdam, 2006

AGI History in the 1990s

The End of Print?

Ben Bos, Amsterdam, 2006

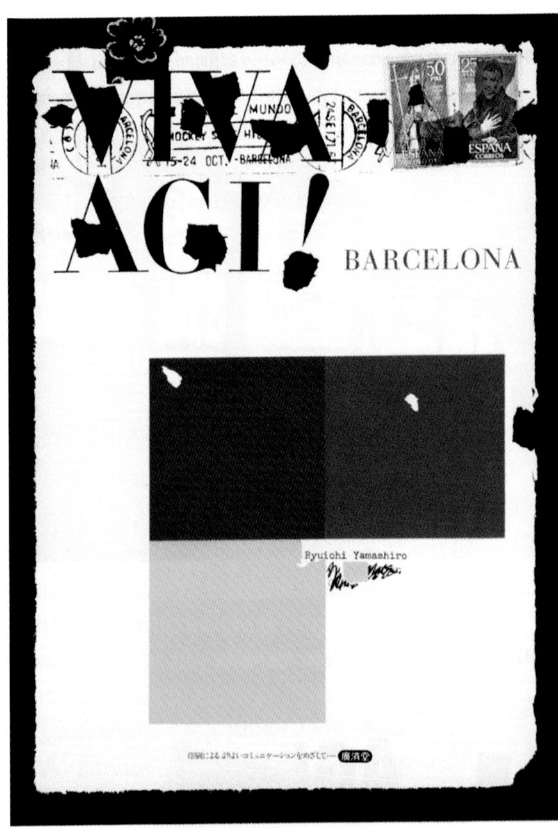

Unofficial poster by Ryuichi Yamashiro.

Despite the rather French origins of the AGI, 23 years went by before the Alliance met again on French soil: Blois, on the Loire, 1990. The congress had an important patron in the person of the Minister of Culture, Jack Lang. His involvement in the large-scale topical projects of Centre Pompidou, La Villette, the Musée d'Orsay and the Louvre and the associated graphic communication, information and education gave great added value to the congress. Grapus handled the organization and ensured a heavily philosophical and political slant to the programme. The enormous, elegant Renaissance château of Blois was the venue. The great courtyard offered plenty of fresh air after the often grave subject matter of the numerous speeches by politicians and authorities. Mime artists peopled the stage to provide distraction in the interim.
An exhibition of members' work had been set up; as usual, posters were in the majority. This region, full of castles and vineyards, is famed for its culinary specialities and fine wines, of which we were privileged enough to partake.

1991 took the AGI to Cairns in Australia for the first time. For many, this was the ultimate far-from-hearth-and-home show. This was reflected in the modest turnout, 52 if you counted everybody. Well,

on the designer/teacher Josef Albers. Richard Hess, Jackie Casey, Max Huber and Bernard Villemot were all commemorated in a silent slide show.

Paul Rand acted as the critical teacher. A highly spectacular part of the programme was the theatre/fashion show by Oscar-winner Eiko Ishioka. This was followed by a round trip around and inside unique houses on the coast of Long Island. AIGA New York organized a presentation at Cooper Union by Ken Cato, Shigeo Fukuda, Werner Jeker, Pierre Mendell and Bruno Oldani.

In 1993, AGI again held an exhibition in New York.

In 1994, the university town of Cambridge received AGI at an academic level! For the occasion, the members were invited to express something of their humour on a postcard. These were bundled together into a thick paperback full of splendid fun, under the title *Humour is a Serious Thing*. A sad coincidence: the *'minimalist'* cartoonist Mel Calman, who had just become president of AGI Great Britain and the man behind the book, had died in the run-up to this congress. Henry Steiner wrote: *'Mel's ghost would have been amused by the fuss he caused when he died instantly from a heart attack while watching a film in a West End cinema.'* Michael Rand talked about Mel at the congress.

The Garden House Hotel on the river Cam was capable of accommodating the entire, rather modest, party. Cambridge lived up to its reputation 100 percent: the wonderful colleges and their grounds, the punts, the omnipresent students, the pubs, the teas, the English breakfasts and the charming rural surroundings. The town offered a great book market and you could have yourself measured for a lawyer's wig or a college tie.

Muriel Cooper presented *'Flying Through Information'*, a virtual space performance by her MIT Media Lab. Then followed the General Assembly, where there were a couple of hard nuts to be cracked. As always, the discussion primarily concerned admission policy and its consequences. Luckily, humour came back in a talk by Peter Brookes and Nick Garland (humour in newspapers) and the presentation by Yarom Vardimon, Pierre Mendell, John McConnell and Italo Lupi on humour in their own countries and a UK advertising guru, John Hegarty. AGI's latest *'acquisition'* Roger Law of *Spitting Image* fitted perfectly with the subject, as did the sponsors Guinness, who like to use humour to present their beer. David Gentleman presented *'The Kite and the Sting'*. We sat in the gothic choir stalls of Trinity College chapel, listening to sacred music and taking a moment to remember Mel Calman. We dined in veritable academic style, by candlelight in Downing College. Well and truly *'warmed'* we returned home, to answer the call of waiting work.

In 1994, an AGI Young Professional Seminar was held in London.

That year saw the passing of Jacques Richez, the eminent and highly respected AGI member whose contribution to AGI and his (unfortunately rather fruitless) struggle for a better design climate in his native Belgium is unforgettable. He once advertised in a Belgian newspaper: *'Serious designer seeks talented client.'* Gilles Fiszman, compatriot and friend, spoke about this exceptionally valuable AGI pioneer at the next congress.

Amalfi, by the Tyrrhenian Sea, to the south of Naples, Vesuvius, Pompeii and Capri. What a fantastic location for AGI 1995! A sun-drenched coastal town, with its back against the mountains. AGI gathered in the port of Naples and sailed to Amalfi, which dates back to the 10th and 11th centuries. The almost 120(!) guests were housed in various lodgings, partly with a view to their budgets. We were asked to bring a design for a pizza, not round, but 40 x 40 cm. Was this perhaps a vague intimation of the future of Italian *cucina*? It was a real shame that the Italian AGI members had stayed at home in their droves. The actual congress took place in the Arsenale, a historic ruin near the harbour, with great vaulted domes and, unfortunately, just too much daylight to do justice to projection. A gentleman from the Bodoni museum in Parma greeted us warmly, only to inform us that it's actually impossible to get into. The rest of the programme included a discussion between the generations, between the digi-nitwits, the designosaurs and the young ones, the computer generation. Massimo Vignelli and April Greiman in the boxing ring, partly as a result of a controversial letter from Paula Scher that should never have been printed. Meanwhile, a spontaneous *'questionnaire'* among the audience was unable to lie: the majority of the AGI members present belonged to the digi-nitwit brigade. AGI was

1993: AGI congress in Montauk, Long Island, USA.

Programme leaflet.

Shigeo Fukuda, integrated with a fish.

1994: AGI congress in Cambridge, England.

Punt Regatta.

Congress members on the university grounds, Kings College.

Creative assignment: 'Humour in Design'. Postcard by Hans Hillmann.

1995: AGI congress in Amalfi, Italy.

Registration of the congress visitors.

The AGI crowd on the steps of Amalfi Cathedral.

1997: *Essays on Design 1*, published by Booth-Clibborn Editions, London

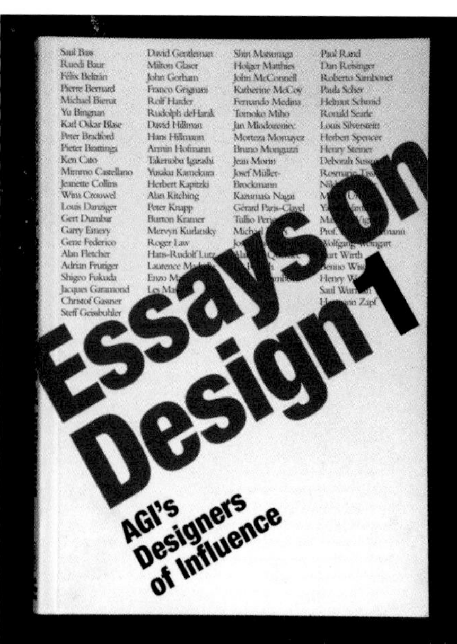

1997: AGI congress in Barcelona, Spain.

Everybody enjoys a lovely lunch.

Peret (Pedro Torrent), one of the congress organizers.

Peter Andermatt, always drawing and painting.

threatening, as in the early 1960s, to become an AGeing I, a bulwark of self-important, rather elderly elitists. And then it was time for lunch...

We visited a delightful local paper-maker's. Some people hired a car and drove to Paestum, where they spent an enjoyable afternoon at the ancient temple ruins and on the winding coastal road.
One evening was spent at sea. The fishermen took us to their far-off fishing grounds where, by the light of the moon, they cooked fish and chips on board, which we washed down with the local wine.
The customary AGI official photo was taken on the high steps of Amalfi Cathedral. The following year, the AGI took a sabbatical from its series of congresses. For contemplation, perhaps?

More sadness: within the space of six months, we lost a number of prominent AGI members: Jock Kinneir, Roberto Sambonet, Bradbury Thompson, Walter Herdeg, Gérard Miedinger, Roman Cieslewicz and Kurt Wirth. There was a worthy commemoration in the *AGI Letter* 5/6.

In 1997, it was Europe again: AGI in Barcelona. Spanish temperament, in the highly capable hands of Javier Mariscal and Pedro 'Peret' Torrent. The fabulous city played the major role (although there were criminal touches here and there, as a number of light-fingered locals helped themselves to quite a few things). But what brilliance, what energy and what creativity we were treated to. The welcome dinner was held in a lively restaurant, Hivernacle, on the completely renovated quay. The congress commenced with a presentation on Spanish culture and design. In the evening, we moved to Peret's big studio. The studio was an almost theatrical revelation, as good as the work he showed. *'Airs of Spain'* entertained us with live music. The next day was AGI day: the assembly and the presentation of new members. A new board also took up its role: Ken Cato, David Hillman, Jean Robert, Ruedi Rüegg, Laurence Madrelle and Uwe Loesch. These IEC members were allotted their own *'ministries'*.

The evening started with *'The Incredible Magic Bus Tour'*. The tour of the city was linked to all kinds of pieces of street theatre, mini operas, fake bullfights and acrobatics. Gaudi received a generous amount of attention, with his Sagrada Familia and the Parc Güell, where we were treated to a surprising concert and fireworks once the sun had made way for the moon. Dinner was on the mountainside. The following morning, Ruedi Baur, George Hardie, Lars Müller and Paula Scher got us to look to the future, *'Inventing the Next Century'*. In the evening, the coach took us to the equally vast Estudio Mariscal, where the young maestro delighted us with his cinematic presentation, *'The History of Colours'*. His often exuberant work bears a very clear signature. The recent AGI acquisitions, Peret and Mariscal, immediately won the hearts of all their colleagues. The farewell party at an industrial site was a whirl of dancing, acrobatics, theatre, lights, fire, music, food and drink: an overwhelming, unforgettable experience for all the senses. Barcelona set some great AGI records.

AGI also unveiled its own *'Oscar'* award, named the *'Henri'*, a typical Peret creation, intended to be awarded annually to members of extraordinary merit. Two were immediately promised in the presence of Henrion's widow, Marion: one for the co-founder Jacques Nathan Garamond and one for Pieter Brattinga (which I later handed to him in Amsterdam during a private viewing at his Print Gallery).

The selection committee for new members in Barcelona (1997) received nominations for no fewer than 80 candidates. Even more astounding is that 50 of them were accepted. If you look at the list of names, it is a qualitatively impressive company (see *AGI Letter* #9 of September 1997). Surely it can't be that the 50 from 1997 were flukes? In 1998, too, there were more than 80 candidates and these generated 47 new members. *Agitate* in March 1999 again demonstrated a solid level of quality.

In 1997 seven prominent French designers wrote a very concerned letter in the *AGI Letter* (#9). They wondered what was left of the ideals and intentions of the AGI founding fathers. *'The history of design is difficult to write. Has it developed independently from history: fascism/socialism/world war/Cold War/fall of totalitarian socialism/triumph of the international financial capitalism?' 'What should be our values as designers today'* and *'What to do and what to teach?'*

We do design to commemorate Hiroshima, to celebrate human rights, to fight child labour and child abuse, to guard against the mistreatment of prisoners, but those are still the proverbial drops in the ocean. We are now 10 years further on and the right answers have still not been given. Certainly, the gap between the insatiable *'haves'* and the *'have-nots'* has widened enormously. There would appear to be no suppressing the greed and the urge to flaunt. Some have two-million-Euro cars, pimped up for the same amount again... and some have daily wages of something like $1 or less.

The themes of AGI Toronto 1998 were *'Confrontation, Collaboration and Congregation'*, with the emphasis on the first. A city of 4.5 million people, dubbed by Peter Ustinov *'New York run by the Swiss'*. The welcome reception was in the Design Exchange (DX), a landmark from the 1930s. Readings and discussions were on the agenda for the second day. A mixture of AGI members, other designers, architects, artists, musicians and people from the theatre world. More confrontations and debates on day 3, when an exhibition of Canadian postage stamps by AGI members also opened. A culinary tour and jazz concluded the day. The final AGI day was reserved for the assembly and the dinner dance.

1999: AGI in Pontresina, Switzerland. 300 students attended the symposium held in Zürich's Art Museum prior to the congress. Bülent Erkmen (Turkey), Irma Boom (The Netherlands), Makoto Saito (Japan), James Victore, Stefan Sagmeister and Dana Arnett were received by an enthusiastic audience. We then travelled on to Pontresina in Oberengadin. It was a gathering of unprecedented size: some 170 participants, including a remarkable number of newcomers. Not so surprising in itself, as the selection procedure in Barcelona had approved no fewer than 50 new members from a candidate list of 80! Hotel Saraz Pontresina houses the *'Rondo'*, a new congress centre built from steel and glass with an unimpaired view of the magnificent snowy mountaintops. It was there that the presentation and discussions were held. The poster exhibition had been set up in the grounds in front of the building. The theme for the piece to bring along was this time a (loose-leaf) 4 Letter Poetry Book. Coffee breaks to catch up with news and look at the pieces we had all brought. After lunch, the coach took us to the Maloja Pass, to the house of the painter, sculptor and poster artist Giovanni Giacometti and his sons Alberto and Diego. Reception in the oldest (former) hotel in the area. Ancient and modern music: a frequent element of this AGI congress, *'orchestrated'* by Niklaus Troxler, mostly on traditional instruments. The hotel's wonderful indoor pool was a great place for long-remembered, moving conversations. On Friday afternoon, the coach took us to the foot of the cable-lift to the Diavolezza glacier, at 3,000 m. A mountain camel and three llamas awaited us at the mountain hut. Four Alp horns *'vied'* with a saxophonist.

There was a presentation by Jörg Zintzmeyer on the design of the new Swiss banknotes and corporate design – about which we like to think that we ourselves know something. Anne-Marie Sauvage, curator of the Bibliothèque Nationale de France, talked about the AGI archive it houses. All this was accompanied by excellent food and drink. The General Assembly, on the last day, was primarily devoted to commemorating the many old and even young friends we had seen leave us: Anton Stankowski, Georges Calame, Franco Grignani, Takashi Kono, Giovanni Pintori. Rick Eiber, AGI founder and lecturer Donald Brun, Gene Federico, plus Tibor Kalman and P. Scott Makela. A sad list. It was a time of constant partings. The last dance on the final evening and tears over breakfast.

After a long series of not-too-pretentious AGI Bulletins and Newsletters, suddenly we had *AGITATE*, the richly illustrated and beautifully designed newsletter devised by Pentagram's David Hillman. Lots of news, good reports and high-quality articles, such as the one on *'Alerting the minds of young designers'* (prompted by the AGIdeas 10th conference in Australia) and an alarming look by Edo Smitshuijzen at the lack of ideals and the role of design in today's chaotic world. And, in an earlier issue, a cri-de-coeur from Pierre Bernard. To quote just one line of his: *'If we want a really international AGI, we must remember that the major part of the world is not that of easy consumerism but rather a planet that is paralysed by troubles where most people suffer far too much to live in harmony.'* Alas, *Agitate* came all too rarely through the letterbox.

1998: AGI congress in Toronto, Canada.

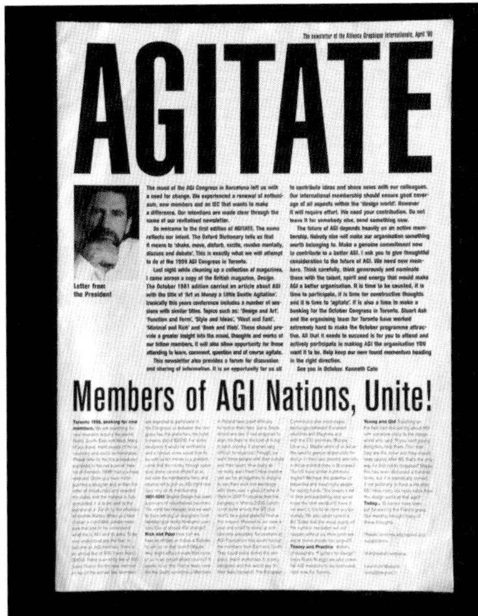

The newsletter of the Alliance Graphique Internationale, April '98

AGITATE

Letter from the President

The mood of the AGI Congress in Barcelona left us with a need for change. We experienced a renewal of enthusiasm, new members and an IEC that wants to make a difference. Our intentions are made clear through the name of our revitalised newsletter.

So welcome to the first edition of AGITATE. The name reflects our intent. The Oxford Dictionary tells us that it means to 'shake, move, disturb, excite, revolve mentally, discuss and debate'. This is exactly what we will attempt to do at the 1998 AGI Congress in Toronto.

Last night while cleaning up a collection of magazines, I came across a copy of the British magazine, Design. The October 1981 edition carried an article about AGI with the title of 'Art as Money a Little Gentle Agitation'. Ironically this years conference includes a number of sessions with similar titles. Topics such as: 'Design and Art', 'Function and Form', 'Style and Ideas', 'West and East', 'Minimal and Rich' and 'Book and Web'. These should provide a greater insight into the mood, thoughts and works of our fellow members. It will also allow opportunity for those attending to learn, comment, question and of course agitate.

This newsletter also provides a forum for discussion and sharing of information. It is an opportunity for us all to contribute ideas and share news with our colleagues. Our international membership should ensure good coverage of all aspects within the 'design world'. However it will require effort. We need your contribution. Do not leave it for somebody else, send something now.

The future of AGI depends heavily on an active membership. Nobody else will make our organisation something worth belonging to. Make a genuine commitment now to contribute to a better AGI. I ask you to give thoughtful consideration to the future of AGI. We need new members. Think carefully, think generously and nominate those with the talent, spirit and energy that would make AGI a better organisation. It is time to be counted, it is time to participate, it is time for constructive thoughts and it is time to 'agitate'. It is also a time to make a booking for the October Congress in Toronto. Stuart Ash and the organising team for Toronto have worked extremely hard to make the October programme attractive. All that it needs to succeed is for you to attend and actively participate in making AGI the organisation YOU want it to be. Help keep our new found momentum heading in the right direction.

See you in October. Kenneth Cato

Members of AGI Nations, Unite!

Dear AGI Colleagues

P Scott and Massimo Agree on Garbage!

Who was there

Madrelle's contribution

3 IEC meeting notes

Who are they

Toronto '98

Congress report, published in *AGITATE*, a special AGI newsletter, produced by David Hillman.

1999: AGI congress Pontresina, Switzerland.

An afternoon at the glacier, with an Alp horn concert and spitting llamas.

Admitted 1990:
Hinrichs, kit
Yagi, tamotsu

Admitted 1991:
–

Admitted 1992:
Baur, ruedi
Lutz, hans-rudolf *
Unger, gerard *
Yu, bingnan

Admitted 1993:
Blatch, bernard
Büttner, Helmut Feliks
Ensikat, klaus
Finger, enzo
Meyer, rudi
Müller, lars •
Rosenbaum, sarah
Scher, paula

Admitted 1994:
Greenberg, bob
Hardie, george
Jones, terry •
Kitching, alan
Law, roger
Madrelle, laurence
Miranda, oswaldo *
Rushworth, john
Saito, makoto

Admitted 1995:
Mariscal, javier
Miho, james n.
Schraivogel, ralph
Torrent (peret), pedro •

Admitted 1996:
Doyle, stephen
Fisher, jeffrey
Kalman, tibor *
Lancashire, david

Admitted 1997:
Aartomaa, tapani
Apeloig, philippe
Balan, franco
Baissait, bernard •*
Bertram, polly
Bohatsch, walter
Boom, irma
Bouvet, michel
Bucher, mayo
Carbone, ken
Crosby, bart
Eiber, rick
Erlbruch, wolf
Eskenazi, mario
Godard, keith
Gutiérrez, fernando
Kan, tai-keung
Karamustafa, sadik
Keaney, siobhan *
Kemming, loek *
Koeweiden, jacques
Lins, rico
Lionni, pippo *
Makela, p. scott
Matsui, keizo
Montalvo Aguilar, germán
Nygaard, finn
Oberholzer, sabina
Ott, nicolaus
Pfüller, volker
Piippo, kari
Pol, santiago
Probst, robert
Reitsma, lex
Rodriguez, carlos •*
Ruiz, david
Schmitz, hans günter
Sködt, finn
Smolan, leslie
Sotillo, alvaro
Stein, bernard
Woodward, fred •*
Zask, catherine
Zintzmeyer, jörg •*

Admitted 1998:
Allemann, hans-ulrich
Anderson, charles spencer
Arnett, dana
Baviera, michael
Boer, michel de
Coates, stephen
Cooper, kyle
Dempsey, mike bernard •*
Erkmen, bülent
Esterson, simon •
Fili, louise
Gaberthüel, martin
Gelman, alexander
Gericke, michael
Goldberg, carin
Grear, j. malcolm
Imboden, melchior
Isley, alexander
Kidd, chip
Kunz, willi
Lévy, jean-benoît
Michael, anthony
Miki, ken
Miller, abbott
Morla, jennifer
Nakajima, hideki
Nash, stephanie
Netthoevel, andreas
Niijima, minoru
Rodriguez Valencia, gabriela
Sagmeister, stefan
Sato, u.g.
Satoh, taku
Schedler, clemens theobert
Sebastian, james
Skolos, nancy
Sommese, lanny
Tartakover, david
Telmet, tiit
Tenazas, lucille
Till, peter
Valicenti, rick
Victore, james •*
Wadden, douglas
Wasilewski, mieczyslaw •*

Admitted 1999:
Ahn, sang-soo
Chaika, vladimir
Hagenberg, helfried
Hyland, angus
Lenz, anette
Logvin, andrey •*
Niemann, christoph
Varga, mihaly

• *no work submitted*
* *no longer member of AGI*

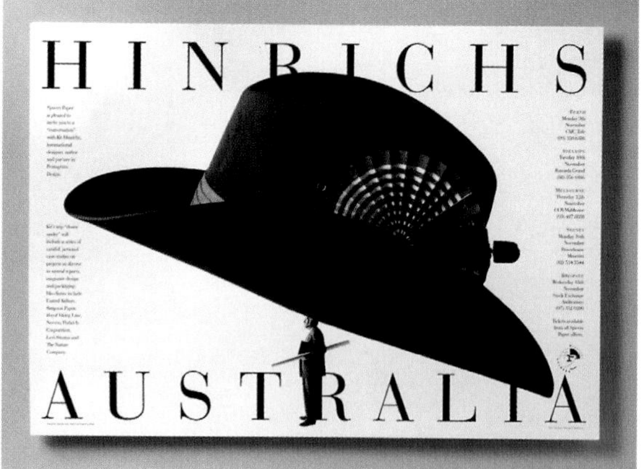

Kit Hinrichs [USA]

1941– born in Torrance, California
Admitted to AGI, 1990

Kit Hinrichs is a partner in the San Francisco office of the international design firm Pentagram, and has been an influential force in graphic design for more two decades. Included among the hundreds of projects that he has design-directed are the Sony Metreon Entertainment Complex interior graphics, United Airlines' *Hemispheres* magazine, The Nature Company identity and catalogue (1980s), and countless annual reports, corporate identities, and packaging, exhibition, editorial, and promotional campaign programmes.

Kit has taught at the School of Visual Arts in New York, the California College of Arts and Crafts in San Francisco, and the Academy of Art in San Francisco. His work has been honoured and widely published internationally and several of his pieces are part of the permanent collection of the MoMA NY and SF and the Smithsonian Institution's Cooper-Hewitt Museum. He is also the co-author of several books on design and a much sought-after guest speaker. He is an AIGA Fellow, past national executive board member and most recently (2004), a medallist of the American Institute of Graphic Arts. Currently, he serves as a trustee of Art Center College of Design and on the Accessions Design and Architecture committee of the SF MoMA.

@issue: Journal of Business and Design, 1994–2006.

Hinrichs Australia, poster for five-city lecture tour, 1990.

Cover for **The Nature Company** direct mail catalogue, 1986.

Grand Hyatt Tokyo, Roppongi Hills, 2003.
Comprehensive design for room amenities, restaurant naming and identity designs.

United Colors of Benetton: Tribu, 1994.
Graphic identity, product design, package design and advertising for Benetton's Tribu fragrance.

C3: identity and package design, 1996–2004.
Corporate identity and package designs for over one hundred products for this Japanese confectionery shop.

Tamotsu Yagi [USA]

1949– born in Kobe, Japan
Admitted to AGI, 1990

In 1984, Tamotsu Yagi brought his 18 years of multi-faceted design experience to California from his native Japan to become the art director for ESPRIT, a San Francisco-based apparel manufacturer. The combination of Japanese sensibilities with West Coast dynamics proved to be successful and influential. The development of the 'ESPRIT Graphic Look' under Yagi's direction was internationally celebrated. He retired from ESPRIT in 1990 and established Tamotsu Yagi Design as an independent multi-disciplinary design studio in San Francisco. With the medium of graphic design at the core, he has worked on a wide range of projects worldwide, including culinary, hospitality, beauty, fashion, exhibition, signage, product and furniture design. Clients include Apple Computers, Intel Corporation, Grand Hyatt Tokyo, Four Seasons Tokyo, and Benetton. Signage direction and design for Yoshio Taniguchi's architecture have been recent projects. Yagi's approach is to design with active curiosity combined with strong aesthetics and artistry. He has been honoured by the induction of over 100 examples of his work to the permanent collection of the SF MoMA. Selected works from this collection were featured in a special exhibit at the opening of the SF MoMA building in 1995.

Ruedi Baur [France]

1956– born in Neuilly sur Seine
Admitted to AGI, 1992

Baur has dual French and Swiss nationalities, and graduated in graphic design from the Zürich School of Applied Arts. After having created BBV (Lyons–Milan–Zürich) in 1983, in 1989 he set up Integral Concept, presently comprising the studios of five independent partners, who are able to intervene jointly on any cross-disciplinary project. Since 1989 in Paris and 2002 in Zürich, Intégral Ruedi Baur et Associés has worked on two- and three-dimensional projects within different fields of visual communication: identity, orientation and information programmes, exhibition design and urban design. Between 1989 and 1994, he coordinated the department of design *'information space'* at the École des Beaux-Arts, Lyons; between 1994 and 1996 he ran a course based on the theme *'civic and design spaces'*. In 1995, he became professor of corporate design at the Hochschule für Grafik und Buchkunst, Leipzig, where he was rector from 1997 until 2000. There he created the Interdisciplinary Design Institute (2id) in 1999. In April 2004 he set up the Design Institute at the Hochschule für Gestaltung und Kunst der Stadt Zürich (HGKZ). He regularly teaches at Laval University, Québec (École de Percée), the CAFA Central Academy of Fine Art of Beijing, China, and the Lu Xun Academy of Shenyang.

Centre Pompidou (x 2), signage system and visual identity.

Cité Internationale Universitaire de Paris, sign system and site identity programme, as part of the renovation of the 34-hectare area, bringing together 38 residences. In collaboration with Eric Jourdan.

Köln-Bonn Airport, visual identity programme and signage system.

Known Faces (x 2).

From **'The Circle as a Visual Theme'**, in *Die Hieroglyphen von Heute*.

Hans-Rudolf Lutz [Switzerland]

1939–1998; born in Zürich
Admitted to AGI, 1992

He made his professional start as a typographer, after training at Orell Füssli Printers and Publishers in Zürich (1955–59). He worked for two years as a typesetter, then studied layout and typography with Emil Ruder and Robert Büchler at the Schule für Gestaltung in Basel. After that, he joined the Parisian atelier of Albert Hollenstein, where he was in charge of the team for typographic expression. Lutz gave evening classes in Paris and worked on covers for *Typographische Monatsblätter* in Sankt Gallen. He taught at the Schule für Gestaltung in Zürich (1966–70) and in Lucerne from 1968.

He was a co-founder of the Swiss Publishers' Association. and assisted in building up an experimental design school, F+F. He also produced graphic work for the multimedia group Unknownmix. Lutz taught in Zürich at the Schule für Gestaltung. David Carson was impressed and influenced by a workshop with him in Rapperswill. Lutz was the author of several books: on graphics in Cuba, *Experiment F+F*, *Typoundso*, design education, and *Die Hieroglyphen von Heute* (*Today's Hieroglyphs*: more than 500 pages of transport symbols, stamps and printed ephemera).

abcdefghijklABCDEFGHI123456
abcdefghijklABCDEFGHIJ123456
abcdefghijklABCDEFGHI123456
abcdefghijklABCDEFGHIJ123456
abcdefghijABCDEFGHIJ123456
abcdefghijABCDEFGHIJ123456
abcdefghijABCDEFGHIJ123456
abcdefghijABCDEFGHIJ123456
abcdefghijABCDEFGHI123456
abcdefghijABCDEFGHI123456
abcdefghiABCDEFGH123456
abcdefghiABCDEFGH123456

ABCDEFGHIJ
KLMNOPQRS
TUVWXYZ&
abcdefghijkl
mnopqrstuv
wxyzæœß§@
Ø(–).:;!?€¥£$
1234567890

Gerard Unger [The Netherlands]

1942– born in Arnhem
Admitted to AGI, 1992

Gerard Unger has been a freelance designer since 1975. He teaches as visiting professor at the department of typography and graphic communication, University of Reading, England, and taught at the Gerrit Rietveld Academy, Amsterdam until 2007. From 2006, he has been professor of typography at the University of Leiden. He has designed some twenty typeface families as well as stamps, coins, magazines, newspapers, books, logos, corporate identities, annual reports and many other projects. In 1984 he was awarded the H.N. Werkman Prize for his typographic work, in particular his digital type designs and the way he reconciles technology and typographic culture. In 1988 he won the Gravisie-Prijs for the concept of the font Swift, and in 1991 he was awarded the international Maurits Enschedé Prize for all his type designs. He has written articles for the trade press, and several larger publications, such as *Landscape with Letters* (1989), linking the usually limited scope of type and typography with a much wider cultural view. In 1995 his book *Terwijl je leest* – about the reading process – appeared in Dutch, and an English edition is in preparation. He lectures frequently in the Netherlands and abroad, about his own work, type design, the reading process, newspaper design and related subjects.

Allianz, type family, 2005.

Capitolium, type design, 1998.

Annual report for the **Dutch Film Fund** (and design of the logo), 2003.

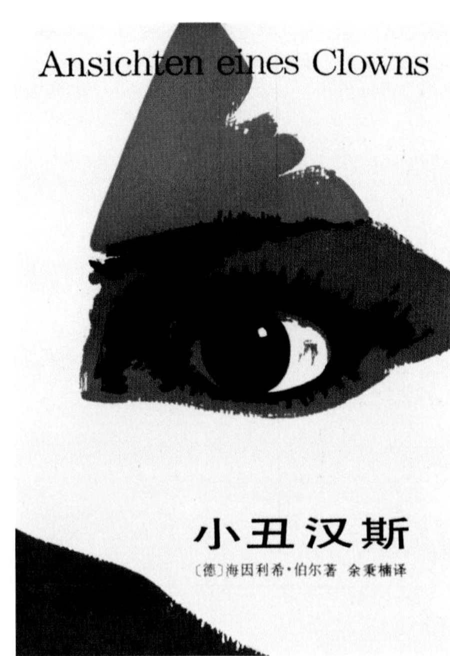

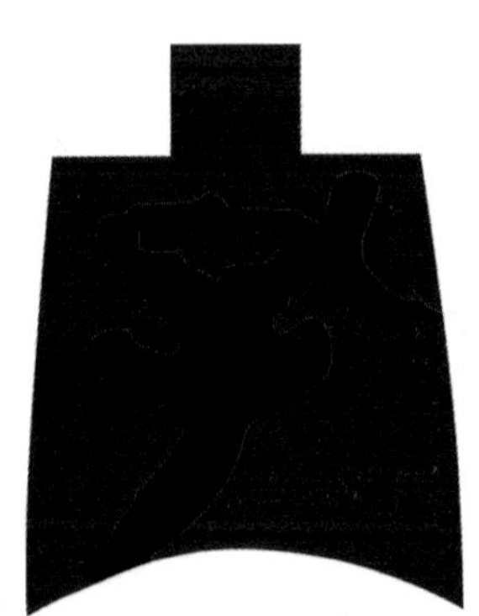

Bingnan Yu [China]

Family, poster. The Chinese character for '*family*' is constructed from the characters for a pig under a roof, a symbol of stable and happy family life.

The reason to choose an eye as the motif of the cover design of **Ansichten eines Clowns** is that this book takes the literary form of a monologue. Readers will be curious about what has this eye seen.

Logo design for **China Confucius Foundation**. The use of the form of a big bell refers to Confucius's concept of awakening mankind to carry forward Chinese culture.

1933– born in Shanghai
Admitted to AGI, 1992

Yu graduated from Lu Xun Academy of Fine Arts in 1956. In 1962, he got his master's degree from the Hochschule für Grafik und Buchkunst, Leipzig. As a professor of the Academy of Arts and Design, Tsinghua University from 1962, he is a member of the academy's science committee, and dean of the book art department. Yu was vice-president of Icograda (2001–2003) and legate of ITC. He won the East German Culture Minister's Award in 1959, The Most Beautiful Books in Germany in 1963, Tokyo TDC Award in 1997 and 1998, Excellence Award in the Deutscher Kinderschutzbund Poster Contest 1998, the special award from the Second China (Shenzhen) International Cultural Fair in 2006 and many other prizes in both local and international design competitions. He has also served on committees and juries for Die Internationale Buchkunst-Ausstellung Leipzig, 1989, OPCW (Organization for the Prohibition of Chemical Weapons) Logo Competition, Morisawa Awards 1993 International Typeface Design Competition, and the Competition for Logo and Poster Design for the 2008 Beijing Olympics. In 1989 he won the Gutenberg Prize from the city of Leipzig for his outstanding contribution to teaching, creation and research in the field of design.

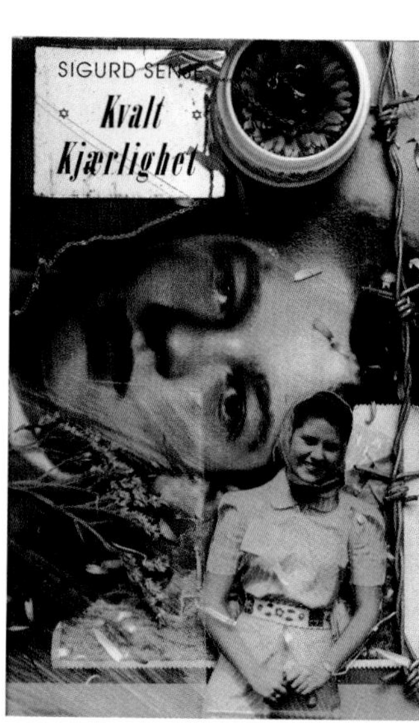

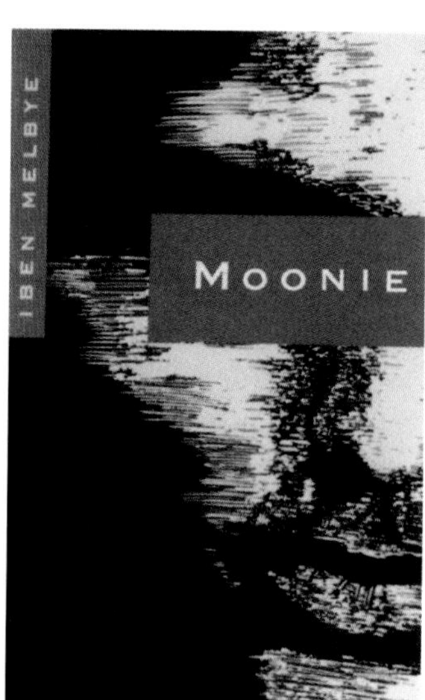

Sarah Rosenbaum [Norway]

1958– born in Ishpeming, Michigan, USA
Admitted to AGI, 1993

Sarah began her professional meandering in the photo department at RISD, but left mid-way and travelled to Norway, ending her studies in design/illustration at the State School for Arts and Crafts in Oslo, 1983. Soon she was an established freelancer, working primarily for book and magazine publishers, and won several awards for book jackets and editorial illustration. She was invited by design director Petter Moshus to join a team of three designers to create the identity programme for the Lillehammer 1994 Winter Olympic Games.
Her popular illustrative pictogram series won a gold award in the European D&AD competition and got her wall space in the Ski Hall of Fame.

She was a partner in Bergsnov, Mellbye & Rosenbaum (1992–2000), a small successful design company, working for a broad range of clients in business, finance, government and culture. In 2001, she joined colleagues to start Making Waves, a company merging competences in design and internet technology. Sarah became increasingly interested in issues concerning healthcare information and left Making Waves in 2004 to begin working for the Norwegian Knowledge Centre for Health Services, executing, managing, and researching design projects with a primary focus on bringing research evidence into healthcare practice.

Lillehammer Winter Olympics 1994, pictogram series (x 2).

Sigurd Senje: *Kvalt Kjærlighet*, book cover.

Iben Melbye: *Moonie*, book cover.

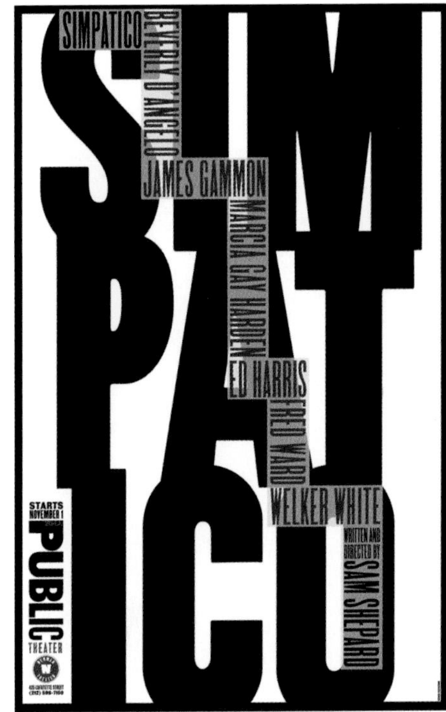

The Public Theater 95–96 Season, poster, 1995.

Environmental graphics for the Children's Museum of Pittsburgh, 2004–2005.
Photo credit: Peter Mauss/Esto.

Simpatico, poster for The Public Theater, 1994.

Paula Scher [USA]

1948– born in Washington, DC
Admitted to AGI, 1993

For over three decades Paula Scher has been at the forefront of graphic design. The images she has created have entered into the American vernacular – at once iconic, smart, and unabashedly populist. Scher has been a principal in the New York office of the distinguished international design consultancy Pentagram since 1991. She began her career as an art director in the 1970s and early 80s, when her eclectic typography for records and books exerted a great influence on the graphic design of the period.

At Pentagram she has created identities, packaging, publications and environments for a broad range of clients that includes The Public Theater, Citibank, Jazz at Lincoln Center and *The New York Times*. She is a recipient of the Chrysler Award for Innovation in Design, a member of the Art Directors Club Hall of Fame, a medallist of the Type Directors Club, and a medallist of the American Institute of Graphic Arts. Scher holds a BFA from the Tyler School of Art and a Doctor of Fine Arts Honoris Causa from the Corcoran College of Art and Design. Her teaching career includes over two decades at the School of Visual Arts. In 2002 Princeton Architectural Press published her career monograph, *Make It Bigger*.

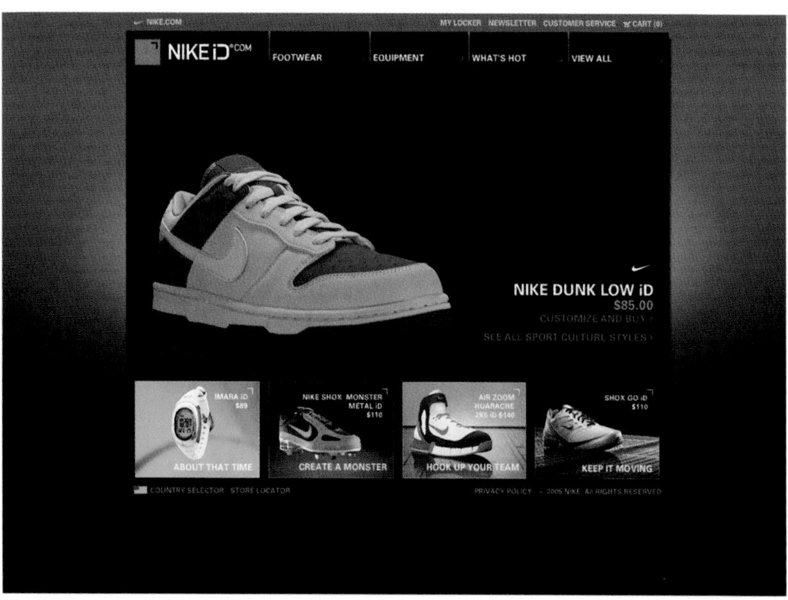

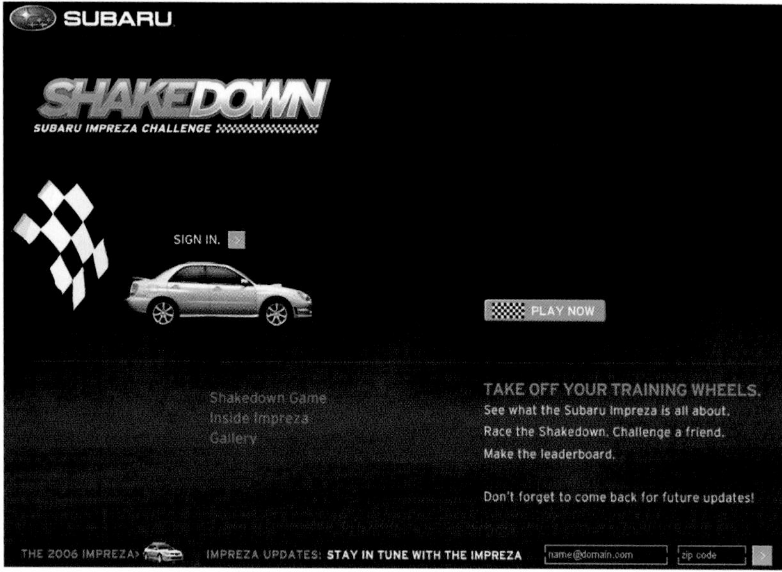

Bob Greenberg [USA]

1948– born in Chicago, Illinois
Admitted to AGI, 1994

Bob leads the vision for R/GA and has been a pioneer in the advertising and communications industry for nearly three decades. R/GA is an agency for the digital age, serving world-class brands such as Avaya, Lowe's, Nike, Nokia, Purina, Reuters, Subaru, Target and Verizon. Bob has won almost every industry award for creativity, including the Academy Award, Clios and Cannes Lions. His most notable awards are the Clio Lifetime Achievement Award in 2006, the Cooper-Hewitt National Design Award for Communications in 2003 and the Chrysler Award for Innovation in Design.

He was the 2004 Cannes International Advertising Festival Cyber Jury President and was a member of the 2005 Titanium Jury. In 2000, there was a retrospective exhibition on R/GA's work at the Art Directors Club in New York. Bob serves on the boards of numerous schools and organizations, including the ADC, the Brooklyn Academy of Music, Dean's Council Advisory Board of Tisch School of the Arts, ITP (Interactive Telecommunications Program), Parsons School of Design and VCU Adcenter. Bob received his BS from Arizona State University in 1970 and has taken graduate courses in mass communications at Northwestern University and Chicago and DePaul University in Business Management.

R/GA created the **Nike iD website**, which lets consumers custom-design and purchase footwear and sports gear. The design process is clean and intuitive, organizing various steps and hundreds of colour choices into a simple four-component sequence.

For the relaunch of **Nike iD**, R/GA created the world's first cellphone-controlled, commerce-enabled interactive experience. Users can customize a shoe live on the Reuters sign in Times Square.

R/GA created the **Subaru Impreza Shakedown Game**, a 3D Flash game to showcase the features of the 2006 Subaru Impreza. The site also includes interviews, driving footage and advice from Subaru Motorsports drivers.

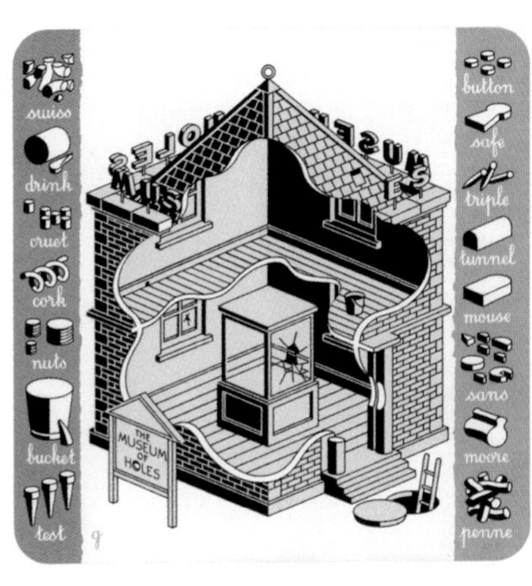

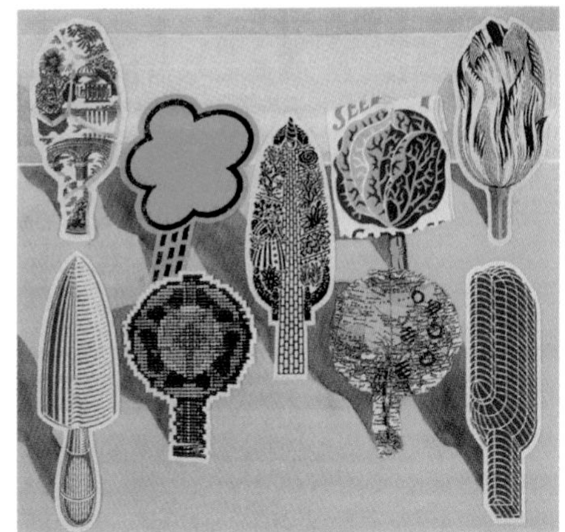

Black Sabbath: *Technical Ecstasy*, album cover (with Hipgnosis), 1976.

The Museum of Holes, calendar illustration for Trickett and Webb, 2002.

The History of English Gardening, invitation for the Garden Show, 1994.

George Hardie [UK]

1944– born in Chichester
Admitted to AGI, 1994

George Hardie trained as a graphic designer at St Martin's and the Royal College of Art in London. He was a partner at NTA studios and designed many legendary record covers (Pink Floyd, Led Zeppelin) with Hipgnosis. He has worked as a jobbing illustrator for some thirty-six years, commissioned to solve problems and make illustrations for a variety of clients in many countries (fourteen to date). His work primarily involves ideas that are carefully composed and crafted into graphic art. As part of a process he describes as *'going amateur'*, he has made and published a number of books, which he explains as *'graphics without clients'*.

George is a Royal Designer for Industry (2005) and a professor at the University of Brighton (1990), where he teaches on postgraduate courses. He has lectured on his work and other subjects in the UK and abroad. In 2006 he toured Australia as the AGDA International Speaker and taught and exhibited at Nagoya University of the Arts as a visiting professor. His ambition: *'To notice things and get things noticed.'*

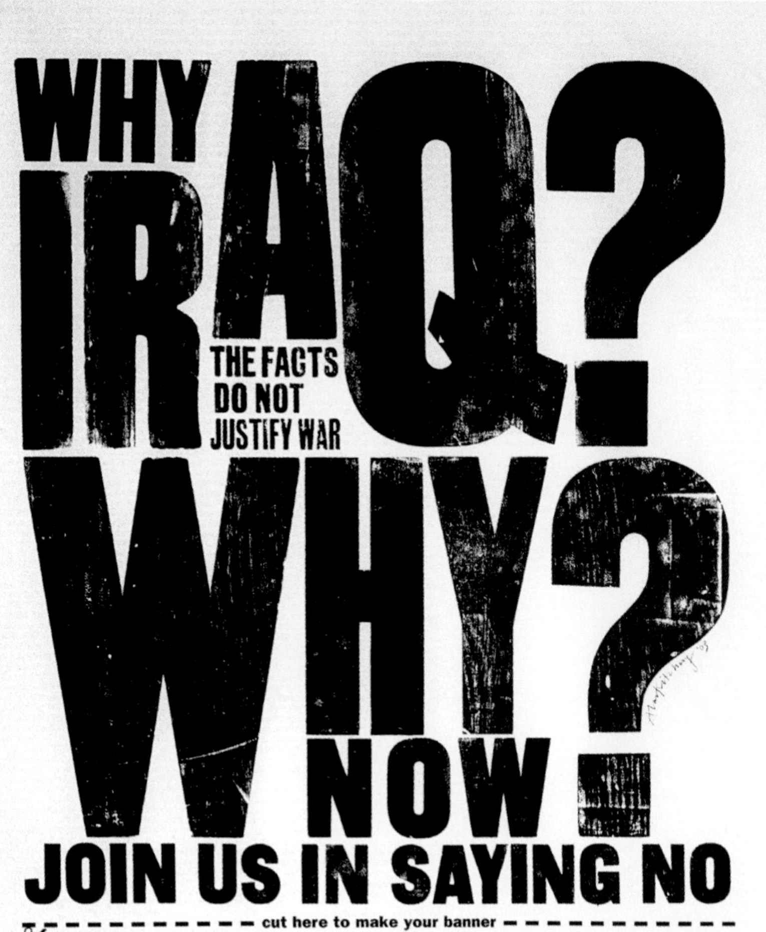

Alan Kitching [UK]

1940– born in Darlington
Admitted to AGI, 1994

Alan Kitching left school aged 14 to become an apprentice compositor with a letterpress printer. He subsequently established his design practice, taught at Central School of Art & Design and became visiting lecturer in typography at the Royal College of Art. In 1989 he returned to his letterpress roots and founded The Typography Workshop, creating typographic visuals for publishing and advertising and making limited-edition prints. Clients and commissions include: Pentagram print ('Monograms') and wine labels; National Theatre posters; Royal Mail stamps; *The Guardian* newspaper typographic mural; The British Council, Design Council and Royal Society of Arts certificates. His work has featured as book covers, magazine illustrations, advertisements, billboards, interior designs, window displays and protest banners. Alan is visiting professor at University of the Arts London, Honorary Fellow of the Royal College of Art and Royal Designer for Industry. He has had solo shows in London and Barcelona, and contributed to group shows at the Centre Pompidou, Paris, the British Library and Barbican Art Gallery. In 1994 Alan and designer Celia Stothard began collaborating on projects and collecting letterpress materials. In September 2005 they launched The Typography Workshop Printroom and Studio in the two London studios where they live and work.

Why Iraq? Why Now? advertisement and banner, 2003. Designed to work as both an ad in the *Guardian* newspaper on 14 March 2003 and a protest banner, the page was used as a personal placard for participants in the 15 March 2003 anti-war rallies.

Imagine ad/promotion, 2000. Image for Scheufelen papers promotional campaign. The original A2 print, hand-inked with just the two Scheufelen colours, black and red, was reproduced on cards and in advertisements.

Magna Carta postage stamp, 1999. Commissioned by Royal Mail for their Millennium issue, the stamp commemorates the forced signing at Runnymede Island of the great charter granting the first rights to English freemen in 1215.

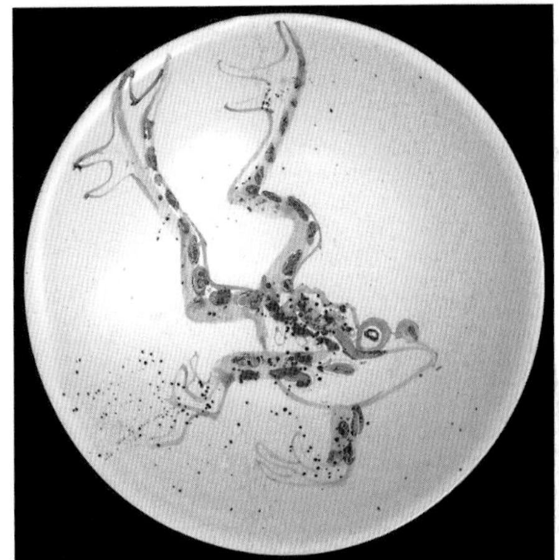

Caricature of the Queen for a publication.

3D caricature of Margaret Thatcher as Marilyn Monroe for a Spitting Image publication.

Plate, black oxide brush drawing on white glazed stoneware.

Roger Law [UK]

1941– born in Littleport, Cambridgeshire
Admitted to AGI, 1994

Roger Law used to be famous. He masterminded the caricature puppets of *Spitting Image*, which erupted onto UK television screens in 1984.
Law was known in the visual arts world long before *Spitting Image*. He studied at Cambridge School of Art where he art-directed *Granta* magazine; moving on to London to draw cartoons in collaboration with Peter Cook. Law worked as an illustrator and caricaturist for *The Sunday Times* for over a decade.

In 1975 he formed a partnership with Peter Fluck – 'Luck and Flaw' – and made caricature effigies for publications worldwide. This work lead directly to *Spitting Image*. The topical, satirical show ran for twelve years. When it closed, Law did the only decent thing he could do – possibly has ever done – he transported himself to Australia. These days Law divides his time between England, Australia and China and keeps busy making drawings and ceramics, celebrating his new life as a wild colonial *'old'* boy.

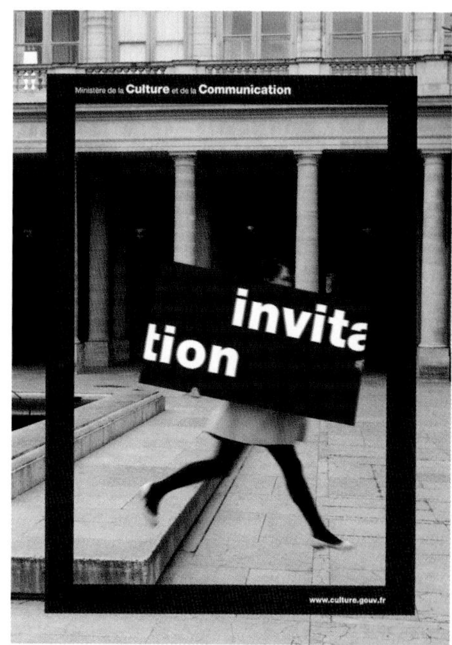

Laurence Madrelle [France]

1946– born in Paris
Admitted to AGI, 1994
International President 2003-2006

Laurence spent seven years away from France in the UK and US. Foreign fellowship at Rhode Island School of Design, 1971. Worked with Malcolm Grear in Providence, RI. Back in Paris in 1974, met Jean-Pierre Grunfeld who shared the same interests: design for the public domain, the citizen rather than the consumer, the subject not the object. Within agencies from Signis to Topologies, which included up to 25 people, she developed identities, signing and campaign for public institutions, cities and more.

In 1987 Laurence started LM Communiquer, her own studio, and continues to work within the same fields with a small team and close to her two architect *'brothers'*, Patrick and Daniel Rubin at Canal studio. LM's subjects range from the fight against Aids to signage for hospitals and cultural institutions. The studio also works on communication for urban renewal projects with Jean-Pierre Grunfeld. LM builds enlarged teams according to the project: writers, architects, product designers, illustrators, photographers, web designers. Laurence has been teaching at architecture schools since 1989.

13e Paris Rive Gauche, communication of an urban project with signs as landmarks, posters and maps (x 2). The primary medium is the city itself. Strategy: Jean-Pierre Grunfeld. LM team: Isabelle Guillaume, Cyrille Fourmy, Marie Pellaton. Perspective drawings: Didier Ghislain. Writer: Agnès Thurnauer. Photographer: Myr Muratet, 2001.

French Ministry of Culture, a red frame on invitations and posters for events organized by the Ministry. This invitation was part of a series of 12. We played with the blue logo designed in 1989 for the Ministry by Pippo Lionni. LM team: Amélie Boutry, Edoardo Cecchin. Photographer: Stéphanie Lacombe, 2004.

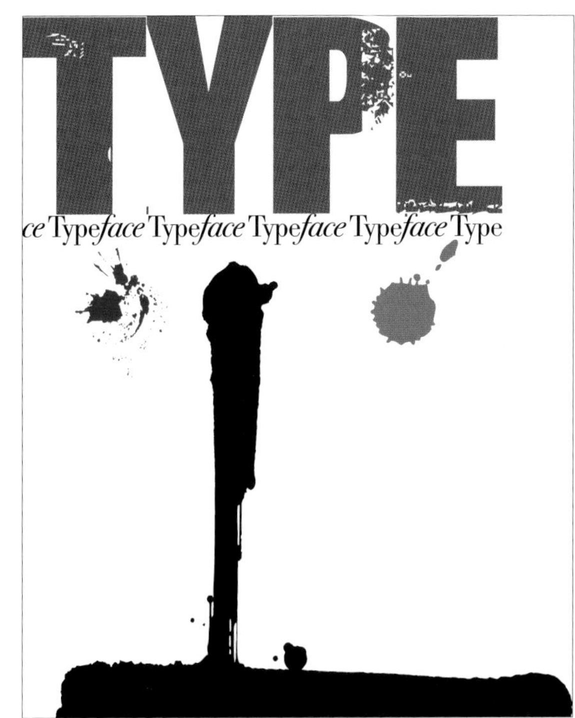

Piet Zwart, poster for an exhibition on De Stijl.

Collage, design for a cover of *Idea* magazine.

Gráfica Special #56. Homage to Milton Glaser in the graphic arts magazine. Art director/designer: Oswaldo Miranda (Miran) and M. André Cunha. Artist: Milton Glaser.

Oswaldo Miranda [Brazil]

1949– born in Paranaguá
Admitted to AGI, 1994

Oswaldo Miranda, known as Miran, is an art director,designer, illustrator and editor of the international graphic arts magazine *Gráfica*. A member of TDC, ADC (NY) and of AGI (1994–2001), Miran has been awarded more than 450 prizes of which 75 percent are international ones. Among the prizes he received in Brazil were 25 gold and 35 silver medals in the CCSP Clube de Criação de São Paulo. He also received the bronze medal at the Brno Biennial and the Silver Pencil at the Buenos Aires Design Biennial of the CAYC Centro de Communicación and awards of excellence in the CA Design annual, NY ADC annuals and in the Society of Illustrators annual.

His work has featured in the magazines *Graphis*, *Idea*, *CA*, *Novum* and in U&LC. Miran's work has been exhibited in Argentina, Brazil, France, Germany, Japan and Sweden. His work is included in the permanent collections of the Cooper-Hewitt Museum, the Centre Pompidou, Paris and the Deutsches Plakat Museum, Essen.

John Rushworth [UK]

1958– born in Yorkshire
Admitted to AGI, 1995

Graduated in 1981 with a first class honours degree in graphic design from Preston College of Art. He began his career with Michael Peters and then worked for Conran Design Group before joining Pentagram in 1983. In 1987 he became Pentagram's first associate and in 1989 he was invited to become a partner. His work spans the development of major, strategically driven identities through to craft-based design programmes. Design consultant to Polaroid for over 12 years, he has also developed long-term relationships with further clients such as the Savoy Group, One&Only, Crafts Council, King's College London and Egon Zehnder International, supporting the management of their brands worldwide. Other recent and current clients include Pantone, Disney, the National Museums of Scotland, the Museum of London, the Dorchester Group, Bulgari, Mothercare and Hewlett Packard. He has exhibited posters in personal and collective shows worldwide, including AOSTA (Italy) and the Tel Aviv Museum of Art. He has received many international awards including a gold medal at the Lahti Poster Biennale and D&AD silver awards for the Crafts Council, the Four Seasons Hotel, Polaroid, and the Berkeley Hotel. John is an external assessor at Falmouth College of Art and the University of Lancashire.

P Magazine is a bi-annual European publication aimed at the professional photographer. Each issue focuses on a single photographic theme: still life, fashion, location, portraiture, etc.

Against Violence, a global outdoor advertising association, together with the United Nations, created a competition to design a single poster that would campaign against all forms of violence.

BFAMI (British Friends of the Museums of Israel), a poster to promote an exhibition at Sotheby's, London called 'Outside In: A Week of Art and the Box', part of a fundraising event.

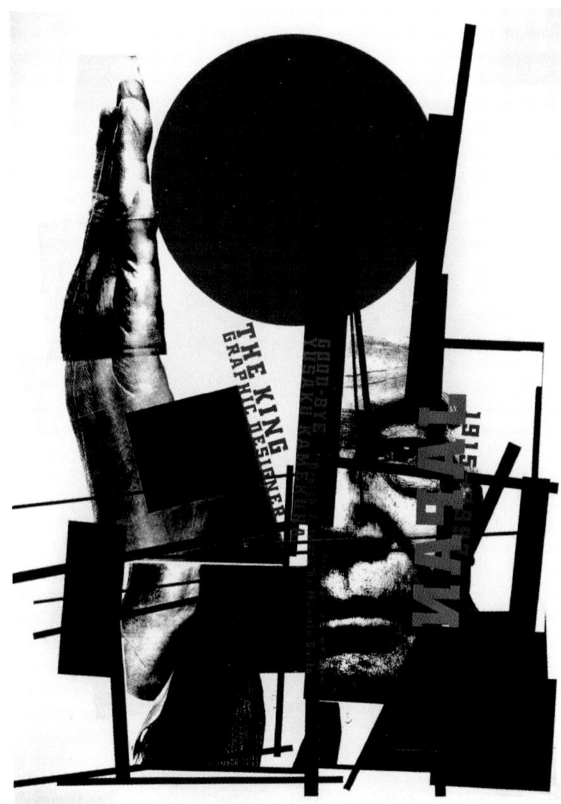

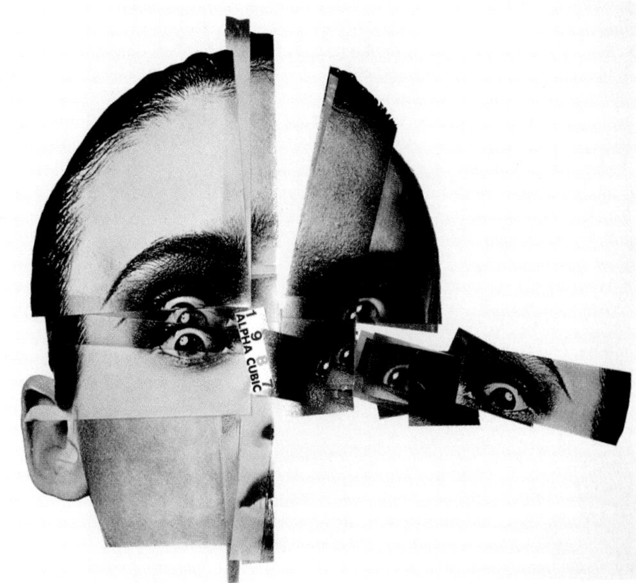

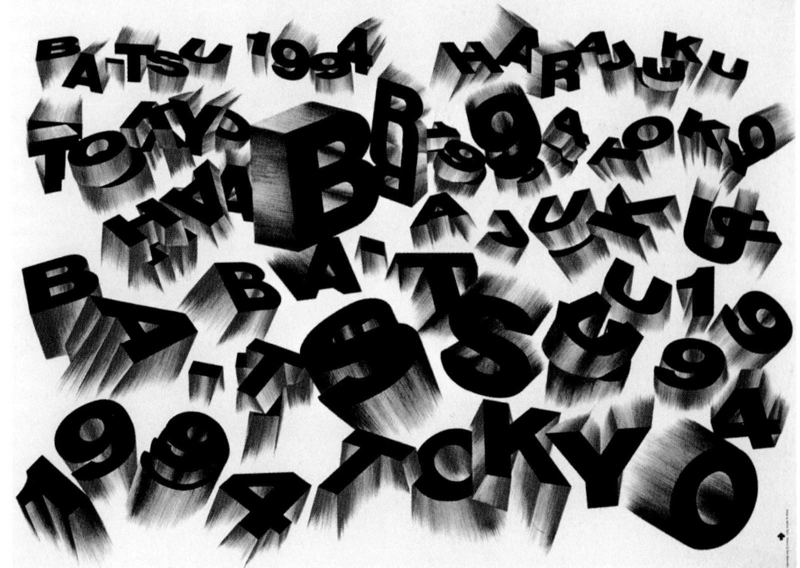

Sunrise Sunset Yusaku Kamekura, 1999. Client: Toppan printing Co., Ltd. Makoto Saito Design Office Inc.

Alpha Cubic, 1987. Client: Alpha Cubic Co., Ltd.

Ba-Tsu, 1994. Client: Ba-Tsu Co., Ltd.

Makoto Saito [Japan]

1952– born in Yame-city
Admitted to AGI, 1995

Makoto Saito is active in various fields as a graphic designer, commercial art/creative director, film director, and also as a product designer. His debut as a graphic designer in the early 1980s was a sensation. His numerous awards include: Gold Prize (twice), Silver Prize and Special Prize (twice) at the International Poster Biennale in Warsaw, Gold Prize (five times) and Silver Prize, and Special Prize (three times) at the ADC International Exhibition in New York, Grand Prize at Lahti International Poster Biennale, Silver Prize and Bronze Prize at the International Biennale of the Poster in Mexico, Gold Prize (three consecutive times), Bronze Prize (three times) at the International Poster Triennial in Toyama, Mainichi Design Award, Grand Prize, ADC Best Award, ADC Award (twice) ADC Member Award (twice) at Tokyo ADC, Good Design Award from the Chicago Athenaeum (four times), Germany Red Dot Award Best of Best (twice), Modern Japanese Art Exhibition Award (13th, 18th), Grand Prize at France International Poster Award, Best Prize at Colorado International Poster exhibition, Second and Third Prizes at Chaumont International Poster exhibition, and other prizes at leading international poster exhibitions. He also lectures frequently at both local and international institutions in the US, France, the Netherlands, Poland, Australia and Hong Kong.

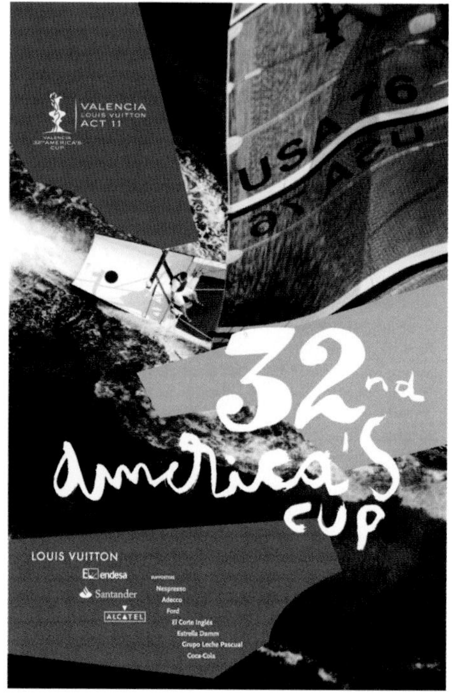

Javier Mariscal [Spain]

1950– born in Valencia
Admitted to AGI, 1995

Born in February, when the midday sun in Valencia feels like a caress, Javier was eventually one of eleven brothers and sisters. They lived in El Parterre park, in the Plaza Alfonso el Magnánimo. In 1957 the river flooded and the shops in Valencia had to be redecorated. Valencia was full of neon, formica and plastic, and pastel colours; the doleful style of the years after the Civil War was ditched. Those were the years of Cola-Cao, Coca-Cola, Choleck, the bikini, and Barrachina, the Sistine Chapel of sandwiches and mixed grills.

In 1969 Mariscal decided to move to Barcelona. In 1981 he became the father of Julia. In 1988 he created Estudio Mariscal. In 1999 he was awarded the National Design Prize. In 2000 he reached his half-century. In 2002 Alma and Linus were born and there were 45 people at the studio. At other times there were 64, or 24. Now the bougainvillea in the studio spans 26 metres and the studio is working on 64 projects, from a 280-metre sculpture to a 4-page book.

In collaboration with Fernando Salas, we did the **interiors of the IKEA restaurant** in Vitoria, Spain. The oak and other local wood combined with the limestone make an atmosphere that turns its back on the rustic style, without renouncing the beauty of the textures of materials.

The **Julián chair** designed for the Me Too collection by Magis has been conceived to help children grow up and awaken their imaginations, so they live better and feel like part of their own world.

America's Cup. For the image and communication design for the last three years' events of the 32nd America's Cup, we gave this avant-garde event an almost artistic treatment, both in typography and image composition.

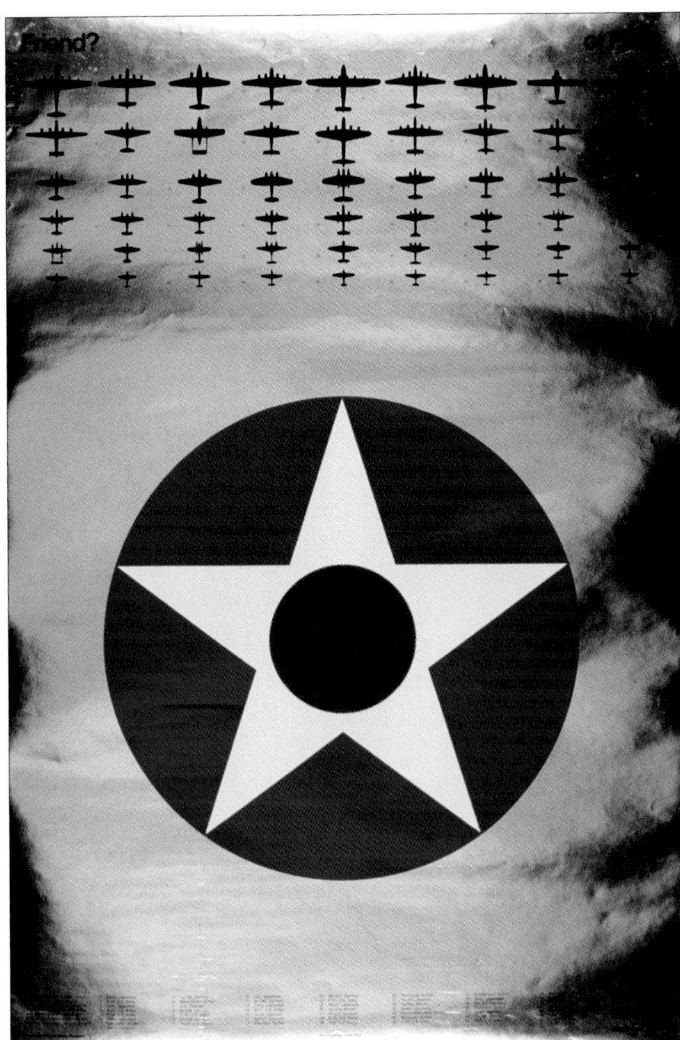

Friend or Foe, poster, 1975. Air and Space Museum. Washington, DC. Copywriter: David Brown. Director: Michael Collins.

Solo exhibition, poster. Tokyo, 1971.

A Second Talent: Painters and Sculptors Who Are Also Photographers, exhibition catalogue, Aldrich Museum of Contemporary Art, Ridgefield, CT, 1985.

James N. Miho [USA]

1933– born in Gridley, California
Admitted to AGI, 1995

James Miho is a graduate of the Art Center College of Design and Woodbury College. He was the Art Director for N.W. Ayer & Son from 1956 to 1965, where he worked on the 'Great Ideas of Western Man' campaign. He was vice-president and creative director for Needham, Harper and Steers in Chicago and New York, 1965–72. As designer and art director for Champion Paper Corporation, he created the Imagination book series, which spanned twenty years and included books on countries, rivers and main streets of the world. In 1988 Miho became the chairman of the Graphic and Packaging Departments at Art Center College and served in this capacity until 1998. Along with freelance work he became the education and design advisor to the Innovative Design Systems Labs (IDS) of Samsung Corporation in Seoul, Korea, 1995–99. Miho has served as an advisor and consultant to several museums and agencies, including the Smithsonian National Air & Space Museum, International Museum of Folk Art, Japanese–American National museum, Museum of Contemporary Art LA, US Information Agency, National Endowment of the Arts, and currently the US Postal Committee.

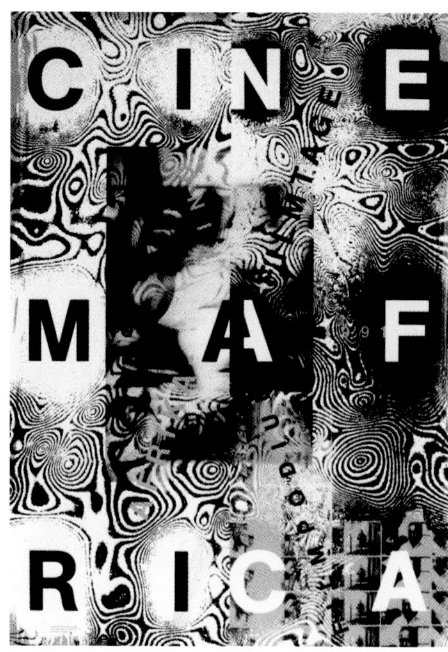

Ralph Schraivogel [Switzerland]

1960– born in Lucerne
Admitted to AGI, 1995

Trained as a graphic designer at the Zürich School of Design from 1977 to 1982. In 1982, upon completion of his studies, he opened his own graphic design studio in Zürich. He has created posters and programmes for the Zürich arthouse cinema Filmpodium since 1983; he has worked frequently for the Zürich Museum of Design since 1984. He has also worked for many other institutions including: the Kunsthaus Zürich, the Theater am Neumarkt, the International Jazz Festival Zürich, the Schaffhausen Jazz Festival, the Solothurn Literature Days, and Cinemafrica: the African Film Festival in Zürich.

From 1992 to 2001 he taught at the Zürich School of Design. In 2001–2002 he was guest professor at the UdK, Berlin. One-man shows were held in Osaka, 1997, Berne, 1998, Tehran, 2002, Paris, 2003, and Zürich, 2004. His posters have been awarded many prizes including: gold medals at the Warsaw Biennial, 1994; Moscow Biennial, Golden Bee, 1994; Chaumont Poster Festival, 1997; Ningbo International Poster Exhibition, 2001, 2003; ADC New York, 2003 and the Grand Prix at the Brno Biennial 1998. His posters are part of various permanent collections including the NY MoMA.

Poster for the **Schaffhausen Jazz Festival**, 2002.

One of many posters he designed for the **Cinemafrica** African film festival in Zürich, 1991.

Poster for a **John Ford retrospective** at the Zürich Filmpodium, 1996.

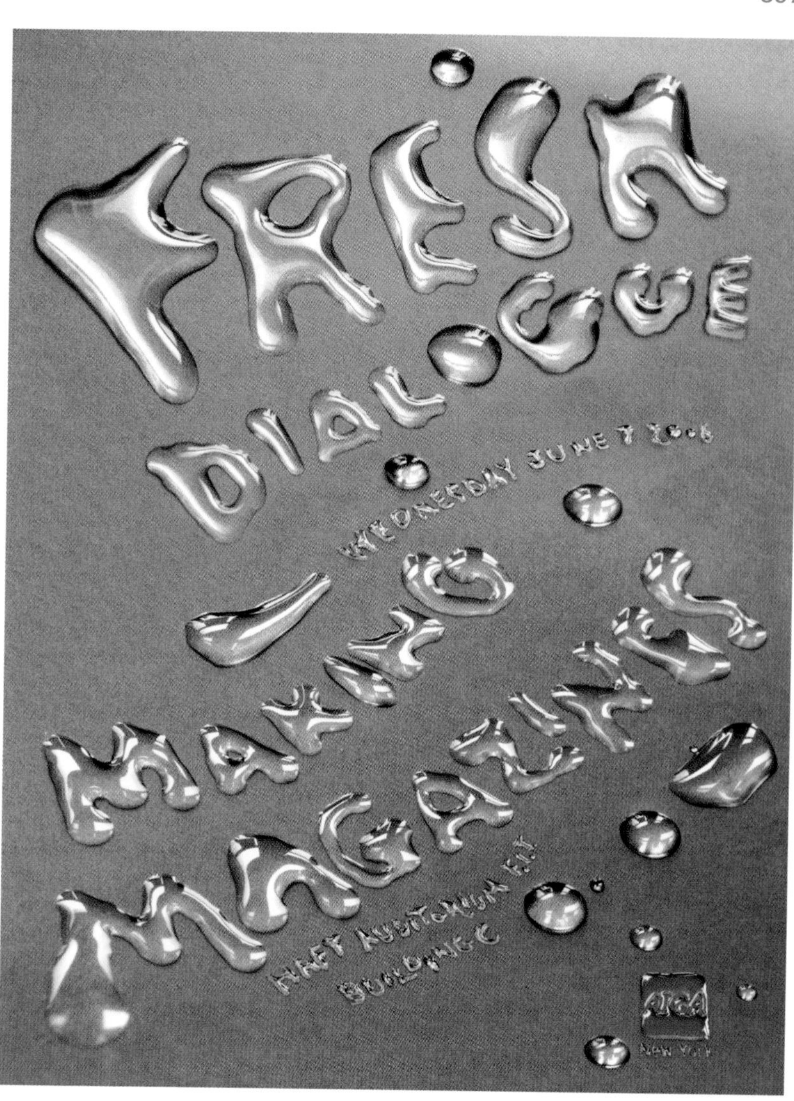

Stephen Doyle [USA]

Norman Spinrad: *The Druid King*, book cover, 2003. Vercingetorix was the first leader of the tribes of Gaul who battled against Julius Caesar. The Druids drew their strength and magical powers from the forest. This led to the idea of rustic type.

Fresh Dialogue, poster, 2006. What could be fresher than water, the source of life on this planet, to signal another *'Fresh Dialogue'* sponsored by the NY Chapter of the AIGA?

19th Amendment Installation, 1996. This installation celebrates and calls attention to the 75th anniversary of the passing of the 19th Amendment to the American Constitution. The text was applied to the floor of the main waiting room in Grand Central Station, NY, in letters eight feet in length.

1956– born in Maryland
Admitted to AGI, 1996

Stephen Doyle is principal and creative director at Doyle Partners, a New York-based design studio known for its expertise in graphic design, communications, and marketing. Founded in 1985, this studio is known for creating communications programmes and engaging design concepts implemented with discipline, imagination, and humour. Doyle, a graduate of the Cooper Union, brings his background in editorial design to play in some unlikely places – from mass-market retail to exhibitions, from corporate communications to packaging. Notable projects include branding and packaging of Martha Stewart Everyday in Kmart; a new identity programme for Barnes & Noble; and a new identity for the global real estate firm Tishman Speyer. Doyle often cites projects from the world of fine art as inspirations as he tries to infuse his design with a sense of humanity and personal engagement. Previously, Doyle was art director of M&Co., and associate art director at *Rolling Stone* magazine and *Esquire*. He is a member of AIGA, SPD. In 1999, he was awarded the prestigious St Gaudens Award from the Cooper Union. His teaching posts have included the graduate programmes at the School of Visual Arts, Yale, the Cooper Union, and NYU.

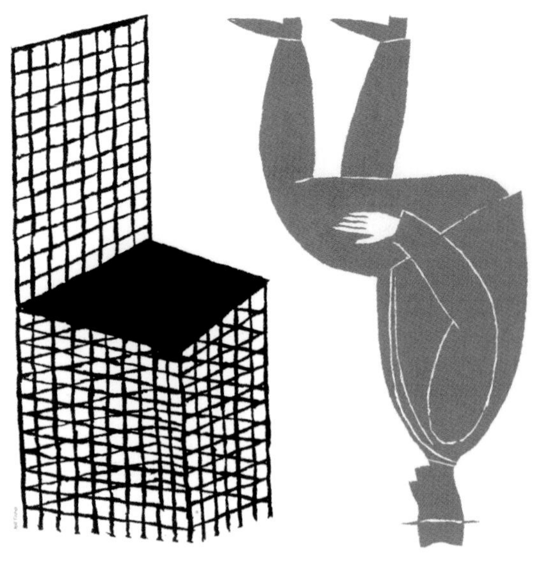

Jeffrey Fisher [UK]

1952– born in Melbourne, Australia
Admitted to AGI, 1996

Illustrator/designer, studied Fine Art/Film and Animation at Preston Institute of Technology, Melbourne, 1971–74. Lived in London 1983–91. Lives in France since 1993. The bulk of his work is in publishing; book covers and book design. Also works widely for design companies, newspapers and magazines. Output also includes posters, postage stamps, his own books and paintings. For some years he has been designing and making chairs with Nicholas von der Borch.

Clients: Bloomsbury Publishing, *New York Times*, United Airlines, 3i, Editora Schwarcz, FLIP Literary Festival Brazil, Rizzoli, Chronicle Books.
Exhibitions: 'Large Paintings', Pentagram, London 1998; 'Free Jeff Fisher', 2000; 'Paintings and Chairs', MRM Partners, Paris, 2003, 'Chairs', Pentagram, London, 2005.
Books: Pass the Cellery Ellery, Stewart, Tabori & Chang, 2000; *How to Get Rich*, Bloomsbury, 2001; *The Hair Scare*, Bloomsbury, 2005; Articles written for *Abitare*, *Print*, *Creative Review*. Magazine cover for *Blueprint*, London, 1993. His work is included in many annuals (*European/American Illustration*, *D&AD*, *Print*, *3x3*).

Design Renaissance, poster for Pentagram London, 1993.

Calendar drawing for Trickett & Webb Design, London, 2000.

Bloomsbury Classics, book covers from a series of 150 titles, Bloomsbury, London, 1994.

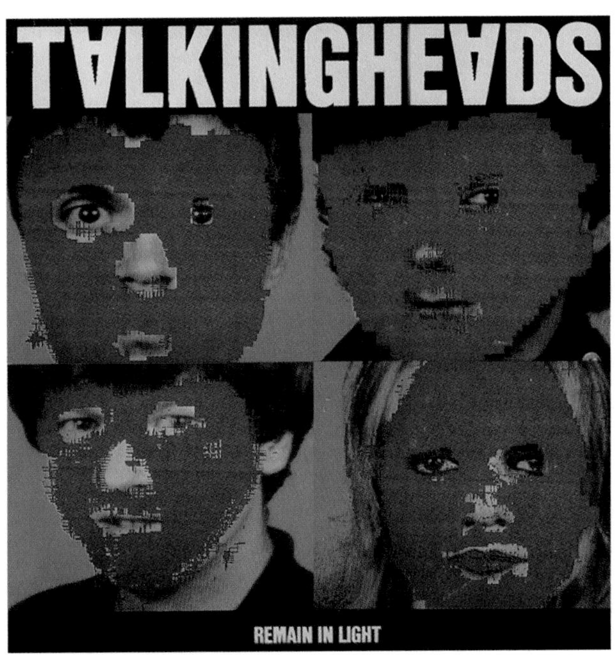

Everybody, installation, Times Square, New York, designed in collaboration with Scott Stowell and Andy Jacobson. Client: 42nd Street Development Corporation/Creative Time, 1993.

Black Queen Elizabeth, image from *Colors* 4, designed in collaboration with Paul Ritter. Client: Benetton, 1993.

Album cover for **Talking Heads: *Remain in Light***, designed with Carol Bokuniewicz. Image: MIT Architecture Machine Group. Client: Talking Heads/ Sire Records, 1980.

Tibor Kalman [USA]

1949-1999; born in Budapest, Hungary
Admitted to AGI, 1996

Aged 7, Tibor immigrated to the USA. As a literature student at NY University, he worked in the local bookstore. Without any training, he took on a job designing the store's displays, advertising and packaging when the regular designer failed to show up. He opened his own design studio M&Co in 1979. Initial success with commercial clients led to more adventurous and highly visible work for the avant-garde band Talking Heads, the small downtown bistro Florent, *Interview* and *Artforum* magazines, and fashion designer Isaac Mizrahi. The work expanded from print to motion graphics, exhibition design, products and large urban installations.

He closed the studio in 1993 and moved to Rome to become the founding editor of Benetton's *'magazine about the rest of the world', Colors*. Kalman was able to exercise his commitment to social change with 12 issues, dedicated to race, religion, and the Aids crisis. Contracting cancer, he returned to NY in 1995, and worked on an equally wide range of projects until his death. About design's mission, he wrote: *'We're not here to help clients eradicate everything of visual interest from the face of the earth. We're here to make them think about design that's dangerous and unpredictable. We're here to inject art into commerce. We're here to be bad.'*

David Lancashire [Australia]

1946– born in Stockport, England
Admitted to AGI, 1996

He studied fine arts at the Circle Studio from the age of eleven, and went into design studios and advertising before emigrating to Australia in 1966. In 1976, he started his own studio in Melbourne, working on packaging, corporate identity programmes and publication design. He had a life-changing experience when he began working with indigenous Australians on visitor centres and museums in 1993, interpreting one of the oldest cultures on earth. This work has taken him to some of the most remote areas of Australia.

His work has appeared in many graphic design publications in Australia and in Europe, such as *Graphis*, *Communication Arts*, *Australian Creative*, *Architectural Review* and *Gebrauchsgraphik*, and has won many awards, including one from the Goethe Institute. He is a past president of the Melbourne ADC, has judged on many awards committees (in Melbourne and nationally), was a member of the Advisory Committee at RMIT Photography Department, the Stamp Advisory Board of Australia Post, the Graphic Design Advisory Committee for the Phillip Institute of Technology and RMIT Graphic Design, and was the Victorian President of the Australian Graphic Design Association 1992–93. He was admitted into the Victorian Government Design Hall of Fame in 1999. He gave masterclasses at the design conference Everything In Between at Swinburne National Centre for Design.

Peace Roo, poster for the 2000 Olympic Games in Sydney, Australia.

Maralinga Roo, poster, making statement about British nuclear weapons testing site, 2004.

Bowali Visitor Centre, Kakadu National Park. Billabong Zone: *'we are a part of the food chain'*, 1993.

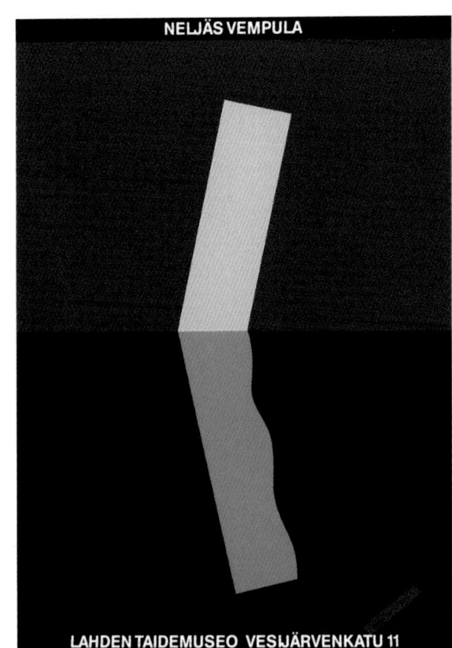

Stop! Committee for Protection of Water, poster, 1971. Photograph by Leo Nieminen.

The Fourth Vempula, exhibition poster, Lahti Poster Museum, 1988.

Alnus Poster, Model 4, exhibition poster, 1993. Chair design by Yrjö Kukkapuro.

Tapani Aartomaa [Finland]

1934– born in Karuna
Admitted to AGI, 1997

Aartomaa started his studies at the Institute of Marketing in Helsinki, at the same time as attending graphic art evening classes at the Institute of Art and Design (Ateneum). Continued studying book design and sculpture in day classes. Started his career as a commercial artist in major advertising agencies in Finland. He has run his own freelance studio since 1963. Taught graphic design at Lahti Design Polytechnic 1972–86. In 1972 he also started as lecturer at the University of Art and Design, where he became a professor in 1986. Over the years he has given lectures and workshops in various countries in Europe, Asia, and North and South America.

He has been awarded for numerous book designs since 1967, most recently in 2005. His poster designs have been honoured both nationally and internationally, including an award at the Colorado Poster Biennial 2005. He was nominated one of the 100 leading graphic designers of the world 1983–93 by *IDEA*/Japan, 1993. He has been a member or head of international and national juries for poster biennials and competitions in Warsaw, Aosta, Moscow, Rzezów and Lahti, and was co-founder of Lahti Poster Biennial, 1975. Collaboration with interior architect Yrjö Kukkapuro since 1989 in design of graphics for chairs. 'Tattooed Chair' exhibitions together with Yrjö Kukkapuro, most recently in Lisbon, 2006.

Philippe Apeloig [France]

1962– born in Paris
Admitted to AGI, 1997

Philippe Apeloig, who grew up in Paris, was educated at the École Supérieure des Arts Appliqués and the École Nationale Supérieure des Arts Décoratifs. After graduating and spending two transformative training periods at Total Design in Amsterdam, he worked as a designer for the Musée d'Orsay in Paris from 1985 to 1987. In 1988, Apeloig received a grant from the French Foreign Ministry to work in Los Angeles with April Greiman. Later, from 1993 to 1994, he was honoured with a research and residency grant at the French Academy of Art in the Villa Medici in Rome.

Apeloig taught typography and graphic design at the École Nationale Supérieure des Arts Décoratifs in Paris from 1992 to 1999, and the Cooper Union School of Art in New York City from 1999 to 2002. He established his own design studio in Paris in 1989 and works on design projects such as posters, logos, typefaces, and communication materials for cultural events, publishers and institutions.

Henry Moore Intime, poster for exhibition at the Didier Imbert Fine Art Gallery, Paris, 1992.

Present-Day South Africa, poster for Aix-en-Provence annual book festival, 1997.

The Roth Explosion, poster for Aix-en-Provence annual book festival, 1999.

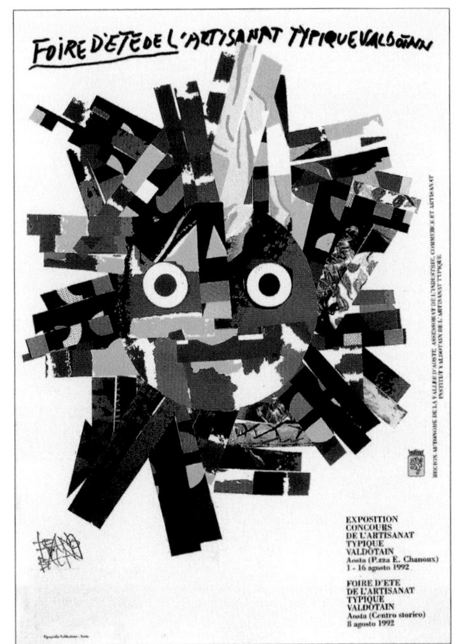

Legend of Franco Balan, *kakejiku* decorative scroll for AGI Congress Tokyo/Kyoto, 2006.

Olympic Winter Games, Turin, screenprinted poster, 2006.

Aosta Valley Summer Craft Festival, poster.

Franco Balan [Italy]

1934– born in Aosta
Admitted to AGI, 1997

Balan has worked on visual communication since the mid-1950s, uniting artistic experience with visual expression. He produces posters, *'combined images'* and pictorial and graphic research projects as well as working on the development and debate of innovative graphic art. Memberships: ADI, (hon.) AIAP, Academy of St Anselm. Works include: posters for Italian and foreign cultural and sports events; logos and coordinated images for Gran Paradiso National Park, Espace Mt Blanc; signage for the Aosta Law Courts; work for IBM Italian Conference, Seville and the Nuova Sias steelworks, Cogne; silkscreen works for Aosta Valley.

He presented the Visual Communication exhibitions at La Salla, Aosta, 1984–94. He has always been involved in education, from primary schools up to (international) academic level. Balan has had numerous exhibitions, in Cogne, Parma, Rome, at the Milan Triennale, Barcelona, and Lecco. He has received many international awards, and specialist magazines from many countries have featured his works. He creates concrete-framed windows and blocks in churches, sports complexes, etc. In 1997 he set up a studio for traditional graphics and multimedia innovations, together with his son Joel.

Polly Bertram [Switzerland]

1953– born in Hamburg, Germany
Admitted to AGI, 1997

Grew up in Lucerne. Graduated 1980 from the University of Art and Design, Zürich. First professional experience in E+U Hiestand studio. From 1981, ran her own studio with Daniel Volkart for eleven years, then with different collaborators, often ex-students. Clients in the culture, politics and public communication sectors. Cooperative projects with photographers and architects. In terms of media, she works mainly with design for print, especially posters. Successful campaign for the Theater am Neumarkt in Zürich 1983–89, published and shown in several exhibitions on graphic design of the eighties and theatre posters.

Started to teach at the university of art and design in Zürich in 1991, then for three years was responsible for the visual communication department at the university of art and design in Lucerne. Since 2002 teaches at the university of applied science in Lugano, where she is responsible for research into design in the visual communication department. Lecturer in workshops, juror and member of commissions at national and international level. *Exhibitions:* 'Mehrwerte–Schweiz und Design: die 80er', Museum für Gestaltung, Zürich 1991.

Invitation for the celebration of a thousand days of marriage by friends in Zürich.

New Year's cards, four examples from a series for the architects Fosco-Fosco-Vogt, Zürich.

Invitation for an exhibition of the work of the designer Claude Fontaine in Luxembourg.

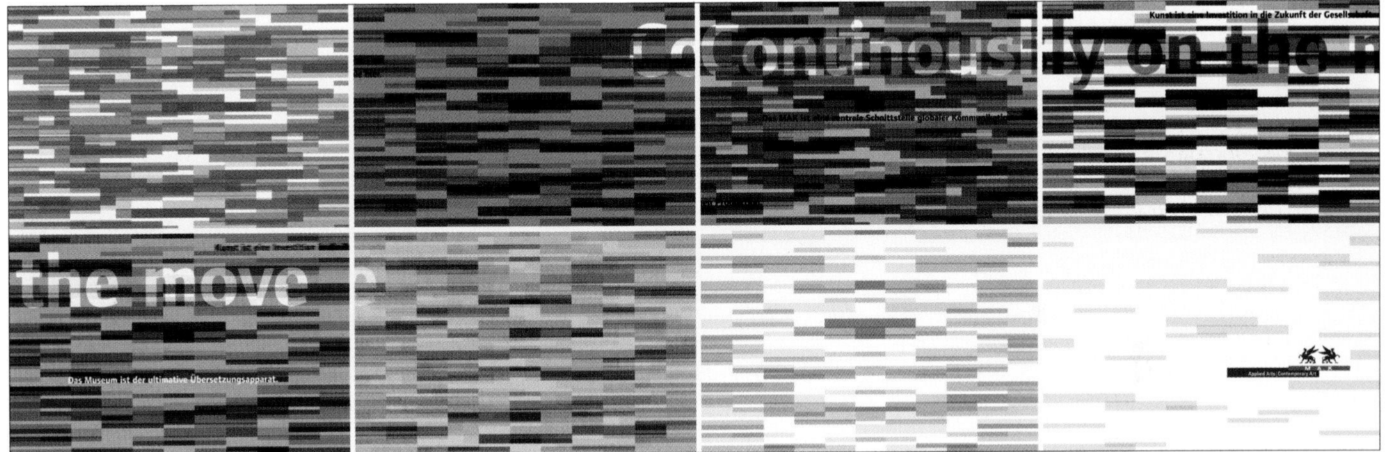

Walter Bohatsch [Austria]

Book: 2 Delugan_Meissl. The pairing of these two books allows complex patterns of legibility; each book has its own strategy for cross-referencing the information that it contains. They bring the architects' conceptual process into a coherent correlation.

Musical Encyclopedia. 424 Austrian composers are documented and presented, together with carefully researched lists of works, discographies, and bibliographies for each. It is not only an excellent reference work, it makes fascinating reading as well.

MAK: Animation. Starting from the relationship between the two bars of the MAK museum logo, methods of subdivision, overlap, partial removal and accumulation are developed, all based on the same system being applicable in all kinds of media.

1949– born in Mürzzuschlag
Admitted to AGI, 1997

Walter Bohatsch began his career as a graphic designer in 1973 in Montreal, Canada, where he worked for John German Inc. and Gottschalk & Ash. From 1978 to 1981 Bohatsch attended the post-graduate course for Structural Film and Graphic Design at the School of Design in Basel, Switzerland. In 1988 he took further courses at Carnegie Mellon University and Harvard University (Electronic Publishing). In 1983 he set up his own office in Vienna, Austria. In 1993 he and his former employee Clemens Schedler established Bohatsch und Schedler GmbH; in 1997 the firm was restructured and renamed Bohatsch Visual Communication GmbH.

He taught experimental and computer-supported typography from 1989 to 1992 at the University for Applied Arts in Vienna and in 1998 'Integral Design' for the 'InterMedia' programme at the University for Applied Sciences in Vorarlberg, Austria. Bohatsch's designs have received prizes at national and international graphic design competitions and have been included in various exhibitions. He also takes part in national and international juries.

Irma Boom [The Netherlands]

1960– born in Lochem
Admitted to AGI, 1997

Irma Boom is an Amsterdam-based graphic designer, specialized in making books. For five years she worked (editing and concept/design) on the 2,136-page *SHV Think Book 1996–1896*, commissioned by SHV Holdings in Utrecht. The Think Book was published in English and Chinese. Irma Boom studied graphic design at the AKI Art Academy in Enschede. After graduation she worked for five years at the Dutch Government Publishing and Printing Office in The Hague. In 1991 she founded Irma Boom Office, which works nationally and internationally in both the cultural and commercial sectors.

Clients include Rijksmuseum Amsterdam, De Appel theatre group, Inside Outside, Museum Boijmans Van Beuningen, Zumtobel, Ferrari, Vitra International, NAi Publishers, United Nations and OMA/Rem Koolhaas, Koninklijke Tichelaar, Camper. Since 1992 Boom has been a critic at Yale University in the US and gives lectures and workshops worldwide. She has been the recipient of many awards for her book designs and was the youngest ever laureate to receive the prestigious Gutenberg Prize for her complete oeuvre.

SHV Think Book, 1996.

Holland Festival, poster, 1990.

Tutti i motori Ferrari, book, 2004.

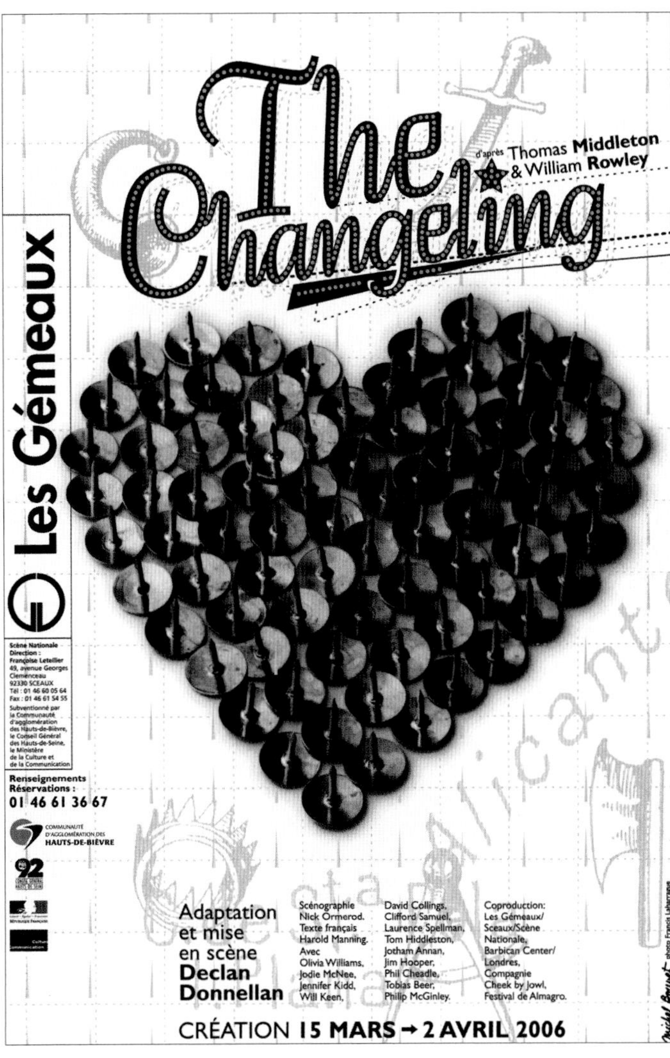

Eldorado, poster, 2006.
Client: Les Gémeaux/Sceaux.
Photo: Francis Laharrague.

The Changeling, poster, 2006.
Client: Les Gémeaux/Sceaux.
Photo: Francis Laharrague.

Michel Bouvet [France]

1955– born in Tunis, Tunisia
Admitted to AGI, 1997

Bouvet graduated from the École Nationale Supérieure des Beaux-Arts de Paris. He lives and works in Paris. His studio works mainly for public institutions: theatres, operas, museums, festivals, dance companies, orchestras, and for publishers in France and abroad. Bouvet has participated as a poster artist and a jury member in international biennials in Warsaw, Lahti, Helsinki, Brno, Fort Collins, Toyama, Mexico, Chaumont, Rzeszow, Sofia, Ogaki, Zagreb, Taipei, Seoul and the Art Directors Club, New York.
Solo exhibitions: France, Netherlands, Germany, Romania, Yugoslavia, Poland, Austria, Portugal, Mexico, USSR, Uruguay, Chile, Finland, India, Philippines, Peru, Cuba, Greece, South Africa, Italy, Czechoslovakia, Argentina, Hungary, Albania, Spain, Japan, Denmark, Turkey, Paraguay, China.
Major awards: Grand Prize for a Cultural Poster, Bibliothèque Nationale, Paris; First Prize, International Poster Biennale, Fort Collins, Colorado; First Prize, International Biennale of Theatre Posters, Rzeszow, Poland; Silver Medal, International Poster Triennial in Toyama; Jan Lenica Prize, International Poster Biennale, Warsaw; Bronze Medal, Brno Biennale; honourable mentions in Warsaw, Lahti, Fort Collins, Moscow and Zagreb. Michel Bouvet is professor at the ESAG/Penninghen, École Supérieure des Arts Graphiques, Paris.

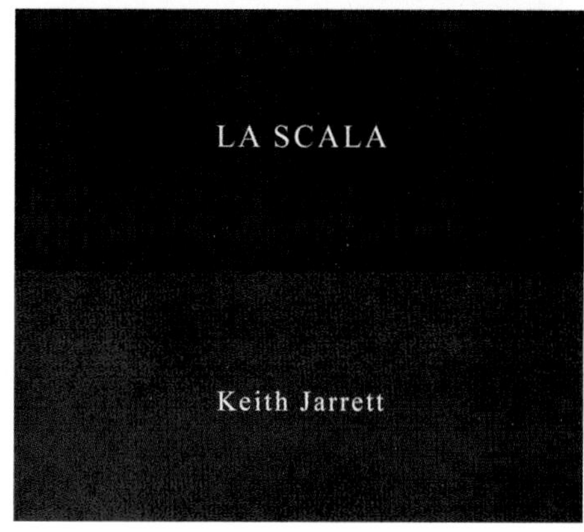

Mayo Bucher [Switzerland]

1963– born in Zürich
Admitted to AGI, 1997

Artist and designer, who studied in the Grafikfachklasse, Academy of Visual Arts HGKZ Zürich (1981–86). Mayo lives and works in Zürich.

Selected exhibitions (2002–2007):
Gallery of the University of Brighton (solo); Centre Pompidou, Paris; Museé Toulouse-Lautrec, Albi; Gallery Lelong, Zürich; Academy of Visual Arts HGB, Leipzig (solo); Metahaus Berlin (solo); Galerie Judin, Zürich (solo); UNO Vienna; Haunch of Venison Zürich/London (solo).

EMME Art and Architecture concept for a public building in Emmenbrücke, Switzerland. Collaboration with Lussi & Halter, Architects, Lucerne, 2000.

Mayo Bucher, exhibition poster, 2002.
Open Sign Academy of Visual Arts Leipzig, HGB

Keith Jarrett: *La Scala*, album cover design in cooperation with ECM, 1997.

Louvre. Ken Carbone created a wayfinding programme which echoes Paris's own *arrondissement* system and accommodates the constant relocation of the museum's collections.

American Craft Museum. A folding sponge *'brick'* provided both an element of surprise and a call to action for the American Craft Museum's capital campaign.

Sesame Workshop. This was part of a cohesive branding programme that leveraged Children's Television Workshop's strongest asset, *Sesame Street*, into a new identity and provided for translation across all media.

Ken Carbone [USA]

1951– born in Philadelphia, Pennsylvania
Admitted to AGI, 1997

Ken Carbone is known for his work in the areas of brand identity, print communications, exhibitions and environmental graphics. Among his accomplishments are a signage and wayfinding system for the Louvre, a brand identity programme for Sesame Workshop and a graphics and display system for the international auction house, Christies. He has also worked with top corporations, such as Morgan Stanley, Tiffany & Co. and Herman Miller, in addition to many celebrated cultural institutions, including MoMA, the High Museum, Hartford Stage and the Cleveland Museum of Art.

An adjunct professor at the School of Visual Arts, Ken frequently speaks to audiences about the role of strategic design and communications in business. His work has been featured in design publications such as *Graphis*, *Communication Arts*, *I.D.*, *Print* and *Idea*. He is the author of *The Virtuoso: Face to Face with 40 Extraordinary Talents*, which explores excellence in art, science and music. In addition to his design career, he has been an avid guitarist for forty years.

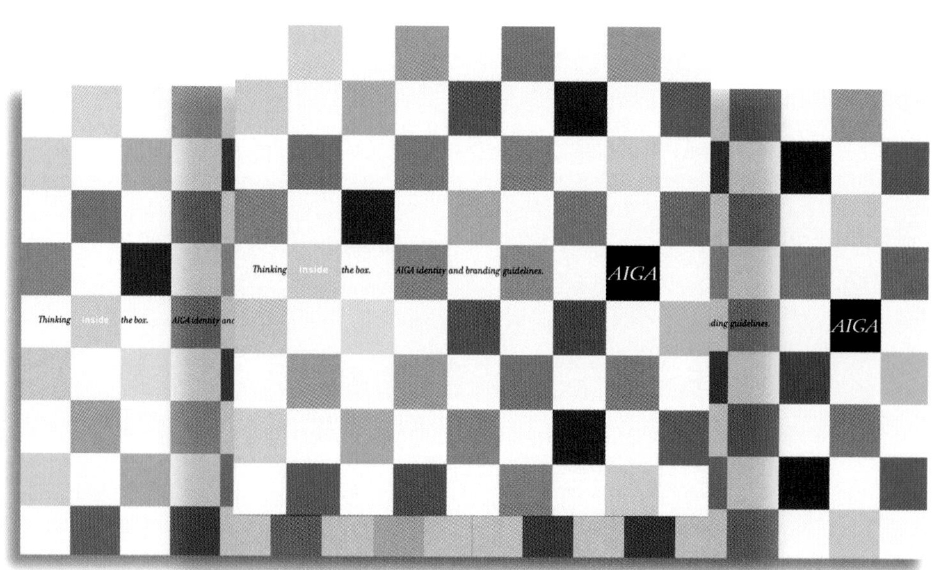

Bart Crosby [USA]

1943– born in Michigan City, Indiana
Admitted to AGI, 1997

Bart founded Crosby Associates in 1979. The firm focuses primarily on the planning and design of organizational, product, event, and initiative identification and branding programmes.
In addition to managing the firm and relationships with clients, he provides strategic and design direction to most of the office's projects and programmes. His work has been recognized by nearly every professional design organization and featured in many national and international design and business publications. Bart has been executive vice president and a director of the American Institute of Graphic Arts and is a founding member and past president of the AIGA Chicago Chapter.

In 2002 he was made a fellow of the Chicago Chapter, and in 2005 he was awarded the AIGA Medal in recognition of exceptional achievements and contributions to the field of graphic design.
A graduate of the American Academy of Art, he is a frequent lecturer at conferences and universities and has served as adjunct associate professor at the University of Illinois at Chicago. Before establishing Crosby Associates, he held leadership positions in Chicago design firms including Design Consultants Incorporated, the Centre for Advanced Research in Design, and RVI Corporation.

City of Chicago Millennium Celebration, identity and branding programme, 1998.

U.S. Canoe and Kayak Team, identity programme and uniform design, 1991.

AIGA, re-branding programme, 1999.

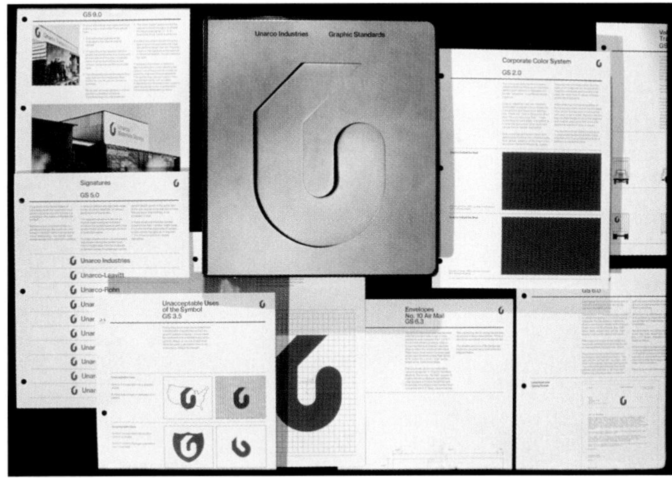

Peace Poster, Toyama Triennial, 1988.

Poster for **The Type Gallery**, a digital typography service.

Identity for **Ardco**, manufacturer of refrigeration equipment, 1993.

Symbol for **Chicago Institute for Psychoanalysis**.

Rick Eiber [USA]

1945-1999; born in Akron, Ohio
Admitted to AGI, 1997

Rick studied architecture and visual communication at Ohio State University. He started his professional career in Chicago. He worked as project director with John Massey at the Centre for Advanced Research in Design, a part of the Container Corporation of America. He then worked for three years as vice-president of the RVI Corporation with Robert Vogele. At the beginning of the 80s, he moved to Seattle where he was on the faculty in Graphic Design at the University of Washington. He founded his own studio RED (Rick Eiber Design) in 1981, first in Seattle, later in Fall City, Washington.

Rick designed posters, marks, logos, identity programmes, catalogues, annual reports and printed communications for museums, corporations, civic and cultural organizations. He worked for Boeing, the Henri Art Gallery, Seattle Symphony and numerous regional businesses. His work was internationally recognized and published in many reviews and awarded from many societies. He wrote articles in *Industrial Design*, *Print and Communication Arts*, and was the author of *World Trademarks: 100 Years*. His motto was: *'We create solutions in response to problems. The more specific the definition of the problem, the more directed the efforts at solving it. Constraints are not your enemy, but your friend.'*

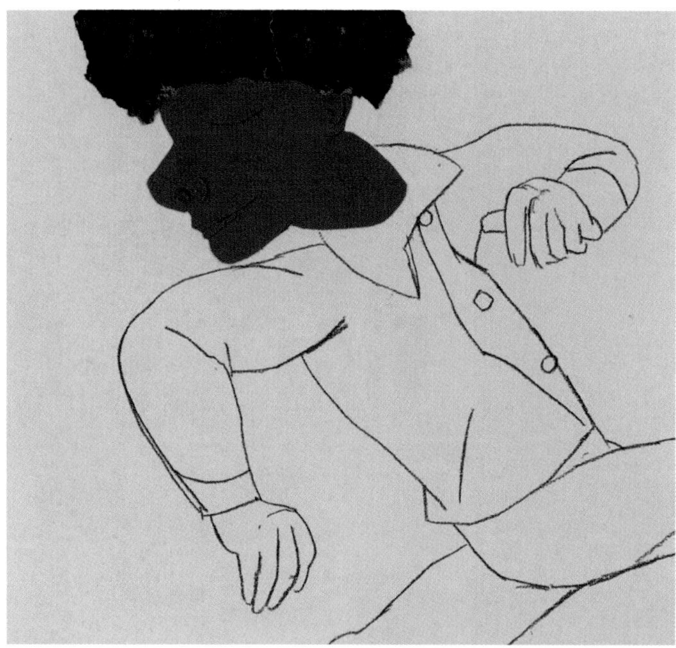

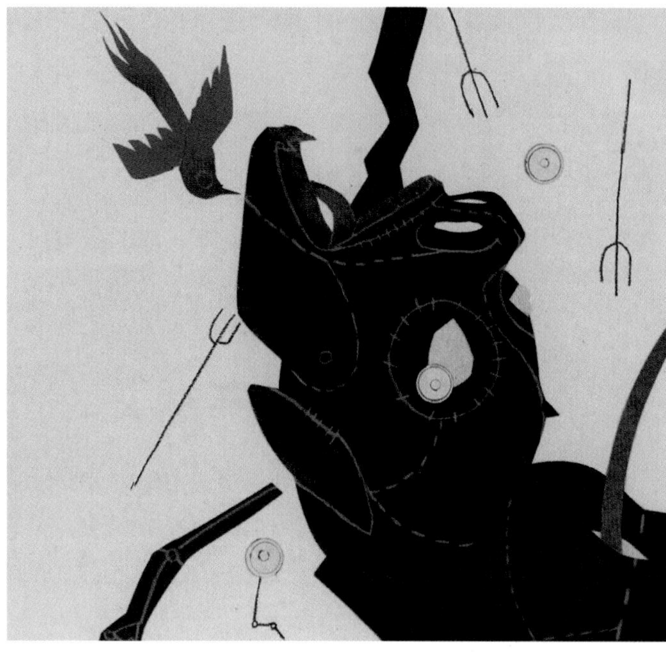

Wolf Erlbruch [Germany]

1948– born in Wuppertal
Admitted to AGI, 1997

I studied at the Folkwangschule für Gestaltung (1967–74), lived in Groningen, Netherlands, from 1970 to 1971, and worked as a freelance illustrator for advertising, animation and magazines in Germany, France and the US. I designed several hundred book covers for many publishers, worked as a costume designer for the theatre, came to children's books in 1990, and I am still very much interested in the medium. I have received lots and lots of awards, the last being the Andersen Award 2006 for illustration.

Illustrations from **Olek schoot een beer**, children's book with text by Bart Moeyaert, Uitgeverij Querido, Amsterdam, 2006.

Erich Fromm: *El arte de amar*, book cover and spread, 2000. Publisher: Ediciones Paidos, Barcelona.

Banco Sabadell, corporate identity, Barcelona, 1997–2006.

CCIB (Barcelona International Conventions Centre), signage, Barcelona, 2004.

Mario Eskenazi [Spain]

1945– born in Buenos Aires, Argentina
Admitted to AGI, 1997

Graduated in Architecture, Universidad Nacional de Cordoba, Argentina, 1971. Member of the design team for TV Canal 10, Argentina (1967–71). Since 1971 has lived and practised in Spain. Professor at Escuela de Arquitectura, Las Palmas, Gran Canaria, 1973–74. Since 1975 has been a visiting lecturer at EINA Design School, Barcelona. Among the design awards he has won are: LAUS (ADG FAD, Barcelona); Awards of Excellence (CA Magazine, San Francisco); Merit Award (NY ADC); Merit Awards (D&AD, London); Premio Nacional de Diseño 2000 (Ministry of Science & Technology and BCD Foundation).

Principal projects include corporate identities for: Banca Catalana, Barcelona, 1975; Grupo Banco Sabadell, Barcelona, 1997–2006; Grupo Tragaluz, Barcelona, 1999–2006; BCNeta: Barcelona City Council waste disposal and cleaning service, 2000. Between 1979 and 2006 he designed more than forty book collections for Ediciones Paidos, Barcelona.

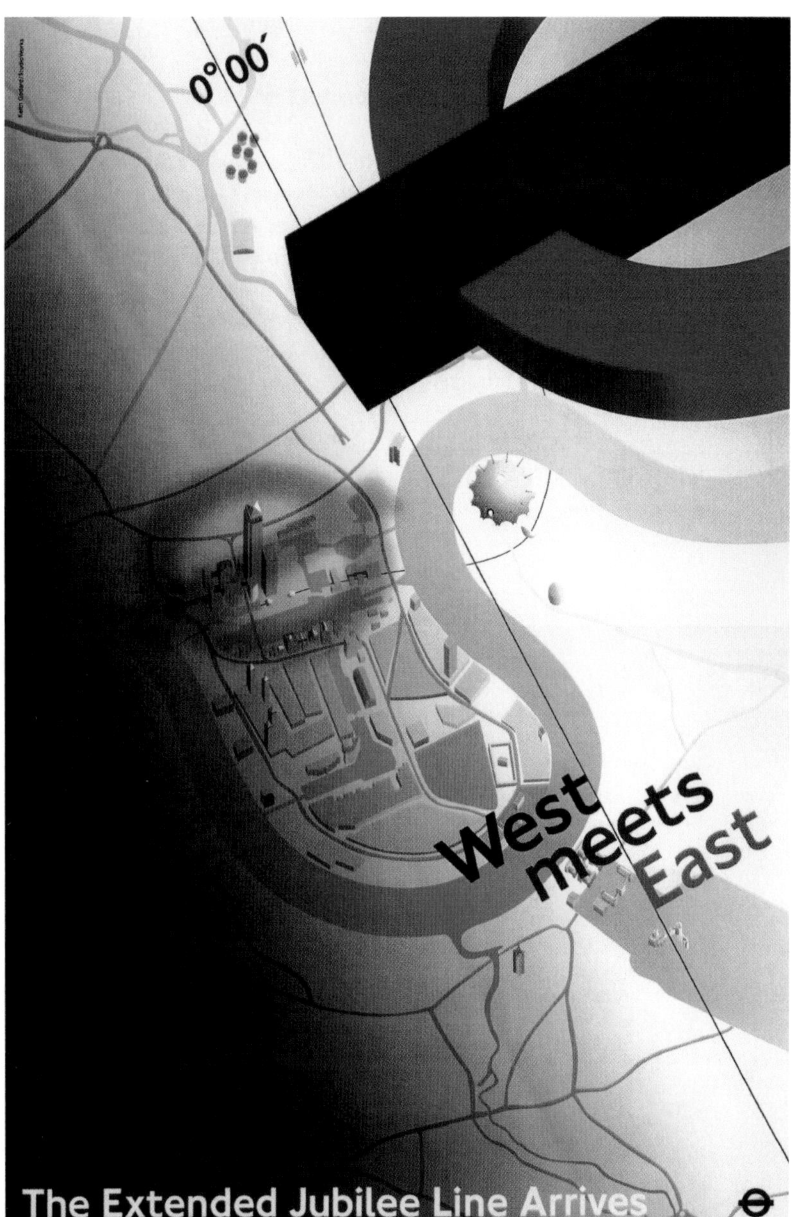

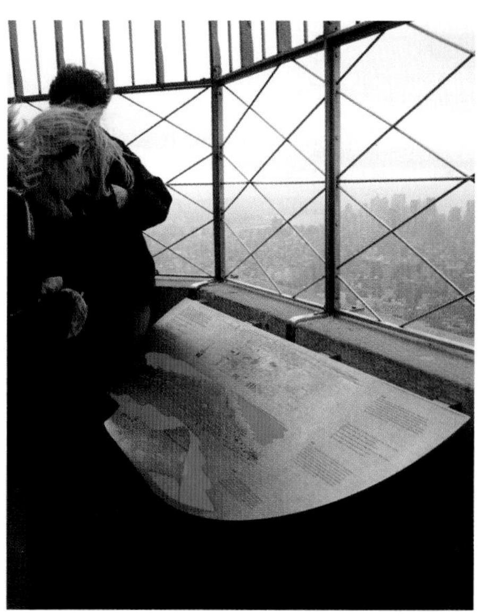

Keith Godard [USA]

1938– born in London, England
Admitted to AGI, 1997

Graduated London College of Printing in 1962, Yale University School of Art and Architecture in 1967. Started Works Design Group with architect partners in 1968. Continued until 1987 with Hans van Dijk and Stephanie Tevonian. Since then, sole proprietor of StudioWorks. Designs exhibitions, wayfinding, print design and publishing, public art and info art. Teaches part time: Philadelphia College of Art, 1968–78; Cooper Union, from 1976–present; from 2000, School of Visual Arts graduate programme; NY State College of Art and Design. *Lecturing and workshops:* RCA London, College of Communications, Dundee University, Yale University, Hochschule für Gestaltung und Kunst, Basel.

Projects: MTA, Arts for Transit, subway murals, Empire State Building observation plaques, exhibitions for UNICEF and UNFPA, banners for Lincoln Centre NY. Design consultant for posters and publications for University of Virginia School of Architecture at Charlottesville. Brooklyn Bridge Centennial Commission, NY Landmarks Conservancy, the P.T. Barnum Museum, MoMA and Getty Museum. *Exhibitions:* 'Images of an Era', 1975; 'Ephemeral Images', Cooper-Hewitt Museum, 1976; 'Images for Survival', Hiroshima Museum, 1985; 'Modern Poster', NY MoMA, 1988; Warsaw Poster Biennales, 1973/2000; 'The World's Most Memorable Poster Competition', 1999; 'this way that way': 30-year retrospective of work at the University of the Arts Philadelphia and Cooper Union Lubalin Center, 2003 and 2005.

West Meets East, poster for London Transport to commemorate the extension of the Jubilee Line. The underground line travels through the meridian. The idea was influenced by Man Ray's 1939 poster.

Grand Central Terminal: City within a City, poster for an exhibition about the station and its importance for being preserved as a landmark. For the Municipal Art Society, NY City.

Plaques for the Empire State Building Observatory. Ten plaques show visitors what landmarks are shown in the vistas as well as telling stories about New York City's past. Etched brushed steel with inlaid colours.

Fernando Gutiérrez [UK]

Prado Museum, new identity and promotional campaign, Madrid, 2003.

Tentaciones, a supplement to the Friday edition of *El País*, the daily Spanish newspaper. Aimed at a young readership, featuring articles on music, cinema, and the arts, 1993–2005.

Colors, the global community magazine sponsored by Benetton, 2000–2003.

1963– born in London
Admitted to AGI, 1997

Fernando Gutiérrez studied graphic design at the London College of Printing, graduating with Honours in 1986. He worked with CDT Design in London, where he became an associate in 1991, and Summa in Barcelona. In 1993 he co-founded Grafica in Barcelona, with Pablo Martín, working on a variety of projects including identity, book publishing, communications campaigns and editorial design. In October 2000 he joined Pentagram where he became a partner in the London office.

In November of 2000 Fernando became the Creative Director of *Colors*, the global community magazine created for Benetton by Oliver Toscani and the late Tibor Kalman. He is currently designer and art director of *Matador*, a literary and photography journal published annually in Madrid. He has worked on a number of editorial projects for the Spanish daily newspaper *El País*. He is presently the consultant creative director for the Prado Museum in Madrid. Other recent projects include: art direction for the Spanish fashion magazine *Vanidad*; identity for the CTA bus and train network operating in the Asturias region of northern Spain; new identity for the official television and radio station of the Asturias region; and a book celebrating the 150th anniversary of Banco Santander.

Tai-Keung Kan [China]

1942– born in GuangChong
Admitted to AGI, 1997

In 1964 Kan began study art and design, and began ink painting in 1970. He was a member of One Art Group and obtained an award from the Urban Council of Fine Art. Starting his career as a designer from 1967, Kan was the first designer/painter elected as one of the 'Ten Outstanding Young People' in 1979; the only designer to receive the Urban Council Design Grand Award in 1984; and Honour of Bronze Bauhinia Star in 1999. Kan's works not only earn him international publicity, but are also collected by local and international museums.

Kan is actively involved in educating and promoting the art and design profession, as dean of the Cheung Kong School of Art and Design, Shantou University, and a member of the Hong Kong Designers Association. He is advisor to the Leisure & Cultural Services Department and Honorary Advisor of Hong Kong Museum of Art. Kan was awarded an honorary doctorate of design by the Hong Kong Polytechnic University.

Graphis, cover design.

Panta Rei Ltd, posters for a furniture store (x 2).

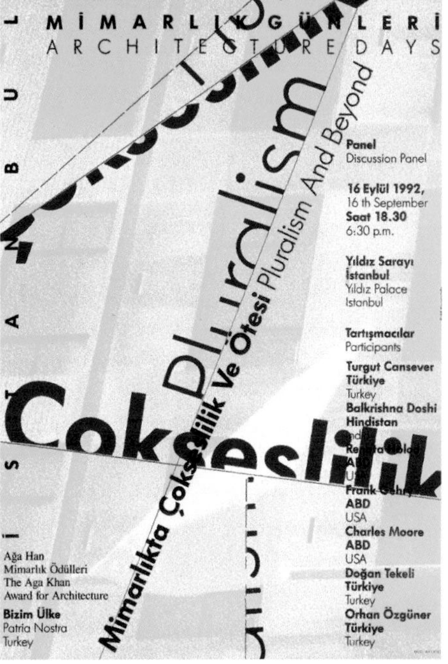

Sadik Karamustafa [Turkey]

America, Bridge, Strike, poster for three plays by a street theatre, Istanbul, 1968.

Miles Davis, concert poster, Istanbul, 1988.

Pluralism and Beyond, poster for a discussion panel on architecture, Istanbul, 1992.

1946– born in Yalikoy, Ordu
Admitted to AGI, 1997

Karamustafa studied graphic design at the Fine Arts Academy Istanbul. Completed MA and PhD studies in Mimar Sinan University and became an associate professor. Teaches at Mimar Sinan Fine Arts University, Istanbul since 1989. 1997: initiated Grafist, an educationally based international graphic design event in Istanbul. 1967–79: worked in publishing companies and advertising agencies. 1979–1999: worked freelance. 2000: founded Karamustafa Design Ltd with his daughter Ayse Karamustafa, active in social and cultural design. He has designed posters, books, magazines, corporate identity programmes, catalogues, environmental projects, exhibitions, fair stands on history, archaeology, photography, literature, fine arts, variable events, political activities for museums, publishers, theatres, art galleries, NGOs and corporations. Solo shows on his works have been organized at: Bibliothèque Pablo Neruda, Grenoble, 1988; Niavaran Cultural Centre, Tehran, 1989; DDD Gallery, Osaka, 2002; GGG Gallery, Tokyo, 2003; Design Museum, Nagoya, 2003. Between 1981 and 2006 he won 46 awards in the annual exhibitions of GMK, the Turkish Society of Graphic Designers. Awarded Special Prize at the Asia Graphic Poster Triennial, Seoul, 2000 and Honorary Diploma at Plovdiv International Posters Exhibition, 2000. He lectures, leads workshops, and is a jury member for international design competitions all over the world. He was vice-president of Icograda, 1995–1999.

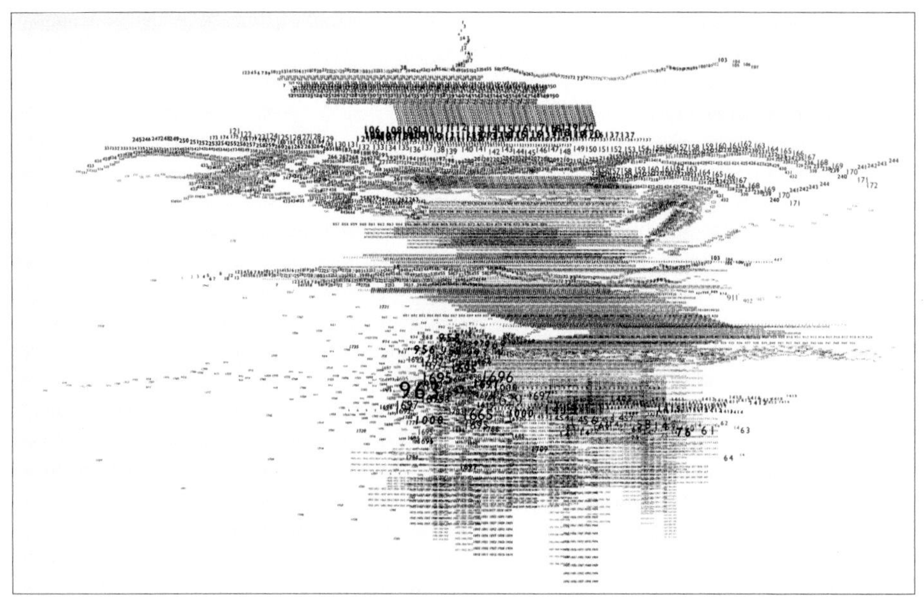

Siobhan Keaney [UK]

1959– born in London
Admitted to AGI, 1997

Keaney graduated from LCP, 1982. She worked briefly for Smith & Milton, Robinson Lambie Nairn and David Davies Associates before setting up her studio in 1985. Her European-influenced graphic methods and independent, even maverick stance, seen in projects for Apicorp, The Mill, Browns and the Royal Mail, soon attracted attention. Two D&AD awards for an Apicorp annual report and Seymour Powell company brochure. Her work has been recognized with invitations to exhibit and lecture in the UK, US, Sweden, Germany, Australia, Thailand, Israel, the Netherlands, Canada, Germany, France and Turkey.

Keaney has been featured extensively in the design press and publishing, and in design-related TV programmes. She has consulted for the BBC Creativity and Learning Opportunities programmes. Has been invited as a juror for several professional design associations. Works are in the permanent collection in the Twentieth-Century Gallery at V&A, London. She is one of forty European designers and architects to have their work featured at the Design Centre, Osaka. She has been a visiting lecturer at the RCA, London, an external examiner for Central St Martin's College of Art and Design, Camberwell College of Arts, Manchester Metropolitan University, Leeds Metropolitan University, and Bath Spa University College.

Royal Mail Yearpack, exterior.

Millennium, poster.

Futuristic, Royal Mail stamp from a series on H.G. Wells.

Made in Holland: Design from the Netherlands, poster, 1994.
(in cooperation with Jenny van Driel).

Maria van Kesteren, catalogue, 1996.

Sottsass bei Krüger, poster, 1995.

Loek Kemming [The Netherlands]

1951– born in Velp
Admitted to AGI, 1997

1969–74: studied at the Academy of Fine Arts, Arnhem, department of graphic design.
1974: co-founder of Vormgeversassociatie (Associated Designers) with Noudi Spönhoff and Jan van den Broek.
1980: co-founder of Designum, producer of home accessories.
1983–95: co-editor of *Items*, Dutch design magazine.
1990–96: teacher and head of graphic design department, Academy of Fine Arts, Arnhem.
2006: co-founder of OfD (Office for Design), with Noudi Spönhoff.

Jacques Koeweiden [The Netherlands]

1957– born in Eindhoven
Admitted to AGI, 1997

Creative partner of Koeweiden Postma.
Education: Royal Academy of Art & Design. University of Utrecht (sound design).
Clients: Ministry of Education Culture & Science, Ramadan Festival, HEMA. Marhaba (Islamic Cultural Centre), European Student Network, MTV, The Dutch Judiciary Council, Leine & Roebana (dance company), Hortus Botanicus and Viacom/NY.
(Group) exhibitions: Stedelijk Museum Amsterdam; Design Museum London; Poster Festival Bergen (Norway); Cooper Hewitt, NY and SF MoMA; also took part in exhibitions in Los Angeles, Chicago, Sydney, Hong Kong, Malaysia, Italy, France and Germany. *Memberships:* BNO, D&AD.

Koeweiden gives lectures and masterclasses in and outside Europe and is co-founder of Mind the Gap, a series of (visually based) lectures that investigates the role of design, art direction and new media in a changing world of communication. KP is also one of the partner agencies of Design2context/The Swiss Institute for Design Research, Zürich.
Awards/nominations: competitions and festivals include the ADCN; Dutch Theatre Year prize; Dutch Design Prize; Dutch Stationery Prize; British D&AD; NY ADC and TDC; ADC Tokyo; TDC Tokyo; The 100 Show (USA); German Design Prize; STD (UK); TIA (USA); Chaumont Poster Festival (France) and the Hong Kong Poster Triennial (China). As a jury member, Koeweiden has been involved in many festivals and competitions worldwide.

In the end it's all about love, poster, 2006.

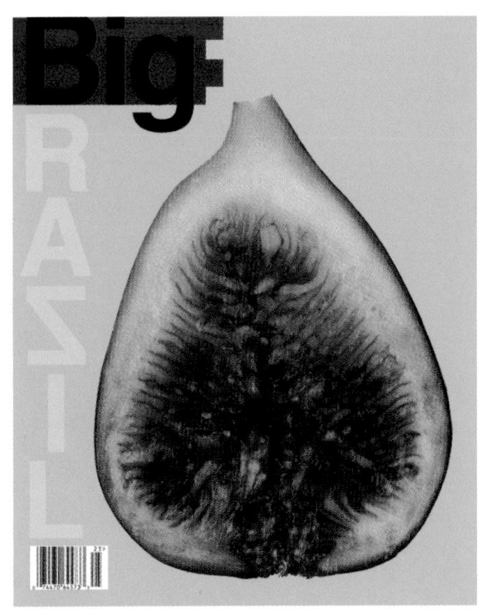

Rico Lins [Brazil]

Poster for **Human Rights**, 1989.
An international group of designers was invited to create a tribute to the Human Rights Bill for the bicentennial of the French Revolution.

Big Magazine, 1999.
First Brazilian issue of this international style magazine. Each edition combines the work of invited artists, photographers, designers, writers and more.

Panamericana 96. Each of 18 invited designers created one image for an international conference on graphic design in Brazil with AGIUSA. The unpredictable was the key element throughout this poster project.

1955– born in Rio de Janeiro
Admitted to AGI, 1997

Studied at ESDI, Rio and the RCA, London and taught at the NY School of Visual Arts, and the Istituto Europeo di Design, São Paulo where he is head of the graphic design masters course. Designer and art director, he works between Paris, London, NY, São Paulo and Rio for fashion, cultural, corporate, advertising and TV clients such as MTV, WEA, *Le Monde*, *NY Times*, *Time*, *Newsweek*, *Big* magazine, Gallimard, Hachette, Random House, Condé-Nast, NY Public Theatre, TV Globo and Natura. One-man shows at Centre Pompidou, Paris; NY MoMA and Museum of Contemporary Art, Brazil. He has taken part in numerous international group shows, projects, biennials and juries.

Awarded at the NY ADC, NY SPD and the ADG and 21st São Paulo Biennials. Elected 'Designer of the Year 2001' in Brazil. Features in the collections of the Musée d'Histoire Contemporaine, Musée de l'Affiche and Bibliothèque Nationale and Chaumont, France; Museum of Contemporary Art, São Paulo and Die Neue Sammlung, Munich. Features in books including: *Non-Traditional Design*, *First Choice*, *All Men Are Brothers* and *Design of Dissent* and magazines such as *Graphis*, *Print*, *Novum*, *AdWeek*, *Creative Review*, *Design*, *Visual*, *Experimenta*, *Art & Design* (Beijing); *Linea Grafica*, *Étapes*, *BàT*, *IDEA*, *+81Tokio*, *Gráfica*, *Tupigrafia*, *Criação* and *a!Mexico*.

Pippo Lionni [France]

1954– born in New York, USA
Admitted to AGI, 1997

Grew up in New York, studied philosophy and mathematics at Portland State University and NYU. He became a designer in the late 1970s. Has lived in Paris since 1981. His work has been shown at several exhibitions: PNCA Portland, Galerie Frédéric Giroux, Artcurial, Espace Modem, Franck Bordas and Brownstone Foundation in Paris, at the Karel de Grote Hogeschool in Antwerp and the Israel Museum in Jerusalem. His oeuvre includes signage, set design, corporate identity programmes and environmental design. *Offices and partnerships:* Pippo Lionni, 1984–89; Integral Concept, 1989–95; Pippo Lionni et Associés, 1995–97; Ldesign (founded in 1997 with Arik Levy). All have done major work for important clients. Lionni has maintained an involvement in design education and research at: Parsons School in Paris, 1986–91; École Nationale Supérieure de Création Industrielle in Paris, 1991–98; International Public Art Symposium, Birmingham, 1990; INCSID/ San José, USA, 1992; University of Industrial Arts, Helsinki, 1992; Bilkent University, Ankara, 1993; École de la Cambre, Brussels, 1993–95; Politecnico d'Architettura, Milan, 1993. He was asked by the French Ministère de l'Industrie to research and create a programme for graduate research into design, 1994–95. Lionni was awarded the distinction of Chevalier de l'Ordre des Arts et des Lettres in 2001.

La Documentation Française, 1990.
Global communication programme.

Ministère de la Culture, 1989–93.
Visual identity programme, signage logo.

Hotlips Pizza, 2005.
Corporate identity programme, poster and product label.

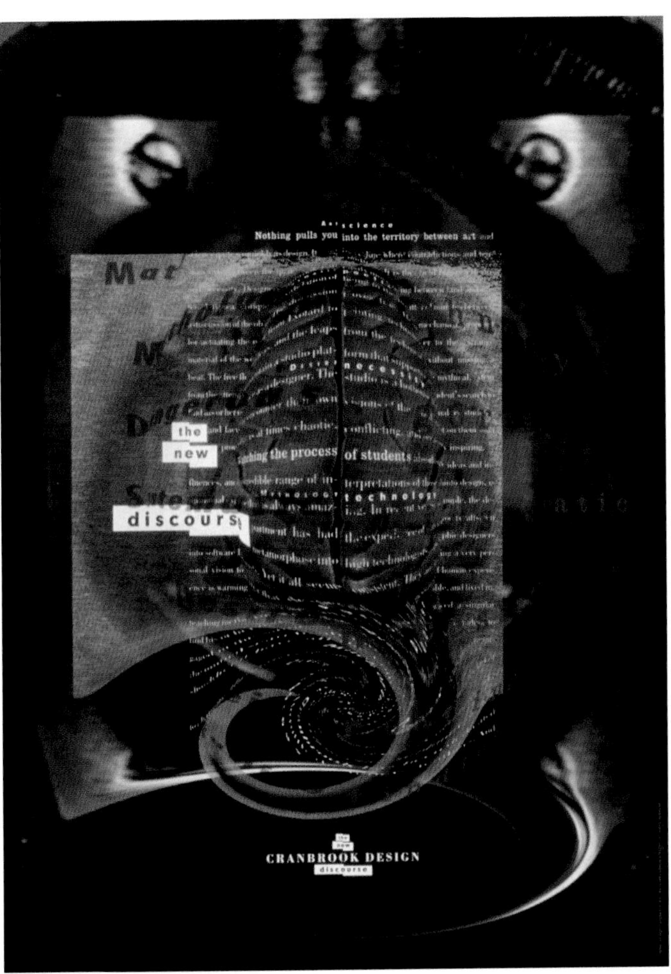

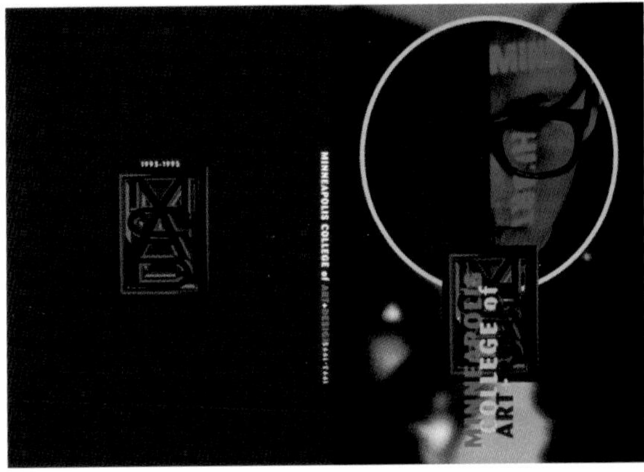

P. Scott Makela [USA]

The New Discourse, poster, 1991. To announce a book and exhibition at Cranbrook Academy, the book's manifesto wraps around a brain superimposed on a mechanical gear – the intersection of organic and inorganic, logic and intuition, rising out of a vortex.

Living Surfaces, conference poster, 1992. A poster announcing the first American conference on communications design for new media, organized by the American Center for Design.

Minneapolis College of Art & Design, catalogue, 1992. To promote this art college to high school art students, a dynamic youthful attitude speaks in the audience's language and greatly increased applications for admission to the college.

1960-1999; born in St Paul, Minnesota
Admitted to AGI, 1997

P. Scott Makela received a BFA from Minneapolis College of Art & Design. In Los Angeles, after time in April Greiman's studio, he formed Commbine and taught at California Institute of the Arts and Otis College of Art & Design. He earned an MFA from Cranbrook Academy of Art in 1991, studying with Katherine McCoy. At Cranbrook, Scott designed the influential font Dead History, and married his design collaborator, Laurie Haycock Makela. Their daughter Carmella was born six weeks before their graduation. Scott founded Words and Pictures for Business and Culture in Minneapolis and quickly became internationally known for his cutting-edge youth-market design for print, multimedia and motion graphics. Scott designed communications for the American Center for Design's first Living Surfaces Conference, the Minneapolis College of Art and Design, Émigré Records, and *Design Quarterly* magazine. In 1996 Scott and Laurie succeeded Katherine McCoy at Cranbrook, as co-chairs of the 2D Design Department. Their successful Cranbrook design studio was expanding into television advertising, when Scott died suddenly from an undiagnosed respiratory virus on a soft spring night in 1999. A moving Buddhist memorial service in the Cranbrook sculpture gardens was attended by Scott's family, Cranbrook faculty and students, and his many design colleagues.

Katherine McCoy

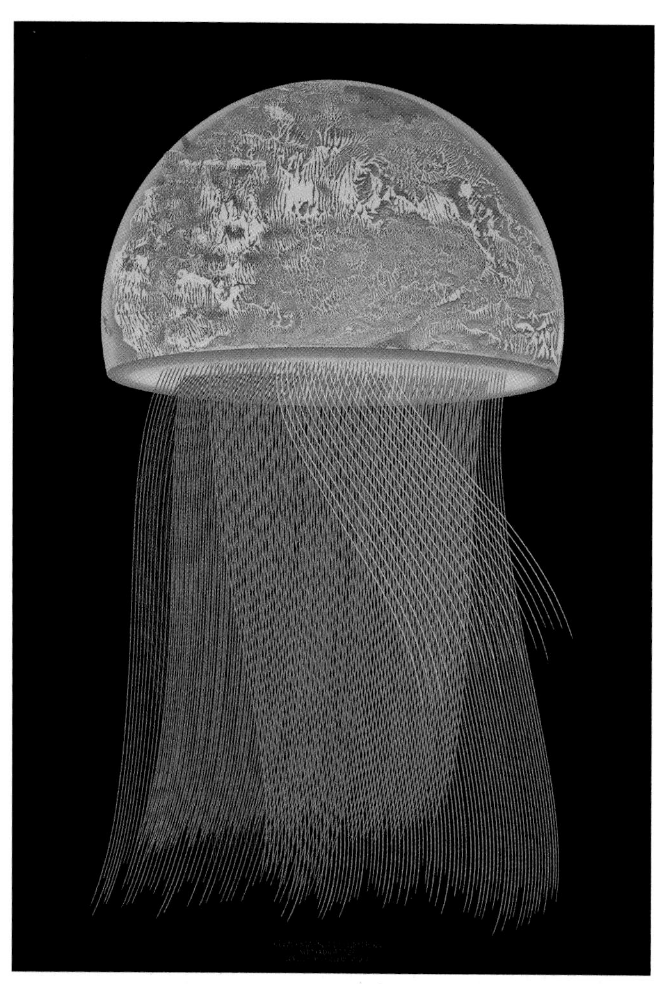

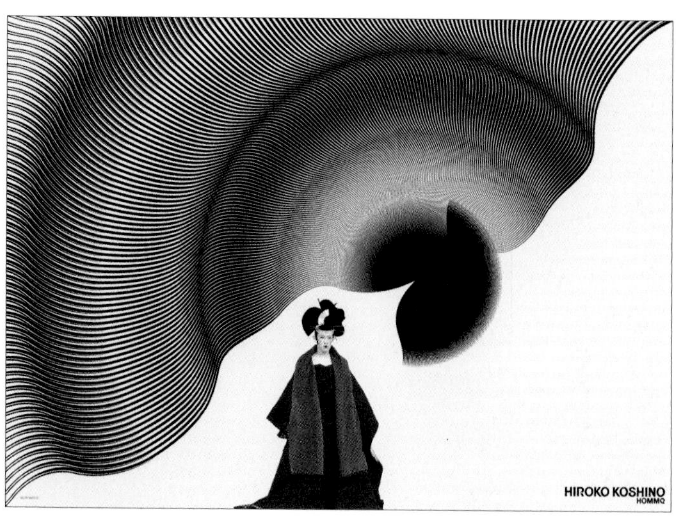

Keizo Matsui [Japan]

1946– born in Hiroshima
Admitted to AGI, 1997

Matsui studied at the Osaka University of Arts.
1984: Hundred Design Inc.
2006: Dramatic Design Institute Designart.
2004: Professor at the Osaka University of Arts Graduate School.
Worldwide design activities include corporate identity, poster design, signage, graphic design, packaging, exhibition design, product development, art and sculpture.

International juror for: Graphic Design in China 96; Helsinki International Poster Biennale 1997; Golden Bee International Graphic Biennale Moscow.
Publications: 'International Graphic Designers' series (GGG, Japan); *3D Graphics* (Japan); *Graphic Designer Matsui Keizo* (China)
Awards: 15th Brno International Graphic Design Biennale (Icograda Excellence Award); New York ADC International Exhibition (silver and bronze prizes); Golden Bee Graphic Biennale Moscow (Golden Bee Award); Japan Package Design Award (gold prize) and more.

Jellyfish, exhibition poster.

Hiroko Koshino Homme (x 2).

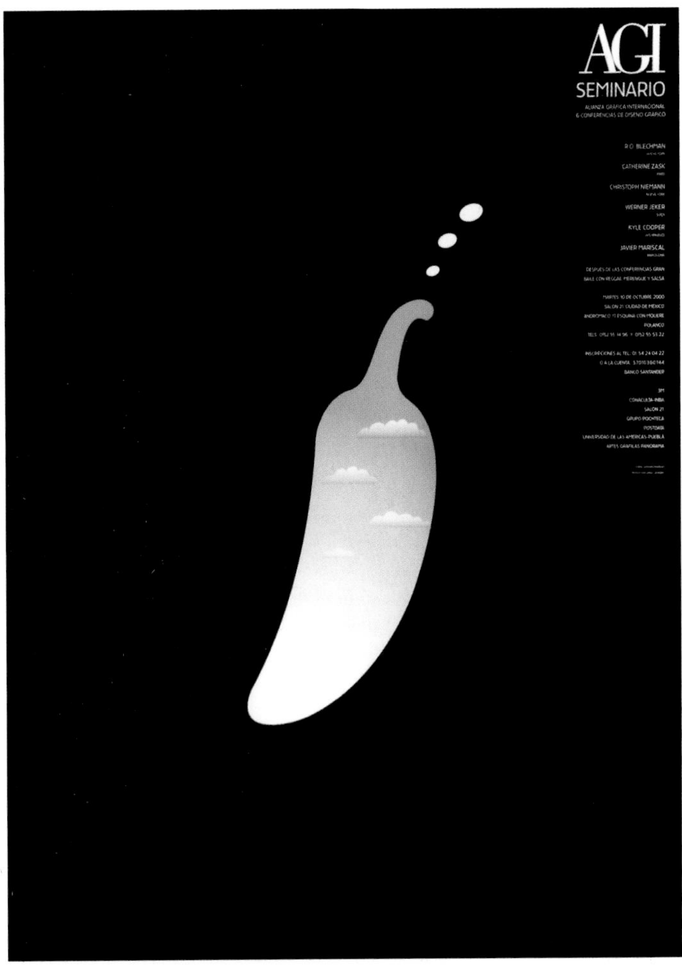

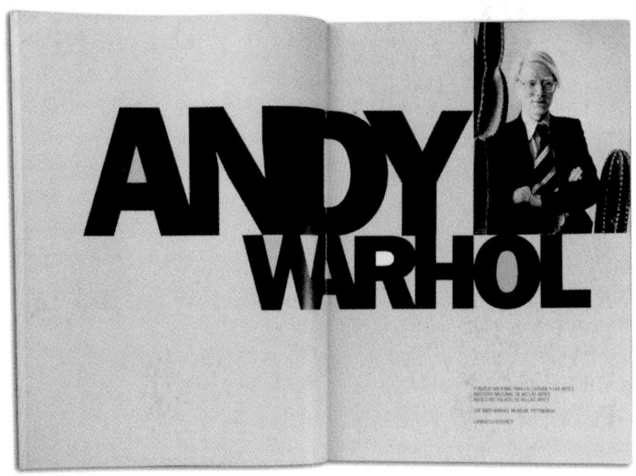

Germán Montalvo Aguilar [Mexico]

AGI Seminario, poster designed for a student seminar, organized by AGI in Mexico City. The chilli pepper and the clouds symbolize the collective imagination that characterizes Mexico.

Andy Warhol. This poster was made for the first exhibition of the American pop art icon's work in Mexico City. The top of the soup can was never used by Warhol; nevertheless, this element represents his work.

Andy Warhol book, spread.

1956– born in Mexico City
Admitted to AGI, 1997

He studied at the Scuola de Libro in Milan, Italy. (1976–77), founded by Albe Steiner. Germán was a teacher at the Universidad de las Americas Puebla (1996–2006). His work is dedicated to cultural design for many institutions.
Awards: 1st place at the Poster Biennale, Fort Collins, Colorado, 1993; Benjamin Franklin Award, Publishers Marketing Association, United States, 1994; Design Award from the Mexican Academy of Design, 1995; Quorum award (1994, 2005).

Poster exhibitions: Milan, 1980; Cuba, 1987; Montreal, 1988; Australia, 1990; Japan, DDD Gallery, 1995; Japan, GGG Gallery, 1997; several Mexican cities.
Publications: Popo-Pop, popular representations of the Mexican volcano Popocatepetl; *Al son de la letra*, children's book; *Las buenas formas*, children's book that teaches shape recognition; *Palabra de tipografía*; *Miguel Prieto diseño gráfico*; *Vicento Rojo cuarenta años de diseño gráfico*; *Coleadas*, children's stories; *Germán Montalvo Diseño Gráfico*, text by Erendira Melendez.

Finn Nygaard [Denmark]

1955– born in Aarhus
Admitted to AGI, 1997

Finn Nygaard studied at the Academy in Aarhus and the Design School in Kolding during the seventies. He established his own studio in 1979. From 1990 to 1995 he was a partner in the famous Danish design group Eleven Danes and the European Designers Network EDEN. Since the beginning he has created posters, illustrations, graphic design and corporate identity programmes and colour consulting for Danish and international companies and organizations, including Egmont, Venstre (the Danish poltical party) and for the EM 2002 Handball for Women. He has created more than 300 posters, for many of which he has received awards. Most famous are those for the Aarhus International Jazz Festival. Finn has had several one-man exhibitions, and his posters and design projects have been shown in major galleries and museums all over the world; several of his posters have found their way into permanent collections. Finn is a frequent guest lecturer to student and professional groups all over the world.

Ode to Toulouse-Lautrec 1864–1901, poster, 2001. Nouveau Salon des Cent.

Poster for the **Aarhus International Jazz Festival**, 1992. A tribute to Ben Webster.

Europe, stamps for Post DK, 2005.

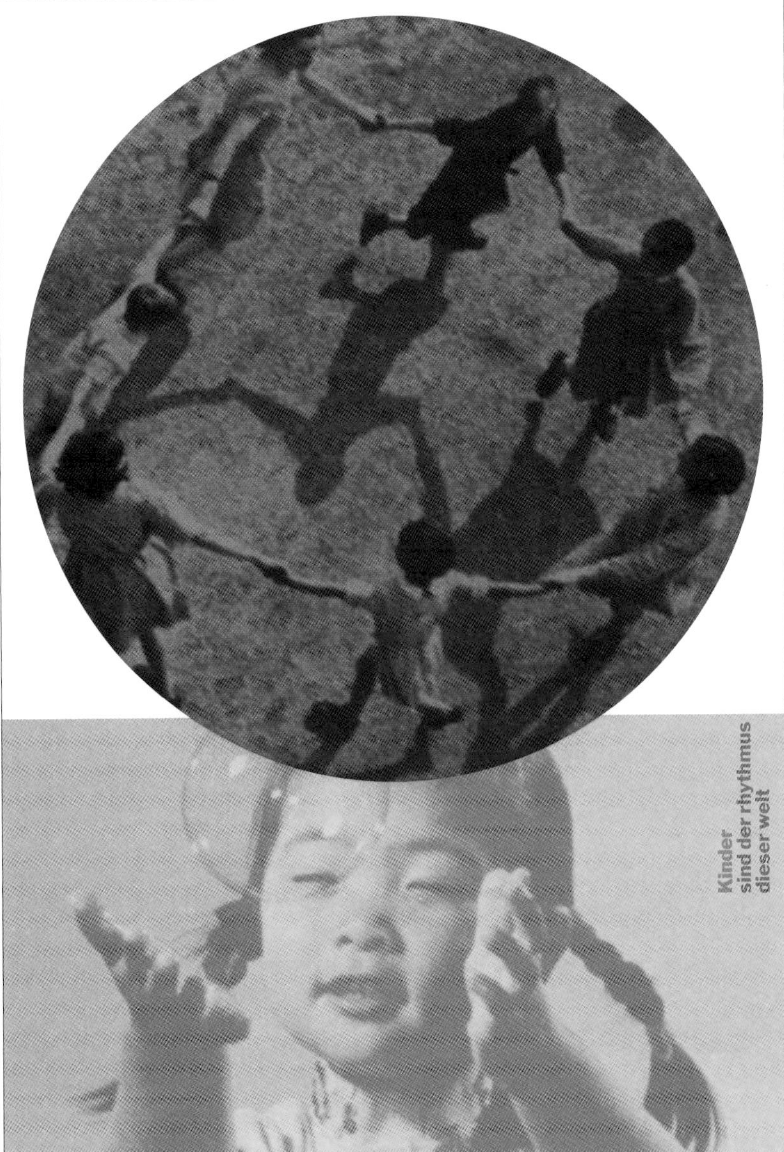
Kinder
sind der rhythmus
dieser welt

Museo
Vela
Ligornetto
HELVETIA
70

Homage to Joseph Beuys, poster, 2004. Museo Communale d'Arte Moderna Ascona.

Children are the rhythm of the world, poster, 2002. Deutsches Plakat Museum Essen and German Child Protection Society.

Museo Vela, Ligornetto, stamp, 1998. Swiss Post.

Sabina Oberholzer [Switzerland]

1958– born in Locarno
Admitted to AGI, 1997

Studied under Bruno Monguzzi at the CSIA in Lugano. In 1983 she founded the Studio di Progettazione Grafica with her partner Renato Tagli in Cevio, in the Italian-speaking region of Switzerland. Oberholzer and Tagli are alive to the relationship between nature and creativity, and sensitive to their responsibilities within the small community in which they live and work. Driven not by economics but rather by a belief in quality and clarity of the message, Oberholzer's design philosophy is based on appropriateness and generally results in the elimination of the superfluous, ornate or artificial.

In 1985, they won the contest for the creation of the corporate identity of the city of Locarno. In 1987, they were responsible for the design of the newspaper *Quotidiano*, for which the following year they won a prize from the Federal Scholarship for Applied Arts, a feat they repeated two years later. They were second in the contest for the best Swiss corporate identity with Ottica Stiefel in 1992.
In 1995 they created the new corporate design for Monte Verità. In 1998, they began work on the corporate design for the Museo Comunale d'Arte Moderna Ascona. In 2005, they were invited by the Swiss National Bank to take part in a competition to design a new series of banknotes.

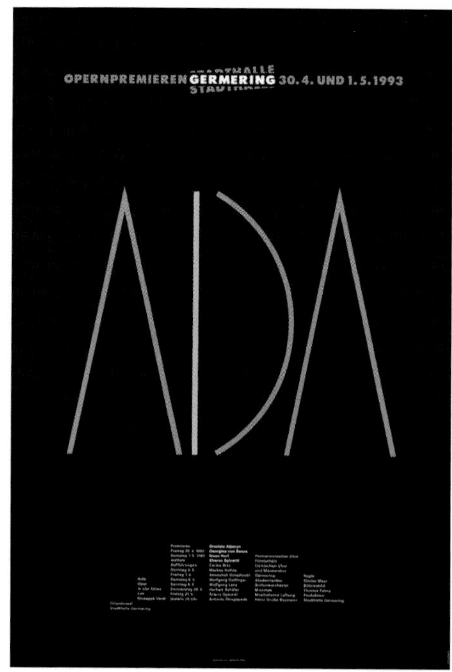

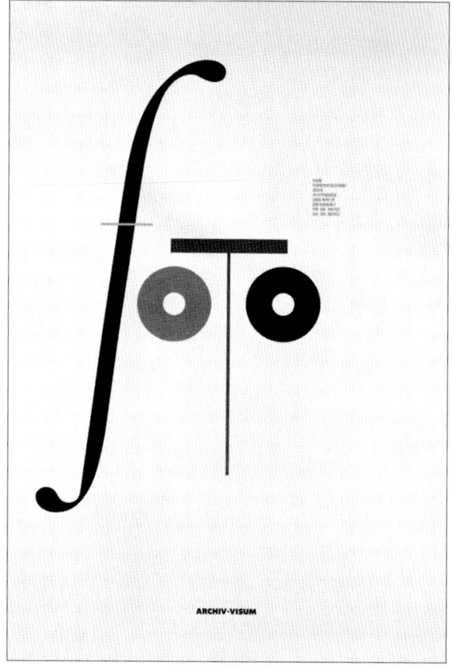

Nicolaus Ott [Germany]

1947– born in Göttingen
Admitted to AGI, 1997

1966: Nicolaus Ott trains as a graphic draughtsman.
1969–74: studies at the Hochschule der Künste under Herbert W. Kapitzki.
1978: Ott+Stein graphic design studio founded in Berlin. They design primarily for cultural institutions and have produced posters, catalogues and typographical logos.
1988: Ott+Stein share a visiting professorship at the Hochschule der Künste Berlin. Since 1996 they have shared a professorship at the Kunsthochschule Kassel.

Exhibitions of their posters include: DDD Gallery, Osaka, 2002; Museum für Kunst und Gewerbe, Hamburg, 2002 and 1992; Aedes East Architectural Gallery, Berlin 1997; Stilwerk, Hamburg, 1996; Deutsches Plakatmuseum, Essen, 1995; International Design Centre, Berlin, 1991 and 1983. In 1992 a book about their poster work, *Vom Wort zum Bild und zurück*, was published by Ernst & Son, with text by Ulf Erdmann Ziegler. In 1998, together with Friedrich Friedl, Ott+Stein published an encyclopedia of typography with the title *TYPO: When, Who, How* (Könemann Verlag).

Diseño, 1989. Poster for an exhibition on Catalonian product design. The exhibition was organized by the IDZ (International Design Centre) Berlin.

Aida, 1993. Poster for the premiere of the Verdi opera, staged at the City Hall of Germering.

Foto, 1990. Poster for Visum Picture Archive. The typography of the poster is designed to resemble a portrait.

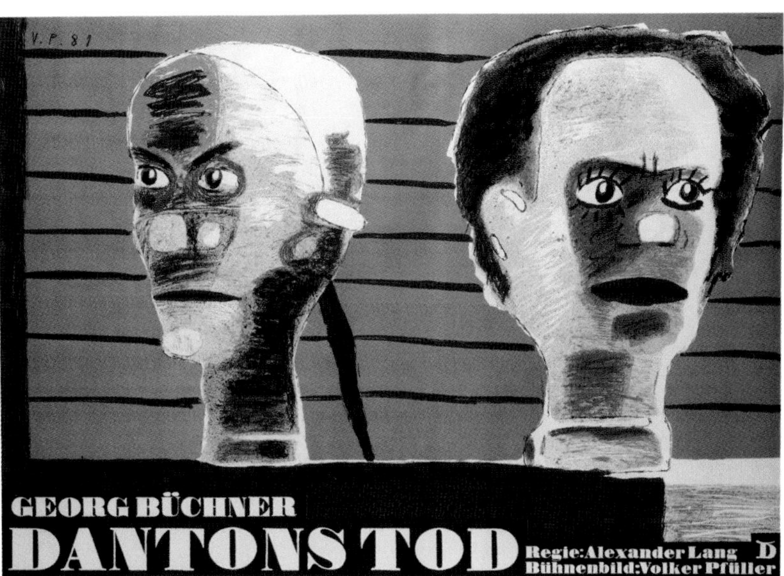

Bertholt Brecht: ***Baal***, theatre poster, 1982. Deutsche Staatsoper Berlin.

Georg Büchner: ***Danton's Death***, theatre poster, 1981. Deutsches Theater Berlin.

Ernst Toller: ***Wotan Unchained***, theatre poster, 841 x 594 mm, 1980. Deutsches Theater Berlin.

Volker Pfüller [Germany]

1939– born in Leipzig
Admitted to AGI, 1997

Volker studied at the Fachschule für angewandte Kunst (technical college of applied arts), Berlin-Oberschöneweide and at the Kunsthochschule Berlin-Weissensee under Professors Klemke, Mohr and Wittkugel. From 1978 he was a teacher of graphic design and set design in Berlin. 1990–91: visiting professor of illustration at GHK Kassel. 1991–97: professor of set and costume design, Kunsthochschule Berlin-Weissensee. 1997–2000: professor of illustration the Academy of Visual Arts in Leipzig.

Works: set and costume designs (Berlin, Florence, Hamburg, Tel-Aviv), exhibition designs, posters, book and illustrations. Participation in numerous exhibitions all over the world as graphic designer and set designer. Since 1975 Volker has had solo exhibitions in Berlin, Chaumont, Chemnitz, Cottbus, Frankfurt, Halle, Leipzig, Munich, Oberursel, Schwerin and Weimar. He has received several awards for poster designs, including: The 100 Best Posters and The Most Beautiful Books in Germany, 1981, 1983 and 1985; *Berliner Zeitung* Critics Award for set design; Silver Medal for costume design at the International Quadrennial for Scenery Design in Prague; GDR Kunstpreis, 1986; Silver Medal, Poster Biennale, Lahti, 1987.

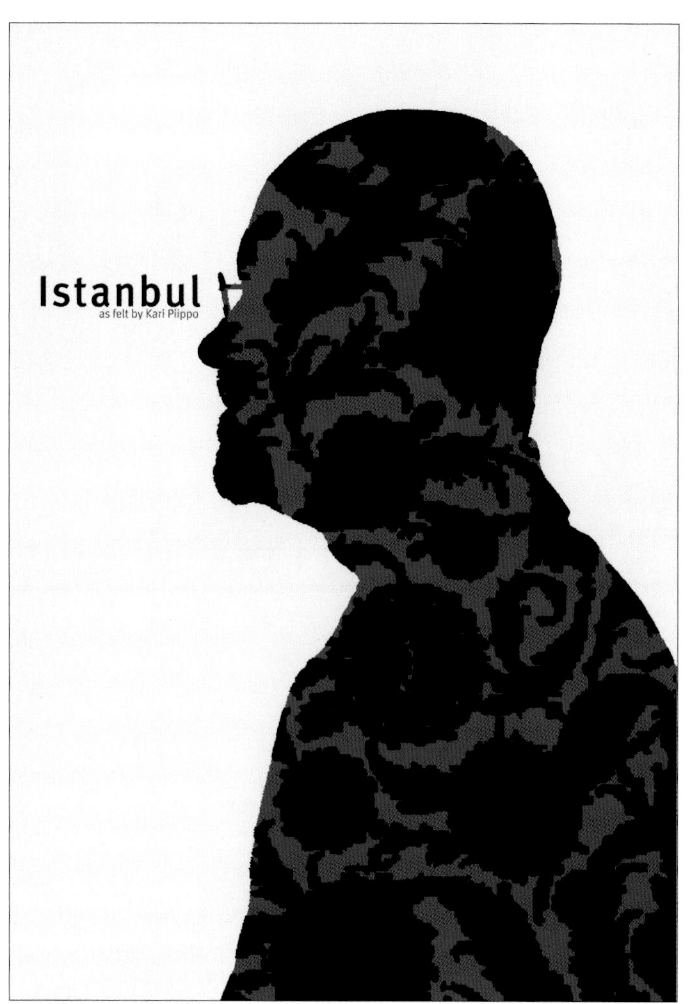

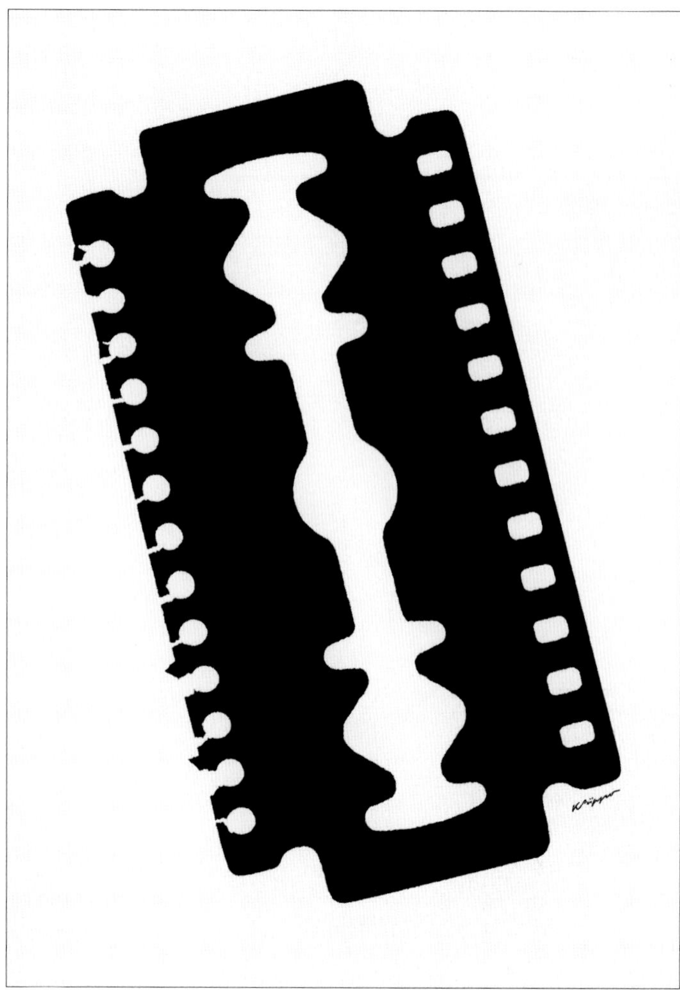

Kari Piippo [Finland]

1945– born in Lappajärvi
Admitted to AGI, 1997

Graduated from the School of Industrial Art in Helsinki in 1967, then became a freelance graphic designer, specializing in illustration and poster design. Founded his own studio in 1987. Lecturer in graphic design at the University of Art and Design Helsinki, 1989–97. Visiting professor at Tama Art University in Tokyo and Shandong University of Art and Design in Jinan, China, since 2004. Has held many individual and group exhibitions at home and abroad. Has given many poster workshops and lectures, in Australia, China, Ecuador, France, Italy, Japan, Mexico, Turkey, USA and elsewhere.

Has taken part in the most important international poster exhibitions since the 1980s and has been a jury member in many national and international competitions since 1989. Major Finnish awards include the State Industrial Arts Award, Graphic Artist of the Year, Platinum Award and four Gold Awards, plus several Best Finnish Poster Prizes. Major international awards: Icograda Excellence Award, Chaumont 1990; 1st Prize, in Mexico IPB, 1990; 2nd Prize, Lahti IPB, 1991; 1st Prize, Rzeszow ITPB, 1993; 1st Prize, Colorado CIIPE, 1999; Grand Prix, Eco Poster Triennial, Slovakia, 2000; Bronze, Graphic Designers Poster Exhibition, Ningbo, 2001; Bronze, Korea International Poster Biennale, 2002; International Poster Art Prize, Germany, 2003.

Istanbul as felt by Kari Piippo, 2006.
Anniversary poster.

Lahti Poster Museum 1975–1990, 1990.
Anniversary poster.

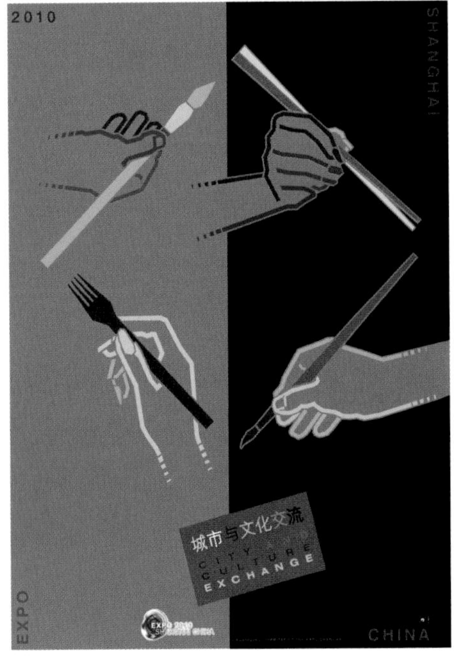

New Mexico Film and Video, poster, 1992.

Expo Shanghai 2010, poster, 2001.

Santiago Pol's Spaces, exhibition poster, 1989.

Santiago Pol [Venezuela]

1946– born in Barcelona, Spain
Admitted to AGI, 1997

Santiago pursued his studies at the Schools of Fine Arts of Caracas and Paris. Some of Pol's works have been presented in solo exhibits in Cuba, Mexico, Brazil, Britain, France and Venezuela. His works have also featured in group shows including the Mexico City Biennial International Exhibition and the Modern Art Museum of Mexico, and at biennials and triennials in Warsaw, Moscow, New York, Lahti, Brno and Toyama. Pol represented Venezuela at the 51st Venice Biennial, 2005. He is a member of the Venezuelan Association of Fine Arts, National Council of Graphic Arts, International Council of Graphic Design of London and Union des Arts Décoratifs de Paris. He has been awarded the Graphic Arts National Prize, and the Golden Dove at the Leipzig International Film Festival. His works are part of important collections in Venezuela and world cities. Some of his works belong to the NY MoMA, the Israeli Museum of Jerusalem, the Museum of Posters of Poland, the Washington DC National Library, the Louvre, and the Carlos Cruz-Diez Print and Design Museum, Caracas. At present, he is the coordinator of academic exhibits at the Integral Design Unit of the Universidad Nacional Experimental de Yaracuy, Venezuela.

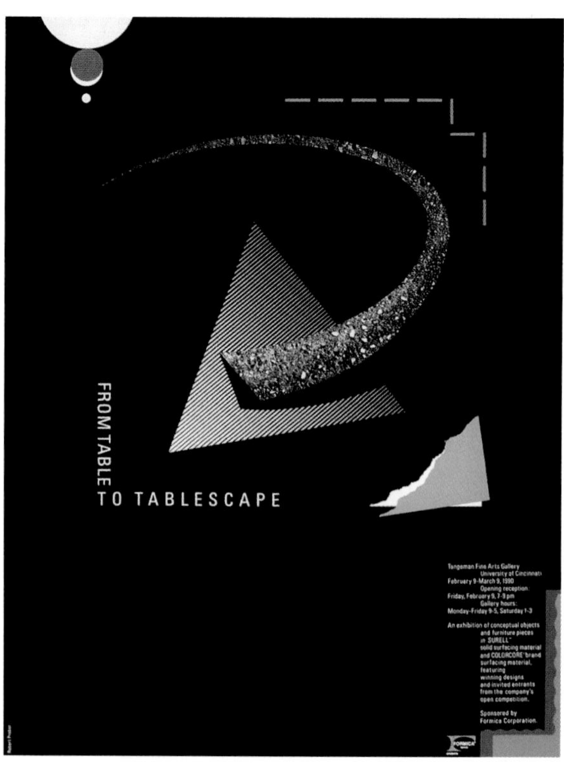

Robert Probst [USA]

1951– born in Loerrach, Germany
Admitted to AGI, 1997

Robert Probst received his design education from the University of Essen, Germany and the College of Design, Basel, Switzerland. In 1975 his professional career began in Otl Aicher's studio for visual communication, Rotis. The scope of his work spans a wide range: from two-dimensional graphics, promotional and identity design, multi-dimensional interpretive exhibition work, architectural signage and environmental design to wayfinding systems and product development. His three decades of practice are based on work for cultural, historical, zoological, medical, educational, and municipal institutions as well as for the private sector.

Since 1978 he has been a professor at the University of Cincinnati; College of Design, Architecture, Art, and Planning; School of Design. In 2001 he was named Director of the School of Design. His work is featured in numerous publications. He has received many awards from professional organizations and has lectured at institutions and conferences in the United States, Mexico, England, Spain, Germany, and Switzerland. He served on the Board of Directors of the Society for Environmental Graphic Design and as President of its Education Foundation. In 1996 he was honoured with the SEGD Fellow Award. He has three children with his wife Alison: Jasmine, Alistair, Lyndon.

Diversity, poster, 2000. Icons developed for Cincinnati Zoo identity programme, 1983. Design collaborator: Heinz Schenker.

Poster for **travelling exhibition of experimental furniture**, Formica Corporation, 1990.

Mural installation for Arts and Science Building at Sinclair Community College, Dayton, Ohio, 1996. Design collaborators: Heinz Schenker, Kelly Kolar, Dariusz Janczewsky.

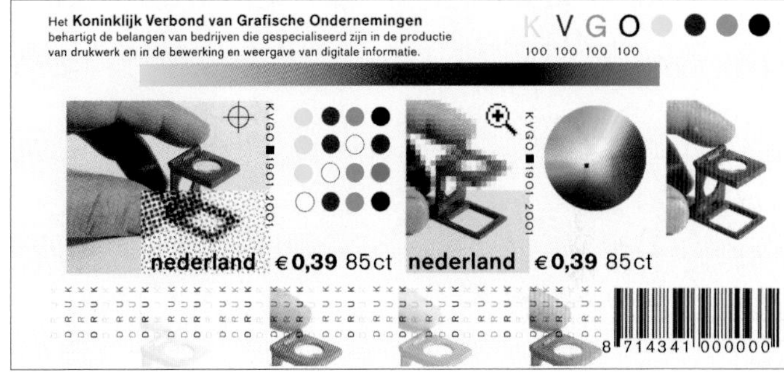

Lex Reitsma [The Netherlands]

Harry Boom, poster for an exhibition at the Haarlem Verweyhal, 1998.

Blikvangers, poster for an exhibition of Dutch film posters, 2005.

100 Years of KVGO, stamps, PTT Post, 2001.

1958– born in Delden
Admitted to AGI, 1997

Lex Reitsma studied graphic design at the Gerrit Rietveld Academy in Amsterdam from 1978 to 1983. He is self-employed. Most of his commissions come from the cultural sphere and many of these publications deal with photography, architecture, art, cinema or the graphic profession. He has designed exhibition catalogues and posters for museums such as Museum Overholland and the Amsterdam Stedelijk Museum. For Dutch Royal PTT he has created postage stamps, diaries and annual reports. As of 1990, he is the regular graphic designer for De Nederlandse Opera.

His opera posters, which often feature his own photographs, balance image, text and empty space to create a total experience and lucidly convey information. His posters are like blown-up stamps, just as his stamps are miniature posters. In 1994, Reitsma won the Dutch Theatre Poster Award. In 2002, he received the H.N. Werkman Award from the Amsterdam Art Fund for his designs for De Nederlandse Opera. Over twenty of his books were included in the annual selection of the Best Book Design by the CPNB. Lex Reitsma has a character trait that dominates his life: he is self-willed, critical and mistrustful of the latest fads.

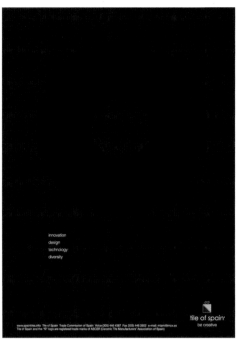

David Ruiz [Spain]

1960– born in Barcelona
Admitted to AGI, 1997

David Ruiz is a creative director, art director and graphic designer. From 1985 to 1993, he worked at the advertising agencies Saatchi & Saatchi, Publicis, GGK and Bassat, Ogilvy & Mather as an art director and creative director. In 1992, based out of this last agency, he created and directed the television show *Jeans, News & Rock & Roll*, sponsored by Levi's. He is the winner of over eighty national and international awards, including the first grand prix for graphic design ever won by Spain at the Clio Festival, held in San Francisco, for a Levi's 501 campaign.

His work has been published in a variety of books and national and international magazines. He has been a member of the jury for the Laus, Eurobest, New York Festival, Art Directors Club of New York and Art Directors Club of Europe awards.

Poster for **Camper stores**.

Be Creative, international advertising campaign for magazines, under the 'Be Creative' concept, for the Spanish association of ceramic tile manufacturers.

Chocolat Factory Tubes, packaging for the company Chocolat Factory.

Martini Frezzio, image design for the new Martini drink, in collaboration with industrial designer Jordi Torres.

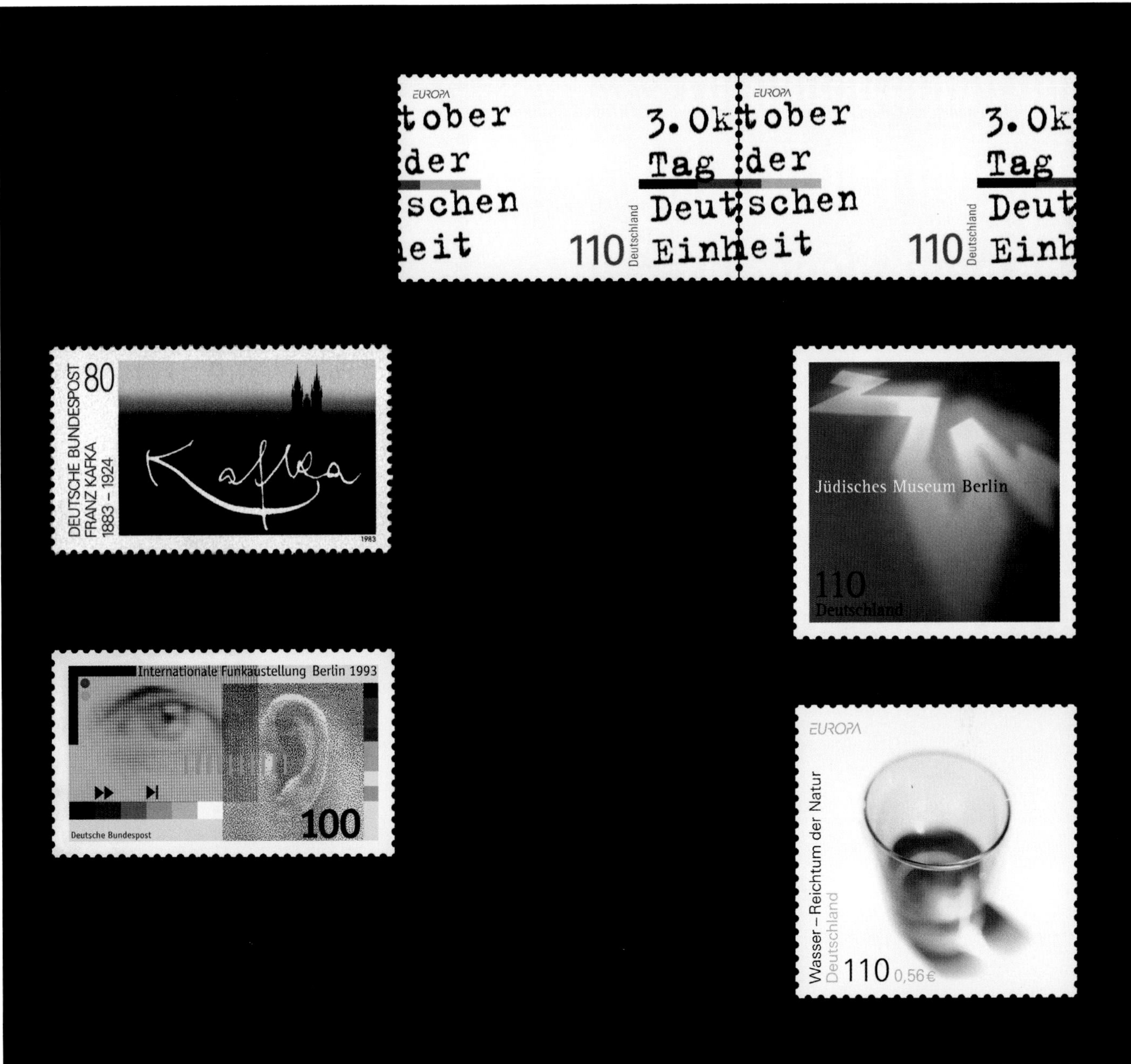

Day of German Unity, stamp.

Franz Kafka's 100th Birthday, stamp.

Jewish Museum Berlin, stamp.

IFA, International Trade Fair Consumer Electronics, Berlin, stamp.

Keeping Water Pure, stamp.

Hans Günter Schmitz [Germany]

1954- born in Stolberg
Admitted to AGI, 1997

Hans Günter Schmitz, founder and owner of Schmitz Visuelle Kommunikation, Wuppertal
His main work is in the field of corporate identity, corporate design and corporate communication. Awards for communication design, web design and product design from the Art Directors Club of New York, Art Directors Club of Germany, Type Directors Club of New York, British Design & Art Direction, Red Dot Design Awards, IF Design Awards. Schmitz has been professor of visual communication at the University of Wuppertal since 1994.

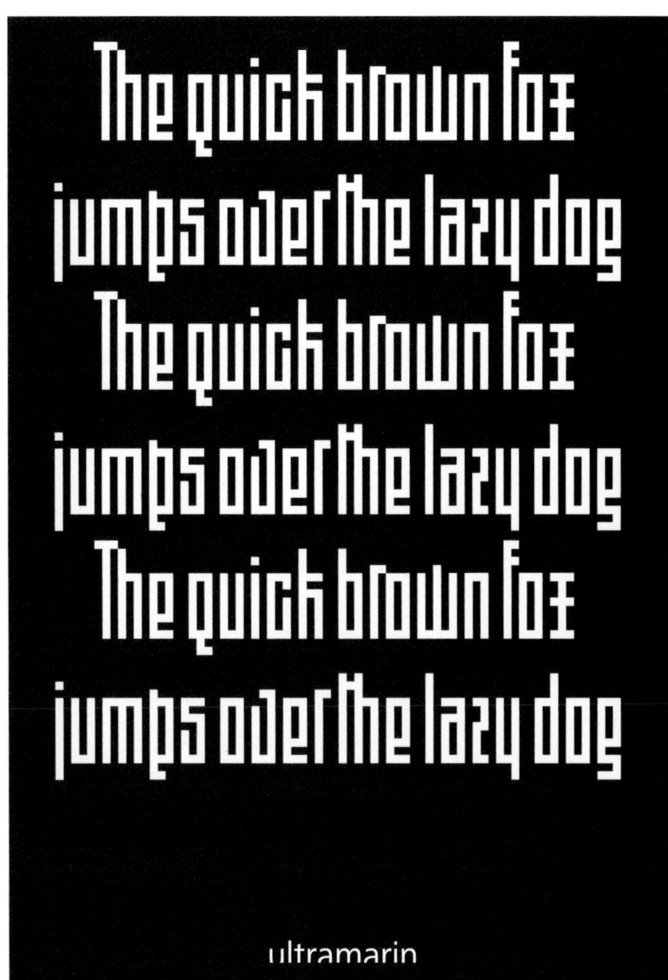
The quick brown fox
jumps over the lazy dog
The quick brown fox
jumps over the lazy dog
The quick brown fox
jumps over the lazy dog
ultramarin

ultramarin

a

Finn Sködt [Denmark]

1944– born in Aarhus
Admitted to AGI, 1997

Designer and painter.
Main interests: Titanium White, Cadmium Yellow Lemon, Naples Yellow, Yellow Ochre, Raw Sienna, Caput Mortuum Violet, Warm Sepia, Indian Yellow, Orange Lake, Vermilion, Burgundy Wine Red, Cobalt Violet Dark, Indigo, Ultramarine Blue Deep, Cyan Blue, Cobalt Blue, Turquoise, Green Gold, Cadmium Green Light, Green Umber, Davy's Grey, Wine Black.

Poster for **Studio Ultramarin**.
One-colour offset print on paper. Font: Q3.

Poster for **Studio Ultramarin**.
One-colour offset print on paper. Font: Strokes.

Letter **a** from the font Mediolanum.

Leslie Smolan [USA]

New York Botanical Garden. Leslie Smolan developed this interpretive signage programme, which combines brightly illustrated signs with easy-to-read text, turning visitors into scientists and educating through interaction and hands-on activities.

Putnam Investments. The comprehensive brand strategy behind Putnam's selling system demystified the investment process for consumers while building trust in financial advisers and set a new standard in the financial field.

Punta Nizuc. This identity, created for a luxury hotel and residential property in Mexico embodies the region's rich Mayan history.

1952– born in New York City
Admitted to AGI, 1997

Leslie Smolan has been internationally recognized for her work in brand identity, publishing and marketing communications. Her passion is to make large amounts of complex information understandable and appealing to a wide audience. A relentless pursuit of a distinct, client-driven aesthetic complements her planning capability and her creative direction is notable for its timeless finesse and carefully nuanced detailing.

Recent projects include a global events identity for Morgan Stanley and a communications programme for its sponsorship of the 'Leonardo da Vinci: Master Draftsman' exhibition at the Metropolitan Museum, New York; a Brand Spirit Book for the developer of Peninsula Papagayo, the first five-star luxury resort development in Costa Rica; and a new interpretive sign system for the Everett Children's Adventure Garden at the New York Botanical Garden, which presents a bug's-eye view of plants. Leslie uses her experience to mentor both clients and designers on the power of strategic design to transform businesses and motivate customers.

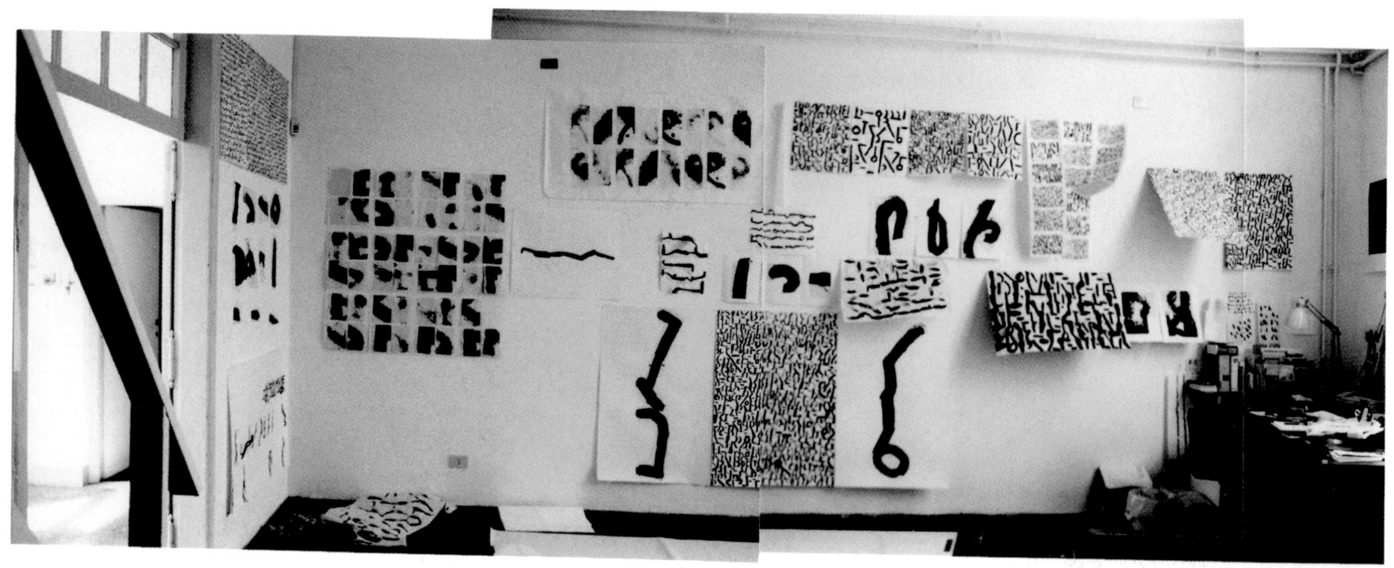

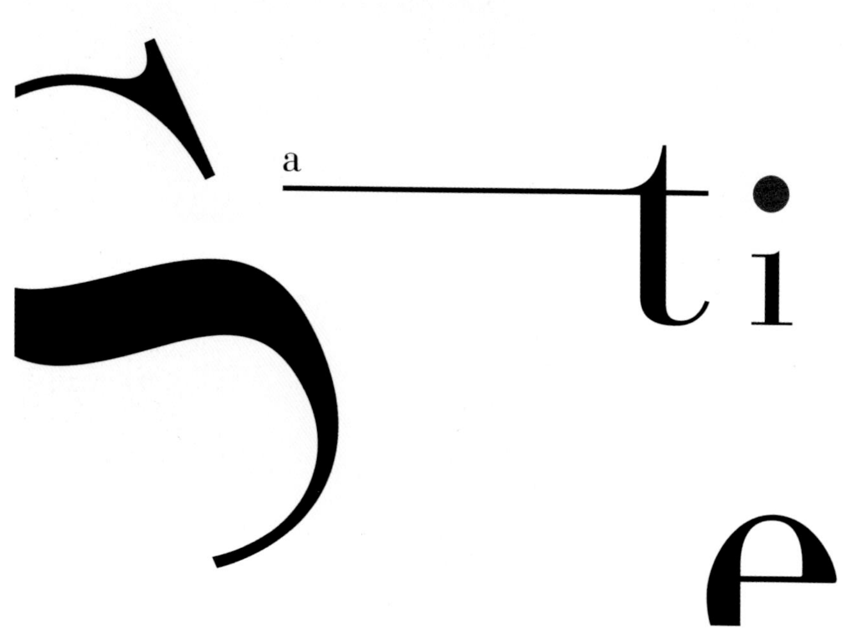

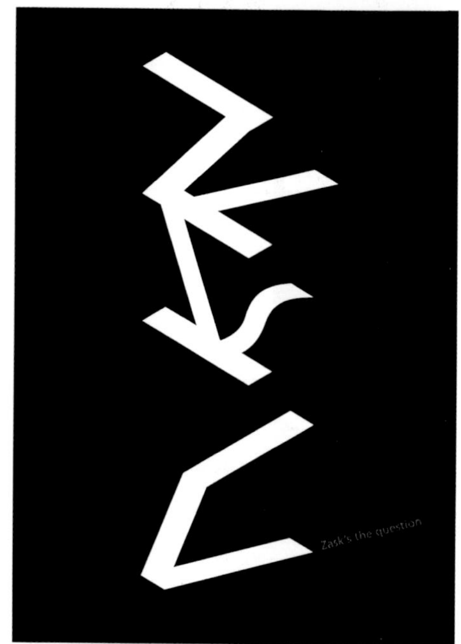

Catherine Zask [France]

1961– born in Paris
Admitted to AGI, 1997

Graphic artist, poster designer, writer – Zask is as multifaceted as the building blocks of her visual language. She graduated from the ESAG, Paris in 1984, and started her career as an independent designer in 1985. She works mainly with cultural institutions: University of Franche-Comté, 1985–2002; Scam, Civil Society of Multimedia Artists, since 1993; L'Hippodrome, national theatre of Douai, 1997–2006; the French Ministry of Culture, since 1998; Université Paris Diderot (Paris VII), since 2006. Her work for the UFC was shown at the Centre Pompidou in 1991.

She taught at the École de Communication Visuelle (1989–90), and at the École d'Art de Besançon (1992–93), and gives lectures and participates in juries in France and abroad. Zask created Alfabetempo in 1993–94, during her residency at the Villa Medici, Académie de France in Rome. This work continues the research she began ten years earlier on letterforms, tracing and signage. A retrospective of her work took place at the Galerie Anatome, Paris in 2004; at the Museum für Gestaltung Zürich in 2005; at Artazart, Paris and at the Design Centre of the Czech Republic, Brno in 2006. Zask has won several awards, including the Grand Prix at the 20th International Biennial of Graphic Design, Brno, 2002.

Catherine Zask's Rome studio, 1993–94.

Satie, spread from a Scam programme, 2001.

Zask's the Question, poster and invitation for Zask's exhibition at the Galerie Anatome, Paris, 2004.

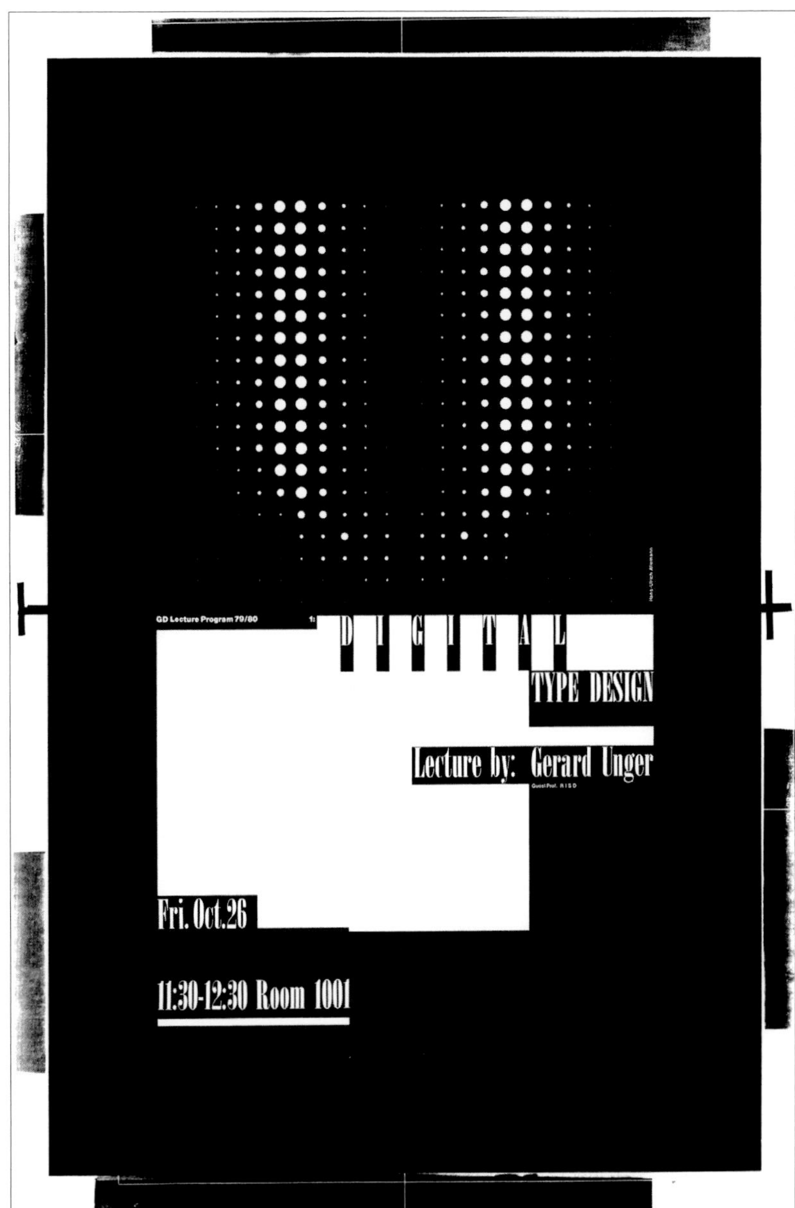

Exposed 2004. Lecture series on graphic design presented by three notable Dutch designers, University of the Arts, Philadelphia, 2004.

Interaction/Motion Exposed, a lecture series featuring three notable American motion graphics designers, University of the Arts, Philadelphia, 2006.

Digital Type Design, poster for a lecture by by Gerard Unger, Philadelphia College of Art, Philadelphia, 1979.

Hans-Ulrich Allemann [USA]

1944– born in Balsthal, Switzerland
Admitted to AGI, 1998

Allemann graduated from the Basel School of Design in 1965 where he studied with Armin Hofmann and Emil Ruder, among others. After his graduation, he worked with Burton Kramer at Halpern Advertising Agency in Zürich. In 1967, Allemann accepted an invitation to teach and help build a new educational programme for graphic design at the Kansas City Art Institute, Kansas City, Missouri. After his return to Switzerland in 1969, he briefly worked with Studio Miedinger and later again with the Halpern Agency, in Zürich.

In 1973, he was offered a full-time teaching position in graphic design at the Philadelphia College of Art (now the University of the Arts), Philadelphia. He also chaired the department for a three-year period. Since 1984, he has been a founding principal of the design and consulting firm Allemann Almquist & Jones. Allemann holds an adjunct professorship at the University of the Arts. His design work has been recognized nationally and internationally by major professional organizations and publications. He is a recipient of the AIGA (American Institute of Graphic Arts) Fellows Award, and the Lindback Award for Distinguished Teaching.

Charles Spencer Anderson [USA]

1958– born in Minneapolis, Minnesota
Admitted to AGI, 1998

Anderson graduated from Minneapolis College of Art and Design (1981) with a major in graphic design and a minor in illustration. Established in 1989, Charles S. Anderson Design Company has produced award-winning packaging, identity, and product design for a diverse range of clients: Nike, Target, Williams-Sonoma, Coca-Cola, Levi's, Sony, Ralph Lauren, Paramount Pictures, *The New York Times*, Turner Classic Movies, Urban Outfitters, Warner Brothers, Taylor Guitars, and The French Paper Company. The company's approach to design is a continuous evolution inspired by the highs and lows of art and popular culture. Their work has been exhibited in museums worldwide including the NY MoMA; Nouveau Salon des Cent, Centre Pompidou, Paris; Institute of Contemporary Arts, London; Museum für Gestaltung, Zürich; and MoMA, Hiroshima. The CSA Archive illustration collection originated in 1975 with the acquisition of Clyde Lewis's original artwork. In 1995, CSA Images was organized as a separate company from Charles S. Anderson Design to concentrate on the distribution and promotion of digital stock image collections. CSA Company's work was featured in the 2003 Design Triennial at Cooper-Hewitt National Design Museum. In 2006, CSA Design Company launched Pop Ink, a brand of licensed products produced in conjunction with French Paper and Laurie DeMartino Design.

AIGA Design Camp, poster announcing an annual weekend conference held in northern Minnesota.

Diet Soap Pads with Hydrochloric Acid, poster for French Paper Company to promote Muscletone, a line of heavyweight packaging papers.

Target stores candy packaging. Part of their extensive Halloween in-store product range and packaging campaign.

One in a series of posters designed for **Harley-Davidson's annual Eaglethon** event.

Playboy Aids Foundation Identity for Playboy Enterprises non-profit Aids Foundation.

Poster promoting **Oak Street Fashion Week**. An event hosted in Chicago's famous retail fashion district.

Dana Arnett [USA]

1960– born in Peoria, Illinois
Admitted to AGI, 1998

Dana is a principal of VSA Partners, leading the firm in the creation of design programmes, film projects, interactive initiatives and brand communications solutions for a diverse roster of clients. His clients have included Coca-Cola, Harley-Davidson, Toyota, IBM, and Nike. Over the course of more than two decades in the field, Dana has been recognized globally by numerous competitions and design organizations, including: Communication Arts, AIGA, Graphis, the Type Directors Club, the American and British Art Directors Clubs, *I.D.*, the LA Film Festival, the AR100 and the American Marketing Association.

Dana holds the honour of being named in the I.D.40 as one of the forty most important people shaping design internationally. He is currently a board member of the American Institute for Graphic Arts. A frequent lecturer and visiting professor, Dana is also active in helping to shape the role of design in society through lectures and published writings.

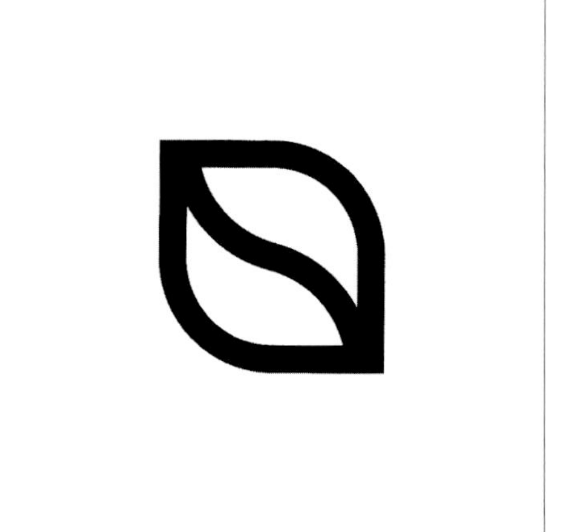

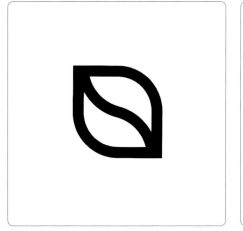

Michael Baviera [Switzerland]

1946– born in Zürich
Admitted to AGI, 1998

1963–68: studies at the Kunstgewerbeschule Zürich.
1964: assistant to Hannes Gruber.
1965: freelance work with Josef Müller-Brockmann.
1967: founds the publishing house Um die Ecke, together with his eldest brother Silvio R. Baviera.
1968: starts Atelier for Corporate Design in Zürich.
1970–92: group and solo exhibitions, various national and international awards, works included in permanent collections and museums in Switzerland and abroad.
1975: co-founder of Wohnflex Inneneinrichtung, president of the Arbeitsgemeinschaft Schweizer Graphiker, judge in various national and international competitions, employee of the magazine *idee...à jour*.
1978: author and publisher of a monograph on Hannes Gruber.
1979–81: awarded art scholarships by the Swiss canton of Zürich.
1981: co-founder of the Atelier BBV in Zürich, Lyons, Milan.
1987: appointed professor by the Institut für Kommunikationsdesign at the Fachhochschule Konstanz, Germany.
1988: author and publisher of the *Monatsbuch Gruber/Baviera*.
1989: publishes the book *Hannes Sils-Chiavenna-Sicilia Gruber*.
1990: new atelier in Barbaresco completed.

Zürich City Park, 1968.

Xyrofin, manufacturer of food additives, 1983.

Aufbruch92, IBM Switzerland, 1992.

Vita, life assurance firm, 1986.

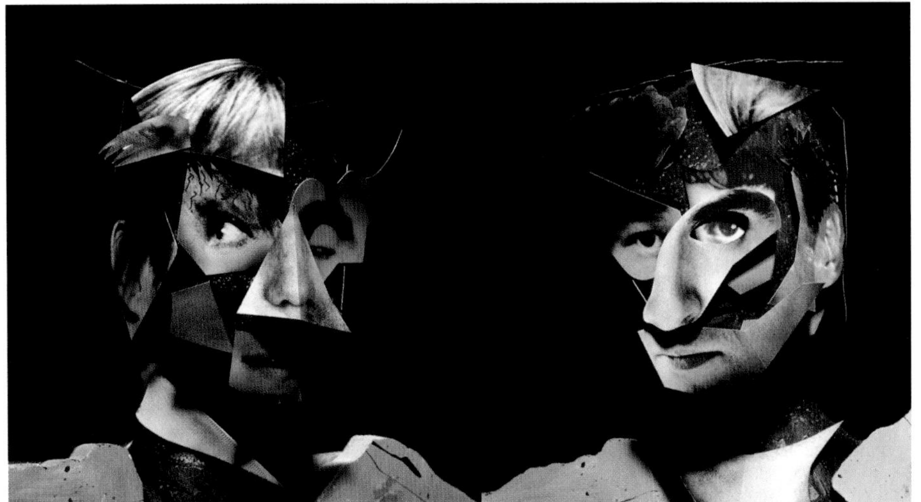

Hollandia Compendium, catalogue for the Rijksmuseum Amsterdam, 1992.

Corporate identity manual for the **Dutch Motoring Association**, the ANWB, 1983.

Illustration for publication **What the Songs Look Like** on the American band **Talking Heads**, 1987. Photography: Lex van Pieterson.

Michel de Boer [The Netherlands]

1954– born in Zaandijk
Admitted to AGI, 1998

Michel de Boer was educated at the Academy of Fine Arts and Higher Technologies in Rotterdam. He worked for two years as an independent designer. In 1980 he became a full-time member of the Studio Dumbar team of designers and in 1989 he became creative managing partner. Within Studio Dumbar Michel de Boer is fully responsible for creative output. He has more than twenty-five years of experience in corporate design and brand identity. He has worked for many clients around the world on projects that require international implementation in the commercial service sector, for non-profit organizations and the public sector.

Michel de Boer has won many awards, amongst them two prestigious D&AD Golden and seven Silver Awards. He has taken part in many international design conferences and has lectured frequently for colleagues and students all over the world. He has been tutor to the design department of the Academy of Fine Arts in Den Bosch and has been a professor of design at IUAV University in Venice, Italy, since September 2004. He is the driving force of the start-up of Dumbar Branding, a new joint venture in Shanghai, which was established in late 2005.

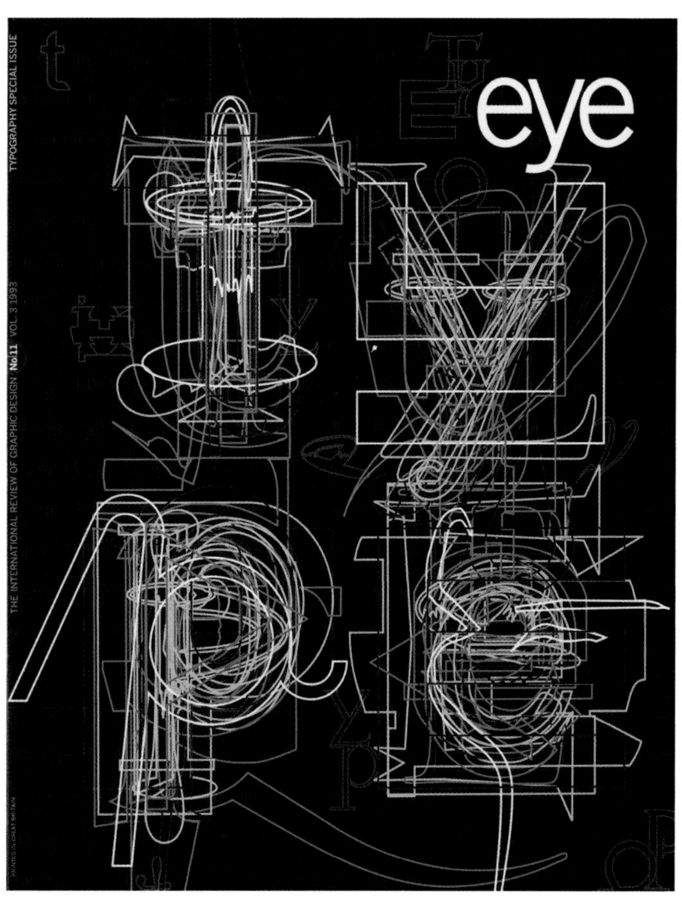

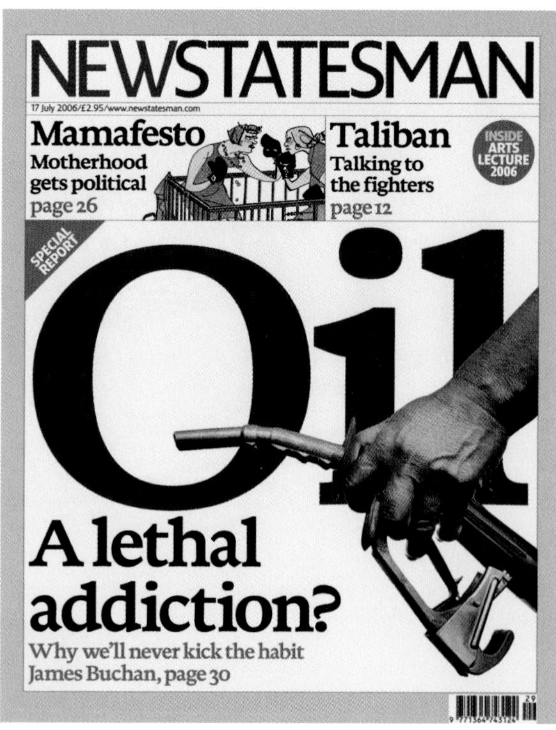

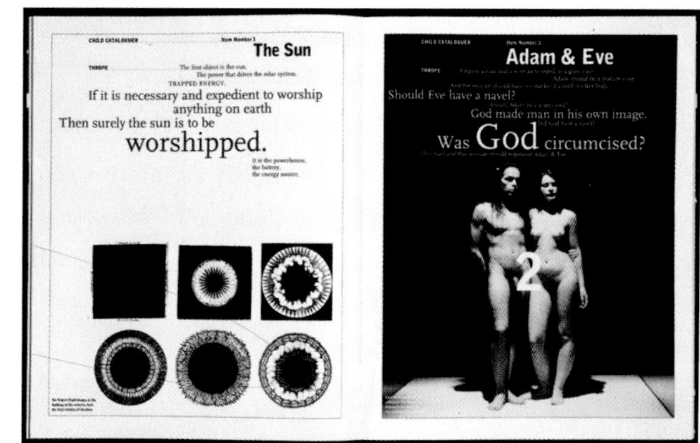

Stephen Coates [UK]

1962– born in St Ives, Cambridgeshire
Admitted to AGI, 1998

Stephen Coates began his career in editorial design in 1984 working alongside Simon Esterson at *Blueprint*, the monthly architecture magazine, which won D&AD awards in both 1986 and 1989. Coates went on to become the founding art director of *Eye*, the quarterly review of graphic design, in 1991 and set up a studio in partnership with Tony Arefin working on catalogues and posters for arts institutions such as ICA London, Serpentine and Tate Gallery. *Eye* won D&AD and Type Directors Club awards in 1993 and a Society of Publication Designers gold award in 1994. He also had spells as art director of *Tate*, the art magazine, and *Sight and Sound*, the magazine of film criticism.

Wanting a more influential role in the editorial conception of his projects, he left *Eye* to launch a publishing imprint and design consultancy called August in 1999. August's output includes books and catalogues on design, architecture and fine arts. Coates completed the redesign of *New Scientist* magazine in 2002, *Music Week* in 2003 and, renewing his collaboration with Simon Esterson, on *Building Design* in 2004 and *The New Statesman* in 2006. His work has been shown in several exhibitions including 'Communicate: British Graphic Design Since the Sixties' at the Barbican, London, 2005.

Cover of **Eye**, typography special issue.

Cover of **New Statesman**, the weekly current affairs magazine.

Spread from **100 Objects to Represent the World**, an opera libretto by Peter Greenaway.

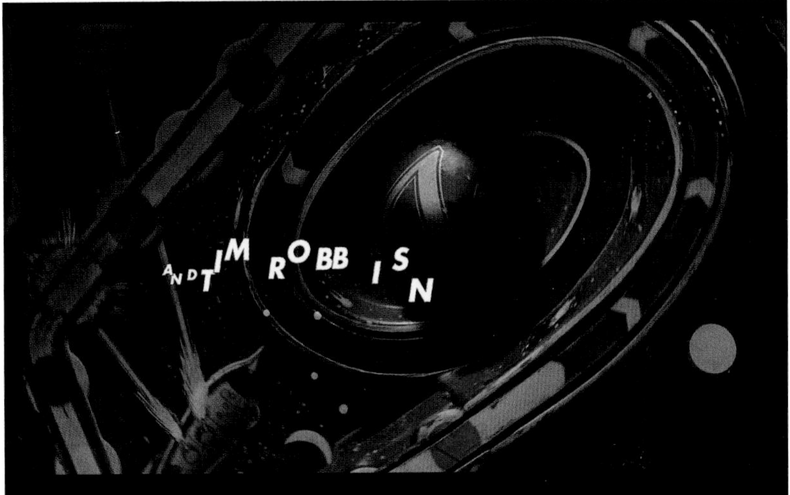

Se7en, 1995. Director, designer.
The juxtaposition of rapid still frames against extreme close-up shots reflects the obsessive and gritty handiwork of the killer, whose hands are the main focus of the sequence.

Dawn of the Dead, 2004. Director, designer.
A bleeding effect on the type is created practically and filmed, yielding a raw presence amid the harrowing portrait of evil grounded in reality and an all-consuming presence.

Zathura, 2005. Director, designer.
Transitions between live action and animation foreshadow the board game coming to life. The camera explores tight shots of the game's tin contours and its mysterious inner workings.

Kyle Cooper [USA]

1962– born in Salem, Massachusetts
Admitted to AGI, 1998

Over the last 15 years, Kyle Cooper has directed more than 100 film title sequences, and has been credited by *Details* magazine with *'almost single-handedly revitalizing the main title sequence as an artform.'* He is the founder of two internationally recognized motion design companies, Prologue and Imaginary Forces. Formed in 2003, Prologue is a Malibu-based design company specializing in film and broadcast. Since its inception, the company has grown to a diverse team of 35 that includes designers, animators, editors, directors and producers – a community with many parts, all performing different functions. With this talented group, Cooper continues to build on a body of work comprising film title sequences, advertising campaigns, and various projects in branding (broadcast, interactive, environmental), entertainment marketing and video game design. Cooper also continues to work on live-action directing for feature films and commercials, special visual effects sequences and second unit direction for features. Prior to starting his companies, Cooper earned a MFA in graphic design from the Yale School of Art, where he studied independently with Paul Rand. He also holds the honorary title of Royal Designer for Industry from the Royal Society of Arts in London.

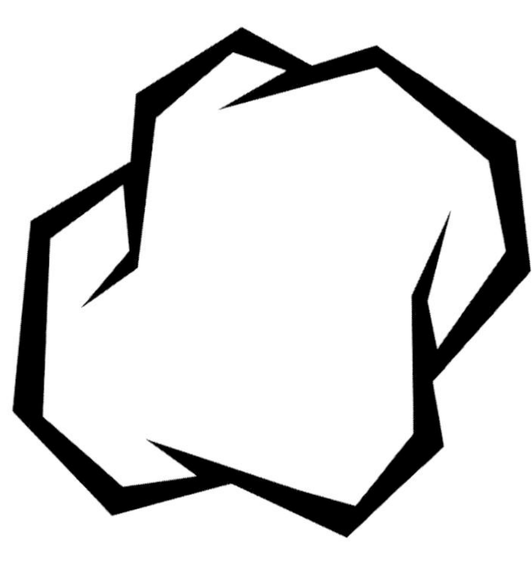

Bulent Erkmen [Turkey]

1947– born in Antalya
Admitted to AGI, 1998

Founder of BEK Design and Consultancy (1994), Bülent Erkmen works with clients across the non-profit to corporate spectrum, specializing in publication design, theatre design, collateral graphics, identity and branding systems, 3D and exhibition design. Erkmen's 'Works 1991 to 2000' and 'Recent Works' have been exhibited in Istanbul. He had a solo exhibition at the Gutenberg Museum in Mainz and the Deutsches Plakat Museum in Essen, Germany. A multimedia exhibit entitled *The Image of Typography, The Typography of Image* was shown at the 7th Forum Typography meeting in Stuttgart.

A film project, *Self-Promotion IV*, was shown at the AGI Seminar 1999 in Zürich. *Awards:* 14th International Lahti Poster Biennial (First Prize); 2nd Trnava Poster Triennial (2nd Prize); Helsinki International Poster Biennial, 1997 (Bronze Medal); 16th International Poster Biennial, Warsaw (Bronze Medal); three 'High Quality Design' awards, German Prize for Communications Design '99; 13th International Poster Biennial, Lahti (Icograda Excellence Award); 10th International Theatre Poster Biennial, Rzeszow (Honorary Award); 70th, 75th, 82th NY ADC Awards (Merit Award).

Poster for the play **Fake Identities**.

Poster for Istanbul State Theatre, **The Stories of Efrasiyab**, 2001–2002 season. A concept is selected for each season, and symbols of that concept are applied in various forms to all posters produced in that season.

Logo for the rock group **Bulutsuzluk Özlemi – Yearning for Cloudlessness**. Is the cloudlessness in rock music turning clouds into rocks?

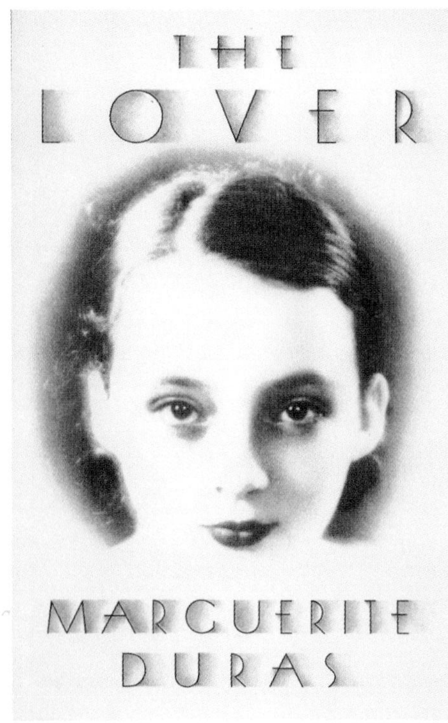

Marguerite Duras: *The Lover*, book jacket, 1983.

Bella Cucina biscotti packaging, 2001.

Bella Cucina aromatic oils packaging, 2001.

Louise Fili [USA]

1951– born in New Jersey
Admitted to AGI, 1998

Formerly senior designer for Herb Lubalin, Louise Fili was art director of Pantheon Books from 1978 to 1989, where she designed over 2,000 book jackets. She has received awards from every major design competition, including Gold and Silver Medals from the New York Art Directors Club and the Society of Illustrators, the Premio Grafico from the Bologna Book Fair, and three James Beard nominations.
In 2004 she was inducted into the Art Directors Hall of Fame. Fili has taught and lectured on graphic design and typography and her work is in the permanent collections of the Library of Congress, the Cooper Hewitt Museum, and the Bibliothèque Nationale de France.

She was the recipient of a National Endowment for the Arts design grant to study the work of W.A. Dwiggins, and is co-author, with Steven Heller, of *Italian Art Deco*, *Dutch Modern*, *Streamline*, *Cover Story*, *British Modern*, *Deco Espana*, *German Modern*, *French Modern*, *Typology*, *Design Connoisseur*, *Counter Culture*, and *Euro Deco*. Louise Fili Ltd, founded in 1989, specializes in speciality food packaging and restaurant identities.

Eine Welt ohne Marken

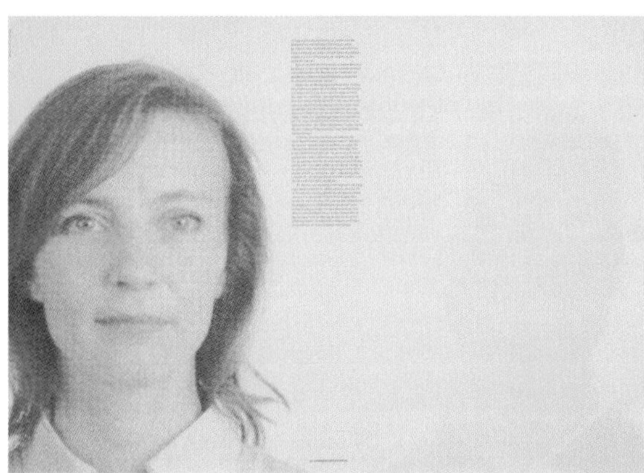

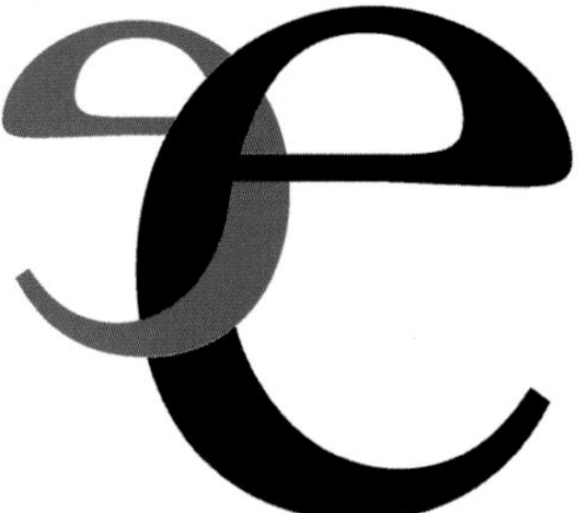

Martin Gaberthüel [Switzerland]

1963– born in Oftringen
Admitted to AGI, 1998

Martin Gaberthüel studied graphic design at the Schule für Gestaltung, Biel, Switzerland (1979–1984) and worked with Jean Widmer (Visual Design) in Paris (1988–91). From 1992–95 he worked at the agency Seiler DDB Atelier Jaquet in Berne, Switzerland. Since August 1995 Martin Gaberthüel has been a partner of the AGI member Andréas Netthoevel at the design studio Second Floor South in Biel, Switzerland. Second Floor South are in constant search of the well-known, combining it with new customer-specific tasks. This way of working has been regularly awarded. Activities include editorials, corporate designs, posters, art in architecture and objects.

The Brand, brochure for the Swiss Federal Institute of Intellectual Property, 1999. Two double pages on the topic of a world without brands. The unnamed product on the left of the page only becomes a branded product by putting the transparency on top.

simultaneity in daylight, poster (for *darkness*, see AGI member Andréas Netthoevel), 2005. Screenprint on the theme of Einstein's text on simultaneity. The left part of the poster is visible with the light on, the right part only appears after switching off the light.

Logo and logotype for the **Theater der Regionen Ensemble**, Biel-Solothurn, Switzerland, 1996. Two cities, two languages: French/German, two sections: operas and plays.

poetry
readings
every
thursday
at biblio's
starting
at 8:30
317 church
new york

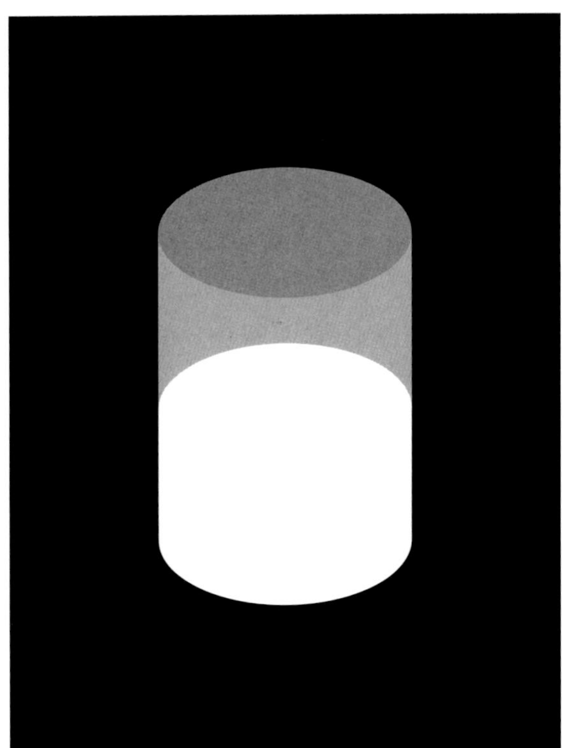

Alexander Gelman [USA]

Biblios, 1995. Poster announcing poetry readings, New York.

Cover for **Subtraction**, 2000. Rotovision, UK.

Side, 1996. Watch design for Swatch 1997–98 collection. Milan–New York.

1967– born in Monaco
Admitted to AGI, 1998

In 2001 the Museum of Modern Art NY listed Alexander Gelman among the *'world's most influential modern and contemporary artists in all media'*. Alexander Gelman (most commonly known as Gelman or Glmn) is a celebrated media artist based in New York, Tokyo and London. His work, extensively shown around the world, has been a subject of private and public acquisitions and is represented in permanent museum collections, including the Smithsonian, the NY MoMA, and Bibliothèque Nationale de France in Paris.

Gelman collaborates with musicians and artists, companies and institutions, he designs products and installations, directs TV commercials and music videos. Some of his most recent collaborations include projects with Apple, Nike, Target and Warp Records in London. A noted thinker on creativity, perception and communication, he also serves as a guest professor with Yale and MIT Media Lab and is the subject as well as author of many books, articles, and monographs. His bestselling book, *Subtraction*, reissued in four languages, has been acclaimed a *'modern day classic'*. His latest project *Infiltrate* (currently in its second printing) has become a milestone in critical journalism.

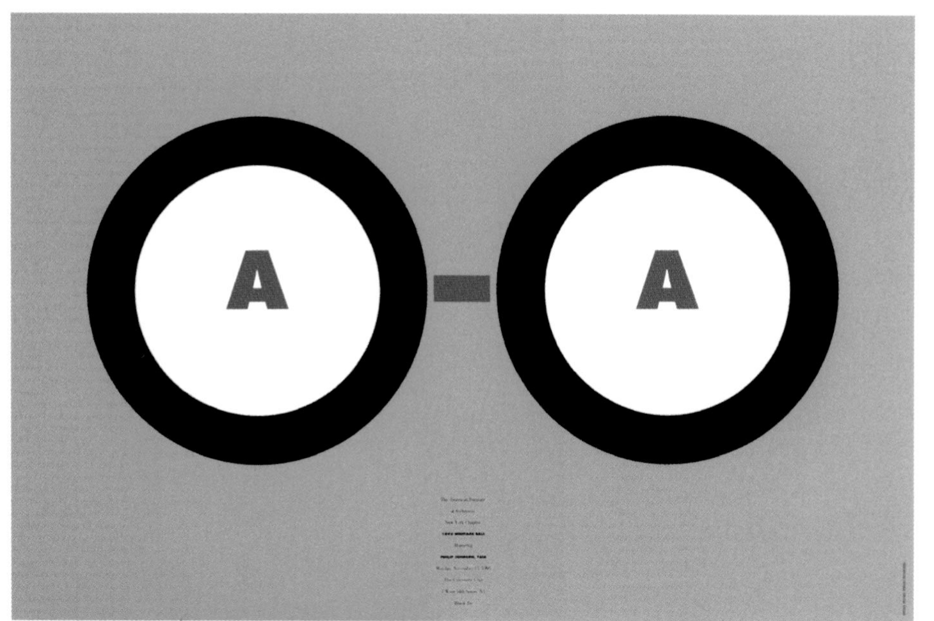

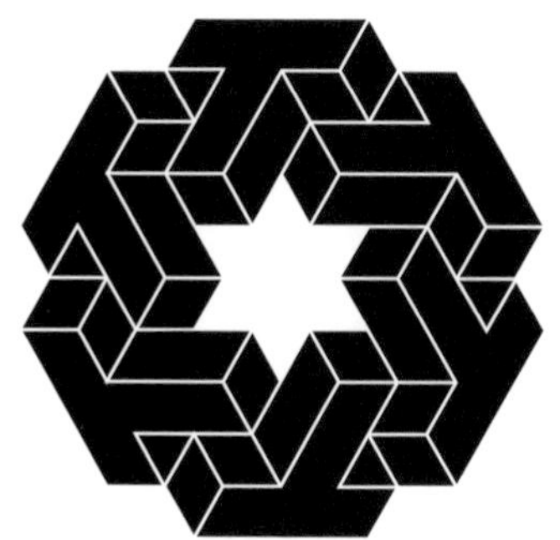

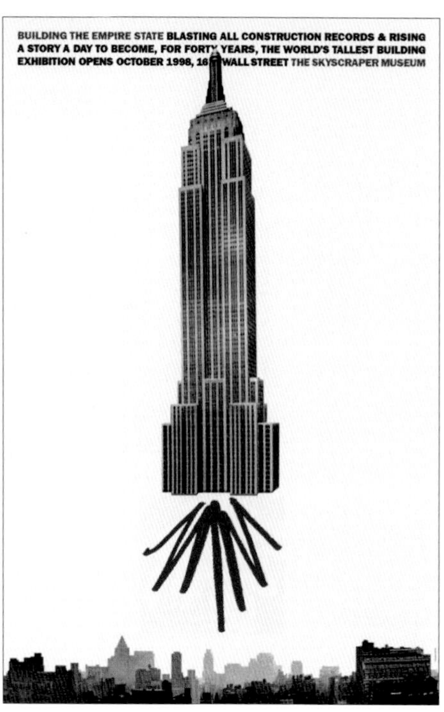

Michael Gericke [USA]

1956– born in Wisconsin
Admitted to AGI, 1998

Michael studied design at the University of Wisconsin. He then moved to Colorado, where he worked for two expatriates of the Charles and Ray Eames office and produced many projects that combined graphics with three-dimensional design. Joined Pentagram's NY office in 1986 and was elected a Partner in 1995. Michael's images and projects are known for their simplicity and clarity, and often portray the essential qualities of the object or topic he is representing. His work encompasses a wide variety of assignments and media, including identity, environmental graphics and communication design. He has been actively involved in the design efforts for the rebuilding of Lower Manhattan. His recent projects have included the Viewing Wall that now surrounds the World Trade Center site; a major information programme for Calatrava's PATH train terminal, and the cornerstone and graphic system for the Freedom Tower. Michael has also produced many comprehensive identity programmes, including CBS's television coverage of the 1992, 1994 and 1998 Winter Olympic Games, the 1994 World Cup soccer championships, New York's AirTrain, and the Arizona Cardinals NFL stadium. He has received numerous accolades and his work is represented in the permanent collections of museums around the world. He is a frequent lecturer and teacher at universities and professional organizations.

American Institute of Architects: Philip Johnson, poster.

Center for Architecture, symbol.

New York Art Directors Club **Call for Entries** poster.

The Skyscraper Museum, Empire State Building, exhibition poster.

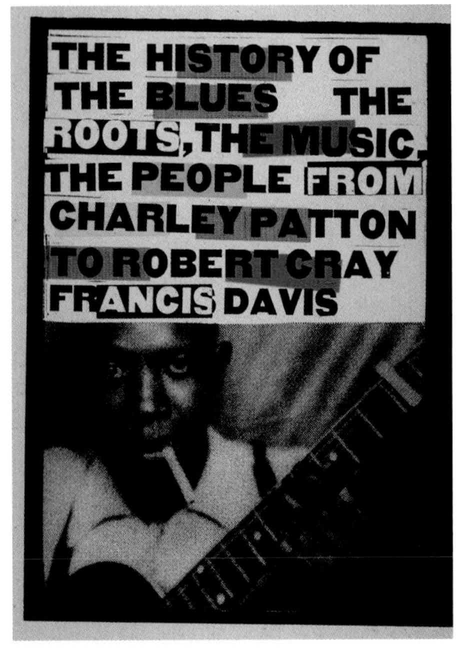

Book design for **Typography 20: The Annual of the Type Directors Club**, published by the Type Directors Club/Watson-Guptill, 1999.

Book jacket for **The History of the Blues**, published by Hyperion, 1995.

Book design and concept for **Catalog**, published by Stewart, Tabori & Chang, 2001.

Carin Goldberg [USA]

1953– born in New York City
Admitted to AGI, 1998

Carin Goldberg studied at the Cooper Union School of Art, graduating in 1975. She began her career as a staff designer at CBS Television, CBS Records and Atlantic Records before establishing her own firm, Carin Goldberg Design, in 1982. Over the following two decades she designed hundreds of book jackets for all the major American publishers, including Simon & Schuster, Random House, Farrar Straus & Giroux, and HarperCollins, and dozens of record covers for labels such as Warner Bros., Motown, Nonesuch, Interscope and EMI. In recent years her work has expanded to publication design and brand consulting; from 2003 to 2004 she was Creative Director at Time Inc. Custom Publishing.

Her work has appeared in major exhibitions including 'Graphic Design in America' at the Walker Art Center (1989), 'Mixing Messages' at the Cooper-Hewitt National Design Museum (1996), and 'Superwoman' at the Hong Kong Heritage Museum (2002). Carin is currently president of the New York Chapter of the American Institute of Graphic Arts and served on its board from 2002 to 2004. She has taught at the School of Visual Arts in New York City since 1983, and is the author and designer of *Catalog* (Stewart, Tabori & Chang, 2001).

J. Malcolm Grear [USA]

1931– born in Kentucky
Admitted to AGI, 1998

Malcolm Grear has played a vital role as designer and educator in the field of visual communication design for forty-six years. After graduating from the Art Academy of Cincinnati he taught in the Rhode Island School of Design's graphic design department from 1960–98. Malcolm Grear Designers was founded in 1960 and has had the distinct honour of having more than 28 solo exhibitions in museums and galleries. Malcolm's book *Inside/Outside: From the Basics to the Practice of Design*, published in 1994, was recognized as one of the 50 best-designed books of the year and has been critically acclaimed in numerous reviews. The second edition, published by the AIGA and New Riders, was published in 2006. The philosophy of the book is that form and structure are the pivotal underpinnings of effective design, rather than the standard reductive design approach found in most modern design education. Over the years Malcolm has been awarded five honorary doctorates and was selected by the National Association of Schools of Art and Design, comprising 190 institutions, to receive the Citation for Distinguished Service in the Visual Arts. In 2005 Malcolm's name was placed in the sidewalk of Lexington, Kentucky where he was honoured as a *'Kentucky Star'*.

Marsh & McLennan Companies, **September 11, 2001 Memorial**. Richard Fleischner, artist.

Malcolm Grear, **Inside/Outside: From the Basics to the Practice of Design**, second edition, 2006.

Trinity Repertory Company, identity programme.

Solomon R. Guggenheim Museum, poster series, 1969.

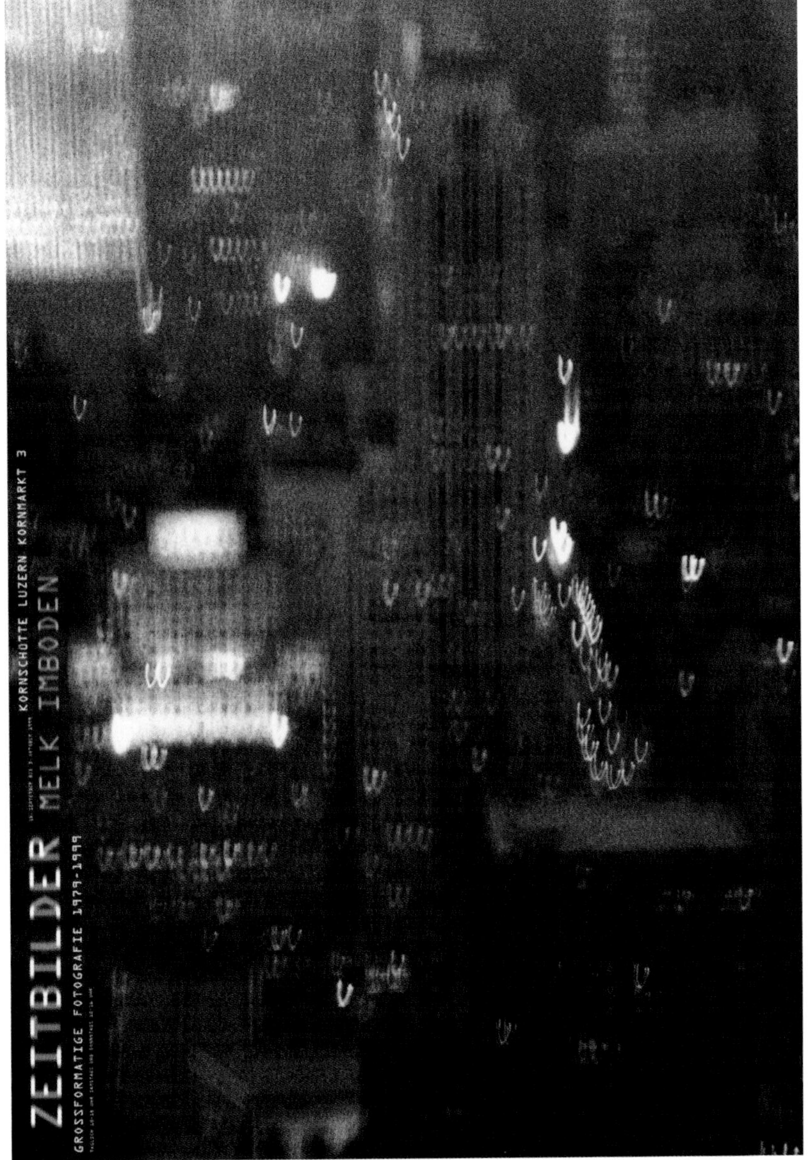

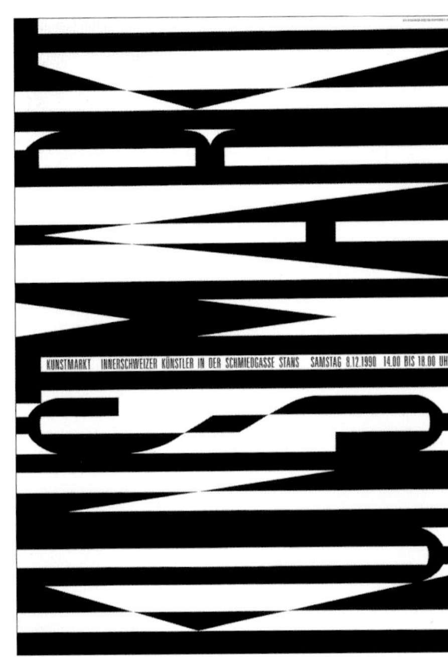

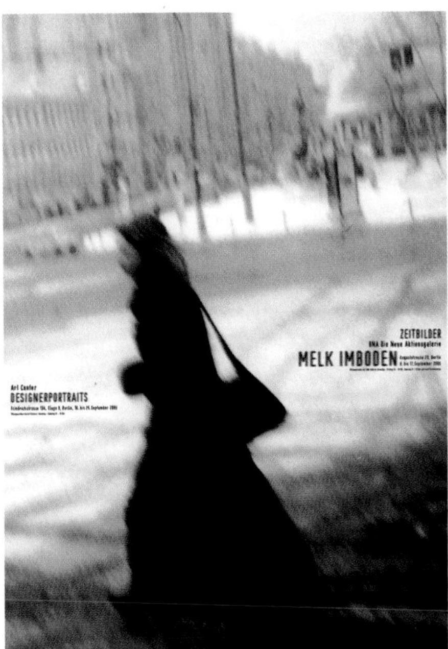

Poster for **solo exhibition in Lucerne**, 1999.

Poster for an **Art Fair with 70 artists from central Switzerland** in Stans, 1990.

Poster for **solo photo exhibition in Berlin**, 2005.

Melchior Imboden [Switzerland]

1956– born in Stans
Admitted to AGI, 1998

Melchior Imboden studied graphic design at the Art School in Lucerne. After practical work in Milan and Basel, he was employed as a designer in Zürich. In 1992 he became a freelance graphic designer and photographer. His main field of activity is in poster, book and catalogue design. He has taken part in several international poster exhibitions. His posters are part of different permanent collections and have been honoured with numerous awards including: Gold Medal, Brno, 1994; IBCC Award Golden Bee, Moscow, 1996; Bronze Medal, Tokyo, 1998; NY TDC Award, 1998; Bronze Medal, Toyama, 2000; NY ADC Award, 2002; Best Design, Brno, 2002; Silver Medal, Mexico City, 2002; Icograda Award, Chaumont, 2003; Grand Prix, Seoul, 2004; Poster Award, Rüttenscheid, 2004; Josef Binder Award, Vienna, 2004; Icograda Award, Taipei, 2005.
As a photographer he has participated in many national and international exhibitions and has received several awards. His photographs are in several museums and private collections.
In 2001–2003 he was a guest professor at the, University for Art and Design, Karlsruhe, and in 2003–2006 he was a guest professor at UdK University for Art and Design, Berlin.

Alexander Isley [USA]

1961– born in North Carolina
Admitted to AGI, 1998

Alex received a degree in Environmental Design from NC State University and a BFA from the Cooper Union in New York City. From 1984–86, Alex was senior designer at Tibor Kalman's M&Co. He then went on to be art director of *Spy* magazine, for which he was awarded gold and silver medals from the Society of Publication Designers.
He founded Alexander Isley Inc. in 1988. Articles showcasing his studio and its work have been published in numerous international books and magazines. He is a frequent lecturer on design.

Alex has been a visiting lecturer at Yale University, NY University, Columbia University and the Walker Art Center. He has served as a professor at the Cooper Union and at the School of Visual Arts in New York City. He has been a critic at the Yale Graduate School of Art since 1996. Alex has served as president of the New York Chapter of the American Institute of Graphic Arts. Alex's firm has received a Federal Design Achievement Award, and in 1993 he was selected as an inaugural member of the I.D. 40, *I.D.* magazine's survey of the USA's leading design innovators.

Rock and Roll Hall of Fame and Museum, Cleveland, Ohio. Architectural signage and wayfinding programme, in collaboration with the signage specialists Calori & Vanden-Eynden Ltd.

A/X Armani Exchange. Packaging, retail design, and merchandising materials for a new line of stores for Giorgio Armani.

Animal Planet. Design of comprehensive packaging and signage for the Animal Planet line of toys, including package designs for over 120 items.

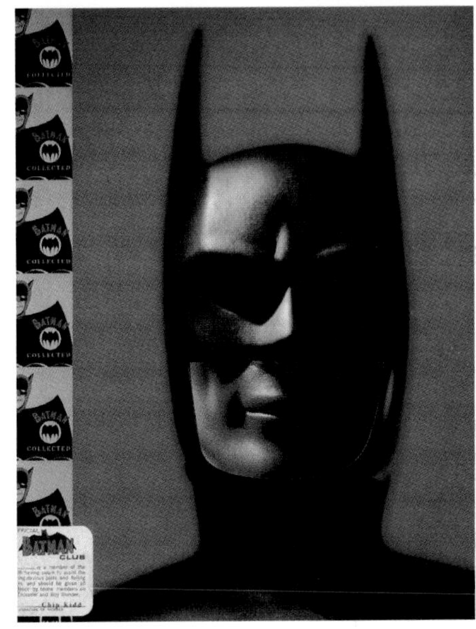

Michael Crichton: *Jurassic Park*, 1990. Knopf.

Chip Kidd: *Book One*, 2005. Rizzoli.

David Sedaris: *Naked*, 1997. Little, Brown.

Chip Kidd: *Batman Collected*, 1996.

Chip Kidd [USA]

1964– born in Reading, Pennsylvania
Admitted to AGI, 1998

'The history of book design can be split into two eras: before graphic designer Chip Kidd and after.' – *Time Out* New York.

Chip is a NY writer and graphic designer. His book jacket designs for Alfred A. Knopf (where he has worked since 1986) helped spawn a revolution in the art of American book packaging. In 1997 he received the International Center of Photography Award for Use of Photography in Graphic Design. He is a regular contributor of visual commentary to the Op-Ed page of the *NY Times*.

As an editor of books and comics for Pantheon, Kidd has worked with some of the most brilliant talents practising today, including Chris Ware, Art Spiegelman, Dan Clowes, Kim Deitch, Charles Burns, Ben Katchor and Alex Ross. *The Cheese Monkeys*, Kidd's first novel, was published by Scribner in 2001 and was a national bestseller and *NY Times* Notable Book of the Year.

A comprehensive monograph of his work, *Chip Kidd: Book One*, was published in 2005. Introduced by John Updike, the 400-page book features over 800 works, spanning two decades from 1986.

In 2006 Kidd was a finalist for the National Design Award for Communications. His work was included in the Cooper-Hewitt Museum's third National Design Triennial.

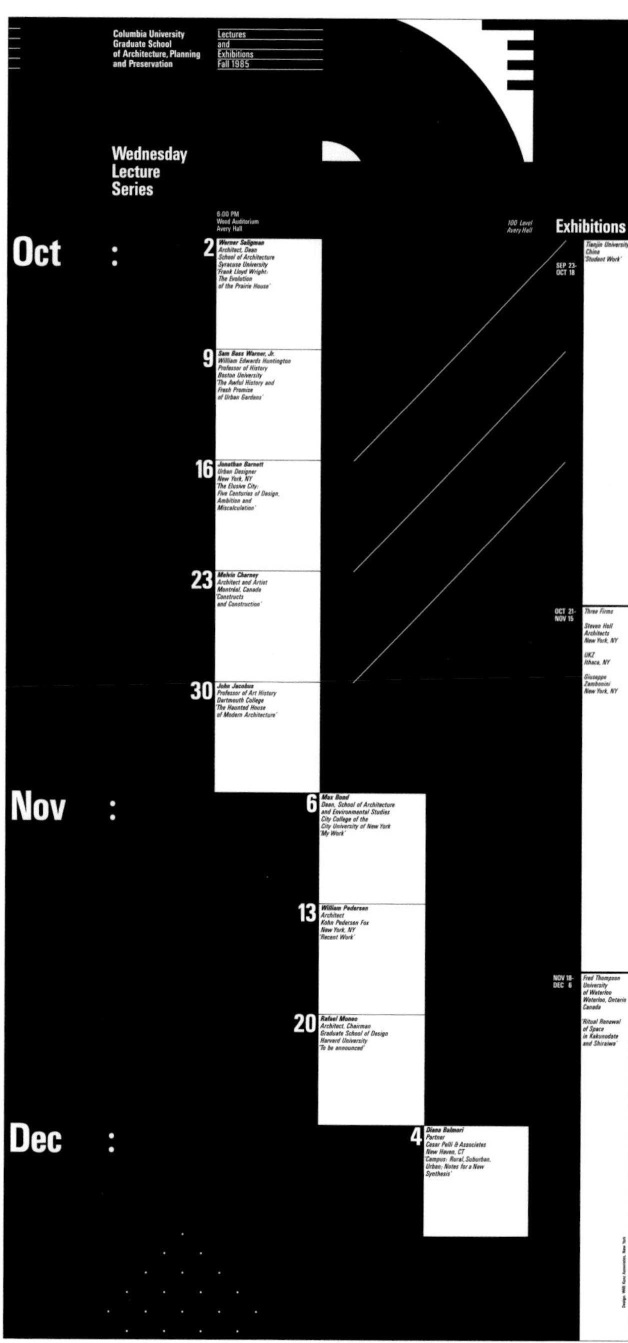

Willi Kunz [USA]

1941– born in Frauenfeld, Switzerland
Admitted to AGI, 1998

Apprenticeship as a typographer with a Swiss national degree. Postgraduate degree in typographic design, Kunstgewerbeschule Zürich. Moved to NY in 1970. Designer at Anspach, Grossman, Portugal. Design director at W.H. Sadlier Inc. Principal of Willi Kunz Associates, a design firm specializing in print communications, visual identity and architectural graphics. Teacher of typographic design at Ohio State University, and the School of Design, Basel, Switzerland. Typographic workshops and lectures in the United States, India, and China.

Winner of numerous national and international awards. Exhibited and published widely in the United States, Japan and Europe. Works included in the collection of the NY MoMA; the Cooper-Hewitt National Design Museum, NY; the Cooper Union Lubalin Center for Typography, NY; the Getty Museum, Los Angeles; the SF MoMA; Denver Art Museum; Museum für Gestaltung, Zürich; Kunstsammlungen Cottbus, Germany; Bibliothèque Nationale de France, Paris; and important private collections in the United States. Author of *Typography: Macro- and Microaesthetics* (1998), with editions in English, German, Spanish and Chinese; and *Typography: Formation and Transformation* (2003).

Merit gasoline stations, identity programme, 1971.

Floor design, black and white marble. Lobby, World Trade Centre Building, Osaka, Japan, 1995.

Poster announcing a **series of lectures and exhibitions at Columbia University**, 1985.

Postage stamp for **the centenary of Einstein's Theory of Relativity**. Swiss Post, Berne, 2005.

Postage stamp design. Priority A-mail stamp with capital A that lasted ten years and became a classic in Switzerland. Swiss Post, Berne, 1995.

The Seam. Poster for the promotion of a graphic club offering visits to 10 design studios in the Bay Area. Photo: Robert Schlatter. Client: AIGA, San Francisco, 2003.

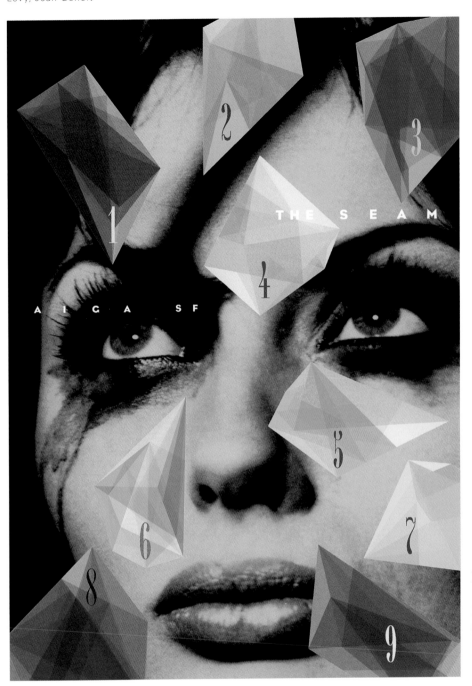

Jean-Benoît Lévy [Switzerland]

1959– born in Pully
Admitted to AGI, 1998

Multi-tasking visual communicator with nomadic aspirations. Visual designer (graphic artist, teacher, global communicator). After his education at the Basel School of Design where he studied under some great names of Swiss typography, JBL opened his own studio in Basel in 1989 called AND. For the next twenty years his studio created graphic design for various local, regional and national companies and organizations in Switzerland, collaborating when needed with other marketing and advertising agencies. Since 2006 he has lived in San Francisco and divides his professional activities between California and Europe.

Beside the everyday jobs of his studio such as the creation of logos, pictograms, collaterals, book designs, presentations, branding, annual reports or websites, JBL is known for his street posters and postage stamp designs and recognized as a multi-disciplinary visual specialist. In parallel to his client work, he has developed personal creations such as a series of moving-word products, a collection of hand signs and a book about non-verbal hand communication. In addition JBL shares his knowledge through educational activities such as exhibitions, workshops and courses in the US, Europe and Asia on topics such as signs, typography and interactive information design, together with his life and work partner Claudia Dallendörfer.

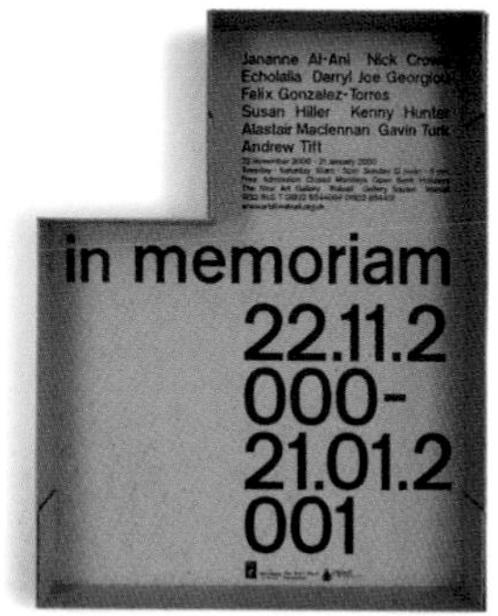

Anthony Michael [UK]

1958– born in Peckham, London
Admitted to AGI, 1998

Anthony Michael and Stephanie Nash studied at St Martin's School of Art, London (1978–81), and formed the partnership Michael.Nash Associates in 1984. Initial work was drawn from the music industry, as Stephanie had worked at Island Records as an in-house designer after graduating. Early projects included Massive Attack, Seal, Neneh Cherry and INXS. Current projects include Sophie Ellis-Bextor and The Rolling Stones.
The client base developed into the world of fashion with clients including Jasper Conran, Issey Miyake, Jil Sander, Philip Treacy, Joyce, and Patrick Cox.

In the early 90s the company was commissioned to design the own-brand packaging for Harvey Nichols Food Hall, an association that continues today, and has embraced the Fifth Floor, OXO and Prism restaurants. Projects have been completed for The National Portrait Gallery, The New Art Gallery Walsall, Louis Vuitton, Marc Jacobs, John Galliano, Alexander McQueen, H&M, Margaret Howell, Egg, Asprey & Garrard, David Morris, Space NK, Ruby & Millie, Toni & Guy, Flos, Cassina, Boots, Phaidon, 4th Estate Books, Schrager Hotels, Marks & Spencer, Heals, and the Royal Mail. There are ongoing projects for many of these clients.

Art direction and design of sleeve and campaign for **The Rolling Stones: *A Bigger Bang***.

Identity for **Walsall Art Gallery**.
Collaboration with Jane.

Harvey Nichols Christmas Pudding.
Winner of a D&AD Silver Award for the Most Outstanding Packaging: Individual Pack.

Identity for Uth. Pictured: Wooden Shirt Box.
Winner of 2001 D&AD Silver Award for the Most Outstanding Range of Brand Packaging.

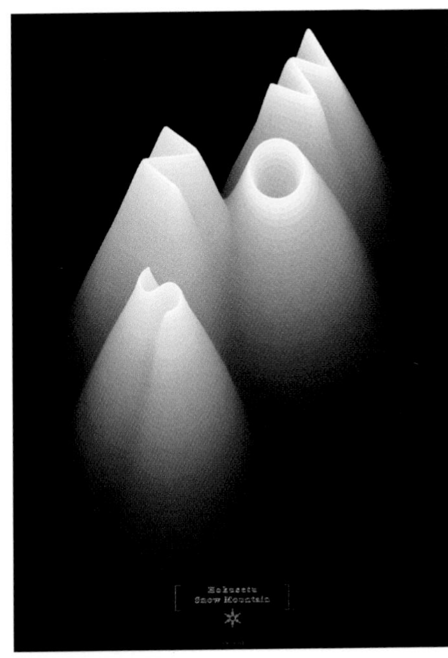

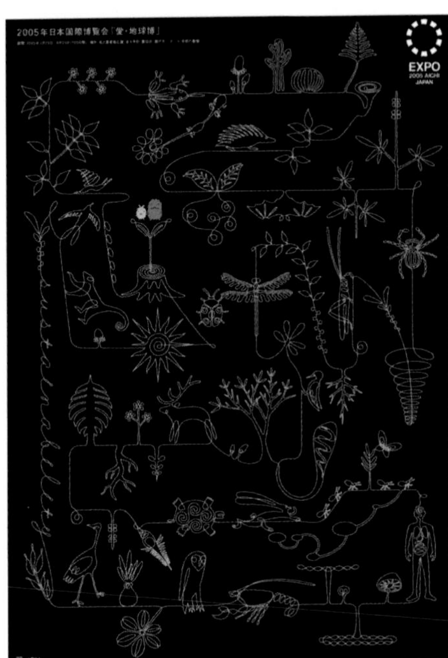

Two Tops, poster for paper promotion.

Snow Mountain, poster for paper promotion.

Sustainability, poster for EXPO 2005 Aichi, Japan.

Ken Miki [(Japan)]

1955– born in Kobe
Admitted to AGI, 1998

'I want to design like we communicate.

I want to bring joy to people around through my rich design skills.

I want most of all to enjoy design myself.'

Work in permanent collections of Suntory Museum, Osaka; Contemporary Art Centre, Toyama; Prefectual Museum Of Modern Art, Japan; Musashino Art University, Japan; Center for Contemporary Graphic Art, Japan; Museum für Kunst und Gewerbe, Hamburg; Regional Council Heritage Museum, Hong Kong; Chicago Athenaeum; Museum fur Gestaltung, Zürich.

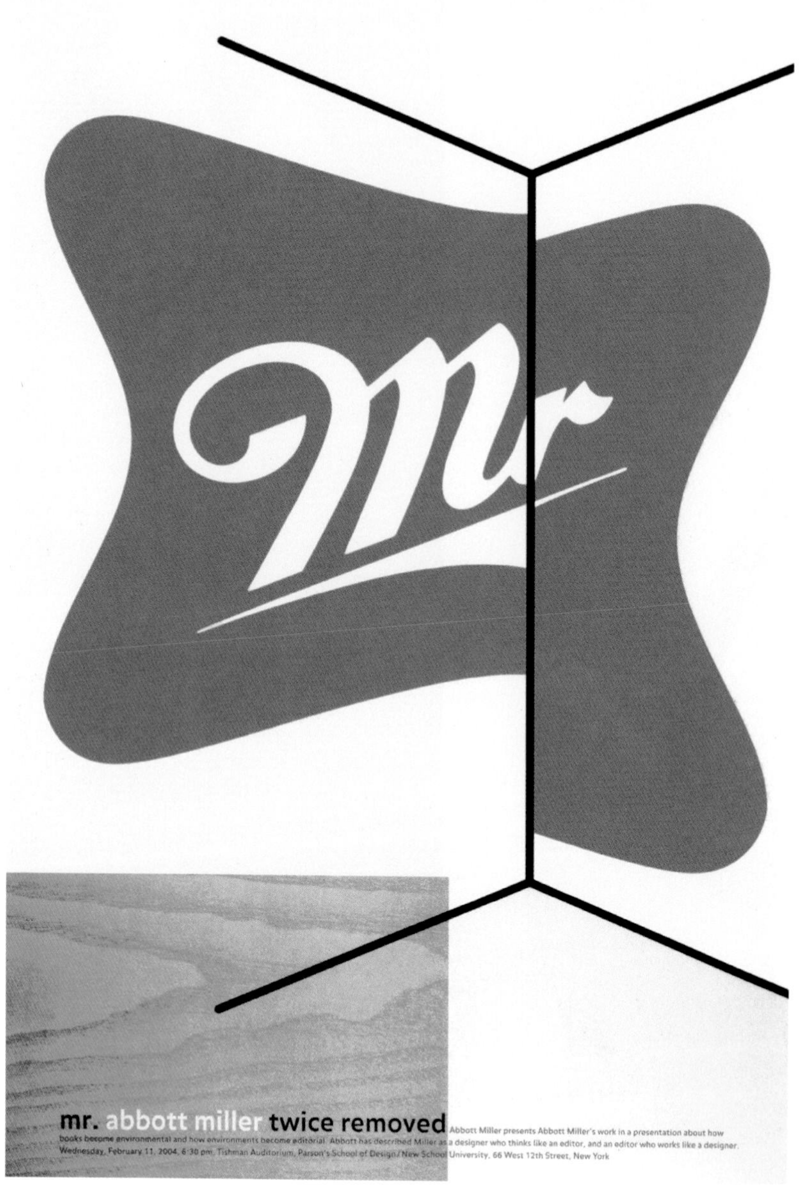

Abbott Miller [USA]

1963– born in Gary, Indiana
Admitted to AGI, 1998

Abbott J. Miller studied graphic design at the Cooper Union School of Art in New York, graduating in 1985. He began his career as a designer with Richard Saul Wurman before establishing the studio Design/Writing/Research with Ellen Lupton in 1989.
The studio pioneered the concept of the *'designer as author'*; undertaking projects in which content and form are developed in a symbiotic relationship. Since 1999 Abbott has been a partner in the New York office of Pentagram, where he has created identities, books, magazines and exhibitions for clients that have included Harley-Davidson, Knoll, Vitra, Geoffrey Beene, the Sigmund Freud Museum, the Whitney Museum of American Art, the Solomon R. Guggenheim Museum, and the Hirshhorn Museum and Sculpture Garden. He is editor and art director of the visual and performing arts magazine 2wice and the creative director of Steuben Glass. He has designed numerous books, magazines and exhibitions, and is co-author with Ellen Lupton of *Swarm* (2005), *Design Writing Research* (1996) and *The Bathroom, the Kitchen, and the Aesthetics of Waste* (1992). In 1994 he was a recipient, with Ellen Lupton, of the first annual Chrysler Award for Innovation in Design. He teaches at Maryland Institute College of Art (MICA) in Baltimore.

Solo exhibition poster for the **American Institute of Graphic Arts** (AIGA), 2004.

Harley Davidson: The 100th Anniversary Open Road Tour, travelling exhibition for the Harley-Davidson Motor Co., 2003–2004.

Geoffrey Beene: A Design Tribute, book for 2wice Arts Foundation, 2005.

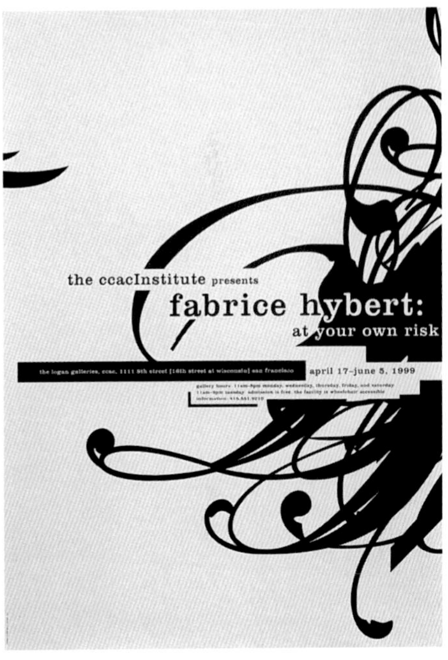

Jennifer Morla [USA]

Benday portrait of Frida Kahlo and the ubiquitous image of Our Lady of Guadalupe, combined with 19th-century Mexican wood block type, to celebrate the **Mexican Museum's anniversary**.

Morla Design was hired to design the product launch image for a new line of **Levi's**. Oversized product, historical and contemporary images are sandwiched between a laminated chipboard cover and bound with a hunky aluminium spiral.

Exhibition poster for the CCAC Institute, one of San Francisco's most experimental art venues. Each poster incorporates letters from each show's title to create dynamic forms that give the installations a unique visual voice.

1955– born in the East Coast
Admitted to AGI, 1998

Jennifer Morla is president and creative director of Morla Design, San Francisco. She has been honoured internationally for her ability to pair wit and elegance on everything from annual reports to retail environments. With over 300 awards for excellence in graphic design, Ms Morla has been acknowledged by virtually every organization in the field. Her work has been published extensively, with showcases in *The History of Graphic Design*, *Graphic Design: America* and *US Design 1975–2000*. She has been featured in numerous magazines such as *Graphis*, *Communication Arts*, *IDEA* (Japan), *Linea Grafica* (Italy), *A Diseno* (Mexico) and *Novum* (Germany). In addition to being displayed at the Grand Palais in Paris, the Brandenburg Art Gallery in Berlin, the Museum of Arts and Design in New York, the Denver Art Museum and the Smithsonian Museum of American Art in Washington DC, Ms Morla's work is a part of the permanent collections of the NY MoMA and the SF MoMA, the Denver Art Museum and the Library of Congress. Ms Morla has had solo exhibitions at the SF MoMA and DDD Gallery in Japan. In addition to teaching at California College of the Arts, she lectures internationally.

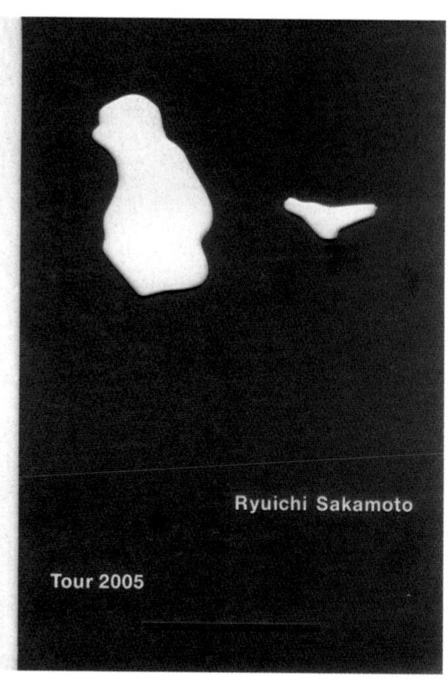

Hideki Nakajima [Japan]

1961– born in Saitama
Admitted to AGI, 1998

After working at *rockin'on* magazine, he established Nakajima Design in 1995. In 1999, he published the anthology *Revival*. Prizes to date include: Art Directors Club Awards (5 Gold, 7 Silver, 1995–2000); Tokyo ADC Award in 1999; Best Design, Books Category, 19th International Biennale of Graphic Design, Brno, 2000; Chicago Athenaeum's Good Design Award, 2001; Tokyo TDC Grand Prize, 2006. Member of the Art Directors Club and Tokyo ADC, and Tokyo TDC.

SEVEN #01, exhibition poster, Hong Kong Arts Centre, 2005.

SEVEN #02, exhibition poster, Hong Kong Arts Centre, 2005.

Ryuichi Sakamoto, tour poster, 2005.

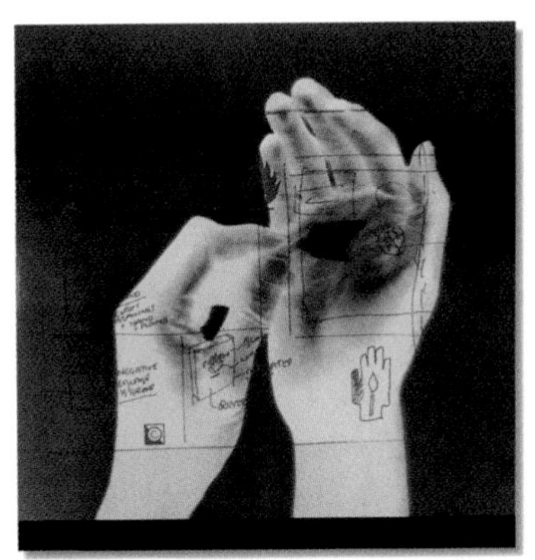

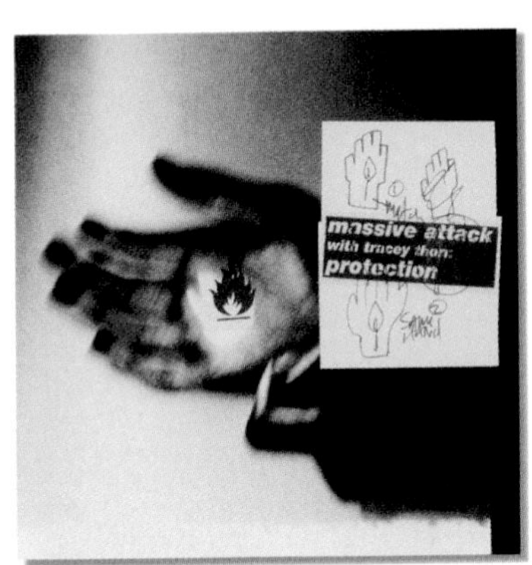

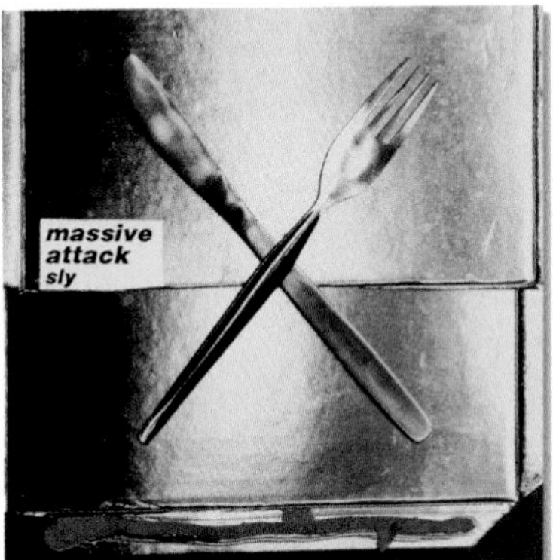

Identity for **Harvey Nichols Food Hall**. Winner of the D&AD Gold Award, New York Festivals Grand Award, Chartered Society of Designers Minerva Award, and the European Art Directors Award.

Massive Attack: *Protection* sleeves. Winner of 1995 D&AD Silver Award for the most outstanding compact disc & record sleeve campaign.

Identity for **John Galliano**. Pictured: boxes for shoes, handbags & gloves. Winner of 2004 D&AD Silver Award for outstanding achievement in brand label: packaging range.

Art direction and design of sleeve & campaign for **Seal**, eponymous album.

Stephanie Nash [UK]

1959– born in Burton on Trent
Admitted to AGI, 1998

Stephanie Nash and Anthony Michael studied at St Martin's School of Art, London (1978–81), and formed the partnership Michael.Nash Associates in 1984. Initial work was drawn from the music industry, as Stephanie had worked at Island Records as an in-house designer after graduating. Early projects included Massive Attack, Seal, Neneh Cherry and INXS. Current projects include Sophie Ellis-Bextor and The Rolling Stones.
The client base developed into the world of fashion with clients including Jasper Conran, Issey Miyake, Jil Sander, Philip Treacy, Joyce, and Patrick Cox.

In the early 90s the company was commissioned to design the own-brand packaging for Harvey Nichols Food Hall, an association that continues today, and has embraced the Fifth Floor, OXO and Prism restaurants. Projects have been completed for the National Portrait Gallery, the New Art Gallery Walsall, Louis Vuitton, Marc Jacobs, John Galliano, Alexander McQueen, H&M, Margaret Howell, Egg, Asprey & Garrard, David Morris, Space NK, Ruby & Millie, Toni & Guy, Flos, Cassina, Boots, Phaidon, 4th Estate Books, Schrager Hotels, Marks & Spencer, Heals, and the Royal Mail. There are ongoing projects for many of these clients.

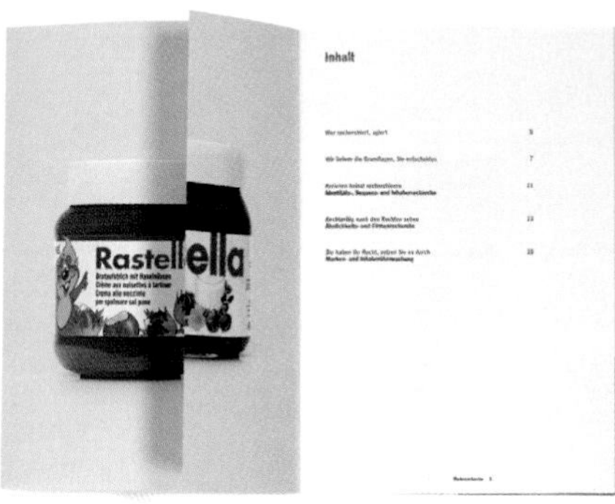

Andréas Netthoevel [Switzerland]

1963– born in Lucerne
Admitted to AGI, 1998

Andréas Netthoevel studied graphic design, colour consultancy and design (International Association of Colour Consultants/Designers: IACC) and photography (1979–86). After several jobs as a graphic designer, Netthoevel founded his own design studio Second Floor South in Biel, Switzerland in 1990, where he has worked together with AGI member Martin Gaberthüel since 1995. Second Floor South is in constant search of the well-known, combining it with new customer specific tasks. This way of working has been regularly awarded.

Activities include editorials, corporate designs, posters, art in architecture and objects. Since 2000 Andréas Netthoevel has also taught at the Hochschule der Künste, Berne, Switzerland.

Simultaneity in darkness, poster (for *daylight* see AGI member Martin Gaberthüel), 2005. Screenprint on the theme of Einstein's text on simultaneity. The left part of the poster is visible with the light on, the right part only appears after switching off the light.

Invitation in a black envelope, 2005. When removing the card, you are only holding a white paper in your hands. Due to the effect of the light, the motif gradually develops. The picture becomes clearly visible after 5 minutes.

Brand Research brochure for the Swiss Federal Institute of Intellectual Property, 2001. Three double pages on the topic of brand names. When the half-pages are unfolded, products with similar names and packages appear.

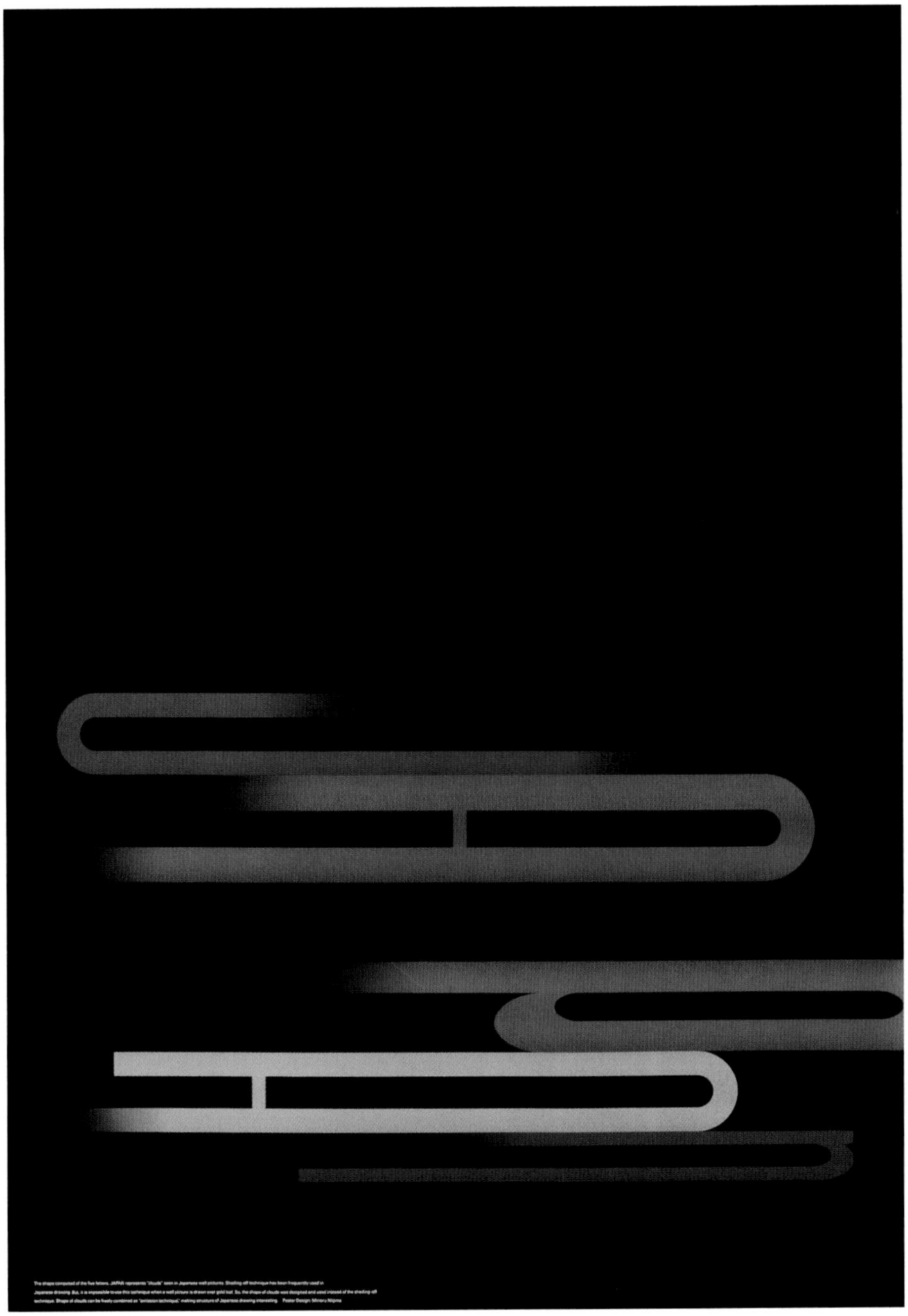

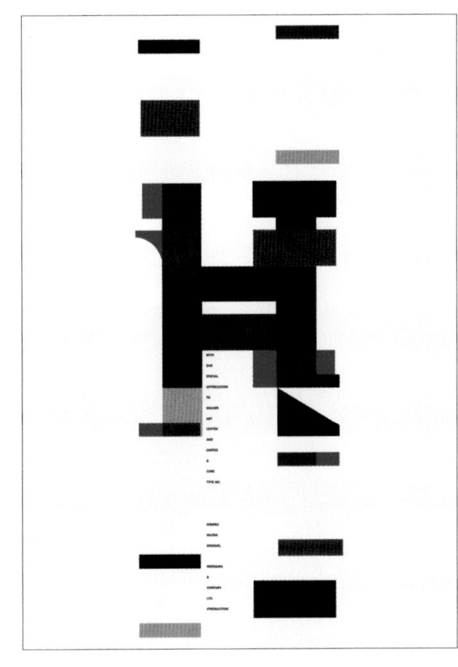

Minoru Niijima [Japan]

Japan, exhibition poster, 1988.

Poster for new typeface, 1997.

Life, exhibition poster, 1994.

1948– born in Tokyo
Admitted to AGI, 1998

Niijima opened his own design studio in Tokyo in 1977. Three years later he travelled to the USA to continue his study of graphic design, typography and book design at the graduate programme at Yale University. He received his MFA in 1983. When he returned to Japan, he held an exhibition in Tokyo and opened Minoru Niijima Design Studio.
He became a committee member of the Japan Typography Association the following year.

In 2003, he held an exhibition called 'Interaction of Colours and Fonts' at Ginza Graphic Gallery (GGG) in Tokyo. He is currently a professor at Musashino Art University, in the Visual Communication and Design Department.

たくさんのふしぎ
Animals and Human Being – From Legs to Arms. Published by Fukuinkan-Shoten, Tokyo.

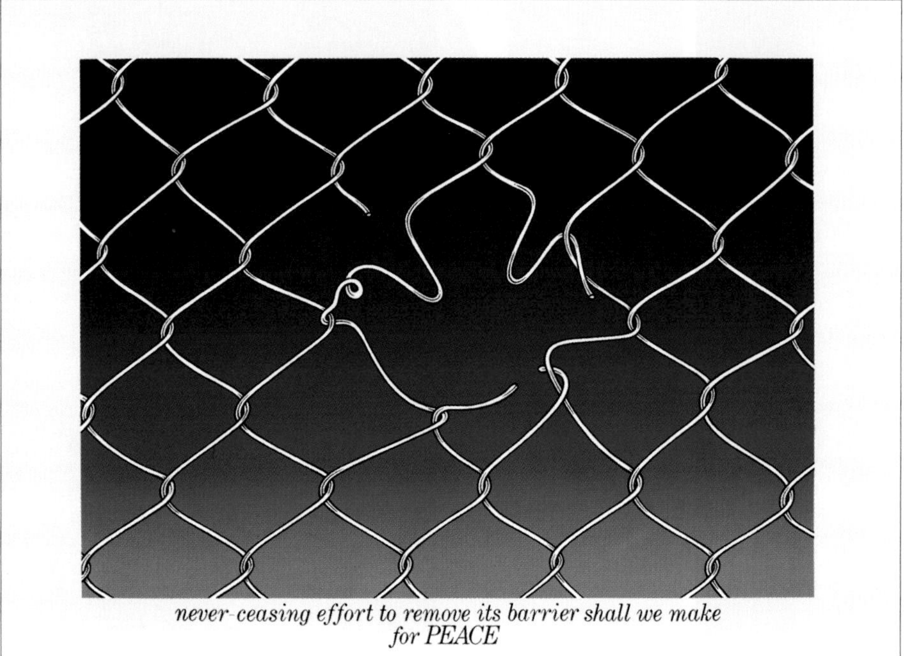

never-ceasing effort to remove its barrier shall we make for PEACE

U.G. Sato [Japan]

1935– born in Tokyo
Admitted to AGI, 1998

After graduating from Kuwasawa Design School in 1960, I began working at Oka Studio in 1961. I established Design Farm Inc. in 1975, and later taught illustration at Kuwasawa Design School (1995–2005). My major fields of design activity are posters, picture books for children, calendars, objects and monuments. In particular, I continue to tackle the subjects of world peace and environmental issues through the use of humour, imagination and satire. In 1995 I organized an anti-nuclear poster campaign by fax in Paris and Tokyo to protest against French nuclear testing.

Over the years I have held numerous solo exhibitions including 'My Theory of Evolution' (Okabe Gallery, Tokyo, 1972), and 'Visual Structure of humor' (International Design Centre, Nagoya, 2003). Among the major awards I have won to date are: Gold Prize, International Biennale of Graphic Design, Brno, 1978; Gold Prize, Poster Biennale, Lahti, 1979; Bulgarian Artists Federation Award for Sculpture, Humour and Satire Biennale, Gabrovo, 1989; Gold Prize, Warsaw International Poster Biennale, 1996; Golden Bee, International Biennale of Graphic Design, Moscow, 1998; Bronze Prize; International Poster Triennial, Toyama, 1997, 2000.

Preserve the Natural Heritage, poster, 1998. Silkscreen.

Animals and Human Being, poster, 1978. Silkscreen.

Peace, poster, 1978. Silkscreen.

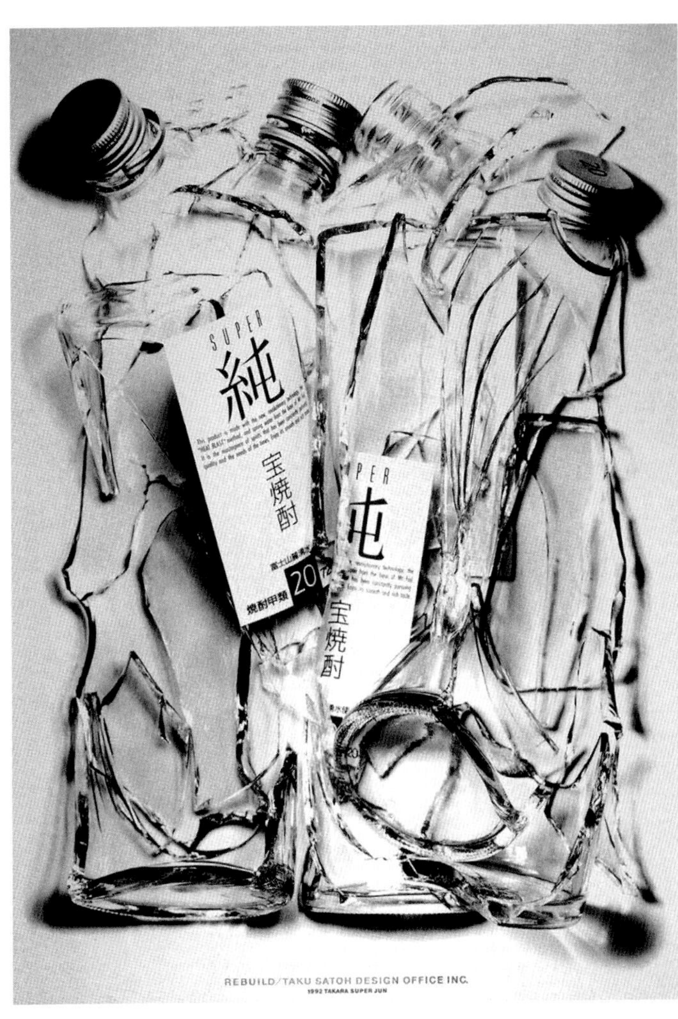

Message for the Twenty-First Century, exhibition poster, 1999.

Lotte Cool Mint, chewing gum package, 1994.

Rebuild, poster, Taku Satoh Design Office Inc., 1993.

Taku Satoh [Japan]

1955– born in Tokyo
Admitted to AGI, 1998

Graduated from Tokyo National University of Fine Arts and Music, majoring in design, in 1979; completed graduate course at the same university in 1981. Initially joined Dentsu, then established Taku Satoh Design Office in 1984. Created graphic designs for Nikka Pure Malt, Lotte Chewing Gum (Mint series), Lotte Xylitol Gum, Taisho Pharmaceutical's ZENA drink, MEIJI Dairies Oishii Gyunyu milk, and NTT DoCoMo P701iD cellular phone. Creative VI for BS Asahi (TV station), 21st-Century Museum of Contemporary Art, Kanazawa, Tokyo Metropolitan University and the Issey Miyake Foundation.

Involved in planning and art direction of *Nihongo de Asobo* (Let's Play), a TV show on the NHK educational channel, and the 'Analysis of Mass-Product Design' project ('dissecting' mass-produced merchandise from a design perspective). Publications to date include *Skelton* (Rikuyo-sha) and the *Analysis of Mass-Product Design* series (Bijutsu Shuppan-sha). Major exhibitions include: 'Neo-Ornamentalism', Tokyo, 1990; 'LUMEN Lurking in the City', Tokyo, 2002; 'Optimum', Tokyo, 2002; 'Invisible Designer', Japanese Canadian Cultural Centre, Toronto, 2002; 'Anatomia do Design: a obra de Taku Satoh', Japanese Cultural Centre, São Paulo, 2002; 'Plasticity', GGG, Tokyo, 2004.

Lakeside
SCIENCE & TECHNOLOGY
PARK

Clemens Theobert Schedler [Austria]

1962– born in Gräfelfing, Germany
Admitted to AGI, 1998

He grew up in the Wild West of Austria, in Vorarlberg. One year of art history studies in Salzburg followed by four years of commercial art in Vienna at the Höheren Graphischen Bundes- Lehr- und Versuchsanstalt: a fun phase of happy-go-lucky roads to nowhere and confusing depressions. 1987: he started as a freelance graphic artist for Walter Bohatsch – his actual basic training. 1989: he married Erika Parits (divorced 1997). 1990: birth of Lisa; founded his own graphic design office. 1992: guest professor at University of Applied Arts, Vienna. 1993: Bohatsch und Schedler, Büro für grafische Gestaltung was founded. 1996: became Büro für konkrete Gestaltung. 1998: marriage to Márcia de Lacerda Guimarães 1999: birth of Tereza. 2000: birth of Elena. 2002: guest professor at the Institute of Architecture and Industrial Design, Linz. He has designed corporate identity programmes for Kunsthaus Bregenz, MoMA Vienna, Carinthian Economic Promotion Fund and Hotel Therme Vals and is well known as a book designer.

'Everything is authentic.

Appearance is essential,
it reveals the essence of a thing.

Not how something looks,
is essential, however,
but how it moves.'

One and One is Eleven, book cover, 2004, published by Lakeside Science & Technology Park.

Logotype for Lakeside Science & Technology Park in Carinthia, Austria, designed 2004.

Craft Strategies: Seven Portraits of Unusual Projects in Europe, book cover, published 2005.

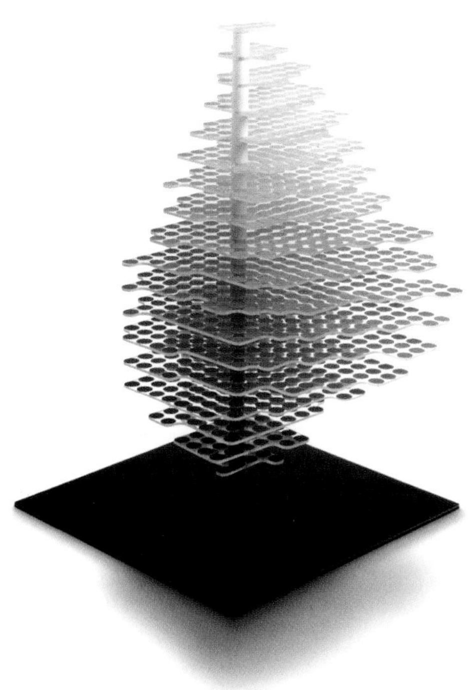

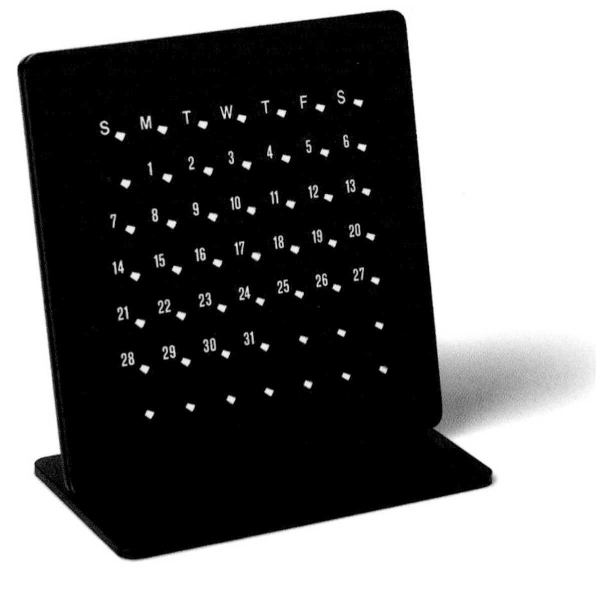

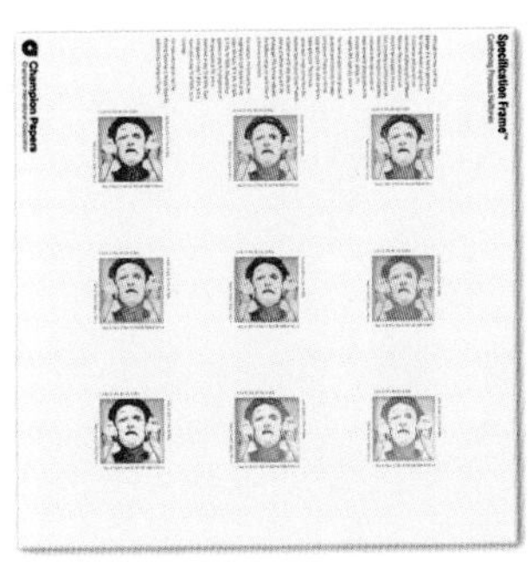

Colorcurve. A model of *'color space'* made possible with the Colorcurve Specification System.

Timeframe. A perpetual calendar for Designframe. Rotating the calendar advances the month.

Specification. Frame examples of duotones, tritones and quadtones. Specification is made easy with a simple turn of the frame.

The Art of Martex. This volume blurs the line between photography and illustration with sets built to deliberately fool the eye.

James Sebastian [USA]

1942– born in Providence, Rhode Island
Admitted to AGI, 1998

Jim Sebastian studied at the Rhode Island School of Design including an internship in 1966 with Karl Gerstner in Basel where he pursued his interest in colour, form and motion. Jim continued his kinetic explorations and invented Timeframe, a perforated surface through which changing information is viewed. In 1976 Timeframe was inducted into the MoMA Design Collection and Jim founded Designframe, a full-service design consultancy. Designframe offered Jim a platform to work with clients in developing new technologies and methods for communication. Created for Champion Papers, the Specification Frame gave designers a tool that expanded their creativity in printing.

Jim's work with Strathmore Paper included the redesign of their complete product offering and promotional material, including the renowned series of books about colour titled *Aspects of Color*. Simultaneously Jim developed the *'Colorcurve'* specification system followed by the Digital Process Tint Guide, a multi-part tool that offers precision colour formulation. Jim also worked with Martex creating and producing thirty books. Each book promoted Martex products, yet was really an exploration and celebration of the arts of image making, photography, printing and binding. The series was coveted by designers for its innovative use of materials and new methods of storytelling.

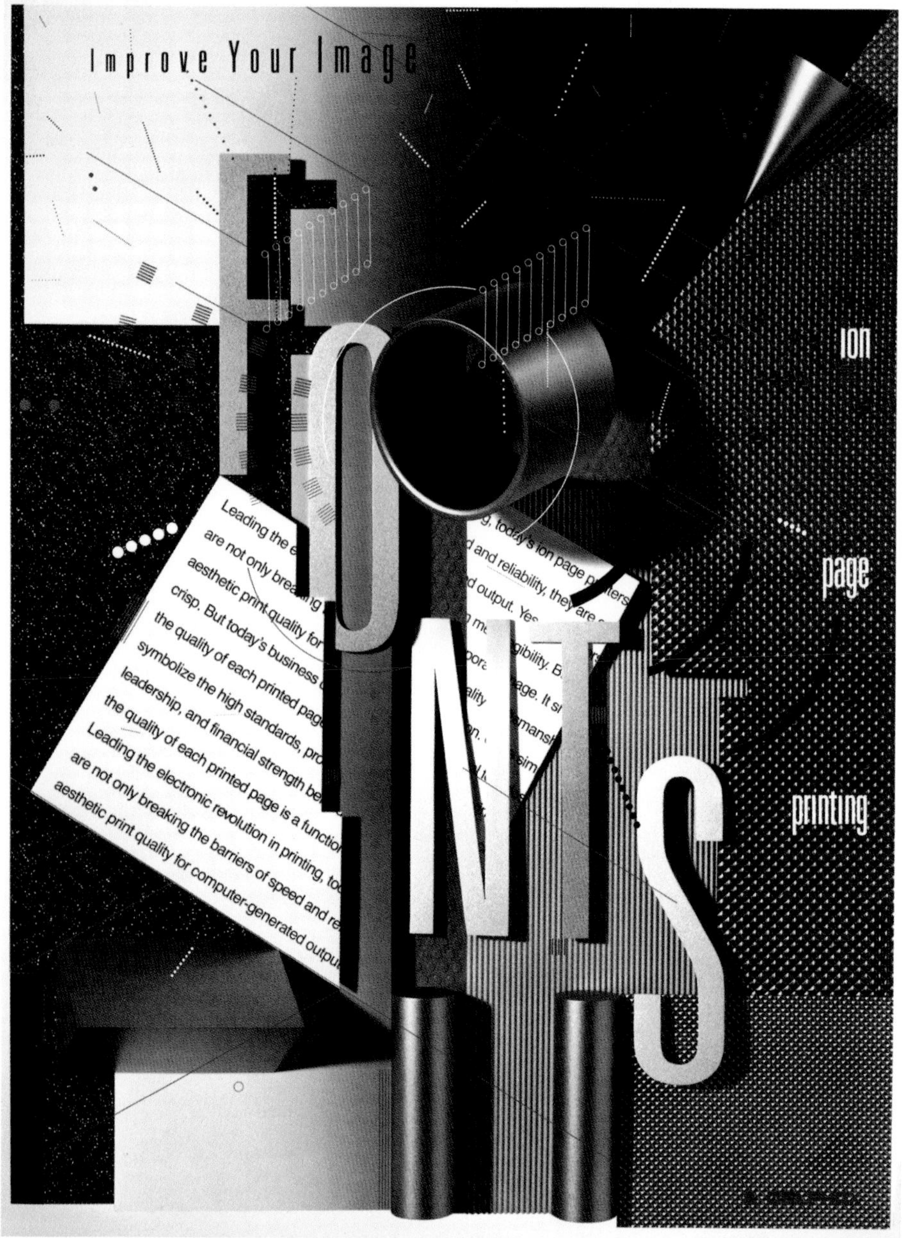

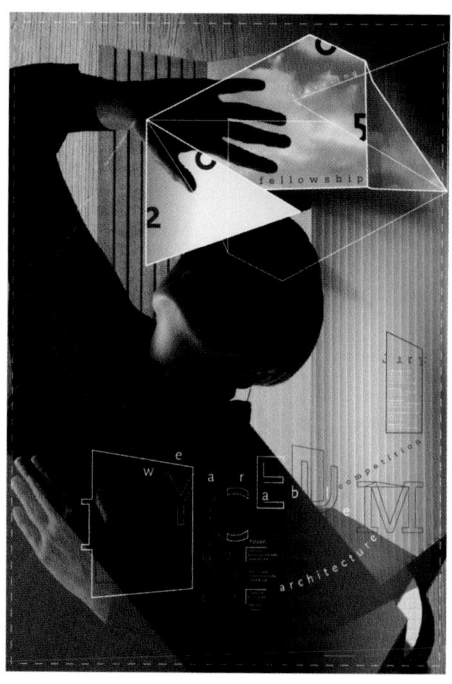

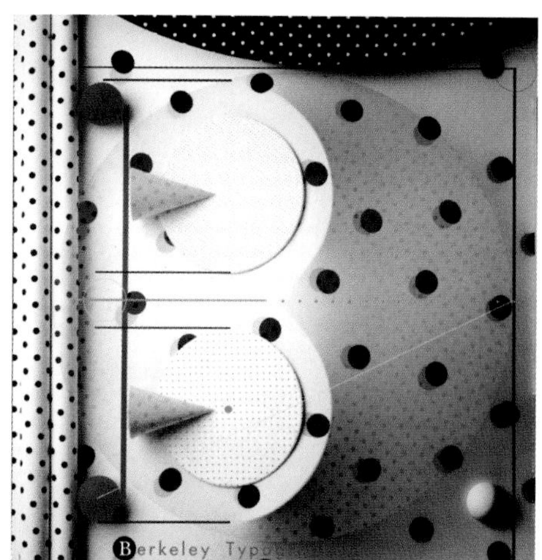

Nancy Skolos [USA]

1955– born in Cincinnati, Ohio
Admitted to AGI, 1998

A native of Ohio, Nancy began her college career in design at the University of Cincinnati in industrial design. After two years of study, she was accepted as one of a few undergraduate students at Cranbrook Academy of Art where she completed her BFA in interdisciplinary design, and then went directly to graduate school at Yale University School of Art and received an MFA in graphic design. Within a year of graduation, she started a practice with her husband, photographer/designer Tom Wedell, whom she met at Cranbrook.

Their early projects developed a visual vocabulary with a complexity of structure and colour that reflected the high-technology and consumer electronics clients they had in Boston such as Digital Equipment Corporation, and Boston Acoustics. In 1983 Nancy won an Award in *Progressive Architecture*'s Conceptual Furniture Competition and in the late 1980s Skolos-Wedell's work was featured in the book *New American Design*. Nancy began teaching in the late 1980s. She was named a Boston AIGA fellow in 2003, and has won many awards with her husband including Silver Prize in Toyama (1985) and Bronze Prize in Lahti (1988). She is currently a professor and has also been head of the department of graphic design at the RISD, Providence.

Delphax Fonts, 1987.
Poster for high-speed office printer type technology.

Berkeley Typography, 1986.
Poster for a typesetting company.

Poster for **Lyceum Fellowship student architecture competition**, 2005.

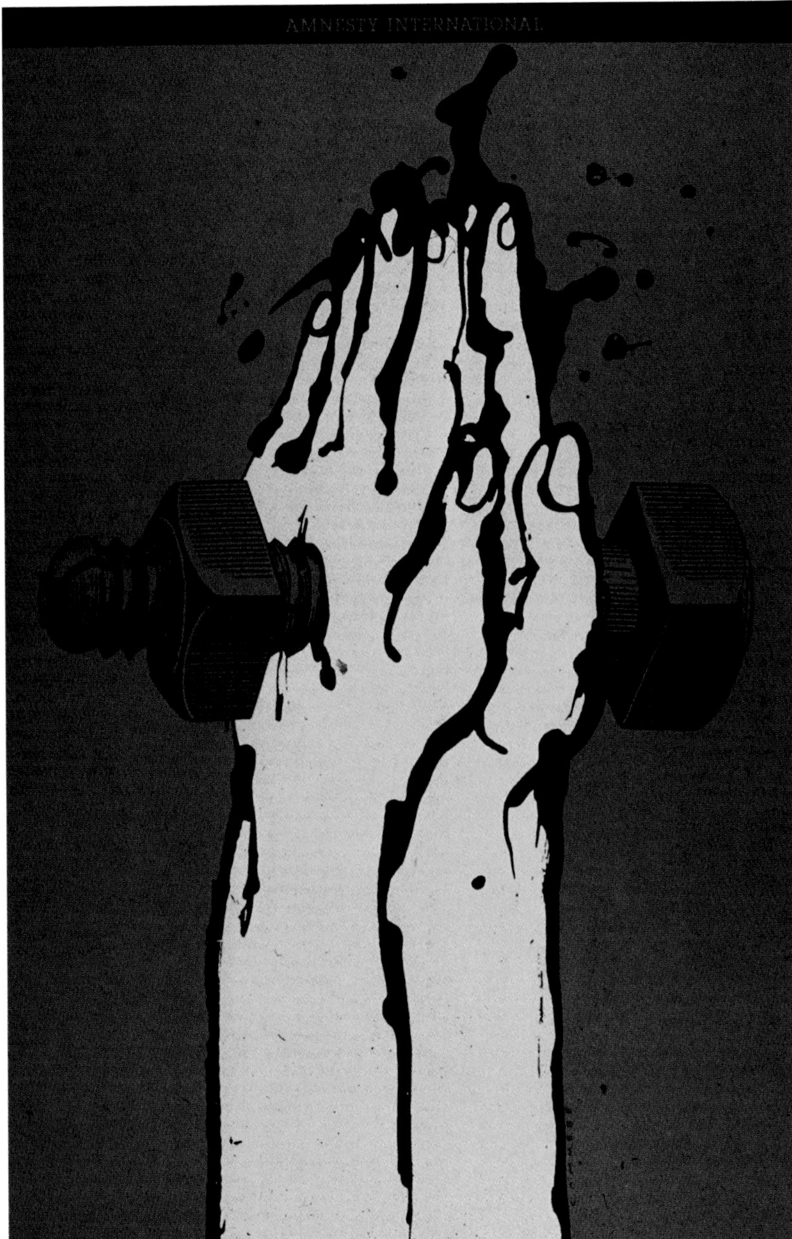

Lanny Sommese [USA]

Amnesty International, poster, 1982.

Poster for a performance of Shakespeare's **Romeo and Juliet**, 1994.

Poster for a performance of the writings of **Bertolt Brecht by the Penn State Readers**, 1978.

1943– born in East Moline, Illinois
Admitted to AGI, 1998

Lanny Sommese studied graphic design and fine arts at the University of Florida (1961–65), and graphic design at the University of Illinois, Urbana (1966–70). His career has taken two tracks. As an educator he developed and shepherded the graphic design programme at Penn State University. As a practitioner he maintained his own design office, Lanny Sommese Design & Illustration, which, in 1988, when his wife Kristin joined him, was renamed Sommese Design. The firm specializes in corporate, print, packaging and poster design as well as illustration for clients on and off campus.

Sommese has had an ongoing engagement with social issues and social responsibility, not only in his work but that of his students as well. Best known for his conceptual posters, which are often witty and full of commentary about the human condition, he has won many awards, highlighted by a gold medal and the José Guadalupe Posada medal for Best Poster at the Biennial of the Poster in Mexico and first prize in the Triennial of the Stage Poster, Sofia. Finally, for more than thirty years Sommese has created posters for the Central Pennsylvania Festival of the Arts, providing the annual event with a unique and internationally recognized reputation.

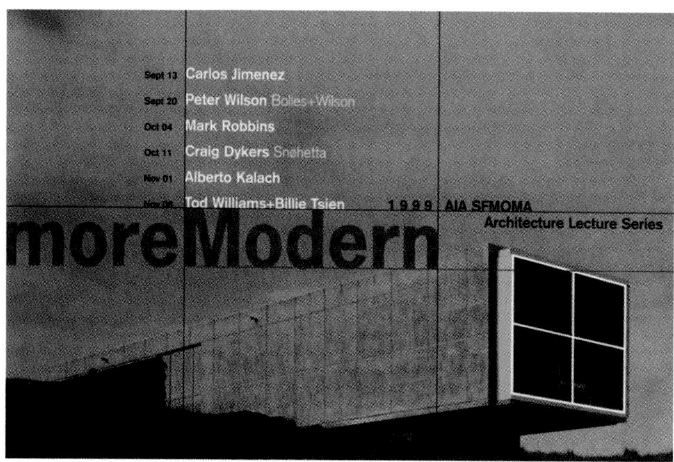

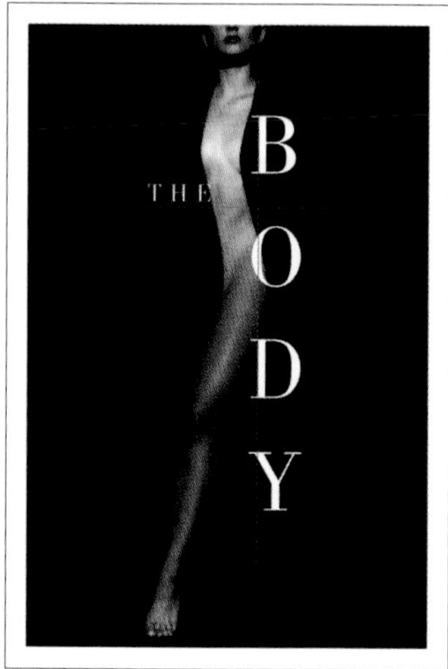

Lucille Tenazas [USA]

1953– born in Aklan, Philippines
Admitted to AGI, 1998

Originally from the Philippines, Lucille came to the United States in 1979 and studied at California College of the Arts (CCA) in San Francisco and Cranbrook Academy of Art, where she received her MFA in Design. After graduating she went to New York, a city she immediately felt at home in because its intensity reminded her of Manila. She established Tenazas Design in San Francisco in 1985, working on identity systems and print materials for cultural and non-profit organizations. Clients include the SF MoMA, Rizzoli and the SF International Airport. Her work has been exhibited in museums including a solo exhibition at SF MoMA.

Lucille has been a design educator for the last twenty years and was the founding chair of the MFA design programme at CCA. She has given lectures and conducted workshops all over the United States and throughout the world – in France, New Zealand, Croatia, South Africa, London, Seoul, Beijing, Sydney, Stockholm and Istanbul. She was the national president of the American Institute of Graphic Arts (AIGA) from 1996 to 1998 and was the recipient of the National Design Award in Communications Design sponsored by the Smithsonian Cooper-Hewitt National Design Museum for 2002.

Poster for **Lecture series** for the SF MoMA/ American Institute of Architects, SF Chapter.

Constructions of Legibility, 1997, poster announcing a lecture series for the SF MoMA/ American Institute of Architects, SF Chapter

The Body, 1994. We designed a two-part case, with the bound book inside a silk-screened translucent slipcase, conceptually relating to the idea of *'undressing'* the book when the contents are taken out by the reader.

CCAC Graduate Show, poster, 2002. *'1111'* is the street address of California College of the Arts in SF and numeral also served as an iconic element for the poster announcing the events during the MFA show.

Illustration for **postcard notifying a change of address**.

September 11, 2001, *Guardian* illustration.

Illustration for article about **the difference between male and female psychology**.

Peter Till [UK]

1945– born in Manchester
Admitted to AGI, 1998

Read English literature at Cambridge University (1964–67). Started making drawings at university and sold some to *OZ* magazine in 1969. Whilst writing and performing in the Flies Revue, a theatre group, he continued to make illustrations for a variety of clients – mostly the underground press. Made an animation, *The Running Man*, which was part of a Flies Revue show at the Cockpit Theatre in London in the early 1970s. Gradually the illustration side of his activities began to take precedence and his clients included *The Radio Times*, *The Sunday Times* and *The Observer*. In 1979 he made a short animated film, *The Beard*, that went on general release with a number of feature films.

In 1979 he formed The Rhumba Brothers and released a record on Big Beat Records. By now he was working for all the English broadsheet newspapers (and some of the tabloids).
He illustrated *The Emperor of the United States and other Great British Eccentrics* (1981) and campaigns for London Transport, Barclays Bank, etc. He has featured in numerous group exhibitions and won the V&A Museum Illustration Award (2005). He contributes a weekly illustration to the *Guardian* and has designed a set of six postage stamps for the Royal Mail.

Rick Valicenti [USA]

1951– born in Pittsburgh, Pennsylvania
Admitted to AGI, 1998

Rick Valicenti is founder and design director of Thirst, a firm devoted to art with function. His passion for design and embrace of new technologies makes for a dynamic marriage of imagery and inspiration. Thirst's strategic and creative versatility continues to lead the discourse and pursue the elusive ideals of intelligence and real human presence within today's world of commerce. In October 2006, Rick was awarded the prestigious AIGA medal for his sustained contribution to design excellence and the development of the profession.

Rick has served as president of the STA (Society of Typographic Art), board member of AIGA's Chicago chapter, and juror for the President's Design Awards National Endowment for the Arts (Bush and Clinton). He has been nominated twice for the prestigious Chrysler Design Awards and selected for the first *I.D.* magazine 40 and 50 top designers. Rick's work has been published in practically every major graphic design publication. In 2005, the Monacelli Press published a 356-page monograph of Thirst work titled *Emotion as Promotion*. The GGG Gallery (Osaka), DDD and Canon Galleries (Tokyo) have exhibited Rick's design and digital imagery. Selected Thirst works are in the permanent collections of the Cooper-Hewitt National Design Museum and the 2006 National Design Triennial.

Print This Moment, 1995.
Client: Gilbert Paper.
Concept/direction: Rick Valicenti.
Design: Rick Valicenti/Linda Q. Valicenti.
Photography: William Valicenti.

Tannhauser, 1988.
Client: Lyric Opera of Chicago.
Concept/direction: Rick Valicenti.
Design: Rick Valicenti/Michael Giammanco.

It's a Beautiful Day in the Neighborhood, 2005.
Client: A commissioned tribute to Mr. Rogers.
Concept/direction: Rick Valicenti.
Design: Rick Valicenti/John Pobojewski.

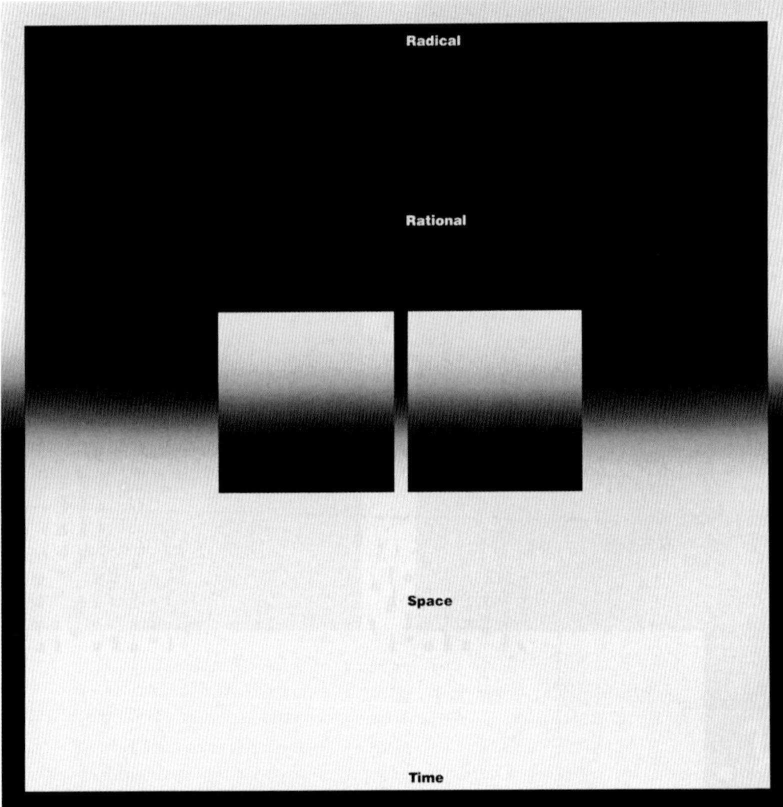

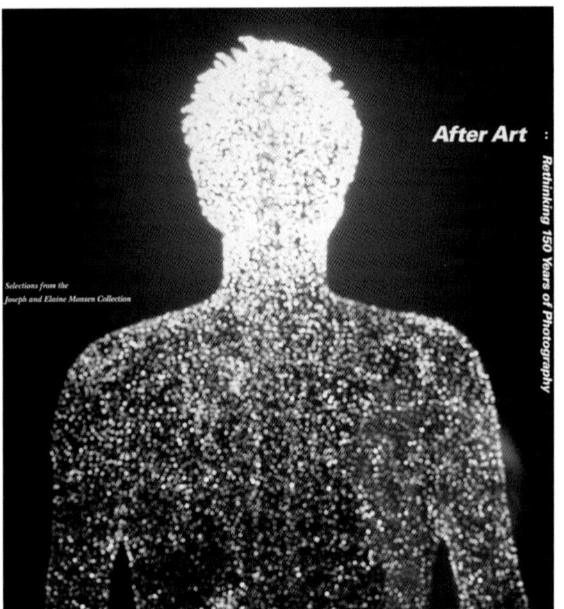

Radical Rational/Space Time, photography exhibition catalogue.

Art Into Life: Russian Constructivism 1914–1932, book cover.

After Art: Rethinking 150 Years of Photography, catalogue cover.

Douglas Wadden [USA]

1946– born in New York City
Admitted to AGI, 1998

Doug Wadden studied both photography and design, first at the Rochester Institute of Technology and then receiving his graduate degree from Yale University in 1970. He initially experimented with printmaking and video before turning his attention exclusively to visual communication design.
As a graphic designer he has worked for museums, corporations, public agencies and institutions, but perhaps most notably as the principal design consultant to the Henry Art Gallery for 25 years.
His books, catalogues, posters and publications have been recognized internationally in exhibitions, competitions and publications and are in the permanent collections of NY MoMA, the Library of Congress in Washington DC and the Walker Art Center in Minneapolis. As an educator, he has been chair of design at the University of Washington in Seattle, teaches design history and professional practice and is currently the Marsha and Jay Glazer Endowed University Professor. He has sought to balance teaching with practice and theory with creativity, whether in the classroom or the studio. He has been on the national boards of the American Institute of Graphic Arts in New York and the American Center for Design in Chicago and has been a juror, panellist and lecturer at numerous competitions and design conferences.

Anette Lenz [France]

1964– born in Eslingen, Germany
Admitted to AGI 1999

After studying in Munich, Anette moved to Paris in 1990, where she worked with Alex Jordan in the well-known cultural-political design group Grapus. Later, as a co-founder of the design collective Nous Travaillons Ensemble, she was involved in designing books, posters and identities for cities and cultural institutions. Since 1993, when she started her own studio, Anette has continued working in the social and cultural field, bringing beautiful, intelligent works into the public space. She draws on her knowledge of German typographic traditions with bold French-influenced imagery for clients such as the City of Paris, the French Ministry of Culture, Radio France, Le Sénat Français, Museé des Arts Décoratifs, Le Monde, and Théâtre d'Angoulême. Anette has won, amongst other prizes, the Gold Medal at the Brno Biennale, 2002; the Honorary Prize in Lahti, 2003; and the Plakatkunsthof Rüttenscheidpreis 2005 for her entire body of work in poster design. Her work on posters for the Théâtre d'Angoulême, in association with Vincent Perrottet, has received the Silver Medal at the Tehran Biennale, 2004, and the Grand Prix at Ningbo, China, 2004. She actively participates in exhibitions, conferences and workshops, and enjoys sharing her passion for design with students in many countries.

Théâtre d'Angoulême 2003–2004 Season, poster, 2003. In collaboration with Vincent Perrottet. Screenprint in 5 colours.

La tête dans les nuages, poster for children's theatre festival, Théâtre d'Angoulême, 2004. In collaboration with Vincent Perrottet. Screenprint in 5 colours.

Théâtre de Rungis, one of 17 posters for the 2000–2001 season. Screenprint in 3 colours.

Cover for **American Illustration Annual**.

Japanese Style Special, cover for *The New Yorker*.

The Legacy of George W. Bush for *Esquire* magazine.

Christoph Niemann [USA]

1970– born in Waiblingen, Germany
Admitted to AGI, 1999

After completing his studies at the Stuttgart Academy of Fine Arts, he moved to New York City, where he has worked as an illustrator, animator and graphic designer since 1997. In that time he has produced numerous covers and illustrations for the *New York Times Magazine*, *The New Yorker*, *Rolling Stone*, *Entertainment Weekly* and *Atlantic Monthly*. He has also been awarded honours from the American Institute of Graphic Arts (AIGA), the Society of Public Designers (SPD), the Art Directors Club (ADC) and American Illustration.

His works have been featured in various design books and magazines. Along with his collaborator, Nicholas Blechman, he is the publisher of the artist's book series, *100%*, which he describes as presenting *'editorial illustration without an editor'*. The latest issue, *100 % EVIL*, was published by Princeton Architectural Press. His first children's book, *The Police Cloud*, will be published by Schwartz and Wade books in spring 2007. Niemann lives in Brooklyn with his wife and two sons.

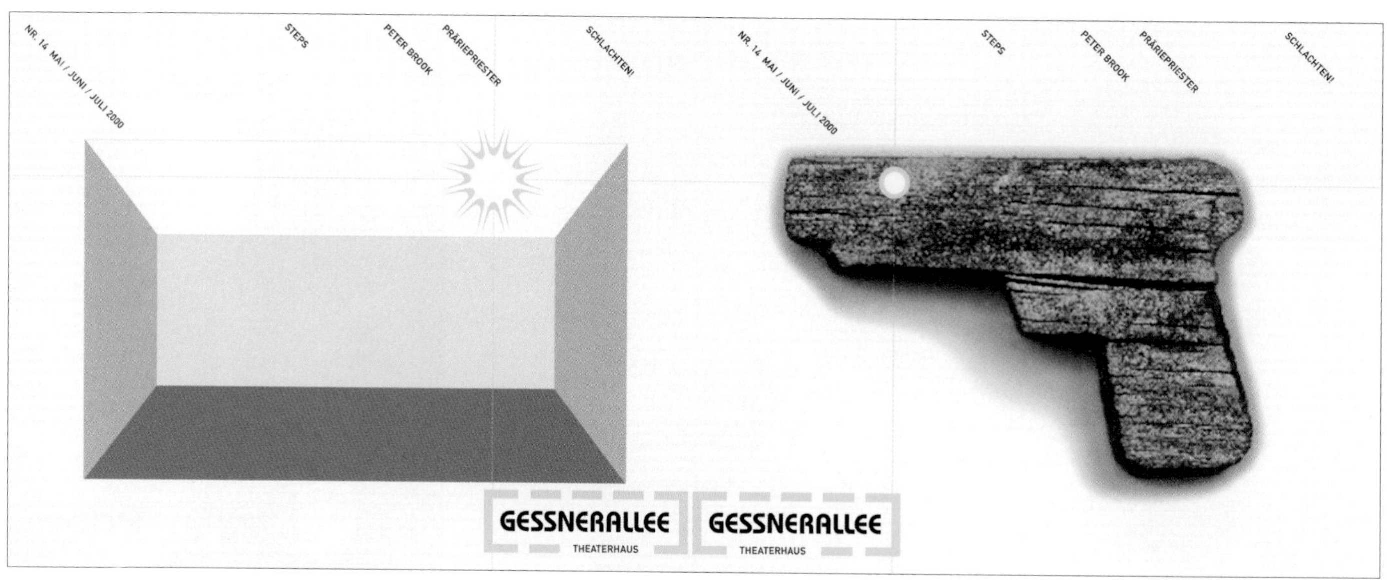

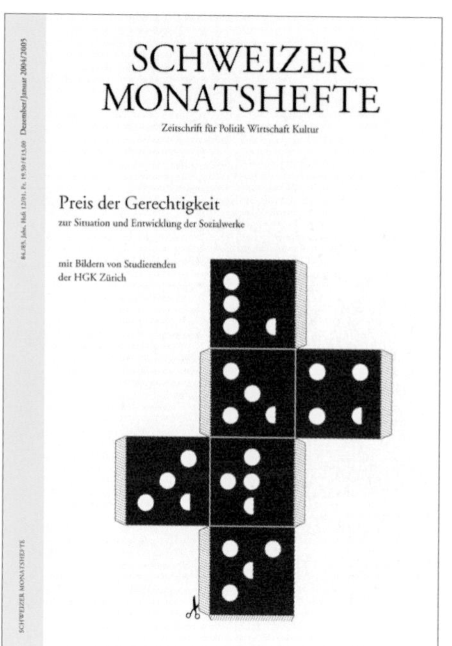

Mihaly Varga [Switzerland]

1957– born in Dunakiliti, Hungary
Admitted to AGI, 1999

1977–80: studies architecture in Budapest.
1985–88: studies graphic design at the HGKZ school of art and design, Zürich.
1988–90: graphic designer in the studio of Lars Müller, Baden.
1990: opens own studio.
1992: teacher at the HGKZ, department of visual communication.
1996: co-founds the multimedia agency Eyekon.

Clients: Zoo Zürich info system, educational guides, 1991–2000; Swiss National Library corporate design and advertising, 1994–2004; Gessnerallee Theatre, Zürich, corporate design and advertising, 1994–2004 (the theatre supports young independent groups from Switzerland and all over Europe); *Schweizer Monatshefte*, magazine, Zürich, redesign and advertising, 2004–ongoing.

Theatre Gessnerallee, Zürich, programme.

Filmpodium Cinema, Zürich, poster.

Schweizer Monatshefte, redesign of Swiss cultural and political magazine.

Swiss National Library, booklet and poster.

R.O. Blechman, USA.

2001

The 21st Century: A New Millennium

There were real doom scenarios written for the Millennium Night. A night that lasted for 24 hours around the globe. Would the computers that watched over our global energy supply, our transport systems and financial transactions all survive that fatal instant in which '99' would become '00'? It was all completely under control. Guinness could book a new record for the number of uncorked champagne bottles, for the wildest fireworks and TV shows. London had treated itself with a Dome and an Eye.

The USA inaugurated George W. Bush and friends, who came into power after a tumultuous election campaign. 300 million Americans elected their new President with a margin of just a few hundred votes. Not exactly an example of a true democratic accomplishment. Al Gore, who didn't use the support of a damaged Bill Clinton, just fell off the stage. These were the times of stock exchanges, capital, sky-high salaries, golden handshakes, bonuses and scandals. With explosive growth among the legion of billionaires and millionaires. And yet also these were also the times of outsourcing, globalization, Aids and poverty.

The new century was still in its earliest years when the tensions between extremist Muslims and the USA led to the fatal, devastating attacks on the New York World Trade Center and the Pentagon. Protracted wars in Afghanistan and, later, in Iraq have lain a heavy burden on the United Nations and the international community. Terrorism-without-borders has become a daily catchword in world politics. It has struck Madrid, Beslan, Bali, Moscow, Grozny, Baghdad, Beirut, London, Sharm-el-Sheikh, Tel-Aviv and numerous other places around the world. It seems we have entered an entirely new and painful chapter in history. Predictions for the future are hard to make. The speed with which we are now writing new chapters in world history seems higher than ever.

The Western world does not yet know how to cope with *'Eurabia'* and the major problems of semi-ghettos, unemployed young masses, refugees, etc. The effects of the changing climate are alarming. If we go on behaving like this, by the end of this century there will be no more ice to be found in Iceland. The US and Australia have declined to sign the Kyoto treaty aimed at reducing CO_2 emissions. An attempt at a new treaty broke down in 2006. The temperature of the ocean waters has risen. 360 natural disasters claimed the lives of at least 100,000 people in 2005; perhaps this is nature's answer to the way we are treating the planet. Hurricane Katrina, in and around New Orleans, was a very serious global warning. Al Gore presented his *Inconvenient Truth*. At a conference (2006, Noordwijk, Holland) Jan-Ernst de Groot, vice-president of KLM, also warned that, without dramatic improvements, airlines and airports would become major sources of the greenhouse effect and find themselves in serious economic trouble.

The war that started in Kuwait (1990) had spread throughout the region, touching the hearts and minds of the whole world: Iraq, Afghanistan, the Taliban, Saddam, Father George and son George W. and their friends, Israel, the Palestinians, the Shiites and the Sunnis, Syria, Al-Qaida, Iran and North Korea are names that reappear every day in the mass media everywhere, filling us with fear and anxiety. The old Cold War has been replaced by a new Long War. The Killing Fields have been revisited. The Polish Pope John Paul II, who played his role in the fall of Soviet Communism, died and got a German successor.

Most countries in the European Union swapped their own currencies for the Euro. The EU was expanded with many new member states. Its territory is now reaching the Russian borders. Once admitted, candidate member Turkey will bring take the European border right into the Middle East. The Internet hype and the rise of various short-lived generations of mobile phones had the whole world in its grip. ITC became a magic concept of fluctuating significance. The new *'capitalistic'* policy of the Chinese Republic resulted in enormous growth figures and rapidly changed the outlook of its big cities. The Chinese demand for oil and steel exerts a great influence on world economics. The British handed back the former Crown colony of Hong Kong without a single shot being fired, either by the British or by the Chinese.

Vladimir Putin came to power. In 2005 he stated that the fall of the USSR *'was a great disaster'* for the population of his Union. NATO and its former Iron Curtain enemies now go on joint manoeuvres. American and Russian astronauts cooperate in space. Disasters with Russian submarines are now being solved by British and US action. ICT industries are upsetting the world economies. The economic heavy weather of the years following 9/11 ruined many companies, large and small, due to their recent investments.

Ben Bos, Amsterdam, 2006

The AGI Steps into the 21st Century

At Almost 50 Years Old...

Ben Bos, Amsterdam, 2006

Alan Fletcher, 'framed' during the dinner at the house of Jennifer Morla.

The location for the opening of the Millennium AGI 2000: Mexico! The new century took us into a new world. The first AGI gathering place was Mexico City, where a student seminar had been organized. Speakers: R.O. Blechman, Catherine Zask, Christoph Niemann, Werner Jeker, Kyle Cooper and Javier Mariscal. The seminar was followed by dinner and dancing in Salon 21. The next morning, there was a visit to the Anthropological Museum and then on to Oaxaca, the congress's host town (where other participants had already arrived). Germán Montalvo and Gabriela Rodríguez, who had only been with the AGI for a few years, were the organizers of this Mexican congress. No simple task. A wonderful hotel, near the cathedral of Oaxaca, accommodated the AGI leaders and was also the venue for the presentations. Other participants had booked into slightly more modest accommodation. The welcome cocktails were served surrounded by the exhibition of Mexican posters and drawings by Fernando Medina.

Mexico is dazzling and sometimes deafening, too. The hours off spent in the city centre of Oaxaca provided colourful merchandise, displayed in the shady market square, beautiful people and children, music, terraces, little shops, balloons, art, religion,

2000: AGI student seminar and congress in Mexico City and Oaxaca.

Posters in folk style.

Creative assignment: design a carpet. Presentation of 80 results in the cathedral square of Teotitlán del Valle, carpet-weaving town.

AGI on the pyramids of Monte Albán.

Papier maché statues, 3.5 to 4.5 m high, everywhere in and around the Santo Domingo Cultural Centre.

2001: AGI *'50'*, Jubilee congress and student seminar in Paris.

Gala dinner in the Hôtel de Ville (City Hall).

Exhibition 'Ode to Henri de Toulouse-Lautrec', organized in Paris by Anthon Beeke.

Spread from the book (creative assignment): 'Paris, seen by AGI' (design by John McConnell).

theatre, kitsch, lots of skeletons, parades, food and drink. And you can take it from me: fried grasshoppers taste perfectly all right, even for breakfast! There were lectures on ancient Mexican art, architecture and history. Mariscal and Trino went into the virtual boxing ring. We visited and climbed the fabulous pyramids and surrounding antiquities of Monte Albán.

We were given the opportunity to provide designs for the carpet weavers who, for once, were able to swap their traditional work for modern graphic design. The results were spread out in the church square in Teotitlán del Valle and were worthy of AGI. Beautiful, innovative graphic carpet art, sometimes terribly elaborate. Unfortunately, the project was not handled entirely correctly and left a number of people with unnecessary heavy losses. The weavers' village then treated AGI to folk dancing, music and culinary specialities. The artists of Oaxaca exhibited their zoomorphic figures for us; there were continual processions through town, preceded by horns, strings, singers and drummers. The final dinner in the Santo Domingo cultural centre was accompanied by an enchanting light show and dancing in a circle accompanied by colourful giants, lots of music, Mexican design and a terrific amount of spectacular fireworks on the square in front of the cathedral. Eastman Kodak experienced some of the richest of its twilight days.

The new century brought a new idea: AGI started publishing *'New Members'* books. Depending on the size of the 'catch' these could be yearbooks or a couple of years with lean harvests could be bundled together. The intention was for AGI to get, and maintain, a grip on its history. By combining the frequent *'illustrated acquisitions'* with this current book, we have managed to make as complete an overview of the membership history as possible. The 2000, 2001–2 and 2003 issues were all made in China, but are bilingual (Chinese/English), as not everyone is equally fluent in Chinese.

Back to our birthplace: the 50-year-old AGI gathered in Paris. It was shortly after 9/11 and people had not recovered from the shock by any means. Is it really safe next to the Eiffel Tower? Our French colleagues had spared no effort. A spry Raymond Savignac played a prominent role. He designed the mascot for the programme, a book cover, and his work was to be seen at the champagne reception in the Bibliothèque Forney. At the following seminar day, at the Centre Pompidou, the chairs were occupied by both AGI members and students. The parade of prominent celebrities included Peret, Irma Boom, Werner Jeker, Koichi Sato, J. Abbott Miller, Gunter Rambow and John Maeda. There was so much to see and enjoy: a true graphic *tour du monde*.

The next day, the national library was the scene for the French contribution. A surprise *'Welcome to Paris'* film by the 20 French members, followed by *'50 Years of AGI'*, a show by Ruedi Baur, Peter Knapp and Rudi Meyer. In the library was an exhibition of AGI work from the years 1997–2001; a subjective selection without any attempt at democracy. The highlight of the day was the reception and gala dinner in the grand 19th-century Paris Hôtel de Ville, seated at a 100-metre-long table, with a little Eiffel Tower for each guest and a large orchestra playing *'Happy Birthday'* for the AGI and my Elly.

The next day, we were back in the National Library. Michel Bouvet led a *'zap'* session: 18 AGI members were each given 5 minutes to present themselves. A number of members appeared on stage to express their opinions and ideas. Alain Le Quernec treated us to the work of his secondary school pupils in Quimper: on drugs, racism and drunk driving. At the end of the afternoon, Galerie Anatome opened the exhibition *'127 AGI Members See Paris'*. An *'Eiffel Tower book'* on the subject was handed out. Dinner was in the classic Hôtel de Sully, with a good glass of Saint-Emilion and a DJ into the bargain. The General Assembly was again held in the library, with the customary commotion. On the final evening, the *Marcel Carné* took us down the Seine to Les Pavillons de Bercy, where the Musée des Arts Forains awaited. An incredible ambiance: antique fairground attractions, fully operational. A buffet, fantastic merry-go-rounds, acrobatics and a farewell turn around the dance floor. As a bonus, one more highlight. On Sunday morning there was a brunch in the Espace Saint-Martin, where the 100 designers Anthon Beeke had selected showed their posters in honour of the centenary of Toulouse-Lautrec's Salon des Cents. That, in itself, was worthy of a book!

'Right Brain/Left Coast' was the slogan for the AGI 2001 congress in San Francisco. Only hoping that 'right' means okay, rather than right in the political

sense, as you will not charm everybody with that by a long chalk. San Francisco is a city to take to your heart: its situation, climate, architecture, international cuisine, its own wines, and lots of friendly people. Pentagram's Kit Hinrichs, continually and extremely competently seconded by Charlene, had planned the student seminar on the first morning and early afternoon at the Yerba Buena Center Forum. Alan Fletcher exhibited his whimsical work, Wang Xu's book and magazine presentation was simply called *'China'*, Jennifer Stirling explained *'How we (don't) sell creative'* and was followed by the inimitable Chip Kidd with his books. We were dropped off at the California College of Arts and Crafts, where we were able to see the students and the students could see us and our work. Jennifer Morla's gigantic home was the dinner venue.

The second day was about the arts: Kyle Cooper showed Left Coast film titles, AGI presented its posters in SF MoMA and the highly acclaimed Wayne Thiebaud projected his Left Coast paintings. This was followed by a cocktail reception for Takenobu Igarashi and a tour of Pentagram, after which we drove on to the open-air restaurant-cum-film theatre Foreign Cinema. Suspense and sensation! On the third morning we met John Bielenberg at Yerba (with a Virtual Telemetrix show) and the innovative Gigi Obrecht and David Karam with their multimedia projects. Day 4 took AGI to the famous Napa Valley. A tour of a winery (listening and tasting), followed by a visit to Niebaum Coppola. That meant even more delicious wine, a little piece of film history, an excellent lunch, and an exchange of wine labels that the congress participants had designed. Then the coach drove back over the famed Golden Gate Bridge. The assembly was held at the W Hotel, followed by an afternoon off and then, in the evening, we met up again in Chinatown for an umpteen-course banquet dinner. AGI S.F. was concluded with a snazzy musical, *'Beach Blanket Babylon'*, and the parting hugs around midnight outside the theatre. A highly-rated AGI week!

Bravo the Finns! Without the customary extensive preparation time, they were thrown into the deep end of their thousands of lakes to organize the next congress (2003). And they did it as if it was the most natural thing in the world. One major, positive organizational fact to start off with: everyone was democratically accommodated in one pleasant hotel in the harbour; this time everyone had the same social rank. For the opening reception, we could all stay put: the bar, on the 10th floor with a panoramic view of the bay of Helsinki, was the gathering point. We then made our way into the centre of Helsinki in groups, for something to eat.

The student symposium was held in the University of Art and Design, a complex that flows almost imperceptibly into the manufacturing halls and showrooms of the Iittala glass and Arabia porcelain company. The reason being that this internationally renowned manufacturer invests a great deal of art and design in its products. In the interval between the readings, it was possible to visit the factory and showroom. Robert Appleton (USA) was the first speaker at the symposium; Robert is an extremely multi-faceted man: designer, artist, musician, photographer and lecturer. Then it was over to Cyan: Daniela Haufe and Detlef Fiedler from Berlin, cultural lecturers and designers. Ruedi Baur is the *'frontman'* for a group of design studios primarily active in identity, orientation, information, urban and exhibition design. Ruedi fulfils numerous functions in design higher education. Jean Benoît Lévy, poster designer, works a lot with photographers. Bruno Monguzzi dealt with *'The Naked Word: Form, Content and Sense'*. A dinner with music was booked at the waterside restaurant, Aqua.

The second day was Finland day. After the opening by AGI chairman David Hillman and Kari Piippo (Finland) there was a talk about the Finns and their roots, 100 years of Finnish architecture and posters (Ulla Aartomaa from the Lahti Museum); Eero Miettinen from Nokia and Lisa Sounio from Iittala talked about their designs. After lunch, the coach took the party to *'the far North'*: Lahti with its sports museum, ski-jumping demonstrations (on artificial grass) and the beautiful Sibelius Concert Hall. After that, the AGI guests visited the 2003 Lahti Poster Biennale and there was a buffet dinner. Late home to Helsinki.

Day 3: AGI day. Niklaus Troxler kicked off, announcing Reza Abedini from Iran: *'Persian Script and Typography'*. Keith Godard followed with a wonderful demonstration of how to transform ideas from 2D to 3D. Jelle van der Toorn Vrijthoff talked about his adventurous stay in Yemen, where he

2002: AGI congress in San Francisco.

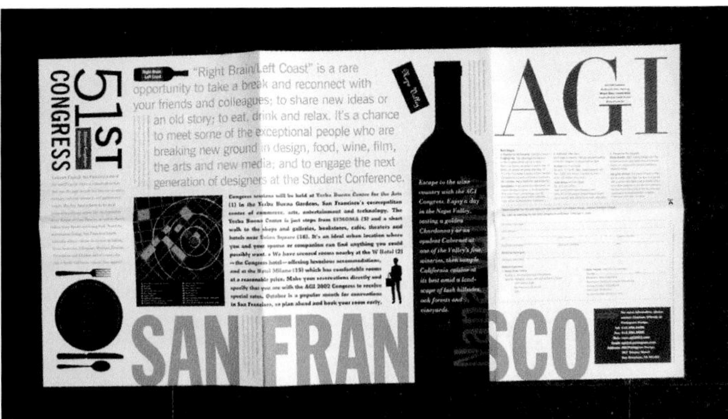

Invitation leaflet, designed by Kit Hinrichs.

Creative assignment: design a Californian wine label.

Creative assignment: decorate a chair, designed by Prof. Yrjö Kukkapuro.

Chair show at the Helsinki City Hall.

2003: AGI congress in Helsinki (Finland).

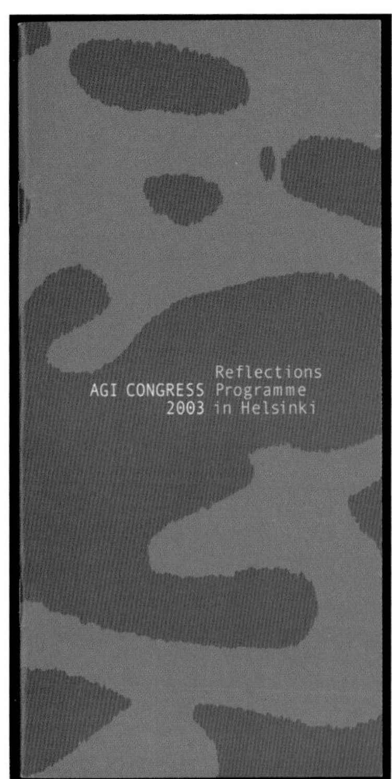

Programme for the AGI congress 2003.

Morteza Momayez.

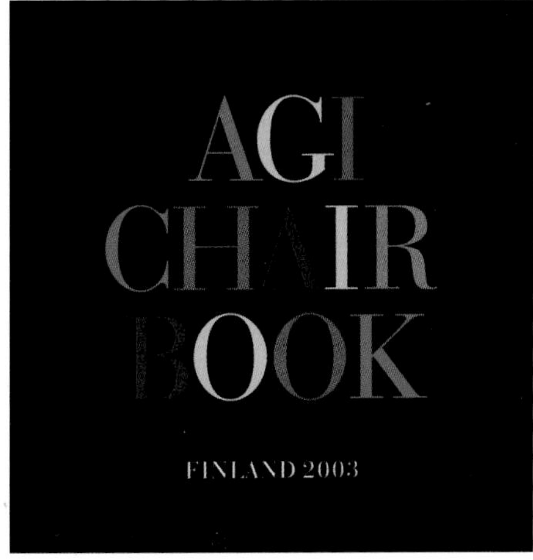

The AGI Chair Book.

2004: AGI congress in Beijing, China.

Congress visitors near the Great Wall.

Creative assignment: 'Breeze in China' (Design a Fan).

Masuteru Aoba.

Santiago Pol.

Kyösti Varis.

worked on a historical museum. Catherine Zask demonstrated her juggling skills with letters.
In the afternoon, we were welcomed to the enormous reception hall of Helsinki's Town Hall where, after a few nice words from the deputy mayor, there was a fantastic display of 76 chairs. The frame was designed by Prof. Yrjö Kukkapuro, the images on the seats and backs produced by AGI minds and fingers. Simple, original, richly decorated, from musical to even fatally electric. Our Finnish friends put them all in a booklet. The Helsinki government provided physical sustenance. In the evening, we travelled by boat to the great historical Suomenlinna fort. And where can you eat better than in 'Valhalla'?

Before the meeting, the following day, the Design Museum was available. The non-members had to *'put up with'* a Jugendstil exhibition, a movement in which Finland was highly influential. Later in the afternoon, the coaches took us via Helsinki's suburbs (and the Rock Church) to Tapiola Garden City and, finally, to the Hvitträsk museum and restaurant, where the atmosphere is extremely pleasant and there is a dance floor to boot.
Many thanks to the Piippos, the Varis family and the Aartomaas. Those who still had time and enough roubles (or dollars) left could take a trip to St Petersburg.

The first AGI member from the Chinese mainland, Prof. Yu Bingnan, joined in 1992. Over the next 12 years, the world changed and China, in particular. In 2004 Beijing received a visit from AGI. In the meantime, a gale-force *'breeze'* had blown China into the centre of global attention. Old Beijing has been flattened by an armada of continually spewing concrete mixers. A lot has been gained for the future, but a lot of the past has been lost forever. The campus of the university where the AGI student symposium was held is the size of a small city. The students are modest, disciplined, hard-working and tremendously interested in foreign visitors.

The Austrian Walter Botasch pleaded for a structure that accommodates all the client's needs. Shigeo Fukuda demonstrated his inexhaustible, astounding imagination. Anette Lenz started her career at Grapus, but then set up her own studio where she works on a wide range of commissions. Poster designer Sato, from Japan, showed the wonderful world of his visual *'jungle'*, which is even reflected in his home environment. Lucille Tenazas, born in Manila but working in San Francisco, brought up the rear of the parade. As a lecturer, she pleaded for the best possible design training: the most experienced designers passing on the torch to the most creative, open-minded talents.

There was a tour of the vast grounds of the Emperor's Summer Palace, after which it was time for a sublime dinner, accompanied by a string trio. Walking back, we saw that Beijing can also be calm and deserted.

The next Chinese congress day, in the old Dongyuan Theatre, Mrs Liang May spoke of the dualism in Chinese culture. Taoism versus Confucianism, like yin and yang, constantly seeking balance. In a lecture on ancient Chinese architecture, Liu Chang showed breathtaking examples of wooden constructions. Then came AGI members Song Xiewei, Wang Yuefei and Kan Tai-Keung, who each threw light onto the graphic design from their own huge regions. Some of the work was of a global level. In the afternoon was the opening of the AGI fan design exhibition. The beautiful catalogue of fans was presented. The hosts had also organized a lovely new edition of the 2001 AGI Eiffel Tower book. Song Xiewei invited a large party to dinner in his studio, situated in a penthouse in a high-rise building.

Day 3, international day, generated 10 *'zapping sessions'*, each of 5 minutes. Katsumi Asaba, Werner Jeker, Etienne Mineur, Finn Nygaard, Dan Reisinger, Arnold Schwartzman, Chen Shaohua, Jelle van der Toorn Vrijthoff, Garth Walker and Song Xiewei. This was followed by a terrific presentation by Robert Massin (France), who attempts to unite typography and music. Edgar Reinhard (Switzerland) exhibited his high-tech trade fair presentations for Toyota, IBM, Dow and other big companies. His floating IBM pavilion in Geneva was sensational. David Tartakover (Israel) produces a lot of (left-wing) political campaigns in his country, to the dissatisfaction of Premier Ariel Sharon, who was obliged to award him with a State Prize. The rest of the day was spent on an extensive visit to the enormous Forbidden City, where Chinese history flows over into a memorial to the great leader Mao Tse Tung. You have to eat Peking duck in Peking. And that became another kind of zapping session, trying all the different varieties.

The last day. The morning was for the AGI assembly. After that it was a heavy climb over the Great Wall. The concluding Congress Gala Dinner was held in a big restaurant, part of a housing project for China's new ultra-rich that had not quite made it. There, too, you are not allowed to build until the permit is in your possession. The spontaneously formed AGI band consisted, for the time being, solely of Robert Appleton. Loud and clear, just the same.

Berlin 2005. The old capital that became the new capital, which a lot of people wanted to see. The congress centre was the Kulturbrauerei: a former brewery complex in the charming (Eastern) Kreuzberg district, which had evidently also been given a new lease of life. AGI chair Laurence Madrelle was waiting for us there, dressed as the Berlin Bear. Behind the bear's back was a hall with the reception and some brilliant student work by illustrators from 7 academies. The brewery complex has a cinema, where the presentations were given every morning. A pitch-black pit. Outside, in the courtyard, the exhibition had been set up: Berlin, seen by AGI in black and white, the entries blown up to a monumental format. A newspaper showed the entire crop of 105 pieces. The sessions in the cinema were continuous and on the long side.

Day 1: Michael Rutschky projected Berlin as a romance. Niklaus Troxler was 'in Jazz': a visual concert of his Willisau posters. Garth Walker (AGI's first South African) had his own style of signature. Paula Scher *'made it Bigger'*, with her images of super-graphics in theatrical settings. Isidro Ferrer, from Spain, turned out to be a 3D mime artist. In the afternoon, there were 12 open studios in Kreuzberg. Wonderful exhibitions of all our German colleagues in often former industrial spaces. The welcome dinner was held in Die Halle, the first sports hall (19th century) in Berlin. Delightful music and performances by, amongst others, Russian singers, skilfully accompanied by Shigeo Fukuda and his assistant Alexander Jordan.

Day 2: Sara Fanelli with her elegant collages, Stanley Wong, Günther Karl Bose, István Orosz with his fantastic Escher-like film work. Makato Saito concluded the line-up. In the afternoon, there was the opportunity to go cycling and a sightseeing tour with a visit to Melk Imboden's designer portraits and the George Grosz archive. With white gloves, holding the smallest masterpieces in your own hand. The Kulturforum Potsdamer Platz (in the former DDR) was hosting *'imAGIne'*, an exhibition of 5.5 decades of selected AGI masterpieces. Not that democratic, but very impressive and still full of posters. There was an accompanying booklet but, unfortunately, without pictures. The curators were Armin Hofmann, Jan van Toorn, Pierre Bernard, Paula Scher and Stefan Sagmeister, who were each responsible in that order for a decade.

The last morning session (Day 3) in the cinema began with an improvisation by Bruno Monguzzi, who, with skill and humour, replaced the originally announced Italo Lupi. Paul Davis II (the new English version!) screened his drawings. One of the highlights was an appearance by Ahn Sang-Soo, who presented a grand rendition of his story of the Korean alphabet (and more) and was greeted with tumultuous applause. Wim Crouwel looked back at his illustrious career. Klaus Theweleit concluded the day but, unfortunately, there were a lot of people too tired to experience it. A gorgeous afternoon on the waters of the Spree and adjoining canals provided a different perspective to the big city with all its greenery, its remarkable buildings and its bridges. An excellent idea, that boat trip. The official photo was taken at the Haus der Kulturen der Welt and then it was sausages on the barbecue.

The impressive Meta-Haus accommodated the general assembly. An enticing presentation by the hosts of ToKyoTo AGI 2006. Shigeo Fukuda and magician Asaba Katsumi, assisted by an engaging lady, tempted the members to make the long trip. The AGI book was presented. The final dinner was given in the Kulturbrauerei's Palais club, with plenty of music and dancing and resounding applause for all the fantastic Berlin crew.

The high-speed Shinkansen bullet train was the linking factor in the ToKyoTo 2006 AGI congress. A short stay in Tokyo followed by slightly more time in Kyoto and then back to Tokyo for the finale. Added to the long distances within the two guest cities themselves, this meant a great deal of sitting in buses and trains. Having said that, there are still plenty of good and beautiful things worth mentioning about hospitable Japan. Soaked to the skin in *'tropical showers'*, the AGI members arrived at the famous Ginza Graphic Gallery (GGG). The registration area was rather over-populated. Sponsors (?), friends, students and registration

2005: AGI congress/seminar in Berlin, Germany

Ahn Sang-Soo's visitors' picture at the Haus der Kulturen der Welt.

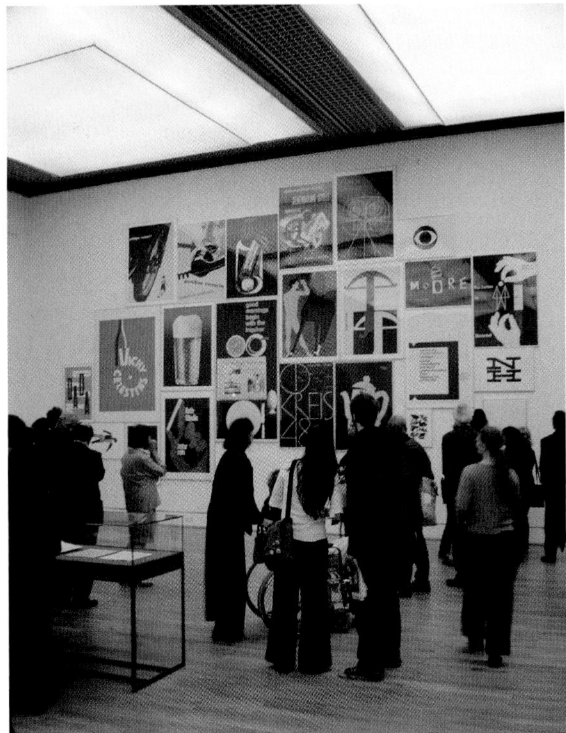

ImAGIne exhibition at the Kulturforum.

Creative assignment: design a poster on Berlin, black/white only. Paper with some of the Berlin posters

AGI on the river Spree.

2006: AGI congress/seminar in ToKyoTo [Tokyo/Kyoto], Japan.

The New Members catalogue, designed by Jianping He.

Kyoto, Enryakuji Temple. AGI members after the Buddhist ceremony.

Dinnertime in the Mori Tower, Tokyo.

tables slightly blocked the view of the exhibition of often surprising *kakejikus* (hanging scrolls) the members had submitted. After the welcome, we braved the showers again en route to the Creation Gallery, where the Japanese AGI members had displayed the posters they had designed partly for the occasion. Magnificent! A few speeches, some drinks and nibbles and then back out with the umbrellas and off in search of a restaurant in the shopping area.

Day 2 was largely the *'international'* day. The Kuwasawa Design School provided a stage for Garth Walker, Wout de Vringer and Ben Faydherbe, Etienne Mineur, André Baldinger, Wang Xu, Leonardo Sonnoli, István Orosz, Detlef Fiedler and Daniela Haufe (Cyan). Two sessions of four lectures, interspersed with culinary treats. There was a good turnout, with a large contingent of students. Toppan Printing Co. has an impressive Printing Museum, with all the trimmings. This sponsor also accommodated an exhibition of 72 contemporary posters by AGI members. These were both presented in miniature in a beautiful portfolio and recorded on a disc, a precious souvenir. There followed a delicate, but lavish Japanese meal, inundated with saki and wonderful wine. The dinner was ritually *'opened'* with the opening of the big saki barrel. Kakujo Nakamura gave an impressive concert on his antique lute, the exotic strains delighting the ears of the visitors.

It was a really early start to catch the 08:03 Shinkansen from Tokyo Station. We swished past an incidentally visible Mt Fuji to Kyoto, where coaches took us straight to Seika University. A student guard of honour ensured that the visitors were ushered unerringly to the auditorium, where a former Korean Minister of Culture held a philosophical speech on making choices in the creative process. After lunch on campus there were demonstrations on such subjects as *'Wrapping Japanese style'* and making woodcuts. Wisdom, aesthetics and skill. On this day, too, there was a big turnout of enthusiastic students. The lovely Enryakuji temple complex is situated several hairpin bends above Kyoto, at the summit of Mt Hiei. Those AGI members lost to us forever were commemorated in a solemn Buddhist service. Slightly lower down the mountain face is the villa, Eizankakuji, which also belongs to Seika University. Here, eight members held mini presentations and there was dancing from the geishas who were to provide charming company at the sumptuous buffet... Asaba Katsumi gave out a beautiful AGI ToKyoTo shawl. The end of a long, long day.

29 September was Kyoto sightseeing day. Due to the hot summer, there was, as yet, no sign of any red autumn finery adorning the trees. The famous Ryoanji temple with its raked rock garden and the Ginkakuji temple, set in stunning gardens, were the highlight of the morning programme. A delicate lunch (*'low to the ground'*) in a chic restaurant was followed by optional visits to various temple complexes and museums. Dinner under your own steam: we, ourselves, ended up in a tiny local restaurant, after which three generations of owners warmly waved us goodbye.

The following morning was reserved for the general assembly. Various changes to the international board. At the highest level: Laurence Madrelle handed over the chairmanship to Jelle van der Toorn Vrijthoff. Resounding applause and some nice words. The new secretary general George Hardie and treasurer Stephan Bundi succeeded Niklaus Troxler and Jelle van der Toorn. The progress of this book was reported on and the Amsterdammer Hans Wolbers showed a short film spontaneously shot in Tokyo as promotion for the 2007 congress in Amsterdam, on the theme of *'Unknown Land'*.

The Shinkansen was again entrusted with the task of transporting us to Tokyo. Then just enough time to don our smart suits and swanky dresses for a grand dinner on the 51st floor of the Mori Tower in Roppongi Hills. This was graced by a thundering performance on the enormous Taiko drums, by maestro Hayashi Eitetsu and his two accompanists. A brief attempt to make use of the dance floor was followed by hugs and kisses and the sayonara: *'See you in Holland!'*

Admitted 2000:
Birnbach, heribert
Bose, günter karl
Deuchars, marion
Fanelli, sara
Ferrer Soria, isidro
Fiedler, detlef
Gassner, reinhard
Hasting, julia
Haufe, daniela
Holland, brad
Ilic, mirko
Kusoffsky, björn
Mabry, michael
Maeda, john •*
Martín, pablo
McGuire, richard •*
Millot, philippe
Mineur, étienne
Moser, peter
Shaohua, chen
Sonnoli, leonardo
Sterling, jennifer •
Stolk, swip
Surkov, yuri
Wang, xu
Woodtli, martin

Admitted 2001:
Abedini, reza
Appleton, robert
Blechman, nicholas
Bundi, stephan
Ebina, tatsuo
Fong, karin
Frost, vince
Gorkin, baruch •
Guarnaccia, steven
Haghighi, ebrahim
Hara, kenya
Kitagawa, issay
Massin, robert
Nagatomo, keisuke
Neale, paul
Sawada, yasuhiro
Shiva, ghobad
Stevens, andy
Sugisaki, shinnoske

Admitted 2002:
Baldinger, andré
Bielenberg, john
Faydherbe, ben
Kisman, max
Lau, freeman
Meshki, saed
Palotai, gábor
Vringer, wout de
Wagenbreth, henning
Walker, garth
Wang, yuefei
Wolbers, hans

Admitted 2003:
Alessandri, cordula
Brade, helmut
Carson, david •
Cox, paul
Davis, paul
Feseke, dieter
Lepetitdidier, michel
Matsushita, kei
Oehler, justus
Orosz, istván
Pesce, giorgio
Reichert, hans dieter
Schmidt, gerwin
Song, xiewei •
Vetta, pierpaolo

Admitted 2004:
Arvanitis, dimitris
Ashton, andrew
Barber, hans-georg
Cao, fang
Dinetz, bob
Dressen, markus
Hickmann, fons
Li, tommy
Magallanes, alejandro
Muir, hamish
Myerscough, morag
Olyff, clotilde
Porter, mark
Wang, min
Warren-Fisher, russell
Wong, stanley
Yu, lu
Zhao, jian

Admitted 2005:
Curchod, ronald
He, jianping
Knip, rené
Lippa, domenic
Pearce, harry
Sahre, paul
Tassinari, paolo
Thomas, patrick

Admitted 2006:
Bi, xuefeng
Bilak, peter
Brook, tony
Dijk, bob van
Farkas, kiko
Jiang, hua
Kasai, kaoru
Kopf, elisabeth
Lu, jingren
Pidgeon, david
Tachibana, fumio
Yount, danny
Yu, garson

• no work submitted
** no longer member of AGI*

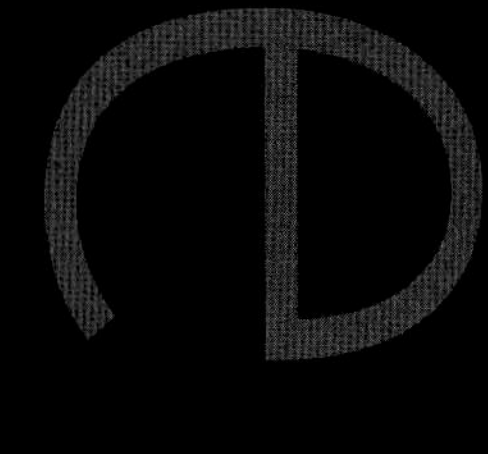

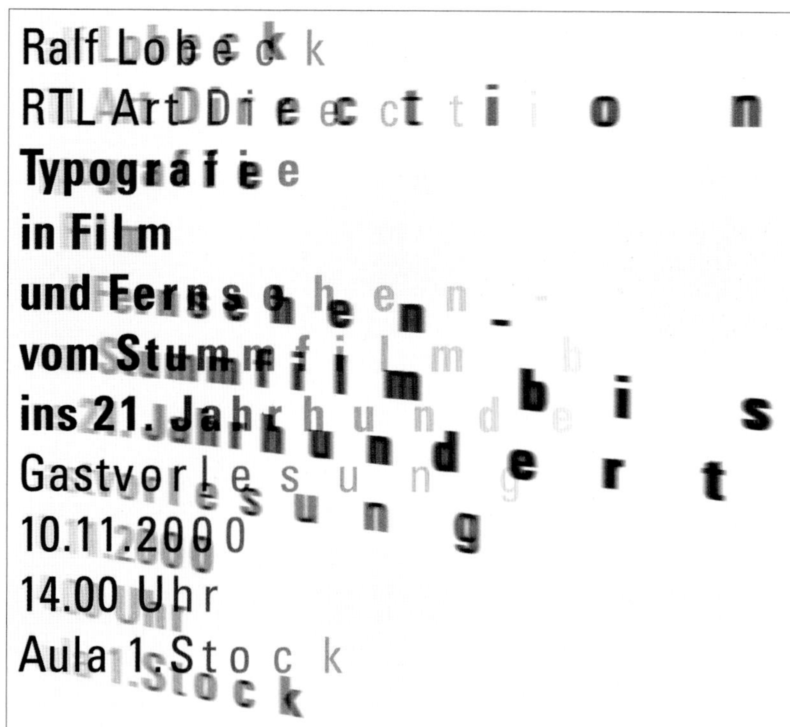

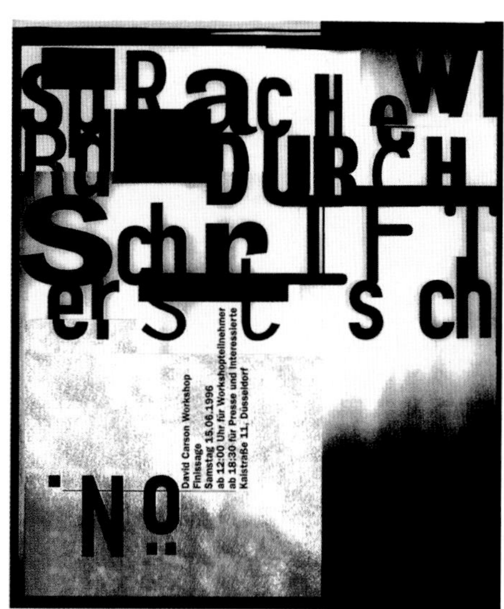

Heribert Birnbach [Germany]

1956– born in Bad Godesberg
Admitted to AGI, 2000

Heribert Birnbach started his studies in political science, history and psychology at the University of Bonn, but turned then to visual communications at the FH Düsseldorf. There he took a postgraduate degree in 1982 and afterwards worked for several years as an employee and later as a freelancer for advertising agencies in Düsseldorf and Cologne. He started his own design office in 1988, working in the fields of corporate communication and corporate design, poster design and advertising.

He has received numerous national and international awards, including: Art Directors Club Deutschland, Grafik Design Deutschland, Typografie Deutschland, Red Dot Award for excellence, The 100 Best Posters and several awards from the Type Directors Club New York. His posters feature in the collections of several German museums. Since 1995 Heribert Birnbach has been professor of graphic design and typography at the University of Wuppertal. In winter 2005–2006 he moved his studio to Bad Godesberg. He is a passionate pilot and enjoys open water diving.

Brochure design for **Bonner Sommer**, a culture festival, 1995.

Poster for a lecture about **typography in film and TV** at Bergische Universität Wuppertal, 2001.

Poster for the opening of the **David Carson Workshop** in Düsseldorf, 1996.

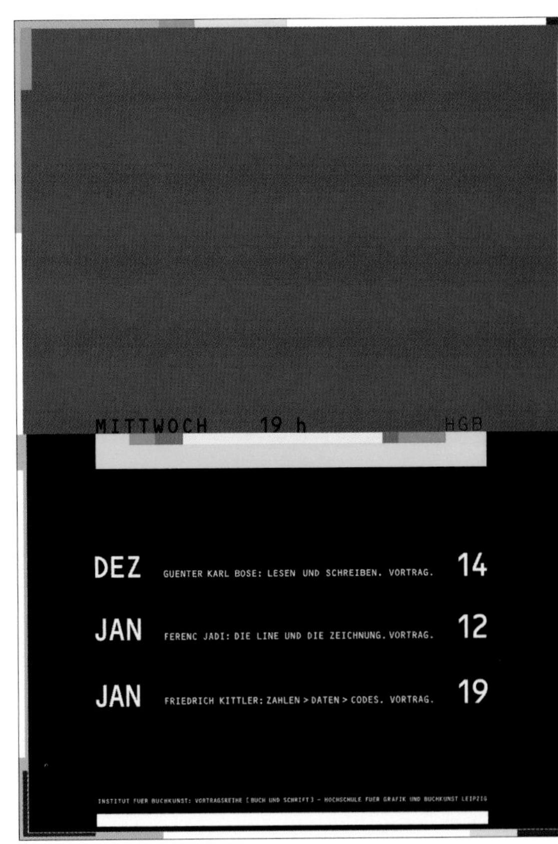

Günter Karl Bose [Germany]

Oulipo, poster, 2003.

Musique concrète, poster, 1998.

Vorträge Institut für Buchkunst, poster, 1998.

1951– born in Debstedt
Admitted to AGI, 2000

He studied German studies, art history and politics at the University of Freiburg, Germany (1970–76), before becoming a publisher in Berlin (1979–96), at Brinkmann & Bose. From 1993 he became professor of typography at the Hochschule für Grafik und Buchkunst, Leipzig, and since 1998 he has been head of the school's Typography Department and Institute for Book Design.
He has owned LMN-Studio in Berlin since 2000.
He lives and works in Berlin and Leipzig as a graphic designer, collector of photography and typography.

Bose is a consultant for Deutsche Oper Berlin, musica viva (Bayerischer Rundfunk), Kunststiftung NRW, Literaturhaus Berlin, Kleist-Museum and Berliner Festspiele.
Selected bibliography: Plakate + andere Drucksachen für musica viva (Munich: Bayerischer Rundfunk, 2005); *Area: 100 Graphic Designers* (New York & London: Phaidon, 2003); *IDEA Magazine* 292 (Tokyo, 2002).
Selected exhibitions: 'Text als Bild', Hamburger Bahnhof, Berlin, 2006; 'Plakate + andere Drucksachen', Munich, 2005; 'Summit. The Best Posters at the End of the 20th Century', PAN Kunstforum, Emmerich, Germany, 2003.

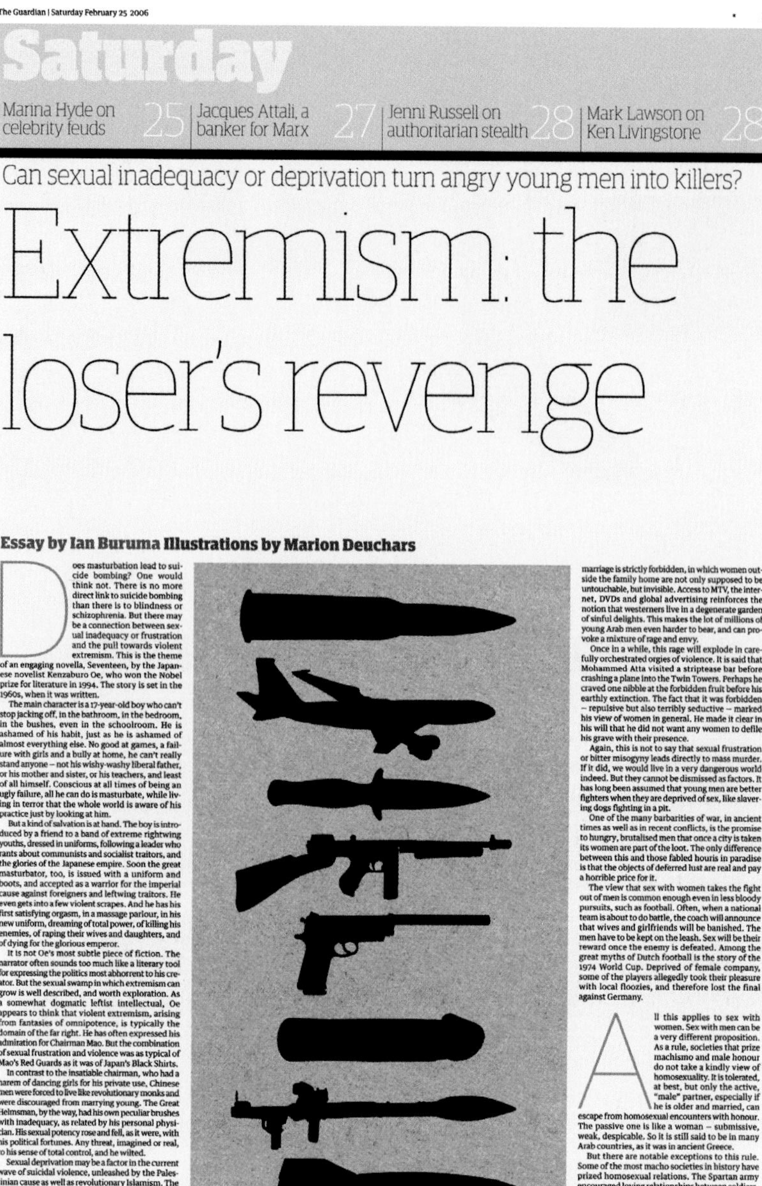

The Guardian | Saturday February 25 2006 23

Saturday

Marina Hyde on celebrity feuds 25 | Jacques Attali, a banker for Marx 27 | Jenni Russell on authoritarian stealth 28 | Mark Lawson on Ken Livingstone 28

Can sexual inadequacy or deprivation turn angry young men into killers?

Extremism: the loser's revenge

Essay by Ian Buruma Illustrations by Marion Deuchars

Does masturbation lead to suicide bombing? One would think not. There is no more direct link to suicide bombing than there is to blindness or schizophrenia. But there may be a connection between sexual inadequacy or frustration and the pull towards violent extremism. This is the theme of an engaging novella, Seventeen, by the Japanese novelist Kenzaburo Oe, who won the Nobel prize for literature in 1994. The story is set in the 1960s, when it was written.

The main character is a 17-year-old boy who can't stop jacking off, in the bathroom, in the bedroom, in the bushes, even in the schoolroom. He is ashamed of his habit, just as he is ashamed of almost everything else. No good at games, a failure with girls and a bully at home, he can't really stand anyone – not his wishy-washy liberal father, or his mother and sister, or his teachers, and least of all himself. Conscious at all times of being an ugly failure, all he can do is masturbate, while living in terror that the whole world is aware of his practice just by looking at him.

But a kind of salvation is at hand. The boy is introduced by a friend to a band of extreme rightwing youths, dressed in uniforms, following a leader who rants about communists and socialist traitors, and the glories of the Japanese empire. Soon the great masturbator, too, is issued with a uniform and boots, and accepted as a warrior for the imperial cause against foreigners and leftwing traitors. He even gets into a few violent scrapes. And he has his first satisfying orgasm, in a massage parlour, in his new uniform, dreaming of total power, of killing his enemies, of raping their wives and daughters, and of dying for the glorious emperor.

It is not Oe's most subtle piece of fiction. The narrator often sounds too much like a literary tool for expressing the politics most abhorrent to his creator. But the sexual swamp in which extremism can grow is well described, and worth exploration. As a somewhat dogmatic leftist intellectual, Oe appears to think that violent extremism, arising from fantasies of omnipotence, is typically the domain of the far right. He has often expressed his admiration for Chairman Mao. But the combination of sexual frustration and violence was as typical of Mao's Red Guards as it was of Japan's Black Shirts.

In contrast to the insatiable chairman, who had a harem of dancing girls for his private use, Chinese men were forced to live like revolutionary monks and were discouraged from marrying young. The Great Helmsman, by the way, had his own peculiar brushes with inadequacy, as related by his personal physician. His sexual potency rose and fell, as it were, with his political fortunes. Any threat, imagined or real, to his sense of total control, and he wilted.

Sexual deprivation may be a factor in the current wave of suicidal violence, unleashed by the Palestinian cause as well as revolutionary Islamism. The tantalising prospect of having one's pick of the loveliest virgins in paradise is deliberately dangled in front of young men trained for violent death. And even those who are not trained to kill and die often live in authoritarian societies in which sex before marriage is strictly forbidden, in which women outside the family home are not only supposed to be untouchable, but invisible. Access to MTV, the internet, DVDs and global advertising reinforces the notion that westerners live in a degenerate garden of sinful delights. This makes the lot of millions of young Arab men even harder to bear, and can provoke a mixture of rage and envy.

Once in a while, this rage will explode in carefully orchestrated orgies of violence. It is said that Mohammed Atta visited a striptease bar before crashing a plane into the Twin Towers. Perhaps he craved one nibble at the forbidden fruit before his earthly extinction. The fact that it was forbidden – repulsive but also terribly seductive – marked his view of women in general. He made it clear in his will that he did not want any women to defile his grave with their presence.

Again, this is not to say that sexual frustration or bitter misogyny leads directly to mass murder. If it did, we would live in a very dangerous world indeed. But they cannot be dismissed as factors. It has long been assumed that young men are better fighters when they are deprived of sex, like slavering dogs fighting in a pit.

One of the many barbarities of war, in ancient times as well as in recent conflicts, is the promise to hungry, brutalised men that once a city is taken its women are part of the loot. The only difference between this and those fabled houris in paradise is that the objects of deferred lust are real and pay a horrible price for it.

The view that sex with women takes the fight out of men is common enough even in less bloody pursuits, such as football. Often, when a national team is about to do battle, the coach will announce that wives and girlfriends will be banished. The men have to be kept on the leash. Sex will be their reward once the enemy is defeated. Among the great myths of Dutch football is the story of the 1974 World Cup. Deprived of female company, some of the players allegedly took their pleasure with local floozies, and therefore lost the final against Germany.

All this applies to sex with women. Sex with men can be a very different proposition. As a rule, societies that prize machismo and male honour do not take a kindly view of homosexuality. It is tolerated, at best, but only the active, "male" partner, especially if he is older and married, can escape from homosexual encounters with honour. The passive one is like a woman – submissive, weak, despicable. So it is still said to be in many Arab countries, as it was in ancient Greece.

But there are notable exceptions to this rule. Some of the most macho societies in history have prized homosexual relations. The Spartan army encouraged loving relationships between soldiers, as it would foster loyalty and courage. Samurai in feudal Japan had a similar attitude. Sex with women was fine, as far as it went, which was to produce children. But honour and nobility were to be found only in relations between men. » page 24

Marion Deuchars [UK]

1965– born in Falkirk, Scotland
Admitted to AGI, 2000

Marion Deuchars is a graphic artist living and working in London. She graduated from the Royal College of Art in 1989. Deuchars has a distinct graphic language that utilizes everthing from pencils and paint to photography and Photoshop. Her work has been described as having a 'deeply attuned spatial Gestalt'. Her strengths are to be able to visually articulate a broad range of subjects and clients with her distinctive artworks.

Her international clients are many and varied, from FIA Formula One, Levi's, Volkswagen, Adidas, Planeta Spain, *The Guardian*, The British Council, Royal Mail, The Barbican, *Harpers* NY, Orange to *Time* Magazine. Recent projects include re-packaging the book covers of classic novelist George Orwell, producing the Design and Art Directors Annual Report (which involved handwriting over 6,000 words of text), to being involved in 'UK in NY', an exhibition of 100 British examples of design excellence. Her Cuba reportage project, recently published in *The Independent*, is part of a larger personal project producing drawings, paintings, photography and writing based on her travels in Cuba and South America.

Hans Jonas: Recuerdos, book cover, Losada.

Extremism, illustration for *The Guardian*.

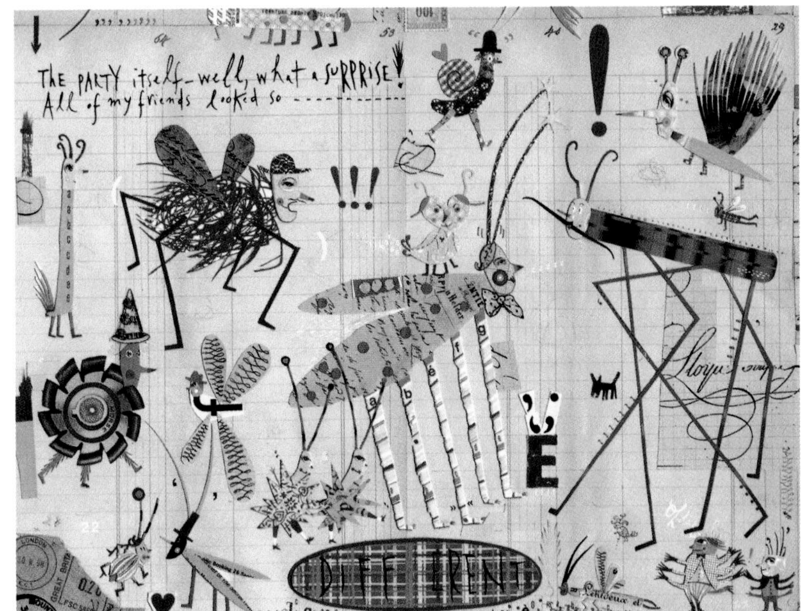

Sara Fanelli [UK]

Muriel Spark: *The Snobs*, book cover, Penguin.

Oisive Jeunesse, personal piece inspired by Rimbaud.

'The Insects' Party' from *Dear Diary*, written and illustrated by Sara Fanelli, Walker Books, 2000.

1969– born in Florence, Italy
Admitted to AGI, 2000

Sara Fanelli came to London to study art and has been working there as a freelance illustrator ever since graduating from the Royal College of Art in 1995. She has worked for a diverse range of clients internationally, dividing her time between general illustration work, books and self-generated projects. Her clients include: *The New Yorker*, Penguin Books, Faber and Faber, Tate Modern, Tate Britain, BBC Worldwide, Ron Arad, the *New York Times* and the Royal Mail. She has also written and illustrated a number of children's books.

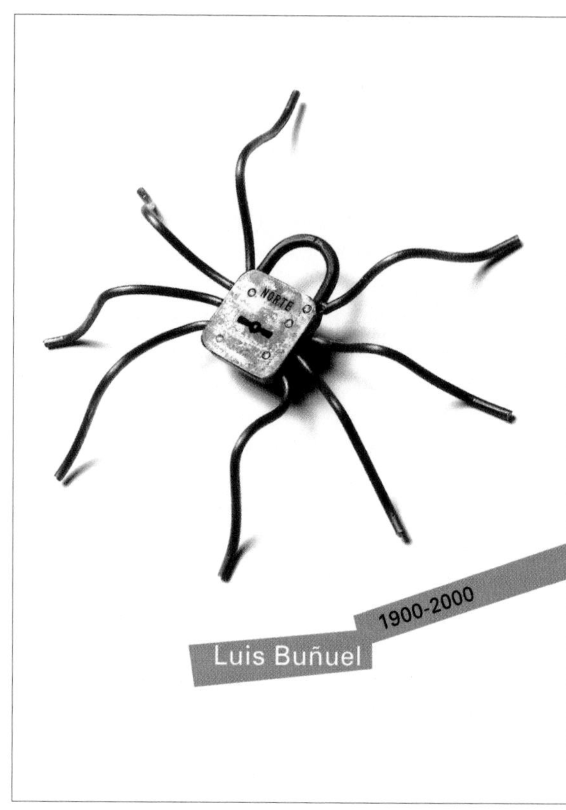

Isidro Ferrer Soria [Spain]

1963– born in Madrid
Admitted to AGI, 2000

Ferrer has qualifications in dramatic arts and scenography, and studied mime and pantomime at Jacques Lecoq's school in Paris. In 1989, he worked at the studio of the graphic designer Peret in Barcelona. After spending time in Zaragoza and Valencia, where he made storyboards for an animated series, he established his own studio in Huesca in 1996. He combines his work as a graphic designer with intense work in the field of illustration, creating comics, animations for television, and publishing over 20 books, some for children, some unclassifiable.

He has won various international awards for his work as a graphic designer and illustrator and his work has been the subject of solo exhibitions in Madrid, Gijon, Lisbon, Rouen, Rijeka, Bogota, Toulouse, Quito, Turin, Paris and Mexico City.

12th Spanish National Design Awards, poster, 2002.

Poster for the events celebrating the centenary of **Luis Buñuel**, 2000.

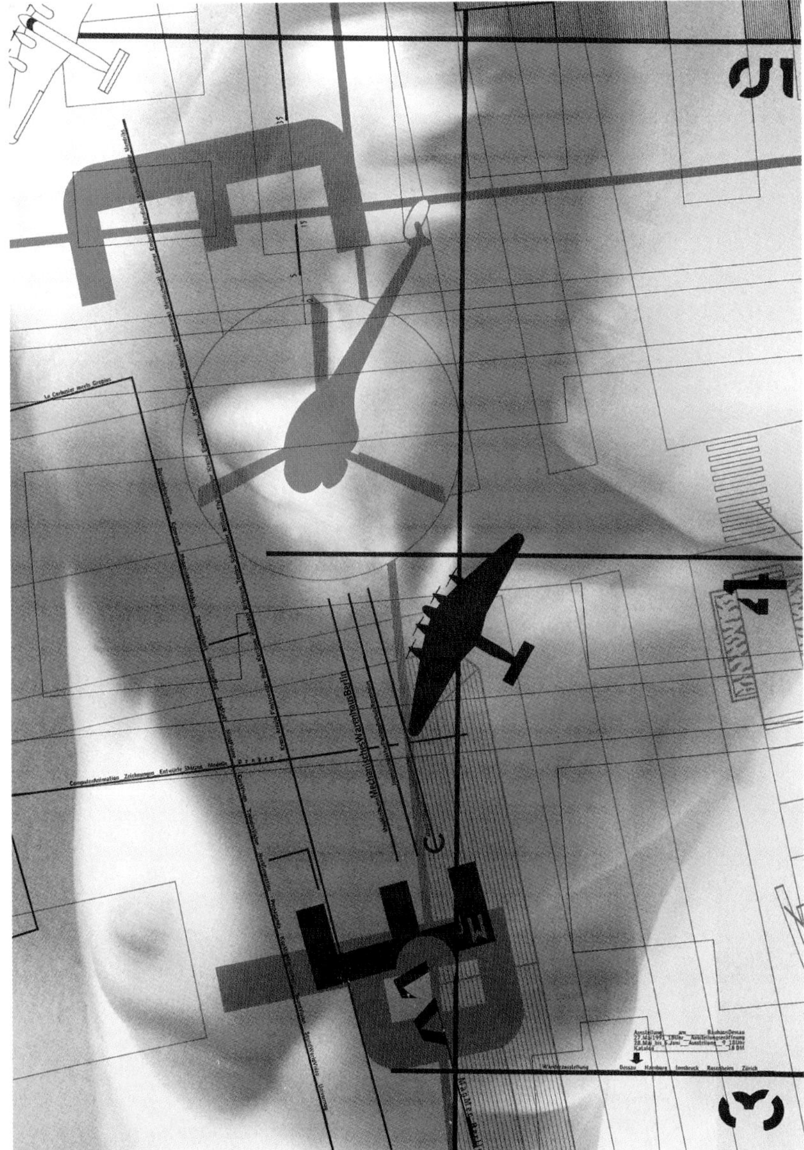

mag mec berlin, poster for an exhibition on futuristic department stores, at the Dessau Bauhaus, created by students of the Rosenheim design school in Bavaria, 1992. Offset print, three colours.

Each day brings everyone the opportunity to refuse, 1991. Anti-war poster, made in reaction to the first Gulf War. Offset print, two colours.

Poster for the 15th anniversary of **Friends of Good Music Berlin**, 1998. Offset print, three colours.

Detlef Fiedler [Germany]

1955– born in Schönebeck
Admitted to AGI, 2000

Detlef Fiedler studied architecture in Weimar. After his studies he worked as a gardener and later as a garden architect. He moved to East Berlin in 1987 and worked as a graphic designer at the advertising agency DEWAG. In 1989 he and four other young designers founded Grappa, the first graphic design group in the GDR. In 1992 he and Daniela Haufe left the group to found Cyan. Together with one to four other designers they create graphic design and corporate identity programmes exclusively for cultural clients such as the Bauhaus Dessau, the State Opera Berlin, the House of World Cultures and various galleries.

From 1991 to 1996 he was co-editor of the critical design magazine *form+zweck* (form+purpose). As a member of the dance company Toula Limnaios he created several films and videos that were projected on stage. From 1996 to 2006 he taught as a professor of graphic design together with Daniela Haufe at the Academy of Visual Arts, Leipzig. He has been invited to exhibit his work and to give lectures and workshops worldwide.

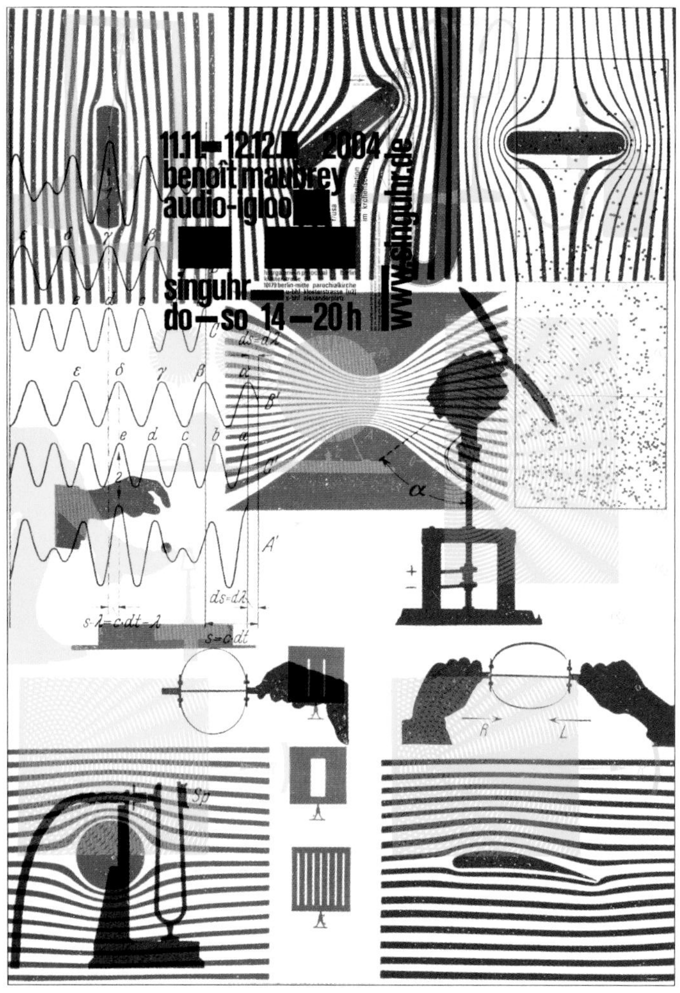

Daniela Haufe [Germany]

1966– born in Berlin
Admitted to AGI, 2000

Daniela Haufe was trained as a manual typesetter and worked as a typographer at a state publishing house in East Germany. In 1988 she started studying graphic design in Berlin, and was strongly engaged in the civil movement for more democracy. After the Wall came down she cancelled her studies and joined the group Grappa. In 1992 she and Detlef Fiedler left the group to found Cyan. Together with one to four other designers they create graphic design and corporate identity programmes exclusively for cultural clients such as the Bauhaus Dessau, the State Opera Berlin, the House of World Cultures and various galleries.

From 1991 to 1995 she was co-editor of the critical design magazine *form+zweck* (form+purpose). As a member of the dance company Toula Limnaios she created several films and videos that were projected on stage. From 1996 to 2006 she taught as a professor of graphic design, together with Detlef Fiedler, at the Academy of Visual Arts, Leipzig. She has been invited to exhibit her work and to give lectures and workshops worldwide.

Singuhr: Sound Gallery at the Parochial Church, Berlin, one of a series of four events posters, 2004. Silkscreen print, black and three fluorescent colours.

One of a series of about 50 event posters designed between 1991 and 1998 for the **Dessau Bauhaus**, 1993. Offset print, two colours.

Better Days, poster for a piece by the dance company Toula Limnaios, 2003. Offset print, two colours.

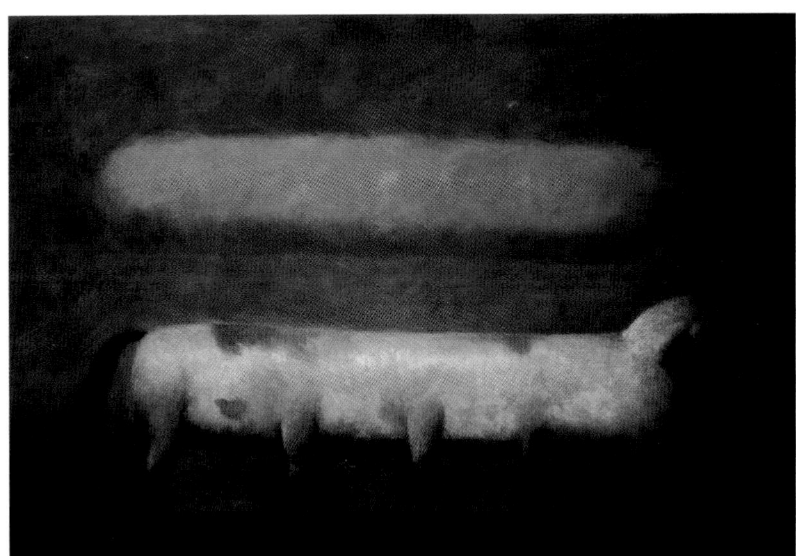

Romeo & Juliet.

Long Horse.

Have Suitcase, Will Travel.

Brad Holland [USA]

1943– born in Fremont, Ohio
Admitted to AGI, 2000

Brad Holland is a self-taught artist and writer and a member of the Society of Illustrators' Hall of Fame. His work has appeared in *Time*, *Vanity Fair*, *The New Yorker*, *The New York Times*, *The Wall Street Journal* and many other international publications. He has received gold medals from the New York Art Directors Club, the Society of Illustrators and the Society of Publication Designers. His recent exhibitions include a 1999 retrospective at the Museé des Beaux-Arts in Clermont-Ferrand, France and a 2005 one-man exhibition at the Torino Atrium, Turin, Italy.

Holland has painted CD covers for Ray Charles, Stevie Ray Vaughn and Billy Joel, and has written articles for *The Atlantic Monthly*, *Texas Monthly*, *Communication Arts Magazine* and other publications. In 1999, he co-founded the Illustrators' Conference (now ICON), and in 2000 he co-founded the Illustrators' Partnership of America, a member of the International Federation of Reproduction Rights Organizations (IFRRO). He lectures internationally, most recently at the AGIdeas Conference in Melbourne, Australia, the Turin International Book Fair and the a! Design Conference in Acapulco, Mexico. In 2006 he testified in defence of US Copyright Law before both houses of the United States Congress.

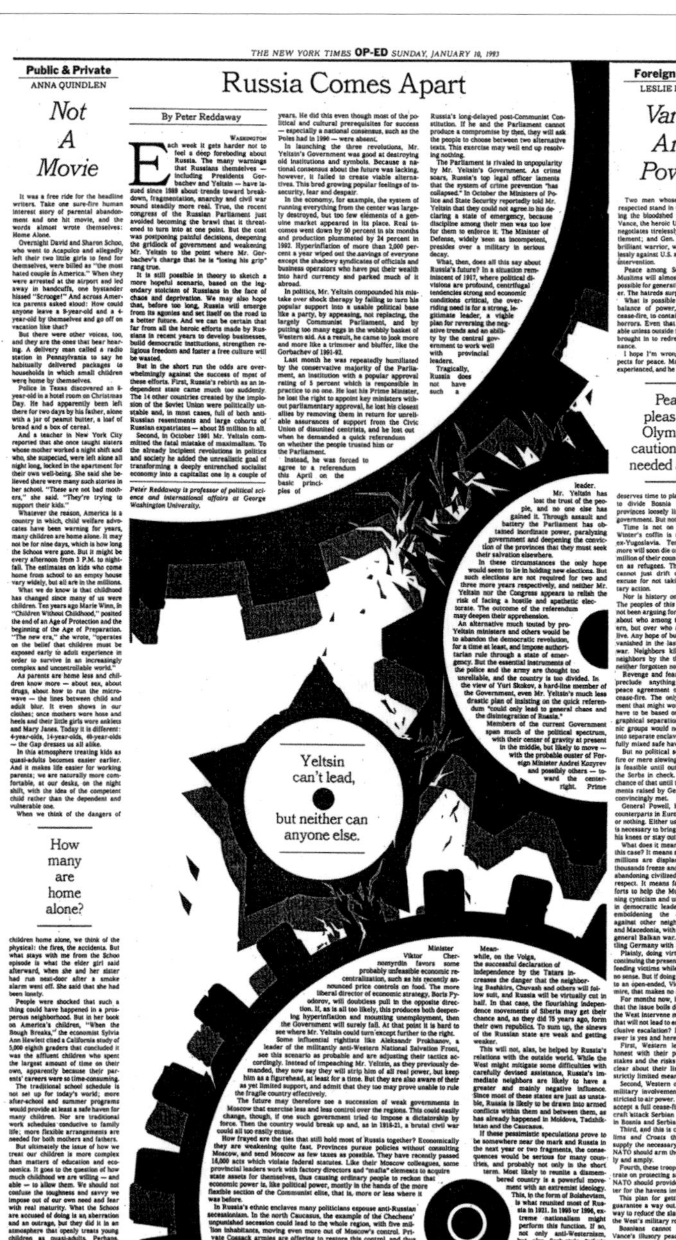

THE NEW YORK TIMES OP-ED SUNDAY, JANUARY 10, 1993 23

Public & Private
ANNA QUINDLEN

Not A Movie

Russia Comes Apart

By Peter Reddaway

Foreign Affairs
LESLIE H. GELB

Vance And Powell

Peace pleas and Olympian caution block needed action.

Yeltsin can't lead, but neither can anyone else.

How many are home alone?

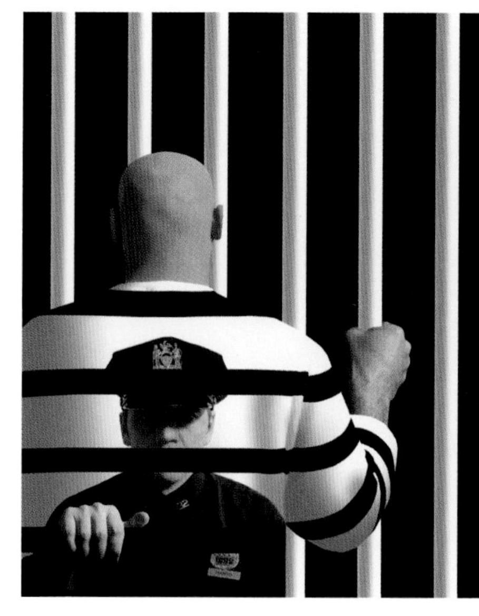

Mirko Ilic [USA]

1956– born in Bijeljina, Bosnia
Admitted to AGI, 2000

In Europe Mirko Ilic has illustrated and art-directed posters, record covers and comics.He arrived in the USA in 1986 and was commissioned as illustrator for many major magazines and newspapers. In 1991 he became art director at *Time* magazine, in charge of the International edition. A year later he became art director of *New York Times* Op-Ed pages. In 1995 Mirko Ilic Corp. was established, a graphic design and 3-D computer graphics and motion picture title studio. Ilic has received awards from the Society of Illustrators, the Society of Publication Designers, the NY ADC, *International Design* magazine, the Society of Newspaper Design, and others. He was vice-president of AIGA New York, 1994–95. Ilic has taught advanced design classes at Cooper Union with Milton Glaser, and teaches masters degree classes in illustration at the School of Visual Arts. He is the co-author of the books *Genius Moves: 100 Icons of Graphic Design* and *Handlettering in the Digital Age* (with Steven Heller), and *The Design of Dissent* (with Milton Glaser), and is currently co-authoring the book *Anatomy of Design* with Steven Heller.

Russia Comes Apart, *New York Times*, 1992. Art director, designer, illustrator: Mirko Ilic.

Impersonating an Officer, *New York Times Book Review*, 2000. Art director: Steve Heller, illustrator: Mirko Ilic.

The Design of Dissent by Milton Glaser and Mirko Ilic, cover design, 2005.

Making Differences, cultural and artistic programme in conjunction with Stockholm International Forum 2004: Preventing Genocide. Art direction and identity, 2004. Pictured: *Making Differences* poster. Photo by Sølve Sundsbø.

Hästens, high-quality bed manufacturer. Design programme; corporate identity, flagship store, retail environment, bed accessories, 2001–ongoing. Project partner: Thomas Eriksson Architects. Pictured: flagship store.

Moderna Museet, design programme; signage, objects for bookshop, printed material, 2004. Project Partner: Teark, Greger Ulf Nilson/Henrik Nygren. Pictured: museum exterior signage.

Bjorn Kusoffsky [Sweden]

1965– born in Stockholm
Admitted to AGI, 2000

Kusoffsky studied at Beckmans School of Design, Stockholm. In 1998 he and Thomas Eriksson founded Stockholm Design Lab, a design company operating in the global marketplace. The concept and goal of SDL is to be a major platform for the creation of quality design that matters and makes a difference. SDL's work includes comprehensive design projects such as corporate identities, retail design, product design, range strategy, packaging solutions, architecture, graphic design and film. *Clients include:* IKEA, SAS Scandinavian Airlines, Askul, Swedish Television, Moderna Museet and Iittala. Member of the Society for Swedish Art. *Collections represented:* the National Museum of Art, Stockholm. *Teaching/lecturing:* Beckmans School of Design, Konstfack, University of Arts, Crafts and Design, HDK, Berghs School of Communication, Royal Institute of Technology, Kuwasawa Design School, Tokyo. *Exhibitions:* Puls Young Swedish Design, Bauhaus Archive, Berlin; Puls Young Swedish Design, Moscow; '1900–2000', National Museum of Art, Stockholm; 'Niemeyer: Modernist Cultural Heritage', Museum of Architecture, Stockholm; 'New Scandinavia', Museum für angewandte Kunst, Cologne; 'Swedish Style', Tokyo; 'Artek-Ruotsi', Helsinki; 'Design in Sweden', London. *Awards include*: 3 Golden and 3 Silver Eggs and 30 Diplomas at the Golden Egg Swedish Advertising Awards; 2 first prizes in Core Design;, 3 times Best Title Sequence, Scandinavian Trailer Award; Design Award, British D&AD.

Michael Mabry [USA]

1955– born in Niles, Michigan
Admitted to AGI, 2000

Michael received his BFA in graphic design from the University of Utah. He worked for SBG Partners as a senior designer and then started his own firm in 1981. He served on the faculty at the California College of Art and guest lectures at many universities and various designer/art directors' organizations. His work has received awards in design competitions including Communication Arts, the American Institute of Graphic Arts, the American Center for Design, Graphis, the NY ADC and the SF Society of Communicating Arts. His work is in the permanent collections of the Library of Congress, SF MoMA, the Hong Kong Heritage Museum and the Center for the Study of Political Graphics. Michael's work has featured in a solo exhibition in Osaka and a group exhibition on California Design at the Museo Fortuny, Venice. He has been included in the *International Design Magazine*'s '40 Design and Technology Innovators on the West Coast'. He was president of the SF chapter of the American Institute of Graphic Arts and on the National Board of Trustees of the American Institute of Graphic Arts. Current clients include: Columbia School of Journalism, Chronicle Books, Hewlett Packard Corporation, The Land of Nod, Lucasfilm, Martha Stewart Omnimedia, the Mellon Foundation, Netjets Europe, *The New York Times* and the Oakland Museum of California.

Stop the Arrogance, poster. Created out of frustration at President George W. Bush's utter disregard of the environment. Hong Kong International Poster Triennial, 2004.

AIGA National Headquarters Membership, poster. American Institute of Graphic Arts, 2000.

Bottle for Camper, 'useful, healthy, friendly', 2005.

Cover and spread of **Miedo** (Fear), a 16-page tabloid black-and-white newspaper that recreates Raymond Carver's eponymous poem. It was distributed for free in 12 subway stations as part of Mapapoetic, a poetry festival held in Barcelona, 2004.

Egyptian-themed cover and page of issue 6 of **TWS** (The Walking Society) magazine, 2003. TWS is published twice a year by the shoe manufacturer Camper and distributed in their shops worldwide.

Pablo Martín [Spain]

1964– born in Barcelona
Admitted to AGI, 2000

Pablo Martín studied graphic design at Eina Design School, where he has now been teaching typography for 15 years. He worked for Eskenazi & Asociados and for Vignelli Associates before setting up his own studio in 1990. In 1993 he founded Grafica. Grafica works mainly in the areas of editorial design and corporate identity, having developed projects for national and international clients such as Camper, Grupo Godó, Metalarte, Grupo Prisa, BMW, IBM, Joyco and BTicino among others.

Philippe Millot [France]

1968– born in Kampala, Uganda
Admitted to AGI, 2000

Millot studied with Rudi Meyer and Jean Widmer at the École Nationale Supérieure des Arts Décoratifs in Paris, and started his career in 1992 as an independent designer. Radio France was an early important client of his; he designed their catalogues, posters and visual identity (1993–2000). Work for Parisian Catacombs and Paris City Music Concerts followed. Book design then became his prime activity. From literature and art to politics, he designed several collections of books for CulturesFrance (Foreign Affairs French Ministry), Le Moniteur (books on architecture), Take Five, Geneva (art), Cent Pages (photography, novels and pamphlets) and the Centre Georges Pompidou.

Philippe Millot lives and works in Paris, sharing his time between teaching at the École Nationale Supérieure des Arts Décoratifs and his professional activities. After the exhibition 'La force de l'art', at the Grand Palais, Paris, a book about his book designs is forthcoming, published by F7.

Poster for the **Parisian catacombs**.

Qui je suis: La tigresse, cover of a children's book published by Paris Musées, based on a sculpture from the Musée Cernuschi.

Gilles Deleuze, book cover with a sophisticated fold. Published by the ADPF (French Foreign Affairs Ministry).

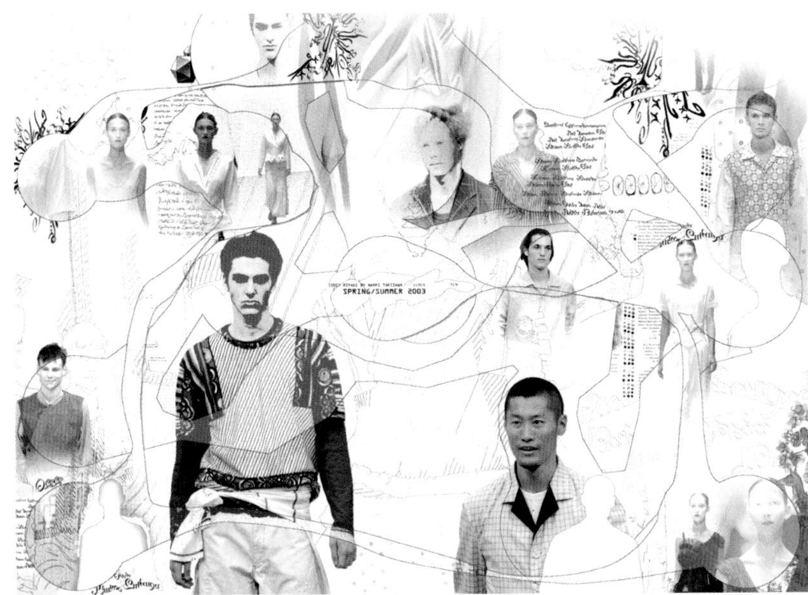

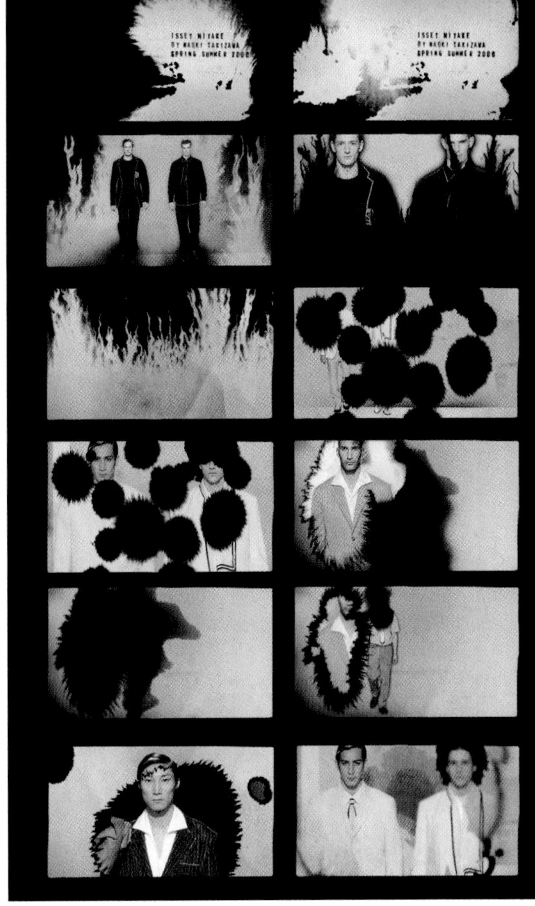

Design and art direction of the **Issey Miyake website**. The site is entirely re-designed four times a year to match the theme that inspires each new collection.

Design and art direction of **Pleats Please, A-POC** and **Issey Miyake by Naoki Takizawa** catalogues.

Étienne Mineur [France]

1968– born in Bordeaux
Admitted to AGI, 2000

Étienne graduated from the École Nationale Supérieure des Arts Décoratifs de Paris (ENSAD) in 1992 and became co-founder and art director of the multimedia company Index Plus. As an independent art director he worked for many agencies such as Hyptique, Paris and Nofrontière, Austria.
In 2001 he became co-founder and art director of Incandescence Studio. For six years he has collaborated with Japanese company Issey Miyake on the design and production of their website, as well as many more of their publishing projects.

Étienne has been a lecturer at the École Nationale Supérieure Louis Lumière (cinema, photography and sound) since September 2003. He has given workshops at Les Gobelins in Paris (multimedia, animation, sound), Beaux Arts in Rennes and Art Décoratifs in Strasbourg. He takes part in lectures at other schools and in many events around the world (China, Switzerland, USA, Austria, Mexico).

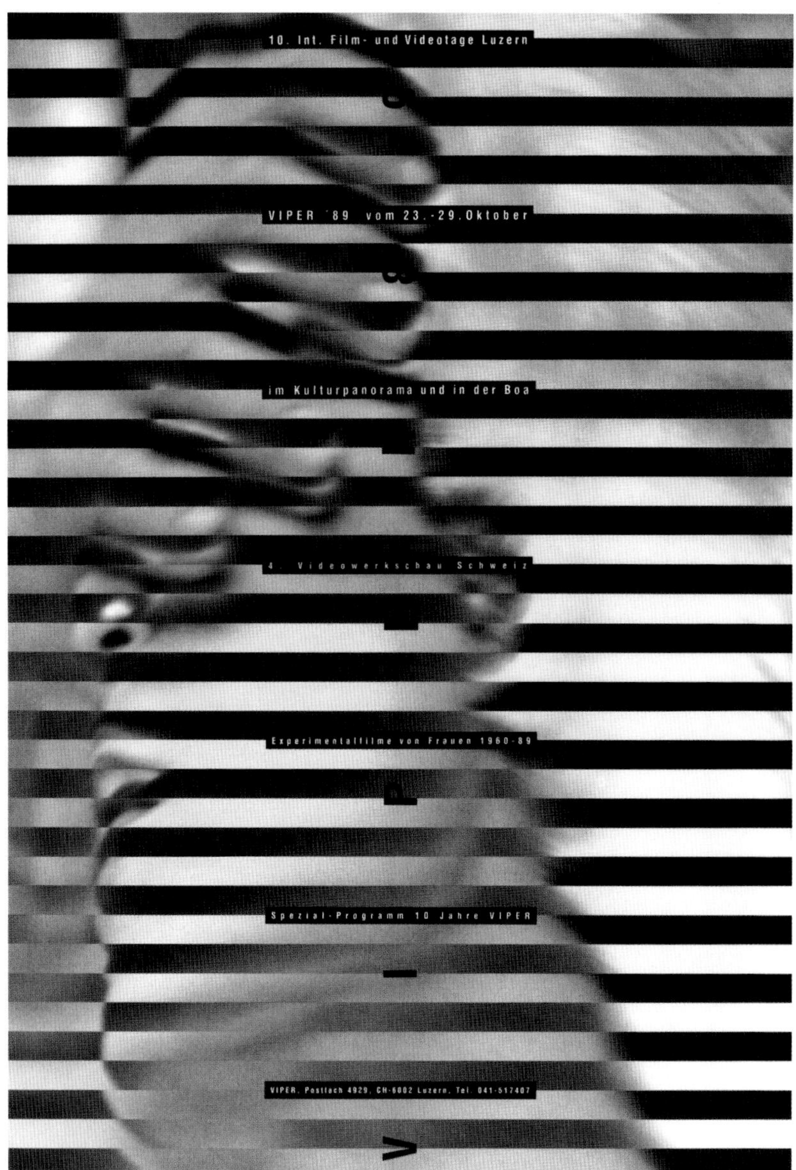

Peter Moser [Switzerland]

1962– born in Lucerne
Admitted to AGI, 2000

Peter Moser trained at the Lucerne School of Design from 1978–83. From 1989–96, he worked for VIPER, International Festival for Film, Video and New Media Lucerne. A new image and graphic concept was created. Until 1996, Peter worked alone in various studio partnerships in Zürich and Lucerne. During this time, he designed posters for the Museum of Design in Zürich. In 1996, he became a member of Velvet Creative Office in Lucerne. Velvet rapidly acquired new customers. Besides working for advertisers such as Völkl Ski and Paiste Cymbals, Peter particularly dealt with customers in the cultural sector.

From 1999, he designed a new image for the Lucerne Theatre, and in the four years that followed, he produced posters, programmes, flyers and their website. In 2004, he started working for the famous Munich Kammerspiele studio theatre, designing a series of posters covering three seasons, focusing on religion, war and society. Once a year, Velvet undertakes a journey. On site, they produce an 'instant journal', using digital cameras and computers. In 1997, for example, Velvet was in Havana, Cuba and in 2003 in Tirana, Albania, to portray the city and a renovated children's hospital. In December 2005, Velvet was in Laos to document a landmine clearance project.

Poster for **VIPER International Festival** for Film, Video and New Media, Lucerne.

Tatort, exhibition poster for the Museum of Design, Zürich, 1998.

The Ten Commandments, poster from a series for the Munich Kammerspiele, 2004.

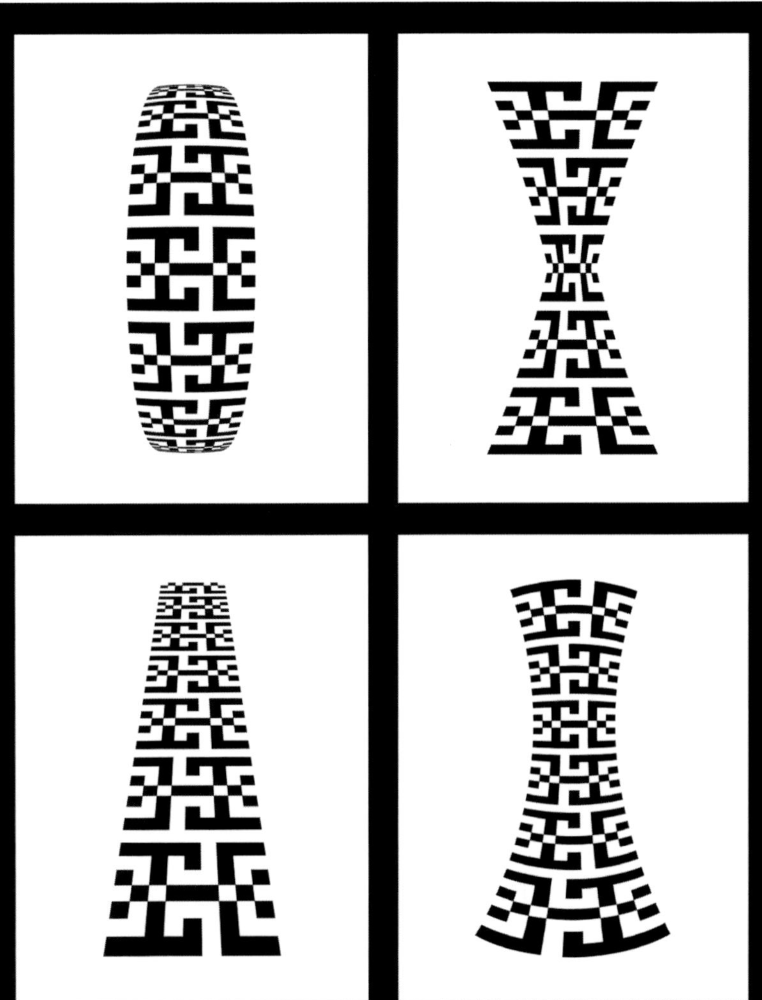

Communication International Poster Exhibition, poster, 1996. The first Chinese poster design exhibition to cross four cities: Shenzhen, Taipei, Hong Kong and Macao. 'Only communication can bring hope and light.'

Beijing 2008 Candidate City, logo, 2000. The logo deconstructs the five Olympic rings to reflect the idea of peace, cooperation, harmony and co-development.

Design Annual Book of China, promotional poster, 2004. The Design Annual Selection, which includes brand logos, advertising, graphic design and packaging design.

Chen Shaohua [China]

1954– born in Zhejiang
Admitted to AGI, 2000

Chen Shaohua is one of the most representative designers in China today. Since he enrolled at the Xi'an Fine Art Academy in 1972, he has participated and led almost all the development and reform of graphic design in modern China. As the earliest professional designer, Chen Shaohua opened the first private commercial design studio in Shenzhen in southern China. Before this career, he worked on exhibitions, advertising and movie graphics. In 1978 he entered the Central Art and Design Academy of Beijing to study traditional Chinese decorative art. After graduation he went back to Xi'an Fine Art Academy to teach and research modern graphic design, and he now trains many graphic designers, who are now the majority group in the field of modem Chinese design. As the first teacher to advocate reform of design education in China, Chen provided Beijing's Olympic Candidate City logo in 2000. He is a visiting professor at several universities and his blog is visited every day by thousands of students and designers. He also puts great effort into working for the benefit of all Chinese designers.

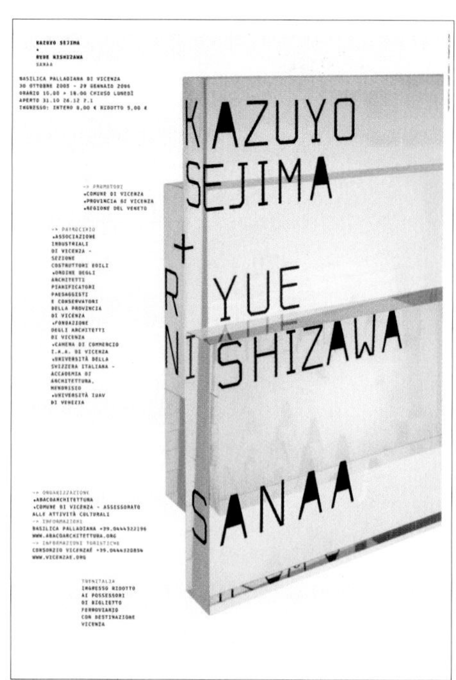

Leonardo Sonnoli [Italy]

1962– born in Trieste
Admitted to AGI, 2000

Sonnoli earned his diploma from the ISIA, Urbino, and did his professional training at the Tassinari/Vetta Studio of Trieste. He worked for the Dolcini Associati Studio from 1990 to 2001. Along with Paolo Tassinari and Pierpaolo Vetta, he founded CODEsign and became a partner in 2002. He is involved with the visual identity of companies in the private and public sectors, and with the design of cultural events and signage systems. He teaches at the IUAV in Venice and at the ISIA in Urbino, living and working between Rimini and Trieste. Along with Tassinari he is the art director of the architectural magazine *Casabella* and Electa architettura publishing house. He designed identities for the 50th Venice Art Biennale and of the Modern Art National Gallery in Rome, and is currently working for the MART Contemporary and Modern Art Museum of Trento and Rovereto. He has won silver medals at the Art Exhibition of Toyama (Japan) and the 2nd China International Poster Biennial in Hangzhou, and received honourable mentions from the 21st Compasso d'Oro/Adi Awards and the New York ADC. His work has been published in books including *Poster Collection 08: Black and White* (2003), *Area* (2005), and *Type, Image, Message* (2006).

Diritti e doveri (Rights and Duties), 1997. Offset, 2 colours + UV varnish. Poster for a conference on civic rights and duties in metropolitan areas.

Pesaro Museum, poster, 1998.

Kazuyo Sejima + Ryue Nishizawa/Sanaa, 2005. Offset, 3 colours. Poster for an exhibition in Vicenza (Italy) on the architects Kazuyo Sejima and Ryue Nishizawa.

From Left to Right and Back, 2005. Offset, 4 colours. Poster designed for an exhibition in Tehran.

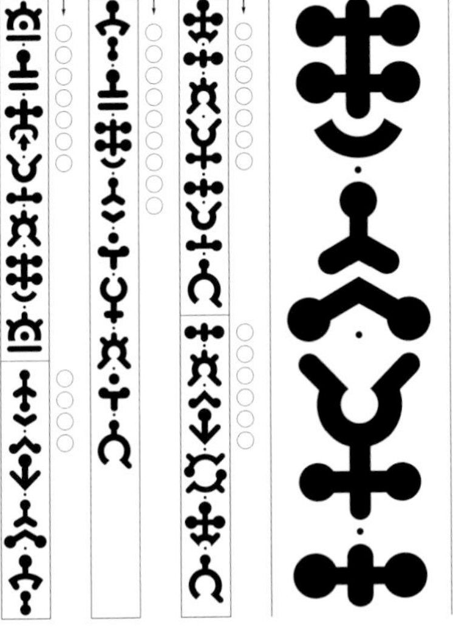
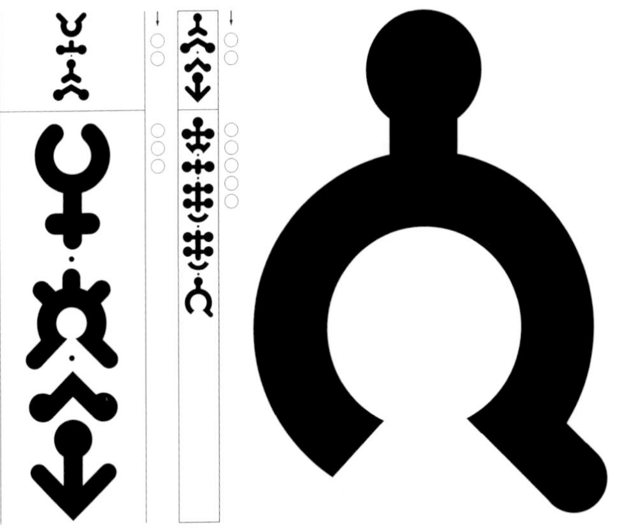
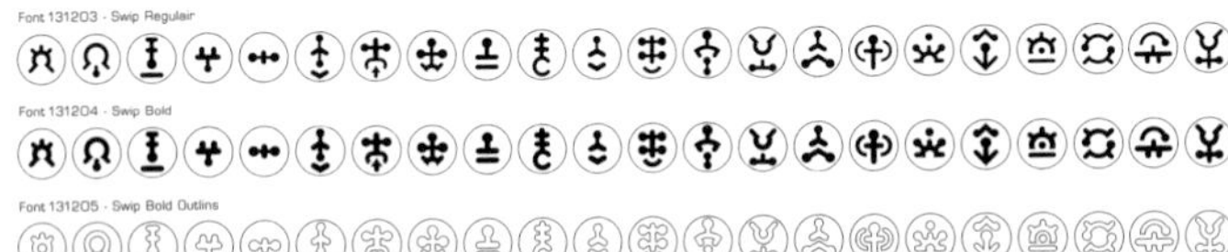

Secret Signs Code, 2003. Start of a series of publications and events all over the world.

BMW Series 1, **Anti Evil Patrol Car**, design for BMW, Germany, 2004. Presented at Palais de Tokyo, Paris. BMW Museum Munich Collection.

Swip Stolk [The Netherlands]

1944– born in Zaandam
Admitted to AGI, 2000

Swip is a self-taught designer who has run his own studio since 1965. He taught graphic design at the AKI Academy, Enschede (1974–79) and Gerrit Rietveld Academy, Amsterdam (1980–87). *Selected projects:* 1968: exhibition architecture and electronic catalogue for 'Environments' exhibition at the Museum Catharijneconvent, Utrecht. 1977–79: art director for VARA Television. 1987–2000: art director for Groninger Museum. 1998: art director of Rembrandt House Museum, Amsterdam. 2002–2006: several Code/Uncode projects. 2003: shop design for Jan Jansen Shoes. 2005: *Geluk/Happiness*, publication in cooperation with Anthon Beeke. 2006: design of rubber and steel objects.

Selected bibliography: V. Krichevski, 'Swip Stolk', in *DA! Design*, no. 4 (1995); Han Steenbruggen and Frans Haks, *Swip Stolk, Master Forever*, Groninger Museum (2000); Alain Weill, 'Radically Swip Stolk', *Graphis* 340 (2002). *Selected exhibitions:* 'Environments', Museum Catharijneconvent Utrecht, 1969; 'Television Design' Groninger Museum, 1979; 'Werkman Award', Stedelijk Museum Amsterdam, 1990; retrospective at Groninger Museum, 2000; 'Rembrandt Series, Paris Photo', Carrousel du Louvre, Paris, 2000; solo exhibition, '106 Poster Designs for Groninger Museum', Chaumont, 2003; 'Curious Wishes, BMW 1 Series, Rubber Car', Palais de Tokyo, Paris, 2004; installation, Museum Het Valkhof, Nijmegen, 2006. He also has works in many national and international museums and collections.

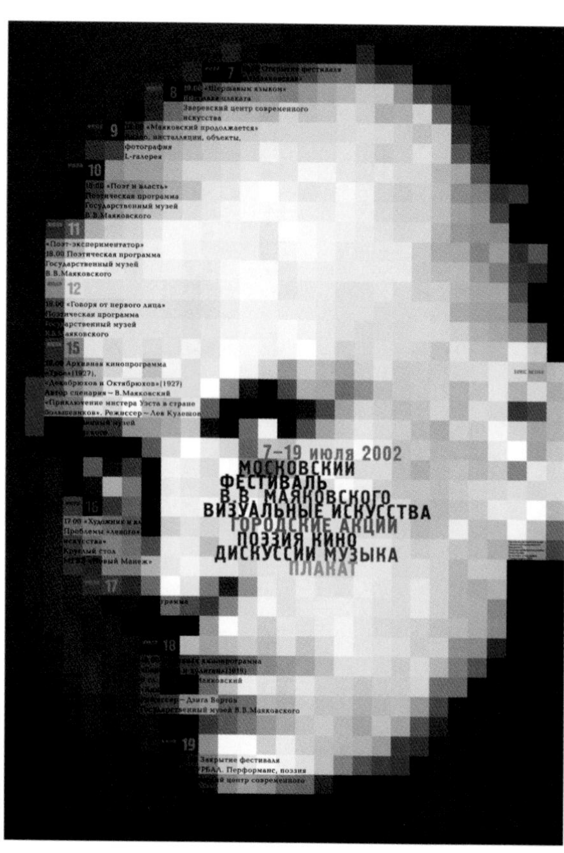

Yuri Surkov [Russia]

1961– born in Moscow
Admitted to AGI, 2000

Education: 1990: graduated from the Moscow Art College in Memory of the 1905 Uprising. 1990–91: assistant art director for *Reklama* magazine. 1992–onwards: independent designer, Suric Design. 2006: jury member, 6th International 4th Block Triennial of Eco Posters. *Teaching:* invited lecturer at High Academic School of Design, Moscow (2003–2005). *Major clients:* Fine Arts Museum of Surgut, World Wide Fund for Nature (WWF), Centre for Russian Environmental Policy, State Tretyakov Gallery, The Open Society Institute, Soros Foundation. *Projects:* 2000: 'Coexistence' poster for international poster project, Museum On The Seam, Jerusalem. 2000: 'Water for Humankind', poster for international poster project, Association pour une Banque d'Images, Paris. 1999 and 2000: Icograda World Graphic Day postcards.
Exhibitions: 'Natura List', solo exhibition, Schusev State Museum of Architecture, Moscow, 2004; 'Trj Bogatyrja', Galerie Anatome, Paris (in collaboration with Vladimir Chaika and Andrey Logvin), 2005; solo exhibition, Academy Gallery, Kharkov, 2005.
Awards: Russian Ministry of Culture award, 1998; two first prizes at the International 4th Block Triennial of Eco Posters, Kharkov, Ukraine, 1997, 2000; bronze medal at the 18th International Poster Biennale, Warsaw, 2002; Golden Bee Awards at the Moscow International Biennale of Graphic Design, 1994, 1996, 2004.

Supremus: The Clitoral Truth, poster for Swiss-Russian art project Supremus, 2003.

Exhibition poster for the **Vladimir Mayakovski Festival**, Moscow, 2002.

Coexistence, poster for international exhibition organized by the Museum On The Seam, Jerusalem, 2000.

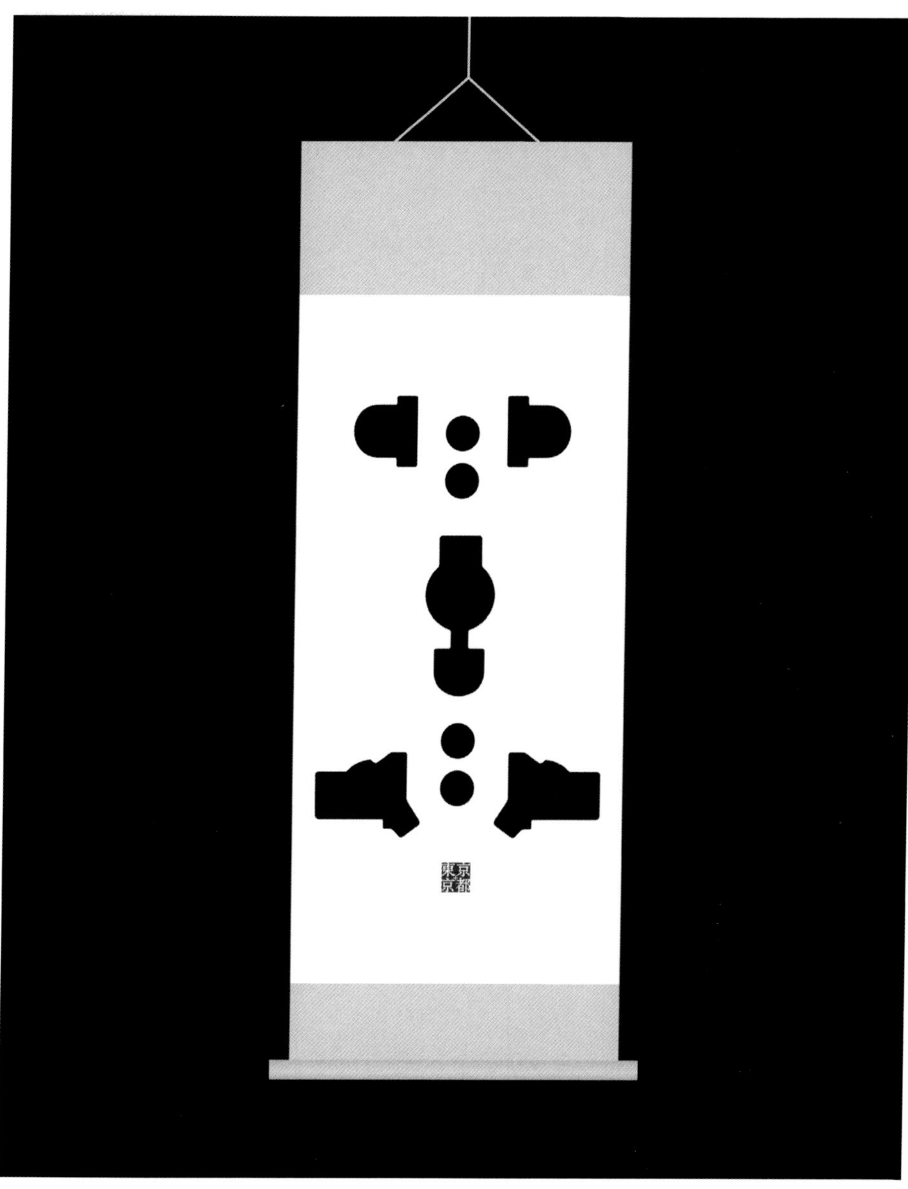

Kakejiku, a work designed for the AGI exhibition of *Kakejiku* (hanging scrolls) at the AGI Congress 2006 in Japan. The congress was held in Tokyo and Kyoto under the theme of 'TO KYO TO (Tokyo + Kyoto): Diversity of Japanese Culture'. This scroll uses the Chinese characters for Tokyo and Kyoto, expressed in the form of an electrical socket, to reflect cultural diversity, the modern and the traditional. The socket also expresses the idea of an electrical charge, a source of energy.

Xu Wang [China]

1955– born in Guangdong
Admitted to AGI, 2000

Xu Wang graduated from the Design Department of Guangzhou Academy of Fine Arts in 1979. He came to Hong Kong in 1986 and worked as a graphic designer until 1995 when he went back to Guangzhou and founded WX Design. Wang is member of the New York Art Directors Club and Tokyo TDC. He is a professor at the Design & Art College of Hunan University, and design director of Guangdong Museum of Art. Wang has received more than 100 international design awards, including the Icograda Excellence Award at the 17th International Biennale of Graphic Design, Brno; winning the Silver Medal twice in the New York Art Directors Club Annual Awards; two Golden Bee Awards at the International Biennale of Graphic Design, Moscow; and the Special Recognition Prize at the Shaw Prize International Design Competition. He has also judged at international competitions such as the 80th and 84th ADC Annual Awards, International Biennale of Graphic Design, Brno, International Competition Poster and Graphic Arts Festival of Chaumont, and Tokyo TDC Awards 2005. Wang has given lectures and speeches on many occasions, has published and designed more than 80 design books and magazines, and has been featured in various publications.

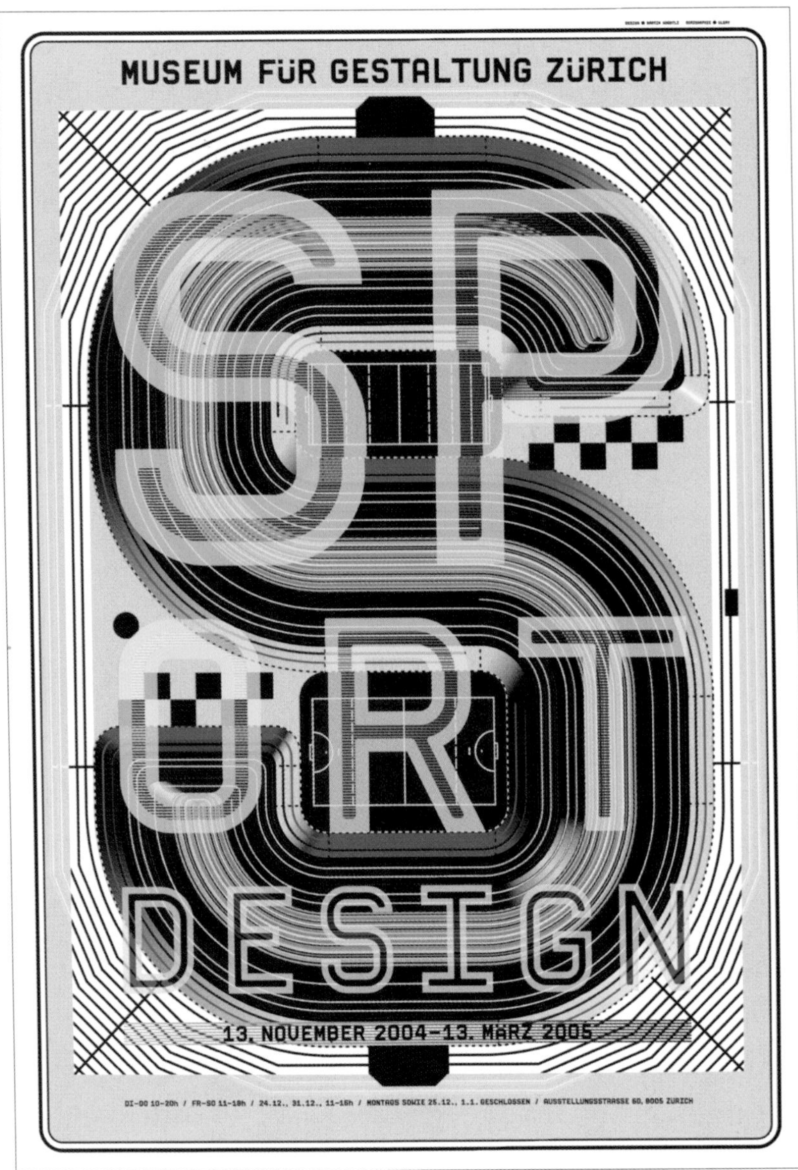

Martin Woodtli [Switzerland]

1971– born in Berne
Admitted to AGI, 2000

Woodtli studied graphic design at the Berne School of Design (1990–95), and visual communication at the Zürich Academy of Art and Design (1996–98). In 1998–99, he lived in New York and worked with Stefan Sagmeister. In 1999, he opened his own studio in Zürich and was awarded the Swiss Federal Design Prize. His works are featured in: *Print* magazine; *International Design* magazine's I.D. Forty (2000); *IDEA* 285, Tokyo (2001); *kAk* magazine, Moscow. The monograph *Woodtli* was published by Die Gestalten Verlag, Berlin in 2001.

Woodtli has taught at the School of Design, Biel, Staatlichen Akademie der Bildenden Künste, Stuttgart, and, since 2002, at the Academy of Art and Design in Lucerne. He also gives workshops at the Academy of Art and Design, Berne. *Awards include:* prize for The Most Beautiful Swiss Books and Jury Book Prize, 2005; first prize at the Chaumont Poster Festival, 2005: second prize, Swiss Bank Design awards, 2005; bronze award, Poster Triennial, Toyama, 2006.

Lichtecht, poster for the Museum für Gestaltung, Zürich, 2004. Silk-screen, four colours.

Trickraum, poster for the Museum für Gestaltung, Zürich, 2005. Silk-screen, four colours.

Sportdesign, poster for the Museum für Gestaltung, Zürich, 2004. Silk-screen, five colours.

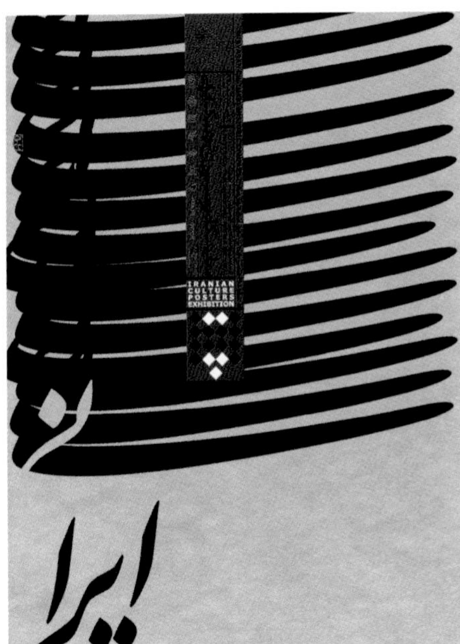

Iranian Culture Posters Exhibition, poster, offset, 2004. A minimalist use of Iranian calligraphy.

Iranian Imaginations, poster, offset, 2006. An attempt to portray a nostalgic concept of Iranian artists living abroad; the single figure was inspired by Qajar art with Iranian calligraphy.

AllOne, poster for an exhibition of selected posters by Reza Abedini, offset, 2006. Here the text and information are designed to complement the whole composition.

Reza Abedini [Iran]

1967– born in Tehran
Admitted to AGI, 2001

Abedini graduated in graphic design from Tehran School of Fine Arts (1985) and earned a BA in painting at Tehran Art University (1992). He founded Reza Abedini Studio in 1993 and has taught at Tehran University since 1996. His works have been shown internationally since 1993, and he is an art critic and editor-in-chief of *Manzar* magazine. *Awards include:* First prize for poster design, International Film Festival, Iran, 1993, 1994, 1996; Film Critics Special Award, Best Film Poster, Iran, 1994, 1996; third prize, Biennial of Iranian Graphic Design, 1999; Special Award for Creativity from the Iranian Graphic Designers Society, 1999; honourable mention, Colorado International Poster Exhibition, 2003; Union of Visual Artists' Award, Brno, 2004; second prize, Chaumont Poster Festival, France, 2004; first prize, Hong Kong International Poster Triennial, 2004; gold medal, International Poster Biennial, Mexico, 2004; silver award, International Poster Biennial, Korea, 2004; first prize, International Islamic World Poster Biennial, Iran, 2004; bronze medal and special awards, China International Poster Biennial, 2003/2005; silver medal, Warsaw International Poster Biennale, 2006; Prince Claus Award, the Netherlands, 2006.

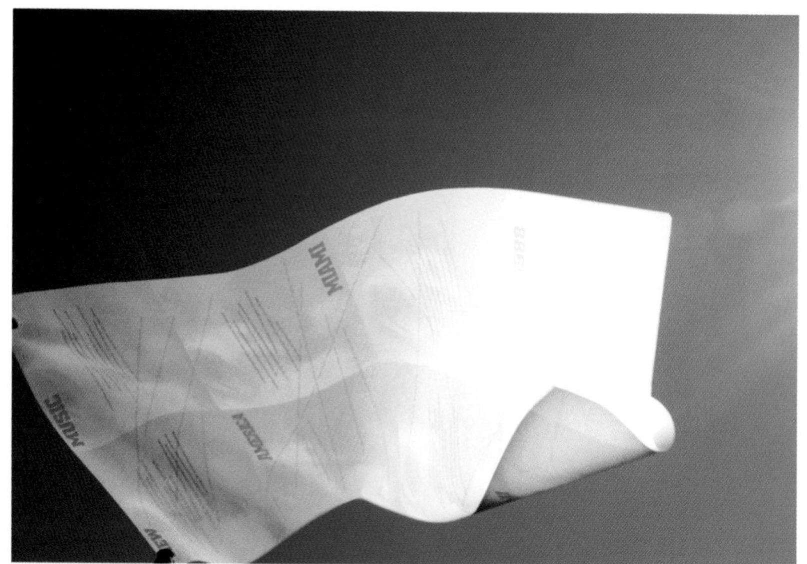

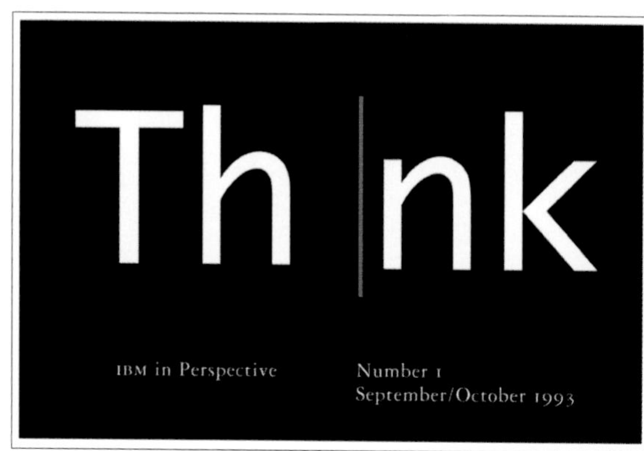

Robert Appleton [USA]

1947– born in Glasgow, Scotland
Admitted to AGI, 2001

Robert Appleton is a graphic designer, artist, photographer, musician and teacher.
After 10 years as an advertising art director, he left Saatchi & Saatchi in 1973 to study fine art at St Martin's in London. A drummer since the age of 14, his percussion studies with Tony Oxley led to performing on the jazz and new music scenes there. After a photo class with Philip Jones Griffiths, he became a photojournalist for BBC Television.
In 1979 he arrived in the US, founding Appleton Design in Connecticut in 1982. After creating the first annual reports on computer for Lotus and Interleaf in Boston, he was invited to New York to develop a new brand identity for IBM.

In music, he worked with John Cage and Ornette Coleman, designing posters, packaging and identity for the Verve Music Group and New Music America. His book *Web Design Now* (Graphis, 1998) was the first international review of the internet as a design medium. He has taught at Parsons School of Design and the University of Minnesota. His original contributions to design vocabulary are documented in his books on design, music and the play instinct, and in his work with jazz composer George Russell.

New Music America, poster, 1987.

Ornette Coleman Festival, mailer/poster, 1987.

IBM Think, logo, 1993.

Cover of **NOZONE X: EMPIRE**, 2004.

Nicholas Blechman, event poster for Syracuse University, 2001.

Cult of Silence, illustration for *Wirtschaftswoche*, 2002.

Nicholas Blechman [USA]

1967– born in New York City
Admitted to AGI, 2001

Nicholas Blechman is the art director of the 'Week In Review' section of *The New York Times*. He began working with the *Times* in 1997, when he art-directed the Op-Ed page and developed the Op-Art feature, a space for artists and cartoonists to contribute their own observations, independent of any article. Blechman publishes, edits, and designs the political underground magazine *NOZONE*. Rallying a coalition of designers, illustrators and cartoonists, *NOZONE* provides a place for social critique through art. He is also principal of Knickerbocker Design, a graphic design and illustration firm in New York. Knickerbocker Design's clients include Greenpeace, *The Nation*, Penguin Books, and the United Nations. His illustrations have appeared in publications including *Newsweek*, *Wirtschaftswoche*, *NY Magazine*, *GQ* and *Dwell*. Blechman has taught at the School of Visual Arts, and led a course in political propaganda at Maryland Institute College of Art. He has lectured and hosted numerous graphic design events, including 'Hell No! Graphic Designers and the War', and his work was included in the 2006 Cooper-Hewitt National Design Triennial. He is the author of *Fresh Dialogue One: New Voices in Graphic Design*, *NOZONE IX: EMPIRE* and *100% EVIL*.

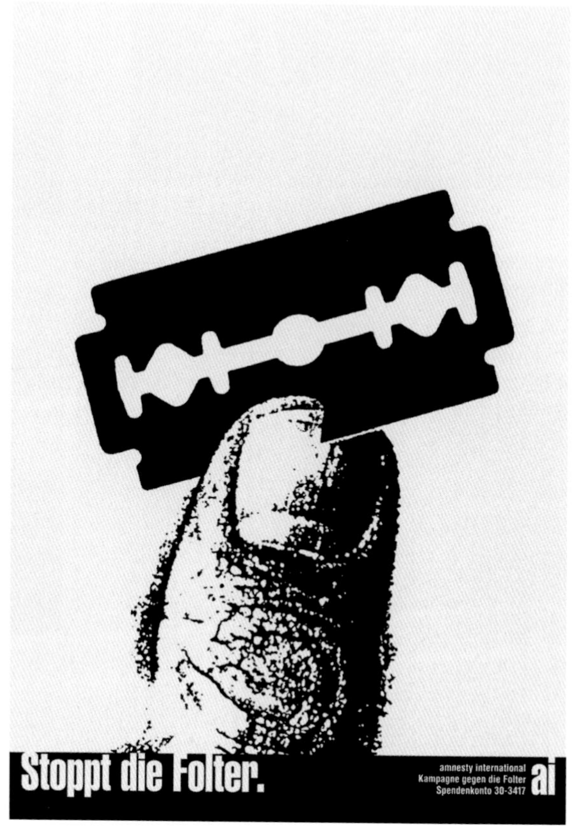

Stephan Bundi [Switzerland]

1950– born in Trun
Admitted to AGI, 2001

Bundi graduated as a graphic designer from the Berne School of Design and trained at the Young & Rubicam agency. He later studied book design and illustration at the Academy of Art and Design in Stuttgart, before going into business for himself. He now works as an art director and designer for publishers, theatres, concert promoters, film producers and museums, and is active in the fields of consumer and investment goods and advertising.

He is a lecturer in visual interpretation (illustration) at the new Berne University of the Arts and is also a guest lecturer and expert at different art and design schools around the world. His work has appeared and been documented in numerous publications. He has won the Swiss national prize for design and several awards for poster, book and CD sleeve design, including gold and silver medals at International Poster Biennials in Belgium and Korea. His latest prize is the Icograda Excellence Award for the 20th International Poster Biennale, Warsaw 2006. *Collections/exhibitions*: BNF, Paris; NY MoMA; Die Neue Sammlung, Munich; Design Museum, Kyoto, among others.

Do Something Impossible: 'View the same face as the same on the same plane at the same time'. Anamorphosis, 1983.

Stop Torture, poster for Amnesty International, 1985.

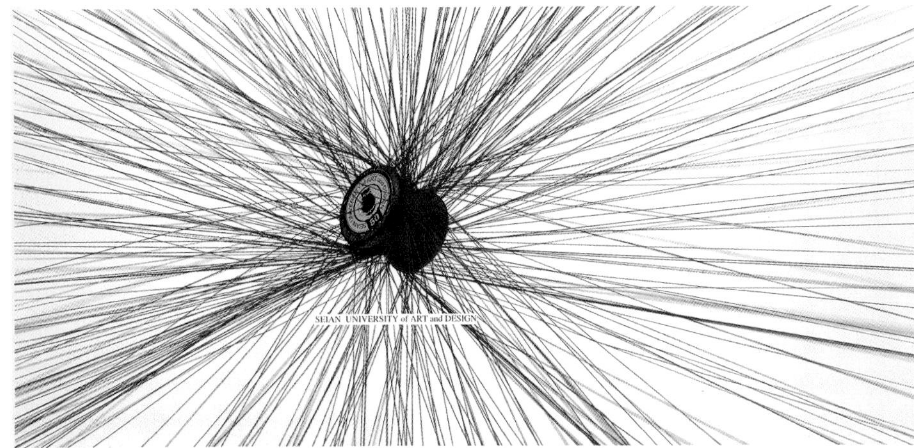

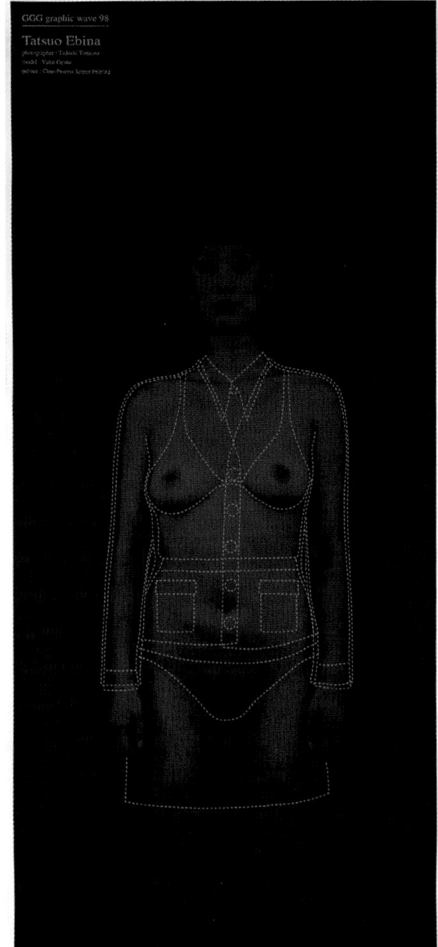

Seian University of Art and Design.

DION, KDDI internet provider.

Ginza Graphic Gallery, **Graphic Wave '98**.

Tatsuo Ebina [Japan]

1960– born in Tokyo
Admitted to AGI, 2001

Ebina founded E Co. Ltd in 1986, joined Satoru Miyata Design Office (now Draft Co. Ltd) in 1987, before reviving E Co. Ltd in 1988. He became a member of JAGDA in 1993, and Tokyo ADC in 1999. *Awards:* JAGDA New Talent Award (1994), Tokyo ADC Awards (1995, 1996, 1997), New York ADC Awards (1999, 2001).

Karin Fong [USA]

1971– born in Canoga Park, California
Admitted to AGI, 2001

Karin Fong directs and designs for film, television and environments. Before joining Imaginary Forces (then RGA/LA) in 1994, she studied art at Yale and worked as an animator at WGBH Boston.
She designed numerous title sequences for feature films, including *Ray*, *Hellboy*, *The Prize Winner of Defiance, Ohio*, *The Cat in the Hat*, *Daredevil*, *Bedazzled*, *The Truman Show*, *The Avengers*, and *Charlie's Angels*. Broadcast work includes the Emmy award-winning main titles for Masterpiece Collection's *American Collection*, and sequences for MTV and Cartoon Network. Karin has also directed commercials for Janus Mutual Funds, Honda, and Chevrolet, as well as promotional films for Herman Miller. Experience design includes show content for the Wynn Las Vegas 'Lake of Dreams', visual entertainment for the 4-block-long screen at Las Vegas's Fremont Street, tour visuals for DJs Sasha and John Digweed, and video and print projects for Malcolm McLaren. She recently designed projections for the LA Opera/Lincoln Center's production of *Grendel*. Personal work includes an art installation, comic-book story and collages based on unusual words. Karin has taught workshops at Art Center, RISD, Cal Arts, and has been a guest critic at Yale. She splits her time between Los Angeles and New York.

The Prize Winner of Defiance, Ohio. A main title sequence created in the style of advertising from the 1950s and 60s, for a feature film about a woman who supports her family through jingle-writing contests. Client: Dreamworks Pictures, Imagemovers, director: Jane Anderson. Designed in collaboration with Stan Lim, Ronnie Koff. Stills courtesy of Paramount Pictures.

Janus Mutual Fund Campaign. Images from 5 of 14 commercials created for a financial company that follow up various investments in unusual ways. Sprinkler, Dial, Oil, Wireless,Underground. Client: Janus Mutual Funds, FCB San Francisco, Tom Rosenberg, Jeff Iorillo CDs. Designed in collaboration with Peggy Oei, Grant Lau, Rafael Macho, Peter Cho. © Janus Mutual Fund Campaign.

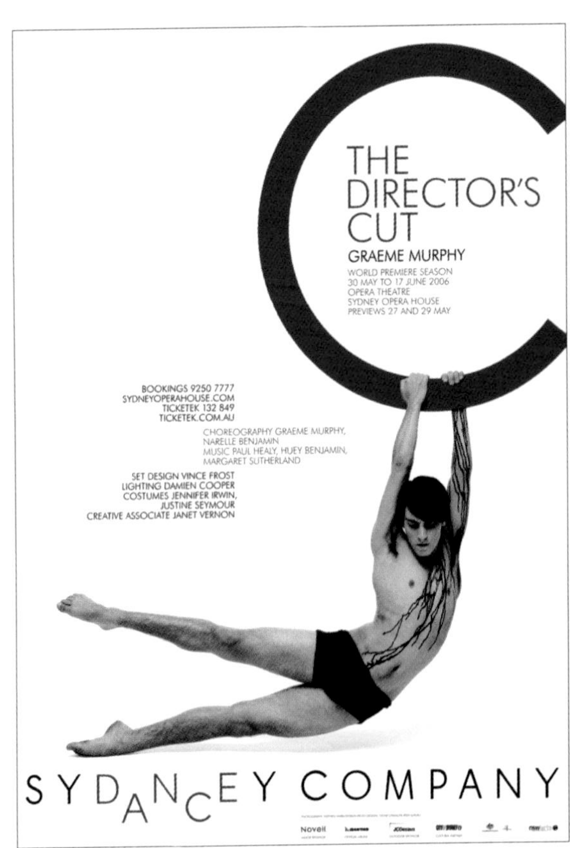

Swiss Re
Centre for Global Dialogue

Vince Frost [UK]

Arte & Frank, identity and interior design for a hair salon (x 2). When designing this identity for my brother-in-law Frank, I realized that the peace sign turned on its side makes a pair of scissors. The identity also appears in lettering on the salon walls.

Director's Cut, poster, Sydney Dance Company. The title 'Cut' was the clue. We used the idea of 'Cut' very theatrically – with dancers hanging off the letter 'C', blood running down their arms. This influenced the costumes for the production.

Swiss Re: Centre for Global Dialogue, identity. Logo consisting of two sets of red quotation marks in Helvetica. Together, the quotation marks and the negative space between them create a Swiss flag.

1964– born in Brighton
Admitted to AGI, 2001

Born in England, raised in Canada, Vince Frost joined Pentagram London in 1989 and three years later became their youngest Associate at 27.
In 1994 he started his own studio, Frost Design, London creating award-winning work for clients from *The Independent* newspaper to Nike. In 2003 Vince relocated to Sydney, Australia, from where he now runs his 25+ creative studio, working on anything from postage stamps to magazines, identities, TV commercials, online projects and the built environment. He continues to work for a range of international clients, including D&AD's magazine *Ampersand*, as well as Warner Music, Macquarie Bank and Sydney Dance Company.

Frost's work was the subject of a retrospective at the Sydney Opera House, January–March 2006. His work is also documented in the 500-page book *Frost*(sorry trees)*, spanning more than a decade of projects. A member of CSD, D&AD, ISTD and AGI, Frost's work has been acknowledged with many awards including golds from the New York Society of Publication Design, D&AD silvers, and other awards from the New York and Tokyo Art Directors Clubs. He has been shortlisted for the BBC Design Awards and won three awards from the Society for Environmental Graphic Design in 2006.

Steven Guarnaccia [USA]

1953– born in Bridgeport, Connecticut
Admitted to AGI, 2001

Steven Guarnaccia is Associate Professor of Illustration and Chair of the Illustration Department at Parsons The New School for Design. He was previously art director of the Op-Ed page of the *New York Times*. During his 30-year career as an internationally recognized illustrator he has worked for major magazines and newspapers including the *New York Times*, *Abitare* and *Rolling Stone*, and has created murals for Disney Cruise Lines, and exhibition drawings for a show of Achille Castiglione's work at the Museum of Modern Art.

He is the author and illustrator of numerous children's books, as well as books on popular culture and design, including *Black and White*, a book on the absence of colour, published by Chronicle Books. Steven has designed watches and packaging for Swatch, and greeting cards for the Museum of Modern Art. He has won awards from the AIGA, the Art Directors Club, and the Bologna Book Fair and has exhibited his work in one-man shows in the USA and Europe.

Drawn and Quarterly, cover of comics anthology.

Busy Busy City Street, cover of children's book, Viking, 2000.

Royal Society of the Arts, magazine illustration.

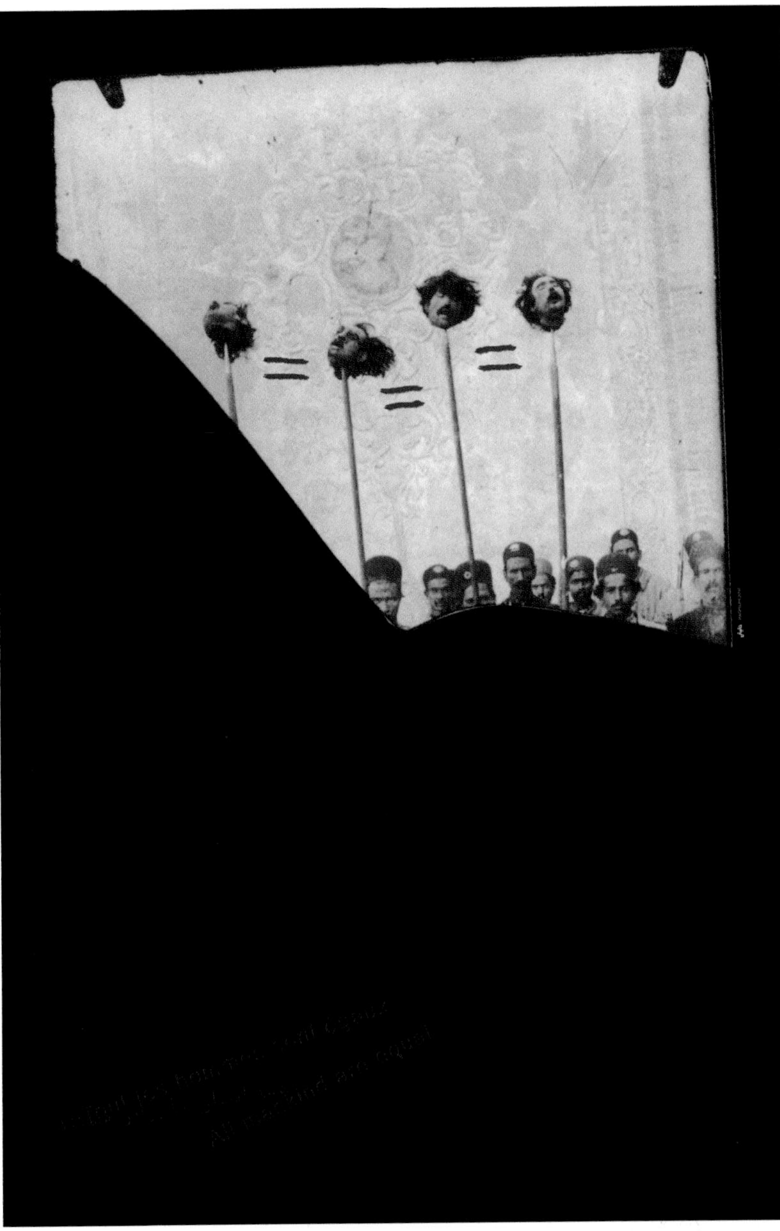

Poster in commemoration of **Reza Mafi**, a contemporary Iranian calligrapher.

All Mankind Are Equal, poster for human rights.

Ebrahim Haghighi [Iran]

1949– born in Tehran
Admitted to AGI, 2001

He has an MA in Architecture from the Faculty of Arts, Tehran University. In 1970, he founded his own studio with his brother, and began his professional activities in graphic art. He has taught graphic arts at Tehran University, Farabi University, University of Art, Tehran, College of Tehran Television and Cinema, and Azad Islamic University of Iran. He is a board member of the Iranian Graphic Designers Society (IGDS), the Iranian Documentary Filmmakers Society, and the Iranian Association for Illustrators of Children's Books.

Ebrahim has had more than 20 solo exhibitions of his paintings and graphic work and has produced title sequences for more than 30 Iranian films and TV series. He was the general secretary of the 8th Tehran International Poster Biennial, 2003.

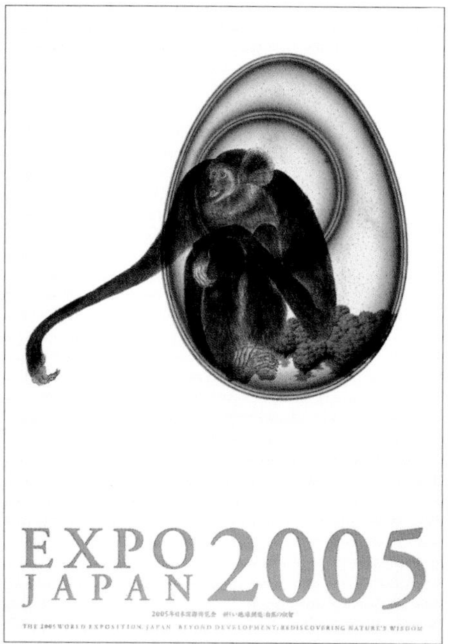

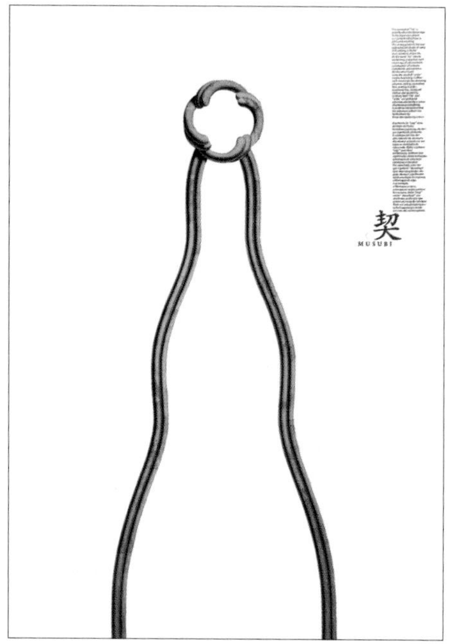

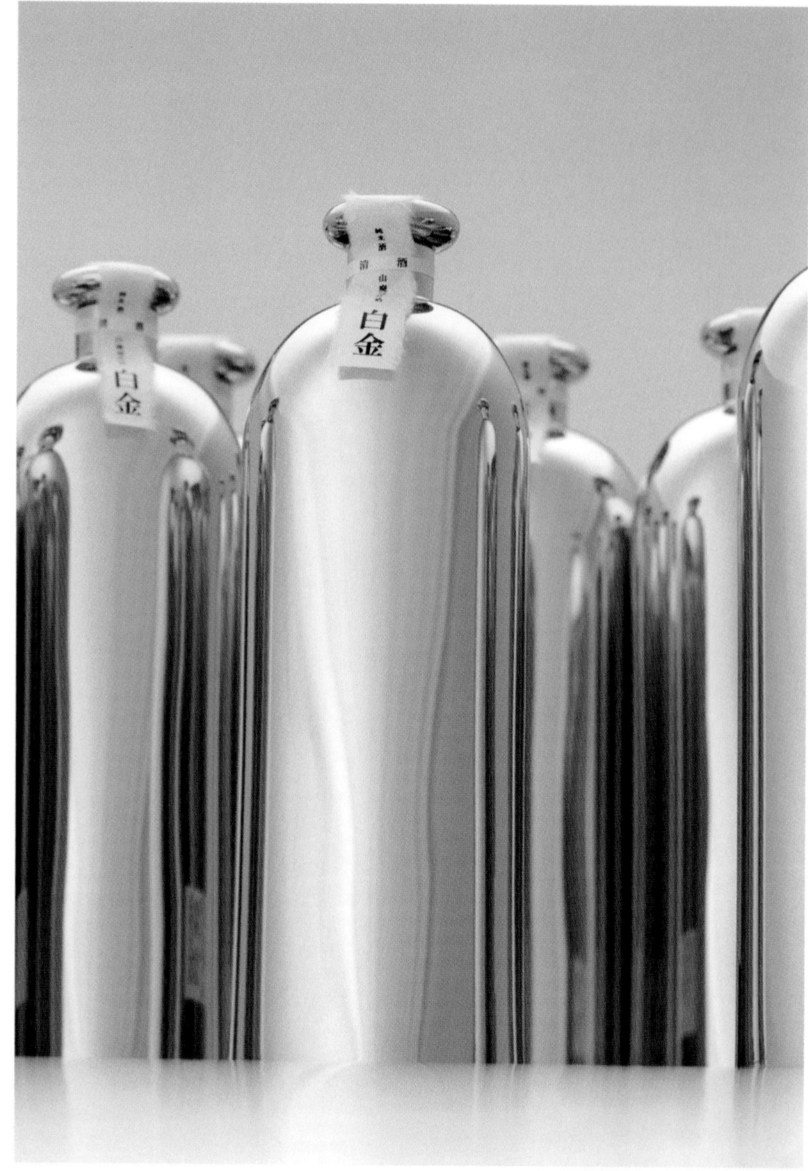

Kenya Hara [Japan]

1958– born in Okayama
Admitted to AGI, 2001

Kenya Hara is an internationally recognized graphic designer. In 2001, he took over as art director of MUJI, where he has helped to balance the company's 'no brand' policy with high quality design. In addition to his recent work at MUJI, he has been a professor at Musashino Art University, and has participated in numerous high-profile projects, among them the Nagano Winter Olympics, the promotion of 2005 Aichi Expo, and the renewal of Matsuya Ginza department store. Hara has also produced numerous design exhibitions, including 'Macaroni Exhibition of Architects', 'HAPTIC: Awakening the Senses' and 'RE DESIGN: The Daily Products of the 21st Century', the last of which toured the world and won him two International Industrial Design Biennale Grand Prizes (for Industrial and Graphic Design) and the Mainichi Design Award (2000). Hara is also the recipient of the Tokyo Art Directors Club Grand Prize (2003) for his MUJI advertising campaign, the Kodansha Publishing Culture Award and the Japan Inter Design Forum Prize, among many others. His books include *RE DESIGN*, *HAPTIC*, and *Design of Design*, a bestseller in Japan.

Promotional poster for **EXPO Aichi 2005**. The theme for the EXPO was 'Nature's Wisdom'. The illustrations are from a natural history book from the Edo period.

Musubi poster. The Musubi series was shown at a poster exhibition at the Contemporary Art Museum of São Paulo in 1995.

Hakkin, packaging design for a Japanese sake brand. The name Hakkin means white gold. The bottles resemble mirrors, and seem to disappear into their environment.

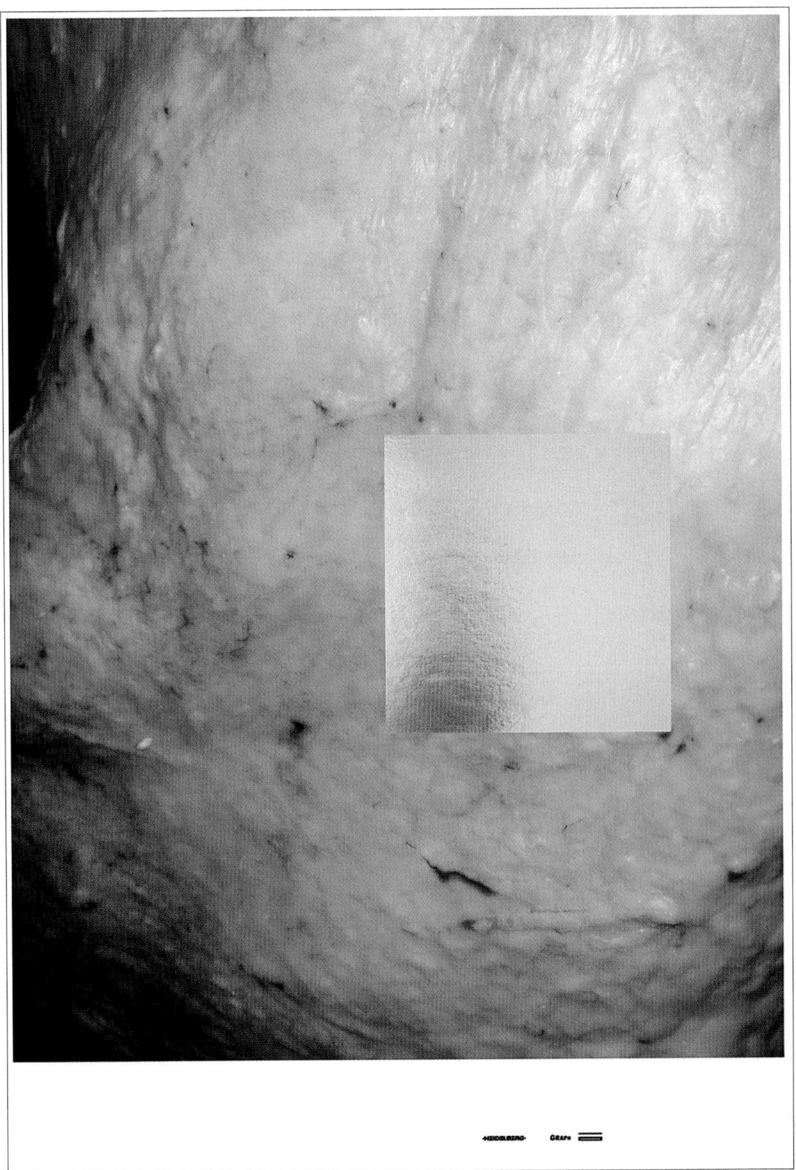

Fukunishiki, sake barrel and bottle.

Meat and Gold, poster on the theme of 'lust'.

Issay Kitagawa [Japan]

1965– born in Hyogo
Admitted to AGI, 2001

He graduated from University of Tsukuba, Japan in 1987, and is now principal designer and president of GRAPH. GRAPH specializes in visual communication by offering graphic design, brand consulting and printing. The strength of GRAPH begins with having three Heidelberg printing machines and two die-cutting machines. New possibilities in printing are found every day. Issay is also a printing director and often immerses himself in the GRAPH printing factory. His graphic design work fuses this knowledge of printing with design. Subtle nuances are shown experimentally and exquisitely.

Issay's designs are also based upon his love of typography. Both English and Japanese typography are often a central part of his visual images.
He has held exhibitions all over the world, including GGG in Tokyo, Elahe Gallery in Tehran and Salone del Mobile in Milan. Kitakawa has judged for Tokyo TDC, D&AD, New York ADC and more, has lectured at many universities, has been appeared in numerous publications including *IDEA* in Japan, *Creative Review* in the UK, and *Etapes* in France, and has been selected for the permanent collection at the Toyama MoMA and the Bibliothèque Nationale de France, among others.

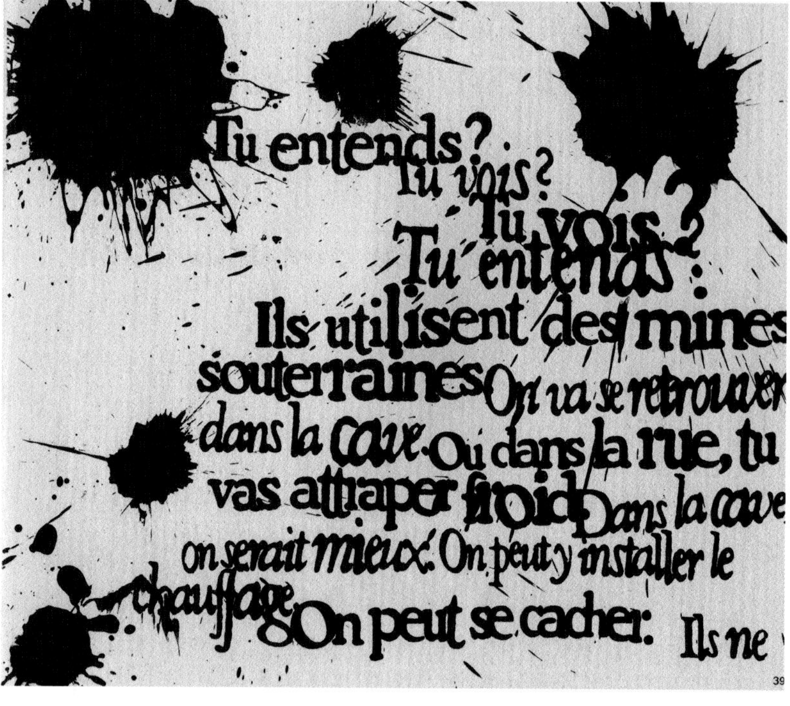

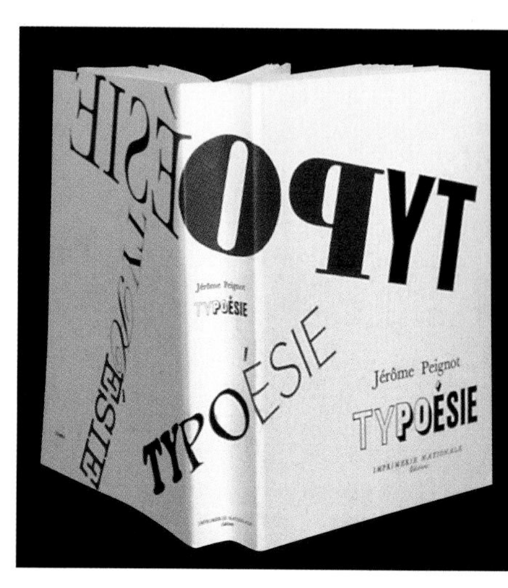

Robert Massin [France]

1925– born in Bourdinière
Admitted to AGI, 2001

Massin started his career in French book clubs, where he became one of the principal figures of the book design revolution of the 1950s. For twenty years, he was the art director of Editions Gallimard, where he created the pocketbook collections 'Folio' and 'L'Imaginaire', and conceived (in collaboration with photographer Henry Cohen) a graphic interpretation of *The Bald Soprano* – the famous Eugene Ionesco absurdist play – for which he received the Leipzig International Book Prize. As an independent graphic artist, he has designed thousands of covers and jackets, and many layouts of books and posters.

In 1970 he wrote and designed the book *Letter and Image*, which has been continually updated and re-issued ever since. His work as a writer includes some thirty volumes, and the city of Chartres has published a catalogue raisonné of his typographical work in three volumes. Under the auspices of UNESCO he has received the International Book Award for his contribution to culture. From New York to Seoul and from Istanbul to San Francisco, dozens of cities around the world have organized retrospective exhibitions of his work. In 2001, he was elected to the Royal Academy of Belgium.

Blaise Cendrars, *L'Or*, bookbinding, Club du Meilleur Livre, 1956.

Arnold Schönberg, *Pierrot Lunaire*, unpublished, 1966–2006.

Jérôme Peignot, *Typoésie*, cover. Imprimerie Nationale, 1993.

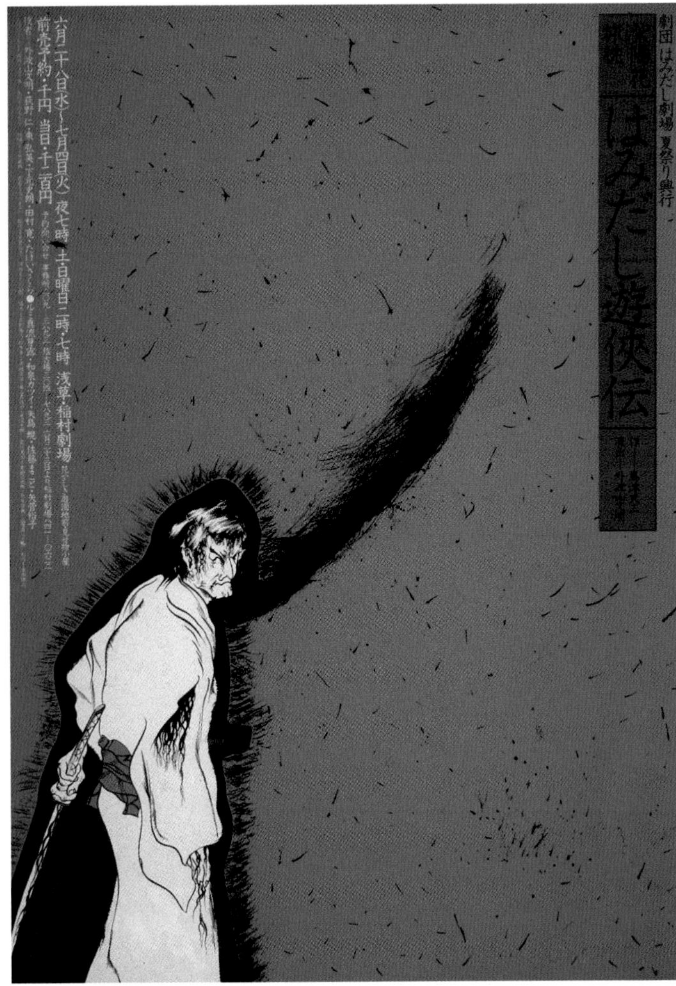

Keisuke Nagatomo [Japan]

Poster for book promotion.

Exhibition poster.

1939– born in Osaka
Admitted to AGI, 2001

Keisuke has illustrated Shizuka Ijyuin's writings for many years. He has also created illustrations for the literary work of Kazuko Hosoki, Jyunji Yamagiwa and many other prominent writers in addition to producing their book and cover designs. He also works as the editorial designer for *Ryukou Tsushin*, *Goro*, *Shukan Gendai* and many other magazines. His essays have been serialized by magazines and he has been a frequent guest of television and radio shows. Additionally, he has created advertising poster designs for major department stores such as Parco and Marui and for theatre plays.

Keisuke is an art director for event and meeting spaces and a special adviser to the Nihon Kougakuin Senmongakou (Nippon Engineering College) Graphic Design Department. He is also a guest professor at Tokyo Zokei University.

Paul Neale [UK]

1966– born in Leicestershire
Admitted to AGI, 2001

Paul Neale and Andrew Stevens have worked together as Graphic Thought Facility (GTF) since graduating from the Royal College of Art, London, in 1990. Working predominantly for cultural and retail clients they have created the identities for The Design Museum, Frieze Art Fair and Habitat amongst others, as well as being known for their exhibition graphics for national and international museums and galleries. GTF is jointly owned by three directors – Paul Neale, Andy Stevens and Huw Morgan.

Andrew and Paul have lectured widely on graphic design at institutions including the Ecole Cantonale d'Art, Lausanne, Switzerland; Jan van Eyck Academie, Netherlands; Fabrica, Italy; Cal Arts & Walker Arts Center, US; and many UK colleges. In 2006 Graphic Thought Facility's work was the subject of a retrospective exhibition at the DDD Gallery, Osaka, Japan.

Digitopolis, exhibition graphics, 2000. Client: The Science Museum. Graphic design: Graphic Thought Facility. Exhibition design: Casson Mann.

Work from London, exhibition poster for the British Council, 1996.

Instant Action, poster, 1994. Client: Antoni + Alison. Photography: Andrew Penketh.

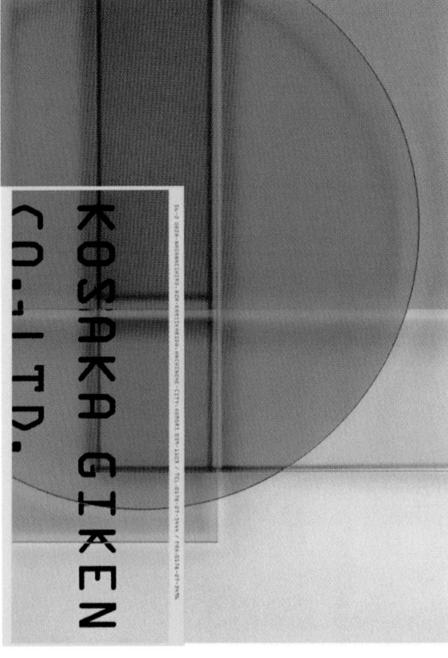

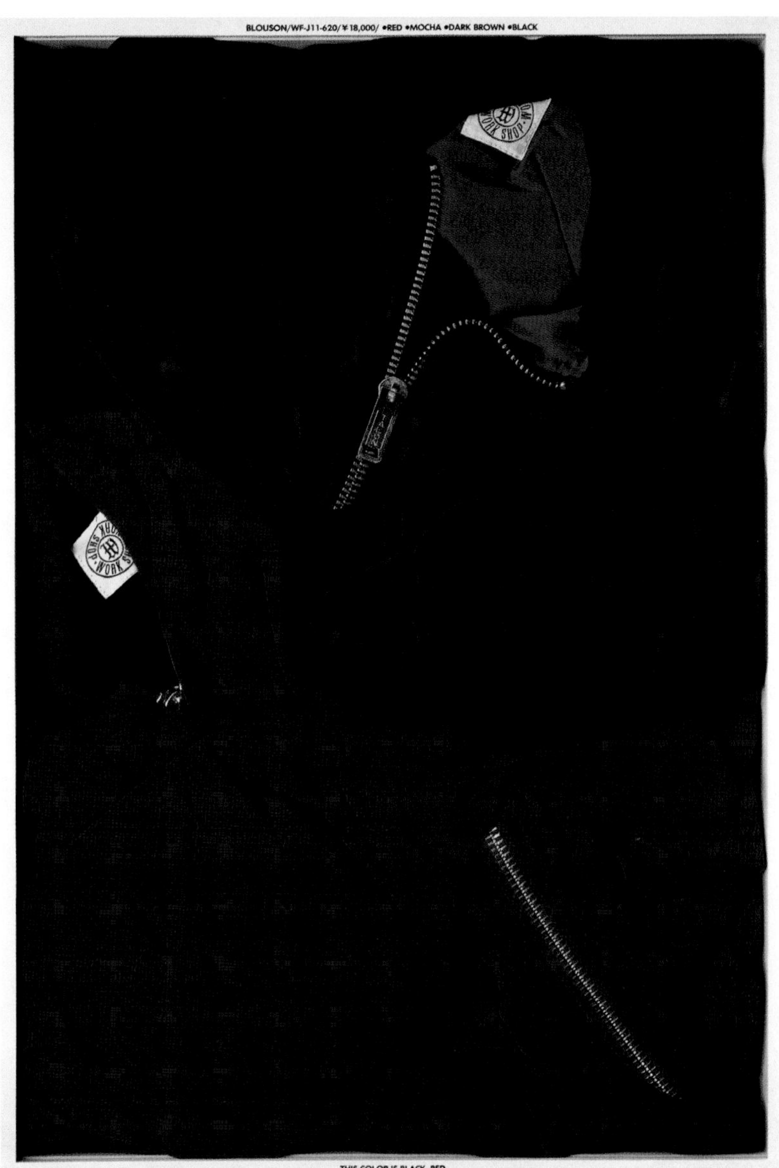

Poster for construction consultancy firm **Kosaka Giken Co.**, Japan, 2004.

Poster for construction consultancy firm **Kosaka Giken Co.**, Japan, 2002.

Large-size catalogue for **'Workshop' brand, Y's for Men**, Japan, 1989.

Yasuhiro Sawada [Japan]

1961– born in Tokyo
Admitted to AGI, 2001

Education: 1981–85: Graphic Design, Tokyo University of Fine Arts and Music. *Career:* 1994–present: assistant professor at Tama Art University, Department of Graphic Design; 1989–present: Sawada Yasuhiro Design Studio; 1985–89: art director, Suntory Creative Department.
Major awards: 2003 Bronze Prize, International Poster Triennial in Toyama; 1994 Bronze Prize, International Poster Triennial in Toyama; 1993 New Designer Award, Japan Graphic Designers Association; 1991 Silver Prize, Tokyo Type Directors Club; 1990 Gold Prize, Japan Magazine Advertising; Tokyo ADC Award; 1989 Grand Prize, Tokyo ADC; 1988 Silver Prize, NY ADC; Bronze Prize, International Poster Triennial in Toyama.
Major exhibitions: 2005, 'Japanese Posters Today', State Museum of Applied Arts and Design, Munich, Germany; 2002, 'Graphic Wave', GGG, Tokyo, Japan); 2001, 'Design Spirit of Japan', The University Art Museum, Tokyo National University of Fine Art & Music; 1997, 'Advertising Art History II 1991–1995', Tokyo Station Gallery; 1995, 'Close-up of Japan', São Paulo Museum, Brazil; 1995, 'Today's Japan', Harbourfront Centre, Toronto, Canada; 1992, Amnesty International Poster Exhibition, Yokohama Museum, Kanagawa, Japan; 1991, Yasuhiro Sawada Exhibition, GGG, Tokyo.

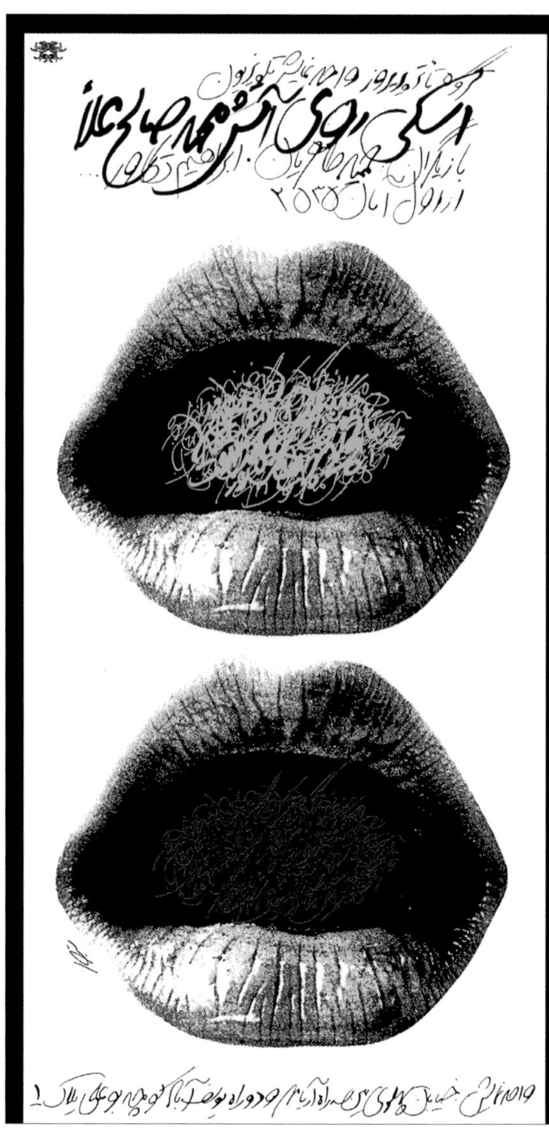

Ghobad Shiva [Iran]

1941– born in Hamadan
Admitted to AGI, 2001

Shiva has a BA in painting from Tehran University (1966) and a Masters in communication design, from Pratt Institute, New York (1980). Over several decades he has created a form of graphic design with a Persian flavour, which has attracted museums and collectors across the world. He set up Iranian TV's graphics department (1968) and the Soroush Press design department (1971), and is co-founder of the Iranian Graphic Designers Society (IGDS). He has been teaching and lecturing in eminent art and design faculties in Tehran since 1976, and is an artistic adviser and jury member for several Iranian graphic design biennials.

For decades he has held national and international exhibitions of his paintings, photographs and particularly of his graphic works. His awards include: Brno Graphic Design Biennale (1978); Shiraz Festival of Arts Poster Competitions (1969, 1970, 1971, 1977); IGDS logo competition (1988, 2001). He has a design studio and is director of the Ghobad Shiva Art & Cultural Institute. Three books are published on his graphic works: *Posters by Ghobad Shiva* (2004), *Ghobad Shiva graphic designer* (2005), *Ghobad Shiva* in 'The Selected Works of Masters of Graphic Design' series (2006).

Shiraz Art Festival, film poster, 1972.

The First Exhibition of Iranian Contemporary Art, in support of cancer patients, poster, 2006.

Skiing on the M. Salehala Fire, poster for an experimental play, 1976.

FRIEZE
ART
FAIR

Mebox, storage boxes, 2002. Self-initiated product.

Visual identity for the **Design Museum**, 2003. Graphic design and art direction: Graphic Thought Facility. Illustrator: Kam Tang.

Visual identity for **Frieze Art Fair**, 2003.

Andy Stevens [UK]

1966– born in Sheffield
Admitted to AGI, 2001

Paul Neale and Andrew Stevens have worked together as Graphic Thought Facility (GTF) since graduating from the Royal College of Art, London, in 1990. Working predominantly for cultural and retail clients they have created the identities for The Design Museum, Frieze Art Fair and Habitat amongst others, as well as being known for their exhibition graphics for national and international museums and galleries. GTF is jointly owned by three directors – Paul Neale, Andy Stevens and Huw Morgan.

Andrew and Paul have lectured widely on graphic design at institutions including the Ecole Cantonale d'Art, Lausanne, Switzerland; Jan van Eyck Academie, Netherlands; Fabrica, Italy; Cal Arts & Walker Arts Center, US; and many UK colleges. In 2006 Graphic Thought Facility's work was the subject of a retrospective exhibition at the DDD Gallery, Osaka, Japan.

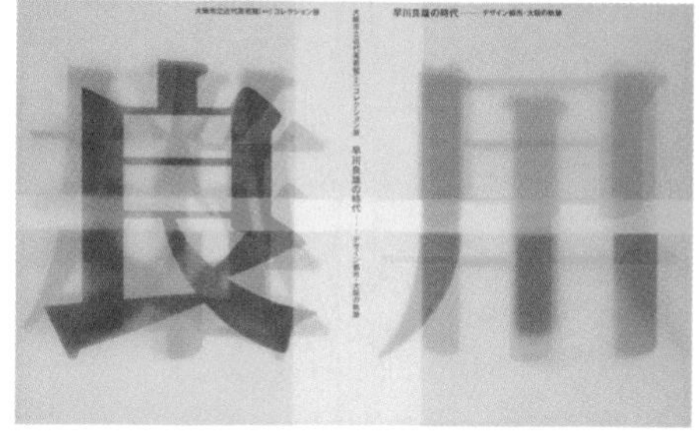

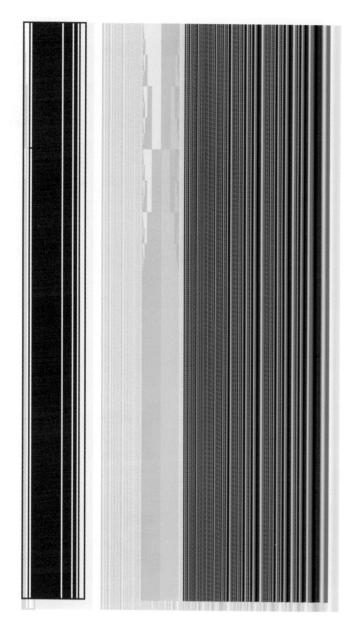

Shinnoske Sugisaki [Japan]

1953– born in Nara
Admitted to AGI, 2001

Shinnoske graduated from the Design Department of Osaka University of Art in 1974. In 1986, he established Shinnoske Inc., where he serves as creative director and president. Sugisaki has designed advertising, identities, graphic and typographic works for some of Japan's largest companies and organizations including Panasonic, Mitsubishi Pharma, Mainichi Broadcasting, Morisawa, Osaka Government, and Suntory. Sugisaki's experimental and private works have been showcased in exhibitions both domestically and internationally, in cities such as Tokyo, Osaka, Beijing, Shanghai, Hong Kong, New York and São Paulo. He has lectured at the Seian University of Art and Design and Kyoto College of Art and Design. Shinnoske has received several prestigious design awards from the NY ADC, the International Poster Triennial in Toyama, the Trnava Poster Triennial, the Graphic Design Biennale Brno, and the Lahti Poster Biennial. His work has been selected for the collections of the Museum für Kunst und Gewerbe, Hamburg; the Regional Council Heritage Museum Hong Kong; Suntory Museum, Tenpozan; and Osaka Contemporary Art Centre. Shinnoske is a member of the Japan Graphic Designers Association (JAGDA), Tokyo Type Directors Club (TDC), Japan Typography Association (JTA) and DAS Designers Association.

Poster design commemorating the **25th anniversary of Manascreen**, a Japanese silkscreen company.

Catalogue design, showcasing works by **Yoshio Hayakawa**, a pioneer of Japanese graphic design, for a large-scale exhibition at Osaka City's Museum of Modern Art.

Cover for the **Swiss Typographic Magazine**, no. 2, 2001.

Promotional poster for the **ANCT**. A work based on research into rhythm and proportion, particularly the Golden Section and Fibonacci.

Edward Bond: *War Pieces I–II*, poster from a series for the Crochet à Nuages theatre company.

André Baldinger [France]

1963– born in Zürich, Switzerland
Admitted to AGI, 2002

Baldinger began his career as a graphic designer in 1987. After three years of practice, he sharpened his skills as a typographer by studying with Hans Rudolf Bosshard in Zürich. After earning his diploma in 1993, Baldinger headed for Paris and joined the Atelier National de Création Typographique. In 1995 he started his own office. His clients range from cultural institutions to a wide range of industries. 'Alternative' projects like set design for the theatre and 3D design projects are key parts of his practice. Baldinger has also established himself as a skilled font designer; his typeface Newut (New Universal Typeface) is notable for its originality and modernity.

Other projects include the type system for the Cité Internationale Universitaire de Paris and a special font for the Eiffel Tower signage project. He has taught at ÉCAL (1995–2003) and Lausanne University of Art and Design and the Berne University of the Arts (2003–2006). He has been awarded grants from both the French and the Swiss governments, and has been honoured by the Japan Type Directors Club (2001, 2003, 2004), the New York Type Directors Club (2004) and the 100 Best Posters, Berlin (2004). In 2005 the Swiss National Bank invited him to join the competition for the design of the new Swiss currency.

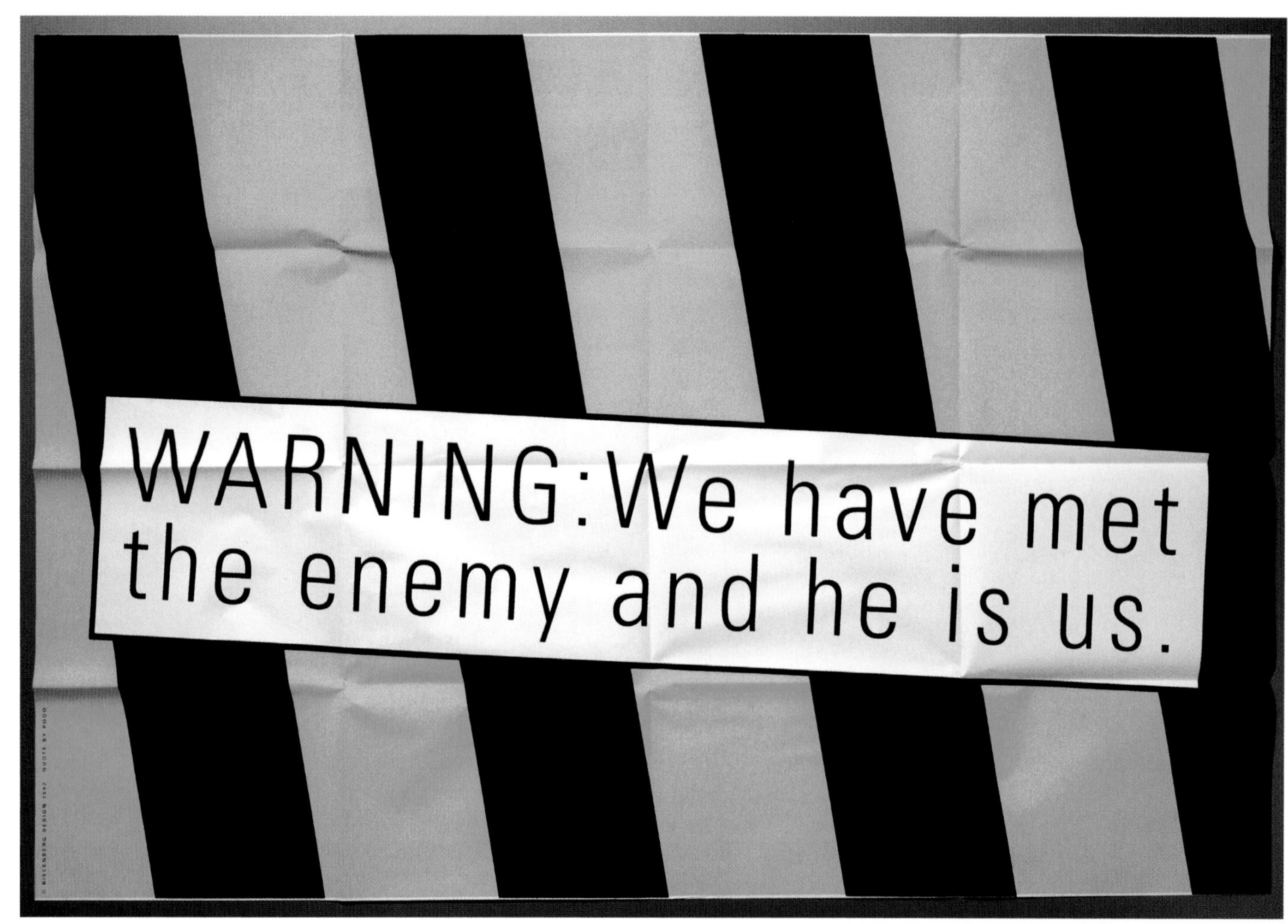

John Bielenberg [USA]

1957– born in Regensburg, Germany
Admitted to AGI, 2002

John is a partner and co-founder of C2, San Francisco, with Greg Galle and Erik Cox, and founder/director of Project M, a summer programme in Maine designed to inspire young designers, writers, photographers and filmmakers by proving that their work can have a positive and significant impact on the world. Since 1991, John has produced an ongoing series of projects under the pseudonym Virtual Telemetrix, Inc., that addresses issues related to the practice of graphic design and corporate America. Projects have included the *Quantitative Summary of Integrated Global Brand Strategy* booklet and video produced for the 1998 AIGA Brand Design Conference, the 1997 *Virtual Telemetrix Annual Report*, a satire on corporate branding, and *Ceci n'est pas un catalogue*, which parodies designer products. The SF MoMA has acquired 6 of the VT projects and staged a Virtual Telemetrix exhibition and mock IPO (Initial Public Offering) in 2000. John has won over 250 design awards and was recently nominated for two National Design Awards from the Cooper-Hewitt Museum. He has served on the AIGA National Board of Directors, taught at California College of the Arts, San Francisco, and written articles on design for *Communication Arts* magazine, *Critique* magazine, *Looking Closer 2: Critical Writings on Graphic Design*, and *Design Issues: How Graphic Design Informs Society*.

Large-scale poster designed in 1991 as a teaser to introduce a self-initiated campaign to the US design community, addressing issues concerning graphic design and corporate America. This poster launched a series of projects under the pseudonym of **Virtual Telemetrix, Inc.**, which culminated in a solo exhibition at the SF MoMA in 2000.

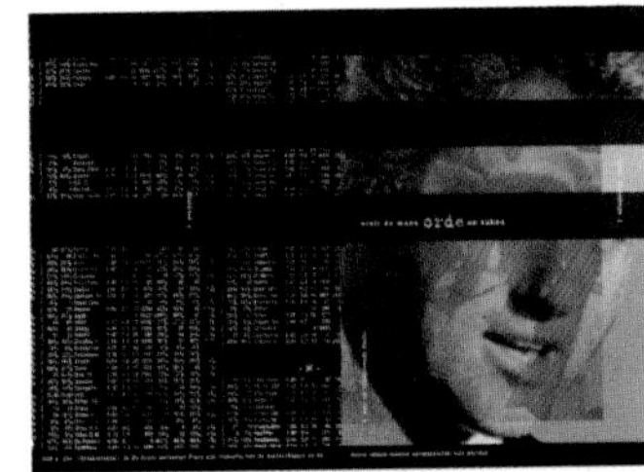

Brush and Liquid, invitation to a exhibition by two artists, 2003.

Z[OO] agenda, double pages from a diary with a story about the future of mankind, 1996.

Film and Architecture, poster for a festival at the Filmhuis Den Haag, 1987.

Ben Faydherbe [The Netherlands]

1958– born in Amsterdam
Admitted to AGI, 2002

He studied at the Koninklijke Academie van Beeldende Kunsten, The Hague (1977–82), then worked at the studio Vorm Vijf (1981–86) with assignments for PTT Telecommunication and Ministry of Welfare, Healthcare and Culture (WVC). In 1986 he formed Faydherbe/De Vringer with Wout de Wringer and designed mostly for cultural clients such as The Hague Summer Festival, Theater aan de Haven and Filmhuis Den Haag, creating a large number of posters. He did more corporate work for government and semi-government bodies, including the Fund for Performing Arts, and designed several books.

From early on in his career Ben has been interested in 20th-century avant-garde design. In his opinion, image complexity, through the use of different techniques like (photo)collage and overprinting, is always of minor importance in comparison with the clear visual language of the design. He won the silver medal at the Brno Biennale in 1986, and has held workshops at St Martin's School of Art, London, and Merz Akademie, Stuttgart. The exhibition 'Looking Back into the Future' was held in the DDD Gallery, Osaka in 1998. Other exhibition venues include the Theater aan het Spui, The Hague (1996) and Hotel van de Velde, Brussels (1999). His work can be found in the collection of NY MoMA and Cooper Union. Faydherbe and De Vringer are the designers of this AGI book.

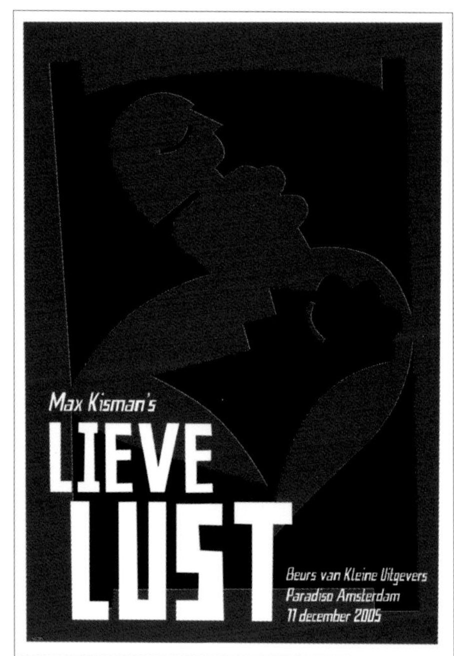

Max Kisman [The Netherlands]

1953– born in Doetinchem
Admitted to AGI, 2002

Kisman studied graphic design, illustration and animation at the Academy for Art and Industry in Enschede and the Gerrit Rietveld Academy in Amsterdam (1972–77). In 1986 he co-founded *TYP/Typografisch Papier*, an alternative magazine on art and typography. At the same time, he pioneered digital technology for *Language Technology/Electric Word* magazine and designed the 1986 Red Cross postage stamps for the Dutch PTT. In 1992 he began designing animations for programme announcements on the progressive Dutch public television broadcasting station VPRO.

In 1996 he received the H.M. Werkman award and the (audience) Design Prize of the City of Rotterdam for his work in television graphics and animation. Kisman taught and teaches at various international art institutes and has been involved in various international projects, like Tribe, Building Letters (UK, USA), AIGA's Spaced Out (USA) and Fleurons of Hope (USA). He lived in California from 1997–2006, worked for Wired Television in San Francisco and founded Holland Fonts, a foundry for his typeface designs. Currently he resides in the Netherlands with a studio in Amsterdam.

Bonjour Toulouse-Lautrec, poster, 2001. Contribution to the 'Homage to Toulouse Lautrec' project.

Bfrika, 2002. Illustrated spread in *i-jusi* magazine (South Africa), 'National Typography' issue.

Lieve Lust, poster from a series of three with images from a limited-edition publication, 2005.

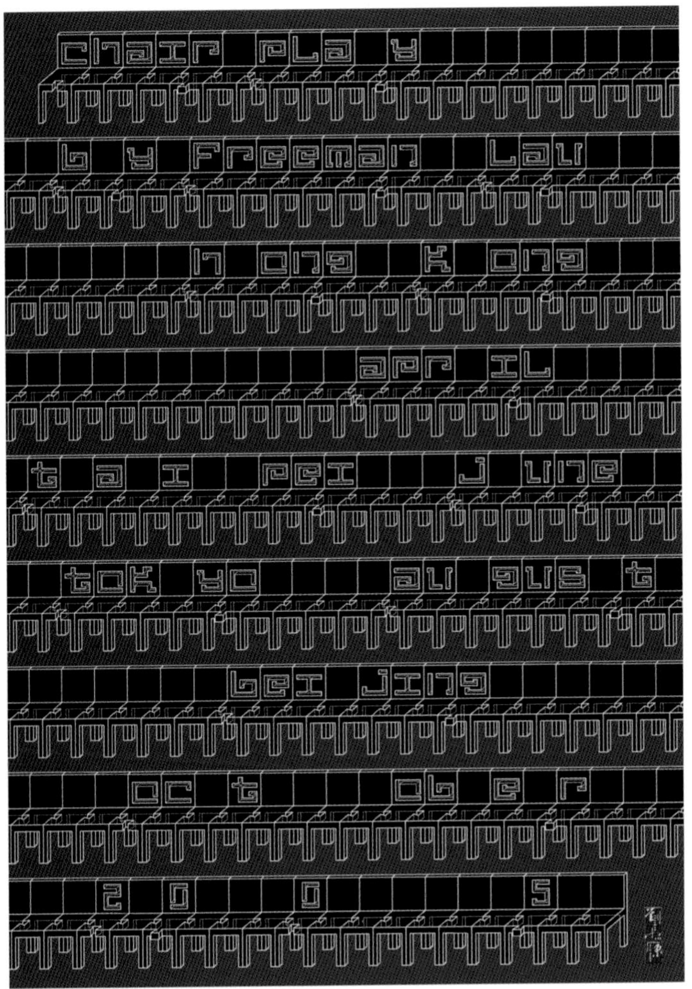

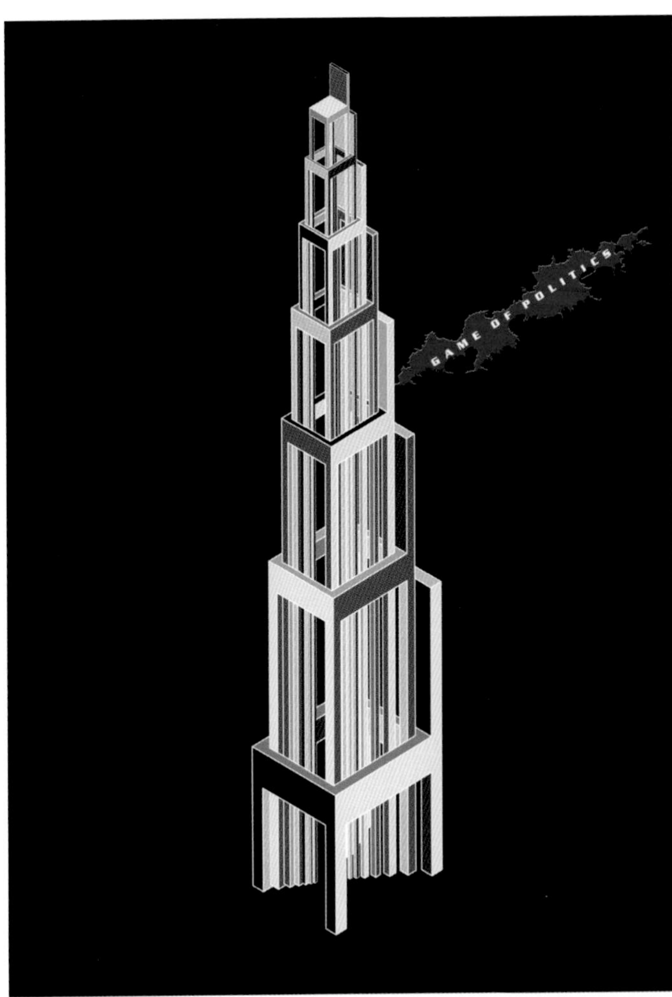

Chairplay, touring exhibition in Taipei, 2005.

Game of Politics, 2000.

Freeman Lau [China]

1958– born in Hong Kong
Admitted to AGI, 2002

Freeman Lau studied at Hong Kong Polytechnic and is now a partner in Kan & Lau Design Consultants. Since 1984, he has won over 250 awards in overseas and local art and design competitions. Most recently in 2004, Freeman's design for Watson's Water won the international *bottledwaterworld* Design Awards. In his design for this bottle, he successfully created a symbiosis between art, culture, design and business acumen; significantly increasing the brand's market share while contributing to the local cultural movement. Apart from his commercial projects, Freeman exerts genuine assertiveness in the fine arts.

In 2004, Freeman's work was awarded 'Chair of the Year' in the Chair Design Competition of Barrie Ho Collections. Last year, the 'Chairplay' travelling exhibition was held in Hong Kong, Japan, Beijing and Taipei. He is now the chairman of the board of directors of the Hong Kong Design Centre, secretary general of the Hong Kong Federation of Design Associations and a member of the Design Management Institute Advisory Council.

Saed Meshki [Iran]

1964– born in Gonabad
Admitted to AGI, 2002

Education: BA in Graphic Design, Faculty of Fine Arts, Tehran University.
Work: graphic designer and art director of Meshki Studio, 1987 to present, working on book design, poster, signage and illustration. Art director of Iranzamin International Theatre Festival, Abadan International Film Festival, and International Festival of Comic Theatre. Graphic designer of publishing imprints including Mahriz, Qoo, Roozgar. Executive manager, art director and graphic designer of *Iranian Contemporary Graphic Designers*, 20 vol. series, and executive manager of *The Book of Signs*. Lecturer in graphic design at the Faculty of Fine Arts, Tehran University.
Member of IGDS (Iranian Graphic Designers Society), board member for *Neshan* (Iranian design magazine), member of 5th Color (Iranian graphic designers group), selection Committee for 7th Iranian Graphic Design Biennial, jury for First Self-Promotional Poster Exhibition, jury for 5th Exhibition of Book Illustration for Children and Young Adults.
Awards: best cover design for children's book, Tehran (1993); special prize, Iranian Graphic Design Biennial (1997); New Talent award, Iranian Graphic Design Biennial (1997); Best Cover Design, Iranian Graphic Design Biennial (1999); special prize, Pearl of Czech Design, Poster Design (2002); first prize for book cover design, First Exhibition of Cover Design in Iran (2003); Icograda Excellence Award at the Warsaw International Poster Biennale (2004).

Saed Meshki, poster for solo exhibition, 2003.

Poster for the **First Exhibition of IGDS Student's & Members**, 2003.

A Little Kiss, poster, 2006.

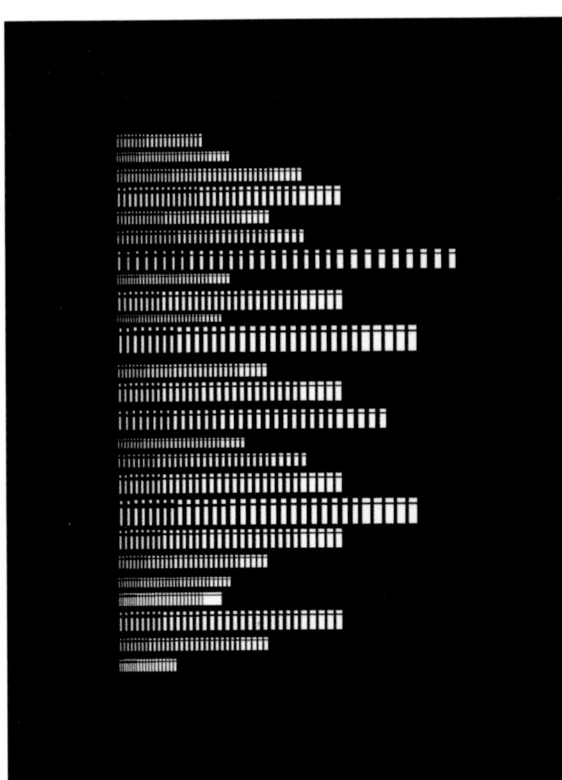

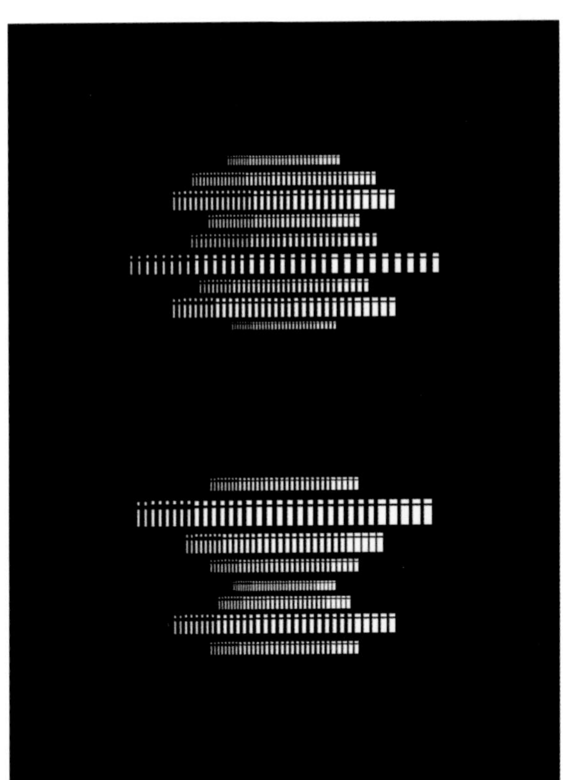

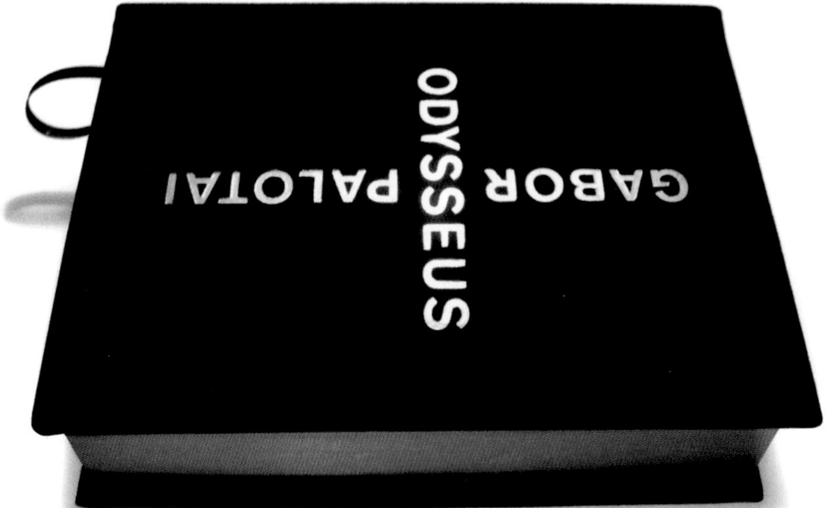

Odysseus, a graphic design novel by Gábor Palotai, 2006. There is nothing to read, only to be seen. The verbal is replaced by the visual. Skirting the surface of the paper, the rhythm of the black and white tells a story in which you become the storyteller: you are your own Odysseus.

Gábor Palotai [Sweden]

1956– born in Budapest, Hungary
Admitted to AGI, 2002

Since 1981 Gábor Palotai has lived and worked in Stockholm, Sweden. He studied graphic design at the University College of Art and Design in Budapest. After receiving his MA, he continued his studies at the Royal Academy of Fine Arts and at the Beckman College of Design in Stockholm. In 1990 he established his own graphic design studio, Gábor Palotai Design, which works on a broad range of design projects. Most of his works from the years 1985–2000 can be seen in his book *Maximizing the Audience* (2000), which also includes a DVD, *The Animated Book*. Gábor Palotai also works with experimental photography, which can be seen in his book *AM MU NA HI* (2001).

In 2006 he published the graphic design novel *Odysseus*. He has received several awards, among them the Red Dot Design Award, the Swedish Golden Egg Design Award and has been nominated for the Design Award of the Federal Republic of Germany. Gábor Palotai has had several solo and group exhibitions, and his works appear in various international publications.

Wout de Vringer [The Netherlands]

1959– born in Rijswijk
Admitted to AGI, 2002

He started his studies in graphic design at the Academie voor Kunst en Vormgeving Den Bosch (1979–84) and was an apprentice at Samenwerkende Ontwerpers, Amsterdam and 2D3D, The Hague. He then began to work as a freelancer and, in 1985–86, for Vorm Vijf, The Hague, and did some print design for PTT Telecommunications. Together with Ben Faydherbe he formed his own studio in The Hague (1986), designing mostly for cultural clients such as The Hague Summer Festival, Theater aan de Haven and Filmhuis Den Haag. He also designed for semi-government institutions including Centrum Beeldende Kunst, Dordrecht and Centrum Beeldende Kunst, Provincie Utrecht. Wout has had one-man exhibitions in The Hague (1997) and at the DDD Gallery in Osaka, Japan (1998) and has taken part in group exhibitions in Europe and the USA. He has given guest lectures at Yale University, New Haven, Bristol, London, Kolding and Detroit and taught graphics at the Evening Academy in Rotterdam. His book *Dolly, A Book Typeface With Flourishes* was selected for the Best Book (2001) in The Netherlands and also for the World's Most Beautiful Book awards, Leipzig. De Vringer and Faydherbe are the designers of this AGI book.

100 Years of Museon, 2004. Poster for Museon, a natural history/science museum for children (and their parents).

Kaguyahime, one of a series of ten posters for NDT, a famous Dutch dance company, 1993.

De Haagse Zomer 1991, poster for an annual cultural summer festival held in The Hague from 1987–92.

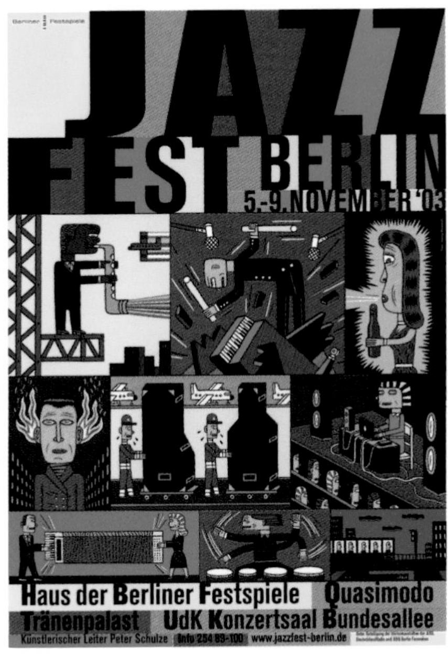

Amerika gibt es nicht (There Is No America), cover illustration for a novel by Daniele Benati, Cologne: Tisch 7, 2005.

Jazzfest Berlin, poster, 2003.

Illustrations for the book **Cry for Help: 36 Scam E-mails from Africa**, 2006.

Henning Wagenbreth [Germany]

1962– born in Eberswalde, East Germany
Admitted to AGI, 2002

Henning Wagenbreth studied at the Kunsthochschule in East Berlin. Before the fall of the Berlin Wall in 1989, he worked for two years as an illustrator and film animator and created posters for various citizens' groups. During the years of political transformation that followed the reunification of Germany, he designed many theatre posters, primarily using illustration and hand-drawn typography. In 1992, he went to Paris where he met many other illustrators, artists, and publishers. In 1994, he returned to Berlin and began his current position as a professor of illustration and graphic design at the University of the Arts.

Henning has illustrated many books for both children and adults, as well as posters, newspapers, magazines and comic strips. He likes to design and digitize hand-drawn typefaces and has developed automated illustration systems. His work shows his interest in combining traditional graphic printing and drawing techniques with modern digital publishing technology. His work has been awarded prizes by poster festivals in Germany, France and Poland and by the German Book Foundation.

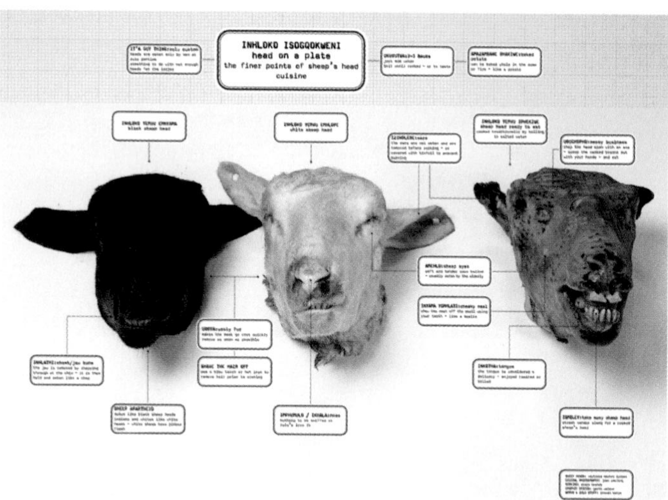

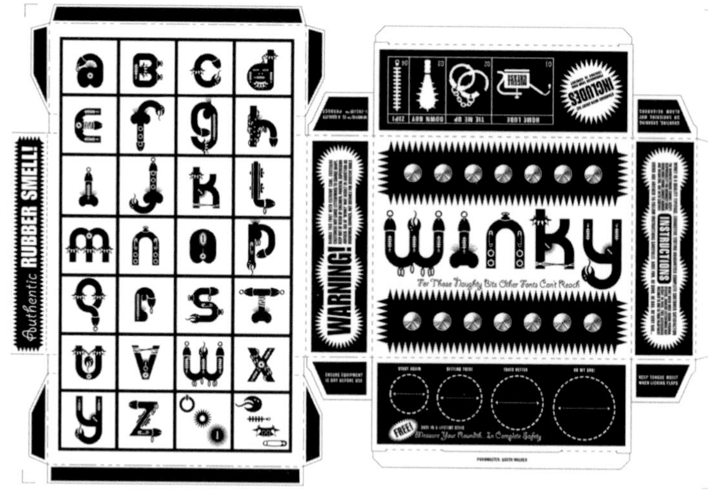

Garth Walker [South Africa]

1957– born in Pretoria
Admitted to AGI, 2002

Garth trained at Technikon Natal, Durban during the 1970s. In 1995 he launched Orange Juice Design in Durban. Many of South Africa's major corporate and consumer brands are among his clients. His projects are too numerous and varied to list, as he states himself. He specializes in branding and identity, literature and packaging. He is the editor and publisher of South Africa's only experimental graphics magazine *i-jusi*. The magazine is non-commercial and exists to create opportunities for designers from different backgrounds and cultures to collaborate and explore their own ideas. He has written articles for various magazines and also several books.

As a teacher, Garth has hosted student workshops in 6 countries. Among the industry awards he has received are: One Show, US (Gold 1998), Art Directors Club, US (Silver 1999), D&AD, UK (1998, 2002, 2005), Type Directors Club, US (1996, 1998, 1999, 2000, 2002, 2004) and Loeries, South Africa (Grand Prix, 6 Gold, 17 Silver 1998–2005).
His works can be found in the BNF, Paris, Victoria & Albert Museum Library, London and the Smithsonian Museum, Washington DC.

Spread from **i-jusi #14** on 'street-style fast food', explaining the finer points of sheep's head cuisine.

Fantasy font based on porn shop graphics and packaging.

Typeface for Constitutional Court of South Africa based on apartheid prisoner graffiti.

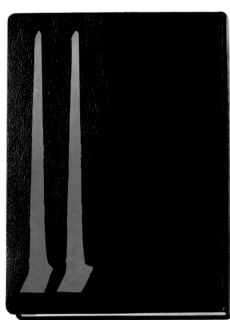

Inspiration from Tibet, book covers.

Rives Paper, promotional book.

Artron Color Printing Co., promotional book.

Yuefei Wang [China]

1956– born in Guangzhou
Admitted to AGI, 2002

Wang is creative director of Shenzhen Wang Yuefei Design Co., a member of NY ADC, scholarship commissioner of Shenzhen Graphic Designers Association and a committee member of Shenzhen Culture Fund Art Evaluation Committee.
He graduated from the Design Department of Guangzhou Academy of Arts in 1979. For many years Wang has devoted himself to the teaching of graphic design in China and in 1992, 1996 and 2005 he held three exhibitions entitled 'Graphic Design in China', which were the first international-style design contests in China and an important landmark in Chinese design history.

Since 1998 Wang has studied Tibetan characters and Buddhist culture, and has combined modern design elements with Tibetan cultural themes to design new Tibetan scripts. He finished the book *Inspiration from Tibet* in 2003 and won the Gold Prize, Shenzhen 03 Exhibition, a Tokyo TDC Prize Nomination 2005 and the NY TDC Excellence Prize 2005. Wang's works have won many prizes and honours, and are featured in the permanent collections of the following institutions: Museum für Kunst und Gewerbe Hamburg; International Corporate Center, New York; Museum für Zeitgenössische Kunst, Germany, Hong Kong Culture Museum and the Danish Poster Museum, Copenhagen.

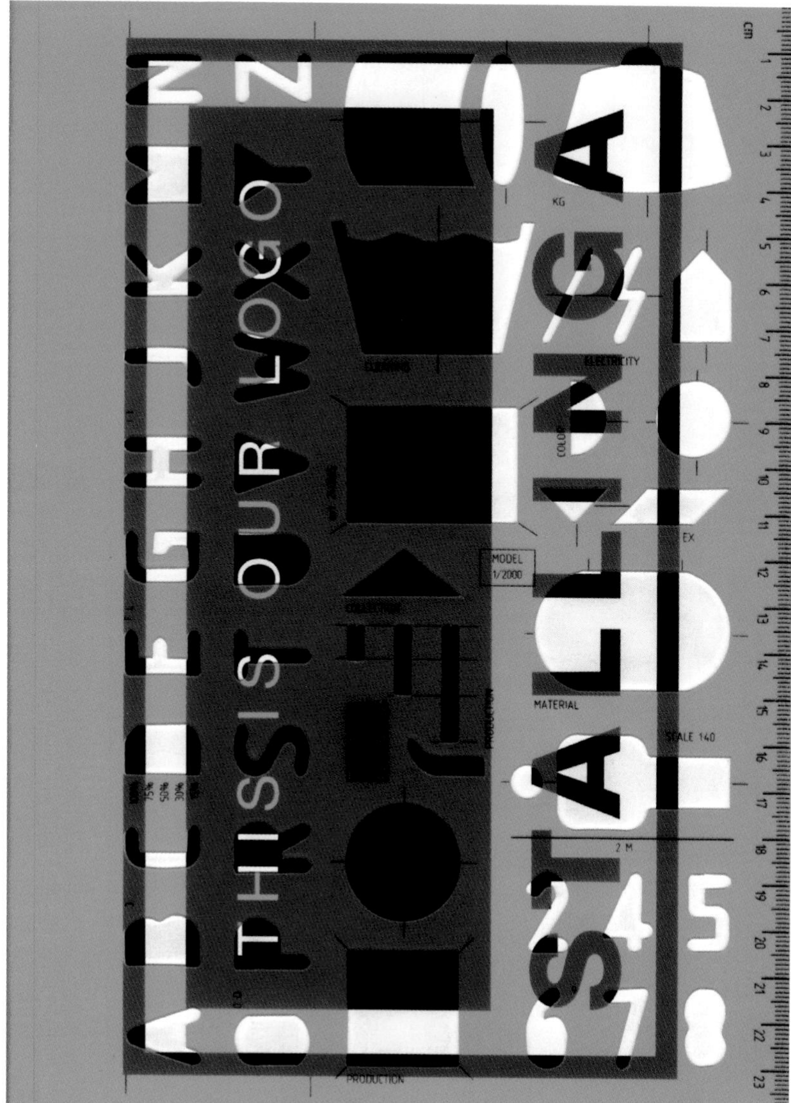

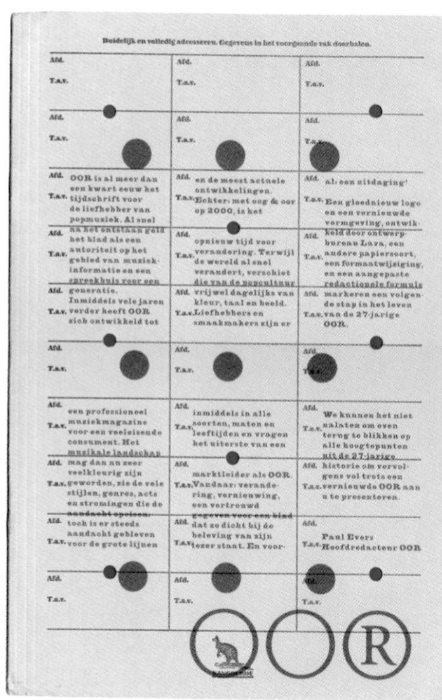

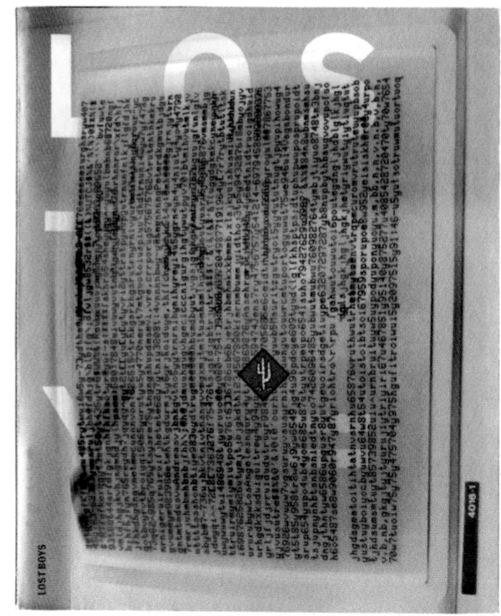

Hans Wolbers [The Netherlands]

1965– born in Oss
Admitted to AGI, 2002

After his studies, Hans Wolbers founded Lava Graphic Design in 1990. Lava is a leading creative studio in Amsterdam, with a variety of national and international clients. Lava does not have a specific visual style, but rather a specific approach to design. Working collaboratively with clients brings Lava closer to the real content, which results in more intelligent design. Lava is as creative in its content thinking as in its design thinking and calls this approach Content-Driven Design.

In 2000 Wolbers was elected Magazine Art Director of the Year in the Netherlands. He has given lectures and workshops throughout the world and his work has been exhibited in various countries. Lava's motto is:
'When you think you've got everything under control, you don't drive fast enough.'
– Alain Prost, former Formula One driver.

Cover for a monograph on **Henk Stallinga**.

Brochure for **Music Magazine OOR**.

Brochure cover for **Lost Boys**.

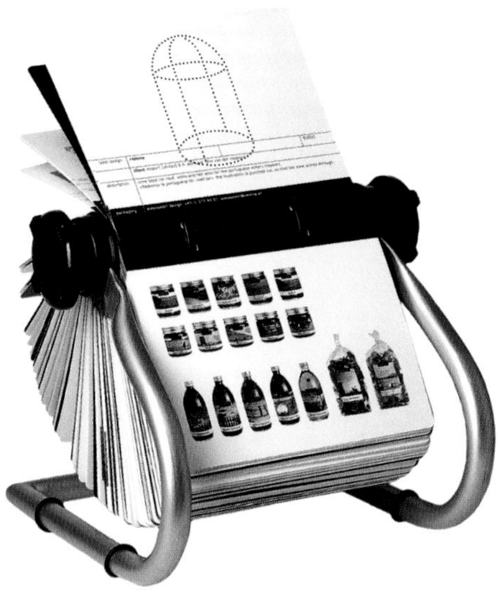

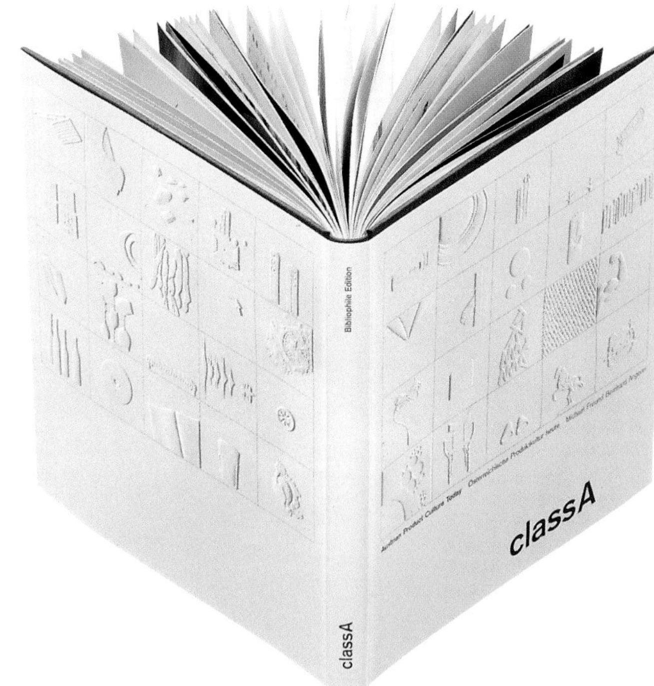

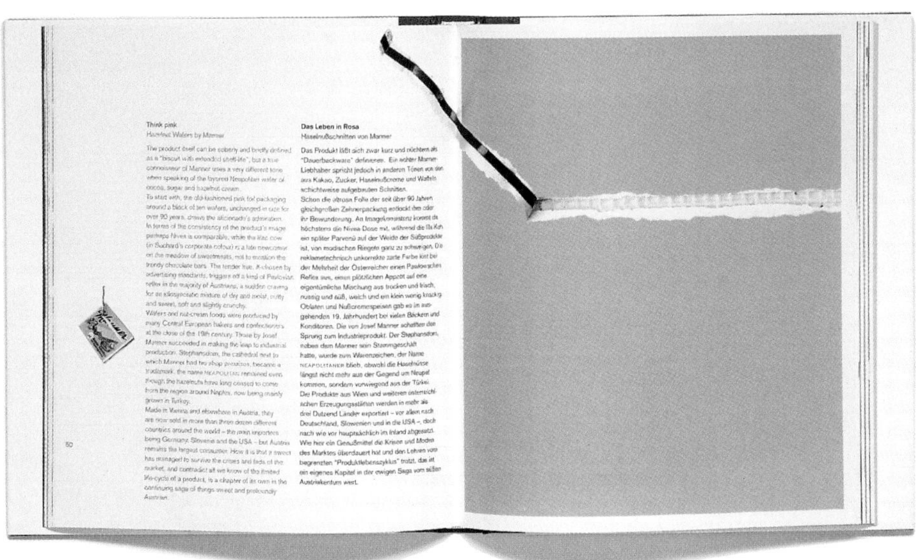

Think pink
Hazelnut Wafers by Manner

The product itself can be soberly and briefly defined as a "biscuit with extended shelf-life", but a true connoisseur of Manner uses a very different tone when speaking of the favored Neapolitan wafer of cocoa, sugar and hazelnut cream.
To start with, the old-fashioned pink foil packaging around a block of ten wafers, unchanged in size for over 90 years, draws the aficionado's admiration. In terms of the consistency of the product's image perhaps Nivea is comparable, while the lilac cow (in Suchard's corporate colour) is a late newcomer on the meadow of sweetmeats, not to mention the trendy chocolate bars. The tender hue, if chosen by advertising standards, triggers off a kind of Pavlovian reflex in the majority of Austrians, a sudden craving for an idiosyncratic mixture of dry and moist, nutty and sweet, soft and slightly crunchy.
Wafers and nut-cream foods were produced by many Central European bakers and confectioners at the close of the 19th century. Those by Josef Manner succeeded in making the leap to industrial production. Stephansdom, the cathedral next to which Manner had his shop premises, became a trademark, the name NEAPOLITANER remained even though the hazelnuts have long ceased to come from the region around Naples, now being mainly grown in Turkey.
Made in Vienna and elsewhere in Austria, they are now sold in more than three dozen different countries around the world – the main importers being Germany, Slovenia and the USA – but Austria remains the largest consumer. How it is that a sweet has managed to survive the crises and fads of the market, and contradict all we know of the limited life-cycle of a product, is a chapter of its own in the continuing saga of things sweet and profoundly Austrian.

Das Leben in Rosa
Haselnußschnitten von Manner

Das Produkt läßt sich zwar kurz und nüchtern als "Dauerbackware" definieren. Ein echter Manner-Liebhaber spricht jedoch in anderen Tönen von den aus Kakao, Zucker, Haselnußcreme und Waffeln schichtweise aufgebauten Schnitten.
Schon die altrosa Folie der seit über 90 Jahren gleichgroßen Zehnerpackung entlockt dem oder der ihr Bewunderung. An Imagekonsistenz kommt da höchstens die Nivea-Dose mit, während die lila Kuh ein später Parvenü auf der Weide der Süßprodukte ist, von modischen Riegeln ganz zu schweigen. Die reklametechnisch unkorrekte zarte Farbe löst bei der Mehrheit der Österreicher einen Pawlowschen Reflex aus, einen plötzlichen Appetit auf eine eigentümliche Mischung aus trocken und frisch, nussig und süß, weich und ein klein wenig knackig.
Oblaten und Nußcremespeisen gab es im ausgehenden 19. Jahrhundert bei vielen Bäckern und Konditoren. Die von Josef Manner schafften den Sprung zum Industrieprodukt. Der Stephansdom, neben dem Manner sein Stammgeschäft hatte, wurde zum Warenzeichen, der Name NEAPOLITANER blieb, obwohl die Haselnüsse längst nicht mehr aus der Gegend um Neapel kommen, sondern vorwiegend aus der Türkei.
Die Produkte aus Wien und weiteren österreichischen Erzeugungsstätten werden in mehr als drei Dutzend Länder exportiert – vor allem nach Deutschland, Slowenien und in die USA –, doch nach wie vor hauptsächlich im Inland abgesetzt. Wie hier ein Genußmittel die Krisen und Moden des Marktes überdauert hat und den Lehren vom begrenzten "Produktlebenszyklus" trotzt, das ist ein eigenes Kapitel in der ewigen Saga vom süßen Austriakentum wert.

50

Cordula Alessandri [Austria]

A standard **Rolodex file** was taken as a model and enlarged, to be used for presentation of the studio's portfolio. This system is easy to present and especially easy to update.

class A: Austrian product culture today (x 2). Images of 40 Austrian products are embossed and arranged in miniature on the front and back cover. Throughout the book the lines of the raster emerge, printed in brilliant varnish.

1960– born in Salzburg
Admitted to AGI, 2003

From 1978 to 1982 Cordula attended the University of Applied Arts in Vienna, where she majored in graphic design with Prof. Herbert Schwarz. Subsequently she got three more years of basic training with her typographic mentor Joey Badian. In 1985, at the age of 24, she became an art director at DDB Needham Worldwide, Vienna. In 1987 she established her own studio Alessandri Design, creating packaging, editorial and corporate design, advertising and financial communications on the forefront of the Austrian design and advertising community. With a team of young outstanding talents always around her, Cordula encourages them to creatively interpret their own ideas.

Numerous national and international awards and publications reaffirm these high standards of quality, Cordula is demanding of herself and her team. From 2003 to 2005 Cordula taught at the University of Arts in Saarbrücken, Germany. Her performances are focused on the communication of 'Sense and Sensitivity in Design'. Cordula has two sons: Tiziano (15) and Lorenzo (9).

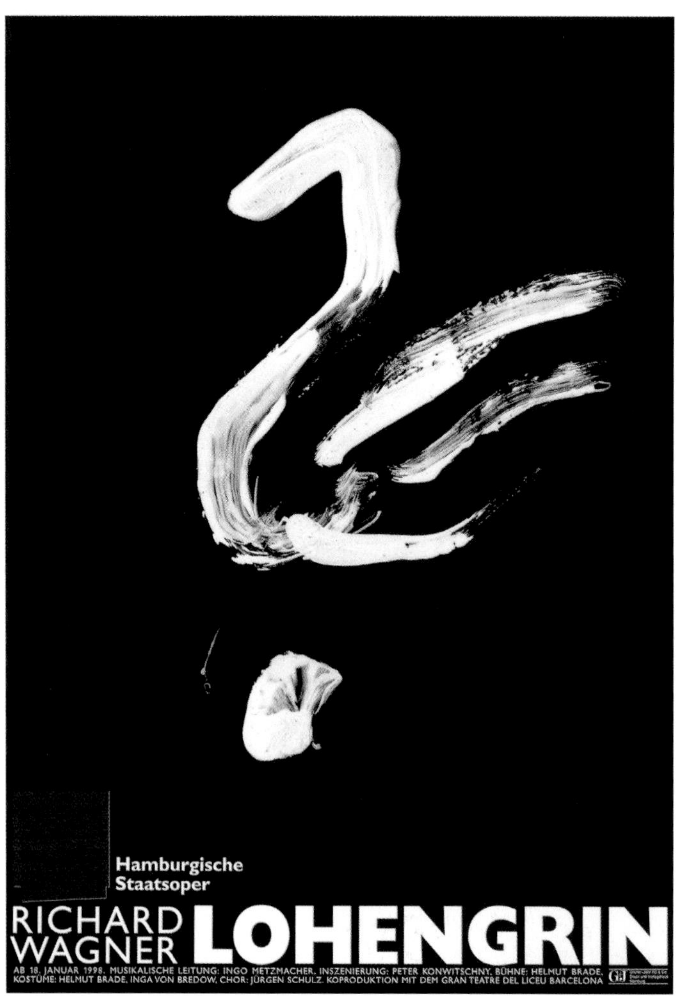

Helmut Brade [Germany]

1937– born in Halle, Saale
Admitted to AGI, 2003

Brade studied ceramic arts, architecture and graphic design at the Hochschule für Formgestaltung, Halle-Burg Giebichenstein. After his studies he started his career as freelancer in various graphic design fields in Halle. He designs posters and books, but specializes in set design for theatre and opera performances in Berlin, Hannover, Budapest, Tübingen, Kassel, Nuremberg, Basel, Leipzig, Hamburg, Paris, Barcelona, Tokyo, Oslo and Copenhagen. He is a professor of graphic design at the College of Arts and Design Burg Giebichenstein in Halle.

He has participated in exhibitions all over the world and was the subject of a retrospective in Halle in 2003 and Berlin in 2004. He won the National Award of the DDR (1983), the Halle Handel Prize (1990) and the Kunstpreis Sachsen-Anhalt (2003). His works feature in several German and international collections.

Richard Wagner: ***Lohengrin***,
poster, 1998.

Hugo von Hofmannsthal: ***Jedermann***,
poster, 2001.

William Shakespeare: ***Timon of Athens***,
poster, 1993.

Sculptures Alphabetiques, 1997.
Painted wood, limited edition: 26 copies.

Jeu de Construction, 2005.
Installation at the Centre Pompidou, Paris,

CD covers, 2001–2003.
Publisher: Editions de Vive Voix.

Paul Cox [France]

1959– born in Paris
Admitted to AGI, 2003

Although he began to learn the violin and was keen to become a musician, Paul Cox soon turned to painting, reassured about his choice by his meeting, as a teenager, with Pierre Alechinsky. A self-taught artist, Cox studied art history and English with a view to earning a living and becoming 'a Sunday painter for whom every day would be a Sunday', in the words of Dubuffet. After writing a thesis on Laurence Sterne and gaining a teaching qualification, he quickly stopped teaching, preferring to design children's books, posters, illustrations for the press, logos, etc., as well as keeping up his painting. He also works for the stage, designing sets and costumes for *L'Histoire du soldat* (Opéra de Nancy, 1997) and *The Nutcracker* (Opéra de Genève, 2005). He has published games and is interested in all printing techniques, which he uses more for experimental production than reproduction – as seen in *A Sentimental Journey*, his recent series of modular maps revisited for one of his collections by Issey Miyake. Cox has begun the regular publication of his work in book form, with the first volume, *Coxcodex I*, being published by Le Seuil in 2004. The Centre Pompidou exhibited his large-scale installation *Jeu de Construction* (*Construction Set*) in 2005.

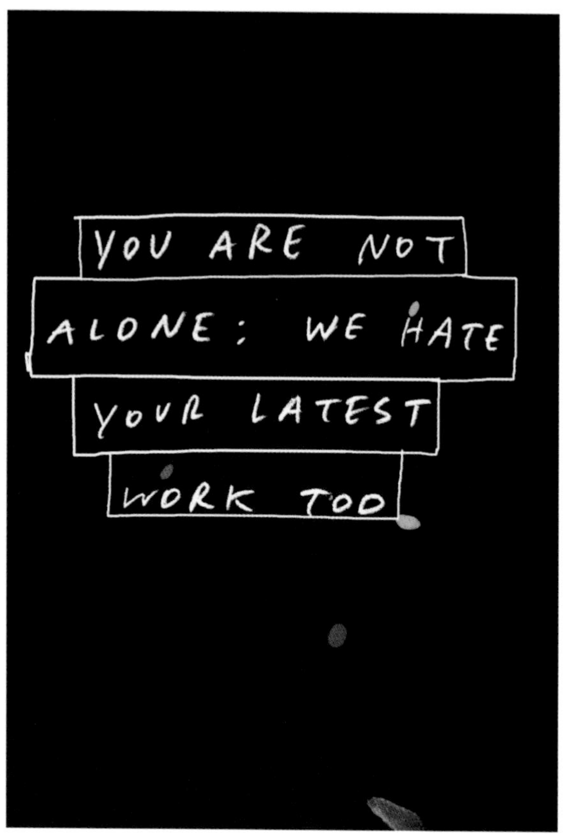

Paul Davis [UK]

1962– born in Somerset
Admitted to AGI, 2003

Work featured in: Creative Review, Time Out, Graphics International, Print (US), *Barfout* (Japan), *Dazed & Confused, Self Service* (France), *Illustration* (Japan), *Bibel* (Sweden), *Doing Bird* (Australia), *Independent on Sunday, iD, Arena, Blueprint, Clear, Eye Magazine, Black Book, 3X3, Esquire, Varoom. Exhibitions:* 2003: 'My Room Somehow, Somewhere', GM Gallery, Osaka; 'The Ganzfeld Unbound', Adam Baumgold Gallery, New York; 'Drawnpaintedprint', Speakfor Gallery, Tokyo; 'New Work', Colette, Paris; 'I love', Brussels; 2004: 'Ballpoint', Pentagram, London; 'Grafitti Meets Windows', Osaka; 'PARC 1', London and Birmingham; 'God Knows', Browns, London; 2005: 'Improved', Rivington Gallery, London; 'Gelman/Davis', Andrew Roth Gallery, New York; Poster Exhibition, Tokyo; 'It's Not About You, The Wapping Project', London; 'CET05', Nihonbashi, Tokyo; 'It's Not About You Again', IID Gallery, Tokyo; 2006: Soi Sabai, Bangkok; 'I'm So Free', Harry's Loft, New York; 'Heidiland-Ku', Nanzuka Underground, Tokyo. *Publications: Blame Everyone Else*, London: Browns with Westerham Press, 2003 (Printed Book of the Year); *Them and Us*, London: Laurence King and Princeton, NJ: Princeton Architectural Press, 2004; *GELMAN/DAVIS*, self-published, 2004; *God Knows*, London: Browns, 2005; *Marketing Photographs*, Zürich: Nieves Books, 2005; *THINK4: The Thinking of Paul Davis*, London: Browns with Howard Smith Paper, 2005.

Invitation to exhibition **I'm So Free** at Harry's Loft, New York, 2006.

Drawing for **Varoom magazine**, 2006.

Spread from **Blame Everyone Else** published by Browns, London, 2003.

Points of Access, poster for Grüntuch Ernst Architects, 2004.

AT – Aki Takase, poster for Deutsches Theater Berlin, 2001.

Silent Film and Music Festival, poster for Kino Babylon, Berlin, 2005.

Dieter Feseke [Germany]

1955– born in Salzwedel
Admitted to AGI, 2003

Feseke graduated from FWG Berlin-Schöneweide and has worked in Berlin since 1986. In the DDR he formed the successful design team Grappa with Baarmann, Franke, Fiedler and Trogisch. From this source originated Cyan, Blotto (Grebin & Trogisch), Umbra (Baarmann) and Dor (Feseke & Döring).
In 2005 Umbra and Dor started a cooperative, together with their friends Frank Döring, Robert Krzeminski, Caroline Winkler and others. They work mainly in Berlin Pankow, as well as elsewhere. Most of their work is for the cultural sector: architecture, art, design, film, photography, music, dance and theatre. Feseke has worked with several of these partners.

His clients include Bauhaus Dessau, Deutsches Theater Berlin, Babylon Berlin, publishing firms, artists and architects; he works on corporate design, posters and books, as well as Project Typomoon (2001–2007). The monograph *Dieter Feseke: from Grappa to Umbra Dor* will be published in China in 2007. From 2003–2005 he taught at the Hochschule für Grafik- und Buchkunst, Leipzig. Solo exhibitions have been held in Carcassonne (France), DDD Gallery Osaka and Grafill Oslo. Awards include Lahti Poster Biennial, 1989; 100 Best Posters, Berlin, 1995; Red Dot Award, Germany, 2002. His works have featured in *Eye*, *Creative Review*, *Who is Who*, *IDEA* and *Type, Image, Message* and in MoMA New York and the Kunstgewerbemuseum Hamburg.

J-ONE

ABCDEFGHI

THE QUICK BROWN FOX JUMPS OVER A LAZY DOG

JKLMNOPQ

RSTUVW

XYZ 12345 <

67890

–

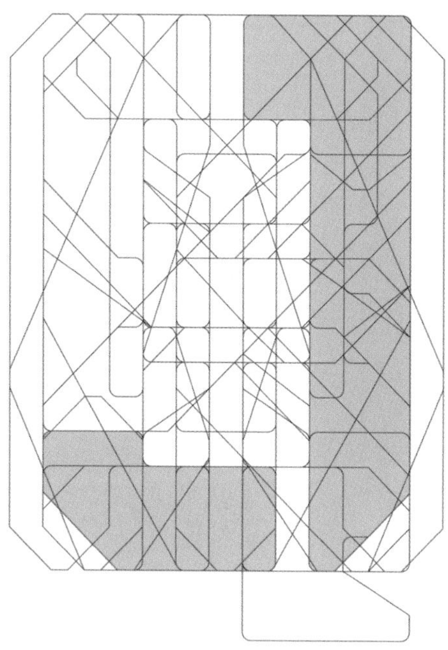

Michel Lepetitdidier [France]

1962– born in Metz
Admitted to AGI, 2003

I haven't figured out if graphic design is my life. Maybe I'll never know, but art may be my reason to live and thus a good reason to work in this direction.

Gently, you enroll in art school, (School of Fine Arts, Metz), 1980 and after five years you graduate and leave. Quietly, you begin to work, (1985) with desire, without certainties but with strength. Slowly, you convince a concert hall (Arsenal Metz), museums (Nicéphore Niépce and Denon in Chalon-sur-Saône, American Art of Giverny, Fine Arts of Dijon, Nancy, Metz), theatres (La Manufacture in Nancy, Jarnisy), publishers (Au Figuré, Paris Musées), a television channel (Arte), from the sidelines. Far from the Paris spotlight you continue alone, then as a pair, as a trio, and then alone again, in a studio which uses your name. Now visible, you begin to teach (School of Decorative Arts, Strasbourg; National School of Fine Arts, Nancy), your works appear in *Graphis* and *Étapes*, you are a jury member for competitions and awards, and you lead student workshops (Échirolles, Art School).

I have been working for more than twenty years, and am both satisfied to have achieved this and unhappy for only having come this far. Although graphic design is not my life, it fills it entirely.

Corporate identity typography for **Jacquet Metals** (x 2), 2006.

Illustration for programme of events 2001–2, Théâtre de la Manufacture, Nancy, 2001.

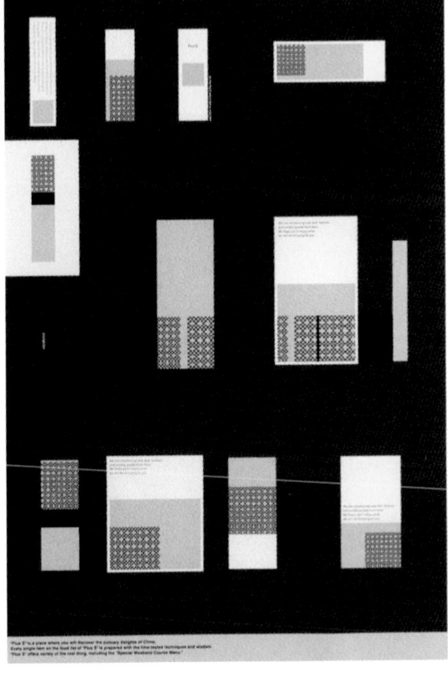

Kei Matsushita [Japan]

+ Silk, work prepared for an annual exhibition held by the paper material dealer Takeo Company Ltd, 2005 (x 2). Inkjet and silkscreen print on paper.

Design News 261 Renewal Kit, a collection of promotional tools designed for a relaunch of a product design magazine, 2003. Offset and inkjet print on paper.

1961– born in Yokohama
Admitted to AGI, 2003

Kei Matsushita graduated in general design from Tokyo National University of Fine Arts and Music, General Design Course in 1985 and then in 1987 completed his postgraduate studies in visual design at the same university. In 1990, he established the Kei Matsushita Design Room. Currently he is an associate professor at the Department of Fine Arts, Tokyo National University of Fine Arts and Music. Prizes include the JAGDA New Designer Awards and Tokyo ADC Awards.

Recent works include a cover design for *Design News* magazine, and overall artistic direction of Benesse Art Site Naoshima (an island art museum) and the Takeo Paper Show 2005. *Membership:* Tokyo Type Directors Club, Japan Graphic Designers Association, Inc.

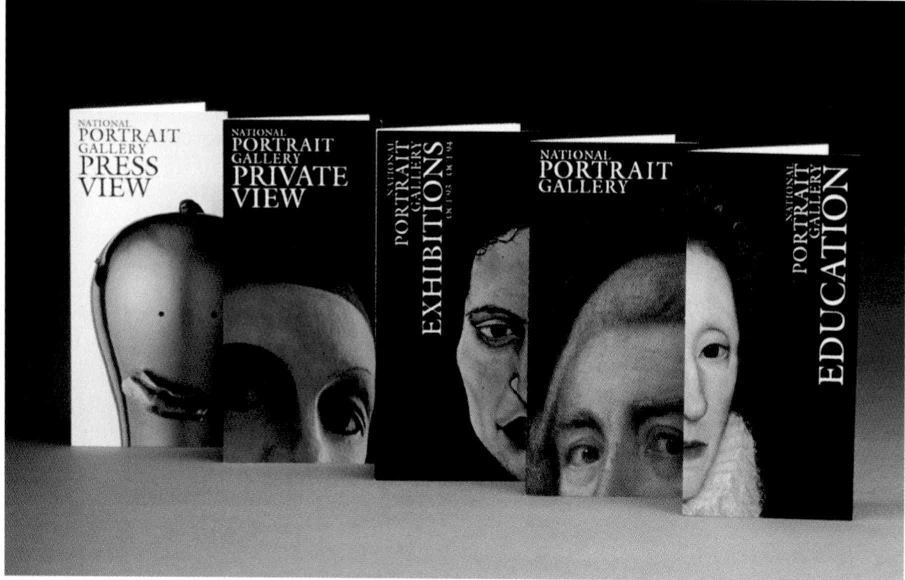

Justus Oehler [UK]

1961– born in Tokyo, Japan
Admitted to AGI, 2003

Justus was born in Japan and grew up in France and Greece. In the early eighties he studied visual communication at the Fachhochschule in Munich. His first job as graphic designer was with Rolf Müller. In 1987 he moved to London and graduated from Central School of Art and Design with a Master's Degree. He joined Pentagram's London office in 1989 and became a partner in 1995. In 2003 he opened the Pentagram office in Berlin.

Justus produces corporate identities, publications, environmental design and visual communication programmes for a diverse array of clients worldwide. His projects have included corporate design work for clients such as the Internet company Tiscali, the Premier Automotive Group, the Philharmonie Luxembourg, the World Economic Forum, the Mozart Haus Vienna and the global airline network Star Alliance.

Naming and corporate identity for **Star Alliance**, a global airline network.

Book design for portrait photographer **Nigel Parry**.

Corporate design for the **National Portrait Gallery** in London.

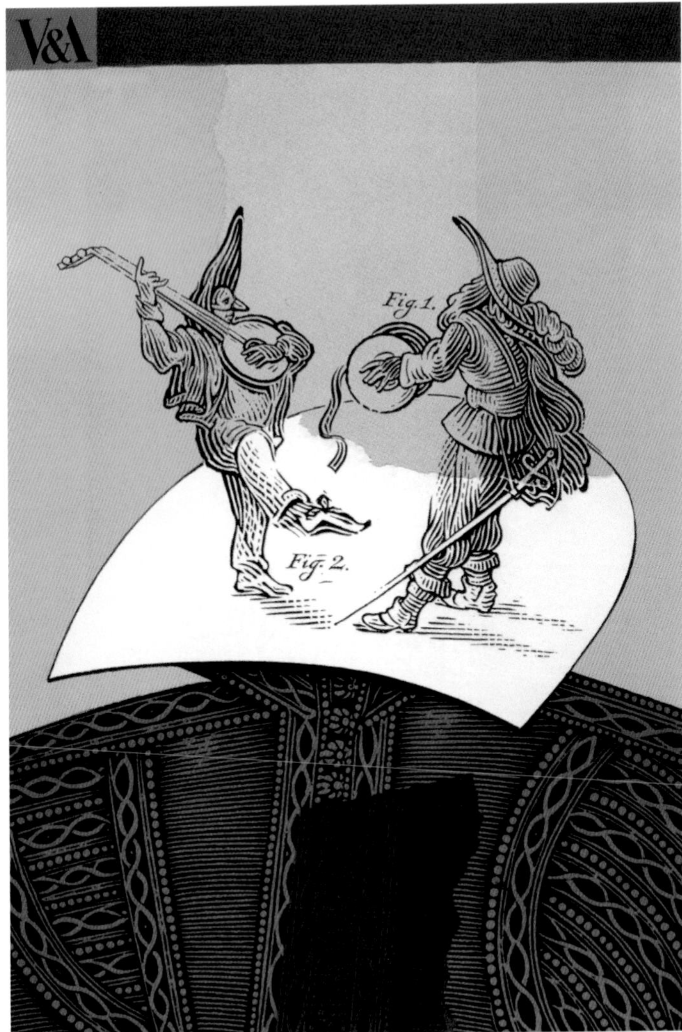

Shakespeare, exhibition poster for Victoria & Albert Museum, 1999.

West Side Story, theatre poster, 1996.

Attila Jozsef Centenary, poster, 2005.

Istvan Orosz [Hungary]

1951– born in Kecskemet
Admitted to AGI, 2003

Istvan Orosz, also known as Utisz, was trained as graphic designer at the University of Arts and Design in Budapest. After graduation, in 1975, he became interested in theatre and film animation and started his career as a stage designer and animation film director. Later he also designed posters, mainly for theatre, movie and exhibitions. During the East European democratic changes he drew some political posters as well. He is known as a painter and printmaker. As an illustrator he is inspired by the Dutch graphic artist M.C. Escher. He likes to use visual paradox and illusionistic approaches while following traditional printing techniques such as woodcuts and etching.

Istvan exhibits in major international exhibitions of posters and graphic art and his animated films are often shown in Hungary and abroad. He is a film director at the Pannonia Film Studio in Budapest, a teacher at the West Hungarian University, a co-founder of Hungarian Poster Association, and a member of the Hungarian Art Academy. Awards include: gold medal at the Biennial of Graphic Design Brno (1990), first prize at the International Poster Biennial, Lahti (1991), Icograda prize at the International Poster Show, Chaumont (1994), gold medal at the Annual Exhibition of Society of Illustrators, New York (2001).

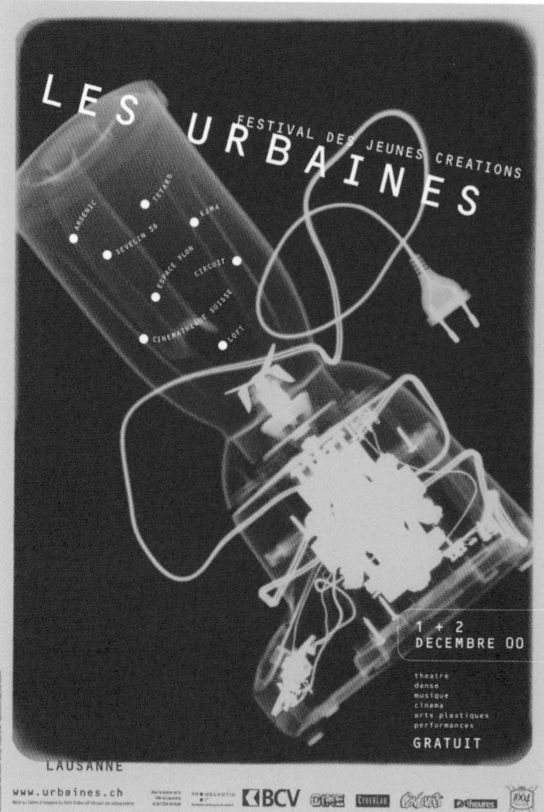

Giorgio Pesce [Switzerland]

1966– born in Lausanne
Admitted to AGI, 2003

Giorgio Pesce studied at the École Cantonale d'Art de Lausanne (ECAL), and on training courses in Spain and France. He worked in New York for a year and was influenced by Tibor Kalman, whom he met there. He opened Atelier Poisson in 1995 in Lausanne. He works mainly in the cultural/institutional domain, on global corporate images from posters to programmes as well on museography and signage. Giorgio is also the illustrator on all his projects, constantly drawing and painting. Attracted to vintage objects, books and signs, he often uses antique inspirations for his new designs. He also eats fish.

Atelier Poisson clients include Arsenic Theatre, La Manufacture school theatre, Lausanne Jardins urban garden festival, Espace des Inventions science museum for kids, Swiss Dance Festival, Alph@ outdoor poster exhibition, Museum Night, *Tracés* architecture magazine, and Lausanne Geological Museum. Numerous works have been awarded by the Type Directors Club NY, Art Directors Club NY, and 100 Best Posters, and published in books on design in the UK, the US and China. His work has also featured in exhibitions at the Bibliothèque Nationale, Paris (2001), and the Centre Culturel Suisse, Paris (2003), and his posters appear in the collection of the Museum für Gestaltung, Zürich.

University Theatre Festival, poster, 1997. The idea was to show that underneath the surface lie many things worth discovering.

Young people's festival of performing arts, poster, 2000. For six years running, x-ray images were used as a basis for the posters, each time on another subject: here, domestic appliances.

Atelier Poisson business card. It has never changed since the opening of the studio.

Arsenic Theatre, seasonal programme. Every year the programme becomes a different object, easy to carry and giving all the essential information.

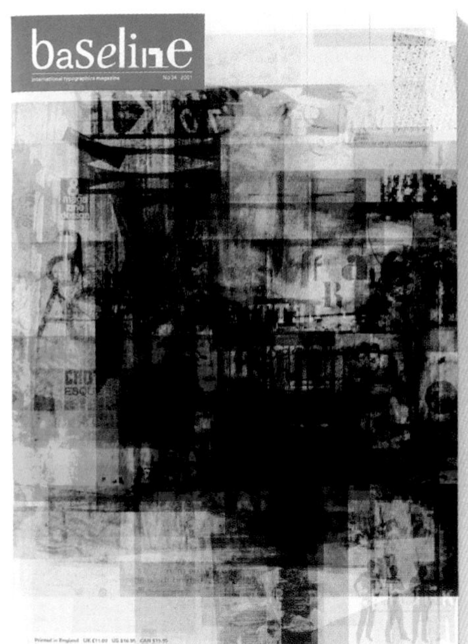

Merz to Emigre and Beyond: Avant Garde Magazine Design of the 20th Century, London: Phaidon, 2003.

Visual identity for **WL** (Werkzeuge Lauer), tool manufacturing company, Germany, 1995.

Baseline magazine '2', # 32, illustration and cover design, 2000.

Baseline magazine 'internal – external' # 34, electronic illustration and cover design, 2001.

Hans Dieter Reichert [UK]

1959– born in Würdinghausen, Germany
Admitted to AGI, 2003

Career: 1977: apprentice compositor. 1982–87: studies graphic design at the universities of Essen, Wuppertal, Basel and London. 1986: first professional experience in Amsterdam at BRS and Total Design. 1987: returns to England and continues professional career with Banks & Miles London. 1993: starts own company, HDR Visual Communication. 1995: co-founds company Bradbourne Publishing Ltd. Works as editor, art director and publisher, and produces the quarterly international typographic magazine *Baseline* as well as small limited-edition publications. HDR Visual Communication works on high-quality projects for a variety of clients in various fields: architecture, banking, car and tool manufacturing, jewelry, publishing and government. 1989–2004: guest lecturer at universities of Bath and Reading. 1998–2002: external examiner at University of Northampton (Nene College). Lectures in Austria, Britain, Switzerland and Germany. Fellow of the International Society of Typographic Designers London (1992), Fellow of Royal Society of the Arts (1992), Honorary Member of Biennale Brno (1996). Honorary Degree from UCCA: University College for Creative Arts (2006). 1999: participated in design competition Kieler Woche 2001. Design awards in New York, England, Germany, France, Czech Republic and Japan. Juror at AOI: Association of Illustrators, London, ISTD: International Society of Typographic Designers, London, D&AD, London, and ADC NY.

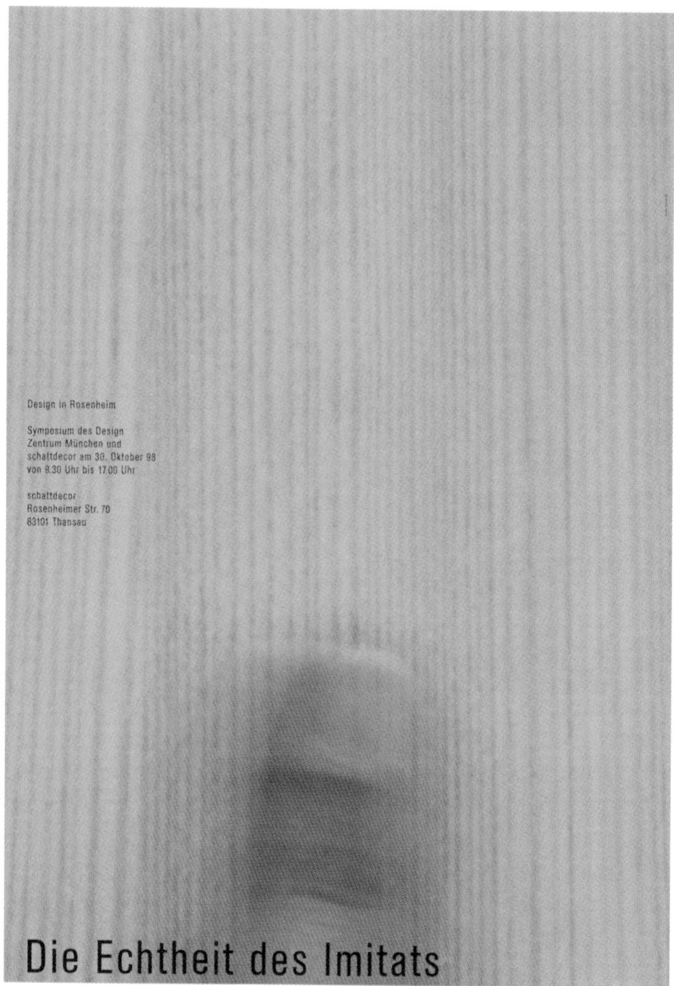

Gerwin Schmidt [Germany]

1966– born in Munich
Admitted to AGI, 2003

1987: graduated from high school in Munich. 1988–89: community service, work with animated cartoons, work for agencies, drawing school. 1990–92: studied graphic-design at Kassel University (Visual Communication Department) under Prof. Gunter Rambow. 1992–97: studied visual communication at design college HfG Karlsruhe under Prof. Gunter Rambow, Kurt Weidemann, Werner Jeker, painting under Prof. Günther Förg. 1993–97: freelance designer in Karlsruhe, Cologne and Munich. Has his own design office in Munich since 1997. Book and poster design, mostly for cultural clients, including: Design Centre Munich, Die Neue Sammlung Munich, Haus der Kunst Munich, Staatsgalerie Stuttgart.Corporate design for cultural events and business clients. Since 1998: graphic design for the film magazine *Revolver*. Since 2001: corporate design for Gaggenau. Mid-1999–2003: guest lecturer at Fachhochschule Vorarlberg, Austria, Intermedia Department. 2000: poster workshop for the Icelandic Design Association in Reykjavik. 2001: guest lecturer at the Icelandic Academy of the Arts (Department of Visual Arts), Reykjavik. Poster workshop at the invitation of the Goethe Institut at the Krakow Academy of Arts, Poland, Graphic Design Department. Since 2003: professor at the State Academy of Art Stuttgart, Visual Communication Department. Awards and prizes in national and international book and poster competitions.

Die Echtheit des Imitats (The Authenticity of Imitation), poster for a design symposium, 1998. Client: Design Centre Munich.

Blickpunkt 1926 (Point of View 1926), poster, 2003. An exhibition of international posters that were first shown at Die Neue Sammlung, Munich in 1926. Client: Die Neue Sammlung, Munich.

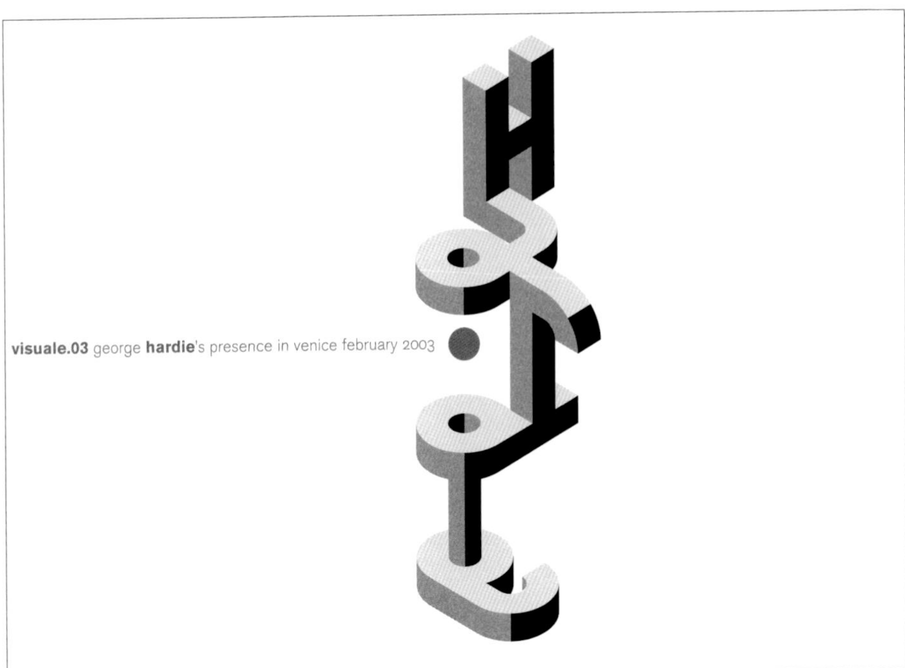

Visuale03: Tradurre tradire condurre condire, poster for lecture at IUAV, Venice, 2003.

Visuale03: George Hardie's Presence In Venice, poster for lecture at IUAV, Venice, 2003.

Pierpaolo Vetta [Italy]

1955-2003; born in Trieste
Admitted to AGI, 2003

Pierpaolo graduated in architecture at the IUAV in Venice, where later he taught editorial design. He started his professional involvement in graphic design by working on Sol Lewitt's installation at the Venice Biennale 1976, followed by the Festival dei Due Mondi in Spoleto, and the exhibition 'Venezia e lo Spazio Scenico' at Aldo Rossi's Teatro del Mondo. With Paolo Tassinari he founded Tassinari/Vetta design office in Trieste in 1980, working mainly in the areas of editorial and exhibition design for cultural institutions in Italy as well as for major publishing houses, and cooperating with architects and designers such as Gae Aulenti, Achille Castiglioni and Massimo Vignelli.

Vetta was art director of *Casabella* architectural magazine from 1996 and of the architecture department of Electa publishing house from 2001. In 2002 together with Paolo Tassinari and Leonardo Sonnoli he founded the Codesign partnership (later merged with Tassinari/Vetta), which was in charge of the visual identity for the 50th Venice Biennale.

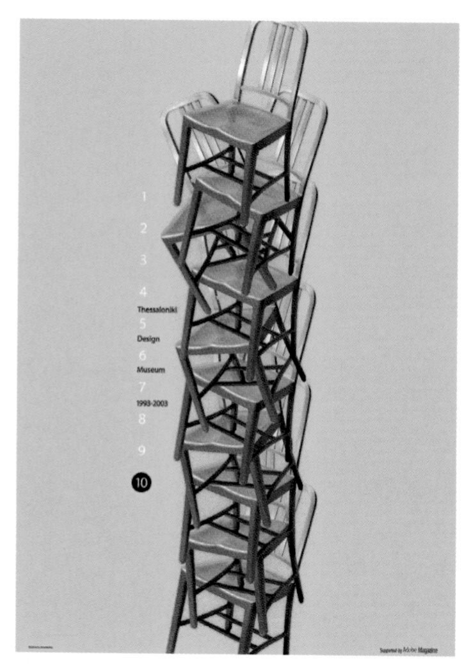

Dimitris Arvanitis [Greece]

1948– born in Halkis
Admitted to AGI, 2004

Arvanitis studied painting and graphic design between 1966–72. From 1976–85 he was art director for EMI Records Greece and from 1986–90 for *Tachidromos* magazine. He also designed the magazines *Jazz*, *Periodiko*, *Minima*, *Diphono*, *Adobe Magazine*, *Ntefi*, *Jazz & Tzaz* and *Kaleidoscopio*.
He is amazingly productive, designing book covers, posters, records sleeves, logos and typography.
He is a member of the Cannibal Fonts company and has his own studio, Espresso Studio.

Arvanitis is one of the few Greek graphic designers who are active on an international level. He writes many articles on design for magazines and newspapers, and has participated in many poster festivals around Europe.

Radio Moscow, film poster, 1995.

10 Years, poster for Thessaloniki Design Museum, 2004.

Hellenic Authors' Society, poster.

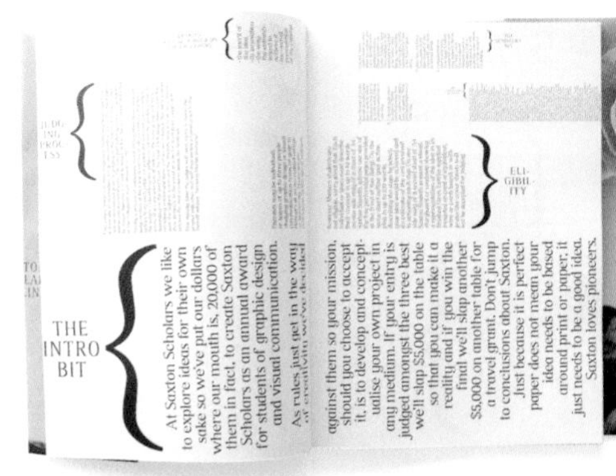

A series of visual diaries investigating fashion and beauty for **Saxton Paper**, 2005.

Christmas poster developed for Precinct Design in 1999, to challenge the Y2K bug, cultural diversity and Christmas.

Andrew Ashton [Australia]

1969– born in Sydney
Admitted to AGI, 2004

Andrew graduated from the Randwick School of Design, Sydney, in 1989. In 1994 he co-founded the graphic design partnership Nelmes Smith Ashton. The partnership had several incarnations over ten years, the last being Precinct Design. During this period Andrew developed a unique body of work in the arts and creative services sectors. In 1999 Andrew relocated permanently to Melbourne. A change in geography saw a shift in Andrew's work that embraced a local vernacular of image, message and form – he called this work 'the beautiful everyday'.

In 2003 Andrew left Precinct Design to establish Studio Pip and Co., a small independent and collaborative practice that works with its clients to bring together strategic thinking, writing, image making and design craft. The Studio executes brand, event, digital and print projects for clients that include: Australian Graphic Design Association, Australian Paper, City of Melbourne, Computershare Limited, Spicers Paper, National Design Centre and Chamber Music Australia. Andrew balances his life in design by blending into the everyday with his wife Pip, and his two young boys Willem and Henry whenever possible.

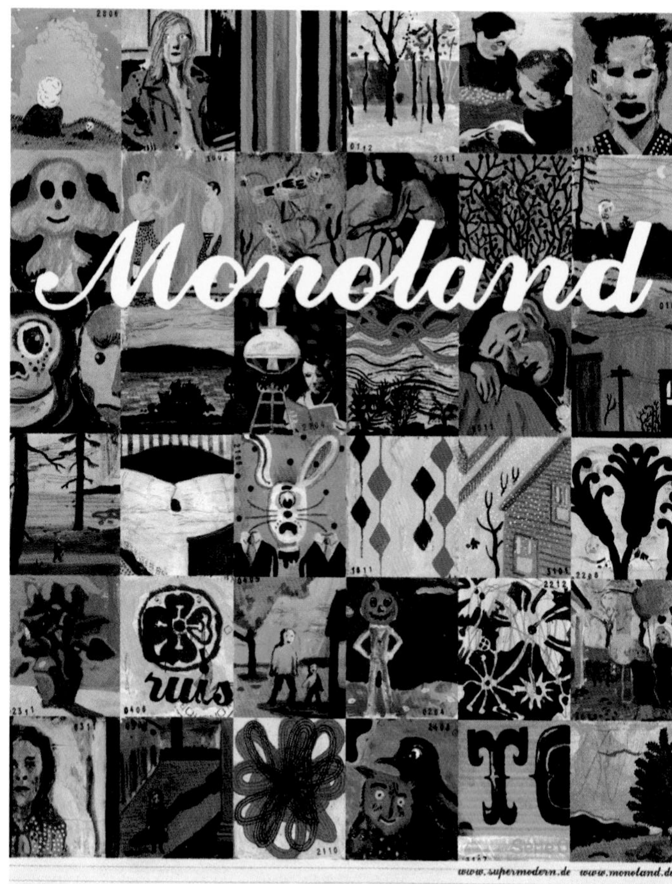

Hans-Georg Barber [Germany]

1967– born in Frankfurt/O
Admitted to AGI, 2004

Barber is an artist and illustrator who lives and works in Berlin, Ghent and Stockholm. He went to graphic design school (1984–86), and studied Visual Communication at the HDK Berlin (1990–95). Since 2002, Barber has taught at art schools in Vienna, Hamburg and Berlin. Since 2006 he has been a professor of illustration at St Lucas Art School in Ghent, Belgium. He works on illustrations for books, magazines and comic books for international publishers. His work has been shown at exhibitions in Paris, Lisbon, New York, Helsinki, Stockholm, Brussels, Kyoto and Zürich.

Monoland, poster for the Berlin-based music group, 2006. Design by ATAK/bax offset.

Gertrude Stein: *Ada*, book cover, 2005. Published by Büchergilde Gutenberg as an original offset print.

Wondertüte #2: Zwischenherbst, 1998. Comic book published by Jochen Enterprises Berlin, offset.

Live Fossil, poster for Chinese Printing Museum.

Playing in the Garden, Suzhou Image, 2004.

Fang Cao [China]

1956– born in Su Zhou
Admitted to AGI, 2004

Fang Cao is a professor at the Nanjing Arts Institute and a member of the Industrial Design Association of China, and has been awarded the title of 'Distinguished Teacher' by Jiangsu Education Bureau. In 1996 she was invited by Aichi Art University, Japan to lecture on the graphic design of Chinese characters, and the same university and the Nanjing College of Arts exhibited her work on the same theme in 1997 (with Shiraki of Japan). From 1999–2005 she published ten design books on different aspects of graphic design and in 1999 she lectured at the Kassel Art Institute in Germany and visited design schools in nine European countries, to study their design courses and work.

She publishes frequently in design journals on topics including logo and book design. From 2000 on she exhibited her *Chinese Characters and Music* series at Hong Kong Heritage Museum, Track 16 Gallery, Santa Monica, and Zürich Design Museum. She won a silver award at the 10th National Art Exhibition and another at the National Packaging Design competition. She has received over 30 national and international prizes.

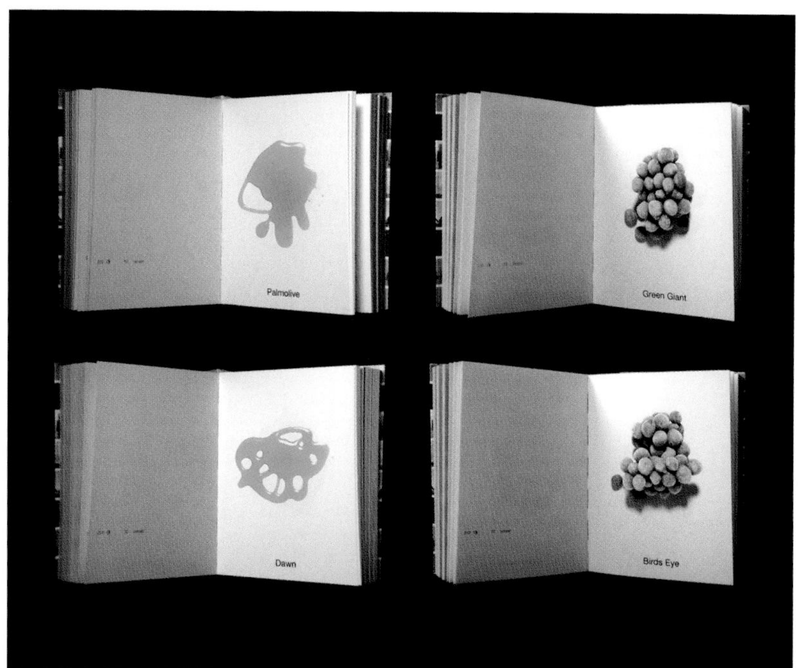

Bob Dinetz [USA]

1963– born in New York City
Admitted to AGI, 2004

Bob Dinetz opened his own studio in 2003. In recent years, projects have included everything from an ad campaign for a brand of cheese to identity programmes to a US postage stamp. Bob's work has been recognized by design competitions and publications including AIGA, American Center for Design, the Clio Awards, Communication Arts, *Graphis*, New York Art Directors Club, and the permanent collections of the Cooper Hewitt National Design Museum, the San Francisco Museum of Modern Art and the Chicago Athenaeum Museum of Architecture and Design. In 1997, Bob won the Marget Larsen Award for design excellence.

From a book for **Stora Enso paper**, this section illustrates undifferentiated markets by comparing brands without using their packaging, logos or commercials.

Logo for a **literary festival** known for its intimate gatherings with well-known authors.

Technology company annual report, depicting the power of the human voice.

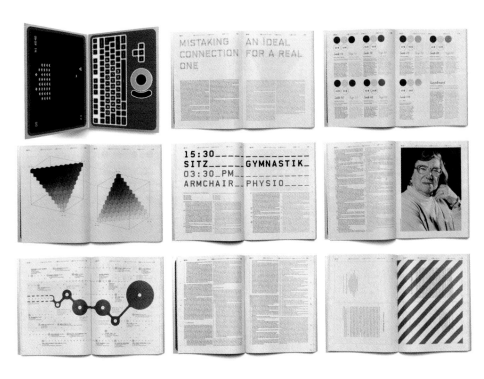

Markus Dressen [Germany]

Printed Matter, design work by Markus Dressen, Spector, Leipzig, 1997–2005.

Dieter Schnebel: *Majakowskis Tod – Totentanz*, poster for the Leipzig Opera, 1998.

Spector cut+paste, issue#2, 2002.
Edited by Markus Dressen, Anne König, Jan Wenzel. 128 pages, 23 x 29.6 cm, offset, brochure, adhesive bond. The Best German Book Design 2002.

1971– born in Münster
Admitted to AGI, 2004

Markus graduated from the Leipzig Academy of Visual Arts & Graphic Design in 1999. Between 1999 and 2002 he taught at the Leipzig Academy of Visual Arts as an assistant lecturer. The collaborative project Spector was founded in 2000 and Markus is co-editor of its magazine outlet, *cut+paste*. What is Spector? It can be an office, a magazine, a network or even a temporary venue in Leipzig. Even so, work on publications on contemporary fine art is still at the core of Spector. Since 2004 he has been senior lecturer for first and second year graphic design at the Leipzig Academy.

The Studio's work includes book designs for contemporary artists; recent examples include projects for Jochen Gerz, Eberhard Havekost, Ramon Haze, Jorg Herold, Christine Hill, Susan Hiller, Jenny Holzer, Ilya Kabakov, Olaf Nicolai, Neo Rauch and Matthias Weischer. Clients include, among others, the Leipzig Museum of Contemporary Art, Leipzig Opera, Dresden Museum of Technology and the Arts Council of the Free State of Saxony. Markus has received numerous national and international awards for his design work, such as the Golden Letter in the competition for The World's Best Designed Books 2004. He has taken part in many national and international exhibitions.

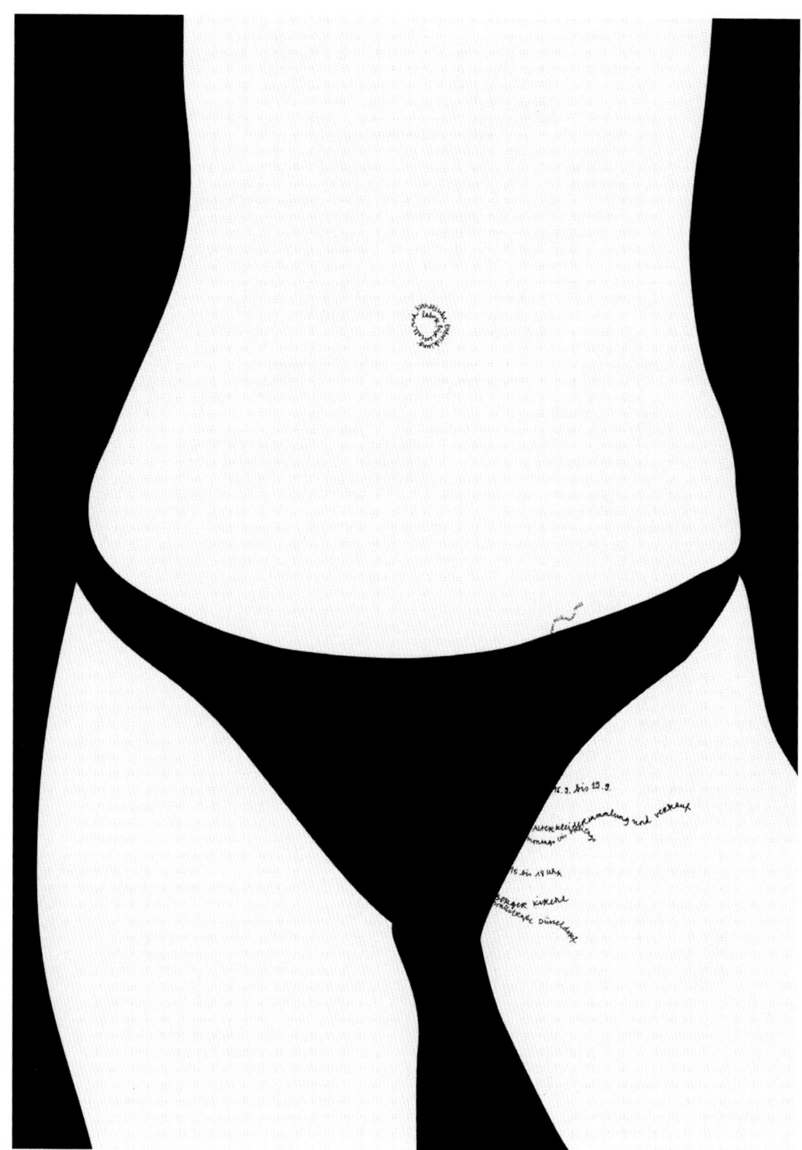

Fons Hickmann [Germany]

1966– born in Hamm
Admitted to AGI, 2004

Fons Matthias Hickmann studied design, photography and philosophy in Düsseldorf. The design studio Fons Hickmann m23 was founded in 2001 by Gesine Grotrian-Steinweg and Fons Hickmann. It varies a lot in size and scope: *'There are seven of us at the moment, sometimes there are four of us, sometimes fourteen,'* says Fons. The crew comes from Austria, Germany and Switzerland. The Berlin studio focuses on the design of complex communication systems, with activities including corporate design, book and poster design, magazine design and digital media.

Hickmann's work is conceptual and analytical, but also has a great sense of humour. Practically all of Hickmann's completed works have been awarded with prizes of international repute. Hickmann has taught at several universities, and holds lectures and workshops around the world. He is a professor at the University of Applied Arts in Vienna and the Berlin University of Arts. His first prize-winning monograph *Fons Hickmann – Touch Me There* was published in 2005.

Clothing Collection. Poster for **Laboratory for Social and Aesthetic Development**. Design is only politically or socially relevant if it takes an independent stand and communicates content. Everything else is just decoration.

When Eyes Could Still Speak. This poster series explores the aesthetics of mistakes in contrast with the perfect portrait. The posters also offer a playful semiotic look at the way information is coded and decoded in the development of communication.

Young and Social. A new design for an old theme, aimed at encouraging young people to formulate social ideas. The posters invited teenagers to send in their concepts to the Diakonie welfare organization.

Heromoism, 2005, posters for solo exhibition, MTR Arttube, Hong Kong.

Tommy Li [China]

1960– born in Hong Kong
Admitted to AGI, 2004

Tommy Li is renowned for his bold originality and prolific work, and was praised by *Agosto*, a high-circulation magazine in Japan, as the only graphic designer with the potential to have an influential impact on Hong Kong in the next decade. Over the years, Tommy has received almost 500 awards. His most distinct achievement to date has been 4 awards from the New York Directors Club, which honours outstanding results among Chinese designers. In Hong Kong, he was the recipient of the Hong Kong Artist of the Year Award in 1997 and many more. These accomplishments have made him a paragon among young designers.

Tommy is one of the few Hong Kong designers to carve out a dual career in both Hong Kong and Japan. He started his career in Osaka as early as 1993 and subsequently moved to Tokyo in 1997. He is the only Chinese designer to be engaged by the Japanese government, to design the emblem of Kaido City, Japan. Tommy Li Design Workshop is now the brand and image consultant for many prestigious corporations in Hong Kong.

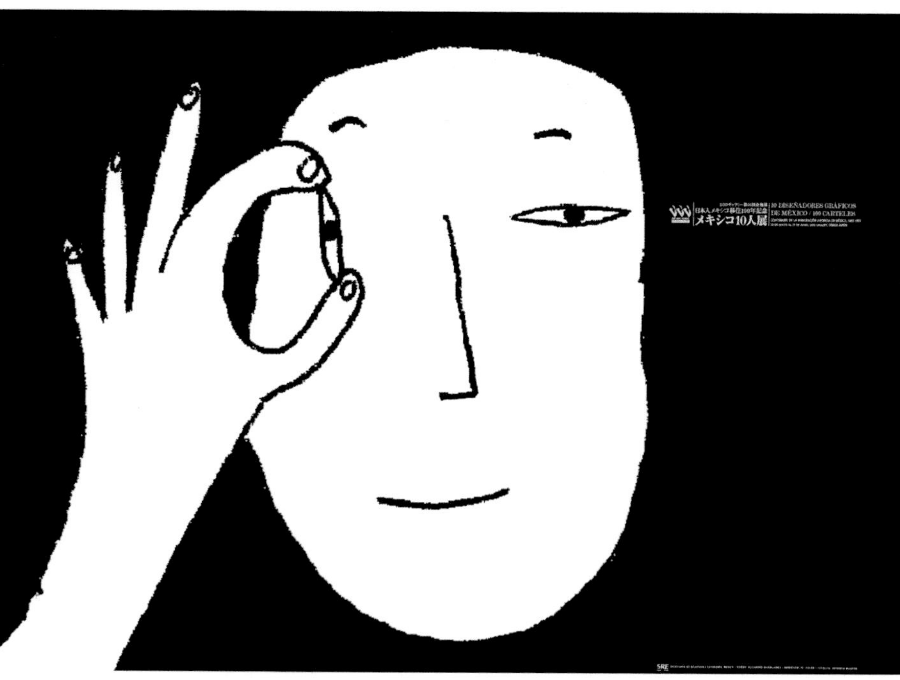

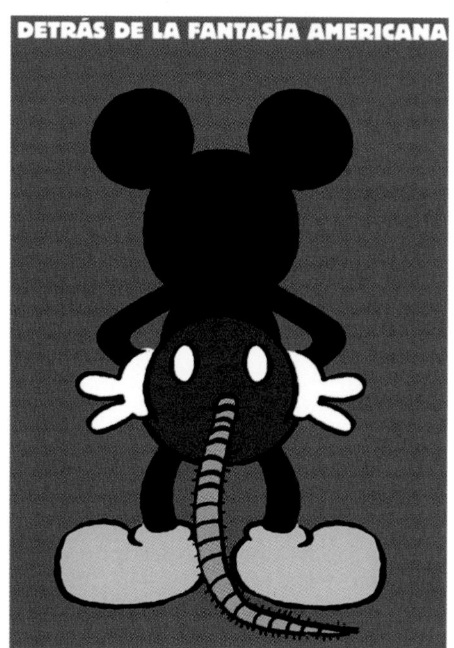

Alejandro Magallanes [Mexico]

1971– born in Mexico City
Admitted to AGI, 2004

Alejandro studied at the National School of Visual Arts, in Mexico City. In 1995 he founded the studio La Máquina del Tiempo, working on cultural and social issues, designing posters, books, illustrations and animations. He was invited to lecture at Alberta University, Canada in 2004, and has led workshops at the 16th International Poster Festival in Chaumont (France, 2005), ItuitLab (France, 2006), and the Université du Quebec (Canada, 2006). He was also invited to be a juror at ESAG Penninghen (France, 2005).

His poster work has won prizes including the Jozef Mroszczak Award, Warsaw Poster Biennale, 1998; third prize at the 4th Block Poster Triennial, Ukraine, 2000; Icograda prize at the Poster Biennale in Mexico, 2000; Golden Bee Prize for brochure design (with Fuera de Registro) at the International Biennale of Graphic Design in Moscow, 2000; first prize at the International Triennale of Political Posters in Mons, Belgium, 2004; first prize at the Latin American Poster Biennial in Bolivia, 2005 and silver medal at the International Poster Biennale in Warsaw, 2004.

Ciudad Juárez, Mexico: 300 women killed, more than 500 women disappeared, poster, 1997.

10 Mexican Graphic Designers at the DDD Gallery, poster, 1997.

Behind the American Dream, poster, 2001.

interact 1
interact 2
interact 3
interact 4
interact 5
interact 6

Edinburgh Fringe, Aug 98
Flux
@Queen's Hall Clerk Street
Fri 14/Sat 15 Spiritualized & Steve Martland. Sun 16 Ken Kesey & Ken Babbs. Fri 21/ Sat 22 Nick Cave. Fri 28 John Zorn. Sat 29 The Creatures.
@Jaffa Cake Grassmarket
Sun 16/Mon 17 The Jesus & Mary Chain. Tue 18 Je t'aime Gainsbourg. Thu 20 Roddy Frame. Fri 21 The Bathers, Pearl Fishers, The Swiss Family Orbison. Sat 22 Arab Strap & The Nectarine No 9. Sun 23 David Thomas & Yo La Tengo. Tue 25 P J Harvey. Thu 27 Asian Dub Foundation.
All doors 8pm
Tickets from £8
Box Office 0131 667 7776
A USP Arts Presentation

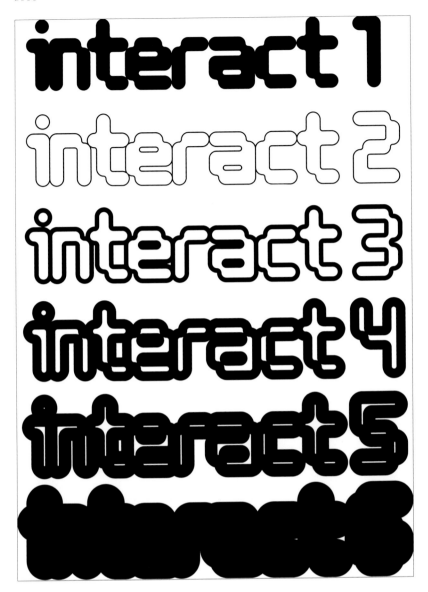

A work in progress: **Interact** font designs, 1994–2006.

Poster for **Flux New Music Festival Edinburgh** (with 8vo), 1998.

Poster for **Flux New Music Festival Edinburgh** (with 8vo), 1997.

Hamish Muir [UK]

1957– born in Paisley, Scotland
Admitted to AGI, 2004

Hamish Muir studied graphic design at Bath Academy of Art in the UK (1976–79) and at the School of Design, Basel, Switzerland (1980–81). He was co-founder (with Mark Holt and Simon Johnston) and principal of the London-based graphic design studio 8vo (1985–2001), and co-editor of *Octavo, International Journal of Typography* (1986–92). 8vo's typographically led design work was produced for a wide range of clients in the UK and Europe, including album covers and posters for Factory Records, Manchester; catalogues and posters for the Museum Boijmans Van Beuningen, Rotterdam; and billing and statement designs for companies such as Thames Water and Scandinavian Airlines. Since 2001, Muir has taught information design at the London College of Communication (formerly LCP). With Mark Holt, he wrote and designed *8vo: On the Outside*, published by Lars Müller, 2005.

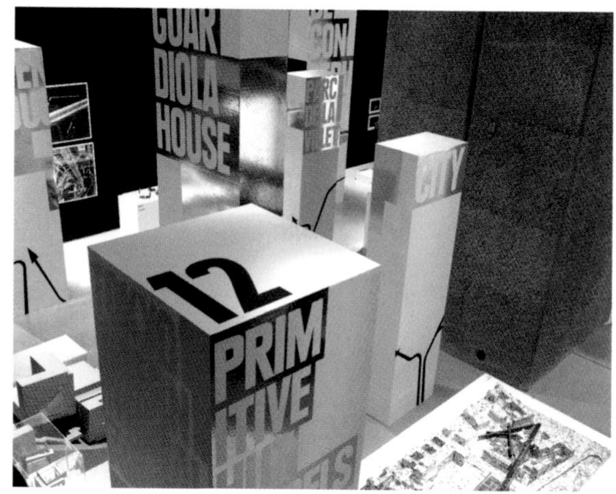

Morag Myerscough [UK]

1963– born in London
Admitted to AGI, 2004

Morag studied graphic design at St Martin's School of Art, London (1983–86) and the Royal College of Art & Design (1986–88). *'It was so fresh, so simple, so witty, we wished we'd done it,'* observed D&AD jury foreman Derek Birdsall, in response to her D&AD award-winning business card for Joe Kerr. The integration of design and its environment is central to her approach, it is a complete approach, not controlled by labels and limitations.
Morag set up her own cross-disciplinary design practice, Studio Myerscough, in 1993. Ever since, Morag has worked with some of the most respected, design-led UK companies, including the Barbican Centre (wayfinding, 2006), Barbican Art Gallery ('Rockstyle', 2000; 'Future City', 2006: exhibition design), the British Council ('Hometime', 2004; British Pavilion, Venice Biennale 2004), DTI (British Pavilion, 'UK State of Play' at E3, Los Angeles 2002–2005; pavilion design), Design Council (Millennium Products exhibitions, 1999), Design Museum ('Webwizards', 2002; 'Somewhere Totally Else', 2003; 'Formula 1', 2006: exhibition design), Science Museum ('Future Face', 2004: exhibition design), RIBA Architecture Foundation ('Greetings from London', 2004: exhibition design), Conran (Bluebird branding and Conran Collection food packaging), the Tate ('Building the Tate Collection: Our Gift to the Future') and Wedgwood (rebranding of all packaging, 2005).

9 Positions, curated by Peter Cook, Archigram, 2004. Graphics and covering building for the British Pavilion at the Venice Biennale, British Council.

New Barbican Centre wayfinding, completed in 2006.

Future City exhibition, 2006. Graphic design, Barbican Art gallery, London.

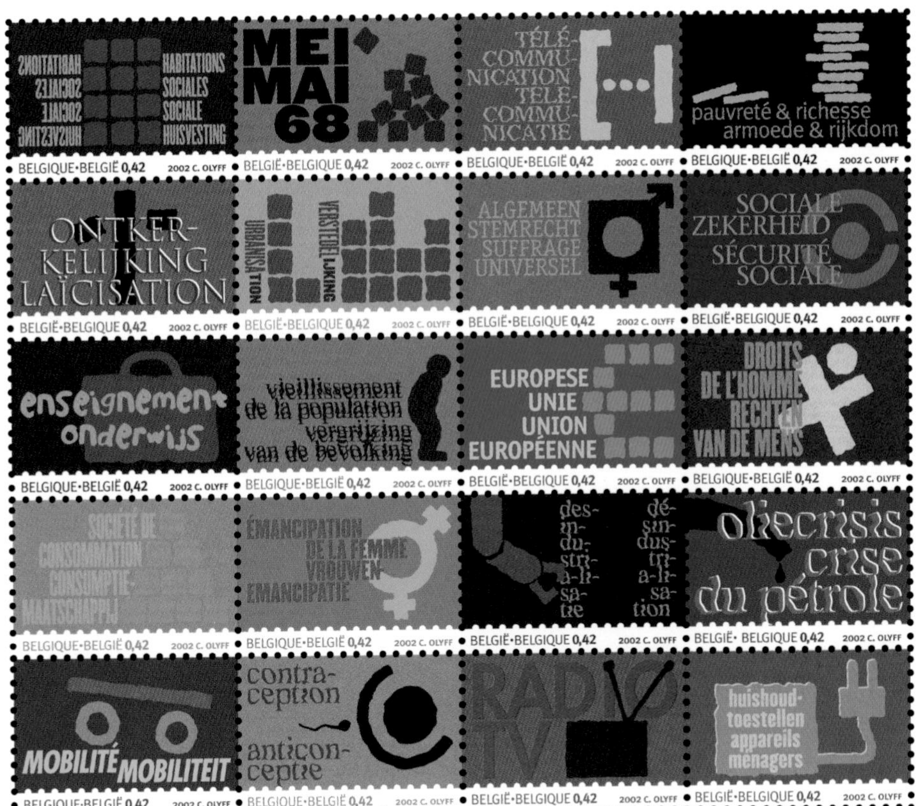

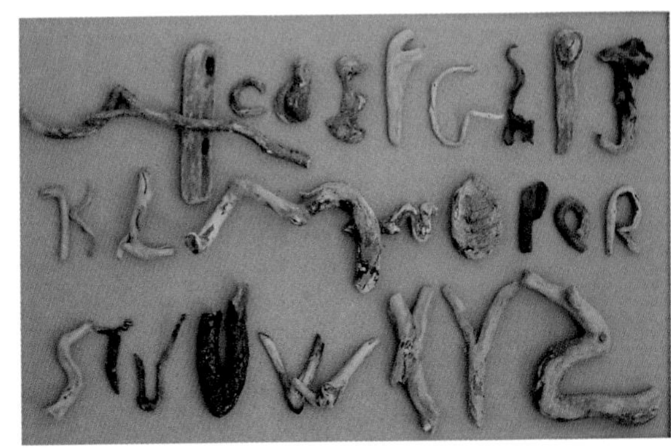

Social Life in the 20th Century, 20 stamps for the Belgian Post Office.

20 years of the Ahn Sang-Soo Studio, contribution to the 2005 calendar.

Wooden alphabet, found on the beach.

Clotilde Olyff [Belgium]

1962– born in Brussels
Admitted to AGI, 2004

Education: 1982–85: silkscreen and graphic design at École Supérieure de l'Image 'Le 75', Brussels. 1985–90: graphic design and typography at La Cambre Academy of Graphic Arts, Brussels. 1987–88: bookbinding workshops at La Cambre.
Teaching: 1992–3002: assistant at Atelier de Design Graphique et Typographique. La Cambre. 1999–2002: lecturer, typography course, Atelier de Design Industriel, La Cambre. 1993 onwards: professor at École Supérieure de l'Image 'Le 75'.
Work: posters, graphic identities, pictograms, stamps (38 stamps for the Belgian Post Office), logotypes, greetings cards; design and production of packaging using book-binding techniques; design and hand-made production of typographic games and type-related sculptures; design amd production of 52 books in the Clotilde Olyff Collection.
Exhibitions: La Cambre, with Michel Olyff, 1991; '10 Years of Work' at the Post Museum Brussels, 2000; 'The Other Letter' at Liège Library, 2000 and St Hubert College Brussels, 2001; 'En corps la lettre, body type', Cultural Centres of Namur and Ottignies, 2001 'Picto'Caro'Blanco' at the Centre d'Art de Rouge-Cloître, 2006; also group exhibitions in Belgium, France and Korea.

Simon Schama: America will never be the same again G2 Page 8

Lady Macbeth, four-letter needlework and learning from Cate Blanchett. Judi Dench in her prime G2, page 22

Chris Patten: How the Tories lost the plot This Section Page 32

Amy Jenkins: The me generation is now in charge G2 Page 2

£0.60 Monday 12.09.05 Published in London and Manchester guardian.co.uk

the guardian

Backlash over Blair's school revolution

City academy plans condemned by ex-education secretary Morris

Patrick Wintour and Rebecca Smithers

Bad'day mate Aussies lose their grip

Shane Warne at the Oval yesterday. Sport

Column five
The shape of things to come

Alan Rusbridger

Continued on page 2

UK link to terror snatches

Ian Cobain and Richard Norton-Taylor

National
Police chief blames Orangemen for riots

Law
Judges may block deportations

International
Israeli troops leave Gaza after 38 years

Financial
Sky's Premiership rights under threat

Bigger isn't always better...

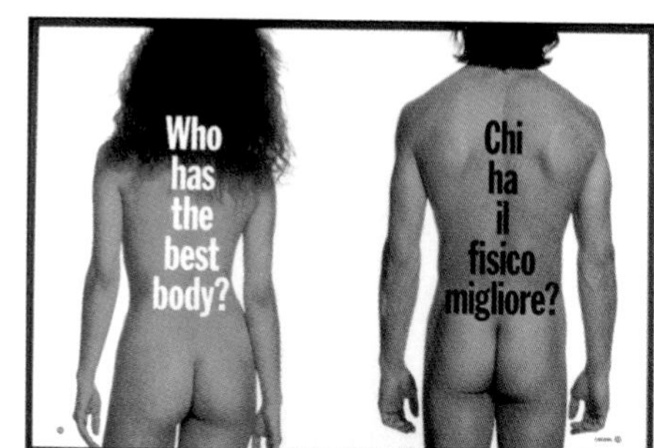

Mark Porter [UK]

1960– born in Aberdeen, Scotland
Admitted to AGI, 2004

Mark Porter is an editorial designer. He was born in Scotland and studied modern languages at Oxford University. Initially self-taught, he learnt from some of London and New York's best art directors. He has worked on a range of award-winning consumer, business and newspaper titles including *Campaign*, *ES* magazine, *Wired*, and *Colors*, and has consulted for newspapers and magazines throughout Europe. Mark joined *The Guardian* in 1995, later becoming head of design and then creative director. In 2005, he led the team which produced the design for the paper's relaunch in the Berliner format.

He has been featured in several exhibitions including: 'Work from London', British Council, touring, 1997; 'Communicate: British Independent Graphic Design since the Sixties', Barbican Art Gallery, London, 2005; and 'Designer of the Year', Design Museum, London, 2006. His work has been recognized at the highest level by many organizations including World's Best Designed from the Society for News Design, a gold medal from the Society of Publication Designers in New York, and a Black Pencil at the D&AD Global Awards. He also lectures and writes on newspaper and magazine design.

The Guardian redesign. A complete overhaul of the newspaper involving a format change, a move to full-colour presses, and the commissioning of over 90 new fonts. These images show the **weekday format** and **Saturday sections**.

Cover for **Shopping issue of Colors**, the multilingual globally published magazine from Benetton.

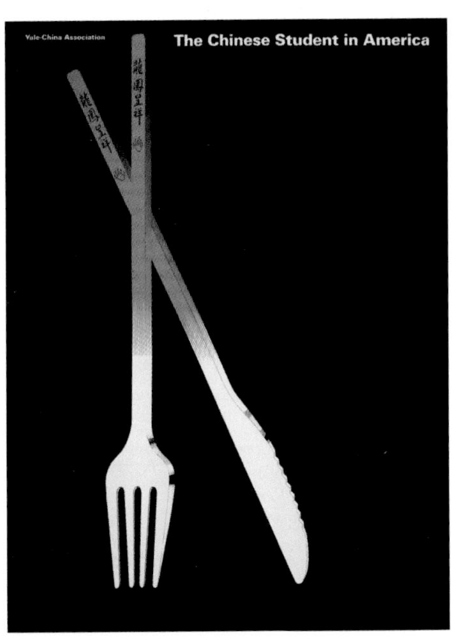

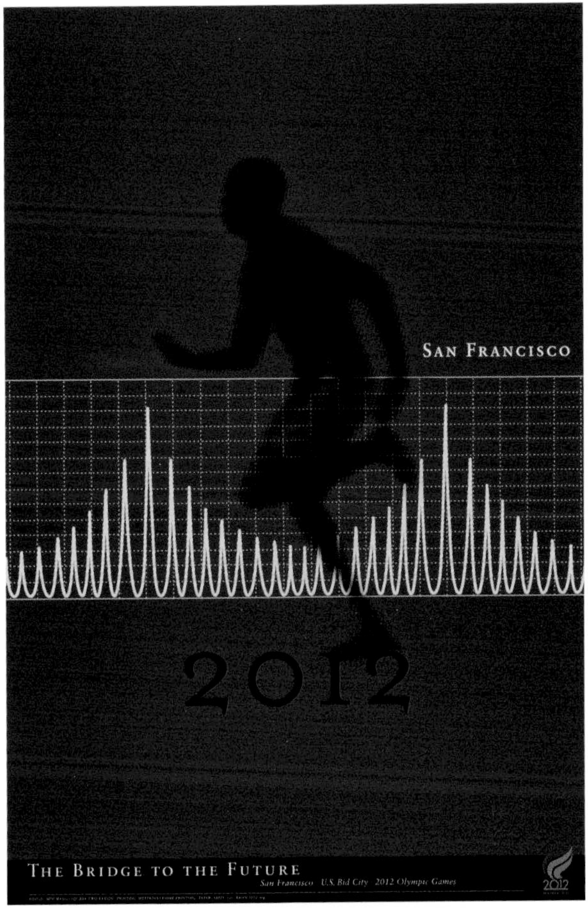

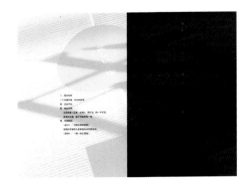

The Chinese Student in America, Yale–China Association, 1987.

San Francisco 2012, poster for San Francisco Olympic Bid, 2002.

Chinese Studies at Stanford University, poster, 2000.

Pages from a book about the design process and cross-cultural design issues.

Min Wang [China]

1956– born in Shandong
Admitted to AGI, 2004

Min Wang is a professor at the China Central Academy of Fine Arts (CAFA). He is currently serving as dean of the School of Design at CAFA and director of the Art Research Centre for the Olympic Games. He also serves as Standing Expert on Image and Identity for the Beijing 2008 Olympic Committee. He received his BA in graphic art from China Academy of Fine Arts and MFA from Yale University School of Art. He is the design director at Square Two Design, which he joined in 1998 after serving eight years as design manager, senior art director and graphic designer at Adobe Systems. He has been a visiting fellow in Germany at Akademie der Bildenden Kunste, Munich and Hochschule der Kunste, Berlin. In 1989, he began lecturing in graphic design at Yale University School of Art, teaching graduate students until 1997. Min's work has been exhibited internationally and is in the collections of the Museum für Kunst und Gewerbe in Hamburg, and the Museum für Gestaltung Zürich Kunstgewerbemuseum, Switzerland. Min has given talks and has been invited to judge design competitions in many countries and was appointed Honorary Professor by Shanghai University Fine Art College. Square Two Design clients include: Adobe, IBM, Intel, and Stanford University.

Russell Warren-Fisher [UK]

1964– born in London
Admitted to AGI, 2004

Russell studied graphic design at the London College of Printing (1983–86) and subsequently at the Royal College of Art (1986–88) under the professorial guidance of Gert Dumbar and Derek Birdsall. A nomination by Gert Dumbar for the Creative Futures award helped launch his independent career, working directly with clients such as the British Film Institute, Theatre de Complicité, Hong Kong Telecom and Decca Records. Taking time away from his east London studio and teaching positions for a sabbatical to China and the Far East in 1993 helped generate new works for solo shows in Tokyo and Osaka.

The space between commercial graphic design and printmaking continues to be the area that he enjoys working in most, and he distributes his time between experimental print projects, teaching and applied graphic design. In 2002 he was invited to the University of Western Sydney, Australia as a course consultant and in 2004 began a 'Print Digital' research project at the Royal College of Art, London. He has won numerous design and print awards and his work has been featured in publications such as *Typography Now*, *Fax You*, *Art & Design: 100 Years of the RCA*, *Graphic Originals*, and *All Men are Brothers*.

Ave Maria, poster for Theatre de Complicité, 1993.

Fly, 2002. Page from an experimental print project entitled 'printed matter no.1'.

Workshop poster, 2006. Promotional literature for Theatre de Complicité workshops. They always have great images to work with!

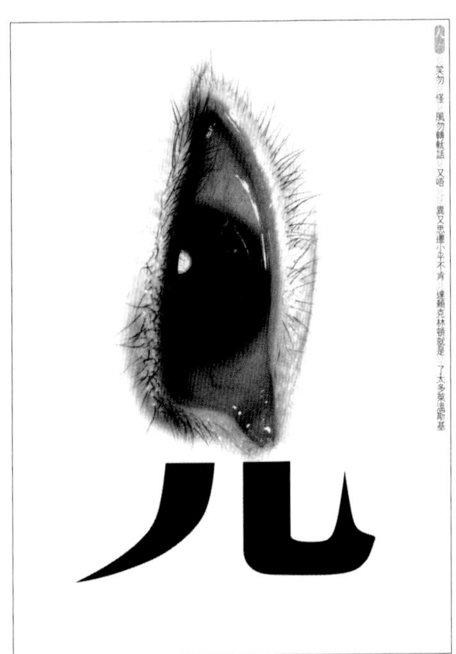

Redwhiteblue/Infinite, poster, 2001.

Redwhiteblue/Here/There/Everywhere, book design, 2006.

People, poster, 2000.

Stanley Wong [China]

1960– born in Hong Kong
Admitted to AGI, 2004

Stanley Wong, also known as 'anothermountainman', graduated from the Hong Kong Technical Teachers' College in 1980. Stanley worked as a graphic designer for 5 years before embarking on what was to become a productive and rewarding career in advertising for 15 years. In 2000, Stanley joined Centro Digital as chief creative officer/film director. There he experienced, for the first time, the joy of directing. Two years later, along with his partner, Stanley set up Threetwoone Film Production Ltd, specializing in advertising film production.

In recent years, his 'Redwhiteblue' works, depicting the spirit of Hong Kong, using the ubiquitous tri-colour canvas, have won critical acclaim both locally and internationally. A selection of his works are in permanent collections at Hong Kong Museums and the Victoria & Albert Museum in London. In 2005, 'Redwhiteblue' travelled to Venice as one of the two art works from Hong Kong presented at the 51st Venice Biennale. Throughout his career, he has won more than 400 awards in graphic design and advertising at home and abroad.

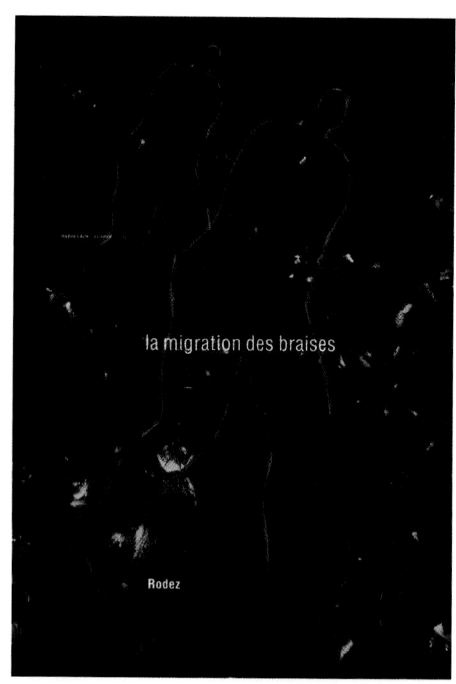

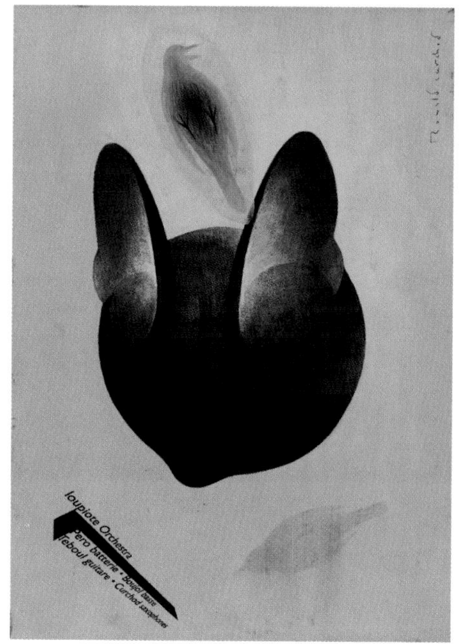

Ronald Curchod [France]

1954– born in Lausanne, Switzerland
Admitted to AGI, 2005

I started working at the age of 17 in a graphic design workshop until my diploma. In 1975 I left for France where I worked as a graphic designer and illustrator for advertising and industry. In 1985 I went freelance to work on cultural events. In 1989 I developed a more personal approach to poster design and illustrations, and worked on some set designs. Since then, I have continued to study the concept of making freely generated images, both for commissioned as well as non-commissioned projects. Images made with oil, clay or watercolours, that have an impact upon each other. The genres even mix together sometimes.

I now work in collaboration with cultural organizations and local, national and international councils. I design event programmes, posters, visual identities, websites and illustrations, and get illustration commissions from newspapers and magazines. I also publish screenprints and books, organize workshops in art schools and exhibit my work in art galleries in France and abroad.
My posters have been selected for international competitions and have won awards at the following events: International Theatre Poster Competition III in Osnabrück, Germany, 1996; bronze award in the International Poster Triennial in Toyama, Japan 2000; first prize at the 13th Poster festival Chaumont, 2001.

Les parchemins du midi, poster, 2003.

La migration des braises, Théâtre² l'Acte, poster, 2000.

Loupiote Orchestra, poster, 2004.

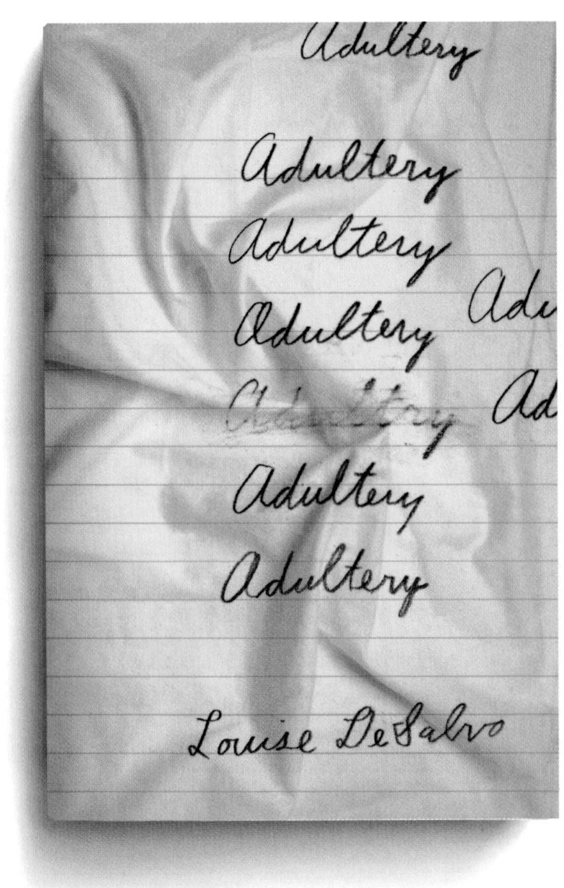

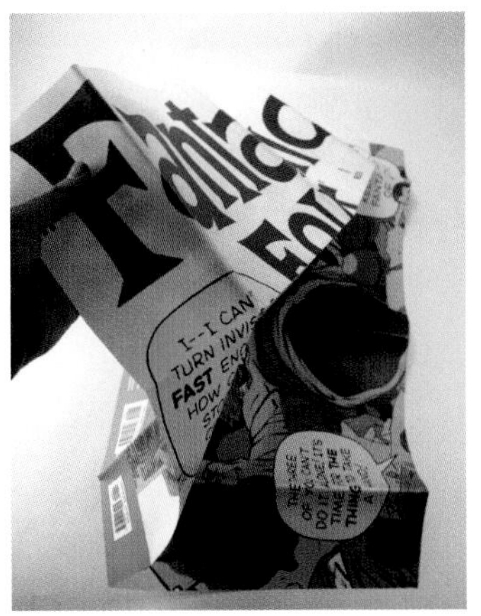

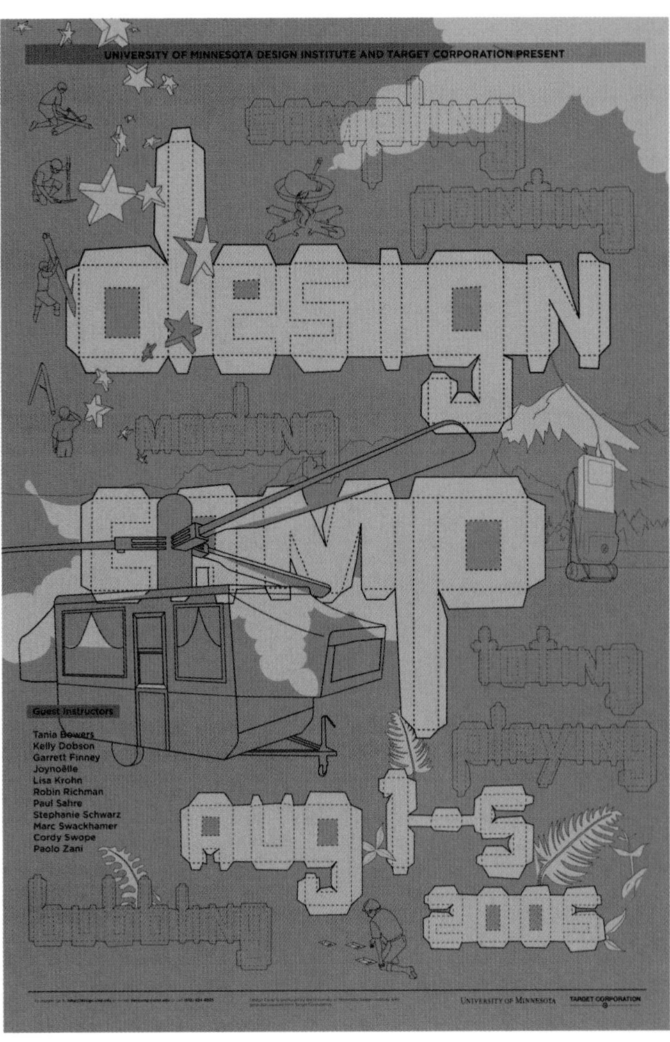

Adultery, book cover. Photographer: Michael Northrup, publisher: Beacon Press.

Design Camp, poster for the University of Minnesota Design Institute.

Maximum Fantastic Four, book. Client: Marvel Comics. In 1961, the first issue of a new comic-book serial created by the team of Jack Kirby and Stan Lee hit the news stands and changed the superhero genre forever. This book is a visual deconstruction of Kirby's dynamic visual syntax.

Paul Sahre [USA]

1964– born in Los Angeles
Admitted to AGI, 2005

Graphic designer, illustrator, educator and author Paul Sahre established his own design company in New York in 1997. Consciously maintaining a small office, he has nevertheless established a large presence in American graphic design. The balance he strikes, whether between commercial and personal projects or in his own design process, is evident in such things as the physical layout of his office – part design studio, part silkscreen lab, where he prints designs and posters for various off-off-Broadway Theatres (some of which are in the permanent collection of the Cooper Hewitt Design Museum). On the other side of the office, he is busy designing book covers for authors such as Rick Moody, Chuck Klosterman, Ben Marcus and Victor Pelevin. Sahre is also a frequent contributor to the *New York Times* Op-Ed page. He is co-author of *Hello World: A Life in Ham Radio*, a book based on a collection of QSL cards, which amateur radio enthusiasts exchange after communication with other operators around the world.

Paolo Tassinari [Italy]

1955– born in Trieste
Admitted to AGI, 2005

Paolo Tassinari studied in Bologna (1975–79), and started his own design practice Tassinari/Vetta with Pierpaolo Vetta in Trieste in 1980, working mainly for cultural institutions and major exhibitions, often side by side with architects and designers such as Aldo Rossi, Achille Castiglioni, and Gae Aulenti.
In 2002 with Pierpaolo Vetta and Leonardo Sonnoli he founded the Codesign partnership, which later merged with Tassinari/Vetta. It is currently involved mainly in communication and identity projects for cultural events, institutions and public companies, as well as the field of book design. Commissions have come from the Venice Biennale and Milan Triennale, Trenitalia, Mondadori, modern and contemporary art museums, regional and local governments among others. Paolo has been art director of *Casabella* architectural magazine since 1996, and of the architecture department of Electa publishing house since 2001. He teaches at the University of Trieste, and is a member of a selection committee for the Compasso d'Oro ADI in Milan.

Installation for the exhibition **4:3, 50 Years of Italian and German Design**, Bonn, 2000.
The installation reinterpreted the work of seventeen masters of Italian design of the 20th century: Antonio Boggeri, Erberto Carboni, Fortunato Depero, Marcello Dudovich, Franco Grignani, Benito Jacovitti, Bruno Munari, Marcello Nizzoli, Aldo Novarese, Edoardo Persico, Giovanni Pintori, Antonio Rubino, Federico Seneca, Albe Steiner, Armando Testa, and Luigi Veronesi.

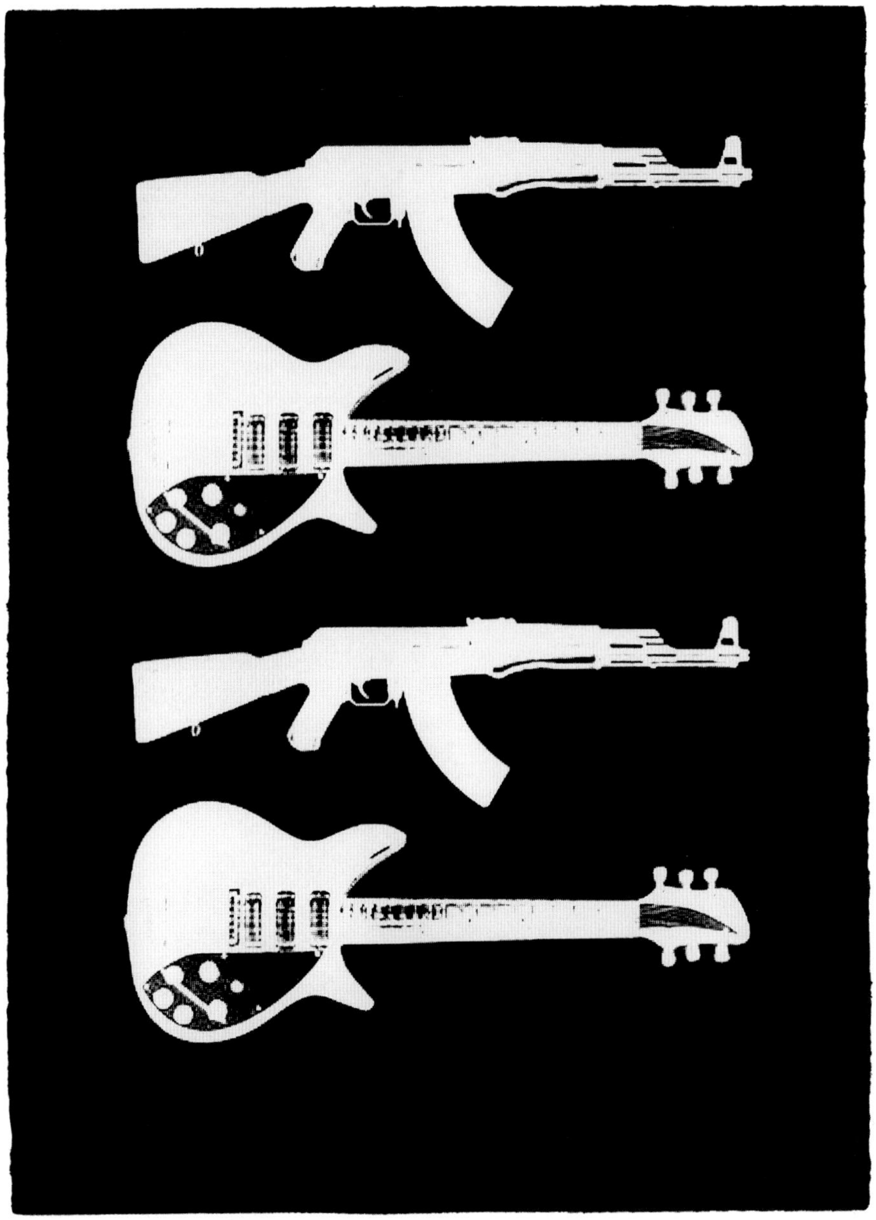

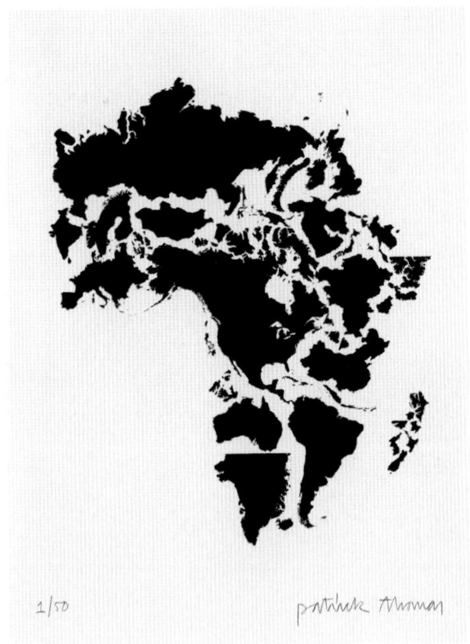

Kalashnikovs & Rickenbackers (Remembering John Lennon), 2006. Silkscreen on Arches 88 paper, 100% cotton. Edition of 50.

Africa, 2006. Silkscreen on Arches 88 paper, 100% cotton. Edition of 50.

Black & White, 2005. A compilation of Patrick Thomas's work for the Spanish press. Publisher: Studio laVista, 148 x 210 x 10 mm, paperback, 96 pages. Edition of 750.

Patrick Thomas [Spain]

1965– born in Liverpool, England
Admitted to AGI, 2005

Studied at St Martin's School of Art and the RCA, London, before moving to Barcelona in 1991. After working freelance for several years he co-founded the multi-disciplinary art/design studio laVista, which has received international recognition. Patrick has won numerous design awards, notably for his on-going collaboration with *Vanguardia* newspaper in Barcelona: a Special Mention from SND-E (Society of News Design, Spain), two consecutive Silver Awards from ADC*E (Art Directors Club of Europe), an Award of Excellence from SND-USA (Society of News Design, USA). His work has been repeatedly selected for the D&AD and ADC*E annuals.

In 2005 he had work selected for *The Design of Dissent*, edited by Milton Glaser and Mirko Ilic. He has exhibited internationally, with recent group exhibitions at the Pentagram Gallery and the Victoria & Albert Museum, London; the School of Visual Arts and the International Center of Photography NY; he is currently preparing exhibitions for Osaka, Mexico City, Boston, Antwerp, Amsterdam and Berlin. In 2004–2005 he was Graphic Research Fellow at Liverpool School of Art & Design, Liverpool John Moores University and is visiting lecturer at EINA and Elisava Schools of Design, Barcelona. In 2005 he published his first book, *Black & White*, documenting his collaboration with the Spanish press.

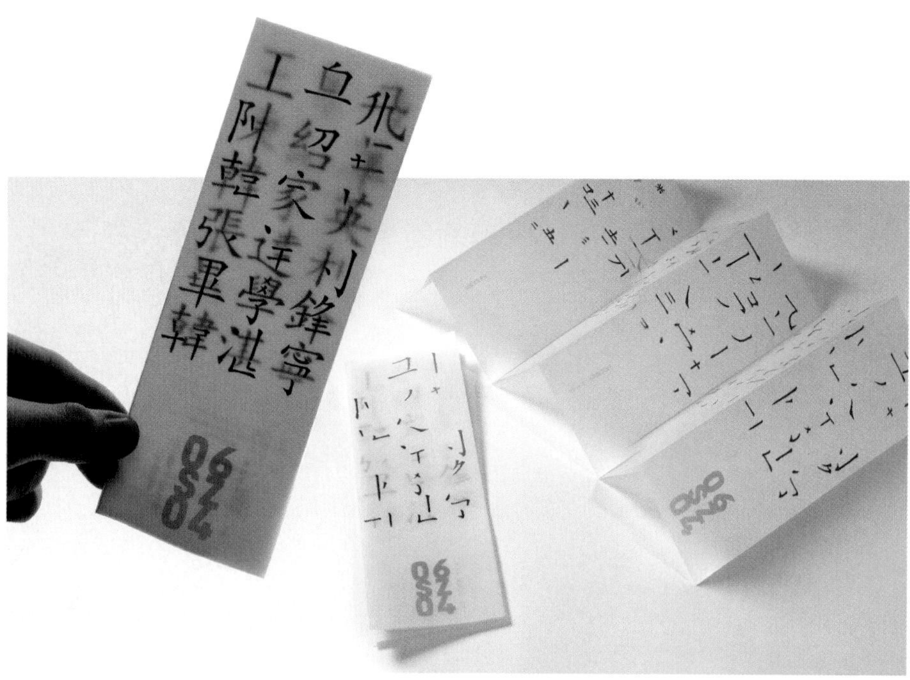

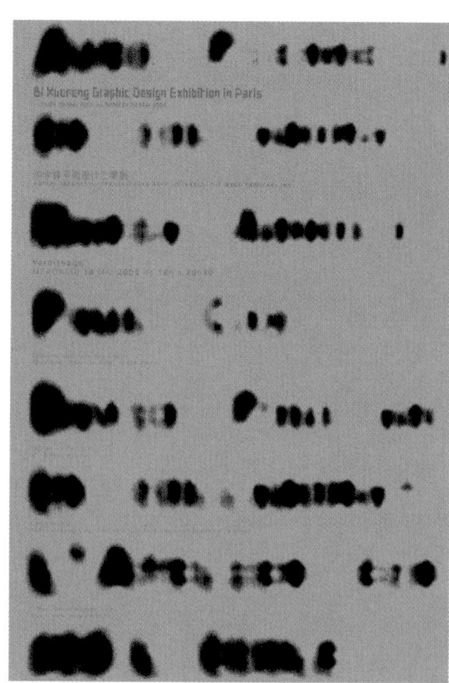

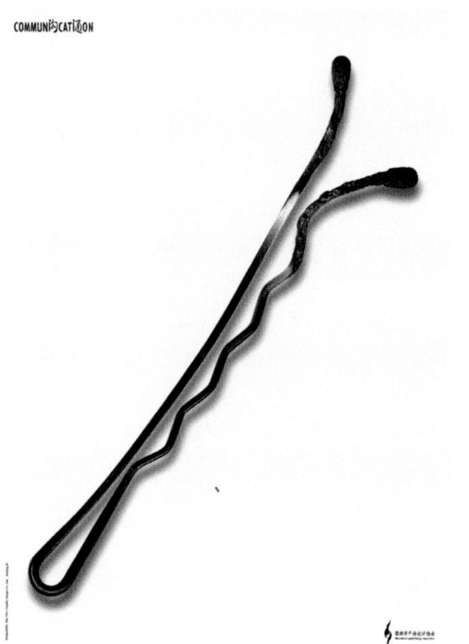

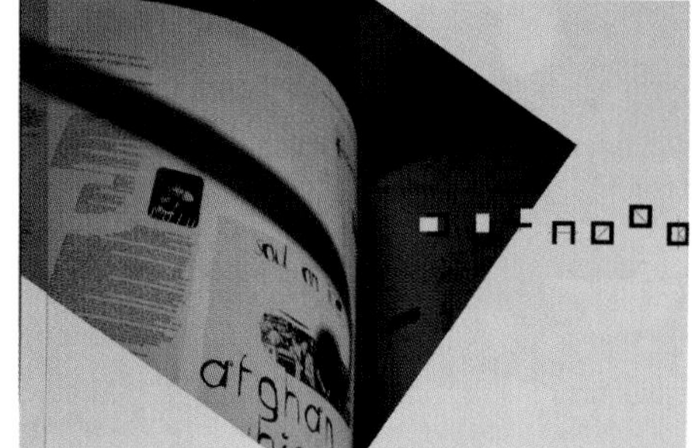

Xuefeng Bi [China]

1963– born in HeBei
Admitted to AGI, 2006

Between 1985–89 he studied at the China Academy of Art, and in 1997 founded IMAGRAM Graphic Design. He is vice-president of Shenzhen Graphic Design Association and has won numerous awards, including: excellence award, Graphic Design in China; gold award, Hong Kong International Poster Triennial, 1997; three consecutive silver awards and excellence awards, Hong Kong Design Show; bronze award, Chinese National Art Exhibition, 1999; silver award and bronze award, Hong Kong Designers Association Awards, 2005.

His work has been selected by the 5th International Triennial of Posters in Toyama, Japan, Helsinki International Poster Biennial 1997, the 18th International Poster Biennial of Graphic Design in Brno, the 16th International Poster Biennial in Warsaw; the 4th & the 6th International Biennial in the Poster in Mexico. For three consecutive years (2004–2006) he had works selected for the TDC Annual Awards.

Promotion design for **Six Designers Show, 06+SZ+04**, 2004. Client: Guangdong Museum of Art. Offset print + screen print.

Communication, poster for Shenzhen Graphic Design Association, 1997. Offset print.

Solo poster exhibition in Paris, promotional poster, 2005. Offset print.

Process, 2004. Offset print + screen print. Size: 150 mm × 205 mm.

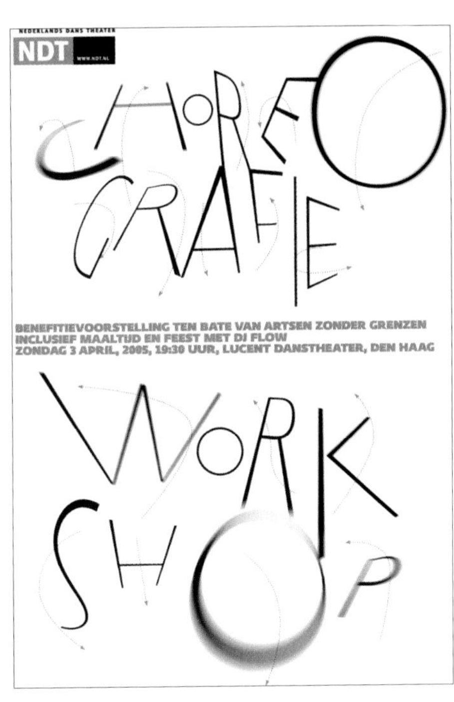

Collage Europe, design of exhibition at NAi Rotterdam, 2004. Collaboration with the house architect of NAi. Client: NAi.

Choreography Workshop, poster for Nederlands Dans Theater, 2005. Client: NDT, The Hague

Eureka typeface family (x 2), 1995–2000. Self-initiated project, published by FontShop International.

Covers of **DOT DOT DOT**, art & design magazine. Founded, edited and designed by Peter Bilak & Stuart Bailey, 2000-2006. Collaboration with Stuart Bailey. Self-initiated project.

Peter Bilak [The Netherlands]

1973- born in Presov, Czechoslovakia
Admitted to AGI, 2006

Peter Bilak studied in Slovakia, the UK and the United States, before getting his MA from Atelier National de Création Typographique in Paris and his postgraduate laureate from Jan van Eyck Akademie in Maastricht. Before starting his studio in The Hague in 2001, he was with Studio Dumbar. He is presently working on a broad range of cultural and commercial projects. Recent projects include: design of the standard stamps for the Dutch Royal mail (TPG Post); a series of dance performances (in collaboration with choreographer Lukas Timulak); design of Arabic fonts (in collaboration with Tarek Atrissi); books and publications for Stroom, The Hague Art Center; exhibition design for the Dutch Architectural Institute; curator of exhibitions for the Biennale of Graphic Design, Brno. He has designed several fonts including FF Eureka (published by Fontshop) and Fedra (published by his own type foundry Typotheque). He frequently contributes writings and designs to books and publications that include *Print*, *IDEA*, *Items*, *Emigre*, *Abitare* and *Page*. He is one of the founding editors of *DOT DOT DOT*, an art and design magazine. Peter teaches at the Royal Academy in The Hague, and lectures internationally.

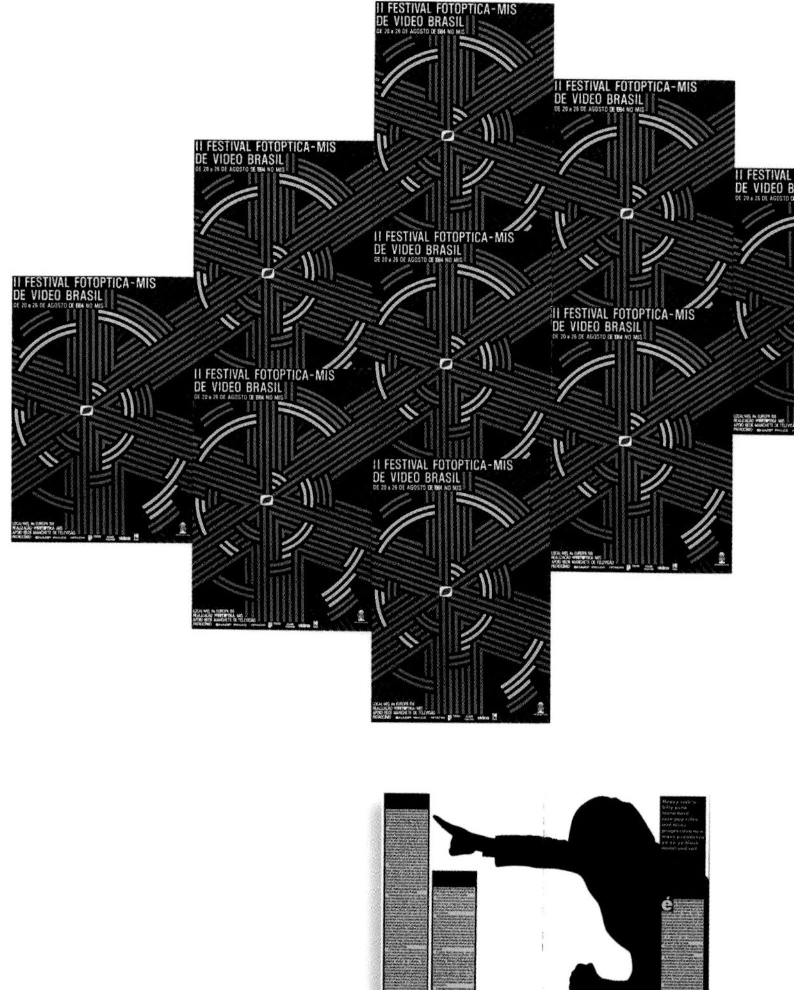

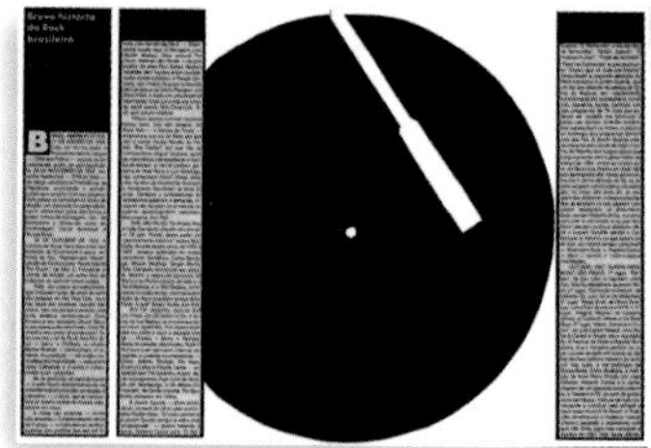

Kiko Farkas [Brazil]

1957– born in São Paulo
Admitted to AGI, 2006

Education and career: 1979: life drawing at Arts Students League, New York. 1982: graduated as an architect. 1987: Founded Máquina Estúdio to work as a graphic designer and illustrator. *Publications: Novum* (June 1991 and October 2000), *Print* (November 1987), *Communication Arts* (April 2005). *International exhibitions:* International Poster Biennial, Colorado, 1991, 1993, 1995, 1997; 14th Poster Biennale, Warsaw, 1994; Poster Triennial, Toyama, 1989; Brno Biennial, 1990; 'New Graphic Design in Brazil', Lisbon; Triennial of the Stage Poster, Sofia, 1997, 2003; Trnava Biennial, 2003; Poster Biennial, Helsinki, 1997, 2002; Special room at 'Brésil à l'affiche', Chaumont, 2004–2005. Working for São Paulo Symphony orchestra since 2003, his posters have been internationally recognized and were the subject of 'Images of Music', his first solo show in São Paulo, 2004. He was curator of the Brazilian contribution to the 'Designmai' exhibition, Berlin, 2006. In 2004 Kiko won a national contest to create the identity for international tourism in Brazil. His children's books have won several prizes, including the Jabuti grand prize for fiction for his book *Um passarinho me contou*. At the 8th ADG biennial (2004, 2006), Máquina Estúdio was the most awarded studio in Brazil. Kiko Farkas is a lecturer, a founder of ADG, the Brazilian association of graphic designers, and an invited teacher at Miami Ad School.

Videobrasil Festival. The poster represents a place of both convergence and radiation. These posters were used also as a decoration for the venue. 50 x 70 cm, offset, 1982.

Encyclopedia of Brazilian Rock, printed in two colours, and sold at newsstands. Illustrated by Kiko on paper cut with scissors to give a 'rough' character. Printed in off-set, two colours, 1987.

Journey to the Centre of the Earth, poster. In an unfinished tunnel under a river in São Paulo, the spectators had to cross an unfinished tunnel in total darkness. Printed in off-set, three colours, 1992.